My Daily BIBLE Companion

Volume 1
OLD TESTAMENT

KEN RAGGIO

My Daily Bible Companion
Volume 1 – Old Testament
A Comprehensive Study Guide And Bible Commentary
More than 4,800 mini-Bible lessons from Genesis to Revelation.

IN TWO VOLUMES
Volume 1 – Old Testament
Volume 2 – New Testament

By Ken Raggio

VOLUME 1:
ISBN-13: 978-1475126921
ISBN-10: 1475126921

For Information, Contact:

Ken Raggio, 3312 Hwy 365, #219, Nederland, Texas 77627
VISIT my major **WEBSITE** at kenraggio.com

Read my **BLOG** at kenraggio.blogspot.com
FOLLOW ME on **TWITTER:** kenraggiocom

FRIEND ME on **FACEBOOK:** Ken Raggio
LIKE my **FACEBOOK FanPage:** Ken Raggio Bible Resources

Table of Contents

LESSONS FROM THE OLD TESTAMENT

Dedication

To the memory of my precious wife, Dixie,
who for thirty-one years, blessed me with her matchless love and devotion…

To my much-beloved children -
my elder son, Brian, and his wife Aimee;
my younger son, Chad, and his wife Ashley;
my precious grandchildren - Ashley, Morgan, Cole and Grant;
and to all of my descendants who may follow -
to them more than anyone else are these multitudinous words written;
that they may quickly know, in time to come,
so many things I have learned about God
through much labor and difficulty over a lifetime…

To my dearly beloved parents, John and Velma Raggio,
who have been the most wonderful, caring parents, never wavering
in their love, encouragement and moral support through the years…

To my beloved Pastor, Rev. John W. Harrell,
who has blessed and encouraged me and countless others through thousands
of days with his utterly awesome preaching, shepherding, and intensive care…

To my beloved aunt and uncle, Norma and Wallace Bedair,
whose kind, generous and loving hearts
have nurtured and encouraged me again and again…

To my dear friend and colleague, Pam Eddings,
whose thorough knowledge of both the Bible and the Chicago Manual of Style
has for years, proofed and edited well over one million of my written words
via the Internet, and with kindred Spirit and zeal for the ministry,
has helped me move continuously forward with my writings
until several books have come into the world, and…

To every hungry soul who longs to rise above the cacophony of this world,
to dabble in the Majestic, and someday see the Face of God…

I dedicate this book.
My Daily Bible Companion

Ken Raggio
April, 2012

"Not seeking mine own profit, but the profit of many,
that they might be saved," 1 Corinthians 10:33.

PREFACE

In the forty-five-plus years since I first entered the ministry, it has become increasingly apparent to me that God ordained me to be a writer. In high school, I studied journalism and learned newspaper editing and publishing. Returning home from Bible College, I became the Editor of a Christian magazine for a national ministry. In my early years of Pastoring, I wrote numerous Christian booklets and articles for a variety of publications. Then I became the Editor of an official Church publication read by thousands of ministers around the world. In the late 1990s, I began writing monthly for a national Prophecy magazine of which I eventually became the Editor, and also became a regular contributor to a national Sunday School publication. Since 1996, I have maintained a major website containing thousands of pages of Bible Studies, Lessons, Resources and Prophecy articles, as well as publishing "TODAY'S BIBLE STUDY," a daily email containing four mini-Bible lessons. To date, tens of thousands of subscribers in 214 nations have received these lessons, and millions in 236 nations have read the Bible studies on my website.

Two years after my wife passed away, and following nearly thirty years of Pastoral ministry, I made an agonizing choice to resign Pastoring and go into full-time writing and publishing. In my heart, I felt that I must not fail to write and publish the marvelous things I have discovered in the Word of God, so that others around the world could learn and know the great Bible Truths that can save their souls. Subsequently, I have written over two million words on Biblical subjects in six years. This book is the first major project to be released from those efforts. Many more books are soon to follow, God willing.

We live in the most ominous of all times. The God of the Bible has known from the beginning of Creation exactly how this age would end. As a serious student of Bible Prophecy since 1972, I have witnessed many breath-taking developments on the world stage that I knew in my heart were the very prophesied acts of God. The cumulative effect of a lifetime of intense Bible study combined with a keen interest in Bible Prophecies leave me feeling like Jeremiah, with "fire shut up in my bones."

There is more about God to tell than any man can tell. Over 4,800 lessons are contained in this book, on every subject from Genesis to Revelation. The wise man said, "Wisdom is the principal thing; therefore get wisdom: and with all thy getting get understanding," Proverbs 4:7. I have also written a book on PRAYER, one on great BIBLE DOCTRINES, a major work on BIBLE PROPHECIES, and several inspirational books. I hope you will read them all.

I want you to know the Lord as I know Him. There is no other pursuit so deserving of your efforts. I earnestly pray that as you peruse these thousands of lessons, the eyes of your heart will be enlightened like Jonathan's eyes when he tasted sweet honeycomb. But even more, I pray that the Word of God will save your eternal soul. In Him alone is life, and that life is everlasting life.

In Jesus' name…

Please keep this book near your favorite easy chair, or on your bedside table.

My Daily BIBLE Companion

A Comprehensive Study Guide and Bible Commentary
MORE THAN 4,800 BIBLE LESSONS
100-Word Mini-Topics Genesis to Revelation
Vol. 1 - Old Testament / Vol. 2 - New Testament
All the lessons in **MY DAILY BIBLE COMPANION**
are equally divided into one of four general categories.

PRAYER
Over 1200 topics pertaining to Prayer, Intercession, Praise, Worship, Conversations with God, God speaking to a man, Words spoken before God.

PRINCIPALS
People, Places, and Things. Principal Characters, Buildings, Cities, Sacred Furnishings, Objects, etc.

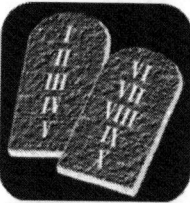

PRINCIPLES
Precepts, Principles and Doctrines. Virtues, Values and Vices. Laws and Lessons of Life.

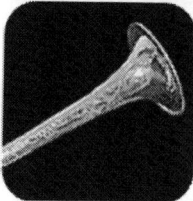

PROPHECIES
Virtually every Prophecy in the Bible, both fulfilled and unfulfilled. Amazing, detailed explanations of every significant prophecy pertaining to the Last Days.

Lessons from the Book of
GENESIS

B | The Book Of Genesis

Genesis is indeed the book of origins, but much more. It defines Creation and the birth of the nation of Israel. This document may be the most hotly contested book on earth. Did God create the worlds? Did Noah build the Ark? Did God favor Israel over Ishmael? Were Jews in bondage in Egypt? Each answer is an unequivocal "Yes!" Genesis tells it like it was. Nobody can prove otherwise. Through faith we understand the worlds were framed by the Word of God.

Genesis 1:1 - "In the beginning God created the Heaven and the earth."

B | The First Day Of Creation

In God's infinite wisdom, He knew that light is a prerequisite to life on earth. Life on earth depends upon light. Light provides energy, warmth, sight, growth and much more. Einstein figured that light is the primary constant in the universe, so time itself is based upon the speed of light. No wonder then, that God created light on the first day. Will not this brilliant God of order also tend to your greatest needs first, too?

Genesis 1:3 - "And God said, Let there be light: and there was light."

B | The Second Day Of Creation

God created a 50-mile-high environment to support all His planned creatures. This "firmament," with water above and water below, is the magnificent atmosphere enveloping our globe. Without the nitrogen, oxygen, argon, hydrogen, helium, carbon dioxide, ozone and all the other elements in the earth's sky, life as we know it could not exist. No other planet in the Universe has an environment as lavish and luxurious as ours. That's not an accident. God wonderfully planned our support and survival.

Genesis 1:8 - "And God called the firmament Heaven."

B | The Third Day Of Creation

God called land out of water. Water is one of the greatest secrets to life on this planet. This biosphere of land, water and air is miraculously regulated by perpetual photosynthesis, respiration, and bacterial regeneration. It supports the life-cycles of everything living. God scattered dry seed everywhere, then raised up a mist to water it and begin endless germination cycles. Great God!

Genesis 1:11 - "God said, Let the earth bring forth grass, the herb yielding seed, and the fruit tree yielding fruit after his kind, whose seed is in itself."

C | Exponential Potential

If I give you one kernel of corn, can you plant every kernel that may ever grow from it? One kernel produces one plant, but one plant produces many ears of corn with thousands of kernels. Here is infinite exponential potential - a world full of corn! Likewise, your godly, obedient act of faith has infinite future potential. Commit a godly act today!

Genesis 1:12 - "And the earth brought forth grass, and herb yielding seed after his kind, and the tree yielding fruit, whose seed was in itself, after his kind: and God saw that it was good."

B | The Fourth Day Of Creation

The light God made on the first day was supernatural - not emanating from a natural source. Without it, the universe was totally dark. The sun, moon, and stars were not created until this fourth day. 24-hour days only began AFTER the fourth day, when 100 billion galaxies with about 100 billion stars apiece were created. The first four days might have spanned aeons.

Genesis 1:16 - "God made two great lights; the greater light to rule the day, and the lesser light to rule the night: he made the stars also."

C | The Eye Of God

The Hubble telescope photographed a Nebula called the "Eye of God." It looks like a beautiful blue eye surrounded by great luminescence. Actually, it is a gaseous tunnel almost one trillion miles deep. Another photo captures one entire spiraling galaxy sitting angular to another spiraling galaxy just behind it - all within a pin-hole view of space. I will live my life any way God's Word tells me for the chance to see the One who created all of that. I have nothing to lose and everything to gain.

Genesis 1:16 - "...he made the stars also."

B | The Fifth Day Of Creation

Yesterday was the last timeless Wednesday. The brand new Solar System gives the earth its first 24-hour day. Thursday evening, God creates every fish, bird, and water mammal. Overnight, the entire earth begins seeing, hearing, tasting, touching and smelling. Totally, inexplicably awesome!

Genesis 1:20,22 - "God said, Let the waters bring forth abundantly the moving creature that hath life, and fowl that may fly above the earth in the open firmament of heaven ...Be fruitful, and multiply, and fill the waters in the seas, and let fowl multiply in the earth."

B | The Sixth Day Of Creation

The second 24-hours. What a day! Jillions of land animals boil up from the ground in species, scattering everywhere. But God's "Grande Finale" that Friday was a single MAN in God's image! Adam, the only truly self-aware creature on earth, saw because HE sees; heard because HE hears; thought because HE thinks; knew because HE knows. First son; first friend of GOD!

Genesis 1:27-28 - "So God created man in his own image, in the image of God created he him; male and female created he them."

B | Let Man Have Dominion Over All The Earth

God brought the animals to Adam for naming. He gave mankind dominion over the earth and all living creatures. God created the earth to benefit and sustain MAN. Man has divine authority and prerogative to use the earth for his benefit, including domestication and cultivation. "Mother Earth" politics elevate animal rights and environmental issues above human rights and give "mother" nature illicit dominion over Father God. Controlling the balance of nature, including global climate, is FAR over our heads. Only God can comprehend and control sustainability.

Genesis 1:26 - "...let them have dominion ...over all the earth."

A | Blessed Without A Prayer

There is no mention of any prayers in the Creation story of Genesis. Nothing is said about prayer until the days of Adam and Eve's grandchildren, when "men began to call upon the name of the LORD," 4:26. But there is a reasonable explanation for the absence of prayer before that time. In the Garden of Eden, Adam and Eve were perfectly blessed. If mankind had never sinned, we would never have needed to pray.

Genesis 1:27 - "So God created man in his own image, ...male and female created he them. And God blessed them."

C | God's Natural Medicine

The old-timers were probably right. Drugs and witchcraft are first-cousins. Nobody can know for sure just what can happen when molecules are manufactured in a laboratory. Harmful side-effects and reactions often result from pharmaceutical drugs. Illicit drugs regularly kill, addict, or sicken. Natural herbs contain God-made molecules that mankind has been accustomed to since the beginning of time. That is God's natural medicine cabinet.

Genesis 1:30 - "I have given every green herb for meat." Ezekiel 47:12 - "...the fruit thereof shall be for meat, and the leaf thereof for medicine."

B | The Seventh Day Of Creation

A light-year is 5.8 trillion miles. Scientists estimate the universe is 28 billion light-years wide containing 100 billion galaxies, each one containing 100 billion stars. Meanwhile, just one human has almost 100 trillion living cells working in perfect synchronization. God invented, created and meticulously oversees every speck. He sanctified a day of rest to view, contemplate and enjoy it all.

Genesis 2:2 - "...on the seventh day God ended his work which he had made; and he rested on the seventh day from all his work which he had made."

B | Adam

A human corpse decomposes into elements just like ordinary dirt. Adam was not a clay sculpture. God used dust. Maybe He transformed dust particles into stem cells, then constituted an embryo, and in a matter of moments quickly advanced it through infancy, adolescence, puberty and adulthood! Who knows? From mere dirt to sophisticated and complex skeletal, muscular, nervous, cardiovascular, digestive and respiratory systems, we are fearfully and wonderfully made!

Genesis 2:7 - "...the LORD God formed man of the dust of the ground, and breathed into his nostrils the breath of life; and man became a living soul."

B | The Creation Of Man

1,400 years before Christ, Moses declared that God formed man from dust. Muslims say that 2,000 years later, the angel Gabriel told Mohammed to recite that Allah created man out of "a mere clot of congealed blood," (Qur'an 96:2 Yusufali translation). So, is Moses a liar, or Mohammed? Judaism and Christianity say Moses was right. So do I.

Genesis 2:7 - "And the LORD God formed man of the dust of the ground, and breathed into his nostrils the breath of life; and man became a living soul."

C | You HAVE A Body, But You ARE A Soul

It was nothing more than a dirt sculpture until God breathed into it. Our bodies are nothing but lifeless elements without the soul that God gave us. The body is a shell that houses a real man. You HAVE a body, but you ARE a soul. Your earthly body is destined for the grave - ashes to ashes, dust to dust. But your SOUL will NEVER die. In the resurrection, God will give His saints a new, immortal body.

Genesis 2:7 - "And the LORD God ...breathed into his nostrils the breath of life; and man became a living soul."

B | The Garden Of Eden

Adam was created before the Garden of Eden was planted. God put Adam in it afterward. Ezekiel 28:13 depicts Lucifer in the garden, too - before he sinned! Satan did not come to the garden from a failed pre-Adamite society of evil angels. He came sinless. All the sins of men and angels began in the garden. Utopias do not prevent sin. Your health, success and prosperity could be your greatest temptation. Beware!

Genesis 2:8 - "...the LORD God planted a garden eastward in Eden; and there he put the man whom he had formed."

B | Adam's Rib

God put Adam to sleep and performed surgery. He removed one of Adam's ribs and made a woman from it. From the bone marrow came Adam's DNA, making her essentially the first clone - a female version of Adam. An identical twin. Same eyes, same hair, same size. "So God created man in his own image, in the image of God created he him; male and female created he them," Genesis 1:27. Two people. One image.

Genesis 2:22 - "And the rib, which the LORD God had taken from man, made he a woman."

D | The Tree Of Knowledge

God did not want Adam and Eve to know evil in any way. He forbade Adam to partake of the Tree of the Knowledge of Good and Evil. God knows that bad lessons cannot be unlearned, and evil knowledge is never an asset but a liability. Whatever you learned from your mistakes would have been much better unlearned. Shun the very appearance of evil.

Genesis 2:17 - "...of the tree of the knowledge of good and evil, thou shalt not eat of it: for in the day that thou eatest thereof thou shalt surely die."

B | Eve

She must have been beautiful. I cannot imagine God creating less. From Adam's rib came his helpmate. Woman. Wo-Man (man with a womb). First wife. First mother. Satan deceived her. She transgressed, then handed a portion of the forbidden fruit to Adam. For that, God cursed womankind with pain in childbirth. Graciously however, the seed of the woman would one day conquer the foul Tempter: God's son, "...made of a woman."

Genesis 3:6 - "...she took of the fruit thereof, and did eat, and gave also unto her husband with her; and he did eat."

C | Obedience

In the Garden of Eden, God pronounced a blessing on Adam and Eve, coupled with commands to fill the earth and rule over it. Before Eve was created, however, God spoke singularly to Adam and commanded him not to eat of the fruit of the Tree of the Knowledge of Good and Evil. Therefore, the first virtue God required man to practice was obedience. Some things never change. Jesus said, "if you love me, keep my commandments." God STILL requires obedience.

Genesis 3:11 - "Hast thou eaten of the tree, whereof I commanded thee that thou shouldest not eat?"

B | The Tree Of The Knowledge Of Good And Evil

Adam and Eve really missed the point. The Tree of Life was standing near the Tree of the Knowledge of Good and Evil. Presumably, if they had eaten of the Tree of Life first, they would have lived forever. God did not want them to taste of the knowledge of evil. They chose evil over life.

Genesis 2:17 - "But of the tree of the knowledge of good and evil, thou shalt not eat of it: for in the day that thou eatest thereof thou shalt surely die."

B | The Forbidden Fruit

People commonly call it an apple, but nobody knows what the forbidden fruit was. It doesn't matter. It might have been anything. Tragically, people always think they will be better off when they get it, but that is NEVER the case. Lucifer tells all kinds of lies to tempt people with anything he can find, but obedience to God is ALWAYS more rewarding.

Genesis 3:5 "And God doth know that in the day ye eat thereof, then your eyes shall be opened, and ye shall be as gods, knowing good and evil."

B | The Serpent

This is not your ordinary snake. He talks. He is subtle. He has a hidden, sinister, diabolical agenda. Lucifer violated that poor mindless creature. How was the first woman on earth supposed to know that snakes do not talk? More importantly, how can YOU or I know when Satan enters into someone to deceive us? Lies. Lucifer's trademark is lies. "Hath God said...?" "Ye shall not surely die." There's your sign. Satan is ruthless and plays by nobody's rules.

Genesis 3:1 - "...the serpent was more subtil than any beast of the field."

Satan's Doom

The very first Bible prophecy was two-fold and awesome. Messiah would come, and Satan would be doomed! "The devil that deceived them was cast into the lake of fire and brimstone, ...and shall be tormented day and night for ever and ever," Revelation 20:10. John clearly said the Serpent was the Devil (Satan) in Revelation 12:9. God had told the serpent,

Genesis 3:14-15 - "I will put enmity between thee and the woman, and between thy seed and her seed; it shall bruise thy head, and thou shalt bruise his heel."

B | Thorns And Death

For Adam's sin, God cursed the ground to bring forth thorns and thistles. But there was more. Adam was sentenced to die and return to the dust from which he was created. Before he sinned, Adam might have lived forever. Now, life is hard, then you die. The great hope is beyond the grave. Are you ready?

Genesis 3:19 - "In the sweat of thy face shalt thou eat bread, till thou return unto the ground; for out of it wast thou taken: for dust thou art, and unto dust shalt thou return."

C | The Man Is Become As One Of Us

God wanted Adam to always be pure, untainted, and innocent. God knew that was the best life. He warned Adam not to eat of the Tree of the Knowledge of Good and Evil. But Lucifer taunted them saying, "Ye shall be AS GODS!" Adam and Eve both yielded. Till then, only God and Satan understood the sickening awfulness of sin. Nothing good comes out of sin. No sin is better than innocence. FLEE temptation!

Genesis 3:22 - "And the LORD God said, Behold, the man is become as one of us, to know good and evil."

D | Tree Of Life

Adam and Eve ate the forbidden fruit of the Tree of the Knowledge of Good and Evil, so God cast them out of the Garden. In the Heavenly paradise of God, the Tree of Life will bear twelve fruits continually for the healing of the nations who keep His commandments and enter the gates of that city (Revelation 22:2).

Genesis 3:24 - "So he drove out the man; and he placed at the east of the garden of Eden Cherubims, and a flaming sword which turned every way, to keep the way of the tree of life."

B | Cherub At The Gate

Apart from Lucifer, the first angels in the Bible were the Cherubims with the flaming sword that guarded the gate to Eden. Angels are said to be ministering spirits for those who shall be the heirs of salvation. Those Cherubs were preserving eternal life for those who will properly have it; for you and me.

Genesis 3:24 - "So he drove out the man; and he placed at the east of the garden of Eden Cherubims, and a flaming sword which turned every way, to keep the way of the tree of life."

A | Your Worship Must Be Doctrinally Correct

Adam and Eve's first son, Cain, voluntarily brought an offering to the LORD - fruit of the ground, a garden harvest. Their second son, Abel, also brought an offering to the LORD - the firstlings of his flock. The LORD respected Abel's blood offering but unexpectedly, He had no respect for Cain's. Cain was furious. God tried to correct him, but Cain would not be corrected. In rage, he murdered his brother. Cain failed to learn that you must worship God in Spirit and in Truth. Doctrinally incorrect worship will be rejected.

Genesis 4:5 - "Unto Cain and to his offering he had not respect."

C | The Risks Of Wrath

Anyone might have congratulated Cain for the beautiful offering of the fruit of his harvest that he presented to the Lord that day. But who could have predicted that God would ignore it and select instead the sacrificial lamb presented by Cain's brother, Abel? God arrested Cain for getting angry and admonished him to try again. But anger got the best of Cain, and he killed his brother. God cursed him. Can you control your anger? If not, sin lies at the door.

Genesis 4:6 - "And the LORD said unto Cain, Why art thou wroth?"

A | If Thou Doest Well, Shalt Thou Not Be Accepted?

Cain only had to look at Abel's sacrifice to quickly learn what was acceptable to God. But he was stubborn. He refused to change his form of worship to please God. Today, multitudes of professing Christians stubbornly refuse to change, even though they are doctrinally incorrect. They intend instead to force God to accept their worship from a heretical environment. But God will refuse it and they will be lost. Change your ways when necessary. Do what is right. Don't be hard-headed.

Genesis 4:7 - "If thou doest well, shalt thou not be accepted? and if thou doest not well, sin lieth at the door."

B | Cain And Abel

The firstborn human on earth became a murderer. How could it be? Cain gave a freewill offering to God; select produce from his crops. His brother, Abel, followed suit, sacrificing an animal from his flock. God loved Abel's blood sacrifice but not Cain's produce. Cain was furious. God said, "if you do well, you will be accepted." If not, sin lies at the door. Cain paid no attention to God's warning admonition. People get crazy and scary when they ignore God.

Genesis 4:8 - "...Cain rose up against Abel his brother, and slew him."

A | The Voice Of Thy Brother's Blood Crieth Unto Me

Cain ignored God's warning and killed his brother. God interrogated Cain, "Where is Abel thy brother?" Cain retorted, "I know not: Am I my brother's keeper?" Abel was already dead. "What hast thou done?" God pressed Cain for a confession, but Cain kept silent. Meanwhile, Abel's innocent blood was crying for vengeance. In Heaven, the souls of martyrs are now praying to be avenged (Revelation 6:10). Obviously, God has given both the blood and souls of martyrs a miraculous ability to pray for vengeance upon their murderers.

Genesis 4:10 - "The voice of thy brother's blood crieth unto me from the ground."

A | A Murderer's Prayer

Cain killed his brother, Abel, in cold blood. For his murderous act, God pronounced lifetime curses on him. Cain felt overwhelmed and feared that men would want to slay him in recompense. He pleaded with God, so God put a mark on him and forbade anyone to harm him. God would have been well-served to destroy Cain for his murder, but instead chose to give him another chance at life. God will have mercy on you, too.

Genesis 4:13 - "Cain said unto the LORD, My punishment is greater than I can bear."

A | Acknowledge God's Judgments

Cain discovered too late that his sins had cost him far more than he ever anticipated. He told God, "Thou hast driven me out this day from the face of the earth; and from thy face shall I be hid; and I shall be a fugitive and a vagabond in the earth; and it shall come to pass, that every one that findeth me shall slay me." If you are in sin, count the cost now, and repent before the price goes even higher.

Genesis 4:16 - "Cain went out from the presence of the LORD, and dwelt in the land of Nod."

B | Seth

Adam and Eve had two sons: Cain and Abel. The bad one killed the good one. Nothing is said about Adam and Eve's grief. But God was good to give them another child to make up for the loss of Abel. God is sensitive to our losses. He may not always provide an identical replacement, but He will always compensate with some act of mercy.

Genesis 4:25 - "Adam knew his wife again; and she bare a son, and called his name Seth: For God, said she, hath appointed me another seed instead of Abel, whom Cain slew."

A | When Men Began To Pray

Adam and Eve lost their second son, Abel, when Cain murdered him. God gave them another son, Seth. This is only the second generation of mankind, and here is where the Bible says men began to pray. Cain, the first murderer, uttered the first recorded prayer, "My punishment is greater than I can bear." God showed mercy. Take heart. Anybody can pray.

Genesis 4:26 - "To Seth, to him also there was born a son; and he called his name Enos: then began men to call upon the name of the LORD."

B | Enoch

The seventh man from Adam, Enoch, walked with God for three hundred years. He prophesied that the Lord would come with ten thousands of his saints to execute judgment and convince all the ungodly of their sins. Long before Noah's flood, Enoch saw Armageddon coming. Then "he was not, for God took him." Before he was translated, he had this testimony, that "he pleased God." Pleasing God is not rocket science. If Enoch could walk with God, so can we.

Genesis 5:24 - "Enoch walked with God: and he was not, for God took him."

A | Enoch Walked With God

What does it mean, "Enoch walked with God..."? Presumably, Enoch lived in continual fellowship with God. Continual communication. Constant contact. Daily devotions. You and I can walk with God, too. "That I may know him, and the power of his resurrection, and the fellowship of his sufferings," Philippians 3:10. Paul instructed us to "Pray without ceasing," I Thessalonians 5:17. "For our conversation is in heaven," Philippians 3:20. Walk with Him. Talk with Him. Have sweet communion with Him daily.

Genesis 5:22 - "And Enoch walked with God after he begat Methuselah three hundred years."

D | Enoch's Prophecy

Enoch was the fellow who walked with God, and God suddenly took him without him ever tasting death. Enoch was only seven generations from Adam, but he saw the great and final battle of Armageddon coming. What a fantastic revelation to have been received over 5,000 years ago! In the Spirit, Enoch foresaw Jesus conquering the world!

Jude 1:14-15 - "Behold, the Lord cometh with ten thousands of his saints, To execute judgment upon all, and to convince all that are ungodly among them of all their ungodly deeds which they have ungodly committed."

B | Methuselah

Methuselah lived longer than anyone else in the Bible. His name meant, "when he dies," suggesting that God may have waited on him for the flood to begin, because the calculations indicate he died the same year as Noah's flood. After the flood, men's lifespans were shortened. Genesis 6:3 says, "And the Lord said, 'My spirit shall not strive with man forever, for he is indeed flesh; yet his days shall be one hundred and twenty years.'"

Genesis 5:27 - "And all the days of Methuselah were nine hundred sixty and nine years: and he died."

B | Sons Of God And Daughters Of Men Bore Human Children

Too much conjecture has been added to this story. A simple statement, that "the sons of God came in unto the daughters of men, and they bare children..." has been amplified to mean that ANGELS had intercourse with WOMEN. Jesus said that in Heaven there is neither marrying nor giving in marriage. Angels do not breed - EVER! An angel cannot impregnate a human. There are no half-breed (half-angel, half-man) creatures on earth. We are all common humans. There is no reason to believe otherwise.

Genesis 6:4 - "The sons of God came in unto the daughters of men, and they bare children to them."

C | The Wickedness Of Man - Their Hearts Are Evil Continually

Who can guess the population of the earth in Noah's day? Hundreds of thousands? Millions? But God could only find one righteous man - Noah. What does that say about the rest of us? Our hearts are predisposed to evil. We are desperately wicked by nature. The "inherent goodness" of man is a delusion. Without God's Word to guide and His grace to forgive, we are all hopeless.

Genesis 6:5 - "And GOD saw that the wickedness of man was great in the earth, and that every imagination of the thoughts of his heart was only evil continually."

A | God Will Not Overlook Your Righteous Ways

"God saw that the wickedness of man was great in the earth, and that every imagination of the thoughts of his heart was only evil continually." Never forget that God is a discerner of your thoughts and intentions. You do not have to verbalize the things that are in your heart. God already knows. But He also knows if you are consecrated to do the right thing. God saw millions of wicked people, but He did not fail to discover the one remaining righteous man - Noah.

Genesis 6:8 - "But Noah found grace in the eyes of the LORD."

D | The Flood Foretold

The Bible does not say how long Noah spent building the ark. He was at least 500 before the commandment came and 600 when he entered the ark. Notwithstanding, anyone can guess that Noah needed many years to build an 800-foot wooden ship. Not coincidentally, the floods came as soon as he finished building. Noah gambled his life on God's Word and won! Likewise, we should heed prophetic warnings for our time!

Genesis 6:13 - "God said unto Noah, The end of all flesh is come before me; ...I will destroy them with the earth."

A | With Thee Will I Establish My Covenant

A man who walks and talks with God will have special favor. When God looked upon the earth, "all flesh had corrupted his way upon the earth." He told Noah, "I will destroy them with the earth. ...every thing that is in the earth shall die." But God had a different plan for Noah. "With thee will I establish my covenant; and thou shalt come into the ark, thou, and thy sons, and thy wife, and thy sons' wives." All this, for doing His will.

Genesis 6:22 - "Thus did Noah; according to all that God commanded him, so did he."

Noah

All the premises in this story are profound. The whole world was evil. God was grieved and angry. He swore to destroy them all. Noah was an isolated righteous man. God had mercy on Noah and made a plan for his salvation. God saved Noah's family along with some of each species of land animals. The flood cleansed the earth. God replenished the earth through Noah. Jesus will also cleanse the earth when He comes.

Matthew 24:37 - "But as the days of Noah were, so shall also the coming of the Son of man be."

A | You Must Hear And Obey The Voice Of God

If you think it is important that GOD hears YOUR voice when you pray, how much more important is it that YOU hear GOD's voice when He speaks? Some people do all the talking, but rarely, if ever, hear God's voice. Noah would not have survived if he had not both heard AND obeyed God's voice. "The LORD said unto Noah, Come thou and all thy house into the ark; for thee have I seen righteous before me in this generation."

Genesis 7:5,16 - "And Noah did according unto all that the LORD commanded him. ...and the LORD shut him in."

B | Noah's Ark

Noah's Ark is among the most controversial of all ancient stories. Today, top-secret government dossiers and political power-mongers deprive the public of evidence that almost certainly exists on Mt. Ararat in Turkey. Noah's Ark landed there. Satellite photos show suspicious objects. Expeditions claim to have seen it. Why is it forbidden to visit? Who built it? Why did he build it? Who planned and designed it? How did it get on the mountain? It was God's doing!

Genesis 7:16 - "they went in... as God had commanded him: and the LORD shut him in."

A | Run Into The Ark: Repent Before The Rains Begin

Peter called Noah "a preacher of righteousness, bringing in the flood upon the world of the ungodly ...making them an ensample unto those that after should live ungodly," 2 Peter 2:5-6. We do not know whether

Noah compelled men to come into the Ark, but his message of righteousness condemned them. Will your Pastor's preaching condemn you on Judgment Day, or will you run into the Ark? Run to Jesus and repent now, before He shuts the Ark.

Genesis 7:21,23 - "All flesh died that moved upon the earth, ...Noah only remained alive, and they that were with him in the ark."

A | God Remembered Noah

If Noah had lived an uneventful life, there would have been nothing for God to take note of. If Noah had ignored his Maker, lived selfishly, and wasted his substance on riotous living as other men had, God would have sentenced him to the same fate. But Noah was a preacher of righteousness. God remembered Noah's righteous words. If you want to be remembered on Judgment Day, speak righteous words.

Genesis 8:1-3,6 - "God remembered Noah ...and the rain from heaven was restrained ...the waters returned from off the earth ...at the end of forty days ...Noah opened the window of the ark."

A | Noah Built An Altar, Gave Offerings, And God Blessed.

Noah sent out a dove, but it found no dry ground. Seven days later, the dove found an olive leaf. Seven days later, the dove found dry ground. God spoke to Noah and told him and his family to leave the Ark. Noah built an altar and gave offerings to the LORD. When God delivers you, you should worship Him lavishly. Noah's offering drew a powerful response from God.

Genesis 8:21 - "The LORD smelled a sweet savour; and the LORD said in his heart, I will not again curse the ground any more for man's sake."

D | Replenish The Earth

God told Noah's sons to replenish the earth. Shem's descendants soon migrated to what is now known as Iran, Syria, Iraq and Turkey - and became the Middle Eastern nations. Ham's descendants are generally believed to have migrated to Africa. Japheth's descendants are principally European Caucasians; For example, Magog is in Southern Russia. Meshech and Tubal were founded in the region of modern Georgia. Ultimately, all nations descend from these three sons of Noah.

Genesis 9:1 - "God blessed Noah and his sons, and said unto them, Be fruitful, and multiply, and replenish the earth."

A | Blessed For Preaching Righteousness

We do not know what Noah preached, only that he was a preacher of righteousness. One solitary man effectively became the savior of the world. In his proclivity to declare righteousness, his words saved him, his family, and the future of humanity. For this, God blessed Noah and his sons. They inherited the entire earth. "By thy words thou shalt be justified, and by thy words thou shalt be condemned," Matthew 12:37. Learn from Noah. Preach righteousness.

Genesis 9:8-9 - "God spake unto Noah, and to his sons ...saying, ...I establish my covenant with you, and with your seed after you."

D | The Rainbow

After the great flood, God made a Covenant with Noah and all his descendants forever that He would never again destroy the world by a flood. He gave the Rainbow as a token and a reminder for perpetual generations. There may be local floods, but never a massive flood as in Noah's day. It won't be water, but fire next time.

Genesis 9:15 - "And I will remember my covenant, which is between me and you and every living creature of all flesh; and the waters shall no more become a flood to destroy all flesh."

B | Shem

The first son of Noah, Shem, is a very significant character. Shem and Japheth intervened to save their father's modesty when Ham discovered him drunk. Noah blessed Shem and Japheth for that. But Ham's descendants, the Canaanites, were cursed to serve the descendants of both Shem and Japheth. That is why Abraham was given the land of Canaan. Abraham descended from Eber (source of "Hebrew") who descended from Shem (source of "Semite"). Jesus Christ descended from Shem.

Genesis 9:26 - "Blessed be the LORD God of Shem; and Canaan shall be his servant."

A | Noah Blessed And Cursed His Descendants

Noah had three sons. All of modern civilization descended from them. "Of them was the whole earth overspread," Genesis 9:19. Noah cursed Ham's son, Canaan. "A servant of servants shall he be unto his brethren." Noah blessed the others through Shem and Japheth. One of

Shem's descendants, Abraham, became the progenitor of the nation of Israel and the spiritual father of all the faithful.

Genesis 9:26-27 - "He said, Blessed be the LORD God of Shem; and Canaan shall be his servant. God shall enlarge Japheth, and he shall dwell in the tents of Shem; and Canaan shall be his servant."

B | Nimrod

Nimrod was called "a mighty one in the earth," and "the mighty hunter before the LORD." His was the first kingdom mentioned in the Bible. It began with the Tower at Babel, then Erech, Accad, Calneh in the land of Shinar. Many outrageous myths exist about Nimrod, but nearly all references to him speak of rebellion. It is fair to say that Nimrod was one of the first to conduct military conquests and to be known as a tyrant dictator.

Genesis 10:8 - "And Cush begat Nimrod: he began to be a mighty one upon the earth."

A | A Mighty Hunter Before The Lord

Nimrod "began to be a mighty one in the earth, ...a mighty hunter before the LORD." Nimrod, presumed to be the driving force behind the Tower of Babel, and ultimately the Babylonian Empire, is one of the most legendary characters in antiquity. Much superstition and mysticism surrounds his name, but Nimrod's real legacy is the tyranny, rebellion and evil mysteries of Babylon. What is heroic in the eyes of men is often abominable in the eyes of God. What is your reputation "before the LORD"?

Genesis 10:9 - "Wherefore it is said, Even as Nimrod the mighty hunter before the LORD."

B | Asshur

Asshur was a person, a city (later called Nineveh), and the ancient Assyrian Empire. Its founders came from Babel and Nimrod, who grievously turned their backs on the God of their forefather, Noah. They worshipped the goddess Ishtar. Assyria eventually became a vicious foe of Israel for centuries. Mosul, Iraq, is now the center of that region, sandwiched between Damascus, Syria and Tehran, Iran. These modern Assyrians are prophetically doomed. In Isaiah 14:25, God swore to destroy an Assyrian Antichrist on His Holy Mount at Armageddon.

Genesis 10:11 - "Out of that land went forth Asshur, and builded Nineveh."

B | Peleg - The Earth Divided

Here is the lineage: Noah, Shem, Arphaxad, Salah, Eber, Peleg. Little is known of Peleg except that in his days the earth was divided. Some say that the continents of earth moved to their present positions then, but that is unfounded speculation. Peleg's birth was near the days of Nimrod and the Tower of Babel. That is where the earth was really divided. God divided their languages.

Genesis 10:25 - "...unto Eber were born two sons: the name of the one was Peleg; for in his days the earth was divided."

A | Let Us Make Brick, Build A City, Make A Name

The ambitions of the people who built the Tower of Babel sound amazingly similar to Satan's ambitions. In Isaiah 14, Satan said, "I will ascend into heaven, I will exalt my throne above the stars of God: I will sit also upon the mount of the congregation, I will ascend above the heights of the clouds; I will be like the most High." Such proud, arrogant words are doomed from the start.

Genesis 11:3-4 - "Let us make brick, ...let us build us a city and a tower, whose top may reach unto heaven; and let us make us a name."

D | The Fall Of Babel

Nimrod spearheaded the project at the Tower of Babel. Their purposes were ambitious: reach Heaven, make a name for themselves, prevent being scattered abroad. Sounds like the Devil's dream, too. But all the purposes of men will be disappointed. All man-made kingdoms will fall to the Kingdom of Jesus Christ at Armageddon.

Genesis 11:4 - "And they said, Go to, let us build us a city and a tower, whose top may reach unto heaven; and let us make us a name, lest we be scattered abroad upon the face of the whole earth."

A | God Spoils The Godless Ambitions Of Men

One of the most deceptive "religious" practices today is "positive affirmation." It revolves around this concept, "If the mind of man can conceive it and believe it, it can achieve it." There is no God in the midst of such thinking. That is humanistic at its core. It is spiritualistic, mind-over-matter arrogance. God will someday come down and destroy everything built on that premise.

Genesis 11:5,9 - "The LORD came down to see the city and the tower, which the children of men builded. ...and from thence did the LORD scatter them abroad upon the face of all the earth."

D | Confusion Of Tongues

One of the greatest ironies of all God's dealings with man is the contrast between the Tower of Babel and the Day of Pentecost. At Babel, God confused their tongues and SCATTERED the people so they could not continue to work together. But on the Day of Pentecost, God caused 120 believers to speak in unknown tongues to EMPOWER and UNIFY them. What is confusion to man is crystal clear to God.

Genesis 11:9 - "Therefore is the name of it called Babel; because the LORD did there confound the language of all the earth."

B | Arphaxad

Born two years after Noah's flood, Arphaxad was the father of Ura and Kesed who founded the ancient city of Ur of the Chaldees (according to an ancient extra-biblical source found among the Dead Sea Scrolls). In 1927, British archaeologist Leonard Woolley discovered the ancient ruins of Ur between Basra and Nasiriyah, Iraq, near Kuwait. Abraham came from there. Discoveries included vast riches of Sumerian artifacts and ruins from the days of Belshazzar and Nebuchadnezzar of Babylon.

Genesis 11:10 - "Shem was an hundred years old, and begat Arphaxad two years after the flood."

B | Terah

Abraham's father took his family from Ur of the Chaldees to Haran, Assyria (modern Turkey) - a prosperous community at that time at the crossroads between Damascus, Nineveh and Carchemish. People there worshipped the moon god Sin. God told Abraham to get out of there. Good advice.

Genesis 11:31 - "And Terah took Abram his son, and Lot the son of Haran his son's son, and Sarai his daughter in law, his son Abram's wife; and they went forth with them from Ur of the Chaldees, ...and they came unto Haran, and dwelt there."

B | Abraham

Abraham was an Iraqi. He migrated to Syria. God called him to Israel. At least that is how it would look on today's map. God called Abraham to raise up a nation that would glorify Jehovah. He might have done it in Iraq or in Syria, but He didn't. God planted Jews in Israel. Abraham would roll over in his grave if he knew all the hatred and warmongering among his grandchildren.

Genesis 12:1 - "The LORD had said unto Abram, Get thee out of thy country, ...unto a land that I will shew thee."

D | A Great Nation

Abraham and Sarai were in their seventies and still childless when God promised that Abraham would become a great nation. Four centuries later, over a million of his descendants marched out of bondage in Egypt and made their way to the very land God promised Abraham. Within another 120 years, Kings David and Solomon would preside over one of the most glorious kingdoms in the history of man.

Genesis 12:2 - "And I will make of thee a great nation, and I will bless thee, and make thy name great; and thou shalt be a blessing."

C | Name Changes

God changed Abram ("Exalted Father") to Abraham ("Father of Many Nations"). He changed Sarai ("Princess") to Sarah ("Princess of All"). God changed Jacob ("Supplanter") to Israel ("Prince with God"). God caused the names of the twelve tribes to be engraved in precious stones on the high priest's garment. Simon ("Reed") became Peter ("Rock"). Saul ("Prayed For") became Paul ("Humble"). In Heaven, God will give His saints a new name written in a White Stone. There the wicked will be forgotten because THEIR NAMES will be BLOTTED OUT.

Genesis 12:2 - "I will bless thee, and make thy name great."

D | Abraham's Blessing

Over 4,000 years ago, God called Abram from Ur of the Chaldees (now in southern Iraq). For forsaking both homeland and family roots, God promised to make a great nation to which He would impart divine blessing. The blessing traced through Isaac and Jacob (Israel). Today, everyone who harms Israel (including the United States) will be cursed for it. If you want God's blessing, bless Israel.

Genesis 12:3 - " I will bless them that bless thee, and curse him that curseth thee: and in thee shall all families of the earth be blessed."

B | Lot

God instructed Abraham to get "out of thy country, and from thy kindred." Why did his nephew, Lot, go with him? Lot's father, Haran, died in Ur. Perhaps Abraham felt responsible for him. But Lot's herdsmen strove with Abraham's. Abraham eventually had to separate. Their collective herds were too large for the land. Abraham had to go to war to protect Lot when Sodom was attacked. Then Lot's wife was destroyed. His daughters committed incest. Maybe Abraham should never have taken Lot with him.

Genesis 12:4 - "So Abram departed, ...and Lot went with him."

D | Shechem

The first Canaanite city Abram visited was Shechem (Sichem) - now known as Nablus. Two mountains there, Gerizim and Ebal are the Mounts of Blessing and Cursing where Joshua read the Pentateuch out loud to the Israelites. Today, it is the headquarters of several Palestinian and Muslim terrorist organizations. God promised it to Abraham, Isaac and Jacob.

Genesis 12:6-7 - "Abram passed through the land unto the place of Sichem, ...and the LORD appeared unto Abram, and said, Unto thy seed will I give this land: and there builded he an altar unto the LORD, who appeared unto him."

D | The Promised Land

God instructed Abraham to "Arise, walk through the land in the length of it and in the breadth of it; for I will give it unto thee." We now call it the "Promised Land." Although many kings, nations, armies and terrorists want to steal this land from Israel, God is the original deed-holder, and every square inch will return to Him when He returns. Those who stole it from Israel will be destroyed.

Genesis 12:7 - "And the LORD appeared unto Abram, and said, Unto thy seed will I give this land."

A | Abram Called Upon The Name Of The LORD

Noah was the first person mentioned who built an altar unto the LORD, and that happened AFTER God saved him from the Flood. Abram was the second person mentioned who built an altar unto the LORD, and that happened AFTER Abram moved into the Promised Land. Before we even think to build an altar and pray, God has already worked countless miracles in our lives.

Genesis 12:8 - "He removed from thence unto a mountain on the east of Bethel, and pitched his tent, ...and there he builded an altar unto the LORD, and called upon the name of the LORD."

A | Abram Practiced Deception

Famine plagued Canaan, so Abram went to Egypt for provisions. Sarai was a beautiful woman, and Abram feared the Egyptians would kill him to take her. "Say, I pray thee, thou art my sister: that it may be well with me for thy sake; and my soul shall live." Predictably, Pharaoh's princes reported her to Pharaoh, who called her to his house. But God plagued Pharaoh's house until he discovered the deception and made her return to Abram. Do not lie. Lies breed trouble. Trust God in perilous situations.

Genesis 12:20 - "Pharaoh commanded his men ...and they sent him away."

A | Abraham's Prayer

God called Abram to forsake all and follow Him. At Bethel, God made great promises that would eventually bring enormous blessings. Meanwhile, a famine drove Abraham down to Egypt temporarily. When he returned to Canaan, he sought out the place where God met him in the beginning. There, he called on the Lord, attempting to restore his original contact with God. Smart move! Always go back to God.

Genesis 13:4 - "Unto the place of the altar, which he had made there at the first: and there Abram called on the name of the LORD."

C | Lot Pitched His Tent Toward Sodom

There is a lot to be said for how you pitch your tent. Our predispositions forecast our destiny. Our attitudes presage our behavior. If we have an eye for the world, we will eventually follow it. If Abraham had kept his mind on his past, he might have gone back to Ur of the Chaldees. Lot was already in trouble by the time he pitched his tent toward Sodom. Be careful which way you face. Shun the very appearance of evil.

Genesis 13:12 - "...and Lot dwelled in the cities of the plain, and pitched his tent toward Sodom."

A | Why Did Lot Not See The Perils Of Sodom?

I can think of nothing more tragic than spiritual blindness. Isaiah spoke of evil men whom God "hath shut their eyes, that they cannot see; and their hearts, that they cannot understand." Isaiah 44:18. Why could Lot not see that Sodom was a TERRIBLE place to move to? Why does this generation move closer and closer to Sodom, when all of history testifies to its debauchery and damnation? Pray that God will never let you become spiritually blind. See the evil and flee from it!

Genesis 13:13 - "But the men of Sodom were wicked and sinners before the LORD exceedingly."

D | Canaan Land

Abraham lived almost 2000 years before Christ. The land was Canaan. Many various tribes dwelled there, but God gave it to Abraham. The earth is the Lord's. He can give it to anyone He wants. Although 4000 years later, God will soon take the entire land by force.

Genesis 13:14-15 - "And the LORD said unto Abram, ...Lift up now thine eyes, and look from the place where thou art northward, and southward, and eastward, and westward: For all the land which thou seest, to thee will I give it, and to thy seed for ever."

D | Hebron

Hebron is 18 miles south of Jerusalem, second-most Jewish city on earth. The king of Hebron launched an offensive against Joshua but lost. Joshua gave Hebron to Caleb. Abraham, Sarah, Isaac, Rebekah, Jacob and Leah are buried there. David ruled there. Today, 166,000 Palestinians and 700 Jews live there. That Israel is giving Hebron away is outrageous! Jesus will recapture it at Armageddon.

Genesis 13:17-18 - "Walk through the land, ...for I will give it unto thee. Then Abram removed his tent, and came and dwelt in the plain of Mamre, which is in Hebron."

A | Abram Worshipped At Hebron After God Promised Land

After Lot departed, the LORD told Abram, "Lift up now thine eyes, and look ...For all the land which thou seest, to thee will I give it, and to thy seed for ever. I will make thy seed as the dust of the earth: ...Arise, walk through the land ...for I will give it unto thee." This was a sacred, historic event. Abram built an altar and worshipped God. Recognize the occasions when God is blessing and worship Him.

Genesis 13:18 - "Abram ...dwelt in the plain of Mamre, which is in Hebron, and built there an altar unto the LORD."

B | Eber The Hebrew

The world knows the Jews as Hebrews. The Hebrew language is the only spoken language ever to return from extinction (in the 19th century), after being eradicated during the Diaspora (dispersion) of Israel. Hebrew has continued to be a major written language since antiquity, largely because of the Old Testament. Today, it is the official language of the State of Israel. The word "Hebrew" derives from Eber, great-grandson of Shem (Noah's son), and grandfather of Abraham. Jesus spoke from Heaven to Saul in the Hebrew tongue.

Genesis 14:13 - "...Abram the Hebrew."

B | First War In The Bible

Lot pitched his tent toward Sodom. It was well-watered like the Garden of Eden, in the green plains of the Jordan River (Genesis 13:10-11). The local cities were under tribute twelve years to Persians (modern Iran) and Chaldeans (modern Iraq). The cities revolted against tribute, but the revolt failed. Sodom was ransacked. Lot was carried away captive. Abraham, with 318 warriors from his household, chased them to near Damascus.

Genesis 14:16 - "And he brought back all the goods, and also brought again his brother Lot, and his goods, and the women also, and the people."

B | Melchizedek

Abraham warred against (Iraq) and (Iran) to avenge their siege on Lot and the city of Sodom. He recovered people and possessions. Melchizedek brought bread, wine and blessings for Abraham, who gave him tithes of everything recovered. This Melchizedek, "King of Salem, Priest of the Most High God," was not Christ, but a type. Both were king and priest of Jeru-Salem. Melchizedek's offering of bread and wine portended Jesus' offering body and blood at Calvary.

Psalms 110:4 - "The LORD hath sworn, and will not repent, Thou art a priest for ever after the order of Melchizedek."

A | The Blessing Of Melchizedek

When Abraham and his men pursued Chedorlaomer, he acted as a savior and redeemer for Lot and his family. For Abraham's good deeds, Melchizedek, King and Priest of Salem, "brought forth bread and wine: ...and blessed him." Melchizedek was NOT Christ, but a profound TYPE of Christ. Melchizedek was a mysterious person with no known lineage. In giving bread and wine, Melchizedek typologically gave Abraham the body and blood of Jesus Christ. A Savior for a savior.

Genesis 14:18 - "Melchizedek king of Salem brought forth bread and wine: and he was the priest of the most high God. And he blessed him."

A | I Have Lift Up My Hand To The Lord

You can live and die without acknowledging God if you so choose. You can do as you please and completely ignore God and His will. But Abraham lived and died before the Lord. From his earliest days, Abram made vows to God and lived by them. In a time when no man considered the Lord, that made Abraham the apple of God's eye.

Genesis 14:22 - "Abram said to the king of Sodom, I have lift up mine hand unto the LORD, the most high God, the possessor of heaven and earth, ...I will not take any thing that is thine."

D | Shield And Reward

After Abraham heroically retrieved the hostages and spoils from the war against Sodom, Melchizedek blessed him. More significantly, the LORD appeared to Abraham in a vision and gave him priceless assurances. God promised to be his Shield. Divine protection! What an amazing guarantee! Better than angelic guardians; GOD HIMSELF would deflect the attacks against Abraham! No wonder his posterity (both Israel and the Church) CANNOT BE ANNIHILATED, no matter how savage their enemies. And the reward? God Himself became his friend. Incomparable!

Genesis 15:1 - "Fear not, Abram: I am thy shield, and thy exceeding great reward."

A | What Will You Give Me?

Sometimes a believer knows in his heart that God will provide, but cannot imagine how that provision will come. Abraham boldly put the question to God, and God answered him very precisely. We should always have peace in our hearts, whether or not God reveals His future plan for our lives, but it is not necessarily wrong to ask God to reveal it to us. Ask!

Genesis 15:2 - "And Abram said, Lord GOD, what wilt thou give me, seeing I go childless, and the steward of my house is this Eliezer of Damascus?"

D | A Son For Abraham

Abraham and Sarai were old and barren, but God can work with anything. He resurrected many barren wombs in Bible days and still does. In choosing Abraham, God was fulfilling a commitment made to the Devil in the Garden - a Seed of the Woman would bruise Satan. God chose Abraham to be progenitor of that Righteous Seed. God's high calling overcomes all obstacles.

Genesis 15:4 - "...the word of the LORD came unto him, saying, This shall not be thine heir; but he that shall come forth out of thine own bowels shall be thine heir."

D | Abraham's Posterity

God told Abraham that his seed would be as countless as the stars. Without doubt, there have been millions of Jews born throughout the centuries since that prophecy. But wait! All born-again believers in Jesus Christ; "...they which are of faith, the same are the CHILDREN OF ABRAHAM," Galatians 3:7. That adds many millions more! God keeps His promises.

Genesis 15:5 - "And he brought him forth abroad, and said, Look now toward heaven, and tell the stars, if thou be able to number them: and he said unto him, So shall thy seed be."

A | Abram Believed In The Lord And Was Counted Righteous

Abram lamented that he had no child, and that his servant, Eliezer, would be his heir. But God said, "This shall not be thine heir; but he that shall come forth out of thine own bowels shall be thine heir." Paul observed that Abram, "staggered not at the promise of God through unbelief; but was strong in faith, ...being fully persuaded that, what he had promised, he was able also to perform, And therefore it was imputed to him for righteousness," Romans 4:21-22

Genesis 15:6 - "He believed in the LORD; and he counted it to him for righteousness."

B | Ur Of The Chaldees

Not all scholars agree, but the prevailing consensus is that Ur was in southern Mesopotamia - Iraq. Skeptics argue that the story of the Garden of Eden and Noah's Flood evolved from ancient Sumerian mythology of that region. Those bizarre myths were concocted after the flood by Noah's godless descendants. Their polytheistic pagan beliefs greatly offended God. That is why He called monotheistic Abram out and blessed him.

Genesis 15:7 - "I am the LORD that brought thee out of Ur of the Chaldees, to give thee this land to inherit it."

A | Whereby Shall I Know?

The terms of your relationship with God are very much up to you. If you want to stay aloof and presume upon His good graces with a never-may-care attitude about what He specifically wants to do in your life, that is your prerogative. But Abraham wanted to know exactly what God was going to do and how He would do it. When God made Covenant with him, Abraham wanted to know all the details. That is the heart of a real Patriarch.

Genesis 15:8 - "And he said, Lord GOD, whereby shall I know that I shall inherit it?"

A | Just Do As You Are Told

Abram asked God for a sign to confirm the Covenant. God called for a three-year-old heifer, a three-year-old she-goat, a three-year-old ram, a turtledove and a young pigeon. Without questioning, Abram prepared all those animals for sacrifice. Most of us would have asked God a thousand questions about why we must do such an odd thing. Abram simply obeyed. God responded profoundly. After you have prayed, just do as you are told.

Genesis 15:12,17 - "A deep sleep fell upon Abram; ...behold a smoking furnace, and a burning lamp that passed between those pieces."

D | Egyptian Bondage Prophesied

Believer, learn the way God operates! From the first, God warned Abraham that his descendants would suffer. We should not count it strange concerning the fiery trials of our lives. God ALWAYS puts His people to the test!

Genesis 15:13-14 - "And he said unto Abram, Know of a surety that thy seed shall be a stranger in a land that is not theirs, and shall serve them; and they shall afflict them four hundred years; And also that nation, whom they shall serve, will I judge: and afterward shall they come out with great substance."

D | Horror Of Great Darkness

Abraham spread a sacrificial offering before the Lord - a goat, lamb, turtledove and pigeon. At sundown, deep sleep and a horror of great darkness fell on him. God revealed a great plan foretelling Egyptian bondage and the birth of a nation.

Genesis 15:13-14 - "Know of a surety that thy seed shall be a stranger in a land that is not theirs, and shall serve them; and they shall afflict them four hundred years; And also that nation, whom they shall serve, will I judge: and afterward shall they come out with great substance."

D | God's Covenant With Abraham

Noah's descendants turned their hearts to other gods who were no gods. God Almighty called Abram away from them to worship and serve one true God. For his obedience, God promised Abraham an impressive earthly inheritance - a VAST HOMELAND for his posterity. Modern enemies oppose it, but God will make it so when Jesus Christ returns.

Genesis 15:18 - "In the same day the LORD made a covenant with Abram, saying, Unto thy seed have I given this land, from the river of Egypt unto the great river, the river Euphrates."

B | The Euphrates River

The Euphrates River flowed through the Garden of Eden. Abraham traversed it from Ur to Haran, Assyria. God promised Abraham's seed would possess everything from the Nile River to the Euphrates, including Lebanon, Syria and Iraq. A World War will break out along the Euphrates - the Sixth Trumpet War of Revelation 9. 1/3 of mankind will die. Kings from the East will cross a dry Euphrates to face Jesus at Armageddon.

Deuteronomy 11:24 - "...from the wilderness and Lebanon, from the river, the river Euphrates, even unto the uttermost sea shall your coast be."

B | Promised Borders

The land promised to Abraham extends from the Egyptian Nile and Mediterranean Sea to the Euphrates River. The Euphrates flows through

Turkey, Syria and Iraq, merging with the Tigris down the Iranian border. Today, Ishmaelites are fighting viciously for it, but God promised it to Isaac (Genesis 26:3) and Israel (Genesis 28:13). This Biblical clash of civilizations is apocalyptic. Jesus and His immortals will slaughter Israel's enemies in "shock and awe" at Armageddon.

Genesis 15:18 - "...the LORD made a covenant with Abram, saying, Unto thy seed have I given this land."

B | Hagar The Egyptian

Some people argue that Arabs are not Ishmael's descendants because they presume that his mother Hagar was a black Egyptian given to Abraham by Pharaoh. But Ishmael's father Abraham was the first Jew. Mohammed corrupted the story of Ishmael, claiming that Ishmael and Abraham built the Kaaba in Mecca. Preposterous! For centuries, Kaaba was a pagan temple of idols. Abraham sent Hagar and Ishmael AWAY to Paran, a wilderness site where Moses and Israel later camped. Neither Abraham, Hagar nor Ishmael ever went to Mecca.

Genesis 16:1 - "...she had an handmaid, an Egyptian, whose name was Hagar."

A | Going Against God's Plan

God promised Abram on numerous occasions that He would give him and Sarai seed as the stars for number. But years passed and Sarai had no children. She sovereignly declared that Abram should bear a child by Hagar, her maid. "Abram hearkened to the voice of Sarai." Just like Sarai, we open our mouths and contradict God, when we should remain silent and wait on God. We taint the miracle and bring future calamities upon ourselves.

Genesis 16:4 - "He went in unto Hagar, and she conceived: and when she saw that she had conceived, her mistress was despised in her eyes."

A | The Lord Judge Between Me And Thee

Sarai made a tragic mistake by giving Hagar to Abram. We have only to consider the Islamic threat to modern society to remind us how one person's mistake can produce horrific results. The Ishmaelites would never have existed except for Sarai's unbelief. But Sarai paid a painful price. From the day Hagar learned she was pregnant, she despised Sarai. Sarai tried to put the blame on Abram for going through with the scheme, but the damage was irreversible. Only God could judge the matter.

Genesis 16:5 - "Sarai said unto Abram, My wrong be upon thee: ...the LORD judge between me and thee."

A | Hagar Talked With The Angel Of The LORD

Because Hagar vehemently despised Sarai, Sarai sent her away. Hagar fled into the wilderness in desperate confusion. The Angel of the Lord visited her. She admitted to him, "I flee from the face of my mistress Sarai." God already knew that. Even in the most complicated situations, God is willing to help, if you will cooperate.

Genesis 16:9-11 - "The angel of the LORD said unto her, Return to thy mistress, and submit thyself under her hands. ...I will multiply thy seed exceedingly, ...[thou] shalt bear a son, and shalt call his name Ishmael; because the LORD hath heard thy affliction."

D | Prophecies To The Ishmaelites

Sarah made a tragic mistake when she gave Hagar to Abraham for a surrogate wife. God fully intended to give Sarah a child but not by Hagar. Hagar and her child had to leave. The Angel of the LORD named him Ishmael and promised he would become an innumerable multitude. Today, the Ishmaelites comprise most of the Arab world, predominately Muslim.

Genesis 16:12 - "And he will be a wild man; his hand will be against every man, and every man's hand against him; and he shall dwell in the presence of all his brethren."

A | Hagar Talked To JEHOVAH

After the Angel of the LORD gave instructions to Hagar, "she called the name of the LORD that spake unto her." The name of the LORD in the 3400-year-old Hebrew manuscript is "JHWH," "Jehovah," which is commonly rendered "LORD" in the Authorized King James Version of the Bible. Hagar believed she had SEEN Him (an angelic theophany). Muslims, take NOTE! Hagar worshipped Jehovah, NOT ALLAH! It is written.

Genesis 16:13 - "She called the name of the LORD that spake unto her, Thou God seest me: for she said, Have I also here looked after him that seeth me?"

D | Father Of Many Nations

God told Abraham that he would be the father of many nations. Through his natural son, Isaac, came the nation of Israel, which later divided into the northern kingdom of Israel and the southern kingdom of Judah. From his surrogate child, Ishmael, it is difficult to say exactly how many nations descended, since Ishmaelites comprise a large segment of the Arab world among the nations of the Middle East. Thirdly, the Gentile CHURCH is a Holy Nation descended from the faith of Abraham.

Genesis 17:4 - "...and thou shalt be a father of many nations."

D | Father Of Many Kings

Abram means "Exalted Father." God changed his name to Abraham, "Father of Multitudes." Four kings, Saul, Ishbosheth, David, and Solomon ruled a united monarchy. Nineteen kings ruled Israel. Twenty kings ruled Judah. When Jesus rules as King of Kings from Jerusalem, multitudes of saints will rule the world as kings under Him - sons of Abraham!

Genesis 17:5-6 - "...thy name shall be Abraham; for a father of many nations have I made thee. And I will make thee exceeding fruitful, and I will make nations of thee, and KINGS SHALL COME OUT OF THEE."

B | Canaan

The significance of the land of Canaan dates back to Noah. Ham discovered Noah drunk then told his brothers. Noah blessed Shem and Japheth for protecting his modesty but cursed Ham and his son Canaan. Canaan would become Shem's servant. As Shem's descendant, Abraham would become Canaan's master. That is why God gave the land of Canaan to Abraham. It included Sidon, Jerusalem, Gaza, Sodom, Galilee, Damascus and much more.

Genesis 17:8 - "I will give unto thee, and to thy seed after thee, ...all the land of Canaan, for an everlasting possession."

D | Circumcision

From the time of Abraham, Jewish males were circumcised in the foreskin of their flesh to confirm their covenant relationship with God. The ultimate purpose of circumcision was to VALIDATE the lineage of the Messiah, proving that He was descended from Abraham. Since Jesus Christ fulfilled the redemption plan, circumcision is no longer necessary. "Jesus Christ was a minister of the circumcision for the truth of God, to confirm the promises made unto the fathers," Romans 15:8.

Genesis 17:11 - "Ye shall circumcise the flesh of your foreskin; and it shall be a token of the covenant betwixt me and you."

D | Ishmael's Circumcision

Even though Abraham circumcised Ishmael when the boy was thirteen years old, Ishmael's descendants do not officially practice circumcision as a matter of their religious faith today. The Koran, which defines the religion of the Ishmaelites, does not actually teach circumcision. A small percentage of Muslims practice circumcision. This is one of many evidences that they are not the true heirs of the Abrahamic Covenant. Messiah Himself had to be circumcised to fulfill the Covenant.

Genesis 17:11 - "Ye shall circumcise the flesh of your foreskin; and it shall be a token of the covenant betwixt me and you."

B | Sarai

The story of Sarai vastly outweighs the story of Hagar, as the story of Isaac outweighs the story of Ishmael. This Biblical story is diabolically perverted by the Koran. All God's promises and dealings with Abraham hinged upon his having a child by Sarai, not Hagar! God's Covenant with Abraham would descend through his proper child, Isaac, not the surrogate child, Ishmael.

Genesis 17:16 - "And I will bless her, and give thee a son also of her: yea, I will bless her, and she shall be a mother of nations; kings of people shall be of her."

A | Abraham Fell On His Face And Laughed At God

God changed Sarai's name to Sarah and told Abraham, "I will bless her, and give thee a son also of her." But Abraham fell on his face and laughed. He was 100! She was 90! Abraham, "Father of the Faithful," was overcome with doubt for the moment, even laughing in God's face. Our carnal minds cannot comprehend God's supernatural abilities. Mercifully, God gives us faith to believe.

Genesis 17:17-18 - "Shall a child be born unto him that is an hundred years old? and shall Sarah, that is ninety years old, bear? ...O that Ishmael might live before thee!"

B | Ishmael

This story is enormously important today. One-fourth of the world's population (Muslims) believe God's Abrahamic Covenant was through

Ishmael, not Isaac. But Ishmael was a surrogate child. His mother despised Sarai. Ishmael mocked Sarai. They both had bad attitudes. That is why they were cast away. God TOLD Abraham to put them away. God said Ishmael's descendants would be many, wild, and against every man. Abraham circumcised Ishmael at age 13, but today the Islamic Koran does not even teach circumcision.

Genesis 17:21 - "But my covenant will I establish with Isaac, which Sarah shall bear unto thee."

D | God's Covenant With Isaac

Mohammed diabolically convinced his followers that Ishmael was the rightful heir to God's Covenant with Abraham. But Ishmael was surrogate-born of Sarah's servant. Isaac was legitimately born of Abraham's proper wife. God explicitly established the everlasting Covenant with Isaac and his descendants. Moses put it in writing 3,400 years ago - 2,000 years before Mohammed was born.

Genesis 17:19 - "God said, Sarah thy wife shall bear thee a son indeed; and thou shalt call his name Isaac: and I will establish my covenant with him for an everlasting covenant, and with his seed after him."

A | Restrict Your Prayers To The Will Of God

God reminded Abram that He still planned to give Sarai a child, but Abram was emotionally attached to Ishmael. He told the LORD, "O that Ishmael might live before thee!" God consented to bless and multiply Ishmael's seed. But 3000 years later, most of Ishmael's descendants are Arab Muslims who call the Bible story a lie. We often breed treacherous outcomes by clinging to people that God wants us to let go of. Let God choose your friends.

Genesis 17:20-21 - "As for Ishmael, ...I have blessed him, ...and I will make him a great nation. But my covenant will I establish with Isaac."

A | He Left Off Talking With Him

God permanently settled the matter with Abraham in two fundamental declarations. ONE, He would bless Ishmael and his descendants. TWO, the Abrahamic Covenant must be THROUGH ISAAC, Sarah's future son. If you have an issue with God, you may freely make your case as Abraham did in behalf of Ishmael. But after God answers, His verdict must stand. Put your arguments and excuses away. The conversation is over. Let God have His way. It is the only wise conclusion. God's ways are higher than yours.

Genesis 17:22 - "He left off talking with him, and God went up from Abraham."

A | Turn Words Into Deeds

You can pray. You can negotiate with God. You can make your case and ask God to do whatever it is that you want or need. But after God answers and reveals to you the terms of His blessing, it is up to you to follow through and do the will of God. For Abraham, the Covenant blessing of God was predicated upon his circumcising every male in his household.

Genesis 17:23 - "Abraham took ...every male among the men of Abraham's house; and circumcised the flesh of their foreskin in the selfsame day, as God had said unto him."

D | Hagar's Exile

Islam viciously contradicts many Biblical truths concretely established for 2,000 years before Mohammed was ever born. The Bible says Ishmael still lived with Abraham and Sarah at THIRTEEN. The Koran says Angel Gabriel took Hagar and SUCKLING BABY Ishmael on a flying horse (Al-Buraq) to a well named ZamZam at Mecca, Saudi Arabia where they say ABRAHAM built the Kaaba (House of Allah) around a meteorite stone on a foundation built by ADAM and EVE! Loathsome lies.

Genesis 17:25 - "Ishmael his son was thirteen years old, when he was circumcised in the flesh of his foreskin."

D | Angels On Assignment

Three angels visited Abraham. One was the Angel of the LORD speaking as the oracle of the invisible God. He declared that Sarah would bear a son within a year. The other two went to judge sinful Sodom. God blessed His favored (Abraham) and cursed His despised (Sodom). God visits those who sacrifice their lives to His purpose.

Genesis 18:2,17 - "...three men stood by him: and when he saw them, he ran to meet them from the tent door, and bowed himself toward the ground. ...and the LORD said, Shall I hide from Abraham that thing which I do?"

A | He Ran To Meet Them And Bowed Himself To The Ground

The angels of God came to visit Abraham. "When he saw them, he ran to meet them from the tent door, and bowed himself toward the ground."

Our generation is almost devoid of such reverence. When is the last time you saw someone bowing on their face or on their knees to pray? Be extremely careful not to be crass or irreverent in the Presence of the Lord. Don't miss your opportunity to make intercession. Run. Bow.

Genesis 18:3 - "My Lord, if now I have found favour in thy sight, pass not away, I pray thee, from thy servant."

B | Dinner With God

When the Angel of the LORD showed up with two other angels at Abraham's door, Abraham showed them extreme hospitality. When Jesus comes to your house, will you welcome Him lavishly? "Behold, I stand at the door, and knock: if any man hear my voice, and open the door, I will come in to him, and will sup with him, and he with me," Revelation 3:20.

Genesis 18:8 - "He took butter, and milk, and the calf which he had dressed, and set it before them; and he stood by them under the tree, and they did eat."

D | The Time Of Life

Sarah was ninety years old when the LORD told Abraham she would conceive. They both laughed. But God had the last laugh. He ordered them to call the baby Isaac - "laughter." God works on a schedule, but we do not always know His schedule unless He chooses to tell us what it is. If God says, "nine months from now," get ready!

Genesis 18:14 - "Is any thing too hard for the LORD? At the time appointed I will return unto thee, according to the time of life, and Sarah shall have a son."

A | Is Any Thing To Hard For The LORD?

You simply cannot afford to forget that God created all of this from NOTHING! His infinite, invisible, eternal Spirit pre-dates everything in the universe. Stars. Galaxies. Planets. Plants. Animals. Humans. Fish. Water. Light. Flowers. Sights and sounds, tastes and smells. Miracles beyond our ability to even catalogue. So the next time you have a need that seems difficult-to-impossible, cast your doubts away. Jesus said, "Whatsoever ye shall ask in my name, that will I do, that the Father may be glorified in the Son," John 14:13.

Genesis 18:14 - "Is any thing too hard for the LORD?"

A | God Exposed Sarah's Unbelief

The LORD asked Abraham where Sarah was, although He certainly already knew. "In the tent," which was behind him. The angel said, "Sarah thy wife shall have a son." Sarah heard it and laughed within herself. "After I am waxed old shall I have pleasure, my lord being old also?" The LORD asked Abraham, "Wherefore did Sarah laugh?" God exposed her private doubts. It is better for God to expose your doubts than allow them to prevent a miracle.

Genesis 18:15 - "Sarah denied, saying, I laughed not; for she was afraid. And he said, Nay; but thou didst laugh."

A | Shall I Hide From Abraham That Thing Which I Do?

Abraham had great stature with God. That is a remarkable fact, especially when you consider that virtually no one else on earth had a relationship with God in those days. What does it take to rank so highly with God? Abraham had been responsive, obedient and exemplary in all his ways toward God. If you talk right, walk right, and do right, God is likely to open the lines of communication widely. Try it.

Genesis 18:17-18 - "The LORD said, Shall I hide from Abraham that thing which I do; Seeing that Abraham shall surely become a great and mighty nation?"

D | For I Know Him

God knew Abraham's heart, and what He knew obviously influenced Him to choose him. You may not even know yourself, but God knows your heart. You may not know how you would respond in a given situation, but God does. If you are driven by wrong motives, God knows. If you have an honest, pure, God-fearing heart, He knows that, too. Be sure that God knows even your thoughts and intentions. Pretenses and phony shows do not fool God.

Genesis 18:19 - "For I know him, that he will command his children and his household after him."

A | He Will Command His Children And His Household

God knew that when he claimed Abraham, He would get Abraham's children and household too. How did He know? Because Abraham understood and practiced spiritual authority. He taught his family and his household the ways of the Lord and commanded them to live by them.

You and I should live like that. Hear what God speaks then speak and reiterate it.

Genesis 18:19 - "For I know him, that he will command his children and his household after him, and they shall keep the way of the LORD, ...that the LORD may bring upon Abraham that which he hath spoken of him."

A | Abraham Stood Yet Before The LORD And Drew Near

Two angels went to Sodom to execute judgment. The third was the Angel of the LORD. He stayed with Abraham. As the other two left, Abraham approached the Angel of the LORD (He is called the LORD because He stood in the LORD's place. Remember, "no man hath seen God at any time," John 1:18). Abraham might have made personal requests, but instead he interceded for his kinfolks, Lot's family. Take advantage of God's presence to intercede.

Genesis 18:22-23 - "But Abraham stood yet before the LORD. And Abraham drew near, and said, Wilt thou also destroy the righteous with the wicked?"

A | Don't Stop Praying Too Soon

God declared His intention to destroy the evil cities of Sodom and Gomorrah. Abraham began to make intercessory prayer for his relatives there. He asked God to save the city if He could find fifty righteous men. Then forty-five, forty, thirty, twenty. Finally, ten. Since there were not ten righteous men in Sodom, Abraham stopped praying. Abraham might have yet saved the city if he hadn't stopped praying.

Genesis 18:24 NAS - "...wilt thou not sweep it away and not spare the place for the sake of fifty righteous that are in it?"

A | I Have Taken It Upon Me To Speak Unto The LORD

We must not allow feelings of unworthiness to prevent us from approaching the LORD. In 1868, Joseph Scriven penned these familiar words: "Oh what peace we often forfeit! Oh what needless pain we bear! All because we do not carry everything to God in prayer!" You may feel like dust and ashes, but God says, "Call upon me in the day of trouble: I will deliver thee, and thou shalt glorify me," Psalms 50:15.

Genesis 18:27 - "Abraham answered and said, Behold now, I have taken upon me to speak unto the Lord, which am but dust and ashes."

A | Shall Not The Judge Of All The Earth Do Right?

Abraham pleaded with God to save Sodom if only "fifty righteous" could be found in the city. "Shall not the Judge of all the earth do right?" Lot's family was the only righteous there. Abraham humbly renegotiated to save Sodom for only forty-five souls. Then forty. "Let not the LORD be angry." Thirty-five. Twenty. "Oh, let not the LORD be angry, and I will speak." Ten! God approved TEN! Apparently, Lot did not have even ten descendants, so why did Abraham stop praying? Ask God for what you need!

Genesis 18:33 - "And Abraham returned unto his place."

D | The Destruction of Sodom

The Contemporary English Bible renders Genesis 19:4-5 thus: "Before Lot and his guests could go to bed, every man in Sodom, young and old, came and stood outside his house and started shouting, "Where are your visitors? Send them out, so we can have sex with them!" God already knew their wicked hearts. That is why the angels came - to destroy it!

Genesis 19:13 - "For we will destroy this place, because the cry of them is waxen great before the face of the LORD; and the LORD hath sent us to destroy it."

B | Lot's Wife

When God delivered Lot and his family from the destruction of Sodom, the angel instructed them not to look back. Tragically, Lot's wife looked back, and "she became a pillar of salt." Our generation would almost certainly fail that test. When God says, "Come out," He says, "touch not the unclean thing." God does not like to see us yearning for the things He delivered us from. Jesus said those who look back are not fit for the Kingdom. Be warned.

Genesis 19:17 - "Escape for thy life; look not behind thee, ...lest thou be consumed."

B | Lot's Daughters

Sodom was destroyed. God told Lot to go to Zoar, but Lot disobeyed. He and his daughters went into a mountain cave. His daughters complained of their isolation. They made their father drunk, and both bore children by him. The older daughter bore Moab. The younger bore Benammi - father of the Ammonites. This pathetic incestuous scenario came about because of Lot's fears. Disobedience always comes at a high price.

Genesis 19:30 - "Lot went up out of Zoar, and dwelt in the mountain, and his two daughters with him; for he feared to dwell in Zoar."

D | Abimelech's Dream

God often speaks prophetically to people in dreams and visions. When Abimelech, King of Gerar, took Sarah from Abraham's household, he was not informed that she was Abraham's wife. But God set the record straight. Every woman in his household was barren as long as Sarah was there. When Abimelech obeyed the dream, the curse was lifted.

Genesis 20:3 - "But God came to Abimelech in a dream by night, and said to him, Behold, thou art but a dead man, for the woman which thou hast taken; for she is a man's wife."

B | Abimelech of Gerar

Abimelech took Sarah from Abraham. God shut the wombs of the women in his household. Then God told Abimelech he was a dead man if he touched Sarah - she was a man's wife. Abimelech asked Abraham why he had said she was his sister. "I thought they would slay me for my wife's sake." Abimelech returned Sarah unharmed, gave Abraham sheep, oxen, menservants, womenservants and a thousand pieces of silver, then said, "my land is before thee, dwell where it pleaseth thee." Divine intervention!

Genesis 20:7 - "...restore the man his wife; for he is a prophet."

D | Pray To Remove A Curse

King Abimelech took Sarah into his household, not knowing she was Abraham's wife. God caused all the women in his household to become barren, and warned him that he was a dead man if he touched Sarah. God ordered the king to have Abraham pray for him to cure the offense. God really does move to protect His chosen people. Even so, He directs us to pray for divine intervention. When Abraham prayed, the women's barrenness was cured.

Genesis 20:7 - "...and he shall pray for thee, and thou shalt live."

B | Hagar

Since God had not given her children, Sarai offered her Egyptian maid to Abraham as a surrogate mother. Hagar despised Sarai after birthing Ishmael. Abraham instructed Sarai to handle Hagar. Sarai dealt harshly with Hagar, so she ran away. God commanded Hagar to return and submit. She stayed thirteen years, until Sarai bore Isaac. The day Sarai weaned Isaac, Ishmael mocked her. After Hagar's despite and Ishmael's mocking, Sarai demanded they be cast out.

Genesis 21:12 - "God said... all that Sarah hath said unto thee, hearken unto her voice; for in Isaac shall thy seed be called."

B | Beersheba

Beersheba is a significant town in south-central Israel - in the Negev desert. It was an important landmark for Abraham, Isaac, Jacob and Joseph. Abraham and Isaac dug water wells there, and made peace treaties with Abimelech of nearby Gerar. Hagar and Ishmael lived in the wilderness near Beersheba. Jacob left there to go to Joseph in Egypt. Today it is a great city of 185,000 people, mostly Jews. "From Dan to Beersheba" meant "all Israel, from north to south."

Genesis 21:33 - "...Abraham planted a grove in Beersheba, and called there on the name of the LORD."

D | Thine Only Son Isaac

For twenty-five years Abraham waited on the prophecy to be fulfilled. Finally, at the age of 100, Isaac was born. The episode with Hagar and Ishmael was completely impertinent to the prophecy. God wrote them out of the story line. Abraham's posterity and blessing would only pass through Isaac. Today, Ishmael's descendants are fighting viciously for Isaac's inheritance. Only God can and will see to its fulfillment.

Genesis 22:2 - "And he said, Take now thy son, thine only son Isaac, whom thou lovest, and get thee into the land of Moriah."

D | Himself A Lamb

When Abraham took Isaac to Mount Moriah to make sacrifice, Isaac wanted to know where the sacrifice was. "God will provide HIMSELF a lamb," his father told him. Surely enough, the angel intervened before Abraham could slay Isaac. A ram (male lamb) appeared nearby as a substitute. This was powerfully prophetic of Jesus Christ. At the Jordan River eighteen centuries later, John the Baptist saw Jesus and exclaimed, "Behold, the Lamb of God!" God Himself a Lamb.

Genesis 22:8 - "Abraham said, My son, God will provide himself a lamb for a burnt offering: so they went both of them together."

□✓

D | Jehovah Jireh – LORD Provider

"The Lord - Provider" is the name God revealed to Abraham on Mount Moriah. Testing his loyalty, God instructed Abraham to sacrifice his ONLY son, Isaac, on an altar. When God saw Abraham's obedience, His angel halted the sacrifice AND provided a ram caught in a bush to sacrifice in Isaac's place. The lamb foreshadowed God again providing salvation for His saints when Jesus returns to Mount Moriah.

Genesis 22:14 - "Abraham called the name of that place Jehovahjireh: as it is said to this day, In the mount of the LORD it shall be seen."

D | Possessing the Enemies' Gates

One promise God gave Abraham was that his descendants would possess their enemies' gates. That pretty much solves the problems of enemies. He said He would curse those who cursed His people. It is best not to fight against God's people because that is a sure guarantee you will be conquered.

Genesis 22:17 - "That in blessing I will bless thee, and in multiplying I will multiply thy seed as the stars of the heaven, and as the sand which is upon the sea shore; and thy seed shall possess the gate of his enemies."

B | Ephron The Hittite - Offered To Donate Sarah's Grave

Sarah died at the age of 127. Isaac was about 36 when his mother died. It was a traumatic event for Abraham. He owned no land to bury Sarah in. "Abraham came to mourn for Sarah, and to weep for her." He told the local sons of Heth that he was a stranger among them and begged a place to bury his wife in the Cave of Machpelah.

Genesis 23:10-11 - "Ephron the Hittite answered Abraham in the audience of the children of Heth, ...the field give I thee, and the cave that is therein, I give it thee; ...bury thy dead."

B | Cave of Machpelah

Sarah died in Hebron about 3700 years ago. There Abraham bought the field and the Cave of Machpelah from the sons of Heth to bury her. Today, the cave sits under a 2,000-year-old building. Around 700 years ago, Muslims turned the place into a Mosque. Israel retook the property in 1967, but Muslims still manage it. It also contains the graves of Abraham, Isaac, Rebekah, Jacob and Leah.

Genesis 23:19-20 - "Abraham buried Sarah his wife in the cave of the field of Machpelah before Mamre: the same is Hebron in the land of Canaan."

D | A Bride for Isaac

Abraham sent his servant to Mesopotamia to find a wife for Isaac. Eliezer wondered what he would do if he could not find one, but Abraham prophesied his success. God's angel delivered. Rebekah came eagerly.

Genesis 24:7 - "The LORD God of heaven, which took me from my father's house, and from the land of my kindred, and which spake unto me, and that sware unto me, saying, Unto thy seed will I give this land; he shall send his angel before thee, and thou shalt take a wife unto my son from thence."

A | Eliezer's Prayer

Abraham's servant was charged with finding a wife for Isaac, and he worried what the consequences would be if he could not find her. He asked God to prosper his mission, even specifying the terms. Amazingly, God did exactly as he asked. At the well, the perfect girl was waiting.

Genesis 24:42-44 - "I came this day unto the well, and said, O LORD God of my master Abraham, if now thou do prosper my way which I go: ...let the same be the woman whom the LORD hath appointed out for my master's son."

B | Eliezer

Abraham sent his eldest servant (presumably his steward, Eliezer) to find a wife for Isaac in the homeland of his grandfather Nahor in Mesopotamia. At one time, Eliezer had been the heir to Abraham's wealth, but after Isaac was born, that changed. Nevertheless, Eliezer was privileged to see God working miraculously for his master. I am thinking of the Prodigal Son who said, "How many hired servants of my father's have bread enough and to spare." Any place in God's service is good.

Genesis 15:2 - "...the steward of my house is this Eliezer of Damascus."

D | Two Nations - Twins!

A major prophecy seemed in jeopardy of failing. Isaac's wife, Rebekah, was barren! But suddenly, God provided - TWINS! Even before they were born, God foretold their future. The elder would serve the younger.

Hundreds of years later, under King David, Esau's Edomites were conquered by Jacob's Israel (2 Samuel 8:14).

Genesis 25:23 - "...the LORD said unto her, Two nations are in thy womb, and two manner of people shall be separated from thy bowels; and the one people shall be stronger than the other people; and the elder shall serve the younger."

D | Sell Me Thy Birthright

Maybe this doesn't look like a prophecy, but think about it. Esau sold his birthright to Jacob for a bowl of beans. Obviously, Esau did not comprehend the true value of his birthright. We are talking about divine posterity - something only Almighty God can assure. Let Esau's descendants rage! Jacob owns the blessing outright. A deal is a deal. Isaac laid his hand on Jacob and transferred it to him irrevocably.

Genesis 25:33 - "And Jacob said, Swear to me this day; and he sware unto him: and he sold his birthright unto Jacob."

D | Heel-Grabber

The birth of Isaac's twins was ominous. Jacob came from the womb grabbing the heel of the firstborn, Esau. Jacob's name means "supplanter: one who usurps or takes the place of another." In time, Jacob did supplant Esau, buying his birthright for a bowl of beans, then tricking his father to lay hands on him for the family blessing. His strong desire for the birthright, which included God's Covenants with Abraham and Isaac, impressed God despite his unscrupulous methods.

Romans 9:13 - "As it is written, Jacob have I loved, but Esau have I hated."

C | A Bowl Of Beans

Look at the modern State of Israel. Then contemplate its 3,600-year history. Scores of large cities. Scores of great kings. Millions of people. The overall impact of Israel on the world stage is inestimable. Great scientists, inventors, financiers, artists, musicians, politicians, etc. Jews have played a major role in nearly every nation on earth. And Esau gave it all up for a bowl of beans.

Genesis 25:34 - "Then Jacob gave Esau bread and pottage of lentiles; and he did eat and drink, and rose up, and went his way: thus Esau despised his birthright."

D | **Go Not Down To Egypt**

Everybody knows about God's promises to Abraham to bless and multiply his seed and inherit the Promised Land. But God made important prerequisites to those prophecies. Isaac must OBEY His commandments, statutes and laws, AND he must NOT go down to Egypt. He must trust God during famine in the land. Likewise, WE must obey God and be in His chosen place before we can claim His promises.

Genesis 26:2 - "...the LORD appeared unto him, and said, Go not down into Egypt; dwell in the land which I shall tell thee of."

B | **Isaac**

Isaac inherited Abraham's divine Covenant blessings. His mother was barren until the age of 90. God used that to prove the power of the Covenant. Isaac's life appears to be relatively non-eventful when compared to many other great characters in the Bible. But his significance cannot be overstated. Totally dismissing Ishmael, God called Isaac Abraham's "ONLY SON."

Genesis 26:3 - "I will be with thee, and will bless thee; for unto thee, and unto thy seed, I will give all these countries, and I will perform the oath which I sware unto Abraham thy father."

D | **God Speaks to Isaac**

Technically, God's promise would never have to be repeated to be valid. God keeps His Word. But God chose to deliver the Abrahamic Covenant first-hand and personally to Isaac. God has no grandchildren. He is Father to every generation, including yours and mine. His Word speaks freshly to us today.

Genesis 26:24 - "And the LORD appeared unto him the same night, and said, I am the God of Abraham thy father: fear not, for I am with thee, and will bless thee, and multiply thy seed for my servant Abraham's sake."

D | **Blessing Time**

Isaac was old and blind, and his days were numbered. He called Esau to prepare a special meal, after which he would give his eldest son the family blessing. But Esau had already despised the Birthright, sold it to Jacob, and married a Hittite woman. Rebekah and Jacob carefully intercepted the blessing. They "pulled out all the stops" for Jacob. If you want the blessing, fight for it.

Genesis 27:4 - "And make me savoury meat, such as I love, and bring it to me, that I may eat; that my soul may bless thee before I die."

B | Rebekah's Intercession

Isaac and Rebekah were grieved by Esau's marriage to a Hittite woman. Rebekah determined that the family inheritance should pass to Jacob. She plotted in Jacob's behalf to get the blessing from dying Isaac. It was a risky venture. What if Isaac discovered he was being deceived? She felt it was worth the risk and was willing to take the blame if it failed. We need more mothers who will fight for righteousness. God loved it.

Genesis 27:13 - "...his mother said unto him, Upon me be thy curse, my son: only obey my voice."

A | Venison For A Prayer

Rebekah and Jacob committed a fraudulent deception against Isaac. She cooked goat meat to taste like Esau's venison. They put goat skins on Jacob's arms to simulate hairy Esau. Jacob blatantly lied to his blind father: "I am Esau..." Jacob wanted Isaac to pronounce the blessing on him. Esau despised it. How far will you go to secure the blessing of God? Isaac's prayer of blessing was the coveted prize.

Genesis 27:28 - "Therefore God give thee of the dew of heaven, and the fatness of the earth, and plenty of corn and wine."

C | Fleeing Esau - Fleeing Trouble

Esau threatened to kill Jacob for stealing the family blessing. Rebekah had pushed Jacob into the situation, then, she had to urge Jacob to flee. Sometimes situations seem to deteriorate before they get better. Nevertheless, Jacob's flight took him to Laban where he met and married his wives and became the father of the "twelve tribes of Israel." It is not uncommon in the will of God for things to get worse before they get better.

Genesis 27:43 - "Now therefore, my son, obey my voice; and arise, flee thou to Laban my brother to Haran."

A | Father's Prayer

As Isaac sent Jacob away, he blessed him with a prayer over him. Jacob was headed to Haran to find his mother's brother, Laban. His first encounter was while he was yet afar off. He met Rachel in a field as she was tending sheep. It was love at first sight. God had everything arranged for Jacob before he ever left home. Even so, our prayers of faith are preparing the way for those we love. Have faith in God.

Genesis 28:3 - "And God Almighty bless thee, and make thee fruitful, and multiply thee."

D | Jacob's Inheritance

Here is a written record, authored by Moses over 3,000 years ago, confirming that Isaac passed Abraham's blessing to JACOB, including the deed to the Promised Land. Islam hotly contests this claim, but it is at least 2,000 years older than Islam. Mohammed's counter-claims are illegitimate. God will confirm Israel's claim to the land originally given to Abraham.

Genesis 28:4 - "And give thee the blessing of Abraham, to thee, and to thy seed with thee; that thou mayest inherit the land wherein thou art a stranger, which God gave unto Abraham."

D | God Visits Jacob

The Lord appeared to Jacob in a dream. The Covenant with ABRAHAM suddenly became the Covenant with JACOB. Even if Abraham had never lived, Jacob now had a promise from God. In his lifetime, Jacob would see his descendants migrate to Egypt, but there was a promise they would be back to the land promised in the Covenant.

Genesis 28:13 - "And, behold, the LORD stood above it, and said, I am the LORD God of Abraham thy father, and the God of Isaac: the land whereon thou liest, to thee will I give it, and to thy seed."

A | Jacob's Vow

After the Lord appeared to Jacob at Bethel, making Covenant, Jacob reciprocated with a vow of his own. Jacob lived his life devoted to the God of his fathers. 3,500 years later, a great nation still witnesses to that relationship.

Genesis 28:20-21 - "And Jacob vowed a vow, saying, If God will be with me, and will keep me in this way that I go, and will give me bread to eat, and raiment to put on, So that I come again to my father's house in peace; then shall the LORD be my God."

D | I Will Not Leave Thee

When God spoke to Jacob in the dream at Bethel, He prophesied of Israel being scattered to the North, South, East and West. Then He said, "I will bring thee again into this land." That was a prophecy for 3,700 years later, fulfilled in 1948 when the modern State of Israel was born. The United Nations, with Resolution 181, fulfilled a divine mandate, opening the door for God's people to return to their homeland.

Genesis 28:15 - "...I will not leave thee, until I have done that which I have spoken to thee of."

B | Bethel

Abraham's first stop in the land of Canaan was a place called Luz (looz), ten miles north of Jerusalem. Jacob saw the ladder reaching into heaven there. Later, Jacob wrestled the angel there, who renamed him Israel. He renamed the place Bethel, which means "house of God" (beth=house, el=God). Samuel confirmed Saul as Israel's first king there. King Jeroboam worshipped a Golden Calf there, an unnamed prophet condemned his altar there, and centuries later, Josiah destroyed the altar and the bones of Jeroboam's false prophets there.

Genesis 28:19 - "And he called the name of that place Bethel."

D | Laban

Jacob's encounter with Laban was a prophetic fulfillment. Although Jacob was forced to flee as a fugitive from Esau's jealous rage, God was working for his good. We must not panic when God forces us out of a comfortable situation into a foreign environment. The steps of a man are ordered by the Lord. Jacob found his wives and the twelve tribes were born. Divine destiny.

Genesis 29:13 - "It came to pass, when Laban heard the tidings of Jacob his sister's son, that he ran to meet him, and embraced him, and kissed him, and brought him to his house."

C | The Deceiver Is Deceived

Jacob offered to serve Laban seven years for Rachel's hand in marriage. Seven years later, the old man pulled a fast one on Jacob. He woke up after the honeymoon to find the older daughter, Leah, instead of his desired Rachel. The beguiler had been beguiled. Years later, Laban continued the deceit and Jacob had to leave. What goes around comes around. If you want truth, deal truthfully.

Genesis 29:25 - "...he said to Laban, What is this thou hast done unto me? did not I serve with thee for Rachel? wherefore then hast thou beguiled me?"

A | Rachel's Distress

Laban made Jacob marry his oldest daughter, Leah, before he could take Rachel, the younger. Leah had four sons, but Rachel was barren. She verbalized her despair to God in prayer. After some time, she gave her handmaiden to Jacob, who then bore Dan. Dan, meaning "judge," became a tribe known for its judges, including Samson. Their homeland was the northern-most territory of Israel, above Galilee, against Lebanon.

Genesis 30:6 - "Rachel said, God hath judged me, and hath also heard my voice, and hath given me a son: therefore called she his name Dan."

C | Little Is Much When God Is In It

Jacob was far from home, fugitive from an angry brother, yet God was with him. His flocks multiplied miraculously. Sometimes our circumstances are mixed - hardship or tragedy on one hand; blessing on the other. Quit your pessimism. If God be for you, who can be against you? What is in thy hand? God will bless and multiply it! Little is much when God is in it.

Genesis 30:30 - "...it was little which thou hadst before I came, and it is now increased unto a multitude; and the LORD hath blessed thee since my coming."

A | Receiving Instructions

Prayer is a two-way street. We pray today. God may speak tomorrow. After Jacob spent twenty years in Laban's household, things went sour. Laban became adversarial. God spoke to Jacob and instructed him to leave. It was a defining moment of Jacob's life. If we want to receive instructions of that kind, we need a heart that desires to hear His voice. We need God's point of view.

Genesis 31:3 - "And the LORD said unto Jacob, Return unto the land of thy fathers, and to thy kindred; and I will be with thee."

C | God Has Been With Me

Jacob had many problems with Laban. After serving seven years to marry Rachel, Laban gave him Leah instead and made him serve seven more for Rachel. Then Jacob negotiated to take the "ring-straked and spotted" livestock and leave the rest to Laban. Laban was enraged when the herds multiplied in Jacob's favor. Troublemakers in our lives just cannot win when God is with us.

Genesis 31:5 - "...I see your father's countenance, that it is not toward me as before; but the God of my father hath been with me."

A | **Here Am I**

Laban was making life difficult for Jacob, so Jacob had to make a deal with him to allow him to have all the "ring-straked and spotted" livestock. As soon as the deal was made, God intervened. Nearly all the cattle began to be "ring-straked and spotted." This was no accident. God clearly spoke with Jacob about the matter, and Jacob affirmed that he and God had discussed it. Conversations with God are profitable.

Genesis 31:11 - "And the angel of God spake unto me in a dream, saying, Jacob: And I said, Here am I."

D | **Manifest Destiny**

When Jacob began to leave Laban after twenty years of service, Laban would have forbid it and would have kept everything including his daughters. But when God pronounces certain destiny over a life such as Jacob's, nothing and nobody can stop it. Blessing and cursing are sovereign irresistible powers of God.

Genesis 31:42 - "Except the God of my father, the God of Abraham, and the fear of Isaac, had been with me, surely thou hadst sent me away now empty. God hath seen mine affliction and the labour of my hands, and rebuked thee yesternight."

B | **The God Of Nahor**

We have heard the phrase, "The God of Abraham, Isaac, and Jacob," but how about the "GOD OF NAHOR"? Nahor was Abraham's grandfather. Nahor was 99 years old when Abraham was born, and died when Abraham was 49. Nahor believed in the one true God, so certainly must have influenced Abraham's faith and calling. Eliezer found Rebekah for Isaac in Nahor's hometown. This scarcely-known grandfather surely had far greater impact than we have realized. Never underestimate your impact on others!

Genesis 31:53 - "The God of Abraham, and the God of Nahor..."

A | Jacob's Prayer

Jacob was plainly terrified of seeing Esau again. Twenty years earlier, Esau had threatened to kill him. Jacob humbled himself and earnestly prayed to God, reminding Him of His promises to return him home safely. He begged God to help him. That night, Jacob met and wrestled with the angel that renamed him "Israel." Everything worked out excellently with Esau after that.

Genesis 32:11 - "Deliver me, I pray thee, from the hand of my brother, from the hand of Esau: for I fear him, lest he will come and smite me, and the mother with the children."

C | Owning Up to Our Flaws

Before the Angel of the LORD would pronounce the blessing upon him, Jacob had to tell the angel his own name. Jacob's name meant "supplanter." Announcing that to the angel was tantamount to confessing, "I am a crook!" Sooner or later, we all have to own up to our flaws. God requires that we confess our faults. There is no point in hiding our sins. God sees everything anyway. Admit it and get on with your divine destiny.

Genesis 32:27 - "And he said unto him, What is thy name? And he said, Jacob."

B | Jacob's Name Change

One of the most notable events in human history is Jacob's name change. Dreading confrontation with Esau after twenty years of exile, Jacob prayed desperately for God's help. That night, an angel wrestled fiercely with Jacob, permanently injuring his thigh joint. Jacob said, "I will not let thee go, except thou bless me." Every day, world headlines republish the name spoken by the angel - ISRAEL.

Genesis 32:28 - "And he said, Thy name shall be called no more Jacob, but Israel: for as a prince hast thou power with God and with men, and hast prevailed."

C | Lead On Softly

By the grace of God, Jacob and Esau reconciled beautifully. Jacob gave him generous gifts, and they blessed each other before parting ways. Jacob's anxiety was relieved. Peacefulness settled over him. From there on, he could relax and head for the Promised Land. They could travel at a leisurely pace for the cattle and children. God diffused the crisis. When we finally see God's hand working, we can relax and travel on.

Genesis 33:14 - "I will lead on softly, according as the cattle that goeth before me and the children be able to endure."

D | Jacob Buys Land At Shechem

God promised Shechem to Abraham and his descendants. Years later, Jacob bought land there for his family. Shechem became a highly significant city throughout Bible days. Joseph visited his brothers there before being sold into slavery. Later, he was buried there. Many Bible stories occurred there, but Palestinians now control it (modern Nablus). Jesus will reclaim it soon at the battle of Armageddon.

Genesis 33:19 - "And he bought a parcel of a field, where he had spread his tent, at the hand of the children of Hamor, Shechem's father, for an hundred pieces of money."

D | Jacob Takes Ownership

Laban and Esau were behind now, so Jacob could take his family and flocks home to the Promised Land. He stopped for a while at Succoth, east of Jordan, and built shelters for cattle. But shortly, he purchased land from Shechem and for the first time, owned part of the Promised Land. Shechem is nestled between Mount Ebal and Mount Gerizim - where Joshua pronounced blessing and cursing. Sooner or later, God's promises always come to pass.

Genesis 33:20 - "And he erected there an altar, and called it Elelohe-Israel [God - the God of Israel]."

C | You Made Me Stink

Jacob settled his family and flocks on Promised Land in Shechem. But his daughter Dinah was raped by the son of the king of Shechem. Enraged, Jacob's sons mindlessly murdered and plundered the entire city. Over-reacting to tragedy doubles the loss.

Genesis 34:30 - "And Jacob said to Simeon and Levi, Ye have troubled me to make me to stink among the inhabitants of the land, among the Canaanites and the Perizzites: and I being few in number, they shall gather themselves together against me, and slay me; and I shall be destroyed, I and my house."

C | Clean Up Your Act

Calamity struck Jacob at Shechem. His daughter was raped by the king's son. His sons murderously retaliated against the Shechemites. They had to flee the region. God called Jacob back to Bethel for spiritual revival.

Genesis 35:2-5 - "Jacob said unto his household..., Put away the strange gods that are among you, and be clean, and change your garments: ...And they gave unto Jacob all the strange gods which were in their hand, and all their earrings which were in their ears; ...and the terror of God was upon the cities that were round about them."

A | An Altar And Offerings At Bethel

After being displaced from Shechem, Jacob returned to the "the house of God," Bethel. He built an altar and made offerings to the Lord. Shortly thereafter, his precious wife, Rachel, died giving birth to Benjamin, and soon his father, Isaac, died. Our inevitable tragedies are much easier to bear when we have already been to the altar beforehand. Why not consecrate today?

Genesis 35:14 - "And Jacob set up a pillar in the place where he talked with him, even a pillar of stone: and he poured a drink offering thereon, and he poured oil thereon."

D | Jacob's Deed

God's Covenant with Abraham passed to Isaac, then to Jacob and his seed. Numerous accounts in the book of Genesis reiterate this fact. This has to be one of the oldest real estate deeds on earth.

Genesis 35:11-12 - "And God said unto him, I am God Almighty: be fruitful and multiply; a nation and a company of nations shall be of thee, and kings shall come out of thy loins; And the land which I gave Abraham and Isaac, to thee I will give it, and to thy seed after thee will I give the land."

B | Leah And Rachel

Marriage laws did not exist prior to Moses' trip to Sinai. Polygamy was commonplace. Jacob married Leah and Rachel. Rachel was initially barren, so she gave her handmaiden, Bilhah to Jacob as a surrogate. Later, Leah "left off bearing," so gave Zilpah, her handmaiden to Jacob. The four wives bore twelve sons to Jacob - the twelve tribes of Israel.

Genesis 35:23-26 - "The sons of Leah; Reuben, ...Simeon, ...Levi, ...Judah, ...Issachar, and Zebulun: The sons of Rachel; Joseph, and Benjamin: And the sons of Bilhah, ...Dan, and Naphtali: And the sons of Zilpah, ...Gad, and Asher."

D | Esau Is Edom

God knew in advance that Esau was not going to work out. Esau went to strange nations to find wives. He settled east of Jordan in the region of Mount Seir. His descendants became known as Edom - the Edomites. When Moses brought the Children of Israel from Egypt, the Edomites would not let them pass through their land. Esau's grandchildren, the Amalekites, were first to declare war on the Children of Israel. Many of Esau's descendants were merciless enemies of Israel.

Genesis 36:9 - "And these are the generations of Esau the father of the Edomites in mount Seir."

B | Joseph

Jacob's favorite son was Rachel's firstborn, Joseph. His brothers were jealous and hostile toward him because he had his father's favor. At seventeen years old, Joseph dreamed two dreams that would eventually catapult him into world recognition for all of time. Think of it! A divinely-ordered, profoundly significant destiny was inaugurated in a seventeen year-old boy. It all began with his father's love. We should take extreme care to pronounce blessings on those we love!

Genesis 37:5 - "Joseph dreamed a dream, and he told it his brethren: and they hated him yet the more."

C | Coat Of Many Colors

Men often resent others who receive special favors. His brothers hated Joseph because he had his father's favor. Korah hated Moses, and Saul hated David because of God's favor. God's favor on a man often provokes others' jealousy or hatred. People commit grievous acts against those who have divine favor. Lucifer killed Jesus in jealousy. That is why true saints have to suffer. "Hated for my name's sake."

Genesis 37:3 - "Israel loved Joseph more than all his children, because he was the son of his old age: and he made him a coat of many colours."

A | "I Pray You..."

The ancient people often used the phrase, "I pray you..." or "I pray thee..." to solicit the kind consideration of their requests of others. It was as if they were either afraid of the other person or were, in effect, begging for merciful consideration. Unfortunately, making a prayerful request of ordinary men does not always elicit a favorable response. Joseph must have hoped his family would rejoice with him, but they did not. Make your prayers to God instead.

Genesis 37:6 - "And he said unto them, Hear, I pray you, this dream which I have dreamed."

C | Deception

If Reuben had not argued in his defense, his brethren would have killed Joseph in rabid jealousy. Instead, they held him captive in a dry well before selling him into slavery. To cover their sins, they deceived Jacob into believing that his son had been killed by a wild animal. If you stand for God, your enemies may use outrageous, diabolical tactics to destroy you. They may deceive others, but they cannot fool God. God judges righteously.

Genesis 37:31 - "And they took Joseph's coat, and killed a kid of the goats, and dipped the coat in the blood."

B | Judah

Judah, fourth son of Jacob, opposed his brothers' scheme to kill Joseph. He suggested that they could sell him as a slave. Throughout history, Jewish rabbis have argued that Judah should have saved Joseph from his brothers and returned him to his father, Jacob. Instead, Judah is blamed for Joseph's plight. Many think the death of Judah's wife and two sons was divine retribution for Judah's behavior.

Genesis 37:26-27 - "And Judah said unto his brethren, What profit is it if we slay our brother, and conceal his blood? Come, and let us sell him..."

B | Onan

Judah had three sons by a daughter of Shuah: Er, Onan and Shelah. Er married Tamar, but God slew him for being a wicked man. Tradition demanded that his brother take the widow and give her children for his brother's posterity. Onan laid with Tamar, but would not give her a child. God slew him for that.

Genesis 38:9 - "And Onan knew that the seed should not be his; and it came to pass, when he went in unto his brother's wife, that he spilled it on the ground, lest that he should give seed to his brother."

B | Tamar

Poor Tamar! Married Er. He died. Judah gave her Onan. He died, too! Judah promised to give his third son, Shelah. She waited childless for years. Judah never delivered. Tamar tricked Judah into lying with her by posing as a wayside harlot. Later, his servants reported that Tamar was pregnant from whoredom. Judah ordered her to be burned until she revealed that HE was the father of her twins - Pharez and Zarah! Pharez became grandfather to Boaz, David, and Messiah.

Genesis 38:26 - "Judah...said, She hath been more righteous than I; because that I gave her not to Shelah my son."

D | Sweet Adversity

When a man is fulfilling his prophetic destiny, even the bad times are good. Although Joseph's brothers hated him and sold him to slave-traders, God's purpose could not be averted. "For we know that ALL things work together for the good..." Like Daniel in Babylon, God never loses track of a faithful man, even in the most evil places. God's blessing follows him.

Genesis 39:4 - "And Joseph found grace in his sight, and he served him: and he made him overseer over his house, and all that he had he put into his hand."

D | Can't Keep A Good Man Down

They threw Joseph in a pit to die, but God pulled him out. Potiphar bought him as a common slave, but God exalted him. Potiphar's wife falsely charged him with attempted rape and he went to prison, but God raised him from prison to Egypt's throne. When prophetic destiny is working, nothing can stand in its way. Hell cannot prevail when God has already defined your future.

Genesis 39:21 - "But the LORD was with Joseph, and shewed him mercy, and gave him favour in the sight of the keeper of the prison."

D | The Butler And The Baker

It is impossible for us to know ahead of time how wonderfully God will work in our lives. Joseph went to prison after being falsely accused of attempted rape. There he met Pharaoh's butler and baker and miraculously interpreted a dream for each. According to the dreams, one would live and one would die. But most importantly, God used that seemingly horrible occasion to exalt Joseph to the throne of Egypt.

Genesis 40:1 - "It came to pass after these things, that the butler of the king of Egypt and his baker had offended their lord the king of Egypt."

A | Prayer Not Needed?

It seems conspicuous that many significant Bible stories make no direct mention of a component of prayer. For example, there are no specific references to particular prayers in the story of Joseph. That does not mean that Joseph did not pray or need to pray, just that God works sovereignly from His Throne and is not hostage to our prayers or our prayerlessness. Anyone who prays and seeks God's will daily will see God lead on, as Joseph did.

Genesis 41:14 - "Then Pharaoh sent and called Joseph, and they brought him hastily out of the dungeon."

A | Joseph's Gift

From his childhood, God spoke to Joseph in dreams and supernatural revelations. God revealed that he would be exalted above his own family. Years later, God interpreted the dreams of Pharaoh's butler and baker to Joseph, and eventually, the dreams of Pharaoh himself. Joseph denied that it was a human ability. Joseph's insights came from his personal and intimate communion with God. We, too, may discover amazing insights in prayerful, contemplative times with Him.

Genesis 41:16 - "And Joseph answered Pharaoh, saying, It is not in me: God shall give Pharaoh an answer of peace."

D | Pharaoh's Dreams

God showed Joseph the meaning of Pharaoh's dreams. Seven lean cows devoured seven fat cows. Seven withered ears of corn devoured seven full ears of corn. It meant that Egypt would have seven years of bounty followed by seven years of famine. God showed Pharaoh and Joseph things to come, and God used Joseph to save multitudes in those days, both Egyptians and Children of Israel.

Genesis 41:32 - "And for that the dream was doubled unto Pharaoh twice; it is because the thing is established by God, and God will shortly bring it to pass."

B | Pharaoh

Pharaoh was almost always antagonistic to the Hebrews. But in the story of Joseph, he was a protagonist. When a man's ways please the Lord, God causes even his enemies to be at peace with him.

Genesis 41:39-41 - "Pharaoh said unto Joseph, Forasmuch as God hath shewed thee all this, there is none so discreet and wise as thou art: Thou shalt be over my house, and according unto thy word shall all my people be ruled: only in the throne will I be greater than thou. ...I have set thee over all the land of Egypt."

D | Corn In Egypt

The famine in Canaan was no accident. God was orchestrating an epic story. God had warned Abraham many years earlier that his descendants would become strangers in a land that was not theirs. Now it was about to begin, but they had not a clue. Israel would be forced to Egypt to survive, but miraculously, Joseph was already there with their salvation. So was God.

Genesis 42:2 - "And he said, Behold, I have heard that there is corn in Egypt: get you down thither, and buy for us from thence; that we may live, and not die."

D | Dreams Remembered

When Joseph's brothers showed up on Egypt's doorsteps, it must have been an awesome sight for Joseph. A million thoughts must have crossed his mind. They did not recognize him. He could have easily avenged himself of all their past cruelties, but he only toyed with their minds. He knew that God was in the whole matter. By God's will, he was their wealthy benefactor.

Genesis 42:9 - "And Joseph remembered the dreams which he dreamed of them, and said unto them, Ye are spies; to see the nakedness of the land ye are come."

C | Reckoning Day

Jacob's sons hated Joseph because of his dreams. The dreams said they would bow to him. They determined that it would never happen. They would kill him if necessary to prevent it. But Judah persuaded them only to sell him to slavery. They thought they were done with Joseph. But God was not through with them. It was all for a purpose. It does not pay to resist God's plan for your life. Sooner or later, reckoning day will come.

Genesis 43:18 - "And the men were afraid, because they were brought into Joseph's house."

B | Benjamin

Joseph's dear mother Rachel was dead, and he had not seen his little brother Benjamin for more than twenty years. He yearned to see him. When the older brothers came to Egypt for corn, Joseph threatened them not to come back without Benjamin, or they would be convicted as spies. Someday, Benjamin would be a very great tribe, but first, Joseph would be his savior.

Genesis 43:29-30 - "And he lifted up his eyes, and saw his brother Benjamin, his mother's son, ...he sought where to weep; and he entered into his chamber, and wept there."

C | Subtle Clues

If we could always see how God is working in our lives, we would never doubt Him. Joseph's brothers marveled that they had been seated at Joseph's banquet table in perfectly chronological order, oldest to the youngest. That was a subtle clue that somebody knew them intimately. They did not yet realize that their host was their long-lost brother, or that God was working magnificently - mercifully - in their behalf.

Genesis 43:33 - "They sat before him, the firstborn according to his birthright, and the youngest according to his youth: and the men marveled one at another."

A | God Hath Found Out The Iniquity Of Thy Servants

Joseph ordered his brothers' money to be secretly placed into their bags of grain AND his silver cup to be hidden in Benjamin's sack. He ordered his servants to pursue them as they returned to Canaan. His purpose was to test his brothers' loyalty to their baby brother, Benjamin. It was time for them to have a heart-cleansing. The whole ordeal forced them to confess that God had found them out. Don't make God chase you down to get a confession.

Genesis 44:16 - "Judah said, ...how shall we clear ourselves? God hath found out the iniquity of thy servants."

D | Thou Art Even As Pharaoh

Way back yonder in Joseph's dream, he saw his brethren bowing down to him. "We were binding sheaves in the field, and, lo, my sheaf arose, and also stood upright; and, behold, your sheaves stood round about, and made obeisance to my sheaf." Genesis 37:7. Many years later in Egypt, Joseph had the mastery over his brothers and could easily have had them destroyed. As humiliated aliens before Pharaoh, they begged for mercy. Prophecy fulfilled.

Genesis 44:18 - "Judah came near unto him, and said, Oh my lord, ...let not thine anger burn against thy servant: for thou art even as Pharaoh."

C | They Had Abused Joseph, But Had To Defend Benjamin

Joseph played some serious mind-games with his brothers. He framed them for crimes they did not commit, although he had no intention of prosecuting them. He only wanted to teach them a long-overdue lesson. They had hated and betrayed him, so Joseph forced them to defend Benjamin.

Genesis 44:20-23 - "We have a father, an old man, and a child of his old age, a little one; and his brother is dead, ...if he should leave his father, his father would die. ...I pray thee, let thy servant abide instead of the lad ...and let the lad go up with his brethren."

C | Enslaved To Save Lives

Joseph sent his brothers away with the money they paid him hidden in their grain sacks. Joseph's silver cup was in Benjamin's sack. Then his servants arrested them and charged them with theft. But Joseph dropped the charges. "I am Joseph," he weepingly confessed. Their old sins against Joseph turned out for everyone's good. Same for us. God has a glorious outcome for all our sufferings.

Genesis 45:5 - "Now therefore be not grieved, nor angry with yourselves, that ye sold me hither: for God did send me before you to preserve life."

B | Goshen

Joseph knew God had put him through his trials in Egypt to preserve the posterity of Israel. "...it was not you that sent me hither, but God: and he hath made me a father to Pharaoh, and lord of all his house, and a ruler throughout all the land of Egypt." Joseph gave them the fertile land of Goshen.

Genesis 45:10 - "And thou shalt dwell in the land of Goshen, and thou shalt be near unto me, thou, and thy children, and thy children's children, and thy flocks, and thy herds, and all that thou hast."

C | God Pays Moving Expenses

If and when God wants you to move, He will make a way. Do not fret the details. God will provide.

Genesis 45:19-21 - "Now thou art commanded, this do ye; take you wagons out of the land of Egypt for your little ones, and for your wives, and bring your father, and come. Also regard not your stuff; for the good of all the land of Egypt is yours. And the Children of Israel did so: and Joseph gave them wagons, according to the commandment of Pharaoh, and gave them provision for the way."

C | Unbelief Will Make You Faint

Unbelief is a killer, and it can kill otherwise great men. Double-minded men are unstable in all their ways. Either God is everything He says He is, or He is a liar. It is up to you to get a hold on the truth of that matter. Nobody else can do it for you. Tell Jacob that Joseph is still alive. Don't doubt it. Rejoice!

Genesis 45:26 - "And told him, saying, Joseph is yet alive, and he is governor over all the land of Egypt. And Jacob's heart fainted, for he believed them not."

B | Seventy Souls

Seventy souls entered Egypt - Jacob's immediate family. Centuries later, they left Egypt as a great nation. 600,000 military-aged men were accounted at Sinai, suggesting a total population of around two million who followed Moses across the Red Sea. Chances are, Israel would never have multiplied intact had they remained nomads in Canaan. God sent them to Egypt to strengthen them for the Promised Land. Do you feel your circumstances do not make sense? Trust God!

Genesis 46:27 - "...all the souls of the house of Jacob, which came into Egypt, were threescore and ten."

B | Cattlemen, Shepherds, Herdsmen In Egypt

Joseph told his brothers to move into Goshen. When they arrived, he instructed them to tell Pharaoh that they were herdsmen (46:34). Commentator Adam Clarke suggested that Joseph knew how Egyptians despised cattlemen and shepherds, so Pharaoh would be happy to keep them far away. That was better for them than living under Pharaoh's scrutinous eye. The strategy worked. Pharaoh homesteaded them in Goshen.

Genesis 47:6 - "The land of Egypt is before thee; in the best of the land make thy father and brethren to dwell; in the land of Goshen let them dwell: ...make them rulers over my cattle."

A | Jacob Blessed Pharaoh (Israel Blessed Egypt)

The premise of this claim seems contradictory to the facts. The facts said that Jacob and his family were out of food, out of pasture, and in need of Pharaoh's help. Still the Bible said, "Jacob blessed Pharaoh." How could a poverty-stricken Jew bless the wealthy King of Egypt? With divine graces, of course. But there is more to the matter than first meets the eye. If it had not been for Jacob's son, Joseph, Egypt would have perished during seven years of famine. The blessing was already at work. Israel BLESSED Egypt.

Genesis 47:10 - "And Jacob blessed Pharaoh."

C | While The World Suffers, God Provides For His Chosen

Judah led the family of seventy, "and they came into the land of Goshen," 46:28. Joseph took his royal chariot to meet Israel his father. They hugged and wept together "a good while." Then Joseph took them to meet Pharaoh, who welcomed them to remain in Goshen. Joseph was the governor of Egypt and had authority over all Egypt's wealth. While Egypt suffered epic famine, God's people were well provided for, receiving amazing, royal favor.

Genesis 47:12 - "And Joseph nourished his father, and his brethren, and all his father's household, with bread, according to their families."

D | Into Egypt, There I Will Make Of Thee A Great Nation

God spoke to Israel (Jacob) in a night vision. "Go down into Egypt; for there I will make of thee a great nation. I will go down with thee into Egypt; and I will also surely bring thee up again," 46:3-4. Jacob obeyed the LORD and took his entire family. "All the souls were threescore and six." God made a great nation from seventy poor souls. That is the power of His prophetic Word.

Genesis 47:27 - "Israel dwelt in the land of Egypt, in the country of Goshen; and they had possessions therein, and grew, and multiplied exceedingly."

B | Ephraim And Manasseh

Joseph's children were born into Egypt's royal household; Manasseh, "causing to forget," and Ephraim, "double fruit." When grandfather Jacob came to Egypt and met his two new grandsons, he adopted them both. Afterward, Joseph's tribe was listed as two tribes - Ephraim and Manasseh. The priestly tribe, Levi, had no land inheritance, therefore there were still twelve tribes listed.

Genesis 48:5 - "And now thy two sons, Ephraim and Manasseh, which were born unto thee in the land of Egypt before I came unto thee into Egypt, are mine; as Reuben and Simeon, they shall be mine."

A | Jacob Blesses Joseph And Sons

You can pronounce a blessing on others with special prayer. When Joseph presented his two sons to Jacob, the old man should have put his right hand on Manasseh the older, but instead he switched them. He gave the first blessing to the younger son, just like his own father had done.

Genesis 48:16 - "The Angel which redeemed me from all evil, bless the lads; and let my name be named on them, and the name of my fathers Abraham and Isaac; and let them grow into a multitude in the midst of the earth."

D | Jacob Prophesies To Joseph

Although God forewarned Abraham that his descendants would suffer bondage for hundreds of years, He never planned for the Children of Israel to stay in Egypt permanently. God raised up a holy nation in the midst of the hostile political climate of Pharaoh, most powerful king in the world at that time. Here is the lesson: This world is not our home. God has a better land for all His children.

Genesis 48:21 - "And Israel said unto Joseph, Behold, I die: but God shall be with you, and bring you again unto the land of your fathers."

D | One Portion Above Thy Brethren

Bible scholars suppose that Jacob left Shechem specifically to Joseph. He is, in fact, now buried there. Jacob bought the land when first returning from Laban, but apparently the Amorites took it from him, and he had to retake it by the sword. Today, it is Nablus, a power-center for Muslim extremists in the Middle East. Jesus will retake it following Armageddon.

Genesis 48:22 - "Moreover I have given to thee one portion above thy brethren, which I took out of the hand of the Amorite with my sword and with my bow."

D | Jacob The Prophet

Jacob was a true prophet - a seer. He knew God's working in his own life, but he could also see what God was doing in his twelve sons. The forty-ninth chapter of Genesis records Jacob's prophetic pronouncements on each of the twelve tribes. Reuben will not excel. Simeon and Levi will divide and scatter. In Judah, scepters, lawgivers, and "Shiloh" (Messiah). Everyone received a prophetic word that day.

Genesis 49:1 - "And Jacob called unto his sons, and said, Gather yourselves together, that I may tell you that which shall befall you in the last days."

D | God Meant It Unto Good

Jacob was dead. The family took him to Hebron and buried him in the Cave at Machpelah. The brothers were afraid that Joseph would now avenge himself of their former sins. They appealed to him for mercy. Joseph assured them that he knew God was working for all their good in that horrific experience. We should remember that in our trials.

Genesis 50:20 - "But as for you, ye thought evil against me; but God meant it unto good, to bring to pass, as it is this day, to save much people alive."

Lessons from the Book of
EXODUS

B | Exodus

This book is, at the outset, a biography of Moses - arguably the most significant human being ever born. Without Moses, there would have been no Bible, no Jews, no Christians, no Muslims, and no rule of law as we know it. What man left his stamp on civilization for all time as Moses? Yet, if there had been no burning bush, no voice of God, no leprous hand, no rod changed to a serpent, we would never have heard of Moses. Without God, there had been no Moses.

Deuteronomy 33:1 - "Moses the man of God"

B | Twelve Tribes

Joseph was the first of the tribal elders to enter Egypt. The eleven brothers came later, in God's time, with their father. The Levites, because they were priests, did not inherit lands, leaving eleven. But Joseph was replaced by his sons, Ephraim and Manasseh. Therefore, the number remained twelve. Twelve seems to be the number of divine government. Israel had twelve Tribes. The Church had twelve Apostles. The city of Heaven has twelve foundations and twelve gates.

Exodus 1:2-5 - "Reuben, Simeon, Levi, and Judah, Issachar, Zebulun, and Benjamin, Dan, and Naphtali, Gad, and Asher. ...Joseph."

C | The Power Of One

Jochebed was only one person, but salvation for all humanity hung by a thread on her actions. If Jochebed had not saved Moses, he would never have told the world about Abraham, Isaac, Jacob or Joseph. The power of one is inestimable. We are indebted to many "ones." Don't YOU fail!

Exodus 2:3 - "And when she could not longer hide him, she took for him an ark of bulrushes, and daubed it with slime and with pitch, and put the child therein; and she laid it in the flags by the river's brink."

C | Pitched Within And Without

Jochebed saved baby Moses by daubing an "ark of bulrushes" with slime and pitch. That made it water-proof and made it float. Noah did a similar thing with the great Ark. "Make thee an ark of gopher wood; ...pitch it within and without," Genesis 6:14. My brother, David, suggested to me that if we want to be saved, we need to be pitched within and without with holiness and righteousness.

Exodus 2:3 - "She took for him an ark of bulrushes, and daubed it with slime and with pitch, and put the child therein."

B | Moses' Early Life

Pharaoh's daughter rescued baby Moses from the Nile River, and his sister, Miriam, offered his mother to her as a wet nurse. God was working wonderfully! Although raised in Egypt's royal household, Moses was a blue-blooded, one-God Hebrew. In his youth, he impulsively killed an Egyptian who was assaulting a Jewish brother. He quickly hid the corpse, but the news spread like wildfire. Moses fled Egypt to the wilderness near Midian.

Exodus 2:15 - "Now when Pharaoh heard this thing, he sought to slay Moses. But Moses fled from the face of Pharaoh."

A | When Slaves Pray

I have often wondered why God told Abraham his descendants must spend time in bondage in Egypt. Typologically, Egypt represents the world of sin. Every man and woman must suffer bondage in the world of sin. But when we earnestly cry out to God, He hears and He delivers.

Exodus 2:23-24 - "...and the Children of Israel sighed by reason of the bondage, and they cried, and their cry came up unto God by reason of the bondage. And God heard their groaning, and God remembered his covenant with Abraham, with Isaac, and with Jacob."

A | "Who Am I?"

There are times when we all feel that we are unworthy to serve the Lord. But God will give us courage to fulfill every task. He never calls us to do a job without empowering us to do it. Moses was VERY reluctant to accept the call of God to deliver Israel from Pharaoh, but God had answers to all his objections. God will surely enable us.

Exodus 3:11 - "And Moses said unto God, Who am I, that I should go unto Pharaoh, and that I should bring forth the Children of Israel out of Egypt?"

A | Moses Interviews God

What do you want to know about God? What do you need to know about His will for your life? Ask Him. It is the glory of God to conceal a thing, but it is the honor of kings to search it out. God delights in our interest in Him.

Exodus 3:13 - "And Moses said unto God, Behold, when I come unto the Children of Israel, and shall say unto them, The God of your fathers hath sent me unto you; and they shall say to me, What is his name? what shall I say unto them?"

B | I AM

Moses asked God His name, so he could tell the people. God said, "I AM." It means "the Self-Existent One." It also means, "the cause."

Nothing else in the universe existed before God, and without Him, nothing would exist. His Spirit nature is the primordial stuff - more elemental than atoms, particles, waves, hadrons, quarks, leptons and preons. God is the basis of all things.

Exodus 3:14 - "And God said unto Moses, I AM THAT I AM: and he said, Thus shalt thou say unto the Children of Israel, I AM hath sent me unto you."

D | Ye Shall Not Go Empty

How on earth could Moses ever evacuate two million Jews from Egypt? How on earth could such a multitude survive such an upheaval and transition? Well, he certainly could not do it if not for the mighty hand of God to work miracle after miracle in their behalf. NEVER underestimate the power of God. Israel left with a vast horde of Egypt's riches.

Exodus 3:21 - "And I will give this people favour in the sight of the Egyptians: and it shall come to pass, that, when ye go, ye shall not go empty:"

C | What Is That In Thy Hand?

I love this vast spiritual principle. God uses whatever you have available. Never underestimate God's ability to use ordinary things mightily. Moses had a stick in his hand. God turned it into a snake. He parted the Red Sea with it. He drew water out of a rock with it. That was the mightiest stick in the history of man, but only because God Almighty made it so. What is that in YOUR hand?

Exodus 4:2 - "The LORD said unto him, What is that in thine hand? And he said, A rod."

A | Aggravating Prayers

Moses actually made God angry by his cop-out, excuse-making prayers. He wanted God to send somebody else to do the job. God promised to send Aaron to help him. He gave Moses some impressive miracle-working powers (turning a rod to a serpent, a hand to leprosy, water to blood, etc.). Sometimes our prayers aggravate God, but He graciously answers anyway.

Exodus 4:10 - "And Moses said unto the LORD, O my Lord, I am not eloquent, neither heretofore, nor since thou hast spoken unto thy servant: but I am slow of speech, and of a slow tongue."

D | I Will Be With Thy Mouth

When God calls a man, He assumes full responsibility for his future. God assured Moses that He would teach him everything he should say to Pharaoh. God also promised that Moses would "do signs" with the rod he carried with him. God foretold Moses of all the plagues He would send to Egypt, and how Pharaoh would respond. Moses simply had to follow God's leading, and he did for forty more years.

Exodus 4:12 - "Now therefore go, and I will be with thy mouth, and teach thee what thou shalt say."

C | Firstborn

God instructed Moses to inform Pharaoh that Israel was God's firstborn. If Pharaoh would not free Israel, God would destroy Pharaoh's firstborn. God claimed Abraham's firstborn - "thine ONLY SON Isaac" (as if Ishmael had never been born). When Esau and Jacob were born, Esau despised his role as firstborn, so God claimed Jacob as his firstborn. This is not saying that Israel was God's first son, "because ALL the firstborn are mine," Numbers 3:13.

Exodus 4:22 - "And thou shalt say unto Pharaoh, Thus saith the LORD, Israel is my son, even my firstborn."

C | A Bloody Husband

Zipporah was Moses' wife, daughter of a Midianite priest whom he met during his personal exile. His name was Reuel, later referred to as Jethro (possibly a priestly title meaning "excellency"). Zipporah was hostile about the Jewish circumcision, apparently refusing to allow Moses to circumcise their two sons, Gershom and Eliezer, until God forced the issue by threatening to kill Moses. Their disagreement was so sharp that Moses sent her back to her father for a while (18:2). The entire family rejoined Moses later.

Exodus 4:26 - "...then she said, A bloody husband thou art, because of the circumcision."

B | Aaron

You have to appreciate the timing of this miracle. Moses had been in the wilderness and had not seen his brother, Aaron, for forty years. But after meeting God at the burning bush, God promised to send Aaron. Moses returned home to collect his wife and children. Aaron suddenly showed up. There was no postal service, telephones, or Internet. The only line of communication between Moses and Aaron was God.

Exodus 4:27 - "And the LORD said to Aaron, Go into the wilderness to meet Moses. And he went, and met him in the mount of God, and kissed him."

A | When Expectations Backfire

Moses did what God told him to do. He and Aaron presented themselves to Pharaoh and delivered the message God gave him. But instead of freeing Israel, Pharaoh punished them harsher. God often allows our enemies to rage before He smites them. It may look like our prayers and obedient actions have totally backfired, but they haven't. Moses complained, but God assured him that judgment was coming for Pharaoh.

Exodus 5:22 - "And Moses returned unto the LORD, and said, Lord, wherefore hast thou so evil entreated this people? why is it that thou hast sent me?"

B | Jehovah - LORD

Whenever you see the word LORD in all capital letters in the King James Version of the Bible, it is rendered thus from the Hebrew "YHWH," otherwise rendered "Jehovah." The Hebrew language contains no vowels as does the English. Many Orthodox Jews refuse to pronounce YHWH, so the word LORD is used. Either way, it means "Self-Existent One." In this verse, "God Almighty" is derived from "El Shaddai."

Exodus 6:3 - "I appeared unto Abraham, unto Isaac, and unto Jacob, by the name of God Almighty, but by my name JEHOVAH was I not known to them."

A | How Shall Pharaoh Hearken?

I probably would have asked the same question. "God, why should I believe the king of Egypt will listen to me?" But God had an answer. "I have made you a god in Pharaoh's eyes. And your brother, Aaron, will be your prophet." God can make a mountain out of a molehill. He can make ordinary men stand before kings and prevail. Stop seeing yourself through YOUR eyes and see yourself through God's eyes.

Exodus 6:30 - "...Moses said before the LORD, Behold, I am of uncircumcised lips, and how shall Pharaoh hearken unto me?"

□✓

D | Futile Signs

Jesus criticized the Pharisees, saying, "an evil generation seeketh after a sign." That did not mean that God is unwilling to give miraculous signs to prove His power and glory. But God knows how fickle and self-possessed most men are. He knows that unless a man has faith toward God, no miracles on earth will save him. Few men ever saw more of the miraculous power of God than Pharaoh. Avoid the fatal trap of unbelief!

Exodus 7:3 - "And I will harden Pharaoh's heart, and multiply my signs and my wonders in the land of Egypt."

C | God's Enemies Provoke Him To Judgments

God is not as cruel as many people accuse Him of being. God never launches the first strike. An offense must first be committed. God's enemies provoke Him by transgressions. He does not destroy the just or the righteous. That is Satan's business. God is longsuffering, but His enemies, by nature, invariably give Him cause to destroy them.

Exodus 7:4 - "But Pharaoh shall not hearken unto you, that I may lay my hand upon Egypt, and bring forth mine armies, and my people the Children of Israel, out of the land of Egypt by great judgments."

B | Pharaoh's Sorcerers' Miracles Were Inferior To Moses' Miracles

Satan has always attempted to steal God's glory. It is his number one desire. He regularly uses plagiarism and mimicry to emulate God. Any time Satan can delude and deceive anyone from true faith in God, he has proudly achieved his objective. Again and again, however, God's true power prevails. Moses' serpent ate Pharaoh's serpents. God's Sword of Truth will always prevail over His enemies' swords of deception.

Exodus 7:11 - "Pharaoh also called the wise men and the sorcerers: now the magicians of Egypt, they also did in like manner with their enchantments."

A | Take Away The Frogs!

The second plague God sent upon Egypt by Moses was frogs. Frogs were everywhere - bedchambers, kitchen ovens, even in bread dough. Pharaoh begged Moses to ask God to "take away the frogs!" Moses said, "WHEN?" Unbelievably, Pharaoh said, "TOMORROW!" Tomorrow?? Even today, people are as foolish as Pharaoh was, ignorantly postponing repentance and obedience even in calamitous times. Why not right now?

Exodus 8:8 - "Then Pharaoh called for Moses and Aaron, and said, Intreat the LORD, that he may take away the frogs from me, and from my people; and I will let the people go."

A | This Is The Finger Of God

Pharaoh promised to let Israel go free if Moses took away the frogs. Moses cried out to God because of the frogs, and God immediately killed the frogs in the houses, villages and fields. They piled them up until the whole land stank. But Pharaoh reneged, so God sent another plague by Moses – FLIES! Pharaoh's magicians tried to copy the miracle to appease Pharaoh, but could not. Ultimately, NOBODY will ever beat God at His game.

Exodus 8:19 - "Then the magicians said unto Pharaoh, This is the finger of God."

D | That Nation Will I Judge

When God visited Abraham during the horror of great darkness, Israel's deliverance from Egypt was prophesied. "They shall afflict them four hundred years; and also that nation, whom they shall serve, will I judge; and afterward shall they come out with great substance." Moses executed ten plagues on Egypt, and the Children of Israel walked out with their jewels.

Exodus 9:14 - "For I will at this time send all my plagues upon thine heart, and upon thy servants, and upon thy people; that thou mayest know that there is none like me in all the earth."

A | Intreat The Lord

God sent ten horrifying plagues upon Egypt. Waters turned to blood. Frogs. Lice. Flies. Diseased livestock. Boils on men and beasts. Hail mixed with fire. Locusts. Black darkness. Death of all firstborn. Little by little, Pharaoh seemed to be humbling. He begged Moses to pray for him. But every time, Pharaoh double-crossed Moses. Do you nullify the force of your prayers by returning to sin?

Exodus 9:28 - "Intreat the LORD (for it is enough) that there be no more mighty thunderings and hail; and I will let you go, and ye shall stay no longer."

C | Phony Promises

What do you call a person who promises to do good as long as there is an impending threat of severe punishment, but as soon as they think they can get by with mischief, they quickly break their promises and return to their old tricks? A con-man? A politician? Pharaoh was more. He was a cold-blooded rebel against God. Sounds like many in our generation.

Exodus 9:34 - "And when Pharaoh saw that the rain and the hail and the thunders were ceased, he sinned yet more, and hardened his heart, he and his servants."

C | When Darkness Shines

When God sent darkness upon Egypt by Moses, the Egyptians could not see each other for days. But the Jews could see! Crossing the Red Sea, a cloud darkened Pharaoh's army, but it shone light on Israel! In the world's darkest hour, God's people have light!

Exodus 10:23 - "They saw not one another, neither rose any from his place for three days: but all the Children of Israel had light in their dwellings." Exodus 14:20 - "It was a cloud and darkness to them, but it gave light by night to these."

D | I Will See Thy Face No More

Back in Noah's day, God said that His Spirit would not always strive with man. Sometimes, God decides that He will not waste any more time with certain people. That is a frightening reality. After Pharaoh played diabolical games with Moses, God said, in effect, "that's all - no more!" God judged all the firstborn of Egypt. Pharaoh's son died. Egypt suffered profound judgment. Beware, lest YOU cross the point of no return.

Exodus 10:29 - "And Moses said, Thou hast spoken well, I will see thy face again no more."

B | No Death Angel

Maybe you heard somewhere that a death angel passed through Egypt, killing all the firstborn. But you heard wrong. God did not send a death angel. HE came down! "And it came to pass, that at midnight the LORD smote all the firstborn in the land of Egypt, from the firstborn of Pharaoh that sat on his throne unto the firstborn of the captive that was in the dungeon; and all the firstborn of cattle," Exodus 12:29.

Exodus 11:4 - "And Moses said, Thus saith the LORD, About midnight will I go out into the midst of Egypt."

D | Passover

Passover marks the BIRTH of the nation of Israel. Until that fateful night, the Children of Israel were slaves to Pharaoh in Egypt. God judged Egypt, but Israel was saved by the blood of the lamb they sacrificed that night. Passover foreshadowed Jesus' saving blood which was shed 1400 years later.

Exodus 12:13 - "And the blood shall be to you for a token upon the houses where ye are: and when I see the blood, I will pass over you, and the plague shall not be upon you to destroy you, when I smite the land of Egypt."

A | Worship At Passover

The Israelites marked their doorposts with blood from the "Passover" lamb. Those who observed the Passover feast were protected when God judged the Egyptians. At midnight, Egypt suffered calamity, as millions of firstborn died. But Israel lost not a soul. They bowed their heads and worshipped God. Thank God for His salvation.

Exodus 12:27 - "That ye shall say, It is the sacrifice of the LORD'S passover, who passed over the houses of the Children of Israel in Egypt, when he smote the Egyptians, and delivered our houses. And the people bowed the head and worshipped."

A | Feast Of Unleavened Bread

The seven days following Passover culminate in the Feast of Unleavened Bread. Jews celebrate their deliverance from slavery in Egypt by the mighty hand of God under Moses' leadership. Wine and flatbread are served around a family table, with men, women and children hearing the story of the Exodus read aloud, and thanksgiving given to God for making Israel a nation. Remembering this example, Christians should also give thanks for salvation through Jesus' blood.

Exodus 13:6 - "Seven days thou shalt eat unleavened bread, and in the seventh day shall be a feast to the LORD."

C | Stand Still

God deterred Israel from escaping through Philistine territory because He wanted them to avoid war. Their route seemed senseless, but God knew what He was doing. Pharaoh pursued them with his full army, and the Red Sea locked them in. But God loves impossible situations. Just stand still and let Him work.

Exodus 14:13 - "And Moses said unto the people, Fear ye not, stand still, and see the salvation of the LORD, which he will shew to you to day: for the Egyptians whom ye have seen to day, ye shall see them again no more for ever."

B | The Red Sea

In the "Song of Moses," the dramatic Red Sea crossing is rehearsed and celebrated. Modern archaeological discoveries seem to confirm the scriptures. Egyptian chariots, wheels, weapons and even skeletons have been discovered at the bottom of the sea. But Israel came out of their water "baptism" alive and well!

Exodus 15:19 - "For the horse of Pharaoh went in with his chariots and with his horsemen into the sea, and the LORD brought again the waters of the sea upon them; but the Children of Israel went on dry land in the midst of the sea."

B | Miriam The Prophetess

God called the whole family into service - Moses, Aaron and Miriam. At the beginning, young Miriam negotiated with Pharaoh's daughter for Moses' mother, Jochebed, to be his nursemaid. Now all three children were leading the new nation of Israel. Miriam played her tambourine and led the multitude in praising and worshipping God for taking them safely through the Red Sea. Families who serve God together will see wonderful, glorious things.

Exodus 15:21 - "Miriam answered them, Sing ye to the LORD, for he hath triumphed gloriously; the horse and his rider hath he thrown into the sea."

A | Bitter Waters

Immediately after crossing the Red Sea, Israel was thirsty. But the waters at Marah were bitter and so were the people. Moses prayed. God showed him what to do. When YOUR waters are bitter, pray immediately. Refrain from murmuring. Do not think that God cannot make your bitter waters sweet. He certainly can.

Exodus 15:25 - "And he cried unto the LORD; and the LORD shewed him a tree, which when he had cast into the waters, the waters were made sweet: there he made for them a statute and an ordinance, and there he proved them,"

D | **None Of These Diseases**

Modern science now knows how dangerous many of the medical practices of the ancient world were. Multitudes died due to unsanitary and misguided medical practices. Israel's health and dietary laws seemed strange, but were divinely insightful.

Exodus 15:26 - "If thou wilt diligently hearken to the voice of the LORD thy God, and wilt do that which is right in his sight, and wilt give ear to his commandments, and keep all his statutes, I will put none of these diseases upon thee, which I have brought upon the Egyptians: for I am the LORD that healeth thee."

C | **God Provides An Oasis**

Elim is only briefly mentioned in Exodus, but it was Israel's first encampment past the Red Sea. It was an oasis of seventy palm trees and twelve wells of water. But immediately after departing Elim, the people began to murmur, in a place called (coincidentally?) the wilderness of Sin.

Exodus 16:1 - "And they took their journey from Elim, and all the congregation of the Children of Israel came unto the wilderness of Sin, which is between Elim and Sinai, on the fifteenth day of the second month after their departing out of the land of Egypt."

B | **The Manna**

When God led the Children of Israel from Egypt into the wilderness, He fed them miraculously with manna. Manna means "what is it?" It was nutritious bread sent by God from heaven daily to over a million people for forty years. It tasted like "wafers made with honey," Exodus 16:31. God instructed them to gather only one day's supply, except on the sixth day, they could gather extra for the Sabbath. Otherwise, it always spoiled overnight. Never doubt God's ability to meet your needs.

Exodus 16:23 - "They gathered manna every morning."

C | **Gluttony Punished**

God would surely have fed Israel promptly enough if they had not been so quick to murmur. But they would not restrain themselves. So God sent manna, with a commandment not to gather more than needed - no hoarding. Not surprisingly, some people could not resist over-indulging. God surprised them by rotting the excess. God disapproves of too much, too fast in just about every area of life.

Exodus 16:20 - "Notwithstanding they hearkened not unto Moses; but some of them left of it until the morning, and it bred worms, and stank: and Moses was wroth with them."

A | Pray When Under Threat

A lot has been said about Moses getting water out of a rock at Rephidim. But we seldom contemplate his circumstances. The people were "chiding" with Moses - that means "grappling," "tossing," "wrangling," "contending," with the poor guy. Most every man of God who ever lived has faced the wrath of people he was called to lead. But God legitimizes His anointed in inconceivable ways. Let the skeptics explain water out of a rock.

Exodus 17:4 - "And Moses cried unto the LORD, saying, What shall I do unto this people? they be almost ready to stone me."

B | The Amalekites

This verse has enormous significance. The Amalekites declared war on Israel in the wilderness. Joshua led the defense. Moses stood on a nearby hill while Aaron and Hur held his hands up to God. Joshua won a great victory. God declared war on these people until the end of time. Saul was stripped of his kingship for failing to annihilate them. Samuel killed their king, Agag. David fought them. Hezekiah fought them. Esther defeated Haman, an Agagite (Amalekite). These descendants of Esau are perennial enemies of Israel.

Exodus 17:8 - "Then came Amalek, and fought with Israel in Rephidim."

B | Jethro

Moses benefited immensely from a godly father-in-law. Jethro led the elders of Israel in making a sacrifice unto the Lord with rejoicing over how God led Israel out of Egypt. When he saw the people burdening Moses heavily with their day-to-day problems, Jethro offered the solution of establishing judges over tens, fifties, hundreds and thousands. The seventy elders of Israel were eventually selected from these.

Exodus 18:5 - "And Jethro, Moses' father in law, came with his sons and his wife unto Moses into the wilderness, where he encamped at the mount of God."

A | Going Up To God

Moses met God in Mount Sinai. That is when and where he received the Ten Commandments. Nothing is said about prayer, but in fact, the entire event was about Moses and God in conversation. Sometimes our conversations with God seem more like business as usual than like prayers, but that is the stuff of relationships. You do not have to be on your knees, or speaking in a sanctimonious tone of voice to have priceless communion with God.

Exodus 19:3 - "And Moses went up unto God, and the LORD called unto him out of the mountain."

D | A Kingdom Of Priests

Even before God revealed the Tabernacle plan to Moses, He said Israel was to be a Kingdom of Priests. A priest is an intercessor between God and men. Israel would be God's ministers-servants on earth. For all of time, Israel would be a message-bearer for the Creator of all men. In good times and in bad, God has a purpose for Israel. It will never be annihilated. Israel bore the great High Priest, Messiah, and the twelve Apostles.

Exodus 19:6 - "And ye shall be unto me a kingdom of priests, and an holy nation."

C | Setting Boundaries

God forbad the congregation to come up into the holy mountain and ordered Moses to set bounds to prevent any intruders. The man of God set the boundary. In today's Church, men of God are responsible for defining borders to keep the Church from transgressions. Men of God who fail this are responsible for senseless casualties.

Exodus 19:12 - "And thou shalt set bounds unto the people round about, saying, Take heed to yourselves, that ye go not up into the mount, or touch the border of it: whosoever toucheth the mount shall be surely put to death."

B | God's Sound And Light Show

Modern rock concerts use pyrotechnics and state-of-the-art light and sound equipment to dazzle their audiences. But when Almighty God presented the Ten Commandments, the mountain quaked, covered in smoke, lightnings, and thunderings. God spoke from a great ball of fire

□✓

surrounded by thick darkness. A heavenly trumpet sounded so loudly that two million people ran far away from the mountain.

Exodus 19:16 - "...there were thunders and lightnings, and a thick cloud upon the mount, and the voice of the trumpet exceeding loud; so that all the people that was in the camp trembled."

B | Mount Sinai

Mount Sinai was in the Wilderness of Sin, (some believe) named after the "moon god," Sin. But it was not a moon god who made it famous. Today, "scholars" could drive you crazy with arguments about where Sinai is, but it does not really matter. What matters is that God spoke to Moses and Israel there, and forever changed the world.

Exodus 19:18 - "And mount Sinai was altogether on a smoke, because the LORD descended upon it in fire: and the smoke thereof ascended as the smoke of a furnace, and the whole mount quaked greatly."

A | The Premise Of Prayer

Prayer is the living connection between you and God. Dialogue, not monologue, is the stuff of relationships. How do you know and bond with others without conversation? Can a husband and wife spend happy years together without meaningful conversations? Can parents and children truly bond without frank and honest discussions? Even so, the bilateral exchanges of my words with God's bind me to Him. I pour out my heart to Him, and He responds compassionately. Prayers are the terms of endearment.

Exodus 19:19 - "Moses spake, and God answered him by a voice."

C | The Ten Commandments

Before God gave Moses the Ten Commandments, He had already done many mighty miracles in behalf of the Children of Israel (i.e., Deliverance from Pharaoh, Red Sea crossing, Manna, Quail, etc.). If they had been grateful, they should have been eager to conform to His commandments. But God had to remind them of His goodness. Let us remember that we owe Him far more than He will ever ask of us.

Exodus 20:2 - "I am the LORD thy God, which have brought thee out of the land of Egypt, out of the house of bondage."

85

C | First Commandment - No Other Gods

What did any other god ever do for you? The God who created everything, including YOU and ME, deserves all the glory. It is a shame that He has to tell us not to worship anybody else. You can call it a commandment if you want, but it begs to be appreciated as a stark reality. There ARE no other gods. Whoever created this universe OWNS it. Worshipping anything else is just plain stupid. That may not be grammatically correct, but it is theologically incontrovertible.

Exodus 20:3 - "Thou shalt have no other gods before me."

C | Second Commandment - No Idolatry

Idolatry existed long before Abraham and his descendants worshipped the one, true God. But God will not share His glory with any other. Certainly, nothing man-made, whether carved, molten (molded) or beaten, could ever hear, and know, and respond like the true and living God.

Exodus 20:4-6 - "Thou shalt not make unto thee any graven image, or any likeness of any thing that is in heaven above, or that is in the earth beneath, or that is in the water under the earth: Thou shalt not bow down thyself to them, nor serve them."

C | Third Commandment - Keep His Name Holy

God demands our respect. He is holy, even beyond our wildest imaginations. He will not tolerate disrespect, sacrilege, mockery, or any kind of insult. God is not mocked. This third commandment instructs us to protect the sacredness of God's name. It is NOT a swear word, nor to be used in making oaths. Be safe. Give maximum honor to the Lord's name.

Exodus 20:7 - "Thou shalt not take the name of the LORD thy God in vain; for the LORD will not hold him guiltless that taketh his name in vain."

C | Fourth Commandment - Sabbath

What a brilliant idea! One day off every week! God thought of it first. Rest! Every person needs rest. This is the only one of the Ten Commandments not taught in the New Testament, because God gives believers rest every day when the Comforter comes in - the Baptism of the Holy Spirit. (See Isaiah 28:11-12.)

Exodus 20:8-11 - "Remember the sabbath day, to keep it holy. Six days shalt thou labour, and do all thy work: But the seventh day is the sabbath of the LORD thy God: in it thou shalt not do any work."

C | Fifth Commandment - Honor Father And Mother

This is the first commandment with a promised blessing. At the very least, your parents have a 15-20 year experience ahead of you. They provided shelter, food and clothing while you were otherwise helpless. But that is only a fraction of countless reasons why we should respect, reverence, esteem, even obey our parents - our elders! Our world would be radically improved if this generation would obey this command.

Exodus 20:12 - "Honour thy father and thy mother: that thy days may be long upon the land which the LORD thy God giveth thee."

C | Sixth Commandment - Thou Shalt Not Kill

Here is a stark warning from the Giver of all life to all the potential Takers of life. DON'T DO IT! There is no greater created miracle in the entire universe than the human creature. Not even the angels have freedom of choice, or the ability to freely partake of both mortality and immortality, including their respective worlds. This marvelous entity called mankind is God's pride and joy. Not one of us should have the arbitrary prerogative to terminate another. And we do not.

Exodus 20:13 - "Thou shalt not kill."

C | Seventh Commandment - No Adultery

An adulterer is someone who is married, but commits sexual intercourse with someone other than their lawful spouse. Strong's Concordance compares adultery to apostasy. An apostate abandons faith, departing former beliefs. Adulterers abandon wedlock - breaking vows and destroying the sanctity of matrimony. Since marriage typifies God's relationship with His holy people, an adulterer grievously trespasses against holy principle. The Hebrew language from which "thou shalt not" comes is "lo, lo, lo," which is "no, no, no" or "never, never, never" commit adultery. God says, "NEVER commit adultery."

Exodus 20:14 - "Thou shalt not commit adultery."

C | Eighth Commandment - Do Not Steal

God supplies all our needs according to His riches. Every person receives what God has appointed to him. According to the talents and abilities that God gives, we earn our daily sustenance. God forbids you and me from taking anything that belongs to others. That is THEIR portion. Imagine the world descended into chaos, where no one could keep that which he has worked to attain; a world without borders, boundaries, privacy or safety. That is the world of thieves. Obedience to God's laws would prevent such a world.

Exodus 20:15 - "Thou shalt not steal."

☐ | Ninth Commandment - No False Witness

God defends the integrity of the individual by forbidding false testimony. Slander is a heinous, grievous sin against anyone. Lives are destroyed by lies, false accusations and misrepresentations. God demands truth and right-doing in our relationships with others. The devastating sinfulness of malicious gossip and scandalous rumor-mongering ranks equally with murder and adultery in this context. If you cannot say something nice about someone, do not say anything at all. Get the stick out of your own eye before assailing them for their splinter.

Exodus 20:16 - "Thou shalt not bear false witness against thy neighbour."

☐ | Tenth Commandment - Do Not Covet

Coveting is a synonym for lust. When Jesus warned that lusting after a woman was adulterous, He spoke of covetous desire. Since the Garden of Eden, God has always forbidden certain things. The desire for ANYTHING that God forbids is covetousness. Learn what belongs to you, and leave everything else alone. The forbidden fruit is NEVER good.

Exodus 20:17 - "Thou shalt not covet thy neighbour's house, thou shalt not covet thy neighbour's wife, nor his manservant, nor his maidservant, nor his ox, nor his ass, nor any thing that is thy neighbour's."

☐ | God Is Specific

God gave Adam everything in the garden except one specific tree. The story of Cain and Abel taught that God insists on a specific offering (blood sacrifices - not garden produce). Later, God even made specific requirements for the altar itself - unhewn stone. Learn a lesson. If you want to receive God's blessings, you have to do everything His specific way.

Exodus 20:25 - "...if thou wilt make me an altar of stone, thou shalt not build it of hewn stone: for if thou lift up thy tool upon it, thou hast polluted it."

C | Sundry Laws

Besides the Ten Commandments, God gave Moses countless "miscellaneous" laws. Every aspect of domestic life was considered. Laws about family, commerce, criminal and civil laws, moral, even sexual codes were defined. God's laws were given to define right and wrong, with a prescription for punishment for non-compliance. Centuries earlier, Hammurabi of Babylon had written sundry laws on the now-famous stele, but his code has mostly perished. Today, in governments and societies around the world, the influence of "Moses'" law is still profound.

Exodus 21:1 (to 22:31) - "Now these are the judgments which thou shalt set before them."

C | Let It Unfold

God never planned for Israel to take possession of the entire Promised Land in one large conquest. He knew there would be enormous challenges and changes to adapt to, even in God's will. Great victories best come in increments. Therefore, we should not fret when improvements in our lives come slowly. A rosebud must unfold gradually. Any effort to force it open will only destroy it. Relax. Be patient - God is!

Exodus 23:30 - "By little and little I will drive them out from before thee, until thou be increased, and inherit the land."

D | By Little And Little

This prophecy is based on a divine principle. Everything God does is progressive. "By little and little I will drive them out..." is God's daily reminder that HE is giving us the land, and that we are not taking the land by our own brilliance or devices. He truly governs our daily progress, sometimes giving more, sometimes giving less than we expect, but always reminding us that He is the benevolent Master of all things.

Exodus 23:30 - "By little and little I will drive them out from before thee, until thou be increased, and inherit the land."

B | The Body Of Heaven

We are forced to reconcile verses that appear to contradict. Again and again, the scripture says that God is invisible. But the seventy elders saw "the body of heaven in his clearness," upon a sapphire foundational stone. The key word here is "clearness." They saw a bright shining light representing God's presence. See, The Oneness of God. Twice, John said, "No man hath seen God at any time," John 1:18; 1 John 4:12.

Exodus 24:10 - "And they saw the God of Israel: and there was under his feet as it were a paved work of a sapphire stone, and as it were the body of heaven in his clearness."

D | The Tabernacle Plan

The Tabernacle plan was as prophetic as anything in the Bible. Virtually everything about the Tabernacle and its furnishings carried a message about the coming Messiah and His plan to redeem men from their sins. If Moses had not followed God's pattern meticulously, a profound message would have been skewed or totally lost.

Exodus 25:8-9 - "And let them make me a sanctuary; that I may dwell among them. According to all that I shew thee, after the pattern of the tabernacle, and the pattern of all the instruments thereof, even so shall ye make it."

D | The Ark Of The Covenant

The first item God commissioned for the Tabernacle was the Ark of the Covenant. Built of shittim wood, roughly about 4ft-L x 3ft-W x 3ft-H, overlaid with and crowned with gold. Staves permanently slid through rings on four corners for carrying by priests. The "testimony" (Ten Commandments) inside was covered by a beaten-golden "Mercy Seat" with two winged cherubims facing each other. It prefigured Jesus Christ; the embodiment and mouthpiece of everything divine.

Exodus 25:22 - "...there I will meet with thee, and I will commune with thee from above the mercy seat."

D | The Table Of Shewbread

The second item prescribed for the Tabernacle was the Table of Shewbread, made of shittim wood and overlaid and crowned with gold. It had rings and staves so the priests could carry it when they traveled. It sat past the altar, before the golden candlestick, and ALWAYS contained a loaf of bread for each tribe of Israel. It foreshadowed Jesus Christ, the Bread of Life. God wanted us to know that there is always bread on His table. Hungry? Jesus will fill you.

Exodus 25:30 - "And thou shalt set upon the table shewbread before me alway."

D | The Golden Candlestick

Jews call it the Menorah. It was a beaten-gold Candlestick with seven branches. Jesus is the Light of the World. The oil that burned in the light represents the Holy Ghost of Jesus Christ burning in the seven original New Testament Churches. Now, His Spirit fills everyone who will receive it. The Candlestick was to burn continuously. This little light of mine, I'm going to let it shine.

Exodus 25:37 - "Thou shalt make the seven lamps thereof: and they shall light the lamps thereof, that they may give light over against it."

D | The Tabernacle Curtains And Boards

God told Moses every detail of the Tabernacle, including the number of boards with their measurements, wood type, and overlayments. He defined all the curtains and coverings by material, color and measurement, and how they were to be placed. The principal colors were blue, purple and scarlet. The metals were gold and silver. The skins were goat and badger. It is inconceivable that a God of such detail doesn't care about the minutiae of our lives.

Exodus 26:30 - "And thou shalt rear up the Tabernacle according to the fashion thereof which was shewed thee in the mount."

D | The Veil

The Veil prevented anyone from entering the Most Holy Place where the Ark of the Covenant was. The Veil was blue, purple and scarlet. Blue is the color of water, and red is the color of blood. Purple is the color of royalty - kingship. By the blood of Calvary and the water of baptism, the Son of Man, prince of peace, Jesus, was exalted to royalty - King of Kings.

Exodus 26:31 - "And thou shalt make a vail of blue, and purple, and scarlet, and fine twined linen of cunning work: with cherubims shall it be made."

D | The Brazen Altar

Everything that happened in the Tabernacle began at the Brazen Altar. Animals were killed and burned. Since the Garden of Eden, God has required death for sin. At the altar, the debt began to be paid, the blood was shed, and remission of sins became possible. Without shedding blood, there can be no remission for sins. This animal blood appeased God until the perfect Lamb was slain - Jesus Christ. ALL remission of sins ultimately comes by HIS blood.

Exodus 27:1,8 - "And thou shalt make an altar... as it was shewed thee in the mount, so shall they make it."

D | The Court

The Tabernacle plan included only one entrance, and that was on the east side. Nearly all the pagan religions worshiped the sun god, facing east. God made them face west when they entered the Tabernacle. The single entrance typifies Jesus Christ, the ONLY door of our salvation. There is salvation in no other. We must turn our backs on all other gods.

Exodus 27:13-14 - "...the breadth of the court on the east side eastward shall be fifty cubits. The hangings of one side of the gate shall be fifteen cubits: their pillars three, and their sockets three."

D | The Priests' Holy Garments

A priest is an intercessor between God and men. From its inception, the priesthood was the highest office a man could occupy. Accordingly, God instructed Moses to dress them appropriately. Holy garments would be glorious and beautiful. Herein is a great precept. Our appearance should reflect our value. The world would have us "dumb down," dressing grungy, sloppily, like worthless creatures. God would have us look holy, glorious, and beautiful. Are you a godly person? Dress the part!

Exodus 28:2 - "And thou shalt make holy garments for Aaron thy brother for glory and for beauty."

B | Bells And Pomegranates

The High Priest's robe had golden bells and woven pomegranates around its hemline. Many theories about their symbolism are mostly mystical, contradictory and unprovable. Pomegranates are perceived as a symbol of the righteousness of the Priesthood. The joyous sound of the bells notified outsiders that the High Priest was still alive after entering the Holy of Holies - he had not died.

Exodus 28:35 - "And it shall be upon Aaron to minister: and his sound shall be heard when he goeth in unto the holy place before the LORD, and when he cometh out, that he die not."

□✓

D | The Consecration Of The Priesthood

The Priesthood was consecrated AFTER the Tabernacle was complete. It took a Tabernacle plan to accomplish the task. The blood sacrifices, unleavened bread, anointing oil, water of washing, garments, ephod, mitre, various offerings - ALL were necessary to make the priests holy. Similarly, the New Testament Church must be assembled before Jesus returns to ascend to His High Priesthood in Jerusalem for 1000 years.

Exodus 29:44-45 - "And I will sanctify the tabernacle of the congregation, and the altar: I will sanctify also both Aaron and his sons, to minister to me in the priest's office."

D | The Altar Of Incense

The Altar of Incense was roughly four-feet-cubed, gold-plated, gold-crowned shittim wood, with horns on the top corners, and rings for the staves with which the priests carried it. It stood before the Veil, immediately outside the Mercy Seat, where the High Priest met God. The Priest offered holy incense morning and evening, perpetually before the Lord. Once annually, a blood atonement was made here. Incense represents the sweet odors of the prayers of the saints.

Exodus 30:1 - "...thou shalt make an altar to burn incense upon: of shittim wood shalt thou make it."

D | The Brazen Laver

After the Priest sacrificed at the Brazen Altar, he had to wash himself at the Brazen Laver before entering the Holy Place. The laver is a typological and prophetic symbol of water baptism in the New Testament. The altar represents repentance. The laver followed, illustrating our need to be baptized for the remission of our sins after we have repented.

Exodus 30:18,20 - "Thou shalt also make a laver of brass, and his foot also of brass, to wash withal... When they go into the tabernacle of the congregation, they shall wash with water, that they die not."

D | The Holy Anointing Oil

God called for a specially concocted holy Anointing Oil to be used in the Tabernacle. The proprietary apothecary formula was forbidden to ANYONE outside the Tabernacle. It had myrrh, cinnamon, calamus, cassia, and olive oil, all in specific measurements. Everything in the Tabernacle had to be anointed (rubbed) with it, including the priests. This

93

oil symbolizes the Holy Spirit which, in the New Testament Church, comes to fill every believer.

Exodus 30:25 - "And thou shalt make it an oil of holy ointment, an ointment compound after the art of the apothecary: it shall be an holy anointing oil."

B | Anointed Craftsmen

God gave Moses explicit instructions for the construction of all artifacts, vessels and furniture in the Tabernacle. Better yet, He called specific men into service and gave them a powerful anointing to do that work. When God wants a thing done, He will bring it to pass. Jesus' parable of the talents indicates that our abilities multiply as we apply ourselves to fulfill His will. You will do an outstanding job. God will enable you!

Exodus 31:3 - "I have filled him with the spirit of God, in wisdom, and in understanding, and in knowledge, and in all manner of workmanship."

B | The Law

God instructed Moses to command the people to eat unleavened bread at the first Passover, before escaping Egypt, saying, "that the Lord's law may be in thy mouth." The bread of God represents His awesome Law, which nourishes us all. God's Word is our life. Manna from heaven nurtured their bodies, but the Law handed down at Sinai gave life to the nation.

Exodus 31:18 - "And he gave unto Moses, when he had made an end of communing with him upon mount Sinai, two tables of testimony, tables of stone, written with the finger of God."

B | The Golden Calf

While Moses was in the mount with God, the Israelites persuaded Aaron to make a Golden Calf which they worshipped as god. When Moses returned, he was outraged and smashed the tablets written by the finger of God. Moses ground the gold to powder and made them DRINK it! God's Spirit would have dwelled in those people, but gold was a bitter-tasting god.

Exodus 32:20 - "He took the calf which they had made, and burnt it in the fire, and ground it to powder, and strawed it upon the water, and made the Children of Israel drink of it."

A | Moses The Intercessor

After meeting God in Sinai, Moses found Israel riotously worshipping a Golden Calf. God started to utterly destroy them, offering to make Moses a great nation instead. But Moses wanted to be blotted out of the Book of Life if God would not save Israel. That was dramatic intercession!

Exodus 32:31-32 - "Moses returned unto the LORD, and said, Oh, this people have sinned a great sin, and have made them gods of gold. Yet now, if thou wilt forgive their sin--; and if not, blot me, I pray thee, out of thy book which thou hast written."

B | Forbidden Ornaments

This is one of the most overlooked and neglected items in the Bible. Aaron and the Children of Israel infuriated God Almighty for creating and worshipping the Golden Calf. It all began with the jewelry they brought from Egypt. After that incident, God utterly hated jewelry on His people. He demanded that they give it to Him. Read my essay on the topic, entitled "Ornaments of Jewelry," and you will see that God spoke to the issue all throughout the Bible.

Exodus 33:6 - "And the Children of Israel stripped themselves of their ornaments by the mount Horeb."

A | Face To Face With God

God punished Israel for worshipping the Golden Calf. Moses' intercession literally saved their lives. Immediately, God again promised to give them a land flowing with milk and honey. But the people were unmoved. Ultimately, it was Moses' profound relationship with God that salvaged the entire project. Israel could easily see that when Moses entered the Tabernacle, the cloudy pillar descended, and the voice of God spoke to Moses. Remember, whole nations can depend on one man's prayers.

Exodus 33:11 - "And the LORD spake unto Moses face to face, as a man speaketh unto his friend."

A | Show Me Thy Glory

God is invisible. Three times, the Bible says, "No man hath seen God at any time." When Moses asked to see God's glory, God showed him His "back parts." That could not possibly mean God's back, buttocks or thighs. He is invisible. Moses saw God's past goodness - the Genesis story revealed! 1400 years later, Moses saw the glory of God in the face of Jesus Christ on the Mount of Transfiguration.

Exodus 33:23 - "I will take away mine hand, and thou shalt see my back parts: but my face shall not be seen."

B | The Stone Tablets

The first set of the Ten Commandments were hewn and written on stone by God Himself. Moses broke them in rage when he found Israel worshipping the Golden Calf. God made Moses prepare new tablets and bring them into the mountain where Moses wrote as God dictated the law. Those tablets were stored in the Ark of the Covenant for centuries.

Exodus 34:1 - "And the LORD said unto Moses, Hew thee two tables of stone like unto the first: and I will write upon these tables the words that were in the first tables, which thou brakest."

C | Jealous God

God promised Israel a holy land, but commanded them to remove every false god. God will not share His glory or tolerate spiritual adultery. Our love for Him must be undivided. Love not the world.

Exodus 34:12 - "Take heed to thyself, lest thou make a covenant with the inhabitants of the land whither thou goest, lest it be for a snare in the midst of thee: But ye shall destroy their altars, break their images, and cut down their groves: For thou shalt worship no other god: for the LORD, whose name is Jealous, is a jealous God."

A | Moses' Fast

Moses spent forty days in the holy mount, presumably without food. God miraculously engraved the Ten Commandments on stone tablets. Moses descended and found Israel sinfully rioting. He broke the tablets in fury, and returned up the mount for another forty days without food and water - a truly miraculous fast. Ordinarily, no man could attempt that and survive. Nevertheless, his fasting yielded supernatural results. Holy fasting will sanctify you unto God with miraculous results.

Exodus 34:28 - "...he was there with the LORD forty days and forty nights; he did neither eat bread, nor drink water."

B | Forfeiting Gold

Nowadays, people do not talk about this much, but it is a big deal in the ancient story. After the Children of Israel offended God so profoundly by worshipping the Golden Calf, they turned in all their gold. Eventually, God commanded that all gold be surrendered either to the Tabernacle or the Kingdom - no privately held gold.

Exodus 35:22 - "And they came, both men and women, as many as were willing hearted, and brought bracelets, and earrings, and rings, and tablets, all jewels of gold: and every man that offered offered an offering of gold unto the LORD."

B | Aholiab And Bezaleel

Two men oversaw the creation and production of the entire Tabernacle and all its furnishings, in a VAST range of workmanship - metalworkers, stone cutters, woodworkers, tailors, weavers, furniture makers, apothecaries, and more. They made everything from incense and oil to the priests' robes, even the Ark of the Covenant. When God gives you a job, He will fully enable you.

Exodus 36:1 - "Then wrought Bezaleel and Aholiab, and every wise hearted man, in whom the LORD put wisdom and understanding to know how to work all manner of work for the service of the sanctuary."

B | The Tabernacle Materials

God instructed Moses to collect a free-will offering from the people to construct and furnish the Tabernacle. Gold, silver, brass, linens, skins, wood, oil, spices, precious stones, and much more. "...whosoever is of a willing heart, let him bring it, an offering of the LORD," Exodus 35:5. Soon, Moses had more than he needed. God's work is the most worthy cause. We should be excited to give all we can to support His work.

Exodus 36:7 - "For the stuff they had was sufficient for all the work to make it, and too much."

D | Wood Overlaid With Gold

The Tabernacle furniture was made of shittim wood, overlaid with gold, silver or brass. The furnishings and walls inside the Holy Place were covered in gold. The Ark represents Christ. Wood symbolized the humanity of Christ; gold, His deity. God said, in Isaiah 13:12, "I will make a man more precious than fine gold." Shittim wood is now obscure. No one knows with certainty what kind of tree it was. The significance of our humanity will be obscured in Heaven after God changes our corruption to incorruption.

Exodus 37:1 - "Bezaleel made the ark of shittim wood."

C | Sweetness

God ordered sweet-smelling oil and sweet-smelling incense to be used perpetually in the Tabernacle. We are so accustomed to the odious and unsavory effects of sin in the world that we forget that everything in God's universe was beautiful beyond our ability to comprehend BEFORE SIN came. God demanded that His earthly house be as beautiful and pleasing as it could be, reminding us that in His presence are pleasures forevermore.

Exodus 37:29 - "And he made the holy anointing oil, and the pure incense of sweet spices, according to the work of the apothecary."

C | Touch Not

Everything in the Tabernacle was portable, because Israel was on a journey. God required them to put rings on the four corners of the holy furniture to slide staves into for the priests to lift and carry the items. The Ark of the Covenant could NEVER be touched by any man, and the staves must never be removed. This teaches reverence and sanctity for the things of God and the ministry. Modern Christians desperately need to re-learn this lesson.

Exodus 38:7 - "...he put the staves into the rings on the sides of the altar, to bear it withal."

B | The Breastplate

The priest's breastplate was attached to the ephod (vestment) by golden rings. It had twelve stones, each representing a tribe of Israel. This dramatized the role of the High Priest as the intercessor before God in behalf of the twelve tribes. Some believe that individual stones became illuminated when God had a special message for a particular tribe. A man of God carries the burden of the people continually over his heart.

Exodus 39:8 - "And he made the breastplate of cunning work, ...It was foursquare; ...And they set in it four rows of stones."

D | Obeying A Mystery

Moses' team created the entire Tabernacle with literally hundreds of intricate details as prescribed by God. The furnishings, the consumables (incense, oil, sacrifices), the garments (robes, mitres, vestments, etc.) and much, much more. There is no way they could have understood the amazing prophetic significance of all those things. In like manner, we must also obey God many times when we have NO CLUE what His purpose is.

Exodus 39:43 - "And Moses did look upon all the work, and, behold, they had done it as the LORD had commanded, even so had they done it: and Moses blessed them."

B | The Glory Cloud

The ultimate purpose of the Tabernacle was to be a place where God manifest His glory to the people. On the first day the first service was conducted, God covered the place with His glory. Jesus built the Church (us) for the same reason - to be a habitation of God's glory.

Exodus 40:34-35 - "Then a cloud covered the tent of the congregation, and the glory of the LORD filled the tabernacle. And Moses was not able to enter into the tent of the congregation, because the cloud abode thereon, and the glory of the LORD filled the tabernacle."

C | Follow The Cloud

From the first day the Tabernacle was in service, for thirty-eight years, God's glory was manifest as a cloud by day and a pillar of fire by night in the sight of all the people. When the cloud moved, they moved. When it stayed, they stayed. Always follow God wherever He leads.

Exodus 40:36-37 - "And when the cloud was taken up from over the tabernacle, the children of Israel went onward in all their journeys: But if the cloud were not taken up, then they journeyed not till the day that it was taken up."

Lessons from the Book of
LEVITICUS

B | Leviticus

Leviticus is a seminal document, in many ways more profound than the United States Declaration of Independence or Constitution. How? First, Leviticus sets in order the priesthood, and by default, organized religion. Secondly, it contains the germ form of a universal code of civil law that now rules not only Israel, but also most of Western civilization. Although Hammurabi's Code (Babylon) predates "Moses' Law," the Judaeo-Christian ethic can be seen far more predominantly in governments everywhere.

Leviticus 8:5 - "And Moses said unto the congregation, This is the thing which the LORD commanded to be done."

D | Sacrificing A Male Without Blemish

God instructed Moses to tell the people to bring sacrificial offerings to the priests so atonement could be made for their sins. Specifically, they had to be male cattle, sheep or goats, without blemish. And they had to be presented voluntarily. All these conditions prefigured Jesus Christ, spotless lamb, who freely offered up His life for our sins.

Leviticus 1:3 - "If his offering be a burnt sacrifice of the herd, let him offer a male without blemish: he shall offer it of his own voluntary will at the door of the tabernacle of the congregation before the LORD."

B | The Meat Offering

The meat offerings were different from the blood sacrifices. "Meat" is a general term the ancients used to refer to all food. The meat offering was a FOOD offering. It had to be unleavened bread (baked, cooked or fried) with oil, and salted. Part was burned on the altar to the Lord, and part became the priests' food. It also symbolized Jesus, the bread of life.

Leviticus 2:8 - "And thou shalt bring the meat offering that is made of these things unto the LORD: and when it is presented unto the priest, he shall bring it unto the altar."

D | Killed By The Beneficiary

It seems somehow ironic that God required each person to slay their own sacrifice before presenting it to the priest for placement on the altar. The murderer would be the beneficiary of the atonement. That is exactly how Jesus' sacrifice was enacted. He was killed by the very people He came to save.

Leviticus 3:2 - "And he shall lay his hand upon the head of his offering, and kill it at the door of the tabernacle of the congregation: and Aaron's sons the priests shall sprinkle the blood upon the altar round about."

B | Five Offerings

Burnt Offerings (Leviticus 1) were primary sacrifices for universal sin. Meat (food) Offerings (Leviticus 2) were gift offerings. Peace Offerings (Leviticus 3) were fellowship offerings shared between God (at the altar), the priest and the donor. Sin Offerings (Leviticus 4) covered sins of ignorance - unknown sins. Trespass Offerings (Leviticus 5) covered sins that were knowingly committed.

Leviticus 4:2 - "...If a soul shall sin through ignorance against any of the commandments of the LORD... then let him bring for his sin, which he hath sinned, a young bullock without blemish unto the LORD for a sin offering."

A | Wordless Prayer

Prayer is defined as a petition, a request, or communion with God. The earliest forms of repentance under the Tabernacle plan involved bringing sacrifices to the Lord. Nothing at all is mentioned about praying, confessing, or asking God's forgiveness. Offering a sacrifice of blood apparently constituted an admission of guilt and was viewed as a petition for God's forgiveness. Sometimes, actions speak louder than words.

Leviticus 4:23 - "Or if his sin, wherein he hath sinned, come to his knowledge; he shall bring his offering, a kid of the goats, a male without blemish."

A | Confessing Sins

This is the first occurrence in the Bible of any requirement for confession. After Moses listed several sins, he called for the guilty party to confess his sin. A precedent for all time was set. As a general rule, the priests confessed all Israel's sins when they offered sacrifices. God requires that we acknowledge our wrong-doing. He is more interested in producing righteousness in us than in punishing our wrongs.

Leviticus 5:5 - "And it shall be, when he shall be guilty in one of these things, that he shall confess that he hath sinned in that thing."

C | Lies And Deceptions

Throughout the Pentateuch (the first five books, written by Moses), an almost countless array of sins are condemned. But among the reasons for the five major offerings for sins, lies, deception and bearing false witness ranked among the worst of all. The God of Truth hates lies, deception and false testimony. Liars are reckoned among the worst of sinners. Only speak truth.

Leviticus 6:2-6 - "If a soul sin, and commit a trespass against the LORD, and lie unto his neighbour... or hath deceived his neighbour; or ...sweareth falsely; ...he shall bring his trespass offering unto the LORD."

D | Compensation For The Priests

God stipulated that the priests should keep a portion of the burnt offerings, meat offerings, peace offerings, sin offerings, and trespass offerings for themselves. Prophetically, this sets a divine precedent that all ministers of all ages should be compensated for their services in the ministry.

Leviticus 7:35 - "This is the portion ...out of the offerings of the LORD made by fire, in the day when he presented them to minister unto the LORD in the priest's office; Which the LORD commanded to be given them of the children of Israel, ...by a statute for ever throughout their generations."

C | Congregation

Once the Tabernacle was fully prepared and Moses had thoroughly given instructions pertaining to all the service of the Tabernacle, he called the people together to the door of the Tabernacle to witness the consecration of the Priesthood. This was the first occasion for all of Israel to attend a holy service at the house of God, but it set a precedent. Even in the New Testament, we are not to forsake the assembling of ourselves together at God's house.

Leviticus 8:3 - "And gather thou all the congregation together unto the door of the tabernacle of the congregation."

D | The Ephod

The High Priest wore an elaborate vestment called the ephod. Two onyx stones on the shoulders contained the names of the twelve tribes of Israel. Twelve precious stones were mounted on the front on blue, red, and white embroidered linen. Also called the Urim and Thummin, when the Priest consulted God before the Ark of the Covenant, the stones illuminated if God blessed, or gave a "yes" answer. Dull stones meant God's cursing, or a "no" answer.

Leviticus 8:7 - "...and he girded him with the curious girdle of the ephod, and bound it unto him therewith."

D | The Cross Leads To His Glory

The Tabernacle furniture was positioned in the pattern of the Cross. BOTTOM - Altar (Repentance). CENTER - Laver (Water Baptism). LEFT, Candlestick (Baptism of the Holy Ghost). RIGHT, Shewbread (The Word - Bread of Life). TOP - Incense (Prayer). They led to the Veil and the Ark of the Covenant. When we repent, get baptized, receive the Holy Spirit, study the Word, and pray, we will discover the glory of God in that holy place.

Leviticus 9:6 - "...Moses said, This is the thing which the LORD commanded that ye should do: and the glory of the LORD shall appear unto you."

B | The Horns Of The Altar

Both the Brazen Altar and the Altar of Incense had horns on the four corners. Horns on a creature are considered its most exalted feature. Several scriptures say the horns of the righteous shall be exalted. Most appropriately, the priests applied the blood of sacrifices to the horns to sanctify them to the Lord. Sanctify your best features to God.

Leviticus 9:8-9 - "Aaron therefore went unto the altar, and slew the calf of the sin offering, which was for himself. ...and he dipped his finger in the blood, and put it upon the horns of the altar."

D | Fire From The LORD

God gloriously validated the new Tabernacle with supernatural manifestations, including fire from Heaven to consume the sacrifices. God sent fire upon consecrated sacrifices numerous times in the Old Testament. Fire is a symbol of the Holy Ghost. 120 New Testament believers consecrated themselves in prayer in the Upper Room at Jerusalem. God sent His Spirit with tongues of fire falling on them all.

Leviticus 9:24 - "And there came a fire out from before the LORD, and consumed upon the altar the burnt offering and the fat: which when all the people saw, they shouted, and fell on their faces."

C | No Booze In The Ministry

Is it too much for God to ask His ministers to stay sober? Why this scourge of drunkenness among professing Christian ministers today? Why should a Pastor's office have a "wet bar?" God demands that preachers stay sober.

Leviticus 10:8-10 - "And the LORD spake unto Aaron, saying, Do not drink wine nor strong drink, thou, nor thy sons with thee, when ye go into the tabernacle of the congregation, lest ye die: it shall be a statute for ever throughout your generations: And that ye may put difference between holy and unholy, and between unclean and clean."

C | Fellowship

The Peace Offering was shared three ways. Part was burned on the altar unto the Lord. Part was given to the priest (the Heave Offering) to eat. The remainder was eaten by the people. It is often referred to as the fellowship offering because it brings the people together with God and the Priesthood.

Leviticus 10:14 - "And the wave breast and heave shoulder shall ye eat in a clean place; thou, and thy sons, and thy daughters with thee: for they be thy due, and thy sons' due, which are given out of the sacrifices of peace offerings."

C | Be Ye Holy

God is holy - "sacred, hallowed, sanctified, consecrated, virtuous." God is one of a kind. Unique. Untainted. The opposite of holy is "profane, foul, vulgar, impure." Someday, He will purge all the universe of everything that was begotten of sin. Only God, His holy kingdom and His holy ones will remain. Put away everything carnal, worldly, and profane. Come out. Be separate. Touch not the unclean thing. Be HOLY.

Leviticus 11:45 - "For I am the LORD that bringeth you up out of the land of Egypt, to be your God: ye shall therefore be holy, for I am holy."

C | Clean And Unclean Foods

So-called "Kosher" laws forbade eating "unclean" foods. The New Testament ended those laws. Paul said of various meats, "...for neither, if we eat, are we the better; neither, if we eat not, are we the worse," 1 Corinthians 8:8. He countermanded teachings to "abstain from meats, which God hath created to be received with thanksgiving," 1 Timothy 4:3.

Leviticus 11:46 - "This is the law of the beasts, and of the fowl, and of every living creature that moveth in the waters, ...the unclean and the clean, ...the beast that may be eaten and the beast that may not be eaten."

B | Childbirth

Under the law, contact with blood made one unclean. Therefore, childbirth rendered the mother unclean - seven days for a male child, two weeks for a female. Her purification process was 33 days for a male, 66 days for a female. After purification, she must bring a sacrificial offering for atonement to the Tabernacle. After Jesus' blood made atonement at Calvary, these laws expired.

Leviticus 12:4 - "And she shall then continue in the blood of her purifying three and thirty days; she shall touch no hallowed thing, nor come into the sanctuary, until the days of her purifying be fulfilled."

B | Leprosy

The King James translators saw the Hebrew "tzaraath" and translated it "leprosy." Compared to our modern definition of leprosy, many of the Biblical symptoms mentioned actually encompassed a variety of diseases The ancients simply did not know what they were dealing with. Only God knew the potential risks to the general population, so these rituals of quarantine and purification were enormously important. Sin was always suspected as the first cause of disease, so religious rites were applied first.

Leviticus 13:9 - "When the plague of leprosy is in a man, then he shall be brought unto the priest."

A | The Wave Offering

When Israelites brought their offerings to the Lord, they were considered sacred tokens in the covenant between God and men. Certain offerings were "heaved" into the air as testimony of their presentation, then eaten by the priests. In other cases, the meat was "waved" before the Lord and was eaten by the worshiper. Today, we wave our hands to the Lord as tokens of surrender to Him.

Leviticus 14:24 - "And the priest shall take the lamb of the trespass offering, and the log of oil, and the priest shall wave them for a wave offering before the LORD."

A | Touching The Unclean

Touch is one of the five senses. As ears hear, eyes see, noses smell, and tongues taste, the body feels. It receives input from anything it touches. It is impacted and influenced by what it touches. God repeatedly told Israel not to touch unclean (forbidden) things. Holy things become defiled and unholy by touch. Only sanctified things may touch the holy. Once defiled, one had to go through a purification process. In the New Testament, one must repent and be washed in Jesus' blood.

Leviticus 15:27 - "And whosoever toucheth those things shall be unclean, and shall wash..."

A | Strange Fire And Strange Incense

God killed Nadab and Abihu for offering strange fire. God ordered Aaron to bring fire from the holy altar of sacrifice, and holy incense. God curses phony sacrifices and phony prayers.

Leviticus 16:12-13 - "...he shall take a censer full of burning coals of fire from off the altar before the LORD, and his hands full of sweet incense beaten small, and bring it within the vail: And he shall put the incense upon the fire before the LORD, that the cloud of the incense may cover the mercy seat that is upon the testimony, that he die not."

D | The Scapegoat

Annually, on the Day of Atonement, the High Priest presented two goats to the Lord. He sacrificed one on the altar for the people. He laid hands upon the head of the second goat and transferred the sins of the people to it. This scapegoat was taken into uninhabited wilderness and abandoned - prefiguring Jesus, our scapegoat. Isaiah 53:4 says, "Surely he hath borne our griefs and carried our sorrows..."

Leviticus 16:22 - "And the goat shall bear upon him all their iniquities unto a land not inhabited: and he shall let go the goat in the wilderness."

D | Atonement

God requires all men to make atonement for their sins. Sins are forgiven, dismissed, purged, and washed away. Offenses are repaired, appeased, compensated, and remedied. People are reconciled, excused, exonerated, acquitted, and sanctified. The blood of an innocent sacrificial animal temporarily bought atonement. The sins of Old Testament supplicants were put off until the precious blood of the spotless Lamb of God perfectly atoned at Calvary. ONLY Jesus' blood truly atones.

Leviticus 16:30 - "...on that day shall the priest make an atonement for you, to cleanse you, that ye may be clean from all your sins before the LORD."

B | Blood Makes Atonement

God sanctified everything about blood. He said the life of the flesh is in the blood. In Leviticus 17, He formally banned all profaning of anything pertaining to blood and forbade people to eat blood. The ONLY sacrifices of blood were to be made unto Him for atonement. He promised to destroy anyone who sacrificed blood to devils.

Leviticus 17:11 - "For the life of the flesh is in the blood: and I have given it to you upon the altar to make an atonement for your souls: for it is the blood that maketh an atonement for the soul."

C | You Shall Not Do After The Doings Of The Land

Immediately before introducing the laws for sexual morality, God commanded Israel NOT to follow the ways of Egypt (from which they came), nor the ways of Canaan (to which they were headed). If ancient Egypt and Canaan were taboo, how much more taboo would our modern vile cultures be? Are you in love with "Egypt"?

Leviticus 18:3 - "After the doings of the land of Egypt, wherein ye dwelt, shall ye not do: and after the doings of the land of Canaan, whither I bring you, shall ye not do: neither shall ye walk in their ordinances."

C | Incest

The law clearly defined what is now called incest. "It is wickedness." A person must never have sexual intercourse with parents or step-parents. A man must never have intercourse with sisters, half-sisters, daughters, granddaughters, aunts, daughters-in-law, or sisters-in-law, and he must not take both a woman and her daughter or granddaughter. God's laws are singularly responsible for the integrity of civilization. Without them, society would have already completely disintegrated.

Leviticus 18:6 - "None of you shall approach to any that is near of kin to him, to uncover their nakedness: I am the LORD."

C | **Homosexuality**

God did not stutter or mince words when He ordered men NOT to lay with other men as they do with women. He said it is an abomination worthy of death. How much plainer could it be?

Leviticus 18:22,30 - "Thou shalt not lie with mankind, as with womankind: it is abomination. ...defile not yourselves therein: I am the LORD your God." Leviticus 20:13 - "If a man also lie with mankind, as he lieth with a woman, both of them have committed an abomination: they shall surely be put to death; their blood shall be upon them."

C | **Sexual Perversions**

God hated the sexual perversions He saw among heathen nations and demanded that His people not engage in any of them. He forbade incest, homosexual acts, acts with beasts, acts committed unto false gods or idols, and acts with anyone who was married to someone else. At the core of these commands was God's insistence that human seed and human sexuality be sacred and undefiled, reserved only for a man and his wife.

Leviticus 18:24 - "Defile not ye yourselves in any of these things: for in all these the nations are defiled which I cast out before you."

C | **Provision For The Gleaners**

God instructed Israel not to thoroughly harvest their fields, but to leave small amounts unharvested around the edges and corners of the fields so the poor could glean and take freely from the remains of the harvest. In the book of Ruth, Boaz instructed his workers to leave "handfuls of purpose" for the young widow, Ruth. God will remember you in your hour of affliction.

Leviticus 19:10 - "And thou shalt not glean thy vineyard, neither shalt thou gather every grape of thy vineyard; thou shalt leave them for the poor and stranger: I am the LORD your God."

C | Love Thy Neighbor

God's word is profoundly good. What would we do, or where would we be without God's word? It is the ancient, historical, DIVINE source of priceless values. Things like: "...don't curse the deaf," "...don't stumble the blind," "...have no respect of persons," "...don't be a talebearer," "...don't hate your brother," and the best of all, "...love thy neighbor as thyself." Thank God for His word!

Leviticus 19:18 - "Thou shalt not avenge, nor bear any grudge against the children of thy people, but thou shalt love thy neighbour as thyself: I am the LORD."

A | Seeking After Wizards

God Almighty is the eternal, omnipotent, omniscient Spirit. He is sovereign and able to do exceedingly above anything we can ask. Understandably, He is completely intolerant of those who put their trust in evil spirits of any kind. You can get the help you need from God. If God will not give it, you do not need it and should not want it. Consulting devils is the ultimate slap in God's face.

Leviticus 19:31 - "Regard not them that have familiar spirits, neither seek after wizards, to be defiled by them: I am the LORD your God."

C | Child Sacrifices

The heathen were known to make child sacrifices by fire to various gods, including Molech, Milcom and Chemosh. One prominent location was the Valley of Tophet, or Gehenna, at Jerusalem. Priests beat drums to drown out the voices of screaming, dying children. God abhors such horrors, pronouncing the death penalty on anyone who practices such.

Leviticus 20:2 - "...Whosoever he be of the children of Israel, or of the strangers that sojourn in Israel, that giveth any of his seed unto Molech; he shall surely be put to death: the people of the land shall stone him with stones."

C | Familiar Spirits

God is the ONLY UNCREATED SPIRIT. All other spirits were created by Him; angels, men, and all living creatures. Angels who sinned became unclean spirits. They are diabolical enemies of God. They keenly observe humans to become FAMILIAR with them that they may falsely pose as God. Foolish men and women confuse familiar spirits with God. God will destroy everyone who consults these evil, familiar spirits.

Leviticus 20:6 - "...the soul that turneth after such as have familiar spirits, and after wizards, ...I will even set my face against that soul, and will cut him off from among his people."

D | The Inheritance-Separation Connection

God could save everybody in the world, but He does not want all He sees. He wants those who forsake the world for Him. His promises are inextricably linked to our consecration. Israel had to separate. If we will not give up Egypt, there is no Promised Land.

Leviticus 20:24,26 - "...Ye shall inherit their land, and I will give it unto you to possess it, a land that floweth with milk and honey: ...And ye shall be holy unto me: for I the LORD am holy, and have severed you from other people, that ye should be mine."

B | Highest Standards For Priests

All of Aaron's male descendants were consecrated for ministry. They had to live by the highest standards. For example, they could not marry a widow, a divorcee, a profane woman or a harlot. They could not adapt other cultural trends pertaining to hair, beards, or markings in their flesh. They had to be in excellent health. Any notable infirmity of the flesh disqualified them from priesthood. Their model was Jesus Christ, the great High Priest, yet to come.

Leviticus 21:1 - "And the LORD said unto Moses, Speak unto the priests the sons of Aaron, and say unto them..."

A | Making A Vow

Jacob made the first vow, promising to pay tithes as God blessed him. Under the law, in the absence of a sacrificial animal, a man could vow to pay later. It is better not to vow, than to vow and not pay. You can negotiate with God, but you must be prepared to live up to your bargains.

Leviticus 22:21 - "...whosoever offereth a sacrifice of peace offerings unto the LORD to accomplish his vow, or a freewill offering in beeves or sheep, it shall be perfect to be accepted; there shall be no blemish therein."

D | Seven Feasts

God set forth seven major feasts which spoke prophetically to Israel. Passover taught the doctrine of salvation by the blood. The Feast of Unleavened Bread taught the broken body of Jesus Christ. The Feast of

Firstfruits taught the resurrection of Christ. The Feast of Pentecost taught the Baptism of the Holy Ghost. The Feast of Trumpets teaches the Second Coming of Jesus. The Day of Atonement teaches redemption through Christ. The Feast of Tabernacles teaches the Kingdom of Christ.

Leviticus 23:4 - "These are the feasts of the LORD, even holy convocations, which ye shall proclaim in their seasons."

B | Passover And Unleavened Bread

The first two annual feasts began in Egypt - Passover and the Feast of Unleavened Bread. Together, they teach the blood and broken body of Jesus Christ, and deliverance from sin and worldly bondage thereby. The lamb was spotless, and the bread was unleavened. Leavening is the yeast that agitates and causes the dough to rise. It is likened to sin. Jesus, bread of life, had no leavening - no sin.

Leviticus 23:5-6 - "In the fourteenth day of the first month at even is the LORD'S passover. And on the fifteenth day ...is the feast of unleavened bread."

B | Feast Of Firstfruits

The first three feasts; Passover (blood of the lamb), Unleavened Bread (broken body), and Firstfruits (new life) were springtime celebrations representing the death, burial and resurrection of Jesus Christ. Israel brought sheaves from their firstfruits with meat and drink offerings on the first day after the Sabbath following Passover. Jesus rose from the dead on that same day - firstfruit from the dead.

Leviticus 23:10 - "When ye be come into the land which I give unto you, and shall reap the harvest thereof, then ye shall bring a sheaf of the firstfruits of your harvest unto the priest."

B | Feast Of Pentecost

"Pentecost" means fifty. Fifty days after Israel escaped Egypt and celebrated the Feast of Unleavened Bread, God gave the Law at Sinai, birthing the NATION on Pentecost. Fifty days after Jesus' body was broken at Calvary, the Holy Ghost was given to 120 believers in the Upper Room, birthing the CHURCH on Pentecost. Old Testament laws were written on stone tablets. New Testament laws are written by the Spirit on our hearts.

Leviticus 23:16 - "Even unto the morrow after the seventh sabbath shall ye number fifty days; and ye shall offer a new meat offering unto the LORD."

B | Feast Of Trumpets

The first four feasts, (Passover, Unleavened Bread, Firstfruits and Pentecost), were in the spring-time and have already been fulfilled prophetically. The Feast of Trumpets, Atonement and Feast of Tabernacles will soon be fulfilled in this end-time. In the book of Revelation, John described **Seven Trumpets**[1] that would sound in the last days. Jesus Christ will return to earth at the Seventh Trumpet.

Leviticus 23:24 - "Speak unto the children of Israel, saying, In the seventh month, in the first day of the month, shall ye have a sabbath, a memorial of blowing of trumpets, an holy convocation."

B | Feast Day Of Atonement

The Feast of Trumpets announced ten days of preparation for the Day of Atonement, now known as Yom Kippur. It was an elaborate event, including fasting, sacrificing, and repentance. This most important ritual ransomed Israel from sin and restored pure fellowship with God. Now, atonement comes by "...the man, Jesus Christ; Who gave himself a ransom for all," 1 Timothy 2:5-6.

Leviticus 23:28 - "And ye shall do no work in that same day: for it is a day of atonement, to make an atonement for you before the LORD your God."

B | Feast Of Tabernacles

The Feast of Tabernacles (also called Sukkot, or Feast of Ingathering) celebrates the final harvest. In late September or early October, various branches are waved before the Lord, presenting the harvest in this "Feast to the Lord." Israelites pitched tents in the fields, remembering the wilderness journey while celebrating the fruit of the Promised Land. In the Millennium of Jesus Christ, all nations will come to Jerusalem annually to celebrate Tabernacles (Zechariah 14:16). It celebrates redemption: God's harvest (ingathering) of mankind after atonement.

Leviticus 23:34,42 - "...the feast of tabernacles...Ye shall dwell in booths seven days."

C | Purity

The services of the Tabernacle required continual supplies of oil for the golden candlestick, flour for the shewbread, and incense. God required the oil and the incense to be pure, and the flour refined. The oil represents the Holy Ghost; the bread, the body of Christ; and the incense, the prayers of the saints. Now, the Church is the Tabernacle of God and functions by the Holy Spirit, the body of Christ and prayer.

Leviticus 24:2,5,7 - "Command the children of Israel, that they bring unto thee pure oil olive beaten for the light, ...fine flour, ...pure frankincense."

A | Blaspheming The Name Of The LORD

The people brought a boy to Moses who had cursed and blasphemed the name of the Lord. Moses asked God what to do with him. God told him to have the people stone him. Why? Cursing God is a very, very serious offense of a mere creature against his Creator. Be careful about mouthing off against God. He gave you your heartbeat, and He can take it away as easily as He gave it.

Leviticus 24:15 - "And thou shalt speak unto the children of Israel, saying, Whosoever curseth his God shall bear his sin."

C | An Eye For An Eye

The Law defined formulas for punishing crime and injuries. God's laws were less harsh and more equitable than older Babylonian laws or subsequent Islamic laws. Most of modern law evolved from Moses' teaching. However, Jesus taught that forgiveness and "turning the other cheek" is better than vengeance.

Leviticus 24:19-21 - "And if a man cause a blemish in his neighbour; as he hath done, so shall it be done to him; Breach for breach, eye for eye, tooth for tooth: as he hath caused a blemish in a man, so shall it be done to him again."

D | A Sabbath Of Rest For The Land

The Sabbath also applied to the land. Every seventh year the land should rest - no crops planted. God promised to bless the sixth year enough to sustain the people throughout an off year. Prophetically, after six millennia, God will soon declare a millennium of rest for the earth while Jesus reigns.

Leviticus 25:1-2 - "And the LORD spake unto Moses in mount Sinai, saying, Speak unto the children of Israel, and say unto them, When ye come into the land which I give you, then shall the land keep a sabbath unto the LORD."

D | Jubile (Jubilee)

After seven Sabbath years (49 years), a Jubile was celebrated. The ram's horn was sounded. The land rested for a year. Leased land returned to its owner. Hired slaves were freed. It was a year of liberty. Jubile corresponds to Pentecost (fifty). It is a reminder that everything belongs to God and will someday revert back to His possession. 2000 AD was the seventieth Jubilee year since Moses' day.

Leviticus 25:10 - "And ye shall hallow the fiftieth year, and proclaim liberty throughout all the land unto all the inhabitants thereof: it shall be a jubile unto you."

D | The Land Is Mine

This single verse would solve the entire Middle East crisis. God says, "the land is mine" and shall not be sold forever. Leviticus listed several real estate laws that were intended to guarantee that the Promised Land would ALWAYS be the homeland of the twelve tribes of Israel. Although God anciently drove Israel out because of their sins, He PROMISED to bring them back - and He did in 1948! Jesus will reclaim every inch of it very shortly.

Leviticus 25:23 - "The land shall not be sold for ever: for the land is mine; for ye are strangers and sojourners with me."

D | I Will Walk Among You

Incentives. People are motivated by incentives. God always offered marvelous incentives. He promised that if His people would love Him and obey His commandments, He would give rain in due season, harvests would increase, trees would bear fruit, their land would have peace, their enemies would be defeated, and so much more. Most valuable is His promise to come and dwell among us. Jesus IS coming. We shall behold Him.

Leviticus 26:11-12 - "And I will set my tabernacle among you: ...And I will walk among you, and will be your God, and ye shall be my people."

D | Seven Times More Plagues

In contrast to God's promised blessings, He promised judgment if they rebelled. Even worse, He promised to multiply their punishment SEVEN TIMES if they did not repent when chastised. This actually happened several centuries later. God sentenced Israel to 70 years captivity in Babylon for their sins. But most did not repent, so the prophet Daniel proclaimed "Seventy Weeks" of years to finish the transgression - 490 years! (Daniel 9:24).

Leviticus 26:21 - "...if ye walk contrary unto me, and will not hearken unto me; I will bring seven times more plagues upon you according to your sins."

A | Averting Judgment By Confession

God threatened horrifying judgments on Israel if they spurned and disobeyed His laws. That was fair enough. He had just delivered them from slavery and was performing one miracle after another to sustain them. So if they rejected him, He would deal severely with them. BUT - if they confessed their wrong-doing, He promised to reverse judgment and reinstate all the blessings. That was more than fair.

Leviticus 26:40-42 - "If they shall confess their iniquity, ...if then their uncircumcised hearts be humbled, and they then accept of the punishment of their iniquity: Then will I remember my covenant..."

B | The Shekel Of The Sanctuary

When men made vows to God, they were obliged to keep them. But, if a man vowed himself, or a family member, or a piece of property to God, he could redeem them by paying an estimated fee in "Temple shekels." If he vowed animals, he could exchange another animal for it. If he delayed to pay a tithe to the Lord, he had to add a fifth part later.

Leviticus 27:23 - "...the priest shall reckon unto him the worth of thy estimation, ...and he shall give thine estimation in that day, as a holy thing unto the LORD."

Lessons from the Book of
NUMBERS

B | Numbers

The Book of Numbers is especially valuable for its historicity. Moses chronicled nearly forty years of wilderness journeying: the census, the camp, the Tabernacle, ordaining Levites, Passover and other ordinances. He reports rebellions, adventures, war, divine interventions and many miracles. Finally, Moses gave instructions for conquering the land of Canaan, including cities for Levites. Anybody who calls this a myth is a hardened skeptic. What other ancient nation has a better documented beginning?

Numbers 36:13 - "These are the commandments and the judgments, which the LORD commanded by the hand of Moses unto the children of Israel."

C | The Poll

God promised Abraham to "make of thee a great nation." At Mount Sinai, Moses counted every male Israelite older than twenty, who was fit for war. There were 603,550 warriors! From only seventy elders who migrated to Egypt, God raised up this powerful infant nation of at least two million souls! God will keep His promise to you, too. Believe it.

Numbers 1:2 - "Take ye the sum of all the congregation of the children of Israel, after their families, by the house of their fathers, with the number of their names, every male by their polls."

D | Pedigrees

We often skim over scriptures that list the "begats" because it is difficult to appreciate the seemingly endless listings of family genealogies. However, many detailed and extensive Bible prophecies are given to specific tribes and families, including tribal inheritances, etc. It is important to establish pedigrees to prove that prophecy is truly fulfilled and that claims are legitimate.

Numbers 1:18 - "And they assembled all the congregation together... and they declared their pedigrees after their families, by the house of their fathers, according to the number of the names, from twenty years old and upward, by their polls."

B | The Levites

Instead of taking the firstborn from every tribe, God took the sons of Levi (including Moses and Aaron) for the ministry of the Tabernacle. They were not added to the census. They received no inheritance as the other tribes. God was their inheritance. They encamped around the Tabernacle. Inside the Promised Land, they dwelled in suburbs of other tribes' cities, similar to Jesus, our Priest, Who had "not where to lay His head." They pitched the Tabernacle. Jesus built the Church.

Numbers 1:47 - "But the Levites after the tribe of their fathers were not numbered among them."

D | Judah Shall First Set Forth

When Israel pitched camp around the Tabernacle, they pitched three tribes on each side. Every tribe posted their standard, their ensign for all to see; three on the east, three on the west, three on the north, three on the south. Judah, the lead tribe, "shall first set forth." This lead tribe would eventually produce Jesus, the Captain of our Salvation, Lion of the Tribe of Judah.

Numbers 2:9 - "All that were numbered in the camp of Judah were an hundred thousand and fourscore thousand and six thousand and four hundred, throughout their armies. These shall first set forth."

D | The Firstborn Are Mine

God claims the firstborn of every generation. If the firstborn is unsuitable, God may sanctify another as firstborn. Jacob (Israel) wrestled God for firstborn status. God made David (youngest son of Jesse) His firstborn (Psalm 89:27.) Joseph's younger son, Ephraim, was called "firstborn." Paul called the entire Church "firstborn," Hebrews 12:23. We are blessed above men to be His firstborn.

Numbers 3:13 - "Because all the firstborn are mine; for on the day that I smote all the firstborn in the land of Egypt I hallowed unto me all the firstborn in Israel, both man and beast."

B | Gershon, Kohath And Merari

Moses' great-grandfather, Levi, begat three sons: Gershon, Kohath and Merari. These comprised the Levitical priesthood. Aaron, the High Priest, and his sons were Kohathites. Kohath's other descendants transported and set up the most holy furnishings of the Tabernacle. Gershon's descendants were responsible for the curtains, cords and hangings.

Merari's descendants attended the boards, bars, pillars and sockets of the Tabernacle. God loves to use families.

Numbers 4:3 - "...From thirty years old and upward even until fifty years old, all that enter into the host, to do the work in the tabernacle of the congregation."

A | Confession With Restitution And A Penalty

Sometimes it is not good enough just to say, "I'm sorry." Sometimes we owe a debt that must be repaid. God instructed Moses to tell the people not only to repay the principal of the trespass, but also to add a fifth-part penalty - a twenty percent surcharge. Words alone are worthless if your deeds contradict them.

Numbers 5:7 - "Then they shall confess their sin which they have done: and he shall recompense his trespass with the principal thereof, and add unto it the fifth part thereof, and give it unto him against whom he hath trespassed."

C | The Law Of Jealousies

If a man suspected that his wife had been unfaithful to him, he could bring her to the priest for judgment. The priest gave her a concoction of bitter water to drink. If certain symptoms developed, she was deemed guilty. If not, she was declared innocent and freed from the accusation. Immorality is wrong, but so is a false accusation. God intervened and put an end to the matter. God always knows the truth from the lies.

Numbers 5:28 - "And if the woman be not defiled, but be clean; then she shall be free, and shall conceive seed."

B | The Nazarite Vow

A Nazarite is one who is consecrated unto the Lord ("nazir" - consecrated). It has nothing to do with the city of Nazareth. Saying "I am a Nazarite," launched a period of 1) abstinence from the fruit of the vine, 2) avoidance from touching the dead, and 3) unshaven hair. At the end of the vow, the hair was shaved and offered as a sacrifice. The general purpose was to consecrate to the Lord during times of distress, affliction, or earnest prayer.

Numbers 6:8 - "All the days of his separation he is holy unto the LORD."

A | Priestly Blessings

God could bless anyone without needing an intercessor. Nevertheless, He instructed the priests to pronounce blessings on the people. Men of God are beneficial to us.

Numbers 6:23-27 - "Speak unto Aaron and unto his sons, saying, On this wise ye shall bless the children of Israel, saying unto them, The LORD bless thee, and keep thee: The LORD make his face shine upon thee, and be gracious unto thee: The LORD lift up his countenance upon thee, and give thee peace. And they shall put my name upon the children of Israel; and I will bless them."

A | The Voice From The Mercy Seat

They finally finished setting up and consecrating the Tabernacle and Priesthood. The tribes brought six wagons full of offerings. Sacrifices were made on the new Altar. Then, Moses entered in, and God spoke to him from the Mercy Seat. Completed acts of obedience lead to great communion with God.

Numbers 7:89 - "...when Moses was gone into the tabernacle of the congregation to speak with him, then he heard the voice of one speaking unto him from off the mercy seat that was upon the ark of testimony, from between the two cherubims: and he spake unto him."

D | Beaten Gold

The Golden Candlestick with its seven lamps represented the Seven Spirits of God in the Seven Churches which were to come (Revelation 1:20). It was made of beaten gold. This is contrasted to a molten (molded) work. Saints of God are not molded. They are beaten into shape. They, like their Savior, are made perfect by the things they suffer.

Numbers 8:4 - "And this work of the candlestick was of beaten gold, unto the shaft thereof, unto the flowers thereof, was beaten work: according unto the pattern which the LORD had shewed Moses, so he made the candlestick."

D | Keeping The Passover

Certain men came to Moses because they had been exposed to dead bodies and were defiled. They wanted to know if God wanted them to keep the Passover in that condition. Moses talked to the Lord, and God said that everyone should take the Passover, even the strangers in their midst. Anyone who "forbeareth to keep the passover, even the same soul shall be cut off from among his people," verse 13. Without the shedding of blood, there is no remission of sins.

Numbers 9:2 - "Let the children of Israel also keep the passover at his appointed season."

A | Rise Up, LORD!

Moses prayed each time they journeyed. The priests carried the Ark of the Covenant ahead of the people, so Moses besought the Lord to dispel His enemies along the way. When they camped, Moses welcomed the Glory back into their midst. Let God arise, and His enemies be scattered.

Numbers 10:35-36 - "And it came to pass, when the ark set forward, that Moses said, Rise up, LORD, and let thine enemies be scattered; and let them that hate thee flee before thee. And when it rested, he said, Return, O LORD, unto the many thousands of Israel."

A | The Fire Of The LORD

God does not like to hear His people complaining. He likes to hear them praising, worshipping and giving thanks. When Israel complained, God set their camps on fire. Moses made intercessory prayer, and God put the fires out.

Numbers 11:1 And when the people complained, it displeased the LORD: and the LORD heard it; and his anger was kindled; and the fire of the LORD burnt among them, and consumed them that were in the uttermost parts of the camp. And the people cried unto Moses; and when Moses prayed unto the LORD, the fire was quenched."

A | God Responds Dramatically To Moses' Prayer

Numbers 11 records a dramatic exchange between Moses and God. The people were tired of manna and wanted meat. Moses was desperate for help. God vindicated Moses with two great miracles. He anointed seventy elders to prophesy over the people, then sent TONS of quail for thirty days.

Numbers 11:30 - "And Moses gat him into the camp, he and the elders of Israel. And there went forth a wind from the LORD, and brought quails from the sea, and let them fall by the camp,...as it were two cubits high upon the face of the earth."

A | Prayer For Divine Healing

Miriam and Aaron spoke against their brother, Moses, criticizing him and challenging his authority. God Himself called all three to the Tabernacle door, where He came in a pillar of a cloud. God was angry and vindicated Moses, smiting Miriam with leprosy. Aaron panicked and pleaded with Moses to have mercy. Moses prayed for God to heal Miriam, and seven days later, she was healed. This first occurrence proves for all time that effective prayer can and will bring divine healing.

Numbers 12:13 - "And Moses cried unto the LORD, saying, Heal her now, O God, I beseech thee."

B | The Grapes Of Eshcol

Have you ever seen a cluster of grapes so large that it took two men to carry it? That is what the spies found at Eshcol. To this day, one of the great symbols in Israel is artwork depicting Joshua and Caleb carrying those grapes. The Bible does not say it was Joshua or Caleb, but the posterity certainly belongs to men of great faith.

Numbers 13:23 - "And they came unto the brook of Eshcol, and cut down from thence a branch with one cluster of grapes, and they bare it between two upon a staff."

C | An Evil Report

At Kadesh Barnea, Moses sent one leader from each tribe to do surveillance throughout the Promised Land prior to its conquest. Except for Joshua and Caleb, they were all afraid to invade it. Even worse, they spread their fears throughout Israel. They sabotaged the work of God. They paid dearly. Learn from their mistake. Spread faith - not fear.

Numbers 13:32 - "And they brought up an evil report of the land which they had searched unto the children of Israel, saying, The land, through which we have gone to search it, is a land that eateth up the inhabitants thereof."

D | Self-Fulfilling Prophecies

Doubt is its own punishment. Nothing good ever came of doubt. No monuments or memorials are built to doubt. When the twelve Hebrew spies surveyed the land of milk and honey, they doubted they could take it - and they DIDN'T! Whether you believe you can or can't, you are right. If you see yourself as a loser, that is what the record will eventually show.

Numbers 13:33 - "And there we saw the giants, the sons of Anak, which come of the giants: and we were in our own sight as grasshoppers, and so we were in their sight."

A | Moses Argues With God And Wins

Poor Moses sent twelve spies to survey the Promised Land, but only Joshua and Caleb had faith. The others turned all Israel against invading, provoking God to disinherit Israel and start anew with Moses' family. But Moses powerfully interceded. God spared them. Intercession sometimes requires heroic determination.

Numbers 14:15 - "Now if thou shalt kill all this people as one man, then the nations which have heard the fame of thee will speak, saying, Because the LORD was not able to bring this people into the land which he sware unto them, therefore he hath slain them in the wilderness."

D | Earth Filled With God's Glory

Modern skeptics dismiss the Bible as a self-serving Jewish fabrication bent on legitimizing the nation of Israel and discrediting its neighboring nations. They deny that it was divinely inspired. But make no mistake about it: Moses did not invent God. God invented Moses and all the rest of us. Men have always doubted God. The fearful spies doubted the land could be conquered, but God swore that He would eventually conquer the whole world without them.

Numbers 14:21 - "But as truly as I live, all the earth shall be filled with the glory of the LORD."

A | Too Late For Repentance

God sentenced every Israelite over the age of twenty (except Joshua and Caleb) to wander in the wilderness forty years because they doubted they could conquer the Promised Land. Everyone panicked and suddenly wanted to repent and go on to war. But it was too late. God's mind was made up. Be careful lest it happen to you.

Numbers 14:40 - "...And Moses said, Wherefore now do ye transgress the commandment of the LORD? but it shall not prosper. Go not up, for the LORD is not among you; that ye be not smitten before your enemies."

C | God Looks Forward

Numbers 14 chronicles the miserable failure of the men of Israel to move into the Promised Land. God rejected them in sore displeasure. Amazingly, Numbers 15 opens with God saying, "WHEN YE COME INTO THE LAND..." followed by a list of offerings, sacrifices, and feasts that He wanted Israel AND the strangers in their midst to perform. God quickly bypassed the failures of one generation and began fulfilling His promises in the next.

Numbers 15:2 - "...say unto them, When ye be come into the land of your habitations, which I give unto you, ...thus shall it be done..."

A | Respect Not Their Offering

Korah, Dathan and Abiram led an epic rebellion of 250 powerful men against Moses. They intended to overthrow Moses. It was a frightful occasion. Moses ordered them to appear with incense at the door of the Tabernacle, then he prayed God not to favor them. God declared He would destroy Korah and company. Moses warned the people to separate themselves from Korah. The earth opened and swallowed Korah's household alive. Fire fell from heaven and consumed all the 250 rebels.

Numbers 16:15 - "And Moses was very wroth, and said unto the LORD, Respect not thou their offering."

A | Declaring The Mighty Works Of God

This does not look like a prayer, but Moses declared a miracle against Korah and 250 rebels. Without knowing how God would judge them, Moses declared an earthquake, and it happened!

Numbers 16:30,32 - "But if the LORD make a new thing, and the earth open her mouth, and swallow them up, with all that appertain unto them, and they go down quick into the pit; then ye shall understand that these men have provoked the LORD. ...And the earth opened her mouth, and swallowed them up, and their houses, and all the men that appertained unto Korah."

B | Aaron's Rod That Budded

Korah and his company tried to usurp Aaron's priesthood. God killed 250 of them. But Israel accused Moses, saying, "Ye have killed the people of the Lord." God told every tribe to lay a wooden rod on the ground.

Overnight, the rod that budded would testify to which tribe God chose. God eventually vindicates His chosen.

Numbers 17:8 - "And it came to pass, that on the morrow Moses went into the tabernacle of witness; and, behold, the rod of Aaron for the house of Levi was budded, and brought forth buds, and bloomed blossoms, and yielded almonds."

B | Covenant Of Salt

Every meat offering made in the Tabernacle was to be seasoned with salt. Salt is a natural preservative. It is contrasted with leavening, which was forbidden in sacrifices. Leavening stirs up and agitates undesirable qualities over time, fermenting and spoiling things. Salt preserves and purifies, inhibiting corruption, even disease. When God makes covenant with His people, it is with salt and purity - nothing about it is corrupt.

Numbers 18:19 - "All the heave offerings of the holy things, ...have I given thee, ...by a statute for ever: it is a covenant of salt for ever before the LORD..."

B | Tithes For Ministers

Abraham paid a tenth of his earnings to Mechizedek the Priest. Jacob vowed to pay tithe continually. Moses called the tithe "holy unto the Lord," Leviticus 27:30. Israel paid tithes to the Levites, and Levites tithed to the High Priest. God appointed tithes to support the ministry.

Numbers 18:26 - "Thus speak unto the Levites, and say unto them, When ye take of the children of Israel the tithes which I have given you from them for your inheritance, then ye shall offer up an heave offering of it for the LORD, even a tenth part of the tithe."

D | The Ashes Of The Red Heifer

The Lord ordered a spotless red heifer to be sacrificed and burned, and its ashes mixed with water to create a "holy water," to sprinkle, for purification, on people and places defiled by touching the dead. In modern times, this purification will be necessary before a newly-built Third Temple can be dedicated. A red heifer is now being raised in Israel for this purpose. It is a type of Christ.

Numbers 19:9-10 - "...gather up the ashes of the heifer, ...for a water of separation: it is a purification for sin. ...for a statute forever."

A | Speak To The Rock

The people needed water. God told Moses to speak to the rock, and it would give water. In frustration, Moses smote the rock twice. It gave water, but Moses angered God for showing unbelief to Israel. God forbade Moses to enter the Promised Land because of it. The works of the flesh hinder the works of the Spirit. Trust God for your miracle, not brute force.

Numbers 20:8 - "Take the rod, and gather thou the assembly together, thou, and Aaron thy brother, and speak ye unto the rock before their eyes; and it shall give forth his water."

B | Eleazar, Aaron's Successor

God forbade Aaron the High Priest to enter Canaan because of the episode with the Golden Calf. As forty years of wandering came to a close, God told Moses to anoint Aaron's son, Eleazar, as his successor. Moses had clothed Aaron in priestly garments long ago. Now he would strip him and give them to Eleazar. God gives. God takes away. We are all expendable. Make the most of your calling while you have time.

Numbers 20:28 - "...Moses stripped Aaron of his garments, and put them upon Eleazar his son; and Aaron died there in the top of the mount."

C | Enemies Cannot Succeed

In one chapter, three wars are documented. In the wilderness journey, Canaanites fought Israel, taking hostages. But Israel fought back and destroyed them at Hormah. Sihon and the Amorites, followed by Og, king of Bashan fought against Israel too, but were soundly defeated. The enemies of God's people often launch unprovoked attacks, but God will never let it go unanswered. Sooner or later, all God's enemies will be defeated. Stay on God's side!

Numbers 21:35 - "So they smote him, ...and all his people, until there was none left him alive: and they possessed his land."

C | Betrayal

The story of the Prophet Balaam and his dealings with Balak, king of Moab, is an unusually long story about a man of God being bribed to side with God's enemies. The world and Satan will pay any price to get you to approve their wrong-doing and betray God or His people. Men quit their convictions and good judgment, to become fools. It happens every day. Don't let it happen to you.

Numbers 22:12 - "And God said unto Balaam, Thou shalt not go with them; thou shalt not curse the people: for they are blessed."

A | Evil Prayers

Balak, king of the Moabites, tried to bribe the prophet Balaam to curse Israel and bless Moab. Balaam refused. Balak raised the bribe until Balaam agreed to pray for him. God was furious! Balaam's donkey rebuked him, and an angel drew a sword against him. Balaam was soon killed by his own troops during wartime. Eleven times the Bible speaks disparagingly of Balaam. Learn a lesson. Don't curse what God has blessed, or bless what God has cursed.

Numbers 23:2 - "...and Balak and Balaam offered on every altar a bullock and a ram."

D | A Star And A Sceptre

Balaam greatly angered God when he capitulated to Balak, king of the Moabites. Nevertheless, his prophetic gift still operated, and he could see the future of Israel under God's blessing. He saw far into the future, a Star and a Sceptre - some say a reference to David, but more accurately to Messiah Himself. About 3400 years ago, Balaam saw the coming Kingdom of Jesus Christ.

Numbers 24:17 - "I shall see him, but not now: I shall behold him, but not nigh: there shall come a Star out of Jacob, and a Sceptre shall rise out of Israel."

D | An Everlasting Priesthood For Being Zealous

Before entering Canaan, many Israelites committed whoredoms with Moabite women, who enticed them to worship their god, Baalpeor. God told Moses to slaughter the whoremongers and idolaters. Even as Moses began, Phinehas (Eleazar's son) caught an Israelite taking a Moabite woman into a tent. With a javelin, Phinehas zealously slew them both. God told Moses to reward Phinehas with a covenant of "everlasting priesthood."

Numbers 25:13 - "...he shall have it, and his seed after him, even the covenant of an everlasting priesthood; because he was zealous for his God, and made an atonement for the children of Israel."

C | Inheriting Your Portion

Moses numbered the men of Israel to determine how the Promised Land would be apportioned once they arrived there. Joshua and Caleb were the only survivors from those who had been twenty years and older at Kadesh Barnea. The younger generation who had NOT sinned received the rich rewards their fathers foolishly lost. If you won't claim God's promises, somebody else will!

Numbers 26:53 - "...To many thou shalt give the more inheritance, and to few thou shalt give the less inheritance: to every one shall his inheritance be given according to those that were numbered of him."

A | Praying About Legal Matters

God will show you how to resolve a legal matter. Moses numbered the men of each tribe just before they were to go over Jordan. The land would be apportioned accordingly. Several women complained because their fathers died without sons to inherit. They wanted an inheritance, too. Moses prayed, and God showed him a plan that satisfied everyone.

Numbers 27:4 - "Why should the name of our father be done away from among his family, because he hath no son? Give unto us therefore a possession among the brethren of our father. And Moses brought their cause before the LORD."

A | Prayer For A Successor

Moses would soon die, so he asked God to provide a new leader for Israel. God selected Joshua. Moses laid hands on him before the priest and congregation. God will answer you, too.

Numbers 27:15-17 - "And Moses spake unto the LORD, saying, Let the LORD, the God of the spirits of all flesh, set a man over the congregation, Which may go out before them, and which may go in before them, and which may lead them out, and which may bring them in; that the congregation of the LORD be not as sheep which have no shepherd."

C | Reminders

Immediately after making Joshua the new leader of Israel, Moses repeated several important commandments concerning offerings, sacrifices, Sabbaths, and feast days. It might have been easy to neglect their service to God while busily making their new homes in the

Promised Land. That is why we need a man of God to remind us to fulfill our duties to God.

Numbers 28:2 - "Command the children of Israel, and say unto them, My offering, and my bread for my sacrifices made by fire, for a sweet savour unto me, shall ye observe to offer unto me in their due season."

B | Holy Convocation

The Sabbaths and Feasts of Israel were generally referred to as convocations. They were "called out" to come together for each event. Once each year, the entire nation was called to the "Holy Convocation," which was a week-long time of fasting and sacrificing for their sins. In that tradition, the modern Church would do well to come together annually for fasting and prayer.

Numbers 29:12 - "And on the fifteenth day of the seventh month ye shall have an holy convocation; ye shall do no servile work, and ye shall keep a feast unto the LORD seven days."

A | Vowing Unto The Lord

God commanded that a man fulfill his vows unto the Lord. If a young girl made a vow, it could be confirmed or voided by her father. If a married woman made a vow, it could be confirmed or voided by her husband. A single woman had to fulfill her vows. God requires us to perform our promises.

Numbers 30:2 - "If a man vow a vow unto the LORD, or swear an oath to bind his soul with a bond; he shall not break his word, he shall do according to all that proceedeth out of his mouth."

D | Spoiling The Midianites

After Sarah died, Abraham married Keturah, who had a son named Midian. His descendants dwelled among Lot's descendants, the Moabites. Both tribes became idolatrous pagans. The Midianites and Moabites solicited the prophet Balaam to curse Israel and bless them. God told Moses to avenge Israel of the Midianites. Israel warred victoriously over them and brought back spoils in great abundance. A precedent was set. God will avenge His saints of their enemies. Jesus will divide the spoils of the whole world with His saints someday (Isaiah 53:12).

Numbers 31:2 - "Avenge the children of Israel of the Midianites..."

C | The Curse Of Holding Back

The tribes of Reuben and Gad loved the pasturelands east of Jordan for their cattle. They wanted to settle there. Moses consented, but he compared them to their fathers who had failed God at Kadesh Barnea. Centuries later, they were the first tribes to apostatize and be taken captive into obscurity. DON'T STOP SHORT of the Promised Land!

Numbers 32:5 - "...let this land be given unto thy servants... and bring us not over Jordan....And Moses said ...wherefore discourage ye the heart of the children of Israel from going over into the land which the LORD hath given them?"

D | The Wilderness Journal

In Numbers 33, Moses documented every leg of Israel's journey from Egypt to the Promised Land, one of the most important events in human history. Many ancient prophecies were fulfilled, but more prophecies lingered. They must decide the outcome. Our journey with God requires unending diligence.

Numbers 33:50-56 - "And the LORD spake unto Moses saying, ...ye shall dispossess the inhabitants of the land, and dwell therein: for I have given you the land to possess it. ...But if ye will not drive out the inhabitants ...I shall do unto you, as I thought to do unto them."

B | The Borders Of Israel

God told Moses "this is the land that shall fall unto you for an inheritance, even the land of Canaan." Then He meticulously defined the borders on the North, South, East and West. It is all right there in Numbers 34. 3500 years ago, Israel took possession of the Promised Land in an irrevocable Covenant with Almighty God. No king or kingdom on earth will EVER get God's title deed to the Holy Land. Let God's enemies be warned. God will fight for Israel.

Numbers 34:12 - "...this shall be your land with the coasts thereof round about."

B | Cities Of Refuge

God gave Israel six "cities of refuge" where accused murderers could run for asylum and find safety until they could get a fair hearing. Even today, Jesus is longsuffering; not willing that any should perish, but that all should come to repentance. Run to Him.

Numbers 35:11-12 - "...ye shall appoint you cities to be cities of refuge for you; that the slayer may flee thither, which killeth any person at unawares. And they shall be unto you cities for refuge from the avenger; that the manslayer die not, until he stand before the congregation in judgment."

C | Marrying Within The Tribe

Some families had no male heirs, and Moses gave the inheritance to the daughters. But if they married outside their tribe, the tribal inheritance would be passed to another tribe. To prevent this, Moses taught the women to marry within their own tribe. The New Testament version of this is "be not unequally yoked together with unbelievers."

Numbers 36:8 - "And every daughter, that possesseth an inheritance in any tribe of the children of Israel, shall be wife unto one of the family of the tribe of her father, ...Neither shall the inheritance remove from one tribe to another tribe."

Lessons from the Book of
DEUTERONOMY

B | Deuteronomy

One year before his death, Moses had thirty-nine years of experience leading Israel. His perspective was mature, and in Deuteronomy (meaning "repetition of this law"), he covered all the bases one more time. This book is very rich. Many primary codes and laws are explicitly documented. Moses emphatically admonished the people that God would bless them if they obeyed the commandments of the Lord, but warned of horrific curses if they rebelled. Even under New Testament grace, that principle still stands.

Deuteronomy 11:26 - "Behold, I set before you this day a blessing and a curse."

D | He Shall Fight For You

In the fortieth year of their wilderness journey, Moses stood before the Israelites and reminded them of their successes and failures since leaving Egypt. Although they were about to engage the Canaanites in many wars of conquest, Moses did not speak of military tactics. Instead, he preached to them about the rewards of trusting God and the evils of doubting God. Then, he prophesied: "God is going to fight for you!" God STILL fights for His people.

Deuteronomy 1:30 - "The LORD your God which goeth before you, he shall fight for you, according to all that he did for you..."

A | **God Hears It All**

God hears more than just the prayers we pray. He hears everything we say. It is possible to say all the right things in prayer, and then nullify them with negative talk. Let your words be "Yes, Yes," or "No, No." Make your everyday conversation support your prayers. Otherwise, your prayers will be rendered worthless.

Deuteronomy 1:34-35 - "And the LORD heard the voice of your words, and was wroth, and sware, saying, Surely there shall not one of these men of this evil generation see that good land, which I sware to give unto your fathers."

C | **I Will Not Give You Their Land**

God rules the affairs of men. God told Moses not to meddle with the descendants of Esau or Lot who dwelled east of Jordan. "I have given..." their lands to them; and "I will not give you of their land." They had a divine posterity. Everyone must find their God-given place and respect everyone else's place, too. You cannot have theirs.

Deuteronomy 2:5 - "Meddle not with them; for I will not give you of their land, no, not so much as a foot breadth; because I have given mount Seir unto Esau for a possession."

A | **When God Says "No"**

Moses desperately wanted to go into the Promised Land, but God's punishment stood. God loves to hear and answer prayer, but we must understand that even prayer must sometimes yield to His greater sovereign purpose.

Deuteronomy 3:24-26 - "O Lord GOD ...I pray thee, let me go over, and see the good land that is beyond Jordan, that goodly mountain, and Lebanon. But the LORD was wroth with me for your sakes, and would not hear me: and the LORD said unto me, Let it suffice thee; speak no more unto me of this matter."

A | **Seek Him, Find Him**

Moses knew that Israel would be sorely tempted by the gods of the heathen. He sternly warned them that if they worshiped idols or images of any kind, or if they worshiped such as the sun, moon or stars, God would drive them out of the land and destroy them. Moses urged them to always quickly turn back to God anytime they erred, and God would save them.

Deuteronomy 4:29 - "But if from thence thou shalt seek the LORD thy God, thou shalt find him, if thou seek him with all thy heart and with all thy soul."

D | **When Thou Art In Tribulation**

Just before the second coming of Jesus Christ, a time will come called "Jacob's Trouble," Daniel 12:1, better known as the Great Tribulation. This will precipitate a national spiritual revival for Israel.

Deuteronomy 4:30-31 - "When thou art in tribulation, and all these things are come upon thee, even in the latter days, if thou turn to the LORD thy God, and shalt be obedient unto his voice; (For the LORD thy God is a merciful God;) he will not forsake thee, neither destroy thee, nor forget the covenant of thy fathers which he sware unto them."

A | **Afraid To Pray**

The Israelites were terrified of the voice of God that spoke from Mount Sinai. They asked Moses to relay their prayers. They promised that they would obey whatever God told Moses to tell them. God knew better. "Oh, that there were such an heart in them!" He promised many, many blessings if they would simply walk in His commandments.

Deuteronomy 5:27 - "Go thou near, and hear all that the LORD our God shall say: and speak thou unto us all that the LORD our God shall speak unto thee; and we will hear it, and do it."

B | **The Lord Is One**

Jehovah is not Allah. **The Koran contradicts the Bible again and again.**[2] Both cannot be true. Let the God of Abraham, Isaac and Jacob be God. He is the only one, true God. He is a singular Spirit, ONE LORD, beside whom, there is no other. Jesus is the bodily incarnation of the one true God. Love Him with all your might.

Deuteronomy 6:4-5 - "Hear, O Israel: The LORD our God is one LORD: And thou shalt love the LORD thy God with all thine heart, and with all thy soul, and with all thy might."

D | In Time To Come

Moses published the Ten Commandments the second time in Deuteronomy 5. He emphasized that God's laws, testimonies, statutes and judgments were the script for a holy nation to come.

Deuteronomy 6:20-25 - "And when thy son asketh thee in time to come, saying, What mean the testimonies...? Then thou shalt say unto thy son, ...the LORD commanded us to do all these statutes, to fear the LORD our God, for our good always, that he might preserve us alive, as it is at this day. And it shall be our righteousness, if we observe to do all these commandments."

C | Men Are Saved By Entering Into Covenant With God

God completely destroyed Noah's hopelessly sinful generation. But He offered a holy covenant to Abraham, promising to show favor and make a great nation of his descendants, Israel, if they would enter into a covenant to keep His commandments. God jealously rules the earth and all mankind, and vows to destroy all nations who hate Him. He will give everything to those who love Him and keep His commandments.

Deuteronomy 7:9 - "Know therefore that the LORD thy God, he is God, the faithful God, which keepeth covenant and mercy with them that love him and keep his commandments."

A | What Does Your Heart Say?

We usually think of prayer as the way we communicate our requests to God. In reality, God is influenced by all our words, spoken or not. He discerns our thoughts and intentions, and acts accordingly. That is why we must be extremely careful of all our thoughts and words. God knows when our hearts are not pure. You do not have to say evil things out loud. God reads you like a book.

Deuteronomy 8:17,20 - "And thou say in thine heart, My power and the might of mine hand hath gotten me this wealth, ...so shall ye perish."

A | Things NOT To Say

God does not want to hear us making proud, false claims. He did not save us because we were good or righteous, but because He hates the wickedness of the heathen and will replace them with people who will sanctify themselves unto Him. Be thankful He considered you.

Deuteronomy 9:4 - "Speak not thou in thine heart, after that the LORD thy God hath cast them out from before thee, saying, For my righteousness the LORD hath brought me in to possess this land: but for the wickedness of these nations the LORD doth drive them out from before thee."

A | **Forty Days Of Prayer**

Most modern believers cannot comprehend a forty-day vigil of prayer and fasting. Nevertheless, it was the crucial key to Israel's survival. God had purposed to destroy the children of Israel for worshipping the golden calf, but Moses pressed hard on God. It worked. You can make excuses for anything, but when things get really critical, nothing works like prayer and fasting.

Deuteronomy 10:10 - "And I stayed in the mount, according to the first time, forty days and forty nights; and the LORD hearkened unto me at that time also, and the LORD would not destroy thee."

A | **Praying To The Wrong God**

Not long before the wilderness journey came to an end, Moses reminded the people of all the mighty works God had done for them in the previous forty years. Then He sternly warned them not to EVER turn toward any other gods. In these modern times, there is no shortage of people who believe in prayer. But the problem lies in WHO they are praying to! Praying to the wrong god stirs God's worst wrath.

Deuteronomy 11:16 - "Take heed to yourselves, that your heart be not deceived, and ye turn aside, and serve other gods, and worship them."

A | **Speak The Word Of God Continually**

Moses taught the people to SPEAK THE WORD OF GOD CONTINUALLY in their homes and around their children, "...that your days may be multiplied, and the days of your children." This is a commandment with a promised blessing attached. Teach your children the Word of the Lord. Speak it in your house continually. Declare the mind and will of God by positive affirmations and prayer.

Deuteronomy 11:19 - "And ye shall teach them your children, speaking of them when thou sittest in thine house, and when thou walkest by the way, when thou liest down, and when thou risest up."

A | Thou Shalt Rejoice

Here is one of the earliest directives for praise and worship. God certainly delights to hear our prayers, but He also wants us to bring our offerings and rejoice about what He has already done. Try that today!

Deuteronomy 12:18 - "But thou must eat them before the LORD thy God in the place which the LORD thy God shall choose, thou, and thy son, and thy daughter, and thy manservant, and thy maidservant, and the Levite that is within thy gates: and thou shalt rejoice before the LORD thy God in all that thou puttest thine hands unto."

B | False Gods And Deceivers

CAUTION! God allows deceivers to test our love for Him, even showing deceptive signs, wonders and miracles. God demanded that anyone who enticed an Israelite to follow another god was to be put to death. False prophets, dreamers, close friends, or even family members had to die. God despises our associating with false religions and perverse doctrines. Stay away from them.

Deuteronomy 13:5 - "...that prophet, or that dreamer of dreams, shall be put to death; because he hath spoken to turn you away from the LORD your God, which brought you out of the land of Egypt."

C | No Markings On Your Flesh

God claims the human body as His property and gives instructions concerning its appearance. "Ye shall not make any cuttings in your flesh for the dead, nor print any marks upon you: I am the LORD," Leviticus 19:28. Markings, cuttings, tattoos, and piercings, etc. were condemned as the ways of the heathen. Consecrate your body in holiness.

Deuteronomy 14:1-2 - "...ye shall not cut yourselves, ...For thou art an holy people unto the LORD thy God, and the LORD hath chosen thee to be a peculiar people unto himself, above all the nations that are upon the earth."

D | Forgiving Loans And Releasing Servants

God commanded Israel to forgive loans and release their servants every seventh year. He called it "the LORD'S release." He promised to bless and prosper those who obeyed this law, and to make Israel a lender and not a borrower; a ruler and not a servant, if they would comply. It reminds me of Jesus' words: "My yoke is easy, and my burden is light." In His coming Kingdom, Jesus will release us from all our debts and oppressions. FOREVER FREE - at last!

Deuteronomy 15:1 - "At the end of every seven years thou shalt make a release."

B | The Men Of Israel

God required the men of Israel to faithfully execute their religious duties three times a year during the feasts of Unleavened Bread, Weeks, and Tabernacles, bringing their sacrifices to the Priests at the Tabernacle. He also instructed them to establish judges and officials in every city, who would judge with just judgment, having no respect of persons, not taking gifts or bribes, nor perverting the words of righteous men, not allowing idolatry in Israel. God is not the God of slackers, but of duty-driven men.

Deuteronomy 16:18 - "Judges and officers shalt thou make thee in all thy gates."

C | Transgressing His Covenant

Christians love talking about "covenant" as if God's covenant means irrevocable blessings. From the beginning, the covenant was God's promise to bless His people IF they would faithfully love and obey Him. So covenant is a two-way agreement. You owe your part to the covenant. Covenant with God is worthless if you still love the world, the flesh or the devil.

Deuteronomy 17:2-3 - "If there be found among you, ...man or woman, that hath wrought wickedness in the sight of the LORD thy God, in transgressing his covenant, And hath gone and served other gods..."

A | Seeking Counsel From Men Of God

Sometimes, God wants us to consult with those men He has ordained as ministers. They walk with God. They study His ways. They know His will. You can pray and search all over the place, but the answer may be in the house of God. They are only men, but God uses men. Men of God certainly know better than laymen. God made it that way.

Deuteronomy 17:9 - "And thou shalt come unto the priests the Levites, and unto the judge that shall be in those days, and enquire; and they shall shew thee the sentence of judgment."

B | Diviners, Witches And Wizards - Abominations

Never forget that God chose to raise up a holy people because He hates the ways of the heathen: paganism, idolatry, spiritualism and that whole lot (including Disney and Potter).

Deuteronomy 18:10-12 - "There shall not be found among you any one that maketh his son or his daughter to pass through the fire, or that useth divination, or an observer of times, or an enchanter, or a witch, Or a charmer, or a consulter with familiar spirits, or a wizard, or a necromancer. ...and because of these abominations the LORD thy God doth drive them out from before thee."

D | A Prophet Like Moses

Moses prophesied that a prophet like himself would come. Paul said that Jesus Christ is that prophet (Acts 3:20; 7:37). Jesus is the greatest prophet of all times, revealing the Kingdom of God.

Deuteronomy 18:15,18 - "The LORD thy God will raise up unto thee a Prophet from the midst of thee, of thy brethren, like unto me; unto him ye shall hearken; ...I will raise them up a Prophet from among their brethren, like unto thee, and will put my words in his mouth; and he shall speak unto them all that I shall command him."

C | Two Or Three Witnesses

The laws of justice wield a heavy blow to a convicted wrong-doer. Because of its enormous power, the law must not be abused. God set safeguards to protect the innocent from unfair accusations and convictions. God would not allow a criminal to be convicted on the testimony of only one man. Multiple witnesses were required.

Deuteronomy 19:15 - "One witness shall not rise up against a man for any iniquity, or for any sin, in any sin that he sinneth: at the mouth of two witnesses, or at the mouth of three witnesses, shall the matter be established."

C | Be Not Afraid

Fear is a subject mentioned in almost every book of the Bible, because fear is deeply ingrained in the fiber of all people. It can become a fatal disease in the absence of faith in God. Trusting God is the antidote to fear. He is the best guardian you can possibly have. Be not afraid.

Deuteronomy 20:1 - "When thou goest out to battle against thine
enemies, and seest horses, and chariots, and a people more than thou,
be not afraid of them: for the LORD thy God is with thee, which brought
thee up out of the land of Egypt."

B | Stubborn And Rebellious Sons

God called Israel to be holy, unlike heathen nations. When sons became
stubborn and rebellious, they provoked God's wrath and judgment.

Deuteronomy 21:18 - "If a man have a stubborn and rebellious son,
which will not obey the voice of his father, or the voice of his mother, and
that, when they have chastened him, will not hearken unto them: Then
shall his father and his mother ...say, ...our son is stubborn and
rebellious, he will not obey our voice; he is a glutton, and a drunkard.
And all the men of his city shall stone him with stones, that he die."

C | Dress Code

The twentieth century was a revolutionary period for gender identity.
Never in history was there such a massive, radical shift in dress codes.
Women in war defense jobs began wearing masculine garments.
Hollywood starlets promoted the trend. Since that time, **sexual
identities**[3] have become muddled and homosexuality is epidemic. God
says men should be men, and women should be women.

Deuteronomy 22:5 - "The woman shall not wear that which pertaineth
unto a man, neither shall a man put on a woman's garment: for all that do
so are abomination unto the Lord thy God."

A | Prayers That Backfire

God is never going to answer a prayer that contradicts His Word, His will,
or His promises. If you ask God to do something that is evil in His sight,
do not be surprised if He does exactly the opposite of what you ask. God
may turn your blessing into a curse, or your curse into a blessing.
Sanctify your prayers by understanding and seeking His will.

Deuteronomy 23:5 - "Nevertheless the LORD thy God would not hearken
unto Balaam; but the LORD thy God turned the curse into a blessing
unto thee, because the LORD thy God loved thee."

C | The Bill Of Divorcement

God requires sexual faithfulness in marriage. Fornication or adultery
betrays a marriage. God allows an innocent person to divorce one who is

an adulterer. But, "...whosoever shall put away his wife, saving for the cause of fornication, causeth her to commit adultery," Matthew 5:32. Jesus added that a woman who puts away her husband and marries another commits adultery (Mark 10:12). What God hath joined together, let not man put asunder.

Deuteronomy 24:1 - "When a man ...hath found some uncleanness in her: then let him write her a bill of divorcement, and give it in her hand."

B | The House Of Him That Hath His Shoe Loosed

If any man in Israel died without leaving children, his brother was to take his widow and bear a child for his brother's namesake. If a man would not do this, the widow reported it to the city elders. They witnessed as she removed the man's shoe and spit in his face. His name was then called, "The house of him that hath his shoe loosed," verse 10.

Deuteronomy 25:6 - "...the firstborn which she beareth shall succeed in the name of his brother which is dead, that his name be not put out of Israel."

A | A Certificate Made By Prayer

Moses required Israel to pray a specific prayer shortly after they settled in the Promised Land. They must bring the first tithes of their crops to the Levites and certify that it was God who brought them into the land and blessed them, that God was their God, and that they were His people. Verbally certify (confirm) your relationship with God occasionally.

Deuteronomy 26:17 - "Thou hast avouched the LORD this day to be thy God, and to walk in his ways, and to keep his statutes, and his commandments, and his judgments, and to hearken unto his voice."

B | Inaugurating The Promised Land

Moses instructed Israel to do several things upon entering the Promised Land. 1) Keep all the Commandments I taught you. 2) When you cross over Jordan, build a stone memorial and write the Commandments on it. 3) Build an altar, offer sacrifices and rejoice. 4) Stand half the tribes on Mount Gerizim and recite the blessings I promised. 5) Stand the other tribes on Mount Ebal and recite the curses I promised if you forsake. 6) Have the Levites curse everyone who breaks the laws of God.

Deuteronomy 27:11 - "And Moses charged the people the same day..."

D | Blessings And Cursing

God's blessings are inextricably linked to obedience. Jesus said, "If you love me, keep my commandments." You have to obey God to be blessed. He curses disobedience.

Deuteronomy 28:1-2,15 - "...if thou shalt hearken diligently unto the voice of the LORD thy God, to observe and to do all his commandments..., ...all these blessings shall come on thee, and overtake thee, But it shall come to pass, if thou wilt not hearken unto the voice of the LORD thy God, to observe to do all his commandments..., ...that all these curses shall come upon thee, and overtake thee."

D | Moses Prophesied Of Nebuchadnezzar

Sometime around 1355 BC, Moses prophesied the invasion and conquest of Nebuchadnezzar of Babylon (ca. 587BC) as consequence for forsaking the LORD. Warnings from God should not be ignored.

Deuteronomy 28:47-52, 63 - "Because thou servedst not the LORD thy God, ...The LORD shall bring a nation against thee from far, ...whose tongue thou shalt not understand; A nation of fierce countenance, ...which also shall not leave thee ...until he have destroyed thee. And he shall besiege thee in all thy gates, until thy high and fenced walls come down. ...and ye shall be plucked from off the land."

D | Shamed Before All Nations

Moses warned the people that if they failed to keep their covenant with the LORD, eventually God would remove them from the Promised Land, and all the nations would know it was because of their backslidings. That prophecy has been profoundly fulfilled. It is a solemn warning to backsliding Christianity, even to a nation like America.

Deuteronomy 29:24-25 - "Even all nations shall say, Wherefore hath the LORD done thus unto this land? what meaneth the heat of this great anger? Then men shall say, Because they have forsaken the covenant of the LORD God of their fathers."

A | The Word Is In Thy Mouth

Moses prophesied lavish blessings on the people if they obeyed God's commandments, but cruel curses if they rebelled. Our divine purpose can only be realized through faithful obedience to God. Disobedience wrecks that. But obedience is entirely possible by believing and speaking the Word of God. Speak the Word daily. Life and blessing is in it.

Deuteronomy 30:11 - "For this commandment which I command thee this day, it is not hidden from thee, neither is it far off, ...But the word is very nigh unto thee, in thy mouth, and in thy heart, that thou mayest do it."

A | **The Song Of Moses**

Sometimes prayer is difficult. It would be wonderful if God would just put words in our mouth. Sometimes He does. God told Moses to write a song for Israel to sing, so that when they found themselves in evil times, they could turn to God and recite all the words Moses had given them. Deuteronomy 32 is that song. Try it yourself.

Deuteronomy 31:19 - "Now therefore write ye this song for you, and teach it the children of Israel: put it in their mouths, that this song may be a witness for me against the children of Israel."

D | **Fire In Hell**

The Old Testament concept of Hell is two-fold. The Hebrew word "sheol" is translated "hell" in more than half the verses it is used, and "grave" in the others. In most cases you can clearly see the references to burning, fire, pain, destruction and punishment. A lifeless human body may rest quietly in its grave, but that person's sinful soul will be tormented endlessly in Hell. Moses taught that God's anger causes the fire that burns in Hell.

Deuteronomy 32:22 - "...a fire is kindled in mine anger, and shall burn unto the lowest hell."

D | **Moses Blesses The Tribes**

Each of the twelve tribes of Israel had a divine posterity. Moses took time to speak to them again before he died. Each tribe received a blessing, except for Simeon. Jacob, their father, had prophesied that Levi and Simeon would be scattered because of the war over Dinah at Shechem. Moses affirmed that Levi would be scattered among all the tribes, but completely ignored Simeon. Over time, Simeon left an erratic history. Blessings and curses are very real.

Deuteronomy 33:1 - "And this is the blessing, wherewith Moses the man of God blessed the children of Israel before his death."

D | **The Death Of Moses**

At 120, Moses viewed the Promised Land from Mounts Nebo and Pisgah, across Jordan, near Jericho. He could see where several tribes would settle. Then he died in the mountain. God buried him in a secret place near Bethpeor. Michael the Archangel contended with Satan over Moses' body, rebuking him in the name of the Lord (Jude 1:9). Peter, James and John saw Moses standing on the mount with Jesus 1400 years later.

Deuteronomy 34:5 - "So Moses the servant of the LORD died there in the land of Moab, according to the word of the LORD."

Lessons from the Book of
JOSHUA

B | Joshua

Moses' protégé, Joshua, is one of the squeakiest-clean characters in the Bible. His testimony was virtually flawless - great faith, courageous, loyal to God and leader. It is no surprise that God handed the reins to him when Moses died. Here is a great lesson for all would-be men and women of God. God rewards obedient faithfulness.

Joshua 1:5 - "There shall not any man be able to stand before thee all the days of thy life: as I was with Moses, so I will be with thee: I will not fail thee, nor forsake thee."

C | Play The Role

A character actor loses his own identity in his role. He disappears into the script. Whether it is Agamemnon at Troy in the Greek tragedy, or Cleopatra in Shakespeare's classic, the actor must not fail the role. God scripts our lives. From the moment we learn His will, we must follow it. Our behavior, speech, dress, hair, our entire countenance - our whole lives are clearly defined in His script (scripture).

Joshua 1:8 - "This... shall not depart out of thy mouth...that thou mayest observe to do according to all that is written therein."

C | Be Strong And Courageous

Joshua made an inspiring "pep talk" to Israel before crossing Jordan. "Have not I commanded thee? Be strong and of a good courage; be not afraid, neither be thou dismayed: for the LORD thy God is with thee whithersoever thou goest," Joshua 1:9. Do you think they would have conquered Canaan if they had been weak and afraid? Of course not! Every person faces weakness and fear eventually, but it has to be overcome. God commands it! Toss out all the self-doubts right now, and move forward.

Joshua 1:18 - "...only be strong and of a good courage."

B | Rahab The Harlot

Joshua sent two spies into Jericho before crossing Jordan. They met Rahab, who revealed that the people were terrified of Israel, because they knew that God was with them since leaving Egypt. Rahab hid the spies from Jericho's king for their promise that she and her family would be saved alive whenever Israel invaded Jericho. Afterward, one of Judah's descendants, Salmon, married Rahab. They begat Boaz, who married Ruth. They were grandparents to King David and ultimately, Jesus Christ.

Joshua 2:9 - "And she said unto the men, I know that the LORD hath given you the land."

D | The Wood Of The Tabernacle

The Ark of the Covenant, Table of Shewbread, Altar of Incense, and everything wooden in the Tabernacle was made of Shittim wood (Acacia Seyal). The last place Israel camped before entering the Promised Land was at a town named Abel-Shittim, which means "Meadow of the Acacias." I think there is some typology there. Wood, hay and stubble represent the temporal, mortal world. We will leave it all behind when we enter our Promised Land - the eternal Kingdom of Jesus Christ.

Joshua 3:1 - "And Joshua rose early in the morning; and they removed from Shittim, and came to Jordan."

C | Step Out By Faith

Jordan was overflowing its banks, but Joshua told the Priests bearing the Ark of the Covenant, to step into the waters. As a sign that God was still among them and would drive out their enemies before them, the waters of Jordan immediately rolled back. If you want the Promised Land, step out by faith and take it.

Joshua 3:17 - "And the priests that bare the ark of the covenant of the LORD stood firm on dry ground in the midst of Jordan, and all the

Israelites passed over on dry ground, until all the people were passed clean over Jordan."

B | Twelve Stones Out Of Jordan

As the priests carried the Ark of the Covenant into the river Jordan, the waters were immediately cut off. They stood on dry ground in the midst of the river while Israel crossed. Joshua instructed twelve men to haul twelve large stones from the river bottom to build a monument. Then he commanded the priests to come ashore. Immediately, the river overflowed its banks again. Keep a souvenir from your miracle to show your family and friends what God has done.

Joshua 4:20 - "And those twelve stones, which they took out of Jordan, did Joshua pitch in Gilgal."

D | Rolling Away The Reproach

Israel miraculously crossed the Jordan River on dry ground. News of what the Lord had done spread fear throughout the cities of Canaan. At Gilgal, God told Joshua to circumcise all males who were not circumcised in the wilderness. Then Joshua announced that God had rolled away the reproach of Egypt from Israel. The next day, the manna ceased falling, and they ate the fruit of Canaan land from that day forward. Faithfulness to God will banish your reproaches.

Joshua 5:9 - "...the LORD said unto Joshua, This day have I rolled away the reproach of Egypt from off you."

A | Shout Unto God

Israel's first conquest inside the Promised Land was at Jericho. They marched around the city wall daily for a week, then seven times on the seventh day. When the trumpets sounded, the people shouted. The wall fell down. That victorious, one-syllable shout was as effective as a 1,000-word prayer. Shout unto God with a voice of triumph.

Joshua 6:16,20 - "...Joshua said unto the people, Shout; for the LORD hath given you the city. ...and the people shouted with a great shout, that the wall fell down flat, ...and they took the city."

A | Prayer Exposes Sin

After a miraculous victory at Jericho, the Israelites were humiliated at war with the men of Ai. Thirty-six Israelites died. Joshua panicked and fell on his face in prayer. God revealed the sins of Achan, who had unlawfully taken precious spoils at Jericho, instead of delivering them to the priests and the Tabernacle. Achan and his family were executed, and God was appeased. Be careful. Your sins can cause much more tragedy than you ever expected.

Joshua 7:10-12 - "...the LORD said unto Joshua, ...Israel hath sinned, ...Therefore the children of Israel could not stand before their enemies."

C | Overcoming Defeat

After a great victory at Jericho, Israel suffered humiliating defeat at Ai because God found a grievous sin in the camp. Once the sins of Achan and his family were dealt with, God told Joshua that he could now go to war against Ai and win. Defeat must never be the end of a story. We all make mistakes, but we should correct them as best we can and fight on.

Joshua 8:1 - "...the LORD said unto Joshua, ... arise, go up to Ai: see, I have given into thy hand the king of Ai, and his people, and his city."

B | The Gibeonites

Gibeonites came to Joshua with old shoes, old garments, old sacks, old moldy bread, and old wine bottles. They pretended to come from AFAR, to trick Israel into making a league with them. Long ago, God said, "...I will deliver the inhabitants of the land into your hand; and thou shalt drive them out before thee. Thou shalt make no covenant with them." Exodus 23:31-32. Do not make peace with the world. Prefer trouble with enemies over trouble with God.

Joshua 9:16 - "...after they had made a league with them ...they heard that they were their neighbours."

A | The Day The Sun Stood Still

Five hostile kings went to war against Gibeon, who called for Joshua to bring Israel to their defense. Joshua assembled his army, and they traveled all night to the battleground. The day wore on, and Joshua asked God for more time. "Stop the SUN!" God did! God can answer bold prayers.

Joshua 10:12-13 - "Then spake Joshua to the LORD... and he said in the sight of Israel, Sun, stand thou still upon Gibeon; and thou, Moon, in the valley of Ajalon. And the sun stood still, and the moon stayed, until the people had avenged themselves upon their enemies."

A | **When God Obeyed A Man**

It does not matter how God made the sun and moon stand still for Joshua, nor that some scientists refute that it ever happened. This epic event is eclipsed by the fact that God obeyed the voice of a man. The CEV version says, "Never before and never since has the LORD done anything like that for someone who prayed." Your problems are no problem for God. Pray on.

Joshua 10:14 - "And there was no day like that before it or after it, that the LORD hearkened unto [obeyed] the voice of a man: for the LORD fought for Israel."

D | **Divine Prerogative**

God did not send Israel to kill good and godly people. God chose their enemies by His own criteria. God sovereignly chooses heathen who have incriminated themselves before giving their place to the righteous. God knows the future of saints and sinners, and as Creator, has **divine prerogative**[4] to take away from one and give to another.

Joshua 11:20 - "...it was of the LORD to harden their hearts, that they should come against Israel in battle, that he might destroy them utterly, and that they might have no favour, but that he might destroy them, as the LORD commanded Moses."

C | **The Divine Premise Of Possessing The Land**

The premise upon which the nation of Israel is founded is God's jealousy over the world He created and His sore displeasure with the sins of heathen nations. God is not arbitrarily prejudiced against any nation, but He certainly hates their worship of false gods, their idolatries, their moral depravities, and more. God does not owe anyone apologies for saying to Joshua and Israel, in effect, "Take this land." It is His land.

Joshua 12:7,24 - "...these are the kings of the country which Joshua and the children of Israel smote... all the kings thirty and one."

B | **Distributing The Inheritance**

Even though Moses was not allowed to enter the Promised Land, he had a pretty good understanding of how the land would be divided and put it in the record before he died. When Joshua took over, God gave him more specific boundaries for dividing the land. We should never discount the divine component of this conquest. It was all written in the mind of God long before it happened. So is OUR inheritance.

Joshua 13:32 - "These are the countries which Moses did distribute for inheritance in the plains of Moab, on the other side Jordan, by Jericho, eastward."

D | Give Me This Mountain!

Joshua and Caleb had been the only two men among 600,000 who really believed they could take the Promised Land. "Moses sware on that day, saying, Surely the land whereon thy feet have trodden shall be thine inheritance, and thy children's for ever, because thou hast wholly followed the LORD my God," Joshua 14:9. At 85 years old, Caleb boasted that God had kept him strong, and he was still ready to take the land. He and his descendants inherited Hebron.

Joshua 14:12 - "Now therefore give me this mountain, whereof the LORD spake in that day."

B | Caleb's Son-In-Law

Joshua 15 contains a tedious description of the land God assigned to the tribe of Judah. Caleb received a portion including a place called Kirjathsepher and offered his daughter as wife for any man who would conquer it. Othniel volunteered, took the city, and won Caleb's daughter, Achsah. Caleb's new son-in-law became a great hero - the first Judge in Israel after Joshua and Caleb died. Heroes tend to inspire other heroes.

Joshua 15:17 - "...Othniel the son of Kenaz, the brother of Caleb, took it: and he gave him Achsah his daughter to wife."

D | Joseph's Inheritance

From his childhood, Joseph seemed to be under the powerful influence of prophetic destiny, due to his favor with God's chosen man, Jacob. Once inside the Promised Land, Joseph's inheritance included some famous places: Bethel - where Abraham and Jacob met the Lord; Jericho - first city taken; and many other cities. This land of Ephraim and Manasseh stretched from the Jordan River to the Mediterranean Sea, lush and well-watered; the choicest of properties.

Joshua 16:1,3 - "And the lot of the children of Joseph fell from Jordan... and the goings out thereof are at the sea."

C | Robbing Bees And Milking Cows

The land given to Ephraim and Manasseh was the choicest of all the lands, but they complained of the Canaanites with their chariots of iron and of the mountains with their heavy woods. Joshua simply told them, "You're a great people. Go and take it!" In this land which flowed with milk and honey, they were about to learn that you have to rob the bees and milk the cows.

Joshua 17:17-18 - "And Joshua spake, ...saying, Thou art a great people, and hast great power... thou shalt cut it down, ...and thou shalt drive out the Canaanites."

A | Casting Lots

To find the will of God, several Bible characters resorted to the equivalent of a "coin toss." Joshua cast lots to decide which tribes inherited which lands. Aaron cast lots between the scapegoat and the goat for atonement. Priests, teachers, musicians and porters cast lots in King David's courts to establish chains of authority. Nehemiah did a similar thing while rebuilding Jerusalem. Jonah's sin was revealed by casting lots. Fulfilling a prophecy of Psalm 22:18, soldiers cast lots for Jesus' garments.

Joshua 18:10 - "Joshua cast lots for them in Shiloh before the LORD: and there Joshua divided the land."

B | How Each Tribe Received The Land

Three tribes, Reuben, Gad and half of Manasseh, settled east of the Jordan River. Inside the Promised Land, God defined borders for every division. Joshua cast lots to give each tribe (except Levi) one division. God guided the lottery. The first lot went to Judah (15:1). Ephraim and Manasseh each received one lot (17:17). Each tribe gave individual cities by lot to Levi.

Joshua 19:1-40 - "...the second lot came forth to Simeon, ...the third lot..., ...Zebulun, ...the fourth lot..., ...Issachar, ...the fifth lot..., ...Asher, ...The sixth lot.. Naphtali, ...the seventh lot..., ...Dan." "...the lot of ... Benjamin," Joshua 18:11.

C | A Fair Trial

In Numbers 35, Moses introduced the plan for cities of refuge, where accused murderers could flee until they could receive a fair trial. When Joshua apportioned the land to each tribe, he also appointed the cities of refuge. This is one of many evidences of God's justice and mercy.

Joshua 20:9 - "These were the cities appointed for all the children of Israel, and for the stranger that sojourneth among them, that whosoever killeth any person at unawares might flee thither, and not die by the hand of the avenger of blood, until he stood before the congregation."

D | Receiving The Promises

After forty years of wandering, Israel finally possessed what God promised to them. God will do all He promised for you, too. Just persevere!

Joshua 21:43-45 - "And the LORD gave unto Israel all the land which he sware to give unto their fathers; and they possessed it, and dwelt therein. And the LORD gave them rest round about, according to all that he sware unto their fathers: ...the LORD delivered all their enemies into their hand. There failed not ought of any good thing which the LORD had spoken unto the house of Israel; all came to pass."

A | What About Your Altar?

The tribes of Reuben, Gad and Manasseh lived east of Jordan, so they built their own altar unto the Lord. All Israel panicked for fear that it was a pagan altar. Phinehas, the Priest, and ten princes of the tribes went to investigate. The three tribes insisted that the altar was unto the true God. Phinehas was appeased. Such matters deserve to be confirmed.

Joshua 22:29 - "God forbid that we should rebel against the LORD, and turn this day from following the LORD, to build an altar..., beside the altar of the LORD our God that is before his tabernacle."

D | Joshua Prophesies Warnings

Modern Israel should read Joshua's prophecies again. His message as he was dying was essentially this: Remember the mighty things God has done for you. He will always defend you if you faithfully obey and serve Him. But if you compromise yourself with heathen nations, becoming like them, the LORD will stop defending you. They will become snares, traps, scourges and thorns to you, and you will perish off the land.

Joshua 23:15 - "...as all good things are come upon you, which the LORD your God promised you; so shall the LORD bring upon you all evil things."

A | When They Cried Unto The Lord

Before Joshua died, he admonished Israel to be faithful to God and warned them against forsaking the Lord. "As for me and my house, we will serve the Lord." He and Caleb were the only believers left from the previous generation. Joshua testified about how Israel cried to God forty years earlier when the Egyptians were pursuing them. We might never backslide if we would faithfully testify how often God has heard our prayers.

Joshua 24:7 - "And when they cried unto the LORD, he put darkness between you and the Egyptians, and brought the sea upon them."

Lessons from the Book of
JUDGES

B | Judges

Both Moses and Joshua could see a time coming when Israel would forsake God's commandments. There would be no king in Israel, and every man would do what was right in his own eyes. Yet, in those times, great men and women stood for God and righteousness, judging Israel in isolated circumstances. Gideon, Sampson, Deborah, Samuel and others were heroic. The moral: even in bad times, one person can save the day.

Judges 2:10 - "...there arose another generation after them, which knew not the LORD, nor yet the works which he had done for Israel."

A | Who Shall Go Up First?

When Joshua died, Israel asked God who should lead in battle against their enemies. The Lord said, "Judah." So Judah led the way, taking the Canaanites, Perizzites, Jerusalem, Hebron, Debir, Hormah, Gaza, Askelon and Ekron. Those victories should be remembered on "World News Tonight." God gave those cities to Israel 3400 years ago. It pays to pray.

Judges 1:1-2 - "...the children of Israel asked the LORD, saying, Who shall go up for us against the Canaanites first, to fight against them? And the LORD said, Judah shall go up: behold, I have delivered the land into his hand."

A | Crying Out For A Deliverer

After Joshua died, the children of Israel began to forsake the Lord and turn to the gods of the heathen. God allowed their enemies to overcome them. From time to time, Israel came to their senses and began to repent and cry out to God for deliverance. The book of Judges recounts how God raised up several anointed judges who brought miraculous deliverance. Surely God yearns to hear our cry when we have sinned.

Judges 3:9 - "And when the children of Israel cried unto the LORD, the LORD raised up a deliverer to the children of Israel, who delivered them..."

A | Othniel, First Judge

It often takes a crisis to make us pray. Such was the case in Israel after Joshua died. The people began worshiping Baalim and groves of idols, so God sent the king of Mesopotamia to rule harshly over them. Finally the people cried unto the Lord for a deliverer, and He sent to them a godly leader: Othniel, the son of Kenaz, Caleb's brother; Israel's first judge.

Judges 3:10 - "And the Spirit of the LORD came upon him, and he judged Israel, and went out to war: and the LORD delivered Chushanrishathaim king of Mesopotamia into his hand."

A | Ehud Conquers Moab

Israel's second judge, Ehud, cleverly gained entrance to the palace of Eglon, king of Moab, by delivering a gift. The king put everyone out of his chambers. Ehud then thrust him through with a dagger and slipped away unnoticed. Eighteen years of evil rule ended as God gave a remarkable deliverance by one man. But deliverance only began when Israel cried out to God for a deliverer. Next victory, be careful to acknowledge God, who heard your prayer.

Judges 3:30 - "So Moab was subdued that day under the hand of Israel. And the land had rest fourscore years."

C | The Woman Gets Honor

Deborah was a godly judge and prophetess in Israel during a twenty-year oppression by the Canaanites. God commanded Deborah to send troops after Sisera, Canaan's army captain. She delivered the word of the Lord to Barak to lead an attack, but he would not go without her. Deborah showed herself a champion, but another woman, Jael, became the heroine who assassinated Sisera that day.

Judges 4:9 - "...I will surely go with thee: notwithstanding the journey that thou takest shall not be for thine honour; for the LORD shall sell Sisera into the hand of a woman."

A | The Song Of Deborah

For twenty years, Canaanites oppressed Israel. Deborah and Barak took an army and miraculously discomfited Sisera, Canaan's captain, who came against them with 900 chariots of iron. Sisera fled to a nearby tent for rest. While he slept, an Israelite woman named Jael drove a nail through his head. By Deborah, Barak and Jael, God delivered Israel that day. The song of Deborah (Judges 5) declared the mighty works of God.

Judges 5:31 - "...let all thine enemies perish, O LORD: but let them that love him be as the sun when he goeth forth in his might."

A | The Call Of Gideon

Once again, Israel did evil, and God allowed their enemies to oppress them. Once again, Israel cried out for deliverance. Once again, God sent a deliverer. This time it was Gideon. The angel said, "The LORD is with thee, thou mighty man of valour." "Why then is all this befallen us?" Gideon asked. "Go in this thy might, and thou shalt save Israel from the hand of the Midianites: have not I sent thee?" Once again, prayer was the solution.

Judges 6:6 - "...Israel was greatly impoverished because of the Midianites; and the children of Israel cried unto the LORD."

B | How Gideon Became Jerubbaal

Gideon's visitor instructed him to place the bread and meat he prepared for him on a rock. The angel touched it with his staff. Instantly, fire consumed it, and the angel vanished. God then commanded Gideon to destroy the local idols and altars to Baal, which he did. Never fear false gods. They are non-existent. Gideon built an altar to the LORD, calling it "Jehovah Shalom," meaning "God is Peace." The locals wanted to kill Gideon, but his father defended him.

Judges 6:32 - "Therefore on that day he called him Jerubbaal, saying, Let Baal plead against him..."

C | Supernatural Confirmations

After Gideon destroyed Baal-worship, Midianites invaded Jezreel. Blowing a trumpet, Gideon called Manasseh, Asher, Zebulun and

Naphtali to war. Laying down a woolen fleece, he prayed, "...if the dew be on the fleece only, and it be dry upon all the earth beside, then shall I know that thou wilt save Israel by mine hand." Next morning, he wrung "a bowl full of water" from the fleece. Still, Gideon wanted ANOTHER sign.

Judges 6:39-40 - "...let it now be dry only upon the fleece, and upon all the ground let there be dew. And God did so that night."

D | The Men Who Lapped

God planned Gideon's success before He ever called him. He would not allow Gideon to have a large army, "...lest Israel vaunt themselves against me, saying, Mine own hand hath saved me." First, God dismissed 22,000 recruits because they were fearful, then sent the remaining 10,000 to the river to drink. Those who knelt down to drink were eliminated. Only three hundred who lapped remained. But God still had plenty.

Judges 7:7 - "And the LORD said unto Gideon, By the three hundred men that lapped will I save you, and deliver the Midianites into thine hand."

D | The Dream That Caused An Army To Flee

God sent Gideon to eavesdrop on the Midianites' encampment. Gideon heard a conversation between a man who had a dream and his fellow who said it meant that God had delivered Midian into Gideon's hands. Gideon worshipped the Lord. God can strike fear in your enemies before you make your first move.

Judges 7:15 - "And it was so, when Gideon heard the telling of the dream, and the interpretation thereof, that he worshipped, and returned into the host of Israel, and said, Arise; for the LORD hath delivered into your hand the host of Midian."

B | The Sword Of The Lord And Of Gideon

Midianites and Amalekites "...lay along in the valley like grasshoppers for multitude." With only 300 men, each bearing a trumpet, a pitcher and a lamp, Gideon surrounded them after midnight. "When I blow with a trumpet, ...then blow ye the trumpets also on every side of all the camp, and say, The sword of the LORD, and of Gideon." No enemy is too big for men with faith in God.

Judges 7:22 - "And the three hundred blew the trumpets, and the LORD set every man's sword against his fellow, even throughout all the host: and the host fled..."

C | Trouble With Family

God enabled Gideon to whip 120,000 Midianites with only 300 men, but his own brethren resisted him. Ephraimites chided him because he did not call them to battle. Men from Succoth and Penuel hatefully refused to feed Gideon's troops as they pursued. Family sometimes causes more grief than sore enemies. Gideon punished the offenders for their insolence and won the hearts of all Israel.

Judges 8:22-23 - "...Rule thou over us, ...for thou hast delivered us from the hand of Midian. And Gideon said unto them, I will not rule over you, ...the LORD shall rule over you."

B | Gideon's Snare

Deuteronomy 7:25-26 says, "Thou shalt not desire the silver or gold that is on them, nor take it unto thee, lest thou be snared therein: for it is an abomination to the Lord thy God. ...but thou shalt utterly detest it, and thou shalt utterly abhor it; for it is a cursed thing." Gideon's family was cursed because he disobeyed, by coveting jewelry from Israel's wars. Gideon had seventy sons. One evil son killed all but one of his brothers.

Judges 8:24 - "...Gideon said unto them, ...give me every man the earrings of his prey. (For they had golden earrings)."

C | Spoiling A Legacy

Gideon refused to be king of Israel. "I will not rule over you, neither shall my son rule over you: the LORD shall rule over you," Judges 8:23. But Gideon sinned with the golden earrings, and his heroic legacy was lost. At Ophrah, where Gideon met the angel of the Lord and built the altar to Jehovah Shalom, he caused Israel to go whoring after the golden ephod. He was buried there. His wicked son, Abimelech, manipulated the Shechemites into crowning him king.

Judges 9:5 - Abimelech "...went unto his father's house at Ophrah, and slew his brethren."

D | The Parable Of The Trees

Gideon's evil son, Abimelech, usurped rule over Israel by killing all his brothers except Jotham, who escaped. Jotham prophesied a parable about trees who wanted a king over them. They asked the olive tree, the fig tree, and the vine. All refused. The bramble (Abimelech) wanted to rule, but he ruled by terror. Jotham prophesied that the people would kill Abimelech.

Judges 9:53-56 - "...a certain woman cast a piece of a millstone upon Abimelech's head, ...and he died. Thus God rendered the wickedness of Abimelech, which he did unto his father, in slaying his seventy brethren."

C | Forsaking The LORD

Gideon, in his backsliding, precipitated gross apostasy in Israel. Although Tola and Jair judged Israel over twenty years each, Israel nevertheless turned to many false gods - Baalim, Ashtaroth, Syrian gods, Zidonian gods, Moabite gods, Ammonite gods, and Philistine gods. Similarly today, multitudes are forsaking Biblical Christianity and choosing wicked belief systems. But the wrath of God will soon be revealed from heaven (Romans 1:18).

Judges 10:6-7 - "And the children of Israel did evil again in the sight of the LORD, ...and forsook the LORD, and served not Him. And the anger of the LORD was hot against Israel."

A | Treasure Your Audience With God

This one is pretty scary. God reminded Israel of a long list of nations He had delivered them from. "Yet ye have forsaken me, and served other gods: wherefore I will deliver you no more. Go and cry unto the gods which ye have chosen; let them deliver you in the time of your tribulation," Judges 10:11-16. Israel went into mortifying repentance, and "they put away the strange gods from among them, and served the LORD." Do not jeopardize your audience with God. Nothing is worse than losing access to Him.

Judges 10:16 "...and His soul was grieved..."

B | Jephthah

Gilead's sons cast out their half-brother, Jephthah, "a mighty man of valour," because he was son of a harlot. But when Ammonites came warring, the elders wanted Jephthah for their captain. The Ammonite king accused Israel of conquering them without justification while fleeing Egypt. But Jephthah argued that Israel was only acting in self-defense against the Ammonites' aggression. Jephthah then launched a massive attack on Ammon and completely subdued it. God often remakes outcasts into heroes.

Judges 11:29,33 - "...the Spirit of the LORD came upon Jephthah, ...And he smote them ...with a very great slaughter."

C | Rash Vows

Jephthah vowed that if God gave him victory over the Ammonites, he would burn a sacrifice of whatever met him first when he returned home. Surely he was thinking about goats, lambs, or calves. But when he returned, his only DAUGHTER met him first! "...he rent his clothes, and said, Alas, my daughter! ...thou art one of them that trouble me: for I have opened my mouth unto the LORD, and I cannot go back," Judges 11:35. It is advisable never to make a vow.

Judges 11:39 - Jephthah "...did with her according to his vow which he had vowed."

B | Trouble With Ephraim

The Ephraimites had ego problems. They troubled Gideon, falsely claiming that he excluded them from war with Midian. Later, they troubled Jephthah, complaining that he did not invite them to war against the Ammonites. Jephthah HAD called them, but they were "no-shows"! Reality check: Ephraim never drove the Canaanites from their own territory, yet wanted superiority over all the tribes. Their ego antagonized Jephthah into civil war with them, and he won handily. "Pride goeth before destruction, and an haughty spirit before a fall," Proverbs 16:18.

Judges 12:6 - "...there fell at that time of Ephraim forty and two thousand."

A | Manoah's Prayer

Again, Israel sinned against God, and oppressors overtook them: Philistines - for forty years. God sent an angel to Manoah's barren wife, informing them that they would have a son (Samson). He would begin to deliver Israel from the Philistines. The angel ordered him to be consecrated a Nazarite, but Manoah wanted to know how they should raise him. He prayed that God would send the angel again to clarify the instructions. Ask God again, when you do not understand.

Judges 13:9 - "...God hearkened to the voice of Manoah; and the angel of God came again unto the woman."

D | Samson

The simple fact of Samson's birth was a fulfillment of prophecy. God declares the end from the beginning. Throughout history, God has sovereignly pre-ordained individuals to come on the scene for a specific time, a specific place and a specific reason. The angel told Manoah's wife she would bear a son who would begin to deliver Israel from the Philistines. As long as God's people cry for deliverance, God will continue to send deliverers.

Judges 13:24 - "And the woman bare a son, and called his name Samson: and the child grew, and Jehovah blessed him."

D | Samson And The Woman At Timnath

God has many rules, but sometimes He makes exceptions to rules. When Samson took an interest in the Philistine woman at Timnath, it seemed to contradict good judgment. But a huge chain of events evolved from that relationship: Samson slew a lion, slew thirty Philistines at Ashkelon, burned the fields of the Philistines, and slew 1,000 Philistines with the jawbone of an ass.

Judges 14:4 - "But his father and his mother knew not that it was of the LORD, that he sought an occasion against the Philistines: for at that time the Philistines had dominion over Israel."

A | Need Water?

Samson miraculously slew 1,000 Philistines with the jawbone of an ass. But when he finished, he was famished for a drink of water. He asked God to provide water.

Judges 15:18-19 - "And he was sore athirst, and called on the LORD, and said, Thou hast given this great deliverance into the hand of thy servant: and now shall I die for thirst, and fall into the hand of the uncircumcised? But God clave an hollow place that was in the jaw, and there came water thereout; and when he had drunk, his spirit came again, and he revived."

A | Samson's Last Prayer

Tragedy befell Samson for compromising his Nazarite vow to Delilah's ploys. She cut his hair while he slept, and the Philistines captured him, put out his eyes, and put him to grinding in prison. But his hair grew again, and Samson renewed his vow. The Philistines mocked him at a feast to their god, Dagon, but Samson prayed God to avenge him. God heard him, and Samson toppled the pillars on which the house stood.

Judges 16:30 - "...So the dead which he slew at his death were more than they which he slew in his life."

B | Micah The Ephraimite

This story is weird. A woman cursed the thief who took her 1100 pieces of silver. Her son, Micah, confessed to taking them, then returned them. As thanks, she dedicated the silver to make a graven image and molten image. Micah set up a house of gods and hired a vagabond Levite to be his private priest. But shortly thereafter, travelers stole away both the priest and Micah's idols. Do not waste yourself on unbiblical religion. It is worthless at best, abominable and cursed at worst.

Judges 17:12 - "...Micah consecrated the Levite, and the young man became his priest."

A | Praying Counsel From Hirelings

One of the most pathetic stories in the Bible is about a vagabond Levite who hired out his priestly services to a man named Micah. Men from the tribe of Dan ignorantly sought his counsel, receiving phony blessings and falling into idolatrous deception. You will be duped if you trust phony ministries.

Judges 18:5-6 - "And they said unto him, Ask counsel, we pray thee, of God, that we may know whether our way which we go shall be prosperous. And the priest said unto them, Go in peace: before the LORD is your way wherein ye go."

C | Complicated Consequences

You can open the Bible almost anywhere and soon find complicated consequences of someone's foolish behavior. Modern culture promotes a delusion that everyone should be free to do whatever is right in his or her own eyes, but history proves that to be the prescription for social chaos, anarchy and disintegration. The woman in Judges 19 who left her spouse to commit whoredoms precipitated a chain of events that drew 400,000 men into war. Over 65,000 people died before the dust settled.

Judges 19:2 - "And his concubine played the whore against him, and went away from him..."

A | Pray For Instructions From God

A Levite and his concubine traveled through Gibeah and lodged overnight with an old man. Locals took the woman, abused, raped, and murdered her. The Levite cut up her body and sent one part to every tribe in Israel to publicize the abominable crime. 400,000 Israelites rose up to punish the perverse Benjamites. Israel sought counsel of God three times, but still lost 40,000 troops before slaying 25,000 Benjamites, defeating them. Sometimes justice requires great sacrifice.

Judges 20:18 - "...the children of Israel arose, and went up to the house of God, and asked counsel of God."

A | Prayer About Family Sins

When the perverse men of Gibeah (who were Benjamites) raped and killed the Levite's concubine, all Israel was inflamed. Phinehas, the high priest, enquired of the Lord whether Israel should declare war on the Benjamites. God said "yes." You have to obey God.

Judges 20:28 - "And Phinehas, the son of Eleazar, the son of Aaron, stood before [the ark] in those days, saying, Shall I yet again go out to battle against the children of Benjamin my brother, or shall I cease? And the LORD said, Go up; for to morrow I will deliver them into thine hand."

A | Restoring A Lost Tribe

The men of Gibeah who raped and murdered the Levite's concubine created a firestorm of trouble. God sent all Israel to war against the tribe of Benjamin. Israel mourned the tragic loss of one whole tribe and asked God what to do. They took 400 virgins from Jabeshgilead and gave them to the few hundred remaining Benjamites, to perpetuate the Benjamite tribe.

Judges 21:6-7 - "...the children of Israel repented them for Benjamin their brother, and said, There is one tribe cut off from Israel this day. How shall we do for wives for them that remain?"

Lessons from the Book of
RUTH

A | Ruth

One of the most heartwarming stories ever - suffering widowhood and poverty in a godless land, Ruth's heart bound to Naomi, her God-fearing mother-in-law. Word of her loyalty, godly devotion and commitment reached Boaz, who became her redeemer-husband. Greater than any Cinderella story! Ruth became Great-Grandmother to Christ!

Ruth 1:16 - "And Ruth said, Intreat me not to leave thee, or to return from following after thee: for whither thou goest, I will go; and where thou lodgest, I will lodge: thy people shall be my people, and thy God my God."

A | Naomi's Prayer

Death dealt devastating blows to Naomi and her daughters-in-law. Her husband and both sons were dead, and Naomi decided that survival depended on returning to Bethlehem. She called her poor daughters-in-law and prayed the blessings of God on them. Prayer is the gift for all occasions and all seasons of life.

Ruth 1:8-9 - "...Naomi said unto her two daughters-in-law, Go, return each of you to her mother's house: Jehovah deal kindly with you, as ye have dealt with the dead, and with me. Jehovah grant you that ye may find rest."

B | Naomi

When she returned to Bethlehem from Moab, her old friends remembered her as Naomi, meaning "pleasant." But Naomi did not feel pleasant, because her husband and both sons had died. She wanted to be called Mara, or 'bitter,' but nobody consented. God had already started a flood of miracles for her and Ruth. We must stop mourning our losses and acknowledge the good things God is doing now.

Ruth 1:20-21 - "...Call me not Naomi, call me Mara: for the Almighty hath dealt very bitterly with me. I went out full, and the LORD hath brought me home again empty."

D | Bethlehem - "House Of Bread"

The legacy of Bethlehem, "house of bread," began when Jacob's beloved Rachel was buried there. Elimelech and Naomi fled from there during days of apostasy and dearth. But in better days, Naomi came with Ruth and found food in the barley fields of Boaz. The whole world would find bread in the fields of Bethlehem, when Jesus Christ, the "Bread of Life," was born there - descended from his famous grandparents: Boaz and Ruth.

Ruth 1:22 - "So Naomi returned, and Ruth the Moabitess, her daughter in law, with her, ...and they came to Bethlehem in the beginning of barley harvest."

D | Ruth And Her "Hap"

Ruth made an epic consecration to be faithful to Naomi and her God, for which she was profoundly blessed. There is no "happen-stance" with God - no accidents! When Ruth went to the fields of Boaz to glean, it was "her hap" to be there. God was scrupulously leading her to Boaz and into the bloodline of the Savior of the world.

Ruth 2:3 - "And she went, and came, and gleaned in the field after the reapers: and her hap was to light on a part of the field belonging unto Boaz, who was of the kindred of Elimelech."

C | A Message For The Gleaners

Although Naomi and Ruth were destitute in their widowhood, God had something special in store for them. His law stipulated that at harvest time, the edges of the fields should be left for the poor to glean in. Boaz carefully instructed the workers to leave plenty for Ruth. Likewise, Jesus says, "he that cometh to me shall never hunger," John 6:35.

Ruth 2:15-16 - "Let her glean even among the sheaves, and reproach her not: And let fall also some of the handfuls of purpose for her, and leave them, that she may glean them, and rebuke her not."

A | Boaz

The law of the kinsman-redeemer required someone near of kin to redeem a childless widow. Ruth did not know who would redeem her, how it would happen, or even IF it would happen. But her faithfulness to God was exemplary, and Boaz assured her good fortune when he pronounced the blessing of God on her in one simple prayer.

Ruth 3:10-11 - "And he said, Blessed be thou of the LORD, my daughter: ...fear not; I will do to thee all that thou requirest: for all the city of my people doth know that thou art a virtuous woman."

D | Bloodline Of Redeemers

Jesus came from a bloodline of redeemers and redeemed, like Judah, who redeemed Joseph from murderous brothers. He descended from Tamar, who was redeemed from playing the harlot. He descended from Rahab the harlot, redeemed to give birth to Boaz, kinsman redeemer for Ruth and Naomi. Women of Bethlehem prophesied to Naomi that Boaz and Ruth's son, Obed, would be famous. He was! Grandfather of King David and Jesus the Redeemer!

Ruth 4:14 - "...the women said unto Naomi, Blessed be the LORD, which hath not left thee this day without a kinsman, that his name may be famous in Israel."

Lessons from the Book of
1 SAMUEL

B | Samuel And The Kings

1 & 2 Samuel and 1 & 2 Kings contain historical tales of Israel during the times of Eli the High Priest, the great prophet Samuel, King Saul, King David, and King Solomon. One man, Samuel, played a central, preponderant role in Israel for forty years. He anointed King Saul, who ruled forty years, and King David, who also ruled forty years. Many of the richest texts in the Bible are contained here - awe-inspiring stories of how God worked through three generations. A must-read.

1 Samuel 3:4 - "...the LORD called Samuel: and he answered, Here am I."

C | The Lord Had Shut Up Her Womb

It is a hard saying, but sometimes barrenness is of the Lord. Elkanah had two wives. Peninnah had many children. Hannah had none. Peninnah tormented Hannah about her barrenness, but it drove her to her knees in desperate prayer. God eventually gave her a son named Samuel, but she gave him back to the Lord. Samuel grew up in the Tabernacle, away from his mother, and became one of the greatest men of God of all times.

1 Samuel 1:6 - "...her adversary also provoked her sore, for to make her fret, because the LORD had shut up her womb."

A | Hannah's Prayer

Hannah was barren, and tormented by that fact. Years went by. In desperation, she went to the Tabernacle at Shiloh to pray. She was so sorrowful that Eli, the priest, accused her of being drunken. But she defended herself, and Eli blessed her. She promised God that if He would give her a son, she would consecrate him to the ministry for life. Soon, God gave her a son. Take your sorrows to God in prayer.

1 Samuel 1:20,27 - "...[she] called his name Samuel, saying, Because I have asked him of the LORD. ...For this child I prayed."

A | Hannah's Song

Hannah blessed the LORD after the sorrow of her barrenness and the torment of her enemy was lifted. Her song in 1 Samuel 2:1-10 declares the everlasting truth that God ultimately favors the righteous over the wicked, no matter how present conditions appear.

1 Samuel 2:6-9 - "The LORD killeth, and maketh alive: he bringeth down to the grave, and bringeth up. The LORD maketh poor, and maketh rich: he bringeth low, and lifteth up. ...He will keep the feet of his saints, and the wicked shall be silent in darkness; for by strength shall no man prevail."

C | You Cannot Outgive God

After many years of barrenness and sorrow, God gave Hannah a son. But she had vowed to the LORD that she would "give him unto the LORD all the days of his life." That was an unimaginable sacrifice for a mother, but she kept her vow. One day, while visiting her son, Samuel, at the Tabernacle, Eli, the priest, blessed Hannah and her husband. God gave her five more children. God will remember your faithful, sacrificial giving and reward you gloriously.

1 Samuel 2:21 - "And the LORD visited Hannah, so that she conceived, and bare three sons and two daughters."

D | Death Of Hophni And Phinehas

Eli was the High Priest at the Tabernacle in Shiloh. His sons, Hophni and Phinehas were scandalous, having shameless greed for the offerings, and lying with the women who visited the Tabernacle. God sent a messenger to Eli with dreadful judgment. Hophni and Phinehas would die in one day. God would raise up a new high priest (Zadok). Sin cannot prevail indefinitely. God will intervene.

1 Samuel 2:35 - "...I will raise me up a faithful priest, that shall do according to that which is in mine heart and in my mind: and I will build him a sure house."

B | The Child Samuel

While the child Samuel ministered to the LORD before the High Priest, God awoke him three times in one night to tell him that Eli would soon be judged severely "because his sons made themselves vile, and he restrained them not." Samuel feared to show Eli the vision, but Eli pressed him. God has often used a child as mightily as any man. Men, take note! You can be replaced.

1 Samuel 3:18 - "And Samuel told him every whit, and hid nothing from him. And he said, It is the LORD: let him do what seemeth him good."

B | Samuel The Prophet

Not just any man can see and know the mind of the LORD. In the days of the Judges, there was "no open vision" in Israel. No particular person had ready understanding of God's doings. But that changed with Samuel. "The LORD revealed himself to Samuel in Shiloh," and everybody knew that he was an anointed prophet.

I Samuel 3:19-20 - "...Samuel grew, and the LORD was with him, and did let none of his words fall to the ground. And all Israel from Dan even to Beersheba knew that Samuel was established to be a prophet of the LORD."

D | Eli Was Cursed, The Ark Was Taken

The prophecy cursed Eli's household and said Hophni and Phinehas must die for profaning the priesthood. The Philistines came to war. Israel foolishly took the Ark of the Covenant into battle for protection, but took a beating. 30,000 died. Hophni and Phinehas were killed. The Ark was taken. 98-year-old Eli heard the news, fell over and died. Phinehas' pregnant wife died delivering "Ichabod."

1 Samuel 4:21 - "...she named the child Ichabod, saying, The glory is departed from Israel: because the ark of God was taken, and because of her father in law and her husband."

C | God Versus Idols

Philistines stole the Ark of the Covenant from Shiloh and set it in the house of their god, Dagon. First night, the idol fell over. They stood it up.

Second night, it fell and broke into pieces. God killed many Philistines and smote the rest with hemorrhoids. They figured, wisely, that they had better return the Ark. NOBODY will ever get by with blaspheming the Holy One of Israel - then or now!

1 Samuel 5:11 - "...[they] said, Send away the ark of the God of Israel, and let it go again to his own place, that it slay us not."

A | Philistines Inquire Of God

God plagued the Philistines for stealing the Ark of God. They asked, "What shall we do to the ark of the LORD? tell us wherewith we shall send it." On a cart pulled by two cows, they put the Ark with a trespass offering. If the cows pulled it unassisted to Bethshemesh, that would prove that God sent the plagues. God speaks to sinners.

1 Samuel 6:12 - "...the kine took the straight way to the way of Bethshemesh, and went along the highway, lowing as they went, and turned not aside to the right hand or to the left."

B | Bethshemesh

God led the Ark to Bethshemesh atop the Philistines' cart. The Levites unloaded it and then burned the cart and cattle as a sacrifice to the LORD. Sinfully, the men of Bethshemesh looked into the Ark, forcing God to smite over 50,000 people. The survivors sent to Kirjathjearim asking them to come take the Ark away from Bethshemesh. When God comes into your midst, you must reverence His holiness or suffer consequences.

1 Samuel 6:20 - "...the men of Bethshemesh said, Who is able to stand before this holy LORD God? and to whom shall he go up from us?"

A | Call A Prayer Meeting

The Philistines captured the Ark of the Covenant, but it was a curse to them. They sent it back on a cart towed by two cows headed straight to Bethshemesh. Sinfully, the men of Bethshemesh looked into the Ark and sorely angered the Lord. God slew many Israelites in anger. Samuel called a nation-wide prayer meeting at Mizpeh. They repented, God heard them, and smote the Philistines in their behalf.

1 Samuel 7:5 - "...Samuel said, Gather all Israel to Mizpeh, and I will pray for you unto the LORD."

C | Filthy Lucre

This is a cursed thing among God's people. The money coming into the ministry becomes their great lust. Eli's sons were greedy for the Tabernacle offerings. God killed them. Samuel set up his sons as judges in Israel, but they too sinned with the money. This very situation precipitated the people's demand for a king. The judges let them down. Lust for money ruins a lot of otherwise good people and destroys once-legitimate ministries.

1 Samuel 8:3 - "[Samuel's] sons walked not in his ways, but turned aside after lucre, and took bribes, and perverted judgment."

A | Israel Gets A King

Samuel's sons were corrupt judges, so Israel's elders demanded a king. Samuel was upset because they would displace God's kingship with a man. He prayed. God gave him a prophetic message. He warned that a king would draft their sons and daughters into his service, and confiscate their flocks, herds, fields and vineyards. They would eventually cry out against his oppression. (That would happen many times - i.e., Rehoboam, Jeroboam). Nevertheless, they insisted on having a king like other nations.

1 Samuel 8:22 - "...the LORD said to Samuel, Hearken unto their voice, and make them a king."

D | The Seer

God gave Samuel an open vision of His will for Israel. Israel knew him as their seer. Saul was looking for a seer to help him find his father's lost donkeys. Samuel was looking for a Benjamite about whom God had informed him the very day before. The two came together by divine arrangement. Saul found his donkeys, and Samuel found his king.

1 Samuel 9:18 - "Then Saul drew near to Samuel in the gate, and said, Tell me, I pray thee, where the seer's house is. And Samuel answered Saul, and said, I am the seer:"

B | God Chooses Saul As King

The LORD told Samuel, "To morrow about this time I will send thee a man out of the land of Benjamin, and thou shalt anoint him to be captain over my people Israel," 1 Samuel 9:16. When Saul arrived, the LORD said, "Behold the man whom I spake to thee of!" God will not always work His will so obviously, but He will always be in control.

1 Samuel 10:1 - "Then Samuel took a vial of oil, and poured it upon his head, and kissed him, and said, Is it not because the LORD hath anointed thee to be captain over his inheritance?"

D | Samuel Prophesies To Saul

After anointing Saul, Samuel prophesied signs that would prove God was with him. Two men at Rachel's tomb would tell him that his father's donkeys were found, and that his father sorrowed for him. At Tabor, three men traveling to Bethel would give him two loaves of bread. Past a garrison of Philistines, a company of prophets would prophesy and play instruments. The Spirit of the LORD would come upon him. He would prophesy and be turned into another man. Lesson? God confirms His word with signs!

1 Samuel 10:9 - "...all those signs came to pass that day."

A | A Kingdom Is Born

Samuel called Israel together to inaugurate King Saul, but he could not be found. "Therefore they enquired of the LORD further, if the man should yet come thither. And the LORD answered, Behold, he hath hid himself among the stuff." They searched and found him. "See ye him whom the LORD hath chosen." The people shouted, "God save the King!" Saul was reluctant to serve, but Samuel drafted the first national constitution, and the Kingdom of Israel was born by a divine mandate.

1 Samuel 10:25 - "...Samuel told the people the manner of the kingdom, and wrote it in a book."

C | Righteous Indignation

Saul shrank back from being king, and many in Israel opposed his appointment. That all changed after Ammonites declared war on Jabeshgilead. When Saul heard the threat, righteous indignation from the LORD rose up in him. He took an army to Jabesh and whipped the Ammonites soundly. At Gilgal, Israel made Saul king, and all the men of Israel rejoiced greatly. God can turn a reluctant participant into a gallant hero, even in the eyes of his detractors.

1 Samuel 11:6 - "The Spirit of God came upon Saul when he heard those tidings, and his anger was kindled greatly."

A | The Sin Of Prayerlessness

The Prophet Samuel was a hands-on man of God. He worked intimately among the people, making intercession for them, and leading them into the will of God as a nation. Because of Samuel's powerful role, two kings, Saul and David, established the kingdom of Israel, and it became a great nation. He was driven by the belief that it was a sin not to intercede. Oh, how we need that same conviction today!

1 Samuel 12:23 - "God forbid that I should sin against the LORD in ceasing to pray for you."

D | If Ye Rebel...

Samuel was deeply disturbed about Israel's untimely demand for a king. He reminded them that God advanced their former leaders - Moses, Aaron, and their judges; but God was always their king. They still wanted an earthly king, so God gave them one, with stern warnings: I will destroy you and your king if you do wickedly. Samuel then called down thunder and rain on them all day - a token demonstration of God's wrath, to make them fear God.

1 Samuel 12:25 - "But if ye shall still do wickedly, ye shall be consumed, both ye and your king."

C | Doing Right Things the Wrong Way

Saul, Jonathan, and 3000 men had smitten a garrison of Philistines. But the Philistines regrouped with 30,000 chariots, 6000 horses, and countless soldiers. Saul prepared to attack them. Samuel was en route, but Saul impatiently and improperly offered burnt offerings without him. Samuel arrived and rebuked Saul for breaking the Law. He prophesied that his kingdom would not pass to his descendants.

1 Samuel 13:13-14 - "...Thou hast done foolishly: thou hast not kept the commandment of the LORD thy God, ...for now would the LORD have established thy kingdom upon Israel for ever. But now thy kingdom shall not continue."

C | Synergy

Jonathan, King Saul's son, was between a rock and a hard place. Huge boulders were on either side, enemies in front of him, and no choice but to retreat or fight. He trusted that God could save either by many or by few. He and his armourbearer put their need before the Lord. The

Philistines made the wrong move, signaling to Jonathan that God was with him. Two men took on an entire garrison of soldiers and won.

1 Samuel 14:14 - "And that first slaughter, which Jonathan and his armourbearer made, was about twenty men."

A | When Your Action Is A Prayer

Jonathan and his armourbearer sneaked away from Saul into a pass overlooking the Philistines. "...it may be that the LORD will work for us: for there is no restraint to the LORD to save by many or by few." Jonathan would attract their attention. If they called him up, it meant God would deliver them into his hands. The Philistines yelled, "Come up to us!" An earthquake shook. Jonathan and his friend slew twenty men immediately. Before sundown, all Israel fought and won a great victory. Sometimes, actions do the praying.

1 Samuel 14:23 - "...the LORD saved Israel that day."

A | God Answered Him Not - Ignored Prayer

Saul's early days as king were fraught with bad behavior. At first, he didn't want to be the king. Then he got impatient with Samuel and burned improper sacrifices. Then he would have killed his own son for eating while unaware of a declared fast. But when Philistines came against him in fury, HE PRAYED! But God would not talk to him. If you want God to answer quickly, behave yourself.

1 Samuel 14:37 - "...Saul asked counsel of God, Shall I go down after the Philistines? wilt thou deliver them into the hand of Israel? But he answered him not that day."

B | Israel Rescues Jonathan From Saul

The Philistines terrified Saul. He called a fast, cursing anyone who ate that day. Jonathan was in battle, so did not know. When Saul learned that Jonathan had eaten, he swore by God, "...thou shalt surely die, Jonathan." But justice vanquishes fools and their folly.

1 Samuel 14:45 - "...the people said unto Saul, Shall Jonathan die, who hath wrought this great salvation in Israel? God forbid: as the LORD liveth, there shall not one hair of his head fall to the ground; for he hath wrought with God this day. So the people rescued Jonathan, that he died not."

B | Saul And The Amalekites

God commanded Saul to utterly destroy the Amalekites. "Slay both man and woman, infant and suckling, ox and sheep, camel and ass." With 210,000 men, Saul smote the city, but captured King Agag and kept the best animals to make sacrifices. God called him stubborn, rebellious and disobedient. That day, God rejected him from being king. Always carefully obey God.

1 Samuel 15:22 - "Samuel said, Hath the LORD as great delight in burnt offerings and sacrifices, as in obeying the voice of the LORD? Behold, to obey is better than sacrifice, and to hearken than the fat of rams."

C | Rebellion Is As Witchcraft, Stubbornness As Idolatry

Samuel told Saul that God chose him to lead Israel when he was little in his own sight. But stubborn disobedience ruined him, and God rejected him. Samuel called for Agag, the Amalekite king, and in front of Saul, cut Agag into pieces - doing Saul's unfinished job. Samuel walked out and never saw Saul again. Stubbornness and rebellion reject God and His word.

1 Samuel 15:23 - "For rebellion is as the sin of witchcraft, and stubbornness is as iniquity and idolatry. Because thou hast rejected the word of the LORD, he hath also rejected thee from being king."

D | I Have Provided Me A King

God took the kingdom from Saul. Samuel said He "hath given it to a neighbour of thine, that is better than thou." God knew all along that Saul would fail. God was angry at Israel for being impatient for an earthly king. Did God intentionally give them a loser to teach them a lesson? God knew that David would someday rule, but they would not trust Him until that day. Do not be impatient. God has a plan.

1 Samuel 16:1 - "...I will send thee to Jesse the Bethlehemite: for I have provided me a king among his sons."

A | Samuel Prays In Fear

Samuel grieved over Saul's failure, but God rebuked him and ordered him to Bethlehem to pick a king from Jesse's sons. Samuel was afraid Saul would find out. He prayed, "How can I go? ...he will kill me." God instructed him to take a heifer and make a sacrifice. "I will show thee what thou shalt do." Even great men of God like Samuel are sometimes gripped with fear. But prayer is still the answer. God wants you to call on Him.

1 Samuel 16:4 - "And Samuel did that which the LORD spake, and came to Bethlehem."

C | The LORD Looketh On The Heart

What is in your heart? God looks into your heart to judge you. Your physical looks, your height, or your appearance cannot deceive God. Lots of people look better outside than they do inside, but God is not fooled. Samuel looked for a king among Jesse's boys, but none had the heart God wanted. He went outside and chose their little brother. What does God see in your heart?

1 Samuel 16:7 - "I have refused him: for the LORD seeth not as man seeth; for man looketh on the outward appearance, but the LORD looketh on the heart."

B | The Boy David

Jesse made seven of his sons to pass before Samuel. But Samuel said, "The LORD hath not chosen these. Are here all thy children?" Many years earlier, this child prophet had "ministered before the LORD, being a child, girded with a linen ephod." Now he was going to anoint a child king who would soon rule all of Israel - the legendary David.

1 Samuel 16:11 - "And he said, There remaineth yet the youngest, and, behold, he keepeth the sheep. And Samuel said unto Jesse, Send and fetch him: for we will not sit down till he come hither."

D | An Evil Spirit From The LORD

When Samuel saw the ruddy little David, the LORD said "Arise, anoint him. For this is he." Samuel took the horn of oil and anointed him king, and "the Spirit of the LORD came upon David from that day forward." You are not sovereign. God controls your destiny according to your heart. He guides the righteous by His Spirit, but if you are wicked, God may loosen Satan to totally wreck your destiny. (See 1 Corinthians 5:5.)

1 Samuel 16:14 - "The Spirit of the LORD departed from Saul, and an evil spirit from the LORD troubled him."

B | David The Musician

An evil spirit from God troubled King Saul. His servants urged him to call a musician to soothe him. Saul consented, so they recommended David who "is cunning in playing, and a mighty valiant man, and a man of war, and prudent in matters, and a comely person, and the LORD is with him." So David came, and Saul loved him greatly. David became his armourbearer. God shrewdly promoted David right into the palace.

1 Samuel 16:23 - "David took an harp, and played with his hand: so Saul was refreshed, and was well, and the evil spirit departed from him."

B | Goliath

For forty days, Goliath stood with the Philistines across a valley from Israel's army, shouting threatenings, insults and dares. Eight to ten feet tall and heavily armored, he dared fight any warrior. The loser's nation must serve the winner's. When David appeared, "the Philistine cursed David by his gods," and said, "I will give thy flesh unto the fowls of the air." In God's name, David killed him instantly. Thus David conquered the Philistines for Israel.

1 Samuel 17:9 - "If he be able to fight with me, and to kill me, then will we be your servants."

C | Is There Not A Cause?

Jesse sent David to the battlefront with meals for his three brothers. David heard giant Goliath shouting threats against Israel and replied, "Who is this uncircumcised Philistine that he should defy the armies of the living God?" David thought somebody should kill Goliath and remove Israel's reproach. His brother rebuked him, but David replied, "Is there not a cause?" Unknowingly, David entered God's Hall of Fame that day. God promotes brave men with righteous convictions.

1 Samuel 17:31 - "When the words were heard which David spake, they rehearsed them before Saul: and he sent for him."

A | Saul Blesses David

David had already slain a lion and a bear, and knew that with God's help, he would slay Goliath, the noisy enemy of God's people. David told Saul, "Let no man's heart fail because of him; thy servant will go and fight with this Philistine." Kings will gladly bless a true Savior.

1 Samuel 17:37 - "The LORD that delivered me out of the paw of the lion, and out of the paw of the bear, he will deliver me out of the hand of this Philistine. And Saul said unto David, Go, and the LORD be with thee."

D | This Day Will The LORD Deliver

David prophesied to Goliath, "This day will the LORD deliver thee into mine hand; and I will smite thee, and take thine head from thee; ...that all the earth may know that there is a God in Israel. And all this assembly shall know that the LORD saveth not with sword and spear: for the battle is the LORD'S, and he will give you into our hands."

1 Samuel 17:57 - "And as David returned from the slaughter of the Philistine, Abner took him, and brought him before Saul with the head of the Philistine in his hand."

A | In The Name Of The LORD Of Hosts

David refused Saul's armor - the brass helmet, the coat of mail, the sword. He had no experience with them. He preferred his sling and five smooth stones. But David did not trust his sling. He trusted the LORD of Israel's hosts. That will get you the victory.

1 Samuel 17:45 - "Then said David to the Philistine, Thou comest to me with a sword, and with a spear, and with a shield: but I come to thee in the name of the LORD of hosts, the God of the armies of Israel, whom thou hast defied."

B | Jonathan

Saul's son, Jonathan, saw David kill Goliath and became David's friend that day. Jonathan was also a brave warrior. They were kindred spirits. Our evil, unbelieving generation slanderously accuses them of having a perverse relationship, but the entire Bible opposes that argument. Wicked minds cannot comprehend genuine brotherly love. Jonathan recognized God's anointing on David and was willing to abdicate his own rights to the throne of Israel so David could fulfill God's will.

1 Samuel 18:1 - "The soul of Jonathan was knit with the soul of David, and Jonathan loved him as his own soul."

C | A Man's Gift

David was a man of war before he played the harp for King Saul. They introduced him as "cunning in playing, and a mighty valiant man, and a man of war, ...the LORD is with him." Proverbs 18:16 says, "A man's gift maketh room for him, and bringeth him before great men." David had at least two gifts; great talent and great courage.

1 Samuel 18:5 - "David went out whithersoever Saul sent him, and behaved himself wisely: and Saul set him over the men of war, and he was accepted in the sight of all the people."

D | Evil Spirits Prophesy

The word "prophesy" means "to bubble forth, to effervesce." Prophecies flow from spirits, holy and unholy. Holy prophecies come from God. Unholy prophecies come from evil spirits. Not all unholy prophecies are false. Some are true, but have evil purposes. Saul prophesied by an evil spirit, while murdering David was on his mind.

1 Samuel 18:10 - "The evil spirit from God came upon Saul, and he prophesied in the midst of the house: and David played with his hand, ...there was a javelin in Saul's hand. And Saul cast the javelin; for he said, I will smite David."

D | Saul Could Not Prevent David's Destiny

The women of Israel sang and danced in the streets after David defeated the Philistines. They said, "Saul hath slain his thousands, and David his ten thousands." This infuriated and frightened Saul. He plotted to kill David. He snared David by offering his daughter, Michal, in marriage. He required the foreskins of 100 Philistines as her dowry, thinking David would surely die in battle. But Saul could not prevent David's prophetic destiny.

1 Samuel 18:27 - "Wherefore David arose and went, he and his men, and slew of the Philistines two hundred men; and David brought their foreskins."

A | Fleeing To The Man Of God

Saul was insanely jealous of David, trying twice to murder him. David fled to the prophet Samuel in Ramah. Saul sent three companies to retrieve David, but the Spirit of God was so strong in the place that nobody could do anything but prophesy. Finally, Saul came. He rent his clothes and prophesied a day and a night. God dwells powerfully among his intercessors.

1 Samuel 19:20 - "When they saw the company of the prophets prophesying, and Samuel standing as appointed over them, the Spirit of God was upon the messengers of Saul, and they also prophesied."

C | The LORD Hath Sent Thee Away

Saul was determined to prevent David from becoming king, but Jonathan knew God was with David. He made a covenant with David in exchange for David's blessing when he became king, and then hid David outside town. Jonathan learned of his father's evil intentions during dinnertime. Shooting three arrows as a signal, Jonathan warned David to flee far away. Jonathan knew God was working. Be sensitive to God's plan in your circumstances.

1 Samuel 20:22 - "If I say thus unto the young man, Behold, the arrows are beyond thee; go thy way: for the LORD hath sent thee away."

C | Exile

Exile is a major Bible principle, if not a doctrine. Virtually every major Bible character suffered a period of exile (Abraham, Jacob, Joseph, Moses, David, the Assyrian captivity, the Babylonian captivity, and many others, including Paul). Why does God ordain His people to be exiled from home or country? Because righteousness and sin cannot dwell together. Sooner or later, they drive each other apart. Exile is a reminder of the ongoing war between good and evil. Exile is a companion to the anointing.

1 Samuel 21:10 - "And David arose, and fled that day for fear of Saul, and went to Achish the king of Gath."

A | Killed For Praying

Saul hated Ahimelech the priest, partly for praying for David. Saul commanded his footmen to kill Ahimelech, but they refused. Like jealous Cain killing righteous Abel, sin lay at Saul's door. "A certain man ...was there that day, detained before the LORD" - Doeg was at Saul's door, killing 85 priests for him. Like Judas Iscariot, God turns evil men over to their devices, and the righteous suffer.

1 Samuel 22:13 - "Saul said unto [Ahimelech], Why have ye conspired against me, ...in that thou hast given him bread, and a sword, and hast enquired of God for him?"

B | **Ahimelech**

Ahimelech was the priest at Nob. David fled to him to escape Saul's assassination attempts. Ahimelech gave David the day-old shewbread and Goliath's sword for David's protection. But Saul's servant, Doeg, betrayed David to Saul. David escaped, but Saul came and ordered Doeg to kill Ahimelech and all eighty-five priests at Nob.

1 Samuel 22:18 - "And the king said to Doeg, Turn thou, and fall upon the priests. And Doeg the Edomite turned, and he fell upon the priests, and slew on that day fourscore and five persons that did wear a linen ephod."

B | **Achish, King Of Gath**

Fleeing Doeg, David fled to Gath. The king's servants recognized him as the brave hero of Israel, about whom people sang and danced. David feared King Achish was allied with Saul, so he feigned madness, scrabbling and drooling, to disguise himself. Achish ran him out of town. But they met again later and became fast friends. Achish donated Ziklag to David for a hometown. Sometimes, crazy situations can yet turn out for the good.

1 Samuel 21:15 - "Have I need of mad men, that ye have brought this fellow to play the mad man in my presence?"

C | **"Mighty" Men – Men In Distress, Debt, And Discontented**

From Saul at Jerusalem, to Ahimelech at Nob, then to Achish at Gath, David kept running to the cave Adullam. There, his family and friends came to his defense. "Every one that was in distress, ...in debt, and ...discontented." What a motley crew! Whatever God gives you, take them. They became David's mighty men (2 Samuel 23:8).

1 Samuel 22:2 - "Every one that was in distress, and every one that was in debt, and every one that was discontented, gathered themselves unto him; and he became a captain over them: and there were with him about four hundred men."

D | **Thou Shalt Be In Safeguard**

God's anointing on David caused him a lot of trouble, but ultimately, it was his best protection. After Saul killed 85 priests for taking sides with David, only one priest, Abiathar, escaped with his life. David regretted the casualties, but assured Abiathar he would be safe with him. David understood he had a divine destiny that no enemy could change. We should have as much confidence in our place with God.

1 Samuel 22:23 - "Abide thou with me, fear not: for he that seeketh my life seeketh thy life: but with me thou shalt be in safeguard."

D | Will They? Yes, They Will.

Philistines attacked a town named Keilah. With his 400 men, David defeated them. But Saul came to Keilah to capture David. Abiathar the priest had the ephod, so David had him enquire of the LORD whether the men of Keilah would betray him to Saul. The LORD said that they would, so David took that warning, and he and his men scattered throughout the countryside. Thank God for His prophetic warnings.

1 Samuel 23:12 - "Then said David, Will the men of Keilah deliver me and my men into the hand of Saul? And the LORD said, They will deliver thee up."

A | Worthless Blessings

The prophet Samuel pronounced doom on King Saul, and anointed David to replace him. Nevertheless, Saul viciously and foolishly pursued David in defiance of God. The Ziphites informed Saul that that they could deliver David into his hands. Saul said, "Blessed be ye of the LORD." But the blessing was worthless. Instead of capturing David, Saul walked directly into David's hands. Nobody can bless you OR curse you contrary to God's righteous, sovereign will. Remember Balaam.

1 Samuel 24:10 - [David said],"Thine eyes have seen how that the LORD had delivered thee to day into mine hand in the cave."

B | The Skirt Of Saul's Robe

God literally delivered Saul into David's hands in a cave in the wilderness of Engedi. While Saul slept, David cut off the skirt of Saul's robe. But he felt guilty about it and refused to touch God's anointed in any way. After Saul awoke, David showed him what he had done and reminded him that he could have killed him, but did not. Saul wept and confessed his shame.

1 Samuel 24:20 - "Now, behold, I know well that thou shalt surely be king, and that the kingdom of Israel shall be established in thine hand."

D | Bound in the Bundle of Life

David sought food for his troops from wealthy Nabal, who responded with a vicious verbal assault. David would have killed him, but Nabal's beautiful wife, Abigail, interceded with a generous supply of food and apologies for Nabal's insolence. She prophesied that God would avenge David without his having to shed blood. God killed Nabal, and David married Abigail.

1 Samuel 25:29 "The soul of my lord shall be bound in the bundle of life with the LORD thy God; and the souls of thine enemies, them shall he sling out, as out of the middle of a sling."

C | Touch Not God's Anointed

David refused to touch God's anointed, King Saul, even though he was very evil against David. Consequently, God delivered Saul into David's hands, and Saul apologized to David. Immediately thereafter, however, David encountered Nabal, who was churlish, evil, insolent, insulting and railing against David. Amazingly, Nabal had a heart attack and died. Was God quick to avenge David because he had refused to harm Saul? Probably so. Touch not God's anointed.

1 Samuel 25:39 - "When David heard that Nabal was dead, he said, Blessed be the LORD, that hath pleaded the cause of my reproach."

A | God Save Me As I Saved You

Ziphites again revealed David's hideout. Saul pursued with 3000 men. That night, David found Saul and Abner in deep sleep from the LORD. Abishai wanted to kill Saul, but David stopped him, refusing to touch God's anointed. Instead, he took Saul's spear and cruse of water. From afar, David taunted Abner for failing to protect Saul. David honored and respected the fallen king. Godly men respect authority.

1 Samuel 26:24 - "As thy life was much set by this day in mine eyes, so let my life be much set by in the eyes of the LORD."

B | Ziklag

After David got the best of Saul in the wilderness of Ziph, Saul promised not to pursue David any more. But David did not trust him. He fled back to Achish at Gath with 600 men. They stayed there sixteen months. David said to Achish, "If I have now found grace in thine eyes, let them give me a place in some town in the country." Ziklag was David's headquarters until God took Saul out of the picture.

1 Samuel 27:6 - "Achish gave him Ziklag that day: wherefore Ziklag pertaineth unto the kings of Judah unto this day."

C | Consulting Familiar Spirits

Saul faced a terrifying conflict with the Philistines. He sought the LORD, but God would not answer. Samuel was dead. Saul sent for a woman with a familiar spirit. She brought up a spirit appearing to be Samuel. The spirit rebuked Saul, reminding him that the curse was from the LORD. The spirit said Israel would lose the battle. Saul and his sons would die that day. Saul fell out on the floor, terrified. Seeking witches or wizards is an abomination to God.

1 Samuel 28:13 - "The woman said unto Saul, I saw gods ascending out of the earth."

B | David Severs Ties With Achish

While Saul's tenure was ending, David's circumstances were changing too. While fugitive from Saul, David had survived with the help of Achish, King of Gath. But Achish was allied with Philistines who were preparing war against Israel. David was obliged to stand with Achish, but the Philistines knew who David was and wanted him to get out of there. God was stirring up David's nest, because big changes were coming for him.

1 Samuel 29:4 - "The princes of the Philistines said unto him, Make this fellow return, that he may go again to his place."

A | Pursue!

The Amalekites which Saul would not destroy came to haunt David. While David and his men prepared for war with Achish, the Amalekites raided Ziklag, capturing the women, children and livestock. When David returned home, he found Ziklag burned to the ground and everyone gone. Abiathar the priest brought the ephod, and David called on God. "Shall I pursue after this troop?" God said, "Pursue." An Egyptian led them to their captives. God can enable you to recover all your losses. Seek His instructions.

1 Samuel 30:18-19 - "David recovered all that the Amalekites had carried away: ...David recovered all."

C | Share Alike

When David recovered Ziklag, he recovered huge additional spoils from other cities of Judah and the Philistines. His men wanted it all for themselves, but David spread the wealth throughout Judah, even sharing with the soldiers who stayed home due to exhaustion from the previous war. Our efforts should be for the good of the entire kingdom of God, not just ourselves.

1 Samuel 30:24-25 - "As his part is that goeth down to the battle, so shall his part be that tarrieth by the stuff: they shall part alike. ...he made it a statute and an ordinance for Israel unto this day."

D | **Saul's Date With Destiny**

The Philistines fought hard against Israel. Many were killed. Archers hit Saul, sorely wounding him. He told his armourbearer, "Draw thy sword, and thrust me through therewith; lest these uncircumcised come and thrust me through, and abuse me. But his armourbearer would not." Saul took his sword and fell on it, but an Amalekite came along and finished him off. The Philistines cut off his head, stole his armour, and flaunted it when they got home. God rules.

1 Samuel 31:6 - "So Saul died, and his three sons, and his armourbearer, and all his men, that same day together."

Lessons from the Book of
2 SAMUEL

D | **God's Timing**

God's timing is perfect. If David had not been forced to sever ties with Achish when he did, he would have been drawn into warfare against his own king, Saul. But David was distracted into pursuing the Amalekites who raided Ziklag while the Philistines were overthrowing Saul. Your circumstances may seem convoluted, but God was in control when your circumstances developed.

2 Samuel 1:1 - "When David was returned from the slaughter of the Amalekites, ...a man came out of the camp from Saul with his clothes rent, ...and he said unto him, ...Saul and Jonathan his son are dead."

B | "I Am An Amalekite"

The messenger told David that he saw Saul fallen in anguish on his own spear. Saul had asked who he was. "I am an Amalekite." "Slay me," Saul demanded. David asked, "How wast thou not afraid to stretch forth thine hand to destroy the LORD'S anointed?" David had him killed then and there. If Saul had obeyed God years earlier, there would have been no Amalekites. Here is a painful lesson. Destroy what God says destroy, or be destroyed by it.

2 Samuel 1:8 - "And he said unto me, Who art thou? And I answered him, I am an Amalekite."

A | Prayer That Got The Kingdom

Fifteen years earlier, Samuel had anointed David to be the next king. So when Saul died in battle, "David enquired of the LORD, saying, Shall I go up into any of the cities of Judah? And the LORD said unto him, Go up. And David said, Whither shall I go up? And he said, Unto Hebron." So David went to Hebron. After suffering many years of demonic opposition, David's prophetic destiny became reality. God will always perform His word.

2 Samuel 2:4 - "The men of Judah came, and there they anointed David king over the house of Judah."

C | Family Ties

Saul's general was his cousin, Abner. David's general was his nephew, Joab. When Saul died, Abner rejected David's kingship, making Saul's 40 year-old son, Ishbosheth, king over Israel. David was king over Judah. Abner proposed a contest against Joab. Each pitched twelve soldiers against each other. But war broke out, and 360 of Abner's men died. Abner's losses were only beginning. It does not pay to resist God's anointing. God's will is more important than family ties.

2 Samuel 2:17 - "There was a very sore battle that day; and Abner was beaten."

D | Abner Defects To David

Abner knew that David was long-ordained of God. So when King Ishbosheth charged him with a fault concerning Saul's concubine, Abner was enraged and defected to David. Abner promised to turn Israel to David and make him king over all. But Joab hated Abner for killing his brother (although in self-defense), and clandestinely murdered him.

David vehemently disavowed the crime and sorely mourned his friend's death.

2 Samuel 3:17 - [Abner said], "Ye sought for David in times past to be king over you: Now then do it: for the LORD hath spoken of David."

A | David Invokes Divine Justice

Despite his untimely death, Abner played a pivotal role in turning Israel to David. Joab was in the wrong for avenging himself of Abner, and David subtly invoked divine justice upon him, saying, "the LORD shall reward the doer of evil according to his wickedness." David memorialized Abner with the highest honors, walking beside his bier, fasting and weeping. The people loved him for it. God can redeem a tragedy to strengthen His anointed.

2 Samuel 3:36 - "And all the people took notice of it, and it pleased them: as whatsoever the king did pleased all the people."

B | The Sons Of Zeruiah

David's sister, Zeruiah, had three sons: Joab, Abishai and Asahel - all warmongers. Asahel died trying to kill King Ishbosheth's captain, Abner. Abishai killed thousands in war. Joab killed Abner, Absalom (David's son), and Amasa (Absalom's captain) - all against David's wishes. Before David died, Joab defected to Adonijah. David advised Solomon to "let not his hoar head go down to the grave in peace." Solomon had him killed.

2 Samuel 3:39 - [David said,] "...the sons of Zeruiah be too hard for me: the LORD shall reward the doer of evil according to his wickedness."

B | The Death Of Ishbosheth

With Abner, his general, dead, King Ishbosheth trembled at his fate. Unexpectedly, two of his own captains, Baanah and Rechab took it upon themselves to assassinate him so the kingdom would fall to David. Entering his home on false pretenses, they murdered him in his bed. They brought his head to David, thinking he would be proud of them. But David was outraged!

2 Samuel 4:12 - "David commanded his young men, and they slew them, ...and hanged them up over the pool in Hebron. But they took the head of Ishbosheth, and buried it in the sepulchre of Abner."

D | The Anointed One Becomes King

With Ishbosheth dead, everything was clear for David to become Israel's king. Suddenly, every tribe rallied to David, saying, "We are your bone and flesh," and "Even when Saul was king, you were the one that led us." God pre-ordains men for particular times and places. Likewise, Jesus will soon be crowned King of Kings in Jerusalem.

2 Samuel 5:2 - "The LORD said to thee, Thou shalt feed my people Israel, and thou shalt be a captain over Israel. So all the elders of Israel came to the king to Hebron; ...and they anointed David king over Israel."

C | Forty Years

Isaac was forty when he married Rebekah. Moses was exiled at forty, for forty years, then led the children of Israel through the wilderness for forty years. Joshua was forty when he spied out Canaan. Othniel, Deborah, Barak, Gideon, and Eli each judged in Israel forty years. Saul, David and Solomon each ruled forty years.

2 Samuel 5:4 - "David was thirty years old when he began to reign, and he reigned forty years. In Hebron he reigned over Judah seven years and six months: and in Jerusalem he reigned thirty and three years over all Israel and Judah."

B | David Takes Jerusalem

Jebusites inhabited Jerusalem, so David and his army took Mount Zion, renamed "the City of David." He promised to promote the man who climbed up the water course, penetrated the walls, and smote the Jebusites. Thus Joab became General (I Chronicles 27:34). David moved into the fort and "grew great, and the LORD God of hosts was with him." Hiram of Tyre sent cedar, carpenters and masons, and built David a house.

2 Samuel 5:12 - "David perceived that the LORD had established him king over Israel, and that he had exalted his kingdom for his people Israel's sake."

A | Sound In The Mulberry Trees

As soon as the Philistines heard that David was King of Israel, they declared war. In a crisis, David always prayed to God for instructions. The LORD said to go after them. David attacked the Philistines. They fled, leaving their idols behind. David burned them. The Philistines regrouped. David prayed again. The LORD told him what to do. David obeyed and smote them soundly.

2 Samuel 5:24 - "When thou hearest the sound of a going in the tops of the mulberry trees, ...bestir thyself: for then shall the LORD go out before thee, to smite the host of the Philistines."

C | Celebrate God's Presence

David brought the Ark of the Covenant from Kirjath-jearim on a new cart. Uzzah handled the tottering Ark, and God angrily killed him. David stored it at Obededom's for three months, then finished the trip. David made sacrifices and danced before the LORD with all his might. Tens of thousands celebrated and played instruments. Moses' Tabernacle had everything else, but no glory. David's Tabernacle had nothing but glory.

2 Samuel 6:17 - "They brought in the ark of the LORD, and set it in his place, in the midst of the tabernacle that David had pitched for it."

D | Cursed For Criticizing

Bringing the Ark to Jerusalem was an epic event. God's glory was finally in the city of David. David demonstrated wildly, dancing in the streets while multitudes celebrated. His wife Michal despised his worship and harshly rebuked him. But God loved it, and David persisted, "It was before the LORD, which chose me ...ruler over the people, ...therefore will I play before the LORD. And I will yet be more vile than thus, and will be base in mine own sight."

2 Samuel 6:23 - "Therefore Michal the daughter of Saul had no child unto the day of her death."

B | David Forbidden To Build A Temple

David wanted to build a house for God, but God forbid him. Instead, God said He would build a house for David. God must build OUR house before we build anything for Him. "Your son will build a house for me." The Father gives His glory to His sons, then they glorify Him. See "**The Spirit of the Father**."[5]

2 Samuel 7:12-13 - "I will set up thy seed after thee, ...and I will establish his kingdom. He shall build an house for my name, and I will stablish the throne of his kingdom for ever."

C | God's People

King David recognized that Israel was a divinely chosen nation. God could easily have spoken to all men everywhere simultaneously when He called Abraham to follow Him. But He didn't. Why didn't He? Abraham found grace in God's eyes like Noah had. God may only select one in a million. He just wants a right heart. Is yours right?

2 Samuel 7:23 - "...what one nation in the earth is like thy people, even like Israel, whom God went to redeem for a people to himself, and to make him a name?"

A | David Worships

God pronounced unprecedented blessings on David. "I will set up thy seed after thee, ...I will establish the throne of his kingdom for ever. ...I will be his father, and he shall be my son. ...the house and thy kingdom shall be established for ever, ...thy throne shall be established for ever." God's promises overwhelmed David. He went in and sat before the LORD, and worshipped.

2 Samuel 7:26 - "Let thy name be magnified for ever, saying, The LORD of hosts is the God over Israel: and let the house of thy servant David be established before thee."

C | Dedicate The Spoils To The LORD

David subdued the nations around Israel - the Philistines, the Moabites, the Syrians, and others. He put garrisons in their cities and collected tribute from them. He collected great spoils of chariots, horses, shields of gold, and of brass, and vessels of gold, silver, and brass. Moses taught that kings of Israel must not take the spoils for themselves, but give them to the LORD (Deuteronomy 7:25; 17:17). Dedicate your victories to the LORD.

2 Samuel 8:11 - "King David did dedicate unto the LORD, ...the silver and gold that he had dedicated of all nations which he subdued."

D | David Becomes A Great King

From the early days, when David was a servant to Saul, David "behaved himself wisely, ...and he was accepted in the sight of all the people." But as the new king of Israel, the anointing was even more evident. David got a name for his greatness. Among other things, he organized the government (Saul never did) and created a powerful cabinet (i.e., Joab -

185

General; Jehoshaphat - Recorder; Zadok and Ahimelech - Priests; Seraiah - Scribe; Benaiah - Overseer; and David's sons - Chief Rulers).

2 Samuel 8:15 - "David reigned over all Israel; and David executed judgment and justice unto all his people."

B | Mephibosheth

David asked Saul's servant, Ziba, if any of Saul's family were still alive. He discovered that the day Jonathan died, a nursemaid fled with his 5-year-old son. She fell down, crippling him for life. Mephibosheth required constant care. David had him brought to Jerusalem and adopted him. David's compassion should inspire us to be compassionate toward the underprivileged.

2 Samuel 9:7 - "I will surely shew thee kindness for Jonathan thy father's sake, and will restore thee all the land of Saul thy father; and thou shalt eat bread at my table continually."

C | Distrust And Suspicion

Nahash the Ammonite king showed some unknown kindness to David. When he died, David showed kindness to his son, Hanun, by sending his servants with condolences. But the Ammonite princes distrusted David and suspected the men were spying to overthrow them. They shaved off their beards, cut off their skirts, sent them shamefully away. They hired mercenaries and declared war on Israel. David sent Joab with an army, who whipped them soundly. Distrust and suspicion cause unnecessary wars.

2 Samuel 10:19 - "When all the kings ...saw that they were smitten before Israel, they made peace with Israel, and served them."

A | Joab's Prayer

The Ammonites hired tens of thousands of Syrians to war with them against Israel. David sent Joab with his mighty men. But they faced Syrians in front and behind. Taking half his army one way, and sending the other half with his brother, Abishai, Joab said, "Be of good courage, and let us play the men for our people, and for the cities of our God: and the LORD do that which seemeth him good." The Syrians lost 40,000 men and 700 chariots.

2 Samuel 10:19 - "So the Syrians feared to help the children of Ammon any more."

B | Bathsheba And Uriah

Bathsheba and Uriah were victims of David's lust. Uriah was at war. His wife had to obey the king. When she discovered she was pregnant, David called Uriah home, so the child would seem to be his. But Uriah refused to sleep with his wife while his brethren were at war. David sent Uriah to the battle front to be killed.

2 Samuel 11:27 - "And when the mourning was past, David sent and fetched her to his house, and she became his wife, and bare him a son. But the thing that David had done displeased the LORD."

C | Thou Art The Man

At first, nobody knew Bathsheba was pregnant or that Uriah was killed on purpose. But God always knows. Nathan came with a story about a man who owned great flocks, but stole a poor man's only lamb to feed his guests. "The man that hath done this thing shall surely die!" David exclaimed.

2 Samuel 12:7 - "Nathan said to David, Thou art the man. Thus saith the LORD, ...I gave thee thy master's house, and thy master's wives into thy bosom, ...thou hast killed Uriah the Hittite, ...and hast taken his wife to be thy wife."

D | David's Sin And Curse

While his armies were off to war, David saw Bathsheba washing herself and ordered his servants to fetch her. He committed adultery with her, then conspired to have her husband killed on the front lines. But Nathan prophesied sorrowful tragedies to come. Beware the awful anguish and high price of sin.

2 Samuel 12:10-12 - "The sword shall never depart from thine house; because thou hast despised me, and hast taken the wife of Uriah the Hittite to be thy wife. Thus saith the LORD, Behold, I will raise up evil against thee out of thine own house."

A | David's Repentance

David's sin with Bathsheba was devastating, and Nathan prophesied grievous punishment. Psalm 51 records David's repentance.

Psalms 51:1 - " Have mercy upon me, O God, according to thy lovingkindness: according unto the multitude of thy tender mercies blot out my transgressions. Wash me throughly from mine iniquity, and cleanse me from my sin. For I acknowledge my transgressions: and my sin is ever before me. Against thee, thee only, have I sinned, and done this evil in thy sight..."

D | The High Cost of Low Living

David had enormous favor with God and men. But when lust took over, his flawless reputation was forever stained. The price of adultery and murder cost him throughout his lifetime. One son betrayed him and tried to overthrow his kingdom. Another raped his daughter and was murdered by a brother. Trouble came in waves, beginning with Nathan's pronouncements. Count the high cost before you engage in sinful behavior.

2 Samuel 12:14 - "Because by this deed thou hast given great occasion to the enemies of the LORD to blaspheme, the child also that is born unto thee shall surely die."

A | David Fasts For The Baby

Nathan prophesied that the baby of David's adultery would die. David fasted and prayed seven days. Still the child died. David washed, dressed, went to the house of God and worshipped. Then he ate. Everyone expected him to mourn, but David wisely accepted both God's mercy and His justice.

2 Samuel 12:22-23 - "I fasted and wept: for I said, Who can tell whether GOD will be gracious to me, that the child may live? But now he is dead, wherefore should I fast? ...I shall go to him, but he shall not return to me."

B | The Birth Of Solomon

David suffered immeasurable consequences for his sins. But he earnestly repented with prayer and fasting, and fully restored his relationship with God. God still loved him and gave David and Bathsheba another child, named Solomon - "peaceful," or Jedidiah - "beloved of the LORD."

2 Samuel 12:24-25 - "David comforted Bathsheba his wife, and went in unto her, and lay with her: and she bare a son, and he called his name Solomon: and the LORD loved him. And he sent by the hand of Nathan the prophet; and he called his name Jedidiah, because of the LORD."

C | The Show Must Go On

Although David nearly destroyed himself with Bathsheba and Uriah, life forced him to move forward. He was still King of Israel. Joab sent news that he was close to taking the royal city of their vicious enemies, the Ammonites. David quickly organized an army and attacked Rabbah, slaughtering its people, and returning victoriously to Jerusalem. Despite your failures, there are victories ahead.

2 Samuel 12:30 - "He took their king's crown from off his head, ...gold with the precious stones: and it was set on David's head. And he brought forth the spoil of the city in great abundance."

D | The Sword Strikes David's House

Nathan prophesied that because of David's sins, the sword would never depart from his house. The first occurrence came whenever his son, Amnon, raped and humiliated his daughter Tamar. Tamar's brother, Absalom, rabidly hated Amnon in silence for two years. Then Absalom invited Amnon to a sheep-shearing with all the king's sons. He instructed his servants to kill Amnon, which they did. Absalom then fled from David for three years.

2 Samuel 13:36 - "The king's sons came, and lifted up their voice and wept: and the king also and all his servants wept very sore."

B | Absalom

Joab knew that David longed to see Absalom. Three years had passed since Amnon died. Joab sent a widow to David, begging mercy for a son who killed his brother. Everyone wanted vengeance. David promised to protect him. She accused David of banishing his own son. David guiltily called Absalom to Jerusalem, but resisted seeing him two more years. Absalom failed twice to get Joab to intercede, finally setting Joab's barley fields on fire, provoking him to reunite them.

2 Samuel 14:33 - Absalom "bowed himself on his face to the ground before the king: and the king kissed Absalom."

A | Deceitful Prayer

Absalom told David that during his exile, he vowed to the LORD that if he ever returned to Jerusalem, "then I will serve the LORD." He immediately asked permission to "pay my vow, which I have vowed unto the LORD, in Hebron." Several Bible commentators suspect that Absalom lied (never made that vow). He was conspiring to win the hearts of the people.

Hebron was a likely place to be crowned king. Some people boast of their praying to legitimize evil schemes.

2 Samuel 15:9 - "The king said unto him, Go in peace. So he arose, and went to Hebron."

C | Conspiracy

Absalom immediately capitalized on David's acknowledgment. He worked the streets feverishly to win friends and influence people. His entourage included fifty men with chariots and horses. He unabashedly wanted to steal the hearts of the men of Israel. He wanted to be king. Evil men MUST conspire to get things they are not supposed to have.

2 Samuel 15:10-12 - "Absalom sent spies throughout all the tribes of Israel, saying, As soon as ye hear the sound of the trumpet, then ye shall say, Absalom reigneth in Hebron. ...the conspiracy was strong; for the people increased continually with Absalom."

D | Evil Out of Thine Own House

David's old sins called for another payday. Nathan's prophecy said, "I will raise up evil against thee out of thine own house." A messenger brought the news. "The hearts of the men of Israel are after Absalom." David told all his servants at Jerusalem to flee, "for we shall not else escape from Absalom." Sin costs so dearly.

2 Samuel 15:23 - "And all the country wept with a loud voice, and all the people passed over: the king also himself passed over the brook Kidron, and all the people passed over, toward the way of the wilderness."

A | Give Your Enemies To God

Absalom conspired hard to overthrow David's government. David fled Jerusalem for safety's sake. Zadok and Abiathar the priests, and the Levites brought the Ark of the Covenant, but David sent them back to monitor the situation and report to him. He learned that Ahithophel, Bathsheba's grandfather and David's counselor, had defected to Absalom. David asked God to turn Ahithophel's counsel to foolishness. God did. Ahithophel was discredited and hanged himself. Give your enemies to God.

2 Samuel 15:31 - "David said, O LORD, I pray thee, turn the counsel of Ahithophel into foolishness."

C | Concurrent Opposition And Support

It looked like David's kingdom was imploding. He and hundreds fled to the wilderness while Absalom and thousands invaded Jerusalem. Two encounters illustrate the good and the bad of anointed living. First, Ziba (Mephibosheth's servant) blessed David with donkeys to ride and food for a multitude. Second, Shimei (kinsman of Saul) cursed and threw stones at David. As you live for God, some will bless you, and others will curse you.

2 Samuel 16:12 - "It may be that the LORD will look on mine affliction, and that the LORD will requite me good for his cursing this day."

B | Absalom Takes His Father's Concubines

When David sinned, the LORD spoke through Nathan, "I will take thy wives before thine eyes, and give them unto thy neighbour, and he shall lie with thy wives in the sight of this sun." Ahithophel probably did not realize that he was fulfilling prophecy when he counseled Absalom. God's awesome power to perform His word is indeed fearful.

2 Samuel 16:21-22 - "Go in unto thy father's concubines, ...So they spread Absalom a tent upon the top of the house; and Absalom went in unto his father's concubines in the sight of all Israel."

D | Hushai Mortifies Ahithophel

David fled with hundreds from Jerusalem as Absalom and Ahithophel betrayed him. But Hushai, David's friend, "defected" to spy on Absalom. Hushai outwitted Ahithophel, who would have killed David, turning his counsel into foolishness (just as David had prayed for). Ahithophel was so mortified, he hung himself. God orchestrates His enemies' defeat.

2 Samuel 17:14 - "Absalom and all the men of Israel said, The counsel of Hushai the Archite is better than the counsel of Ahithophel. For the LORD had appointed to defeat the good counsel of Ahithophel, to the intent that the LORD might bring evil upon Absalom."

B | David's Informants

Hushai secretly relayed Absalom's war plans to priests Zadok and Abiathar. They sent the messages by a local girl to their sons, Jonathan and Ahimaaz at Enrogel. Someone told Absalom, who tried to intercept them, but Bahurim hid them in a well in his courtyard. Word finally reached David to prepare for war. David moved quickly beyond Jordan to buy some extra time.

2 Samuel 17:22 - "Then David arose, and all the people that were with him, and they passed over Jordan: by the morning light there lacked not one of them that was not gone over Jordan."

A | Evil Counsel Defeated By Prayer

Ahithophel's defection to Absalom was an enormous threat to David, because Ahithophel knew everything about David, and was likely to use it against him. But David prayed that God would turn all his counsel to foolishness, and God did. You can always ask God to undermine the enemy's efforts against you. He is able.

2 Samuel 17:23 - "And when Ahithophel saw that his counsel was not followed, he saddled his ass, and arose, and gat him home to his house, to his city, and put his household in order, and hanged himself, and died, and was buried."

C | God's Ground Support Coalition

In God's economy, there are times for peace and times for war. It was time for David to face Absalom in war. Suddenly, ground support came from a coalition of outside nations. Shobi of Rabbah, Machir of Lodebar, and Barzillai of Rogelim presented David with beds, basons, vessels, wheat, barley, flour, corn, beans, lentiles, honey, butter, sheep, cheese, and more. Then David organized for war. If God sends you to battle, He will supply.

2 Samuel 18:1 - "And David numbered the people that were with him, and set captains of thousands and captains of hundreds over them."

D | Absalom's Forces Whipped

David organized three companies of soldiers under Joab, Abishai, and Ittai. The people forbade David to go with them. "Thou art worth ten thousand of us." David asked them to "Deal gently with Absalom." But Absalom intended to overthrow David's house, and God had sworn to bless it. Absalom had to go.

2 Samuel 18:6-7 - "So the people went out into the field against Israel: and the battle was in the wood of Ephraim; Where the people of Israel were slain before the servants of David, and there was there a great slaughter that day of twenty thousand men."

A | Blessing God For Avenging

David tried to defend him, but Absalom's warmongering provoked God. Riding under an oak tree, Absalom caught his head. Joab arrived and killed him there. The war was suddenly over; the coup was thwarted.

2 Samuel 18:19,28 - "Then said Ahimaaz the son of Zadok, Let me now run, and bear the king tidings, how that the LORD hath avenged him of his enemies. ...he fell down to the earth upon his face before the king, and said, Blessed be the LORD thy God, which hath delivered up the men that lifted up their hand against my lord the king."

C | Suffering Losses To Win

From the day he murdered his brother, Absalom was estranged from his father. David loved him, but never trusted him. Absalom betrayed him cruelly and had to be destroyed to preserve God's anointed king. Sometimes, we suffer incomprehensible pain when those we love oppose the will of God.

2 Samuel 19:4-5 - "The king cried with a loud voice, O my son Absalom, O Absalom, my son, my son! And Joab came into the house to the king, and said, Thou hast shamed this day the faces of all thy servants, which this day have saved thy life."

D | Remembering Divine Destiny

Joab constrained David to get a grip on his grief concerning Absalom's death and show the people that he appreciated their heroic efforts to save the kingdom. After we have fought our worst battles and taken our most painful losses, we must nevertheless return to perform the purpose of God that was irrevocably ordained for us.

2 Samuel 19:8, 11 - "The king arose, and sat in the gate. ...And king David sent to Zadok and to Abiathar the priests, saying, Speak unto the elders of Judah, saying, Why are ye the last to bring the king back to his house?"

A | A Model For Repentance

Shimei cursed fleeing David, throwing stones and dust at him. But when David returned, Shimei rushed to repent, a thousand Benjamites with him. Shimei fell before the king, begging,

2 Samuel 19:19-20 - "Let not my lord impute iniquity unto me, neither do thou remember that which thy servant did perversely the day that my lord

the king went out of Jerusalem, ...For thy servant doth know that I have sinned: therefore, ...I am come the first this day of all the house of Joseph to go down to meet my lord the king. ...[David said], Thou shalt not die."

B | Mephibosheth Welcomes David Home

Although Absalom was defeated, David wanted to know that Israel wanted him back in Jerusalem. Thousands came to meet him at Gilgal, where Joshua brought Israel from wandering, and God rolled away their reproach. Mephibosheth, though lame, came explaining that Ziba betrayed him and left him behind. Joyfully, he exclaimed, "My lord the king is as an angel of God." When God finishes your exile, He arranges a glorious reunion.

2 Samuel 19:15 - "So the king returned, and came to Jordan. And Judah came to Gilgal, to go to meet the king, to conduct the king over Jordan."

C | Spill-Over Blessings

At 80, Barzillai furnished food and supplies for David's defenders against Absalom. After David won, Barzillai came to escort him back home. David asked Barzillai to move into the palace with him, so he could care for him in his old age, but he respectfully declined, preferring to die in his own home. Barzillai offered his servant, Chimham, to David, who received him kindly. Great men leave spill-over blessings to their descendants.

2 Samuel 19:38 - "The king answered, Chimham shall go over with me, and I will do to him that which shall seem good unto thee."

D | Sin's Recurring Effects

Nathan's old prophecy promised that the sword would never depart David's house. Joab was David's nephew and captain. But after Joab killed Absalom, David promised to give Joab's room to Amasa, Absalom's former captain, and David's second cousin. But Joab was jealous and would not surrender his title to Amasa, so he chased him down and killed him - sin's recurring effects.

2 Samuel 20:10 - "Amasa took no heed to the sword that was in Joab's hand: so he smote him therewith in the fifth rib, ...and he died."

B | Sheba Attempts Another Coup

Sheba, a man of Belial (a devil), condemned and disowned David, trying again to overthrow him after Absalom died. David said that Sheba would "do us more harm than did Absalom." He sent his new captain, Amasa, in pursuit. Joab followed, too, but killed Amasa first, then pursued Sheba. Joab besieged the town called Abel, and a woman inside negotiated to throw Sheba's head over the wall to prevent their destruction.

2 Samuel 20:22 - "They cut off the head of Sheba the son of Bichri, and cast it out to Joab. ...Joab returned to Jerusalem unto the king."

A | Paying For Breach of Contract

A three-year famine came to Israel in David's time, so he enquired of the LORD. God told him that it was because Saul had slain many Gibeonites. (Moses taught Israel to make no leagues with their enemies, but Joshua had made a league of peace with the Gibeonites, "and the princes of the congregation sware unto them.") David had to make atonement with the Gibeonites. They wanted blood.

2 Samuel 21:6 - "Let seven men of his [Saul's] sons be delivered unto us, and we will hang them up unto the LORD, ...And the king said, I will give them."

C | Divine Payback

When David first became a hero in Israel, Saul promised him his oldest daughter, Merab. But Saul reneged and gave her to Adriel. They had five children. Saul gave David his daughter Michal, who cursed David, and consequently, never bore any children. Michal raised the five children of Merab and Adriel. But God made David atone with the Gibeonites for Saul's sins. They demanded seven of Saul's sons be hanged - two by his concubine, and guess "who else"?

2 Samuel 21:8 - "...the five sons of Michal the daughter of Saul, whom she brought up for Adriel."

D | The Giant-Slayer Retires

Moses prophesied, "The LORD your God he shall fight for you." As David grew old, he "waxed faint" in battle with the Philistines. His men took over. Abishai smote Ishbibenob, a massive giant intent on killing David. Sibbechai slew Saph, another giant. Elhanan and Jaareoregin slew Goliath's brother. Finally, David's nephew, Jonathan, slew a fourth giant from Gath. When your strength fails, God will take care of you.

2 Samuel 21:17 - "The men of David sware unto him, saying, Thou shalt go no more out with us to battle, that thou quench not the light of Israel."

A | The Song Of David

Our first introduction to David's songs and poetry is in 2 Samuel 22. (The same song is published in Psalm 18.) David follows the examples of Moses, Miriam, Hannah, Deborah and others, each of whom created poetry and sang their praises unto the LORD for His goodness and His wonderful works. Every person should create his own song unto the LORD.

2 Samuel 22:1 - "David spake unto the LORD the words of this song in the day that the LORD had delivered him out of the hand of all his enemies, and out of the hand of Saul."

B | David's Mighty Men

David's mighty men were "in distress, ...in debt, and ...discontented," 1 Samuel 22:2. Adino slew 800 men at once. Eleazar slew so many Philistines "his hand clave unto the sword." Shammah defended a crop in a field from an entire army. Three men penetrated enemy lines to fetch a drink of water for David. Abishai slew 300 with a spear. Benaiah slew a lion in a pit in a snowstorm, then killed a fierce Egyptian with his own spear. Thirty brave heroes in all.

2 Samuel 23:8 - "These be the names of the mighty men whom David had."

C | When God Commissions Satan

God and Satan moved David to number Israel. 1 Chronicles 21:1 says, "Satan stood up against Israel, and provoked David to number Israel." A similar thing happened at the Crucifixion. Satan entered Judas Iscariot to betray Christ. Jesus said to him, "That thou doest, do quickly." Satan was God's puppet executing divine purpose. God commissioned Satan to test Job. Job, Christ and David ultimately overcame Satan. Regardless of Satan's mission, he is always under God's limitations.

2 Samuel 24:1 - "The anger of the LORD was kindled against Israel, and he moved David against them."

D | A Choice Of Judgments

God always met David's needs, regardless of his numbers. Numbering Israel meant proudly trusting in his armies - the arm of the flesh. The prophet Gad brought the word of the LORD. David must choose a judgment: famine, war, or pestilence. "Let me not fall into the hand of man." David ruled out war. Let God choose between famine or pestilence. "Let us fall now into the hand of the LORD; for his mercies are great." Always trust God.

2 Samuel 24:15 - "So the LORD sent a pestilence upon Israel, ...and there died of the people ...seventy thousand men."

A | Repentance Stops The Angel Of Death

God was angry when David spent over nine months numbering his valiant men, exposing his pride, self-trust, and confidence in man. The angel of the LORD destroyed 70,000 men before meeting David at the threshingplace of Araunah the Jebusite in Jerusalem. David pleaded, "I have sinned greatly in that I have done: ...O LORD, take away the iniquity of thy servant; for I have done very foolishly."

2 Samuel 24:16 - "...the LORD repented him of the evil, and said to the angel that destroyed the people, It is enough: stay now thine hand."

B | Moriah - The Temple Mount

God sent Abraham with Isaac to build an altar on a mountain in Moriah. Centuries later, the angel of God met David right there. The prophet Gad instructed David to build an altar there. David purchased the land from Araunah (Ornan the Jebusite). With the purchase, David received oxen to sacrifice unto the LORD. Years later, Solomon built the great Temple, with the Holy of Holies on that site. GOD chose the Temple Mount.

2 Samuel 24:24-25 - "So David bought the threshingfloor and ...built there an altar unto the LORD, and offered burnt offerings and peace offerings."

A | The LORD Was Intreated

Among David's last words was this statement: "He that ruleth over men must be just, ruling in the fear of God. And he shall be as the light of the morning, ...even a morning without clouds." David was brilliantly aware that leaders must be a shining light to the people. When did you last see your King or President intreating God at an altar?

2 Samuel 24:25 - "David built there an altar unto the LORD, and offered burnt offerings and peace offerings. So the LORD was intreated for the land, and the plague was stayed from Israel."

Lessons from the Book of
1 KINGS

C | Usurpers

In David's old age, Absalom's brother, Adonijah, repeated his brother's folly in attempting to take the throne from his father. Joab and Abiathar the priest abdicated with Adonijah, but Zadok the priest and Nathan the prophet remained with David, knowing that Solomon was his sworn heir. Nathan urged Bathsheba to persuade the king to quickly install Solomon. If you want to inherit God's promises, prepare now to contend with usurpers - throne-stealers.

1 Kings 1:29 - "The king sware, and said, As the LORD liveth, ...Solomon ...shall reign after me, and he shall sit upon my throne in my stead."

D | Solomon's Divine Destiny

The prophet called Solomon, "Jedidiah," "beloved of Jehovah." David knew that God chose Solomon to reign and build the Temple. "He hath chosen Solomon my son to sit upon the throne of the kingdom of the LORD over Israel," 1 Chronicles 28:5. Adonijah could not succeed. All thrones belong to God.

1 Kings 1:38-39 - "Zadok the priest, and Nathan ...caused Solomon to ride upon king David's mule, ...the priest took an horn of oil out of the tabernacle, and anointed Solomon. And they blew the trumpet; and all the people said, God save king Solomon."

B | David Charges Solomon

Here are two of the most revered men in all human history - David and Solomon. The old king is passing the torch to his son. "I go the way of all the earth: be thou strong therefore, and shew thyself a man; And keep the charge of the LORD thy God, to walk in his ways, to keep his statutes, and his commandments, and his judgments, and his testimonies, ...that thou mayest prosper in all that thou doest." Every man needs to hear words like that from his father.

1 Kings 2:10 - "So David slept with his fathers, and was buried in the city of David."

C | House-Cleaning Time

King David felt Solomon should dispose of some old problems. David remembered how Joab killed Abner and Amasa in cold blood. "Let not his hoar head go down to the grave in peace." Solomon sent Benaiah to execute Joab. David also reminded Solomon of Shimei's cursing the king. "Hold him not guiltless." Solomon promised Shimei that if he ever left Jerusalem, he would die. He did, so Solomon ordered him slain. Sooner or later, righteousness demands a house-cleaning.

1 Kings 2:12 - "Then sat Solomon upon the throne of David his father; and his kingdom was established greatly."

D | Asking For Trouble

Adonijah should have recognized how fortunate he was to be alive after attempting to steal his father's [and his brother's] throne. But he did not. He foolishly asked Bathsheba to petition Solomon to give him David's concubine, Abishag. That was the last straw. Solomon sent Benaiah to execute him. Not reverencing Solomon's prophetic destiny was a fatal mistake.

1 Kings 2:15 - "Thou knowest that the kingdom was mine, and that all Israel set their faces on me, that I should reign: howbeit the kingdom is turned about, and is become my brother's: for it was his from the LORD."

D | Abiathar Was Deposed Prophetically

Abiathar the priest had loyally supported David ever since giving him holy shewbread decades earlier. But Abiathar foolishly joined Adonijah, who tried to overthrow David. A long-forgotten prophecy made by Samuel was fulfilled when Solomon banished Abiathar.

1 Kings 2:26-27 - "...thou art worthy of death: but I will not at this time put thee to death, because thou barest the ark of the Lord GOD before David my father, ...so Solomon thrust out Abiathar from being priest unto the LORD; that he might fulfil the word of the LORD, which he spake concerning the house of Eli in Shiloh."

A | Solomon Prays In A Dream

"Solomon loved the LORD," and offered a thousand burnt offerings to the LORD in the high place at Gibeon. At night, the LORD appeared in a dream to Solomon, saying, "Ask what I shall give thee," to which Solomon answered, "Give therefore thy servant an understanding heart to judge thy people, that I may discern between good and bad: for who is able to judge this thy so great a people?" God responded generously. Some dreams come from God and have authentic prophetic meanings.

1 Kings 3:10 - "And the speech pleased the Lord, that Solomon had asked this thing."

B | God Gives Wisdom To Solomon

In a dream, God asked Solomon what he desired. Solomon asked for wisdom to judge the people. God noticed that Solomon did not ask for long life, riches for himself, nor for the life of his enemies. God delights in granting your petitions that are according to His good pleasure.

1 Kings 3:12-14 - "Behold, ...I have given thee a wise and an understanding heart; so that there was none like thee before thee, neither after thee shall any arise like unto thee. And I have also given thee that which thou hast not asked, both riches, and honour."

C | Dreams and Visions

God spoke to many Bible characters in dreams and visions: Abraham, Abimelech, Jacob, Laban, Joseph, Pharaoh's Butler and Baker, Pharaoh, Gideon's enemies, Samuel, Nathan, Isaiah, Ezekiel, Obadiah, Nahum, Nebuchadnezzar, Daniel, Zacharias, Joseph of Nazareth, Pontius Pilate's wife, Peter, Ananias, Paul, John and many others. "I am against them that prophesy false dreams, saith the LORD," Jeremiah 23:32. "Your old men shall dream dreams, your young men shall see visions," Joel 2:28. A dream from God can be life-changing. Take it seriously.

1 Kings 3:15 - "Solomon awoke; and, behold, it was a dream."

D | Solomon's Wisdom Fulfilled

Two harlots approached Solomon. One's baby died overnight "because she overlaid it," but she secretly swapped it with the other's living baby. They argued about whose baby it was. Solomon called for a sword and commanded that the child be cut in two - half for each mother. One begged him not to. The other was smugly pleased. Solomon gave it to the first, knowing she was the true mother.

1 Kings 3:28 - "All Israel heard of the judgment which the king had judged; and ...they saw that the wisdom of God was in him, to do judgment."

B | Solomon's Administration

Solomon's princes included Azariah, son of Zadok, prime minister; Elihoreph and Ahiah, scribes; Jehoshaphat, recorder; Benaiah, captain; Zadok and Abiathar, priests; Zabud, son of Nathan, principal officer and close friend; Ahishar, household governor; Adoniram, tax collector. Twelve food-service officers (one per month) prepared the king's tables and provided food for his horses and camels. Solomon wisely kept most of his father's key men (or their sons), which greatly strengthened his hand and reputation.

1 Kings 4:1-2 - "So king Solomon was king over all Israel. And these were the princes which he had."

C | An Established House

God stopped David from building the Temple because He wanted David to have a well-established house first. David's kingdom became very strong. Absalom and Adonijah would have destroyed David's kingdom and started from scratch, but Solomon built on his father's strong foundation with his father's good blessings. That made all the difference. Sometimes, change is needed, but not always. Sometimes, the status quo is better.

1 Kings 4:25 - "Judah and Israel dwelt safely, every man under his vine and under his fig tree, from Dan even to Beersheba, all the days of Solomon."

A | Solomon's Proverbs And Songs

Solomon continued in the tradition of David his father, writing proverbs and songs which glorified God. In all, he spoke three thousand proverbs and one thousand and five songs, each a proof of the gift of God upon his life. His wisdom exceeded that of all the other kings and wise men of his day, and his fame spread far and wide. Kings and queens all over the earth heard of Solomon's legendary wisdom, and many came to see and hear him.

1 Kings 4:29 - "And God gave Solomon wisdom and understanding exceeding much, and largeness of heart."

D | Solomon's Temple

King David wanted to build a glorious Temple, a permanent structure to replace the tent-like Tabernacle. God refused to give David permission, because he had been such a bloody man of war, but He prophesied to

David that his son would build the Temple. Solomon fulfilled that prophecy.

1 Kings 5:5 - "And, behold, I purpose to build an house unto the name of the LORD my God, as the LORD spake unto David my father, saying, Thy son, whom I will set upon thy throne in thy room, he shall build an house unto my name."

A | Hiram Blesses The LORD

Hiram, King of Tyre, was a friend to David. He furnished most of the material for David's palace. When Solomon became king, he notified Hiram that he intended to build a great Temple. Hiram was delighted and committed to trade Lebanese cedar and fir timbers for Israeli wheat and oil. Hiram also provided much gold for the Temple. God often sends blessings by outsiders when necessary.

1 Kings 5:7 - "When Hiram heard the words of Solomon, ...he rejoiced greatly, and said, Blessed be the LORD this day, which hath given unto David a wise son over this great people."

B | Solomon Begins Temple Construction

Solomon drafted thirty-thousand men to prepare building materials in Lebanon. Ten thousand at a time spent thirty days there, followed by two months vacation. Seventy thousand bore burdens. Eighty thousand hewed great, costly stones from mountains for the foundation of the house. 3,300 foremen directed almost 200,000 men working on the Temple. Within seven years it was the most magnificent structure in the world, built to the glory of God.

1 Kings 5:18 - "Solomon's builders and Hiram's builders did hew them, and the stonesquarers: so they prepared timber and stones to build the house."

D | No Noise

No hammer, axe, or iron tool was to be heard during construction of the Temple. All noisy work was finished off-site, to keep the Temple holy unto the LORD. This speaks, typologically, of the Church of Jesus Christ - made on earth of "lively stones," for the glorious moment when all saints will assemble "finished" in Heaven.

1 Kings 6:7 - "The house, when it was in building, was built of stone made ready before it was brought thither: so that there was neither

hammer nor axe nor any tool of iron heard in the house, while it was in building."

B | Solomon's Kingdom Comes of Age

The tribes of Israel grew "as the sand of the sea in multitude." Israel's borders expanded from Egypt to the surrounding rivers of the Middle East. Solomon's kingdom was rich in food-stuffs, cattle, oxen, sheep, harts, roebucks and fallowdeer. His stalls were filled with forty thousand horses, tended by twelve thousand horsemen. The king's palace was thirteen years in the building. But the Temple complex was the focal point.

1 Kings 6:2 - "The inside of the LORD's temple was ninety feet long, thirty feet wide, and forty-five feet high," (Contemporary English Version).

C | I Will Dwell Among Them

The Word of the LORD came to Solomon saying, "Concerning this house which thou art in building, if thou wilt walk in my statutes, and execute my judgments, and keep all my commandments to walk in them; then will I perform my word with thee, which I spake unto David thy father." God magnificently promised to dwell in the new Temple. Isaiah saw God's Throne in the Temple [6:1]. When Israel backslid, Ezekiel saw the Throne leave [10:1,18].

1 Kings 6:13 - "I will dwell among the children of Israel, and will not forsake my people Israel."

D | Delayed Gratification

God said to Abraham, "Get thee out of thy country, ...unto a land that I will shew thee: And I will make of thee a great nation." The Exodus from Egypt began 430 years later. Then, in 480 more years, Solomon began building the Temple. After seven more years, it was dedicated. If you have not yet waited 917 years for your promise to be fulfilled, don't panic.

1 Kings 6:1 - "In the four hundred and eightieth year after the children of Israel were come out of the land of Egypt, ...he began to build the house of the LORD."

A | The Oracle

The very heart and soul of the Temple was the Oracle [some commentators call it the Shrine]. The Holy of Holies is where the Ark of the Covenant sat. In the old Tabernacle, Moses often stood before the

Ark of the Covenant and listened to the voice of God on important matters. Therefore, the place where the High Priest met God is called the Oracle - the mouthpiece of God. God's Word is the heartbeat of the universe.

1 Kings 6:19 - "The oracle he prepared in the house within, to set there the ark of the covenant of the LORD."

C | Stone and Wood Overlaid With Gold

The stonework of the Temple was magnificent without precedent, and impressive by itself. But Solomon laminated all the walls and ceilings with cedar, and the floors with fir. The sweet smell and beauty of cedar would also have been impressive. But stone and wood speak only of things temporal and earthly. Gold speaks of things eternal and divine. Solomon had everything inside the entire Temple overlaid with gold. Awesome!

1 Kings 6:9,22 - "So he built the house, and finished it; and covered the house with beams and boards of cedar, ...and the whole house he overlaid with gold."

B | The Cherubims

Two golden cherubims spread their wings across the Mercy Seat covering the Ark of the Covenant. Cherubims decorated all the Tabernacle curtains. Inside the Holy of Holies in Solomon's Temple, two gigantic cherubims (about twenty feet tall) stood side-by-side, each made of olive wood overlaid with gold. The wings between them touched. Their outer wings touched the walls. All were constant reminders that God dwells between the heavenly cherubims.

1 Kings 6:29 - "He carved all the walls of the house round about with carved figures of cherubims and palm trees and open flowers, within and without."

D | Solomon's Palace

Hiram built Solomon's palace of the finest stonework and woodwork. The main House of the Forest was cedar-lined, three stories, twelve doors, 150' x 75'. The Porch of Judgment contained the throne room. The King and Queen (Pharaoh's daughter) had separate houses that looked identical to the Porch of Judgment. An outer Porch of Pillars was 75' x 45'. Nathan's prophecy to David said, "I will set up thy seed after thee, ...and I will establish his kingdom."

1 Kings 7:1 - "Solomon was building his own house thirteen years, and he finished all his house."

C | The Two Pillars

Hiram placed two enormous, free-standing bronze pillars in front of the Temple entrance. Each was about 27 feet tall, 6 feet across, with huge ornamental caps, about seven and a half feet high. The ornaments were seven rows of chains and two rows of pomegranates, capped again with ornamental lilies. The south pillar was called "Jachin," meaning "established." The north pillar was called "Boaz," meaning "strength." Everyone who enters the House of God can plainly see the "established strength" of Jehovah.

1 Kings 7:21 - "He set up the pillars in the porch of the temple."

B | The Molten Sea

The Brasen Sea was an amazing fifteen feet across (45 foot circumference) and over seven feet deep, holding about 11,000 gallons of water. It was a gigantic brass bowl in which the priests washed and purified themselves before entering the Temple. It sat in the southeast corner of the Temple atop twelve bronze bulls facing outward, three each facing north, south, east and west. The water purification rite prefigured the New Testament doctrine of water baptism. Jesus said, "I have a baptism to be baptized with," Luke 12:50.

1 Kings 7:23 - "And he made a molten sea."

C | Frequent Washing

The priests immersed themselves in the Brasen Sea for purification [symbolizing water baptism]. But Solomon added ten bronze bowls, each four and a half feet high, six feet square, containing 230 gallons of water, and decorated with lions, bulls and winged creatures. They sat five to the south, five to the north of the Temple entrance, on large bronze stands having four bronze wheels on axles. The priests washed frequently as they performed sacrifices. Likewise, we all need frequent "washing of water by the word," Ephesians 5:26.

1 Kings 7:38 - "Then made he ten lavers of brass."

D | I Will Build My Church

The prophet foretold that Solomon would build the Temple, and it happened just like the prophet said. Centuries later, Jesus said, "I will

build my church; and the gates of hell shall not prevail against it,"
Matthew 16:18. A world full of atheists and devils cannot stop the Church
from fulfilling all prophecy. God's Word NEVER fails.

1 Kings 7:40, 51 - "So Hiram made an end of doing all the work that he
made king Solomon for the house of the LORD. ...So was ended all the
work that king Solomon made for the house of the LORD."

B | The Holy Vessels

King Hiram of Tyre generously supplied materials for the Temple and
king's palace. But another Hiram, a widow's son from the tribe of
Naphtali, was a brilliant artificer in metals. He created brass, bronze and
golden items for the Temple. Out of bright brass, he crafted lavers,
shovels, basons, and other vessels - never weighed for measure
because there were so many. The holy furnishings: Altar of Incense,
Shewbread Table, Candlesticks, bowls, snuffers, basons, spoons,
censers, even door hinges - were all gold.

1 Kings 7:45 - "All these vessels, ...Hiram made to king Solomon for the
house of the LORD."

A | Bring Your Gifts To The Altar

Solomon wrote, "A man's gift maketh room for him, and bringeth him
before great men," Proverbs 18:16. Before Solomon dedicated the
Temple in prayer, he was careful to present all the gifts that had been
dedicated by his father, David, into the treasury of the House of the
LORD. Before you make your prayers and requests, give your all to God.

1 Kings 7:51 - "Solomon brought in the things which David his father had
dedicated; even the silver, and the gold, and the vessels, did he put
among the treasures of the house of the LORD.

A | Bringing In The Ark

Without the Ark of the Covenant, Solomon's Temple would have been
like a lifeless corpse. The Holy of Holies was a meaningless room. But
with the Ark, it became the Oracle - the voice of God to the people. With
God in the Temple, there is life. We can converse and have relationship.
Without His presence and His glory, we only have dead religion.

1 Kings 8:6 - "The priests brought in the ark of the covenant of the LORD
unto his place, into the oracle of the house, to the most holy place, even
under the wings of the cherubims."

C | The Cloud Of The Glory Of The LORD

Solomon instructed the priests and Levites to fetch the Ark and all the holy vessels from the Tabernacle and carry them into the gorgeous new Temple. The people sacrificed countless multitudes of sheep and oxen. The priests placed the Ark between the Cherubims.

1 Kings 8:10-11 - "And it came to pass, when the priests were come out of the holy place, that the cloud filled the house of the LORD, So that the priests could not stand to minister because of the cloud: for the glory of the LORD had filled the house of the LORD."

A | Solomon's Testimony

Solomon stood before God, the Temple, and a standing multitude. "The LORD said that he would dwell in the thick darkness. I have surely built thee an house to dwell in, a settled place for thee to abide in for ever. ...I am risen up in the room of David my father, and sit on the throne of Israel, as the LORD promised." We should likewise recall God's promises and celebrate their fulfillments in our lives.

1 Kings 8:20-21 - "...I have set there a place for the ark, wherein is the covenant of the LORD."

A | Solomon Dedicates The Temple

Picture this. The King of Israel is kneeling before the altar in front of the spectacular new gold-plated Temple. As multitudes look on, he raises his hands toward heaven and worships and blesses God for keeping His promises, and prays one of the most powerful prayers in history in behalf of his people. Oh, for such a king today.

1 Kings 8:54 - "When Solomon had made an end of praying all this prayer and supplication unto the LORD, he arose from before the altar of the LORD, from kneeling on his knees with his hands spread up to heaven."

B | The Temple Dedication

The people came from the north and south of Israel. Solomon sacrificed 22,000 oxen and 120,000 sheep. The new Brasen Altar was too small, so Solomon hallowed the entire middle court for peace offerings, burnt offerings and meat offerings. They celebrated seven days of feasting with the dedication, through the Feast of Tabernacles.

1 Kings 8:62-66 - "The king, and all Israel with him, offered sacrifice before the LORD, and ...Solomon held a feast, ...On the eighth day he sent the people away: and they blessed the king, and went unto their tents joyful and glad of heart."

A | I Have Heard Thy Prayer

After offering 142,000 sacrifices that day, Solomon begged God to dwell in His new Temple. "Will God indeed dwell on the earth? behold, the heaven and heaven of heavens cannot contain thee; how much less this house that I have builded?"

1 Kings 9:2-3 - "The LORD appeared to Solomon the second time, ...And the LORD said unto him, I have heard thy prayer and thy supplication, that thou hast made before me: I have hallowed this house, which thou hast built, to put my name there for ever; and mine eyes and mine heart shall be there perpetually."

C | Consequences Of Backsliding

Several modern archaeologists brashly contend that the absence of any ruins from Solomon's Temple proves the Bible is a myth. Quite the opposite is true. God explicitly warned Solomon that if Israel abandoned Him, He would cut them off from the land and cast the Temple out of His sight. That is exactly what He did.

1 Kings 9:6-7 - "If ye shall at all turn from following me, ...Then will I cut off Israel out of the land which I have given them; and this house, which I have hallowed for my name, will I cast out of my sight."

D | Because They Forsook The LORD Their God

One of the most important prophetic fulfillments ever was the dispersion of Israel. Their deliverance from Egypt had been divinely orchestrated and completely miraculous. Taking the Promised Land and establishing the Davidic Kingdom were acts of God. After these, the penalties for rejecting God must be severe. From a glorious kingdom to a non-existent one.

1 Kings 9:7-8 - "...and Israel shall be a proverb and a byword among all people: ...and they shall say, Why hath the LORD done thus unto this land, and to this house? And they shall answer, Because they forsook the LORD their God."

C | Paying For The Temple And Palace

After twenty years of building the Temple and Palace, Solomon gave Hiram twenty Galilean cities to pay off the balance due. Hiram visited them, but was not pleased, calling them worthless. He sent another 120 talents of gold (over 15,000 pounds, worth over $380 million in 2012 dollars). Solomon had to levy a special tax on Israel to pay for it. Divine work deserves good buildings, so accept responsibility. Pay the bills.

1 Kings 9:15 - "This is the reason of the levy which king Solomon raised; for to build the house of the LORD, and his own house."

B | Solomon Builds Cities And Military

Solomon gave twenty cities to Hiram to pay off the Temple and Palace. Then he restored several cities that were in ruins from previous wars; Gezer (he gave to Pharaoh's daughter), Millo, Hazor, Megiddo, Bethhoron, Baalath, and Tadmor. Some became storehouse cities, and some became stable cities for horses and chariots. Foreigners did common labor. Citizens constituted the military. He built a great navy on the Red Sea, which acquired half a billion dollars in gold.

1 Kings 9:28 - "And they came to Ophir, and fetched from thence gold, four hundred and twenty talents, and brought it to king Solomon."

A | The Queen Blesses The LORD

Solomon's wisdom and wealth overwhelmed the Queen of Sheba (modern Yemen). She had to see it for herself. Her camel train brought gifts: spices, very much gold, and precious stones. God pours out His blessings on us, intending that everyone will glorify Him.

1 Kings 10:7,9 - "Howbeit I believed not the words, until I came, and mine eyes had seen it: and, behold, the half was not told me: thy wisdom and prosperity exceedeth the fame which I heard. ...Blessed be the LORD thy God, which delighted in thee, to set thee on the throne of Israel."

B | Solomon's Throne

Contrast Solomon's throne with Abraham's tents, Jacob's exile, Joseph's prison, and Moses' wilderness. The king's house had pillars; harps and psalteries for singers; 300 golden shields; 200 golden targets. The ivory throne was overlaid with the best gold. Fourteen golden lions surrounded it. Drinking vessels were gold. His navy brought gold, silver, ivory, apes, and peacocks from afar. 1400 chariots and 12,000 horsemen attended. God's chosen king earned about $1 billion annually.

1 Kings 10:14 - "The weight of gold that came to Solomon in one year was six hundred threescore and six talents of gold."

D | The Queen of Sheba

The LORD told Solomon, in his first prophetic dream, "I have also given thee that which thou hast not asked, both riches, and honour: so that there shall not be any among the kings like unto thee all thy days." The Queen of Sheba came to visit and was astonished and awestruck at Solomon's wisdom and riches and honour.

1 Kings 10:23-24 - "So king Solomon exceeded all the kings of the earth for riches and for wisdom. And all the earth sought to Solomon, to hear his wisdom, which God had put in his heart."

C | Never Satisfied With Enough

Solomon's unspeakable wealth was not enough. He wanted more. The Garden of Eden was not enough. Adam and Eve wanted the forbidden thing. The flesh always lusts against the Spirit. Solomon wanted women that God had forbidden: Egyptians, Moabites, Ammonites, Edomites, Zidonians and Hittites. 700 wives. 300 concubines. They turned his heart to their gods: Ashtoreth, Milcom, Chemosh, Molech, and others. Many wise people have become fools by unrestrained lust.

1 Kings 11:9 - "The LORD was angry with Solomon, because his heart was turned from the LORD God of Israel, which had appeared unto him twice."

D | Solomon's Demise

Solomon threw away the greatest blessings any man had ever received from God. He turned to evil women and false gods. Before it was over, Solomon built altars and idols to just about every imaginable god. Temptation can destroy ANYONE, with shocking results! Beware!

1 Kings 11:11,14 - "The LORD said unto Solomon, Forasmuch as this is done of thee, and thou hast not kept my covenant and my statutes, which I have commanded thee, I will surely rend the kingdom from thee, and will give it to thy servant. ...And the LORD stirred up an adversary unto Solomon."

A | The Absence Of Prayer

The presence of prayer (or the absence of prayer) in a story is a pretty reliable indicator as to the future state of its characters. In the early days of Solomon's reign, his great prayers defined him. Solomon's prayers got him and Israel enormous favor with God. But pagan women enticed him, and his heart forgot God. Suddenly, there are no more stories of Solomon praying. His wisdom and wealth turned to reproach and ruin.

1 Kings 11:31 - "And [Ahijah the prophet] said to Jeroboam, ...Behold, I will rend the kingdom out of the hand of Solomon."

D | Israel Divided

David conquered the enemies of Israel, bequeathing hard-won peace and prosperity to Solomon. But Solomon betrayed it with abominable sins. For David's sake, God allowed Rehoboam (Solomon's son) to keep Jerusalem and the tribes of Benjamin and Judah. But the ten northern tribes fell to Jeroboam. One man's sin shattered an entire kingdom. What harm will YOUR sin cause?

1 Kings 11:13 - "I will not rend away all the kingdom; but will give one tribe to thy son for David my servant's sake, and for Jerusalem's sake which I have chosen."

B | Solomon's Adversaries

David waged war for most of forty years to win the peace of Israel. Consequently, Solomon inherited a wonderfully peaceful and prosperous kingdom. He was respected by kings and queens throughout the region. But outrageously, Solomon fell in love with paganism! God raised up adversaries against him. When God shuts out your enemies, keep the door shut!

1 Kings 11:14,23,26 - "The LORD stirred up an adversary unto Solomon, Hadad the Edomite; ...And God stirred him up another adversary, Rezon the son of Eliadah, ...And Jeroboam the son of Nebat ...lifted up his hand against the king."

B | Jeroboam

Solomon became enslaved to his abominations, so God chose one of his mighty men, Jeroboam, to replace him. Ahijah prophesied that Jeroboam would rule ten tribes. (For David's memory, Solomon's son, Rehoboam retained Jerusalem, with the tribes of Judah and Benjamin.) Solomon wanted to kill Jeroboam, but he escaped to Egypt until Solomon died.

God wanted to sanctify and renew Israel by Jeroboam. Tragically, Jeroboam's sins ultimately rivaled Solomon's.

1 Kings 11:35 - "I will take the kingdom out of [Solomon's] son's hand, and will give it unto thee, even ten tribes."

C | God's Big "IF"

When Solomon failed, Ahijah prophesied over Jeroboam, offering blessings "if thou wilt hearken" to the LORD. "Hearken" means to "to listen, to give attention to." Anybody can find favor if he will hearken to God's commandments. God will build you a sure house if you will hearken.

1 Kings 11:38 - "If thou wilt hearken unto all that I command thee, and wilt walk in my ways, and do that is right in my sight, to keep my statutes and my commandments, as David my servant did; that I will be with thee, and build thee a sure house."

D | The Cause Was From The LORD

Solomon died, and his son, Rehoboam, went to Shechem to be made king. But Jeroboam confronted him. "Thy father made our yoke grievous: now therefore make ...his heavy yoke ...lighter, and we will serve thee." Rehoboam wanted three days to consider. His older counselors advised him to deal kindly with the people, but younger counselors urged him to be more severe. Rehoboam swore to be more severe, so Israel rejected him. Ahijah's prophecy concerning Jeroboam's rise to power came true.

1 Kings 12:15 - "The king hearkened not unto the people; for the cause was from the LORD."

A | The Prayer That Might Have Been

Rehoboam expected to rule all Israel after Solomon died. But he treated the people with so much contempt, they disowned him and followed Jeroboam. Much worse, they disowned their inheritance in David. If they had asked God, "What portion have we in David?" He might have reminded them of all His promises to David. But after they forsook Jerusalem, they never had another righteous king. The northern kingdom eventually perished in captivity.

1 Kings 12:16 - "When all Israel saw that the king hearkened not unto them, the people answered the king, saying, What portion have we in David?"

C | You Cannot Have What God Will Not Give

God was in complete control of Solomon, Rehoboam and Jeroboam. Solomon wanted to kill Jeroboam to prevent his gaining the throne, but Jeroboam hid in Egypt until Solomon died. Then Rehoboam wanted to kill Jeroboam, but he could not. Rehoboam assembled 180,000 chosen warriors to take back the kingdom from Jeroboam, but the word of the LORD came to the prophet Shemaiah, forbidding war. Stop wanting what God will not give.

1 Kings 12:24 - "Ye shall not go up, nor fight against your brethren the children of Israel: return every man to his house; for this thing is from me."

A | Calling Upon Idols

Jeroboam finally became King of Israel, but not in Jerusalem. Shechem was his capital. He worried that the House of the LORD in Jerusalem would draw the people back to Rehoboam, King of Judah, and "they shall kill me." Therefore, Jeroboam built two golden calves, set them up in Bethel and in Dan, and told the people, "Behold, thy gods, which brought thee up out of the land of Egypt!" What a heinous offense! Calling upon man-made idols - false gods!

1 Kings 12:30 - "This thing became a sin: for the people went to worship before the one."

B | Jeroboam, Who Made Israel To Sin

At Shechem, Jeroboam made two golden calves and told Israel that these newly-made idols were their gods! He made altars in high places to these no-gods. He made priests out of the lowest people and burned offerings and incense to these dumb calves. Words cannot describe the gross folly of ANY king of Israel to forsake the LORD God and the Holy Temple in Jerusalem. Twenty times, the Old Testament writers derided "Jeroboam, the son of Nebat, who made Israel to sin."

1 Kings 13:1 - "And Jeroboam stood by the altar to burn incense."

D | Cursed Altars

King Jeroboam built altars and burnt incense to two golden calves. God was enraged! He sent a prophet to curse the altars and declare that a descendant of David, named Josiah, would burn the bones of his false priests on the ruins of these altars. 323 years later, King Josiah fulfilled that prophecy precisely.

1 Kings 13:2 - "...a child shall be born unto the house of David, Josiah by name; and upon thee shall he offer the priests of the high places that burn incense upon thee, and men's bones shall be burnt upon thee."

C | Eat No Bread, Drink No Water

A prophet prophesied against Jeroboam's idolatrous altar. Furiously, Jeroboam reached out to assault him, but his arm withered. He begged for mercy, so the prophet prayed, and God healed him. The king said, "Come home with me," for a reward. He refused. Holy men on holy missions must not compromise.

1 Kings 13:8-10 - "If thou wilt give me half thine house, I will not go in with thee, neither will I eat bread nor drink water in this place: For so was it charged me by the word of the LORD, saying, Eat no bread, nor drink water."

B | The Old Prophet in Bethel

God told the prophet who cursed Jeroboam's idolatrous altar not to eat or drink with anyone while on his mission. We must obey God, even when we do not know why.

1 Kings 13:15-17 - "[The old prophet in Bethel] said unto him, Come home with me, and eat bread. And he said, I may not return with thee, nor go in with thee: neither will I eat bread nor drink water with thee in this place: For it was said to me by the word of the LORD, Thou shalt eat no bread nor drink water there."

C | Obedience Negated By Disobedience

This story is sobering. The prophet who rebuked Jeroboam at first resisted the temptation to eat and drink with the evil king. But an old prophet lied and persuaded him to eat and drink with him. He passed the first test, but failed the second. His error was fatal. The old prophet rebuked him for disobeying God. A lion met him on his journey and killed him. NEVER follow advice that contradicts the word of the LORD - even from old brethren!

1 Kings 13:29 - "The old prophet came to the city, to mourn and to bury him, ...saying, Alas, my brother!"

D | The Sayings Shall Surely Come To Pass

The prophet died for his disobedience, but the word of the LORD which he spoke would still come to pass. The old prophet who buried him declared, "The saying which he cried by the word of the LORD against the altar in Bethel, ...shall surely come to pass." Sadly, "Jeroboam returned not from his evil way." His son died shortly afterward, ending a dynasty before it ever began. God must judge disobedience. He vowed to cut off the house of Jeroboam.

1 Kings 13:34 - "...and to destroy it from off the face of the earth."

A | Audacious, Indefensible Prayer

Jeroboam was excoriated for burning incense to idols. His evil altar was scattered. But when his son became sick, he wanted blessings from the prophet Ahijah. Jeroboam feared him, so sent his wife stealthily, anonymously with bread, cakes and honey. God revealed their deception to Ahijah. Their desire was ignored. The child died.

1 Kings 14:6 - "When Ahijah heard the sound of her feet, as she came in at the door, that he said, Come in, thou wife of Jeroboam; why feignest thou thyself to be another? for I am sent to thee with heavy tidings."

B | Rehoboam

Rehoboam, son of Solomon, ruled Judah from the ages of 41 to 58. Rehoboam and Jeroboam warred all their days. Rehoboam tolerated rampant idolatry and sodomy (male homosexuality) - the same sins for which God destroyed many heathen nations. Consequently, Shishak, king of Egypt, attacked Jerusalem, and stole the priceless treasures of the House of the LORD and the king's palace. Solomon's backsliding destroyed his sons, his posterity, and his nation for generations to follow. DON'T BACKSLIDE!

1 Kings 14:31 - "Rehoboam slept with his fathers, and was buried with his fathers in the city of David."

A | A Lamp For David's Sake

David said, "For thou art my lamp, O LORD: and the LORD will lighten my darkness," 2 Samuel 22:29. Many of David's descendants were evil: Solomon, then Rehoboam, then Abijam. The northern tribes never had another righteous king, but for David's sake, God preserved two tribes at Jerusalem. What if David had never prayed? Your descendants may become completely godless if you neglect to pray.

1 Kings 15:4 - "Nevertheless for David's sake did the LORD his God give him a lamp in Jerusalem, to set up his son after him, and to establish Jerusalem."

C | Revival

Revival is the great hope against the threat of extinction. Sin abounds, but grace much more abounds. Although David's descendants backslid, God periodically raised up revivalists. In darkest nights, there is hope that some man of God will rise up and call people back to Him. "Wilt thou not revive us again?" Psalms 85:6.

1 Kings 15:11-12 - "And Asa did that which was right in the eyes of the LORD, as did David his father. And he took away the sodomites out of the land, and removed all the idols that his fathers had made."

A | Dedicating Our Vessels

David precipitated a national revival when he brought the Ark to the Tabernacle in Jerusalem. Solomon initiated a revival when he sanctified the holy vessels in the new Temple. While Rehoboam was backslidden, Egyptians stole the holy vessels. Rehoboam's grandson initiated a revival when he dedicated new vessels to the Temple. Our bodies are chosen vessels unto the LORD. During apostasy, vessels are profaned. Revival begins when we sanctify and rededicate them.

1 Kings 15:15 - "[Asa] brought in the things which his father had dedicated, and the things which himself had dedicated, into the house of the LORD, ...vessels."

D | Jeroboam's Posterity Terminated

God raised up Jeroboam to lead a revival in Israel following Solomon's backsliding. Instead, he led the people into idolatry and vile apostasy. God abhorred him. His son Nadab ruled for two years, but "did evil in the sight of the LORD, and walked in the way of his father." God totally terminated that family line.

1 Kings 15:27,29 - "Baasha the son of Ahijah, of the house of Issachar, ...smote [Nadab]. ...He left not to Jeroboam any that breathed, until he had destroyed him, according unto the saying of the LORD, which he spake by his servant Ahijah the Shilonite."

B | Baasha Of Israel Versus Asa Of Judah

Baasha, King of Israel, gained his throne by assassinating Nadab, evil son of Jeroboam. Baasha was evil like Jeroboam. He warred continuously with Asa, King of Judah, who "was perfect with the LORD all his days." Asa paid Benhadad of Syria to break league with Baasha and help him defeat Baasha. The prophet Jehu condemned Baasha. Evil men only succeed temporarily. The righteous will ultimately prevail.

1 Kings 16:3 - "Behold, I will take away the posterity of Baasha, and the posterity of his house; and will make thy house like the house of Jeroboam the son of Nebat."

D | Baasha's Posterity Terminated

After Asa, King of Judah, overthrew evil Baasha, his son, Elah, became the next king of Israel. There is little to say about Elah except that he died drunk. He reigned less than two years. One of his captains, Zimri, smote him while he was drunk. That terminated the household of Baasha, according to the prophecy of Jehu. Beware, lest you frustrate the grace of God. He can and will destroy.

1 Kings 16:12 - "Thus did Zimri destroy all the house of Baasha, according to the word of the LORD, which he spake against Baasha by Jehu the prophet."

C | Power Struggles

The northern kingdom was not guided by righteousness, but by misguided egomaniacs. Jeroboam's son, Nadab, was overthrown by Baasha. His son, Elah, was treasonously overthrown by Zimri. The people rejected Zimri, so he committed suicide, burning down the king's house. Half of Israel followed Tibni. Half followed Omri. King Omri defeated Tibni, bought the hill of Shemer, and founded the city of Samaria. King Omri was the father of wicked Ahab. Wickedness breeds wickedness.

1 Kings 16:25 - "Omri wrought evil in the eyes of the LORD, and did worse than all that were before him."

C | When Spouses Corrupt

Eve offered forbidden fruit to Adam. Moses' wife wickedly opposed his practicing circumcision. Delilah betrayed Sampson to the Philistines. Michal scathed David for worshipping the LORD. Solomon's wives allured him to worship a multitude of false gods. But none was ever worse than Jezebel. The word Jezebel is now in the dictionary as a common noun meaning, "wicked or shameless woman." Sanctify your relationship with God from the devices of an evil spouse.

1 Kings 16:31 - "As if it had been a light thing for him to walk in the sins of Jeroboam, ...he took to wife Jezebel."

A | Ahab Worships Baal

Prayer and worship express intimate affections for God. So when King Ahab built altars and idols, and worshipped Baal, he committed contemptuous spiritual adultery. Like a jealous husband whose wife has been unfaithful, our Creator is frighteningly jealous of our affections. "Thou shalt not bow down thyself to them, ...for I the LORD thy God am a jealous God."

1 Kings 16:32-33 - "He reared up an altar for Baal in the house of Baal, ...and Ahab did more to provoke the LORD God of Israel to anger than all the kings of Israel that were before him."

D | A Curse For Rebuilding Jericho

Long ago, after Jericho's walls fell, and God destroyed the city, Joshua said, "Cursed be the man before the LORD, that riseth up and buildeth this city Jericho: he shall lay the foundation thereof in his firstborn, and in his youngest son shall he set up the gates of it." Never restore sin's old habitat. It may curse you.

1 Kings 16:34 - "In his days did Hiel the Bethelite build Jericho: he laid the foundation thereof in Abiram his firstborn, and set up the gates thereof in his youngest son Segub, according to the word of the LORD."

B | Elijah Defies Baal

King Omri's evil son, Ahab, married Jezebel, a worshipper of Baal - known in history as a god of storms and rain. King Ahab forsook Jehovah and worshipped Baal. The great prophet Elijah came on the scene, not just to rebuke Ahab and Jezebel, but to utterly defy their so-called god of storms and rain. First thing, he proved that his God, Jehovah, controls storms and rain - NOT Baal!

1 Kings 17:1 - "As the LORD God of Israel liveth, before whom I stand, there shall not be dew nor rain these years, but according to my word."

A | Engaging God

Elijah prophesied to King Ahab that there would be no dew or rain in Israel except by his word only. Elijah's verbal initiative engaged Almighty God. When we verbalize our beliefs, God performs miracles that will affirm our faith. God sent the drought, and also protected Elijah from Ahab and Jezebel.

1 Kings 17:5 - "So he went and did according unto the word of the LORD: for he went and dwelt by the brook Cherith, that is before Jordan. And the ravens brought him bread and flesh in the morning, and bread and flesh in the evening."

C | When The Brook Dries Up

After Elijah declared the drought against Ahab's idolatrous kingdom, God told him to flee to the brook Cherith for water to sustain him. While Israel suffered, God sent ravens to the man of God twice daily with bread and meat. Eventually, the brook dried up. But worsening circumstances do not befuddle God. He always has refreshing alternatives if you will continually obey him. The word of the LORD spoke to Elijah.

1 Kings 17:9 - "Arise, get thee to Zarephath, which belongeth to Zidon, and dwell there: behold, I have commanded a widow woman there to sustain thee."

B | The Widow Of Zarephath

During drought, God sent Elijah to a poor widow who was gathering firewood to cook her last meal. He insisted that she feed him first, although she had only a handful of meal and a little oil. He prophesied, "Thus saith the LORD God of Israel, The barrel of meal shall not waste, neither shall the cruse of oil fail, until the day that the LORD sendeth rain upon the earth." God will reward sacrificial giving.

1 Kings 17:16 - "The barrel of meal wasted not, neither did the cruse of oil fail, according to the word of the LORD."

D | Signs Of A Prophet

The widow who fed Elijah during famine lost her son to an illness. She felt cursed for some past sin. But Elijah took the dead child into his loft, stretched across him three times, and cried unto the LORD for the child's soul to return. Amazingly, the child revived. She then knew that Elijah was a true prophet. God will confirm His word with miraculous signs.

1 Kings 17:24 - "The woman said to Elijah, Now by this I know that thou art a man of God, and that the word of the LORD in thy mouth is truth."

A | God Responds To Elijah's Boldness

Elijah daringly pronounced a drought on Ahab's evil world. At Elijah's word, God sent a devastating drought. God proudly responds to those who plead His righteous cause with their bold prayers and declarations of faith. Afterward, God called Elijah for several more extraordinary tasks. So speak and pray boldly according to God's will. God is always looking for people who have great faith in Him.

1 Kings 18:1 - "The word of the LORD came to Elijah in the third year, saying, Go, shew thyself unto Ahab; and I will send rain upon the earth."

B | Obadiah, Ahab's Governor

King Ahab desperately wanted to capture Elijah for prophesying drought and famine in Israel. Ahab and his governor, Obadiah, were desperately searching for grassy lands to feed their livestock when Obadiah ran into Elijah, who demanded to see Ahab. Obadiah was a God-fearing man who hid 100 prophets from Ahab, but he feared that Ahab would kill him if he promised, then failed to deliver Elijah. So Elijah vowed to show. Unrepentant Ahab was doomed to suffer even greater losses.

1 Kings 18:16 - "So Obadiah went to meet Ahab, and told him: and Ahab went to meet Elijah."

C | Who Is Troubling Who?

After a long desperate search, Ahab finally laid eyes on Elijah. "Art thou he that troubleth Israel?" Ahab blamed Elijah for all the woes of drought and famine. But Elijah reminded him that it was Ahab's rebellions and idolatries that troubled Israel. The same things happen nowadays. People rail against the Church and preachers, and blame Bible believers for making life miserable for them. But the opposite is true. Sin causes a ton of trouble.

1 Kings 18:17 - "Ahab said unto him, Art thou he that troubleth Israel? And he answered, I have not troubled Israel; but thou."

D | Elijah Calls Down Fire

Elijah condemned Jezebel's 850 prophets on Carmel, challenging them to build an altar to Baal. He built an altar of twelve stones to the LORD. "The God that answereth by fire, let him be God." They screamed, slashed themselves and begged Baal to send fire. Nothing happened. Elijah soaked his altar with twelve barrels of water, then prayed. Fire from God consumed the sacrifice, wood, dust, water, even the stones. Elijah had all the false prophets killed.

1 Kings 18:39 - "When all the people saw it, they fell on their faces: and they said, The LORD, he is the God!"

A | Pray For Rain

Elijah destroyed Jezebel's 850 false prophets. Everyone confessed that the LORD, not Baal, was God. Their punishing drought could end. Elijah told Ahab to get up, "Eat and drink; for there is a sound of abundance of rain." Elijah cast himself down on the top of Mount Carmel and put his face between his knees. After his servant went out seven times looking for rain clouds, he finally saw a little cloud out of the sea, "like a man's hand." Suddenly,

1 Kings 18:45 - "The heaven was black with clouds and wind, and there was a great rain."

B | Elijah's Forty-Day Fast

Elijah called down fire from heaven and slew 850 of King Ahab's false prophets. But Queen Jezebel was furious and demanded he be killed. Elijah fled, but became depressed and suicidal, asking God to kill him. Instead, God sent an angel to feed him. He ran forty days, fasting, to Horeb, mount of God. God said, "What are you doing here?" and made him return to anoint two kings and a prophet. Elijah's fast renewed him to dynamic ministry.

1 Kings 19:9 - "...and he said unto him, What doest thou here, Elijah?"

C | Get Out Of Your Cave

Elijah fled from Jezebel's threatening all the way to Horeb, mountain of God - about 200 miles! He stayed in a cave and waited for the LORD to speak. A storm blew, an earthquake shook, and a fire raged, but Elijah heard no voice. Then a still small voice told him to get out of the cave and go anoint a new king in Syria, a new king in Israel, and a new prophet in his place. Things may be bad, but God is not finished with you.

1 Kings 19:15 - "And the LORD said unto him, Go."

D | A New Prophet Prophesied

At Mount Horeb, Elijah complained that he was the only one left in Israel who was still jealous for the LORD's righteous cause. But God said, "I have left me seven thousand in Israel, all the knees which have not bowed unto Baal." God ordered him to go anoint Elisha to be the next prophet in Israel. This is no time to despair. The work of God must carry on.

1 Kings 19:19 - "So he departed thence, and found Elisha the son of Shaphat, who was plowing, ...and Elijah passed by him, and cast his mantle upon him."

A | Who Shall Order The Battle?

After the drought, Benhadad, King of Syria, brought thirty-two kings against Ahab to besiege Samaria. He demanded all Ahab's silver, gold, wives and children. But a prophet of the LORD prophesied that God would deliver Benhadad's multitude into Ahab's hands. "By whom?" Ahab enquired. "By the young princes of the provinces of Israel." "Who shall order the battle?" "Thou." Ahab numbered 232 young princes and 7000 warriors who miraculously defeated Benhadad. You cannot lose when the LORD of Hosts directs your battle.

1 Kings 20:20 - "They slew every one his man: and the Syrians fled."

B | The God Of The Valleys

Benhadad attacked Ahab again, one year after being defeated. His servants said that Israel's God was God of the hills, but not of the valleys, so they attacked Israel in the plains. But they were wrong. Jehovah is God of hills AND valleys. He will be with you wherever you are.

1 Kings 20:28 - "Because the Syrians have said, The LORD is God of the hills, but he is not God of the valleys, therefore will I deliver all this great multitude into thine hand, ...and the children of Israel slew of the Syrians an hundred thousand footmen."

C | The Enemy Is Not Your Brother

When Ahab's forces killed 100,000 Syrians, King Benhadad hid himself in an inner chamber at a town named Aphek. His servants urged him to put on sackcloth, humble himself before Ahab, and beg for his life. He did, and Ahab spared him saying, "He is my brother." Immediately, a prophet condemned Ahab for the act. Do not call the enemy your brother!

1 Kings 20:42-43 - "Because thou hast let go out of thy hand a man whom I appointed to utter destruction, therefore thy life shall go for his life, and thy people for his people."

D | Jezebel's Death Was Prophesied For Naboth's Death

Ahab was jealous for Naboth's vineyard, which lay next door to his palace in Samaria. Naboth would not sell it because it was his family inheritance. But Jezebel scandalized Naboth, raising up false witnesses with false charges, and Naboth was sentenced to death by stoning. The word of the LORD came to Elijah, prophesying death to Ahab and Jezebel for the act. Ahab repented, but Jezebel never did. Elijah's prophecy was fulfilled in her death.

1 Kings 21:23 - "And of Jezebel also spake the LORD, saying, The dogs shall eat Jezebel by the wall of Jezreel."

A | Ahab's Radical Repentance

Jezebel had Naboth killed so Ahab could have his vineyard. But Elijah had a fatal word from the LORD. And not just because of Naboth. "There was none like unto Ahab, which did sell himself to work wickedness in the sight of the LORD, whom Jezebel his wife stirred up." God sentenced Ahab and Jezebel to death. But Ahab went into radical repentance, and God forgave him. If God will forgive Ahab, He will forgive you.

1 Kings 21:27 - "Ahab ...rent his clothes, and put sackcloth upon his flesh, and fasted, and lay in sackcloth, and went softly."

B | Prophets Who Say Whatever You Want To Hear

Ahab asked Jehoshaphat, King of Judah, to go to war with him against Ramothgilead. Jehoshaphat insisted they enquire at the word of the LORD. Ahab called four hundred spurious prophets who ALL said, "Go up!" But Jehoshaphat knew they were phonies and demanded a true prophet. If you really do not want to hear the Truth, there will always be somebody to tell you anything you want to hear.

1 Kings 22:6 - "The king of Israel gathered the prophets together, about four hundred men, ...and they said, Go up; for the Lord shall deliver it into the hand of the king."

A | Do Not Tell God What To Say

Ahab did not want to hear the word of a true prophet concerning his ambition to take Ramothgilead. When his messengers fetched Micaiah, they said explicitly, "the [false] prophets declare good unto the king with one mouth: let thy word, I pray thee, be like the word of one of them, and speak that which is good." If you want to know God's will, don't tell Him what to say. Why pray that someone will lie to you? Micaiah retorted,

1 Kings 22:14 - "As the LORD liveth, what the LORD saith unto me, that will I speak."

C | Lying Spirits

It was high drama when Jehoshaphat prevailed with Ahab to call a true prophet of the LORD. 400 false prophets did not convince Jehoshaphat. But the prophet Micaiah was annoyed with Ahab's self-deception and played mind games with him. Jehoshaphat pressed him, and Micaiah prophesied the death of the King of Israel. Suddenly, Zedekiah, speaking for the opposition, played an elaborate pantomime to prove that Micaiah was wrong. But Micaiah knew the Truth.

1 Kings 22:23 - "The LORD hath put a lying spirit in the mouth of all these thy prophets, and the LORD hath spoken evil concerning thee."

C | Grit

If you are going to stand for God, you have to have grit - "firmness of character; indomitable spirit." Micaiah told Ahab, "I saw all Israel scattered ...as sheep that have not a shepherd: and the LORD said, These have no master," then added, "A spirit ...stood before the LORD, and said, I will be a lying spirit in the mouth of all his prophets." Zedekiah slapped Micaiah in the face, and Ahab sent him to prison until he returned from war.

1 Kings 22:28 - "Micaiah said, If thou return at all ...the LORD hath not spoken by me."

D | The Prophecies Of Micaiah

Ahab wanted to conquer Ramothgilead and asked Jehoshaphat, King of Judah to go to war with him. But it was not the will of God. 400 false prophets said, "GO!" but the prophet Micaiah prophesied that Ahab would die if he went to war. Ahab defiantly went to battle anyway, disguised as an ordinary soldier, intending to prove the prophet wrong. But the prophet was right. You cannot beat God at His game. Do not try.

1 Kings 22:34,37 - "...a certain man drew a bow at a venture, and smote the king of Israel... so the king died."

D | The Dogs Lick Ahab's Blood

Ahab was determined to defy the Word of the LORD. "I will disguise myself, and enter into the battle." But "a certain man drew a bow at a venture, and smote the king of Israel, ...and the blood ran out of the wound into the midst of the chariot." Ahab died, and they buried him in Samaria. The forgotten prophecy of Elijah came to pass.

1 Kings 22:38 - "One washed the chariot in the pool of Samaria; and the dogs licked up his blood; and they washed his armour; according unto the word of the LORD which he spake."

B | Jehoshaphat

Jehoshaphat ascended to the throne of Judah in the fourth year of King Ahab's rule in Israel. They reigned concurrently for seventeen years. Two kings could hardly have been more opposites. Ahab was the worst king Israel had ever had. Jehoshaphat earnestly sought to please God. In the days of his righteous reign, "the remnant of the sodomites [homosexuals], ...he took out of the land."

I Kings 22:43 - "And he walked in all the ways of Asa his father; he turned not aside from it, doing that which was right in the eyes of the LORD."

Lessons from the Book of
2 KINGS

A | Death For Enquiring Of Other Gods

King Ahaziah of Israel was a foolish Baal-worshipper like his parents, Ahab and Jezebel. When he became sick after a fall, he sent messengers to enquire of Baalzebub whether he would recover. Ahaziah flouted the commandment, "Thou shalt have no other gods!" The angel of the LORD ordered Elijah to confront the king's messengers. "Is it not because there is not a God in Israel, that ye go to enquire of Baalzebub?"

2 Kings 1:4 - "Thus saith the LORD, Thou shalt not come down from that bed on which thou art gone up, but shalt surely die."

B | Elijah Condemns Another Evil King - Ahaziah

Ahaziah's messengers reported that a man prophesied his death for seeking Baalzebub. Ahaziah knew it was Elijah. He sent a captain with fifty soldiers to fetch Elijah. "Man of God... come down!" they said. "If I am a man of God, let fire come down from heaven and consume you!" It did. Ahaziah sent fifty more. More fire. He sent another fifty. That captain begged for his life. The angel of the LORD sent Elijah to personally deliver the curse to Ahaziah.

2 Kings 1:17 - "[Ahaziah] died according to the word of the LORD which Elijah had spoken."

C | A Double Portion Of Thy Spirit

Eventually, the torch must be passed. The sons of the prophets at Bethel and at Jericho reminded Elisha that "the LORD will take away thy master from thy head to day." Crowds came to watch. Elijah smote the Jordan River with his mantle, and it parted. The two crossed on dry ground. Elijah offered Elisha one last request. "A double portion of thy spirit be upon me." Ask, and it shall be so.

2 Kings 2:10 - "Thou hast asked a hard thing: nevertheless, if thou see me when I am taken from thee, it shall be so unto thee."

D | Passing The Mantle

The fiery "chariot of Israel and the horsemen thereof" took Elijah up from Elisha in a whirlwind. Elijah's mantle fell down onto Elisha. The anointing was transferred. Anointing is transferable. True believers have Christ's anointing.

2 Kings 2:14-15 - "He took the mantle of Elijah that fell from him, and smote the waters, and said, Where is the LORD God of Elijah? and ...they parted hither and thither: and Elisha went over. And when the sons of the prophets ...saw him, they said, The spirit of Elijah doth rest on Elisha. ...they came ...and bowed themselves to the ground before him."

A | Men Of Jericho Pray For Water

Fifty prophets saw the whirlwind carry Elijah away. Elijah was gone, but they searched in vain for him in the surrounding mountains and valleys for three days. Elisha said, "Did I not say unto you, Go not?" From then on, the people knew Elisha was in the place of Elijah. They prayed he would remedy the undrinkable waters in Jericho. He called for a cruse of salt and cast it into the waters.

2 Kings 2:21-22 - "Thus saith the LORD, I have healed these waters; ...So the waters were healed unto this day, according to the saying of Elisha."

B | Elisha And The Valley Full Of Ditches

The Moabites paid hefty tributes to Ahab, but rebelled against his son, Jehoram. Jehoram recruited Jehoshaphat and Edom for war against Moab. Three armies started a seven-day journey, but famished for water. Jehoshaphat called Elisha, and the prophet said, "Make this valley full of ditches." At sunrise, water filled the valley, and the sun's reflection looked like blood. Moab thought Israel was fallen in bloody battle and moved in to take a prey.

2 Kings 3:24 - "When they came to the camp of Israel, the Israelites rose up and smote the Moabites, so that they fled before them."

C | God Will Fill Your Vessel

A prophet's widow begged help from Elisha. She had no money, and her creditors were going to take her sons for slaves. Elisha asked what she had. "A pot of oil." He told her to borrow all the vessels she could find and pour the oil into them. Miraculously, she filled every single vessel. Then the oil stayed. God can work with anything you have to meet your need. Just bring an empty vessel to God.

2 Kings 4:7 - "And he said, Go, sell the oil, and pay thy debt, and live thou and thy children of the rest."

D | Thou Shalt Embrace A Son

A great woman at Shunem often provided meals for Elisha as he passed by. She persuaded her husband to build a chamber for the prophet, with a bed, a table, a stool and a candlestick. For their kindness, Elisha asked what favor could be done for them. His servant, Gehazi, informed him that they were childless. God rewards those who support His work.

2 Kings 4:16-17 - "He said, About this season, according to the time of life, thou shalt embrace a son. ...And the woman conceived, and bare a son at that season that Elisha had said unto her."

A | Elisha Raises The Dead

The once-barren Shunammite raised the son that Elisha had prophesied to her. But after a few years, he fell sick and died. She carried the corpse into Elisha's chamber and quickly rode a donkey to Mount Carmel to fetch Elisha. He came and found the dead child in his bed. He shut the door "and prayed unto the LORD," then lay across the child until he became warm. Elisha walked around the house, then stretched across him again. Extraordinary faith in God produces extraordinary results.

2 Kings 4:35 - "The child sneezed seven times, and the child opened his eyes."

B | Elisha Feeds 100 Men Miraculously

Elisha fed pottage to 100 sons of the prophets, but someone unwittingly added poison herbs. "Man of God, there is death in the pot!" Elisha cast meal into it, and it was cured. Someone brought 20 loaves of barley and ears of corn. Elisha told him to feed the prophets. "Should I set this before an hundred men?" Elisha said, "Thus saith the LORD, They shall eat, and shall leave thereof." God can multiply your resources.

2 Kings 4:44 - "So he set it before them, and they did eat, and left thereof, according to the word of the LORD."

C | Honor Your Master

"Naaman, captain of the host of the king of Syria, was a great man with his master, and honourable, because by him the LORD had given deliverance unto Syria." Naaman's maidservant was a captured Israelite who wanted him to go to Elisha for healing. Someone told Naaman, "thus said the maid that is of the land of Israel." We should honor our masters, even if they are enemies.

2 Kings 5:3-4 - "She said unto her mistress, Would God my lord were with the prophet that is in Samaria! for he would recover him of his leprosy."

D | A True Prophet Knows What Will Happen

Naaman, a Syrian, needed to see Elisha for healing. His king sent gifts to Israel, requesting the king to receive Naaman and heal him. The King of Israel said, "Am I God, ...to recover a man of his leprosy?" But Elisha heard, invited Naaman to his home, and instructed him to wash seven times in Jordan. Naaman indignantly refused, but his servant persuaded him to obey the prophet. He was healed.

2 Kings 5:15 - "He returned to the man of God, ...and he said, Behold, now I know that there is no God in all the earth, but in Israel."

A | Naaman Seeks Pardon

Naaman glorified God and tried to reward Elisha for his healing, but Elisha refused. "As the LORD liveth, before whom I stand, I will receive none." As a Syrian captain serving the King, Naaman was forced to accompany his King into the house of the false god Rimmon. He begged forgiveness in advance from God, since he could not possibly be excused. Thankfully, God is merciful during our dilemmas.

2 Kings 5:18-19 - "When I bow down myself in the house of Rimmon, the LORD pardon thy servant in this thing. And he said unto him, Go in peace."

B | Gehazi's Folly

Elisha refused any gift from Naaman, but his servant ran after Naaman, lying. "My master hath sent me, saying, There be come to me from mount Ephraim two young men of the sons of the prophets: give them, I pray thee, a talent of silver, and two changes of garments." Naaman gave him much more. But when he returned, Elisha asked where he went. "Nowhere." Elisha knew the truth. Greed and lies are cursed.

2 Kings 5:27 - "The leprosy therefore of Naaman shall cleave unto thee, ...And he went out from his presence a leper as white as snow."

C | The Iron Did Swim

The sons of the prophets acquired Elisha's approval to build a community dwelling near Jordan. Each man took boards, and they went to work building. One man was cutting down timber when the axe head fell into the water. He cried out, because it was borrowed. Elisha came on the scene, cut down a stick, and threw it in the water. "The iron did swim." If God can make an axe head float, He can salvage your loss.

2 Kings 6:7 - "Therefore said he, Take it up to thee. And he put out his hand, and took it."

D | Revealing Bedchamber Conversations

The Syrians made war against Israel. But the man of God received revelation from God about the movement of the troops. Elisha sent word again and again to the King of Israel, so he was able to remove out of the path of trouble. The Syrian king was sore distressed, thinking a traitor was betraying him. But it was God. He sees all and hears all.

2 Kings 6:12 -"One of his servants said, None, my lord, O king: but Elisha, the prophet that is in Israel, telleth the king of Israel the words that thou speakest in thy bedchamber."

A | Open His Eyes That He May See

Elisha prophetically discerned the Syrian battle plans and warned the King of Israel. The Syrian king, Benhadad, sent a huge army with horses and chariots overnight to Dothan to surround and capture Elisha. In the early morning, Elisha's servant saw them, and cried, "Alas, my master! how shall we do?" Elisha prayed, "LORD, ...open his eyes, that he may see." He saw the mountain full of horses and chariots of fire around Elisha. God's invisible army surrounds His people.

2 Kings 6:16 - "Fear not: for they that be with us are more than they that be with them."

B | The Syrian Army Blinded

God opened Elisha's servant's eyes to see His invisible army. Then Elisha prayed that the Syrian army would be smitten blind. God answered. Elisha led a blind army from Dothan to Samaria, to the King of Israel. He prayed again, and God opened their eyes. God has power over your vision, to open or close your eyes, to serve His purpose. The king asked Elisha, "Shall I smite them?" He said,

2 Kings 6:22 - "Set bread and water before them, that they may eat and drink, and go to their master. ...and they went to their master."

C | The Grievous Depravity Of Sin

In Deuteronomy 28:53, Moses prophesied that if Israel forsook the LORD, "Thou shalt eat the fruit of thine own body, the flesh of thy sons and of thy daughters, ...in the siege, ...wherewith thine enemies shall distress thee." That is EXACTLY what happened following the God-hating generation of Ahab and Jezebel. Benhadad, king of Syria laid siege to Samaria. People were starving to death. The King of Israel was horrified to learn that women were cannibalizing their own children for survival.

2 Kings 6:30 - "The king ...rent his clothes; and ...had sackcloth [for mourning] within upon his flesh."

D | Elisha Prophesies To His Would-be Assassins

The King of Israel blamed Elisha for the famine and the Syrian siege on Samaria. The prophet, at home with several elders, discerned the king's plans to behead him. Challenging the king, Elisha prophesied that there would be food in abundance within 24 hours in the gates of Samaria.

2 Kings 7:2 - "A lord on whose hand the king leaned answered the man of God, and said, Behold, if the LORD would make windows in heaven, might this thing be? And he said, Behold, thou shalt see it with thine eyes, but shalt not eat thereof."

B | Four Lepers Instigate A Miracle

Four lepers sat outside Samaria, starving. "Why sit we here until we die?" They decided to enter the camp of Syrians who were besieging Samaria. "If they kill us, we shall but die." Miraculously, the Syrians heard chariots and horses of a great host, and fled - leaving everything behind; food, clothes, treasures, livestock. The lepers bequeathed their riches to Samaria. Elisha's prophecy was fulfilled.

2 Kings 7:16 - "The people went out, and spoiled the tents of the Syrians. So a measure of fine flour was sold for a shekel, ...according to the word of the LORD."

C | Do Not Trivialize Prophecy

At the time when Elisha prophesied abundance in Samaria within one day, "a lord on whose hand the king leaned answered the man of God, and said, Behold, if the LORD would make windows in heaven, might this thing be? And he said, Behold, thou shalt see it with thine eyes, but shalt not eat thereof." This fellow saw the prophecy fulfilled the very next day, but was killed before he could eat of the spoils.

2 Kings 7:20 - "And so it fell out unto him: for the people trode upon him in the gate, and he died."

A | A Prayer Partner Helps You Intercede

Elisha advised the Shunnamite woman to live with Philistines during Israel's seven-year famine. When she returned, she discovered that the king had confiscated her property. She went to him and cried for her house and land. Gehazi, Elisha's servant, "happened" to be in the king's chamber right then and interceded for her. "O king, this is the woman, and this is her son, whom Elisha restored to life."

2 Kings 8:6 - "The king [said], ...Restore all that was hers, and all the fruits of the field since the day that she left the land."

D | Elisha Foresees Benhadad's Assassination

Elisha visited Damascus while King Benhadad was sick. Benhadad sent Hazael with forty camel-loads "of every good thing in Damascus" to ask the prophet whether he would recover from his disease. "He may recover from his disease, but he will surely die." Elisha wept. The LORD showed him that Hazael would murder Benhadad, take the Syrian throne, and devastate Israel.

2 Kings 8:15 - "It came to pass on the morrow, that he took a thick cloth, and dipped it in water, and spread it on [Benhadad's] face, so that he died: and Hazael reigned in his stead."

B | King Jehoram Of Judah - The Wimp

Jehoram, son of Jehoshaphat, married Athaliah, evil daughter of Ahab and Jezebel. After becoming King of Judah at 32, Jehoram murdered his six brothers, plus many Israelite princes. The Edomites and the town of Libnah revolted against him because he forsook the LORD. He lost all his battles - his armies retreated. Philistines, Arabs and Ethiopians ransacked his palace and kidnapped his family (except his youngest son, Jehoahaz). Elijah accurately prophesied that he would die of a bowel disease. His name, "yoram," is now a colloquialism in Israel, meaning "wimp."

2 Kings 8:18 - "He did evil in the sight of the LORD."

C | Don't Repeat Your Parents' Mistakes

Israel's King Ahab begat Ahaziah, who begat Joram. Judah's King Jehoshaphat begat Jehoram, who begat another Ahaziah. So Ahaziah of Israel appears shortly before Ahaziah of Judah. Unfortunately, both Ahaziahs had evil hearts like Omri, Ahab, Jezebel, and their daughter, Athaliah. Remember how Ahab died for disobeying God at Ramothgilead? Ahab's son, Joram, was critically injured in another battle at Ramothgilead. Elisha commanded Jehu to destroy Joram of Israel and Ahaziah of Judah. If only they had learned from their parents' mistakes.

2 Kings 9:7 - "Smite the house of Ahab, ...For the whole house of Ahab shall perish."

D | Jezebel's Demise

Elisha sent a prophet to anoint Jehu as King of Israel. He commanded Jehu to clean up after Ahab, Jezebel, and their son, Joram. He prophesied, "the dogs shall eat Jezebel in the portion of Jezreel." Jehu drove his chariot furiously to Jezreel. He killed Joram in the field Ahab stole from Naboth. He chased and killed Ahaziah of Judah. Then he called three eunuchs to throw Jezebel out the palace window. She died, and dogs ate her body.

2 Kings 9:35 - "They found no more of her than the skull, and the feet, and the palms of her hands."

B | King Jehu Of Judah

Elisha picked Jehu to be the King of Judah, to thoroughly purge Israel and Judah of its evil leadership. In Israel, Jehu ordered the death of the seventy surviving sons of Ahab, plus all of Ahab's near-of-kin. In Judah, Jehu purged forty-two of Ahaziah's brethren. Jehu shrewdly called all Baal worshipers and prophets of Baal together for a major sacrifice. As soon as they offered one offering to Baal, he had them all slaughtered. Everyone who might have sustained idolatrous Baal-worship was eliminated.

2 Kings 10:28 - "Thus Jehu destroyed Baal out of Israel."

C | An Incomplete Consecration

Israel rarely ever saw a king "clean house" like Jehu did. He destroyed all of Ahab and Jezebel's descendants, forty-two brothers of evil Ahaziah of Judah, AND all the prophets and worshippers of Baal. Nevertheless, Jehu left Jeroboam's golden calves (idols) in Bethel and Dan. Apparently, the massive purge was more to eliminate his own competition than to sanctify the LORD God in Israel. Why waste your time doing only half of God's will?

2 Kings 10:31 - "Jehu took no heed to walk in the law of the LORD God of Israel with all his heart."

D | Jehu's Posterity Prophesied

God rewarded Jehu for removing so many evil leaders in Israel and Judah by promising him that his descendants would continue on his throne for four generations. God often rewards those who tend to His business, even though they may have failures in other areas.

2 Kings 10:30 - "And the LORD said unto Jehu, Because thou hast done well in executing that which is right in mine eyes, and hast done unto the house of Ahab according to all that was in mine heart, thy children of the fourth generation shall sit on the throne of Israel."

B | Athaliah's Rise And Fall

Jehu eliminated evil King Ahaziah and his brethren. Ahaziah's ambitious mother, Athaliah, "destroyed all the seed royal," and made herself queen. But Jehosheba secretly hid Ahaziah's baby son, Jehoash, in the house of the LORD. Jehoiada, the priest, devised an elaborate security plan to keep him safe until he could be made king. Seven years later, he brought Jehoash out, crowned him and cried, "God save the king!" Athaliah screamed, "Treason!" But the guards killed her outside the Temple. All justice needs is time.

2 Kings 11:21 - "Seven years old was Jehoash when he began to reign."

C | The Secret Of Godly Leadership

After years of chaos in Jerusalem, the child king, Jehoash, established his throne in righteousness. The principal reason for this is that he was constantly advised by Jehoiada, the High Priest. Jehoash raised an offering to completely restore the house of the LORD. They gave the money to carpenters, builders, masons, stoneworkers, and bought timber and hewed stone. The work of God prospers under righteous leaders who follow the counsel of men of God. God, give us such leaders!

2 Kings 12:15 - "They delivered the money to be bestowed on workmen: for they dealt faithfully."

D | The Prophetic Significance Of Baby Jehoash

Jehu purged Israel of two royal families - Ahab's and Ahaziah's. Then, Ahaziah's mother, Athaliah, killed all Ahaziah's children so she could be queen. But Jehosheba secretly saved Ahaziah's infant son, hiding him in the house of the LORD for six years, protected by Jehoiada the High Priest. If Jehosheba had not saved baby Jehoash, the royal bloodline of David would have ended. But divine prophecy cannot fail.

2 Kings 12:21 - "[Jehoash] died; and they buried him with his fathers in the city of David: and Amaziah his son reigned in his stead."

A | Jehoahaz Delivers Israel From Syria By Prayer

Jehoahaz, fifteenth King of Israel, succeeded notoriously wicked people: Jeroboam, (who caused all Israel to sin), Omri (worst ever in his day), Ahab and Jezebel (still worse than Omri), and Jehu, who "took no heed to walk in the law of the LORD." God finally sent Syrian King Hazael to sack Israel. He almost took Jerusalem, but Jehoash, King of Judah, gave him the priceless hallowed treasures of the House of the LORD and of the king's house to appease him.

2 Kings 13:4 - "Jehoahaz besought the LORD, and the LORD hearkened unto him. ...[and] gave Israel a saviour."

B | Chronicles, Not Chronological

Stories in Kings and Chronicles are often not chronological. The narrative covers two kingdoms (ten tribes of Israel in the North, two tribes of Judah in the South), and two lines of Kings. The stories are necessarily back and forth. Some kings ruled more than 30 years, others, only a few. Many characters have duplicate names. Several characters have multiple names. Many foreign characters appear. Chronicles includes details not in Kings. Diligent study cures confusion.

2 Kings 13:8 - "The rest of the acts of Jehoahaz, ...are they not written in the book of the chronicles of the kings of Israel?"

C | Do It With Thy Might

Before dying of a sickness, Elisha said to Joash, King of Israel, "Take bow and arrows. Open the window eastward. Shoot." And he shot. And he said, "The arrow of the LORD'S deliverance from Syria." And he said, "Take the arrows. Smite upon the ground." And he smote thrice. Elisha was wroth with him. Ecclesiastes 9:10 says, "Whatsoever thy hand findeth to do, do it with thy might."

2 Kings 13:19 - "Thou shouldest have smitten five or six times; then hadst thou smitten Syria till thou hadst consumed it: whereas now thou shalt smite Syria but thrice."

D | God Restrains Hazael And Benhadad

Anyone should know that Israel's persistent backsliding was the reason why they were finally taken away as captives by the Assyrians and the Babylonians. But for hundreds of years, God postponed their dispersion, giving them countless undeserved opportunities to renounce their sins. God sovereignly prevented Hazael, king of Syria, and his son, Benhadad, from defeating and conquering Israel.

2 Kings 13:23 - "The LORD was gracious unto them, and had compassion on them, and had respect unto them, because of his covenant with Abraham, Isaac, and Jacob, and would not destroy them, neither cast he them from his presence as yet."

A | Asking For A Double Portion

Before Elijah rode the chariot into Heaven, he granted Elisha one request. Elisha prayed, "let a double portion of thy spirit be upon me." That recalls the blessing of the firstborn in each family. Every heir received an equal portion except the eldest, who received a double portion. Elisha stood first in line for Elijah's heritage. Surely enough, Elijah had seven recorded miracles, but Elisha had fourteen. The last miracle happened after he died.

2 Kings 13:21 - "When the man was let down, and touched the bones of Elisha, he revived, and stood up on his feet."

B | Amaziah Started Right, Finished Wrong

Amaziah, son of Joash, became King of Judah at 25. He did mostly right in the sight of the LORD. He killed his father's assassins and organized 300,000 volunteers and 100,000 mercenaries to conquer Edom. A prophet advised him against the mercenaries, so he fired them. Amaziah defeated Edom, but foolishly brought home their idols and burned incense to them. He arrogantly challenged Jehoash, King of Israel, who called him a "thistle" attacking a "cedar." Jehoash attacked and humiliated Amaziah and stole his treasures.

2 Kings 14:19 - "They made a conspiracy against him: ...and slew him."

C | Saved By An Evil King

Azariah (better known as Uzziah) succeeded his father Amaziah as King of Judah. Jeroboam II ruled Israel. Uzziah was the greatest and most famous king since Solomon, but Jeroboam II was as wicked as his namesake predecessor. "The LORD saw the affliction of Israel," who suffered bitterly because of idolatry and sin. Nevertheless, God, in longsuffering, can still save, even if He has to use an evil ruler.

2 Kings 14:27 - "The LORD said not that he would blot out the name of Israel from under heaven: but he saved them by the hand of Jeroboam."

D | God Sends Uzziah To A Leper Colony

Azariah (Uzziah) ruled Judah for fifty-two years, doing "right in the sight of the LORD." But Uzziah outrageously entered the Temple and offered incense with a censer. Azariah and eighty other consecrated priests commanded him to leave immediately. Uzziah got mad. "While he was wroth with the priests, the leprosy even rose up in his forehead before the priests in the house of the LORD," 2 Chronicles 26:19. Always stay in your God-ordained place.

2 Kings 15:5 - "The LORD smote the king, ...he was a leper unto the day of his death, and dwelt in a several house."

B | Jehu's Royal Lineage

For his role in purging Israel of Ahab, Jezebel and Amaziah, God promised that Jehu would have descendants on the throne of Israel for four generations. His son, Jehoahaz, was followed on the throne by his son, Jehoash, then his son Jeroboam II, then his son, Zachariah. The fifth generation king was Shallum - no kindred to Jehu. When God speaks to you, believe His Word.

2 Kings 15:12 - "The word of the LORD which he spake unto Jehu, saying, Thy sons shall sit on the throne of Israel unto the fourth generation. And so it came to pass."

C | Longsuffering Expires, Punishment Begins

Jehu's lineage ended when Shallum killed Zachariah and took his throne in Samaria. One month later, Menahem killed Shallum, and ruled for ten years. His son, Pekahiah succeeded him for two years, but was assassinated and succeeded by Pekah, for 20 years. God gives evil generations a season and opportunity for repentance. But none of these ever repented. Finally, the Assyrians began carrying away the first Israelites into permanent exile.

2 Kings 15:29 - "In the days of Pekah king of Israel came Tiglathpileser king of Assyria, and took ...the land of Naphtali, and carried them captive to Assyria."

B | King Jotham Of Judah

Jotham ruled Judah in proxy until the death of his father, Uzziah, who was smitten with leprosy for usurping the Temple Priest's office. At 25, Jotham became king and ruled righteously for sixteen years, alongside the great prophets Isaiah, Hosea, Amos and Micah. "Jotham became mighty because he prepared his ways before the LORD his God," 2 Chronicles 27:6. Jotham is proof that a son can and should rise above his father's failure.

2 Kings 15:38 - "Jotham slept with his fathers, and was buried with his fathers in the city of David his father."

C | Stupidity: Trusting Everybody Else, Spurning God

King Ahaz of Judah, son of Jotham, scorned the great prophets Isaiah, Hosea and Micah, and contemptuously sacrificed to idols, burnt his son to Baal, and gave the Temple gold and silver to Tiglath-Pileser, King of Assyria, for protection from his enemies. Ahaz copied an altar from

Damascus, placed it in the Temple, made offerings to Syrian gods, and desecrated the Holy Temple furnishings. His was nauseating folly. Crowned at 20, dead at 35, "they brought him not into the sepulchres of the kings."

2 Kings 16:12 - "The king approached to the altar, and offered thereon."

D | Northern Kingdom Ends Under Hoshea

The timeline on the nation of Israel ended sooner than that of Judah. The Northern Kingdom never had a righteous king after Solomon, so God was eventually forced to send them to judgment. Israel began to go into Assyrian captivity in the days of Pekah. He was assassinated by Hoshea, who was king when the Northern Kingdom finally ended. For 328 years, from Saul (1050 BC) to Hoshea (722 BC) the prophets had warned Israel against their sins.

2 Kings 17:6 - "In the ninth year of Hoshea the king of Assyria took Samaria, and carried Israel away into Assyria."

D | God Works By The Prophets

We owe it to ourselves to contemplate God's modus operandi. "The LORD testified against Israel, and against Judah, by all the prophets, and by all the seers, saying, Turn ye from your evil ways, and keep my commandments and my statutes." You can run from God, but you can't hide. He will always have the last word. Israel ignored Him to their damnation.

2 Kings 17:23 - "Until the LORD removed Israel out of his sight, as he had said by all his servants the prophets. So was Israel carried away out of their own land to Assyria."

B | Samaria

Samaria was the name of a city and a region. After Solomon died, Jeroboam ruled ten tribes from Samaria with godless government, an imitation temple, and perverted religion - a despicable alternative to Jerusalem. Jeroboam made all Israel to sin with pagan worship, including two golden calves. Eventually, Assyrians carried the Jews away and placed heathen citizens in Samaria, with one Jewish priest per city. Today, it is illicitly called the Palestinian West Bank. Jesus will soon reclaim it.

2 Kings 17:24 - "The king of Assyria brought men from Babylon, ...Cuthah, ...Ava, ...Hamath, ...Sepharvaim, and placed them in the cities of Samaria."

C | God + Other Gods = Does Not Add Up

After the Assyrians carried the Jews out of Israel, Assyrians filled the newly acquired cities. Once-Jewish cities became heathen communities. "Therefore the LORD sent lions among them, which slew some of them." They believed the lions came because they "knew not the manner of the God of the land." The Assyrian king sent Jewish priests BACK to live among the heathen and teach them how to fear Jehovah. Sounds like too many modern Christians. They fear God, but still love their "American Idols."

2 Kings 17:41 - "So these nations feared the LORD, and served their graven images."

C | "Nehushtan" - Copper Serpent

God-sent fiery serpents were biting the Israelites because of their murmuring. God instructed Moses to make a brazen serpent and have the people look upon it for their healing. Amazingly, almost twelve generations later, King Hezekiah found Jews burning incense to that brazen serpent! Idolatry! Hezekiah destroyed it, and God sent revival. Got any dead religious traditions you need to destroy?

2 Kings 18:4 - "He... brake in pieces the brasen serpent that Moses had made: for unto those days the children of Israel did burn incense to it: and he called it Nehushtan."

B | King Hezekiah Of Judah

Hezekiah championed one of the greatest revivals in Israel's history. At a time when the apostate northern tribes had been hauled off into Assyrian captivity, and his father, Ahaz, had recently been the most wicked of all Judah's kings, Hezekiah single-handedly turned the people back to God, removing high places, breaking images, destroying groves of idols, smiting Philistines all the way to Gaza, and trusting God like no king before him. Anybody can have a revival. Just do what it takes.

2 Kings 18:7 - "The LORD was with him; and he prospered whithersoever he went forth."

D | The Prophetic Implications Of Obedience

Both obedience and disobedience have prophetic implications. When the Psalmist said, "The steps of a good man are ordered by the LORD," the word "good" is not in the Hebrew text, suggesting that the steps of ALL men are ordered by the LORD. Whether or not you do His will, God predetermines your destiny. If you do well, you will be accepted. If you do not well, sin lies at your door.

2 Kings 18:11 - "The king of Assyria did carry away Israel unto Assyria, ...Because they obeyed not the voice of the LORD their God."

A | Give Your Problem To God

King Hezekiah received a vicious letter from the Assyrian king threatening to take control of Israel. Hezekiah had no might against Assyria, so he took the letter into the house of God and asked God to read the letter. That night, the angel of the Lord killed 185,000 Assyrian soldiers. God has solutions we can't even imagine.

2 Kings 19:14 - "And Hezekiah received the letter of the hand of the messengers, and read it: and Hezekiah went up into the house of the LORD, and spread it before the LORD."

C | When Your Enemies Are God's Enemies

The Assyrians carried away the ten northern tribes of Israel. So when Rabshakeh brought threatenings from Assyrian King Sennacherib, Hezekiah called the prophet Isaiah. He told Hezekiah not to be afraid of the Assyrians. He reminded Hezekiah that Sennacherib had not merely blasphemed Israel, but the Holy One of Israel. God destroyed Sennacherib. His own sons killed him.

2 Kings 19:36-37 - "So Sennacherib king of Assyria departed, ...and dwelt at Nineveh. And it came to pass, as he was worshipping in the house of Nisroch his god, that Adrammelech and Sharezer his sons smote him with the sword."

A | Hezekiah Prayed And Was Healed

King Hezekiah was dying, and Isaiah came to tell him to set his house in order. But Hezekiah turned his face to the wall and prayed to the LORD, weeping sorely. The word of the LORD told Isaiah to turn back and tell Hezekiah, "I have heard thy prayers. ...I will add unto thy days fifteen years." Isaiah said, "This sign shalt thou have." The shadow would go backwards ten degrees. Isaiah cried unto the LORD: and he brought the shadow ten degrees backward. Never accept defeat without a prayer of faith.

2 Kings 20:7 - "And he recovered."

D | Guard Your Precious Treasures

Hezekiah showed the king of Babylon's son all the precious treasures in the king's palace. Immediately, Isaiah prophesied, "All that is in thine house, ...shall be carried into Babylon: nothing shall be left, saith the LORD. and ...thy sons ...shall be eunuchs in the palace of the king of Babylon." (That was fulfilled in Daniel 1:3.) Hezekiah cast his pearls before swine. Jesus warns, "They will trample them under their feet and turn again and rend you."

2 Kings 20:19 - "Then said Hezekiah unto Isaiah, Good is the word of the LORD which thou hast spoken."

B | Manasseh Corrupts Judah, Provokes God

Manasseh reversed the good his father, Hezekiah, had done. For 55 years, he rebuilt high places, built altars to Baal (even in the Temple), made groves of idols, consulted familiar spirits and wizards, worshipped and served the host of heaven, burnt his sons in the fire, seduced Israel to do more evil than the nations whom the LORD destroyed, and "wrought much wickedness in the sight of the LORD, to provoke Him to anger."

2 Kings 21:12,14 - "Thus saith the LORD, ...I will forsake the remnant of mine inheritance, and deliver them into the hand of their enemies."

C | Following A Horrible Example

When Amon took the throne of Judah at 22, "he did that which was evil in the sight of the LORD, as his father Manasseh did. And he walked in all the way that his father walked in, and served the idols that his father served." Why waste your life following someone else's bad example? A godly life is its own reward. Had he followed God instead, Amon probably would not have been murdered at 24.

2 Kings 21:26 - "He was buried in his sepulchre in the garden of Uzza: and Josiah his son reigned in his stead."

A | The Reading Of The Law Causes Josiah to Pray

King Josiah restored the Temple after Manasseh desecrated it. Hilkiah, the High Priest, found the book of the Law. Shaphan, the scribe, read it out loud to the king. Josiah rent his clothes, exclaiming, "great is the wrath of the LORD ...because our fathers have not hearkened to the words of this book." He sent Hilkiah to enquire of the LORD. Hilkiah consulted Huldah the prophetess, and she prophesied over Josiah.

2 Kings 22:20 - "Thou shalt be gathered into thy grave in peace; and thine eyes shall not see all the evil which I will bring upon this place."

D | A Long-Prophesied King - Josiah

Around 920BC, Jeroboam built abominable altars and offered sacrifices to false gods. An unnamed prophet prophesied against Jeroboam's evil altar, foretelling a day when "a child shall be born unto the house of David, Josiah by name; and upon thee shall he offer the priests of the high places that burn incense upon thee," 1 Kings 13:2. In about 600BC, over three centuries later, that prophecy was fulfilled.

2 Kings 23:16 - "As Josiah turned himself, he spied the sepulchres that were there in the mount, ...and took the bones out of the sepulchres, and burned them upon the altar."

B | Josiah's Great Reformation Fails

Josiah called the elders, priests and prophets of Judah, and conducted an extreme purge of Judah's abominations. He killed the idolatrous priests and wizards, destroyed altars, images, vessels, groves, incense, high places, everything pertaining to Baal, Ashtoreth, Chemosh, Milcom, Molech, sun, moon, planets, familiar spirits, houses of sodomites, and horses and chariots consecrated to the sun. He commanded the people to keep the Passover unto the LORD. But Josiah could not change the hearts of the people.

2 Kings 23:26 - "Notwithstanding the LORD turned not from the fierceness of his great wrath, wherewith his anger was kindled against Judah."

C | Pernicious Sin

Huldah prophesied correctly. Josiah died before judgment fell on Judah. "There was no king before him, that turned to the LORD with all his heart, ...neither after him arose there any like him." But despite his heroic attempts to save Judah, Josiah could not change their wicked souls. His son, Jehoahaz, ruled wickedly and died within three months, followed by Jehoiakim (Eliakim) who ruled wickedly for eleven years. Judgment began. The end was near.

2 Kings 24:2 - "The LORD sent against him bands of the Chaldees, ...Syrians, ...Moabites, ...children of Ammon, ...against Judah to destroy it."

D | Nebuchadnezzar Takes Jerusalem

Josiah intercepted an Egyptian invasion of Assyria, and was killed at Megiddo, fulfilling Huldah's prophecy. Pharaoh Necho put Judah under tribute until Nebuchadnezzar conquered Egypt and imposed rule on Judah for three years. Jehoiakim died, and his son, Jehoiachin, ruled. Nebuchadnezzar seized Jerusalem. He took ten thousand captives, including all princes and men of valor. Israel's golden age was over.

2 Kings 24:15 - "And he carried away Jehoiachin to Babylon, and the king's mother, and the king's wives, and his officers, and the mighty of the land, those carried he into captivity from Jerusalem to Babylon."

D | Moses Prophesied Of Nebuchadnezzar

Sometime around 1355 BC, Moses prophesied the invasion and conquest of Nebuchadnezzar of Babylon (ca. 587BC) as consequence for forsaking the LORD. Warnings from God should not be ignored.

Deuteronomy 28:47-52 - "Because thou servedst not the LORD thy God, ...The LORD shall bring a nation against thee from far, ...whose tongue thou shalt not understand; A nation of fierce countenance, ...which also shall not leave thee ...until he have destroyed thee. And he shall besiege thee in all thy gates, until thy high and fenced walls come down," verse 63, "...and ye shall be plucked from off the land."

A | Zedekiah Calls On Jeremiah To Pray

As the end drew near for Jerusalem and Judah, Zedekiah wanted Jeremiah the prophet to enquire of the LORD what the outcome would be. Jeremiah was not nice. He prophesied copiously against Zedekiah - that God would utterly foil his efforts to fight Nebuchadnezzar, and "I myself will fight against you with an outstretched hand and with a strong arm, even in anger, and in fury, and in great wrath." Oh, don't wait too late to pray!

Jeremiah 21:7 - "And afterward, saith the LORD, I will deliver Zedekiah king of Judah ...into the hand of Nebuchadrezzar king of Babylon."

B | Jerusalem Falls Under Nebuchadnezzar

Nebuchadnezzar captured King Jehoiachin and exported nearly everyone from Jerusalem to Babylon. He installed Jehoiachin's 21-year-old uncle, Mattaniah, as a puppet king, and changed his name to Zedekiah. In his ninth year, Zedekiah rebelled against Nebuchadnezzar, so Nebuchadnezzar attacked Jerusalem. He killed Zedekiah's sons before his eyes, then put his eyes out, bound him, and carried him hostage to Babylon.

2 Kings 25:9 - "He burnt the house of the LORD, and the king's house, ...and every great man's house burnt he with fire, and ...brake down the walls of Jerusalem round about."

C | Sin Brings Total Ruin

Once Nebuchadnezzar conquered Jerusalem and hauled off most of its citizens, some soldiers remained to finish the plunder, raiding the treasures in the house of the LORD, and cutting to pieces the holy furnishings of gold, silver and brass. He left poor people to be vinedressers and husbandmen. He installed Gedaliah as governor, but he was quickly assassinated. Most of the survivors finally fled to Egypt. Back in Babylon, the king released Jehoiachin from prison and gave him a permanent allowance as a dignitary in Babylon.

2 Kings 25:21 - "So Judah was carried away out of their land."

Lessons from the Book of
1 CHRONICLES

B | The Chronicles

Like the old stereoscope viewers, Chronicles adds a "third dimension," an additional spiritual and religious aspect to the books of Samuel and Kings. Ezra compiled about forty parallel stories and twenty-eight chapters of supplemental information, including extensive genealogies. This 3,500-year saga retells the stories of Samuel, Saul, David, Solomon, construction of the great Temple in Jerusalem, the divided kingdom, captivity in Babylon, the return from exile, up to the days of Ezra and Nehemiah.

1 Chronicles 9:1 - "So all Israel were reckoned by genealogies; and, behold, they were written in the book of the kings of Israel and Judah."

C | Obscure People

Why does God put so many "boring" genealogies in the Bible? Follow the path of the ancients, both winners and losers. Why publish the lineage of Noah's cursed son, Ham; or of Abraham's illegitimate son, Ishmael; or of Abraham's concubine, Keturah; or of Esau, who sold his birthright? God keeps records we may not expect. God keeps track of saints and sinners; He follows both His friends and enemies. Even you. Even me. Nobody is obscure to God.

1 Chronicles 1:28 - "The sons of Abraham; Isaac, and Ishmael," verse 32, "...the sons of Keturah, Abraham's concubine."

C | Genealogies

We often skim genealogies as though they are unimportant and insignificant. But genealogies are extremely important in the Bible. Blessings, cursings, and prophecies often follow family lines. Inheritances are validated or invalidated, based on genealogies. Genealogies furnish some of the best proofs that God keeps His promises. Bible genealogies are not always comprehensive (skipping minor characters); nevertheless, they are reliable. The first nine chapters of Chronicles provide genealogies from Adam to the Babylonian captivity, with many sub-strings, including obscure descendants of Abraham, Ishmael, Esau, the twelve tribes of Israel, and several royal families.

1 Chronicles 1:29 - "These are their generations:"

B | Nahshon, Prince Of Judah

The most comprehensive genealogy of the twelve tribes is that of Judah, father of Israel's royal line. His eldest son by Tamar, Pharez, fathered Ram, who fathered Amminadab, who fathered Nahshon, the "prince of the children of Judah." Jewish tradition says Nahshon was first to cross the Red Sea. He was captain of Judah when Moses pitched the Tabernacle and gave the first offering at its dedication. Aaron married Nashon's sister. His exemplary life is probably why he was a chosen progenitor of Christ.

1 Chronicles 2:11 - "Nahshon begat Salma, ...Salma begat Boaz, ...Boaz begat Obed, ...Obed begat Jesse. ...Jesse begat ...David."

D | **David's Son, Nathan**

The genealogies in Genesis and Chronicles agree from Adam to Abraham. From Abraham to David, Chronicles, Matthew, and Luke agree. From David to Zerubbabel, Chronicles and Matthew agree. But from David to Jesus Christ, two different genealogies appear. Chronicles and Matthew agree, but Luke does not. Why? Luke traces the royal line to Jesus from David through Nathan (not Solomon), to Mary. Joseph descended from David through Solomon. Joseph was Jesus' legal father, but not biological.

1 Chronicles 3:1,5 - "Now these were the sons of David, ...born unto him in Jerusalem; Shimea, and Shobab, and Nathan, and Solomon."

A | **The Prayer Of Jabez**

A descendant of Judah, Jabez, prayed a noteworthy prayer. Some have tried to make it a formulary prayer, one that never fails, but if you are looking for a model prayer, I suggest the Lord's Prayer.

1 Chronicles 4:9-10 - "And Jabez was more honourable than his brethren: ...And Jabez called on the God of Israel, saying, Oh that thou wouldest bless me indeed, and enlarge my coast, and that thine hand might be with me, and that thou wouldest keep me from evil, that it may not grieve me! And God granted him that which he requested."

A | **Soldiers Should Pray**

The tribes of Reuben, Gad, and half of the tribe of Manasseh were valiant men, able to bear buckler and sword, to shoot with bow, and skilful in war. 44,760 made war against the Hagarites. "They were helped against them," because they prayed to God for help. They took rich spoils, including 50,000 camels, 250,000 sheep, 2,000 asses, and 100,000 men. If anybody should pray, soldiers should.

1 Chronicles 5:20,22 - "For they cried to God in the battle, and he was intreated of them; because they put their trust in him. ...because the war was of God."

C | **Ancient Occupations**

In the genealogies of Chronicles, several interesting tidbits of information emerge about ancient Jews. For example, the sons of Shelah, grandson of Judah, "wrought fine linen." Some were "potters, and those that dwell among plants and hedges: there they dwelt with the king for his work," - the king's domestic help. The sons of Simeon "found fat pasture and good, and the land was wide, and quiet, and peaceable." The three sons of Levi - Gershon, Kohath, and Merari, were full-time musicians.

1 Chronicles 6:32 - "They ministered before the dwelling place of the tabernacle of the congregation with singing."

B | Shechem And Gaza

Many prominent cities now claimed by the Palestinian Authority were key Israelite cities for hundreds of years. Not only do the first nine chapters of the book of I Chronicles furnish us with extensive genealogies of the tribes of Israel, but they also document many cities and towns where Israelites lived. Nowadays, the "anti-Zionist" crowd regularly denies Israel's true history, refuting that Israel ever controlled Jerusalem or ever had a Temple. But God knows the truth.

1 Chronicles 7:28 - "Their possessions and habitations were, Bethel. ...Shechem, ...Gaza. ...In these dwelt the children of Joseph the son of Israel."

D | The Lost Tribe Of Dan

The tribe of Dan is never mentioned in the genealogies of Chronicles. In the book of Numbers, it was the largest tribe, but Jeroboam placed a golden calf in Dan, leading them into idolatry. They were the first to go into captivity. But Ezekiel 48 prophesied "a portion for Dan" in the coming millennial kingdom of Messiah. Some Ethiopian Jews claim to be Danites. Modern Danites may not know their identity today, but God does. Ancient genealogies are in the Bible. Future genealogies are in the mind of God.

1 Chronicles 8:28 - "These were heads of the fathers, by their generations."

B | Those Who Returned From Babylon

Skip seventy years from where II Kings ended. If you read the Bible from Genesis to Revelation, you find this roll-call of repatriates - those who made it back home from Babylon - BEFORE the story of the captivity is even told. Your trial (captivity) is not the big story. Your triumph over it is.

1 Chronicles 9:2-3 - "The first inhabitants that dwelt in their possessions in their cities were, the Israelites, the priests, Levites, and the Nethinims. And in Jerusalem dwelt of the children of Judah, and of the children of Benjamin, and of the children of Ephraim, and Manasseh."

C | **God's House Before My House**

The Temple in Jerusalem was totally desecrated with idolatry and the worship of false gods by several kings before God removed the Jews to Babylon by Nebuchadnezzar. After seventy years of punishment, God brought the Jews back to Jerusalem. The very first thing they did was restore the Temple and establish true worship of God. They learned a hard lesson. Put God first.

1 Chronicles 9:13-27 - "...very able men for the work of the service of the house of God. ...priests; ...Levites; ...porters; ...keepers of the gates of the tabernacle: ...chief porters, ...lodged round about the house of God."

D | **The Prophetic Destiny Of Transgressors**

It may not appear to be a prophetic subject, but being punished for one's sins is truly a prophetic fulfillment. When King Saul disobeyed God by sparing the Amalekites and consulting the witch of Endor, he sorely transgressed against God. We all have prophetic destiny; a reward if we have obeyed the Gospel, or eternal punishment if our sins remain unforgiven.

1 Chronicles 10:13 - "So Saul died for his transgression which he committed against the LORD, ...and also for asking counsel of one that had a familiar spirit, ...And enquired not of the LORD: therefore he slew him."

B | **Water Of The Well Of Bethlehem**

David bunkered in the cave of Adullam while fighting Philistines in the valley of Rephaim and Bethlehem. He thirsted and longingly said, "Oh that one would give me drink of the water of the well of Bethlehem, that is at the gate!" Three men risked their lives, penetrated enemy lines, and brought David water. He was humbled. When men honor you, give God the glory.

1 Chronicles 11:18-19 - "David would not drink of it, but poured it out to the LORD, and said, shall I drink the blood of these men that have put their lives in jeopardy?"

C | **Help Will Come On Time**

After many fugitive years, David's exile was over. It was time for prophecy to be fulfilled. Armed and mighty men began to show up from every tribe in Israel to help David - from Benjamin, Judah, Ephraim,

Manasseh, Simeon, Levi, Gad, Issachar, Zebulun, Naphtali, Dan, Reuben, and Asher. God will turn your captivity. Help will come.

1 Chronicles 12:22,38 - "Day by day there came to David to help him, until it was a great host, like the host of God. ...All these men of war ...came with a perfect heart to Hebron, to make David king over all Israel."

A | They Enquired Not In The Days Of Saul

Here is a conspicuous Biblical phenomenon. Most stories about righteous men include some account of prayer. Stories of evil men almost never mention prayer. It is a warning signal, like a canary in a coal mine. If the canary dies, miners know that oxygen levels are low and evacuate the mine. When prayer levels get too low, it is time to pray or evacuate. That was Saul's weakness. David immediately rectified that problem.

1 Chronicles 13:3 - "Let us bring again the ark of our God to us: for we enquired not at it in the days of Saul."

D | Prophetic Anointing

The anointing of God is incomprehensibly powerful. When Samuel first saw the boy David, the LORD said, "Arise, anoint him: for this is he." Samuel took the horn of oil and anointed him. The Spirit of the LORD came upon David. Nobody could have imagined how profoundly God would use David.

1 Chronicles 14:2,17 - "David perceived that the LORD had confirmed him king over Israel, for his kingdom was lifted up on high, because of his people Israel. And the fame of David went out into all lands; and the LORD brought the fear of him upon all nations."

A | "We Sought Him Not After The Due Order"

Since Moses, men enquired of the LORD before the Ark of the Covenant. But Philistines captured it, then returned it, and it was stored away for nearly eighty years. David started to move it to Jerusalem, but the priests were not sanctified properly, and Uzzah died when he touched it. People often handle holy things recklessly, but God is holy and must be approached on His terms.

1 Chronicles 15:13 - "Because ye did it not [sanctify yourselves] at the first, the LORD our God made a breach upon us, for that we sought him not after the due order."

B | The Tabernacle Of David

In the Tabernacle of David, David praised God with boisterous singing, music, even dancing. He ordered harps, psalteries, timbrels, cornets, trumpets, cymbals and choirs of singers. Amos 9:11 prophesied, "In that day will I raise up the tabernacle of David that is fallen." In Acts 15:16, James identified the New Testament Church as the revived Tabernacle of David. Sing! Play! Dance! Worship!

1 Chronicles 15:16 - "David spake to the chief of the Levites to appoint their brethren to be the singers with instruments of musick, psalteries and harps and cymbals, sounding, by lifting up the voice with joy."

C | Bring Back The Glory Of God

The Ark of the Covenant was absent from the Tabernacle of Moses for almost a century. The Tabernacle was impertinent without it. Rituals are useless when the glory of the LORD departs. Levites "brought the ark of God, and set it in the midst of the tent that David had pitched for it: and they offered burnt sacrifices and peace offerings before God." David wrote a beautiful song for Asaph and choir to sing.

1 Chronicles 16:37 - "He left there before the ark of the covenant of the LORD Asaph and his brethren, to minister before the ark continually."

D | "I Will Ordain A Place For My People Israel"

David told Nathan that he wanted to build a house for the LORD. But God spoke to the prophet and said He did not want David to build it. God already had plans for David and Israel. Nathan uttered a great prophecy. God ordained a place for Israel. Today, no UN Resolution or terrorist organization can ever define Israeli borders.

1 Chronicles 17:9 - "I will ordain a place for my people Israel, and will plant them, and they shall dwell in their place, and shall be moved no more; neither shall the children of wickedness waste them any more."

A | Praise And Worship - Prelude To Victory

David pitched the Tabernacle for the Ark because he wanted to bring back the glory of God to Israel. He choreographed a truly epic event with massive sacrifices, lavish offerings, prayers, praise, worship, exultant music, feasts and celebrations. Is it any surprise then, that Almighty God quickly gave David dominion over the greatest nation that ever existed in that territory? Almost overnight, David ruled from Egypt to Syria to the Euphrates. Praising God is a prelude to victory.

1 Chronicles 17:19 - "O LORD, for thy servant's sake, and according to thine own heart, hast thou done all this greatness."

B | David's Exploits

Shortly after David was established as king, he set out to subdue his enemies round about. He smote the Philistines, took Gath, Moab, Edom, Ammon, and Amalek. From King Hadarezer of Zobah, David took 1000 chariots, 7000 horsemen, 20,000 footmen, plus shields of gold, and very much brass. When Syrians tried to intervene, David slew 22,000, and conquered Damascus. All these people became David's servants, and the spoils of gold, silver and brass, David dedicated to the LORD.

1 Chronicles 18:14 - "So David reigned over all Israel, and executed judgment and justice among all his people."

C | When People Misjudge Your Motives

David's sent condolences to Hanun, king of Ammon, over the death of his father, but Hanun's princes accused David of spying on them. To make a long story short, Hanun hired Syrian and Mesopotamian mercenaries and declared a massive war on David. David sent Joab and his mighty men against them, and they whipped them soundly. People who misjudge your motives can cause you lots of trouble, but cannot defeat you.

1 Chronicles 19:18 - "The Syrians fled before Israel; and David slew of the Syrians seven thousand men which fought in chariots, and forty thousand footmen."

D | "I Will Subdue All Thine Enemies"

In Nathan's prophecy (1 Chronicles 17), the LORD said to David, "...Moreover I will subdue all thine enemies." Many adversaries arose. Ammonites from Rabbah came, but David won "exceeding much spoil" from them. Philistines attacked almost continuously, but lost again and again.

1 Chronicles 20:6-7 - "There was war at Gath, where was a man of great stature, whose fingers and toes were four and twenty, six on each hand, and six on each foot: and he also was the son of the giant. But when he defied Israel, Jonathan the son of Shimea David's brother slew him."

A | A National Tragedy Turned Into A National Treasure

David angered God by numbering Israel, so he repented. "I have sinned greatly, ...I have done very foolishly." An angel smote 70,000 men. David prayed again, "Let thine hand, I pray thee, O LORD my God, be on me, ...but not on thy people." God required David to build an altar and make sacrifices where the angel stood. David bought the place, and Solomon eventually built the Temple there. Prayer turned a national tragedy into a national treasure.

1 Chronicles 21:27 - "And the LORD commanded the angel; and he put up his sword again into the sheath thereof."

B | David Prepares For The Temple

God forbid David to build the Temple, so David prepared abundantly before his death; wrought stones, cedar trees, an hundred thousand talents of gold, a thousand talents of silver; brass, iron, timber and stone. He also provided cunning workers in every craft. David's example says, "Do everything you possibly can for God."

1 Chronicles 22:5 - "David said, ...the house that is to be builded for the LORD must be exceeding magnifical, of fame and of glory throughout all countries: ...Then he called for Solomon his son, and charged him to build an house for the LORD God of Israel."

C | That They May Dwell In Jerusalem Forever

David fought valiantly and worked obsessively to build a nation and a religion that would glorify God for ages to come. He returned the Ark to its central role. He called Levites to keep the charge of the Tabernacle. He provided extensively for a new Temple. He established officers, judges, musicians, singers - key people in key roles everywhere. May God make us valiant to build righteous homes, churches, and nations for God and our children.

1 Chronicles 23:25 - "David said, The LORD God of Israel hath given rest unto his people, that they may dwell in Jerusalem for ever."

D | Aaron's Posterity Recertified

God told Moses, "In the tabernacle of the congregation ...Aaron and his sons shall order it from evening to morning before the LORD: it shall be a statute for ever unto their generations." Exodus 27:21. Three hundred years later, David ordained the descendants of Aaron's sons, Eleazar and Ithamar, as overseers of the house of God. No matter how long ago God made a promise to you, it is still valid.

1 Chronicles 24:5 - "Thus were they divided by lot, one sort with another; for the governors of the sanctuary, and governors of the house of God."

A | Prophesying With Instruments

The Hebrew word, "naba," is translated "prophesy," and means "speak or sing by inspiration." David assigned the sons of Asaph, Heman and Jeduthun to prophesy with harps, psalteries and cymbals. Others were "to lift up the horn." They "prophesied according to the order of the king, ...to give thanks and to praise the LORD." Twenty-four courses of twelve musicians created a 288 member orchestra and choir.

1 Chronicles 25:6 - "All these were under the hands of their father for song in the house of the LORD, with cymbals, psalteries, and harps, for the service of the house of God."

B | Treasures In The House Of God

In addition to the ministry of the priests, the house of the LORD in Jerusalem housed tithes and offerings from the people, priceless Temple treasures, and vast spoils of war brought home by Israel's armies. David organized "strong" and "mighty" men called "porters," grouped by family clans, to guard the doors and gates of this veritable "treasure house." About 1700 men in all managed and protected the treasures around-the-clock. Their salaries were derived from the spoils.

1 Chronicles 26:27 - "Out of the spoils won in battles did they dedicate to maintain the house of the LORD."

C | National Government

Every month, a fresh, new staff of 24,000 men over the age of 20 served the king. His captains oversaw the king's treasures, storehouses in the fields, cities, villages and castles, vineyards, olive and sycamore groves, cattle herds, camels, asses, and flocks. He also had scribes, counselors, wise men, "king's companion" and an army general.

1 Chronicles 27:1 - "The chief fathers and captains of thousands and hundreds, and their officers that served the king in any matter of the courses, which came in and went out month by month, ...of every course were twenty and four thousand."

D | The Pattern Of The Temple

God gave Moses the explicit pattern for the Tabernacle in the wilderness (Exodus 25:9). God also gave David explicit plans for the Temple. Although we speak of the Temple of Solomon, it is more accurately the Temple of David, because David provided EVERYTHING pertaining to the Temple, including the laborers. Solomon only followed David's "pattern of all that he had by the spirit."

1 Chronicles 28:11,19 - "David gave to Solomon his son the pattern, ...All this, said David, the LORD made me understand in writing by his hand upon me, even all the works of this pattern."

A | David Prayed An Epic Prayer For Solomon

David called all Israel to Jerusalem to inaugurate Solomon. This epic event also launched construction of the new Temple. The people greatly rejoiced and made countless offerings to the LORD. David prayed one of the greatest prayers ever prayed by a ruler. I recommend you read it completely.

1 Chronicles 29:19,25 - "Give unto Solomon my son a perfect heart, to keep thy commandments, thy testimonies, and thy statutes, and to do all these things, and to build the palace, for the which I have made provision. ...And the LORD magnified Solomon exceedingly in the sight of all Israel."

Lessons from the Book of
2 CHRONICLES

C | Wisdom and Knowledge Is Granted Unto Thee

After his inauguration, Solomon led the people five miles north of Jerusalem to the Tabernacle of Moses on the high place at Gibeon. He burnt a thousand offerings on the Brazen Altar. That night, God said, "Ask what I shall give thee." "Give me now wisdom and knowledge." Ask. Ye shall receive.

2 Chronicles 1:11-12 - "God said to Solomon, ...Wisdom and knowledge is granted unto thee; and I will give thee riches, and wealth, and honour, such as none of the kings have had that have been before thee, neither shall there any after thee have the like."

D | The Temple - An Ordinance Forever

"Solomon determined to build an house for the name of the LORD."
David called it "a palace for the LORD God." Built on a divine pattern,
virtually every aspect of the Temple had prophetic meaning - a sermon
that never stops preaching.

2 Chronicles 2:4 - "I build an house to the name of the LORD my God,
...to burn before him sweet incense, and for the continual shewbread,
and for the burnt offerings morning and evening, on the sabbaths, and on
the new moons, and on the solemn feasts of the LORD our God. This is
an ordinance for ever to Israel."

B | Construction On The Temple Begins

David delivered the God-given Temple plans to Solomon, donating
enormous supplies of timber, stone, gold, silver, brass, iron, and more.
David even contracted many of the workers. Solomon spent four years
accumulating the rest of the materials and laborers.

2 Chronicles 3:1-2 - "Solomon began to build the house of the LORD at
Jerusalem in mount Moriah, where the LORD appeared unto David his
father, in the place that David had prepared in the threshingfloor of
Ornan the Jebusite. And he began to build in the second day of the
second month, in the fourth year of his reign."

A | Mount Moriah - God's Altar And House Of Prayer

ALL ON MOUNT MORIAH: Melchizedek. Salem. Jerusalem. Abraham.
Altar. Isaac. Angel. Covenant with Abraham. "Jehovahjireh - Mount of the
LORD." Threshingfloor of Ornan. David. Altar. Tabernacle of David. Ark
of the Covenant. Temple of Solomon. "Them will I bring to my holy
mountain, and make them joyful in my house of prayer: their burnt
offerings ...shall be accepted upon mine altar," Isaiah 56:7. Crowds
cheered, "Hosanna!" Jesus scourged. Eastern Gate. Second Coming.
Antichrist's demise, Millennial Temple. Holy Place.

2 Chronicles 3:1 - "Solomon began to build the house of the LORD at
Jerusalem in mount Moriah, where the LORD appeared unto David."

B | God Designs His Own House

"These are the things wherein Solomon was instructed for the building of
the house of God." The pattern God gave David was extremely detailed.
Measurements of the porch and house. Gold overlayments. Ceilings.
Garnishments. Beams. Posts. Walls. Doors. Engravings. Weight of nails.

Golden Cherubims. Blue, purple and crimson linen vail. Pillars. Brazen Altar. Molten sea. Lavers. Golden Candlesticks. Courts. Pots. Shovels. Basins. Vessels. Golden Altar. Table of Shewbread. Snuffers. God controls details in His present temple, too - our lives!

2 Chronicles 4:11 - "Huram finished the work that he was to make for king Solomon for the house of God."

C | The Glory of the LORD

The house of the LORD was finished. The priests moved all the holy furnishings inside. Solomon offered thousands of sacrifices. At last, the Ark came, with "two tablets which Moses put therein at Horeb." Singers and musicians jubilantly heralded the moment. Suddenly, "the house was filled with a cloud." Here is the crowning glory of all things religious. GOD'S PRESENCE! Few have ever seen it. Ask God. "Show me Thy glory!"

2 Chronicles 5:14 - "The priests could not stand to minister by reason of the cloud: for the glory of the LORD had filled the house of God."

D | David's Throne Established

God would not allow David to build the Temple in his day, but Nathan prophesied that his son, Solomon, would build it, and that God would establish David's throne through Solomon. Adversaries tried diligently to prevent Solomon from becoming king, but at the Temple dedication, Solomon declared the prophecy fulfilled. God's word will never fail.

2 Chronicles 6:10 - "...for I am risen up in the room of David my father, and am set on the throne of Israel, as the LORD promised, and have built the house for the name of the LORD God of Israel."

A | Dedicatory Prayer

When Solomon dedicated the new Temple, his prayer was an awe-inspiring communion with God - a model template for all time. Acknowledging God's infinite sovereignty, his words flowed with truest worship, heartfelt contrition, and earnest intercession for God's best blessings upon the people. God's response was mind-blowing. Want to see God move like that? Pray like that!

2 Chronicles 7:1 - "...when Solomon had made an end of praying, the fire came down from heaven, and consumed the burnt offering and the sacrifices; and the glory of the LORD filled the house."

A | All The People Worshipped

The new Temple was a breath-taking showpiece of unprecedented wealth and beauty, but when God filled the house with His glory, nobody could even go inside. "The priests could not enter into the house of the LORD, because the glory of the LORD had filled the LORD'S house." Everyone fell on their faces and worshipped God.

2 Chronicles 7:3 - "When all the children of Israel saw how the fire came down, and the glory of the LORD upon the house, they bowed themselves with their faces to the ground upon the pavement, and worshipped, and praised the LORD."

A | The Lord Hears

Our Creator listens. The Spirit who made the worlds is attentive to our voices and hears every word we speak. We all have times when it seems "the heavens are brass," but don't you believe it! Not a word escapes Him. He who knows the number of the stars and calls them all by name, who sees every sparrow fall, and knows the number of the hairs of your head - He hears you!

2 Chronicles 7:12 - "The LORD appeared to Solomon by night, and said unto him, I have heard thy prayer."

A | The Promise Of Prayer

Abraham Lincoln said, "I have been driven many times to my knees by the overwhelming conviction that I had nowhere else to go." God promises faithfully to hear the prayers of His people. Who else in the world guarantees to care and intervene? Abandon all others, but seek the Lord!

2 Chronicles 7:14 - "If my people, which are called by my name, shall humble themselves, and pray, and seek my face, and turn from their wicked ways; then will I hear from heaven, and will forgive their sin, and will heal their land."

B | The House Of Prayer

God was pleased to call Solomon's Temple a house of prayer. "I have heard thy prayer, and have chosen this place to myself for an house of sacrifice." "If my people, which are called by my name, shall humble themselves, and pray, and seek my face, and turn from their wicked ways; then will I hear from heaven, and will forgive their sin, and will heal their land."

2 Chronicles 7:15-16 - "Mine eyes shall be open, and mine ears attent unto the prayer that is made in this place. For now have I chosen and sanctified this house."

C | The Choice Is Up To You

God granted Solomon's prayer and said, "Now have I chosen and sanctified this house, that my name may be there for ever: and mine eyes and mine heart shall be there perpetually." But God warned, "If ye turn away, and forsake my statutes and my commandments, which I have set before you, and shall go and serve other gods, and worship them;" everything would come to naught. The choice is up to you. Obey God or lose everything.

2 Chronicles 7:20 - "This house, which I have sanctified for my name, will I cast out of my sight."

D | They Labor In Vain

Psalms 127 was written for Solomon: "Except the LORD build the house, they labour in vain that build it: except the LORD keep the city, the watchman waketh but in vain." Solomon built a glorious Temple and Palace, plus many cities throughout Israel. But despite great accomplishments, Solomon condemned himself when he began marrying many idolatrous women who corrupted him.

2 Chronicles 8:11 - "Solomon brought up the daughter of Pharaoh ...unto the house that he had built for her: for he said, My wife shall not dwell in the house of David king of Israel, because the places are holy."

A | No More Spirit In Her

When the Queen of Sheba saw Solomon's divinely-endowed wealth and wisdom, "there was no more spirit in her." Solomon's "ascent by which he went up into the house of the LORD" took her breath away. If we whole-heartedly, faithfully enter into His gates with thanksgiving and into His courts with praise, men might be similarly awestruck by our ascent into the house of the LORD.

2 Chronicles 9:5,8 - "She said to the king, ...because thy God loved Israel, to establish them for ever, therefore made he thee king over them, to do judgment and justice."

B | Solomon Reigned Over Kings

Solomon inherited great stature from his father, David, and for years, greatly honored God in words and deeds. While he did, God exalted him above all the other kings of his time. No man can take as much honor as God can give. Honor God, and He will honor you.

2 Chronicles 9:23,26 - "And all the kings of the earth sought the presence of Solomon, to hear his wisdom, that God had put in his heart. ...And he reigned over all the kings from the river even unto the land of the Philistines, and to the border of Egypt."

C | Kindness Is Better Than Cruelty

When Rehoboam became king of Israel, his elders advised him, "If thou be kind to this people, and please them, and speak good words to them, they will be thy servants for ever." But younger men foolishly urged him to be cruel. Why? Terrorism and cruelty are good for nothing! God is kind, even to the unthankful and evil (Luke 6:35). Effective leaders must treat people kindly.

2 Chronicles 10:10,19 - "Young men ...spake unto him, saying, ...say unto them ...'My little finger shall be thicker than my father's loins,' ...and Israel rebelled against the house of David."

D | Revival For Obeying The Prophet

God ordained for Israel to forsake king Rehoboam for his cruelty. But Rehoboam declared war on those who fled. God sent Shemaiah, commanding him to abandon his war plans. When Rehoboam obeyed the prophet, God granted amnesty to Rehoboam. Shortly thereafter, Jeroboam sent the priests and Levites back to Jerusalem, and all the God-fearing Jews who wanted no part of Jeroboam's golden calves returned to Jerusalem.

2 Chronicles 11:17 - "So they strengthened the kingdom of Judah, and made Rehoboam the son of Solomon strong, three years: for three years they walked in the way of David and Solomon."

A | Saved By Humbling Themselves

After three blessed years, Rehoboam and the people forsook the Law of the LORD. For their transgressions, God sent Shishak, king of Egypt, to oppress them. Shemaiah came again to Rehoboam and the princes of Judah and said, "Thus saith the LORD, Ye have forsaken me, and therefore have I also left you in the hand of Shishak." Rehoboam went into the Temple and humbled himself before the LORD. Repentance works.

2 Chronicles 12:12 - "When he humbled himself, the wrath of the LORD turned from him, that he would not destroy him altogether: and also in Judah things went well."

B | Abijah Overthrows Jeroboam

Rehoboam's son, Abijah, courageously challenged the legitimacy of Jeroboam, the idolatrous king of Israel. "The LORD is our God, and we have not forsaken him; ...but ye have forsaken him." Jeroboam ambushed Judah, but "the men of Judah gave a shout: and as the men of Judah shouted, it came to pass, that God smote Jeroboam and all Israel ...so there fell down slain of Israel five hundred thousand chosen men."

2 Chronicles 13:18,20,21 - "Judah prevailed, because they relied upon the LORD God of their fathers. ..the LORD struck [Jeroboam], and he died. But Abijah waxed mighty."

C | God-Given Rest

Asa succeeded his father, Abijah, as king of Judah. The land was quiet for ten years. Asa did good and right in the sight of the LORD, taking away altars and high places of strange gods, breaking down images, cutting down groves, and commanding Judah to seek the LORD. Ethiopians launched an attack, but Asa cried unto the LORD, and God smote the Ethiopians. The surest formula for rest and quiet is to do what is right in the sight of the LORD.

2 Chronicles 14:6 - "He had no war in those years; because the LORD had given him rest."

D | Your Work Shall Be Rewarded

King Asa won great spoils after chasing away a huge army of Ethiopians. The prophet Azariah said, "The LORD is with you, while ye be with him; ...but if ye forsake him, he will forsake you. ...Be ye strong therefore, and let not your hands be weak: for your work shall be rewarded." Asa "took courage," and became one of the great reformers in Israel's history - even dethroning his mother for her idolatry!

2 Chronicles 15:12 - "And they entered into a covenant to seek the LORD God of their fathers with all their heart and with all their soul."

A | The High Cost Of Neglecting To Pray

Asa was a godly king, blessed of God for thirty-five years. But when Baasha of Israel laid siege to Judah, Asa turned to Syria for help instead of seeking the LORD. Hanani the prophet rebuked him for foolishly relying on the Syrians. "From henceforth thou shalt have wars." Later, disease struck Asa, and again, he did not seek the LORD, but instead turned to physicians. Consequently, he died. God wants us to call on Him first. In times of trouble, pray!

2 Chronicles 16:12-13 - "In his disease he sought not to the LORD, but to the physicians."

B | The LORD Was With Jehoshaphat

Nowadays, a president faces the wrath of the media and political suicide if he says that God tells him what to do. But in Bible days, kings were duty-bound to obey God. When Jehoshaphat inherited the kingdom of Judah, he immediately set about to restructure the nation by the will of God. We should ardently support leaders who strive to live and rule by the Bible.

2 Chronicles 17:3-5 - "The LORD was with Jehoshaphat, because he ...sought to the LORD God of his father, and walked in his commandments, ...Therefore the LORD stablished the kingdom in his hand."

C | Teachers Teach The Book Of The Law

Jehoshaphat made an unprecedented move to educate the people of Judah in the ways of the LORD. He sent a "power-team" of princes, Levites and priests "to teach in the cities of Judah. ...and had the book of the law of the LORD with them." Sixteen of the best-learned men went "throughout all the cities of Judah, and taught the people." Our generation perishes for the lack of the knowledge of God. Teach them!

2 Chronicles 17:10 - "The fear of the LORD fell upon all the kingdoms of the lands that were round about Judah."

D | Chenaanah Versus Micaiah

400 false prophets urged Ahab to conquer Ramothgilead. Chenaanah made horns of iron and said, "Thus saith the LORD, With these thou shalt push Syria until they be consumed." But Jehoshaphat called Micaiah, a true prophet, who prophesied Ahab's utter failure. Chenaanah slapped Micaiah in the face and asked. "Which way went the Spirit of the

LORD from me to speak unto thee?" Ahab threw Micaiah into prison, "until I return in peace." But he never returned.

2 Chronicles 18:27 - "Micaiah said, If thou certainly return in peace, then hath not the LORD spoken by me."

B | Jehoshaphat Sets Up Judges

Jehu the prophet rebuked Jehoshaphat for his alliance with evil Ahab. So Jehoshaphat went across the land turning people "back unto the LORD." In each city, he set up godly judges under the chief priest, Amariah. He told the judges, "Judge not for man, but for the LORD, ...let the fear of the LORD be upon you." May God give us judges throughout our land who will judge for the LORD!

2 Chronicles 19:9 - "Warn them that they trespass not against the LORD, and so wrath come upon you. ...Deal courageously, and the LORD shall be with the good."

A | The King Prays For God's Help

Huge armies from Moab, Ammon and Mount Seir threatened Judah, so Jehoshaphat proclaimed a fast. People came into Jerusalem from every direction to seek the LORD. Jehoshaphat stood in the Temple and prayed, "We have no might against this great company, ...neither know we what to do: but our eyes are upon thee." Jahaziel prophesied, "Thus saith the LORD, ...Be not afraid nor dismayed by reason of this great multitude; for the battle is not yours, but God's. ...stand ye still, and see the salvation of the LORD."

2 Chronicles 20:18 - "All Judah ...fell before the LORD, worshipping the LORD."

C | Praise The Beauty Of Holiness

After Jehoshaphat prayed for God's help, a host of Levites stood and loudly praised the LORD. Jehoshaphat's faith soared. "Hear me, O Judah, ...Believe in the LORD your God, so shall ye be established; believe his prophets, so shall ye prosper." He "appointed singers unto the LORD, and that should praise the beauty of holiness, as they went out before the army." As they sang and magnified God, their enemies slew each other. Dead bodies lay everywhere. "None escaped."

2 Chronicles 20:28 - "And they came to Jerusalem with psalteries and harps and trumpets unto the house of the LORD."

D | Elijah Prophesies Jehoram's Fatal Disease

Jehoshaphat's eldest son, Jehoram, was an evil king. He killed all his brothers and many princes in Israel. His wife was a daughter of Ahab and Jezebel. Elijah wrote a letter to Jehoram, condemning his evils. "Behold, with a great plague will the LORD smite thy people, ...And thou shalt have great sickness by disease of thy bowels, until thy bowels fall out." God simply will not tolerate sin indefinitely.

2 Chronicles 21:19 - "And it came to pass, ...after the end of two years, his bowels fell out by reason of his sickness: so he died of sore diseases."

A | Prayer's Good Reputation

When Jehoram died, Ahaziah, his youngest son, became king of Judah. His mother was the daughter of Ahab and Jezebel. "They were his counsellors," so he emulated their evil ways. Like Ahab, he attempted to take Ramothgilead, and like Ahab, he failed. Jehu, who slew Jezebel, slew Ahaziah, too. Ordinarily, kings who died disgracefully did not receive a proper burial, but in honor of his prayerful grandfather, Jehoshaphat, Ahaziah was buried.

2 Chronicles 22:9 "When they had slain him, they buried him: Because, said they, he is the son of Jehoshaphat, who sought the LORD with all his heart."

B | Ahab's Wicked Influence Finally Dies

Ahab and Jezebel's wicked son, Jehoram (Joram) became king of Israel. Their wicked daughter, Athaliah, married the king of Judah, also named Jehoram. He died, and wicked son, Ahaziah, became king. God told Elijah to anoint Jehu king of Israel, who immediately executed both kings Joram and Ahaziah. Athaliah murdered her sons and claimed queenship. But Joash, her baby, was saved alive by her daughter, Jehosheba (and son-in-law, Jehoiada, the High Priest). Eventually, soldiers killed Athaliah and Joash became king of Judah.

2 Chronicles 23:21 - "The people of the land rejoiced: ...after that they had slain Athaliah."

C | "Preacher Religion"

Some people only do right while the preacher holds them accountable. Joash was counseled extensively most of his life by Jehoiada the High Priest. "Joash did that which was right in the sight of the LORD all the days of Jehoiada the priest." He restored the Temple and vessels profaned unto Baalim. "But Jehoiada waxed old, ...and died." Joash was quickly enticed into evil by the princes of Judah. He forsook the house of God and served idols. Even if the Preacher dies, you are still accountable to God.

2 Chronicles 24:18 - "And wrath came upon Judah and Jerusalem for this their trespass."

D | Zechariah's Rebuke

When Jehoiada the High Priest died, King Joash and Judah slid into idolatry. But Jehoiada's son, Zechariah, stood up and rebuked their sins. The people angrily stoned him to death, but as he was dying, he said, "The LORD look upon it, and require it." Shortly afterward, Syrians attacked Judah and caused devastating losses of men and properties. Joash paid dearly for his backsliding. In the end, all backsliders will.

2 Chronicles 24:25 - "His own servants conspired against him for the blood of the sons of Jehoiada the priest, and slew him on his bed, and he died."

A | Foolish Prayers To The Losers' Gods

Amaziah ruled Judah for twenty-nine years. At first, he heeded the prophets, but after a great military victory, "he brought the gods of the children of Seir, and set them up to be his gods, and bowed down himself before them, and burned incense unto them." Such dumbfounding foolishness cannot be explained - worshipping gods who lost the battle; and rejecting God who gave victory.

2 Chronicles 25:15 - "The anger of the LORD was kindled against Amaziah, and he sent unto him a prophet, which said unto him, God hath determined to destroy thee, because thou hast done this."

B | Uzziah - The Strong Man Transgresses

Uzziah became king of Judah after God destroyed Amaziah. Uzziah did right in the sight of the LORD. Zechariah the prophet advised him. He prevailed against the Philistines and Ammonites, and his kingdom flourished. "But when he was strong, his heart was lifted up to his destruction: for he transgressed against the LORD his God, and went into the temple of the LORD to burn incense upon the altar of incense." God smote him with leprosy. You are never too old for pride to destroy you.

2 Chronicles 26:21 - "Uzziah the king was a leper unto the day of his death."

C | Learning From Others' Mistakes

Jotham began reigning in Judah before Uzziah, his father, died of leprosy. "He did that which was right in the sight of the LORD." "Howbeit, he entered not into the temple of the LORD." That statement means more than what appears at first glance. God smote Uzziah with leprosy for committing sacrilege. He entered the holy place of the Temple and trespassed the Priests' office by offering incense. Consequently, Jotham "entered not into the temple." Are you smart enough to avoid repeating others' mistakes?

2 Chronicles 27:6 - "Jotham became mighty, because he prepared his ways before the LORD his God."

D | Predictable Punishments

King of Judah at 20, dead at 35, Ahaz's sins included molding images for Baalim, sacrificing and burning incense practically everywhere, and burning his children in fire. Because of their shocking sins, God delivered Judah to their enemies again and again. Syrians took multitudes captive. The King of Israel killed 120,000. Edomites came and took captives. Philistines raided dozens of towns and villages. Your defiant, provocative sins enrage God to your great hurt.

2 Chronicles 28:19 - "The LORD brought Judah low because of Ahaz king of Israel; for he made Judah naked, and transgressed sore against the LORD."

A | Making A Covenant To Restore Sanctity

When Hezekiah inherited the throne of Judah, his apostate father, Ahaz, had profaned everything. The Temple was abandoned. The doors were shut, the lamps were out, the Altar of Incense was forgotten, and God was angry with the people. Hezekiah called the priests and Levites together. "It is in mine heart to make a covenant with the LORD God of Israel, that his fierce wrath may turn away from us." The first step to spiritual revival is a return to holiness by cleansing.

2 Chronicles 29:16 - "The priests went into the inner part of the house of the LORD, to cleanse it"

B | Hezekiah Tries To Save The Northern Tribes

Hezekiah made a magnanimous effort to save the northern tribes of Israel from their backsliding. He was not even their king! Many were already in Assyrian captivity, and Israel had not kept Passover for decades. Hezekiah sent letters calling all Israel to the house of the LORD at Jerusalem to keep Passover. Many mocked him, but many returned to the LORD. Intercessor, be encouraged! Some sinners only need a nudge!

2 Chronicles 30:8 - "Enter into his sanctuary, which he hath sanctified for ever: and serve the LORD your God, that the fierceness of his wrath may turn away from you."

A | Repenting for Someone Else

Who would you pray for if you knew YOUR prayers would prevent harsh judgment for sins? Hezekiah repented for the people's failures, and God showed mercy.

2 Chronicles 30:18-20 - "...had not cleansed themselves, yet did they eat the passover otherwise than it was written. But Hezekiah prayed for them, saying, The good LORD pardon every one that prepareth his heart to seek God, the LORD God of his fathers, though he be not cleansed according to the purification of the sanctuary. And the LORD hearkened to Hezekiah, and healed the people."

C | Prescription For Revival

Hezekiah successfully turned Judah and many in Israel back to God in one of the greatest reformations in the Bible. He destroyed all the images, high places and pagan altars, then carefully re-instituted the priesthood by genealogy. He totally cleansed the Temple and instructed the people to bring their firstfruits (tithes). Revival demands casting out the wrong and magnifying the right.

2 Chronicles 31:21 - "In every work that he began in the service of the house of God, and in the law, and in the commandments, to seek his God, he did it with all his heart, and prospered."

D | Hezekiah Prophesies Victory Over Assyria

Israel's revival inflamed Assyrian king Sennacherib, who had plundered Israel. He laid siege against several Judean cities. Hezekiah quickly protected the water supply in Jerusalem and encouraged his people, saying, "With him is an arm of flesh; but with us is the LORD our God to help us, and to fight our battles." Sennacherib boasted that no God could stop him, but the LORD sent an angel to cripple Sennacherib's army. He returned home shamefully and was murdered.

2 Chronicles 32:22 - "Thus the LORD saved Hezekiah and the inhabitants of Jerusalem from the hand of Sennacherib."

A | A Most Evil King Saved By Prayer

Manasseh was so wicked, he made Judah "worse than the heathen." He perverted the Temple of the LORD with altars to Baalim and all the host of heaven. He burnt his children in fire, used enchantments, witchcraft, familiar spirits, and worse. God judged Manasseh. Assyrians carried him into Babylonian captivity. Amazingly, Manasseh "besought the LORD his God, and humbled himself greatly before the God of his fathers." God hears even scoundrels when they repent.

2 Chronicles 33:13 - "And prayed unto Him: and He was intreated of him, and heard his supplication, and brought him again to Jerusalem into his kingdom."

B | Josiah - Righteous King Among Unrighteous People

Josiah was a noble reformer. He repaired the Temple, rediscovered the Law, consulted the prophets, overthrew idolatry and false worship, and commanded the Law be taught to the people. Unfortunately, his people resisted reform. Huldah the prophetess prophesied evil upon the people, but grace to Josiah for his heroic efforts. God will reward you for living righteously among sinners.

2 Chronicles 34:33 - "Josiah took away all the abominations out of all the countries that pertained to the children of Israel, and made all that were present in Israel to serve, even to serve the LORD their God."

C | You Will Miss A Righteous Man When He Is Gone

Josiah re-instituted the Passover in Judah and tried his best to turn Judah back to righteousness. But they refused to abandon their pagan practices. Huldah, the prophetess, prophesied that Josiah would go to his grave in peace, "neither shall thine eyes see all the evil that I will bring upon this place." God spared Josiah from seeing His judgments on the rebels. Shortly afterward, Josiah became senselessly embroiled with an Egyptian army en route to Syria and was killed. You will miss a righteous man when he is gone.

2 Chronicles 35:24 - "All Judah and Jerusalem mourned for Josiah."

D | The Demise, Captivity and Revival Of Judah

Josiah's sons and grandsons were wicked. King Jehoahaz was taken captive to Egypt. Kings Jehoiakim and Jehoiachin were taken captive to Babylon by Nebuchadnezzar. Lastly, King Zedekiah, saw his sons killed, then was taken, blinded, and carried to Babylon. Jeremiah accurately prophesied 70-years of captivity for the Jews, followed by a return. Cyrus fulfilled Jeremiah's prophecy when he commissioned the Jews to rebuild the Temple in Jerusalem.

2 Chronicles 36:22 "That the word of the LORD spoken by the mouth of Jeremiah might be accomplished, the LORD stirred up the spirit of Cyrus king of Persia."

Lessons from the Book of
EZRA

B | Cyrus Liberates The Captives

When, in all of world history, did a nation return to its homeland after nearly a century in exile? Name one, besides Israel! Yet Jeremiah prophesied it, and Almighty God made it so. Miraculously, Cyrus king of Persia, announced, "The LORD God of heaven hath given me all the kingdoms of the earth; and he hath charged me to build him an house at Jerusalem." He gave back the stolen Temple treasures and sent the Jews home.

Ezra 1:3 - "Who is there among you of all his people? his God be with him, and let him go up to Jerusalem."

D | Isaiah Prophesies To Cyrus Centuries Before He Was Born

Cyrus the Great received a divine mandate to send the Jews in Babylon back to Jerusalem to rebuild their Temple. The great historian, Josephus, wrote that Cyrus discovered it when he read his name in a prophecy in the Book of Isaiah - written 200 years earlier!

Isaiah 45:1-4 - "Thus saith the LORD to his anointed, to Cyrus, ...I, the LORD, which call thee by thy name, am the God of Israel. For Jacob my servant's sake, and Israel mine elect, I have even called thee by thy name: I have surnamed thee, though thou hast not known me."

C | God Frees Captives According To His Promises

Once the Jews' seventy-year "sentence" was over, Babylon fell to the Medes and Persians, led successively by Cyrus, Darius, and Xerxes (Ahasuerus). Zerubbabel led the first Jews back to Jerusalem in 538 BC and restored the Holy Temple. Ezra led the second wave in 457 BC and revived the priesthood ministry. Nehemiah came to rebuild the city and its walls in 444 BC.

Ezra 1:5 - "Then rose up the chief of the fathers of Judah and Benjamin, ...with all them whose spirit God had raised, to go up to build the house of the LORD which is in Jerusalem."

D | Documenting Prophetic Fulfillment

Ezra 2 provides a genealogical record of the migration and repatriation (in 538 BC) of 42,360 Jews and 7,337 maids and servants from Babylonian captivity to their native homeland in and around Jerusalem. Let the world take note that God fulfills His promises. That includes His promises to you and me.

Ezra 2:1 - "Now these are the children of the province that went up out of the captivity, of those which had been carried away, whom Nebuchadnezzar the king of Babylon had carried away unto Babylon, and came again unto Jerusalem and Judah, every one unto his city."

B | Sheshbazzar - Zerubbabel

His Chaldean name was Sheshbazzar, honoring their sun-god. But his Hebrew name was Zerubbabel, "born in Babylon." He was the key prince of Judah who Cyrus selected when he sent the Jews and their treasures back to Jerusalem. Zerubbabel became the "Tirshatha" - governor - of the new state of Israel. He rebuilt the altar, laid the foundation and began constructing the second Temple. He put away all priests who could not certify their genealogy.

Ezra 2:62 - "These sought their register among those that were reckoned by genealogy, but they were not found: therefore were they, as polluted, put from the priesthood."

D | The Prophetic Significance Of Zerubbabel And Jeshua

Zerubbabel descended from King Jeconiah through Shealtiel (Salathiel), thus a rightful heir to the throne of David. Jeshua, son of Jozadak, descended from Aaron, thus qualified to be High Priest. These two provided, as it were, both a legitimate King and a Priest to reclaim Jerusalem and the Temple. God remembers details men might never think about.

Ezra 3:2 - "Then stood up Jeshua the son of Jozadak, ...and Zerubbabel the son of Shealtiel, ...and builded the altar of the God of Israel, to offer burnt offerings thereon, as it is written in the law of Moses the man of God."

A | Prayer And Praise Return To Jerusalem

Within seven months, Jews returning from Babylon settled into the cities of Judah and began donating money to rebuild the House of God. By today's values, over a million dollars was quickly raised. They gathered in Jerusalem, built an altar, and burnt offerings to the LORD. By the second year, construction began. Following David's examples, priests and Levites played musical instruments, sang and praised the LORD.

Ezra 3:12 - "Many ...ancient men, that had seen the first house, when the foundation of this house was laid before their eyes, wept with a loud voice; and many shouted aloud for joy."

C | Enemies Always Try To Stop The Work Of God

As soon as Zerubbabel started rebuilding the house of God, old Syrian adversaries came, supposedly wanting to help. But Zerubbabel considered Temple work a sacred duty of Jews and refused outside help. Consequently, they fought against them, ultimately writing slanderous letters to Persia, accusing the Jews of rebellion, sedition and insurrection against the Persian king. Any time you take sides with God, His enemies become your enemies. For a while, they totally shut down the building project. But persevere! Right will prevail in the end.

Ezra 4:24 - "Then ceased the work of the house of God which is at Jerusalem."

D | Prophets Haggai And Zechariah Help Zerubbabel

When Zerubbabel started to rebuild the house of God in Jerusalem, trouble-making Syrians repeatedly asked the Persian authorities to stop Temple construction. But the prophets Haggai and Zechariah prophesied to Zerubbabel, who then appealed to Darius the king. Darius found Cyrus' original decree and sent his blessings to Zerubbabel. If God is for you, who can be against you?

Ezra 5:17 - "Let there be search made in the king's treasure house, which is there at Babylon, whether it be so, that a decree was made of Cyrus the king to build this house of God at Jerusalem."

A | Darius Of Persia Asks The Jews To Pray For Him

Zerubbabel asked Darius to find the decree issued by Cyrus authorizing the Jews to build the Temple. Darius found it and added his own decree, ordering all adversaries to leave the work alone and let them speedily build the House of God. He donated sacrifices for the God of Heaven, then added, "Pray for the life of the king, and of his sons."

Ezra 6:12 - "And the God that hath caused his name to dwell there destroy all kings and people, that shall put to their hand to alter and to destroy this house of God which is at Jerusalem."

B | Zerubbabel Finishes And Dedicates The Temple

Darius communicated with his governors beyond Jordan to cooperate with the Jews as they built the Temple. It took about 18-20 years. Kings Cyrus, Darius and Artaxerxes of Persia all supported the Jews, and Haggai and Zechariah prophesied the Word of the LORD as they built. Finally, His house was finished. Similarly, Jesus is now building His Church, but soon, He will be finished. Joy comes in the morning!

Ezra 6:16 - "And the children of Israel, the priests, and the Levites, and the rest of the children of the captivity, kept the dedication of this house of God with joy."

C | Blessed By The Hand Of The LORD

If you want to see what it is like to have the good hand of the LORD on your life, read Ezra 7, when Artaxerxes, king of Persia blessed Ezra to return to Jerusalem. Artaxerxes furnished him with incredible riches to rebuild and restore Jerusalem. "And whatsoever more shall be needful for the house of thy God, which thou shalt have occasion to bestow, bestow it out of the king's treasure house."

Ezra 7:6 - "Ezra went up from Babylon; ...and the king granted him all his request, according to the hand of the LORD his God upon him."

✓□   *My Daily Bible Companion*

B | Artaxerxes Underwrites Ezra's Mission

During Babylonian and Persian captivity, Ezra was a scribe in the law of Moses. Artaxerxes, king of Persia (modern Iran) genuinely feared the God of Israel. He generously supported Ezra's mission to teach the statutes and judgments of God, and "to beautify the house of the LORD which is in Jerusalem." Men of all nations should fear and worship God.

Ezra 7:23 - "Whatsoever is commanded by the God of heaven, let it be diligently done for the house of the God of heaven: for why should there be wrath against the realm of the king and his sons?"

A | Ezra Prays For A Safe Return To Jerusalem

Ezra and the Jews had to cross enemy territories while returning to Jerusalem from Babylon. He called a fast to seek God for safe passage. "I was ashamed to require of the king a band of soldiers and horsemen to help us against the enemy in the way: because we had spoken unto the king, saying, The hand of our God is upon all them for good that seek him; but his power and his wrath is against all them that forsake him."

Ezra 8:23 - "So we fasted and besought our God for this: and he was intreated of us."

C | God Protects Those Who Trust Him

Artaxerxes contributed great quantities of silver and gold to Ezra for the Holy Temple. Ezra was greatly concerned about getting it safely from Persia to Jerusalem without robbery. He entrusted the silver and gold to the priests and Levites until they could weigh them "at Jerusalem, in the chambers of the house of the LORD." They fasted and prayed for divine protection.

Ezra 8:31-32 -"...and the hand of our God was upon us, and he delivered us from the hand of the enemy, and of such as lay in wait by the way. And we came to Jerusalem."

D | Every Generation Must Answer The Prophets

Ezra had difficulty getting enough priests and Levites to return to Jerusalem. When he arrived, he was distraught to realize that most of them had married pagan wives, disqualifying themselves from the ministry. Ezra went into travail. "O our God, ...we have forsaken thy commandments, which thou hast commanded by thy servants the prophets." Even today, the prophets still speak to us.

Ezra 9:12 - "Give not your daughters unto their sons, neither take their daughters unto your sons, ...that ye may be strong, and eat the good of the land, and leave it for an inheritance to your children for ever."

A | **Prayer Sometimes Produces Painful Results**

Ezra knew that God would not allow him to use priests or Levites who had married heathen wives. He and the people spent much time in agonizing prayer, weeping sorely. The people realized they had sinned and promised to do whatever God required of them. Ezra administered a covenant oath committing the priests to put away their pagan families. It took great courage, but it had to be done.

Ezra 10:18 - "And among the sons of the priests there were found that had taken strange wives: ...And they gave their hands that they would put away their wives."

Lessons from the Book of
NEHEMIAH

B | **Nehemiah**

Nehemiah returned to Jerusalem 94 years after Zerubbabel arrived, and thirteen years after Ezra restored the priests and Levites. Nehemiah was cupbearer to Ahasuerus (Artaxerxes) in Shushan the palace where Esther was queen. Nehemiah asked his brethren how things fared for Jews in Jerusalem and learned that Jerusalem was in great affliction. The walls were broken down, and its gates burned. God heard Nehemiah's prayers and sent him to rebuild Jerusalem.

Nehemiah 1:4 - "When I heard these words, that I sat down and wept, and mourned certain days, and fasted, and prayed before the God of heaven."

A | **Praying Day And Night**

Nehemiah faced enormous difficulties after returning from captivity to Jerusalem to rebuild the fallen city. Cruel adversaries waged psychological warfare against him. Nothing but relentless heart-rending prayer got him through trying times. The people worked with a weapon in one hand and a tool in the other. Nehemiah never stopped praying until the walls were rebuilt, and the city was safe again.

Nehemiah 1:6 - "Let thine ear now be attentive, and thine eyes open, that thou mayest hear the prayer of thy servant, which I pray before thee now, day and night."

A | Nehemiah's Request

Nehemiah was cup-bearer for a pagan king, but he was alienated from the life he truly craved back home in Jerusalem. He was depressed, and the king noticed it. "What's bothering you, Nehemiah?" "How can I be happy when the land of my fathers is in ruins?" "What can I do for you?" God opened a dramatic door for Nehemiah. His prayer was ready. Within days, he was in Jerusalem, rebuilding the walls.

Nehemiah 2:4 - "...the king said unto me, For what dost thou make request? So I prayed to the God of heaven."

B | Rebuilding The Gates On The Walls Of Jerusalem

Nehemiah found the gates of Jerusalem needing repair: the sheep gate, fish gate, old gate, valley gate, dung gate, fountain gate, water gate, horse gate, east gate, and the gate Miphkad. Almighty God sent Nehemiah to Jerusalem to rebuild the walls and the gates. I pray that God will send mighty men to rebuild the walls of truth and righteousness and holiness in this generation.

Nehemiah 2:12 - "I arose in the night, I and some few men with me; neither told I any man what my God had put in my heart to do at Jerusalem."

C | The God Of Heaven Will Prosper Us

Nehemiah answered Ahasuerus, "Send me unto Judah, ...that I may build it." Nehemiah requested letters for safe passage and a letter for timber and stones for the gates and walls. The king granted all. After only three days in Jerusalem, Sanballat and Tobiah showed themselves enemies of the project. But Nehemiah secretly toured the city and its walls by night to appraise the situation. He called the people. "Come let us build up the wall of Jerusalem." People of God: BUILD!

Nehemiah 2:20 - "The God of heaven, He will prosper us, therefore we His servants will arise and build."

C | The Sheep Gate

If you take a close look at each of the gates of Jerusalem, you might see some typology. For instance, the first broken-down gate that Nehemiah repaired was the sheep gate, through which the people brought sheep to sacrifice in the Temple. This foreshadows the Lamb of God that takes away the sins of the world. The plan of salvation is completely void without the Lamb for sinners slain. We restore the sheep gate when we preach Christ!

Nehemiah 3:1 - "Then Eliashib the high priest rose up with his brethren the priests, and they builded the sheep gate."

B | The Fish Gate

The second gate that was repaired along the walls of Jerusalem was the fish gate. It is where the fish market was. When Nehemiah built up the fish gate, he helped to restore the fish trade. This reminds me of Jesus telling Peter and Andrew at Galilee, "Follow me, and I will make you fishers of men." Jesus was "fishing" for the souls of men for His eternal kingdom. Jesus told us to go into all the world and preach the Gospel to every creature. Let there be "fish!"

Nehemiah 3:3 - "The fish gate did the sons of Hassenaah build."

C | The Old Gate

The old gate was third to be repaired. Why rebuild the old gate? Jeremiah preached, "Thus saith the LORD, Stand ye in the ways, and see, and ask for the old paths, where is the good way, and walk therein, and ye shall find rest for your souls." Isaiah prophesied of great ones who would build again the old waste places and restore the old paths. The old way was a good way. All God's original works should speak to us continually. Never dismiss the lessons of your forefathers.

Nehemiah 3:6 - "Moreover the old gate repaired Jehoiada."

D | The Valley Gate

King Uzziah built a tower on the valley gate, overlooking Kidron Valley. Kidron is famous for many past and future conflicts, including Armageddon. We refer to our trials and tribulations as valleys. But David said, "Though I walk through the valley of the shadow of death, I will fear no evil, for Thou art with me." God told Ezekiel to prophesy to a valley full of dry bones, and they were all resurrected to become a mighty army. Nehemiah rebuilt the valley gate. We all must go in and out at the valley gate.

Nehemiah 3:13 - "The valley gate repaired Hanun,"

B | The Dung Gate

Each gate that Nehemiah repaired seemed to have a symbolic message for us. Such is true about the dung gate. The people of Jerusalem carried their trash, refuse, and dung out to the Tyropoeon Valley where there was a garbage dump. In every one of our lives, there are things that must be disposed. This is the message of repentance. Repentance not only renounces sin, it also puts it away. "Dearly beloved, let us cleanse ourselves from all filthiness of the flesh and spirit, perfecting holiness in the fear of God."

Nehemiah 3:14 - "But the dung gate repaired Malchiah."

C | The Fountain Gate

Nehemiah repaired the fountain gate, near the pool of Siloam. A fountain is a spring. Jesus said, "He that believeth on me, as the scripture hath said, out of his belly shall flow rivers of living water. (But this spake he of the Spirit, which they that believe on him should receive.)" Again, He said, "The water that I shall give him shall be in him a well of water springing up into everlasting life." This doctrine of the baptism of the Holy Ghost is the New Testament fountain gate.

Nehemiah 3:15 - "The gate of the fountain repaired Shallun."

D | The Water Gate

The water gate required no repairs. That is keen typology for the Word of God. "All the people gathered themselves together ...before the water gate; ...And Ezra the priest ...brought the law before the congregation ...And he read therein ...before the water gate from the morning until midday." Paul said that Jesus Christ sanctifies the Church, in part, by the washing of water by the word. The Word of God NEVER needs repair. It is forever settled in Heaven. Not one jot or tittle of it will fail.

Nehemiah 3:26 - "..to the place over against the water gate."

B | The Horse Gate

Nehemiah rebuilt the horse gate, where horses entered the king's palace. It is where wicked Queen Athaliah was slain. Jeremiah prophesies a day when this gate will be holy unto the LORD and will never be thrown down again. That could only occur in the millennial kingdom of Jesus Christ. Anciently, horses represented warfare. Prophetically, four evil horses patrol the earth in the last days until Jesus returns on His white horse to conquer all armies at Armageddon. The horse gate presupposes a militant Church. Child of God, fight on!

Nehemiah 3:28 - "From above the horse gate repaired the priests."

C | **The Gate Miphkad**

Nehemiah repaired the gate Miphkad, north of the Temple. "Miphkad" is variously translated "muster, gather, assign, appoint." Merchants gathered in the nearby markets. Workmen aggregated there when David prepared materials for the new Temple. Nethinims (Temple servants) established a community there. Most significantly, crowds of Roman soldiers carried out harsh judgments on Jesus there. The greatest "muster-gathering-appointment" of all is our final judgment. "It is appointed unto men once to die, but after this the judgment." What have you profited, if you gain the whole world and lose your soul?

Nehemiah 3:31 - "...the gate Miphkad."

D | **The East Gate**

The east gate, at the Temple entrance, welcomes Jesus Christ to return. As Israel went into captivity, Ezekiel saw cherubims carry the Throne of God from the Temple across the east gate. He prophesied that the eastern gate would later be shut until the Prince returns and enters it. (It has been shut since 1541 AD.) "His feet shall stand in that day upon the mount of Olives, ...before Jerusalem on the east," Zechariah 14:4. The Shekinah glory of the LORD will return to Jerusalem through the east gate as Jesus enters, following Armageddon.

Nehemiah 3:29 - "...the east gate."

A | **Nehemiah Overcomes Sanballat By Prayer**

Sanballat and Tobiah were vicious enemies of Nehemiah's restoration of Jerusalem, mocking and reproaching the workers. But the people had a mind to work, so continued building. Then the enemies conspired to make war against Jerusalem. "Nevertheless we made our prayer unto our God, and set a watch against them day and night." Through great determination, the Jews carried their weapons as they worked and finished the wall. Live for God and work for God, but always stay prepared for battle.

Nehemiah 4:17 - "Every one with one of his hands wrought in the work, and with the other hand held a weapon."

D | Will God Shake You Out Of His Lap?

Jews who returned to rebuild Jerusalem reclaimed the lands of their forefathers, but mortgaged them because they were poor and needed cash to survive. Some of their own brethren loaned them money, but took their sons and daughters as servants in foreclosure. Nehemiah was very angry and persuaded the lenders to promise to release the people's collateral so they could survive. Nehemiah prophesied divine punishment if they reneged.

Nehemiah 5:13 - "I shook my lap, and said, So God shake out every man from his house, ...that performeth not this promise, even thus be he shaken out, and emptied."

A | Should Such A Man As I Flee?

Sanballat and Tobiah tried desperately to stop Nehemiah from rebuilding the walls of Jerusalem, but failed. On their second attempt, they accused him of rebelling against the king. Then they tried to entice him outside the walls to capture him. Next, they sent a false prophet to scare him into hiding in the Temple. But Nehemiah said, "Should such a man as I flee?" Resist the devil, and he will flee from you.

Nehemiah 6:14 - "My God, think thou upon Tobiah and Sanballat according to these their works, and on the prophetess ...that would have put me in fear."

A | God Put It In My Heart

Twice, Nehemiah said, "God put it in my heart." First, it was to rebuild the walls of Jerusalem. Second, it was to gather the nobles, rulers and others to verify their genealogy. Certainly, the future of Jerusalem ultimately depended much more on the integrity of the people than with the integrity of the walls. If Nehemiah had only prayed, and not listened to God, Jerusalem's fate might have been vastly different. God IS speaking. Are you hearing?

Nehemiah 7:5 - "My God put into mine heart to gather together the nobles, and the rulers, and the people."

A | Corporate Worship

As repairs to Jerusalem progressed, Ezra called the people together into a street by the water gate for a reading of the Word of God. He stood on a pulpit of wood above all the people (the only pulpit mentioned in the Bible) surrounded by other priests. When he opened the book, all the people stood up. "Ezra blessed the LORD, the great God. And all the people answered, Amen, Amen, with lifting up their hands." Corporate worship is a glorious exercise.

Nehemiah 8:6 - "And they bowed their heads, and worshipped the LORD with their faces to the ground."

A | **The Joy Of The LORD Is Your Strength**

When Ezra first read the Word of God aloud to the citizens of Jerusalem, everyone wept greatly. The priests ministered to the people so they could understand the words they heard. They admonished everyone not to weep or mourn. "This is a holy day unto the LORD." Celebrate! Have a feast! Do not grieve! Everyone gathered branches and made booths, and celebrated the Feast of Tabernacles which had not been celebrated in decades. Sorrow weakens. Joy strengthens. Rejoice!

Nehemiah 8:10,17 - "Neither be ye sorry; for the joy of the LORD is your strength. ...And there was very great gladness."

B | **The People Make A Covenant At Jerusalem**

Israel celebrated the Feast of Tabernacles with rejoicing. But shortly afterward, the priests called a day of fasting and prayer in sackcloth. One fourth of the day, they listened to the reading of the Word. One fourth of the day, they spent confessing their sins. Then they stood and loudly prayed and worshipped the LORD. The Levites rehearsed the story of the Exodus, then called everyone to make a covenant to serve the LORD.

Nehemiah 9:38 - "Because of all this we make a sure covenant, and write it; and our princes, Levites, and priests, seal unto it."

C | **A Curse And An Oath To Walk In God's Laws**

The long, hard work of Zerubbabel, Ezra and Nehemiah at last culminated in a real revival of the fear of God. The people wrote and sealed a covenant to serve the LORD according to His laws. They promised to separate themselves from the ways of their heathen relatives. They promised not to allow their children to marry the heathen. And they promised to pay tithes and give offerings to support the Temple and the work of God.

Nehemiah 10:29 - "They clave to their brethren, their nobles, and entered into a curse, and into an oath, to walk in God's law."

D | **Casting Lots For Their Destiny**

Would you toss a coin to decide where you will live for the rest of your life? That is essentially what the Israelites did. Some volunteered to live in Jerusalem. The rest were chosen by casting lots. One of ten would dwell in Jerusalem. The other nine parts would dwell in other cities. The idea is not unusual. Generations of priests consulted the Urim and the Thummin to decide the will of God. Nothing is by chance.

Nehemiah 11:1 - "The rest of the people also cast lots, to bring one of ten to dwell in Jerusalem the holy city."

A | **Employed To Minister And Lead Worship**

While the Jews were in captivity, the names of the chiefs of the fathers, the priests and Levites were recorded. Their descendants then entered the ministry by pedigree. "At the dedication of the wall of Jerusalem they sought the Levites out of all their places, to bring them to Jerusalem, to keep the dedication with gladness, both with thanksgivings, and with singing, with cymbals, psalteries, and with harps." From Moses' day, God has ordained for full-time ministers to be paid.

Nehemiah 12:47 - "All Israel ...gave the portions of the singers and the porters, every day his portion."

B | **Nehemiah Sets The People In Order**

Nehemiah made an exemplary stand for righteousness. As he read the book of Moses aloud to the people, he saw things they were doing wrong and immediately acted to correct them. He ran off the Ammonites and Moabites who lived among them. He cast out Tobiah who was staying with Eliashib the high priest. He sanctified the Sabbath and disciplined the unclean priests. Nothing substitutes for obedience. Just do it.

Nehemiah 13:14 - "Remember me, O my God, concerning this, and wipe not out my good deeds that I have done for the house of my God."

Lessons from the Book of

ESTHER

C | God Can Remove Anyone Who Is In His way

God prepared the way for Esther to save Israel from genocide long before her time. Ahasuerus was king over a vast empire in the Middle East, extending from India to Ethiopia. Queen Vashti scandalously refused the king's request to appear at a state dinner at Shushan the palace. The king's wise men urged him to banish her. He did. Esther soon became the queen. God can remove anyone who hinders you from doing His will.

Esther 1:20 - "When the king's decree which he shall make shall be published, ...all the wives shall give to their husbands honour."

D | Esther Was Chosen Above All The Women

After King Ahasuerus had rid himself of Queen Vashti, the search was on for a new queen. Inside the palace, a captive Jew named Mordecai heard the news and brought his uncle's daughter Hadassah (Esther) to the keeper of the women. Mordecai warned her to keep her Jewish identity secret. Before anyone else knew, God knew that Haman would soon plot to exterminate all Jews. God was promoting Esther to save His people.

Esther 2:17 - "The king loved Esther above all the women, ...so that he set the royal crown upon her head, and made her queen instead of Vashti."

B | God Gave Mordecai Favor With King Ahasuerus

King Ahasuerus did not know that Queen Esther was a Jew. Mordecai had told her to keep silent about it. One day, while sitting in the king's gate, Mordecai overheard a conspiracy to assassinate the king. He quickly informed Esther, who told the king. The would-be assassins were caught and executed. Meanwhile, powerful men in the palace plotted to kill the Jews. But God was working to save His people. Mordecai's favor to the king was recorded. God orchestrated Mordecai's future defense.

Esther 2:23 - "It was written in the book of the chronicles before the king."

C | Enemies Would Destroy All God's People

King Ahasuerus promoted Haman above all the princes. Everyone bowed to Haman, except Mordecai. That infuriated Haman, so he decided to kill ALL Jews. Haman persuaded the king that Jews threatened his kingdom and must be destroyed. The king said, "do with them as it seemeth good to thee." Never underestimate your enemy's intentions.

Esther 3:13 - "Letters were sent by posts into all the king's provinces, to destroy, to kill, and to cause to perish, all Jews, both young and old, little children and women, in one day, ...and to take the spoil of them for a prey."

A | A Loud And Bitter Cry

When Mordecai saw Haman's decree announcing a date to exterminate all Jews, "he rent his clothes, put on sackcloth with ashes, and went out into the midst of the city, and cried with a loud and a bitter cry." He wore sackcloth into the king's gate, which was forbidden. Esther was exceedingly grieved and sent raiment to Mordecai, but he refused it. She sent a chamberlain to query Mordecai. Mordecai sent Esther a copy of the genocide decree. His loud and bitter cry arrested the queen.

Esther 4:9 - "Hatach came and told Esther the words of Mordecai."

D | You Have Come To The Kingdom For Such A Time As This

By law, anyone entering the king's chamber unbidden must be put to death, unless the king holds out his golden scepter. Esther feared, but Mordecai insisted that if she held her peace, "thou and thy father's house shall be destroyed: and who knoweth whether thou art come to the kingdom for such a time as this?" Esther knew she had to go. Mordecai called the Jews in Shushan to fast three days. Sometimes, the will of God is simply "Do or Die."

Esther 4:16 - "So will I go in unto the king, ...and if I perish, I perish."

A | A Three-Day Fast For Esther

Esther literally risked her life to appear in the inner court of the king's house. She had not seen the king in thirty days. If he did not raise his golden scepter toward her, by law, she must die. But a multitude of Jews fasted three days in behalf of Esther, and God gave her favor in the king's sight. He held out the golden scepter, and his offer was completely awesome.

Esther 5:3 - "What wilt thou, queen Esther? and what is thy request? it shall be even given thee to the half of the kingdom."

A | Esther's Petition

Haman negotiated with Ahasuerus, King of Persia and Media, to have all Jews in his kingdom killed on the 13th of the month. Mordecai saw the decree posted and sent word to Esther that she must intervene. All the Jews fasted and prayed for three days with great consternation. Esther and her maidens fasted likewise. Miraculously, the King totally reversed his decision because of Esther's intercession.

Esther 5:6 - "What is thy petition? and it shall be granted thee: and what is thy request? even to the half of the kingdom it shall be performed."

B | Esther Planned To Trap Haman

Ahasuerus happily received Esther to his throne and offered to fulfill her for request up to half his kingdom. All Esther wanted was for the king and Haman to come to a banquet she planned to prepare. Haman's ego swelled because he was invited with the king. But Haman's delight soured when he saw Mordecai in the king's gate. His wife and friends said, "Build a gallows a hundred feet high, and ask the king to hang him tomorrow!"

Esther 5:14 - "The thing pleased Haman; and he caused the gallows to be made."

C | God Can Force Your Enemy To Bless You

King Ahasuerus was sleepless, so called someone to read aloud from his book of chronicles. He heard about Mordecai foiling a plot to kill the king. "What honour and dignity hath been done to Mordecai for this?" "Nothing, sir." God was about to deliver Mordecai and all the Jews from annihilation. With shrewd irony, God used the very man who wanted most to kill Mordecai, to set him free.

Esther 6:4 - "The king said, Who is in the court? Now Haman was come ...to speak unto the king to hang Mordecai on the gallows. ...the king said, Let him come in."

D | Blindness To God's Will Is Fatal

Haman wanted permission from the king to execute Mordecai. But God had other plans. Mordecai, Esther and a multitude of Jews had been fasting, because they knew Haman planned to kill them all. Haman was totally ignorant of the plan and purpose of Almighty God. He expected to be honored, and Mordecai to die. Instead, Mordecai would be exalted, and Haman would die. It is dangerous not to know God's prophetic will.

Esther 6:6 - "Haman came in. And the king said unto him, What shall be done unto the man whom the king delighteth to honour?"

B | God Turns The Table On Haman

King Ahasuerus asked Haman what he thought should be done for "the man whom the king delighteth to honour." Haman vainly expected the king wanted to honor him and spelled out a lavish public ceremony. Ahasuerus then shocked Haman. "Do even so to Mordecai the Jew."

Esther 6:11-12 - "Then took Haman the apparel and the horse, and arrayed Mordecai, and brought him on horseback through the street of the city, and proclaimed before him, Thus shall it be done unto the man whom the king delighteth to honour. ...But Haman hasted to his house mourning, and having his head covered."

A | Esther Intercedes For The Jews

Haman despised Mordecai and was mortified as he escorted him through the city streets on the king's horse. His wife and friends warned him that if Mordecai was a Jew, he would never prevail - he would surely fall before him. Haman attended a banquet with the king and queen. Esther bravely announced, "We are to be destroyed, to be slain," and begged the king for the lives of her and her people. "Who presumes to do this to you?" the king asked. Esther indicted Haman.

Esther 7:6 - "And Esther said, The adversary and enemy is this wicked Haman."

C | You Will Pay Dearly If You Persecute God's People

When Esther revealed Haman's plot to exterminate the Jews to her husband, King Ahasuerus, Haman was terrified. Ahasuerus was so angry, he stood up and walked outside. While he was out, Haman fell on a bed where Esther was and pleaded with her for his life. Then the king accused him of attempting to force his wife. One of the chamberlains informed the king that Haman had built a gallows 100 feet high to hang Mordecai on.

Esther 7:10 - "So they hanged Haman on the gallows that he had prepared for Mordecai. Then was the king's wrath pacified."

D | The Enemies of God's People Are God's Enemies

God promised "I will be an enemy unto thine enemies," Exodus 23:22. God put down Haman. Ahasuerus removed Haman's ring and gave it and his entire estate to Mordecai. Then Esther asked the king to reverse Haman's decree to exterminate the Jews. The king gave the task to Mordecai.

Esther 8:8 - "Write ye also for the Jews, as it liketh you, in the king's name, and seal it with the king's ring: for the writing which is written in the king's name, and sealed with the king's ring, may no man reverse."

A | Great Rejoicing After Haman's Demise

Haman planned to hang Mordecai on the gallows, but God helped Esther expose his plot to exterminate the Jews, so the king ordered Haman hanged on the gallows instead of Mordecai. The king ordered Mordecai to publish an order through all provinces for Jews to resist every assault or attempt to spoil them, post-haste.

Esther 8:16-17 - "The Jews had light, and gladness, and joy, and honour. And in every province, and in every city, whithersoever the king's commandment and his decree came, the Jews had joy and gladness, a feast and a good day."

B | The King Of Persia Defends God's People

Persian law forbade Ahasuerus from reversing his own law. Haman's genocide order could not be nullified. To countermand it, Ahasuerus ordered Mordecai to command the Jews to defend themselves. When the Jews mustered, everyone feared them. "The day that the enemies of the Jews hoped to have power over them, ...the Jews had rule over them."

Esther 9:2 - "The Jews gathered themselves together in their cities throughout all the provinces of the king Ahasuerus, to lay hand on such as sought their hurt: and no man could withstand them; for the fear of them fell upon all people."

C | Great Tragedies Can Be Averted By One Intercessor

Mordecai became great in the king's house, and the rulers throughout Persia favored him and showed favor to the Jews. Ahasuerus ordered the Jews to fight against anyone who tried to harm them. Their casualties included ten of Haman's sons, 500 in Shushan the palace, and 75,000 others nationwide. The Jews faced extermination in Persia until Mordecai intervened. Will YOU stand up for God's people?

Esther 9:5 - "Thus the Jews smote all their enemies with the stroke of the sword, and slaughter, and destruction, and did what they would unto those that hated them."

D | The Feast Of Purim Celebrates "Hidden Miracle"

After Mordecai and Esther intervened to prevent genocide of the Jews, and 75,000 enemies died, the Jews celebrated two days of feasting and gladness. Since Haman cast lots (or "Pur") for the date of their execution, the Jews called the holiday the Feast of Purim. God is never mentioned by name in the book of Esther, but He is called the "hidden miracle" in their victory.

Esther 9:28 - "These days should be remembered and kept throughout every generation, every family, every province, and every city; and that these days of Purim should not fail from among the Jews."

B | Esther And Mordecai Rule In Persia

In the end of the story of Esther, the queen issued a decree that all Jews should celebrate the Feast of Purim throughout every generation. Her decree was written into Persian law. Mordecai became the second most powerful man in the Persian Empire - the largest empire in antiquity. You never know how far God might promote you if you do your best.

Esther 10:3 - "For Mordecai the Jew was next unto king Ahasuerus, and great among the Jews, and accepted of the multitude of his brethren, seeking the wealth of his people, and speaking peace to all his seed."

Lessons from the Book of
JOB

A | Job Offers Sacrifices To Sanctify His Children

The book of Job was probably written by Moses before the book of Genesis, making it the oldest book in the Bible. It tells the trials of Job, "perfect and upright, one that feared God, and eschewed evil." The first specific behavior mentioned of Job was that he made intercession for his children every day. Therefore, the first godly behavior ever identified in the Bible was INTERCESSION for children!

Job 1:5 "Job ...rose up early in the morning, and offered burnt offerings ...for Job said, It may be that my sons have sinned, and cursed God in their hearts."

B | The Devil

George Barna's 2006 survey showed that 68% of Catholics, 45% of Evangelicals, and 55% of Americans deny Satan's existence. But don't kid yourself. Unless you are prepared to burn your Bible, you'd better believe there is a devil. The Bible mentions "the devil" 61 times, "devils" 55 times, and "Satan" 55 times. Jesus said, "I beheld Satan."

Job 1:7 - "And the LORD said unto Satan, Whence comest thou? Then Satan answered the LORD, and said, From going to and fro in the earth, and from walking up and down in it."

C | God Will Let Satan Take Everything You Have

Satan ("the adversary") stood before God, after walking to and fro in the earth. God asked, "Have you considered my servant Job? That there is none like him in the earth, ...perfect, upright, ...fears God, ...hates evil?" Satan snapped, "He does not serve you without reasons." He contended that Job would curse God to His face without His protection and benefits. God let Satan take everything from Job to prove him wrong.

Job 1:12 - "The LORD said unto Satan, Behold, all that he hath is in thy power; only upon himself put not forth thine hand."

D | God Knew Job Would Not Curse Him

Satan had a license to kill. He killed Job's cattlemen, his shepherds, his camel tenders. He stole his oxen, asses, and camels, and killed his sheep. He killed Job's seven sons and three daughters.

Job 1:20-22 - "Job arose, and rent his mantle, and shaved his head, and fell down upon the ground, and worshipped, And said, Naked came I out of my mother's womb, and naked shall I return thither: the LORD gave, and the LORD hath taken away; blessed be the name of the LORD. In all this Job sinned not, nor charged God foolishly."

A | God Will Let Satan Afflict Your Body

Did God answer Satan's prayer? He came before the LORD again. He had been to and fro in the earth. Again, God said, "Have you considered my servant Job?" But this time, Satan said, "Put forth thine hand now, and touch his bone and his flesh, and he will curse thee to thy face." Again, God knew Job would not curse Him.

Job 2:6-7 - "The LORD said unto Satan, Behold, he is in thine hand; but save his life. So went Satan forth ...and smote Job with sore boils from the sole of his foot unto his crown."

B | Job Denounced His Wife's Evil Counsel

Satan threw everything he could against Job. All his possessions and family were gone. Only his wife survived. Then boils erupted from his head to his toes. He sat in ashes and scraped himself with a potsherd. His wife said, "Do you still have your integrity? Curse God, and die." But real saints never stop trusting God.

Job 2:10 - "He said unto her, Thou speakest as one of the foolish women speaketh. What? shall we receive good at the hand of God, and shall we not receive evil? In all this did not Job sin with his lips."

C | Sometimes, Friends Cannot Help

Job was experiencing a horrible personal tragedy. His three friends made an appointment to come and mourn with him and comfort him. But when they saw him, his boils had so disfigured him, they did not even recognize him. They rent their clothes, threw dust on their heads, and wept loudly. Then, silence. When God is trying you, you may have to face things alone, even among friends.

Job 2:13 - "They sat down with him upon the ground seven days and seven nights, and none spake a word unto him: for they saw that his grief was very great."

D | When The Prophetic Purpose Is Hidden

Poor Job. He was so low and his trial so agonizing that he cursed the day he was born. He wished he had been stillborn. He felt his birth had been untimely. He yearned for the quietness of death. But Job could not possibly understand that over 3,000 years later, his name would be a household word in every nation on earth, and his unyielding confidence in God would become one of the greatest inspirational stories of all time.

Job 3:23 - "Why is light given to a man whose way is hid, and whom God hath hedged in?"

B | Satan Used Job's Friends

Job was a son of Issachar and grandson of Jacob (Genesis 46:13). He lived in the days of Joseph, his young uncle. Joseph suffered in Egypt. Job suffered in the land of Uz. Job had three friends who came to comfort him - Eliphaz, Bildad and Zophar. Both Joseph and Job were tormented by family and friends. Remember, Satan designs your trial to destroy you. He will even use your friends against you.

Job 4:1,8 - "Then Eliphaz the Temanite answered and said, ...Even as I have seen, they that plow iniquity, and sow wickedness, reap the same."

A | What Kind Of Friend Tells You Not To Pray?

Job's "friend," Eliphaz, believed Job's problems were simple to explain. Job was reaping what he had sown. Job was evil, and God was punishing him for it. His analysis was wearisome. Be careful not to get lost in Eliphaz' criticisms. He was dead wrong. It is lethal to mix wisdom with foolish conjecture. He even went so far as to suggest that Job need not pray anymore, because nobody would hear him. What a lie.

Job 5:1 - "Call now, if there be any that will answer thee; and to which of the saints wilt thou turn?"

C | What Does Your Arguing Reprove?

I do not know how Job kept his sanity after listening to Eliphaz' harangue. His reply certainly indicated that Eliphaz had done no good for him. Job bemoaned his situation again and begged God, "that it would please God to destroy me; that he would let loose his hand, and cut me off! Then should I yet have comfort." Then he scathed his friend.

Job 6:14-15,25 - "To him that is afflicted pity should be shewed from his friend; ...My brethren have dealt deceitfully as a brook, ...How forcible are right words! but what doth your arguing reprove?"

D | Every Man Has An Appointment

Job's skin was broken and loathsome. His flesh was "clothed with worms and clods of dust." His friend smothered him with criticism. He wanted to die. "Is there not an appointed time to man upon earth? are not his days also like the days of an hireling? ...as an hireling looketh for the reward of his work." Yes. It is appointed unto man once to die, and afterward the judgment.

Job 7:11,16 - "I will speak in the anguish of my spirit; I will complain in the bitterness of my soul. ...I loathe it; I would not live alway."

A | Prayers Of The Righteous Can Be Hindered

Job's friend, Bildad, asserted his misguided opinion. To paraphrase, he said, "If your kids had not sinned, they would not be dead." "If your heart was pure, your prayers would be answered." WRONG. Paul spoke of a great open door for ministry, "but there are many adversaries." This is not the Garden of Eden. The thief steals, kills and destroys indiscriminately. Consequently, righteous men often suffer great losses.

Job 8:5-6 - "If thou wouldest seek unto God betimes, and make thy supplication to the Almighty; If thou wert pure and upright; surely now he would awake for thee."

D | The Daysman

Job responded to Bildad by arguing that God is Sovereign and does as He pleases. But cynicism was in his voice. Job could not understand why God allowed him to suffer. He felt powerless to persuade God to change his circumstance. He yearned for a "daysman" - an intercessor between him and God. Job would have rejoiced to meet our daysman - Jesus Christ.

Job 9:32 - "He is not a man, as I am, that I should answer him, and we should come together in judgment. Neither is there any daysman betwixt us, that might lay his hand upon us both."

C | The Unadvisable Propensity For Self-Pity

We act too much like Job. We get weary of life. We want to know why things do not go better than they do. We are tempted to complain that God is not giving us a fair treatment. But we must learn from Job's mistakes. Job said a lot of things that should not have been said, and God eventually rebuked him for them. Self-pity will get you into a lot of trouble. Practice keeping your mouth shut.

Job 10:1 - "I will leave my complaint upon myself; I will speak in the bitterness of my soul."

A | Zophar Prods Job To Repent

Finally, Zophar articulated his opinion. He accused Job of lying and mocking God. "Oh that God would speak, and open his lips against thee." He said that Job deserved more punishment than he was getting.

He called Job to stretch out his hands to God and put iniquity far away from him. Like so many people, Zophar could easily see sin in his friend's life, but could not see his own disgusting self-righteousness. Who are you judging?

Job 11:15-16 - "For then shalt thou lift up thy face without spot; ...thou shalt forget thy misery."

B | The Hand Of The LORD Hath Wrought This

Although Job was sick and tormented, he sparred with his "friends." They relentlessly accused him of wrongdoing. Job sarcastically retorted, "No doubt but ye are the people, and wisdom shall die with you. But I have understanding as well as you; I am not inferior to you" He declared that God rules all creatures - men and beasts, and is supremely wise, making great and powerful men look like fools. Job argued that God does many things that are contradictory to human understanding.

Job 12:9 - "Who knoweth not in all these that the hand of the LORD hath wrought this?"

D | He Increaseth The Nations, And Destroyeth Them

If you remember that the book of Job is the most ancient of all scriptures, then Job, who lived in primitive times, was quite prophetic in these statements. His insights were exceedingly far reaching - all the way to our generation. As great nations fall, and evil men rule, remember that God is in control.

Job 12:18-19, 21,23 - "He looseth the bond of kings, ...He leadeth princes away spoiled, and overthroweth the mighty. ...He poureth contempt upon princes, and weakeneth the strength of the mighty. ...He increaseth the nations, and destroyeth them: he enlargeth the nations, and straiteneth them again."

C | Though He Slay Me, Yet Will I Trust In Him

Job fired back at Zophar. Let me paraphrase it in common words. "What you know, I know. I would speak to God. I would reason with Him. But not you. You are liars - incompetent doctors. I wish you would just stop talking. You grossly misrepresent God. He will reprove you. Why aren't you afraid of Him? Just be quiet and leave me alone." At last, he declared his unflinching intention to trust God, no matter how difficult his trial.

Job 13:15-16 - "Though he slay me, yet will I trust in him: ...He also shall be my salvation."

C | There Is Hope Of A Tree

I once saw a pecan tree that had been blown down by a storm many years earlier. After the storm, it was cut off, leaving a huge stump lying sideways along the ground. Over the next twenty years, another massive tree sprouted out of the side of that stump and became a very fruitful pecan tree again. God can do the same thing with you or me.

Job 14:7 - "...there is hope of a tree, if it be cut down, that it will sprout again, and that the tender branch thereof will not cease."

C | The Hope That Is In God's Grace

Job deserves some credit for discerning the hope that is in God's grace. He said, "Man that is born of a woman is of few days, and full of trouble, ...Who can bring a clean thing out of an unclean? not one." That sounds like Paul, who said, "O wretched man that I am! who shall deliver me from the body of this death? I thank God through Jesus Christ our Lord." Job knew his only hope was to give his sins to God.

Job 14:17 - "My transgression is sealed up in a bag, and thou sewest up mine iniquity."

A | Eliphaz Accuses Job Of Prayerlessness and Evil Talk

Eliphaz launched another round of attacks on Job, accusing him of unprofitable talk, no-good speeches, uttering iniquity, and speaking with a crafty tongue. "Your mouth condemns you. Your lips testify against you." He contradicted himself, insisting that no man is clean or righteous, yet only wicked suffer and oppressors die young, indicting Job. He said his elders were older and wiser than Job's elders. He accused Job of not fearing God or praying. Why should any saint or sinner have to listen to such unbridled character assassination?

Job 15:4 - "Yea, thou castest off fear, and restrainest prayer before God."

A | Pure Prayer

Unless you live isolated in a cave, somebody will eventually accuse you of impure motives. Job's friends stared at his suffering for seven days before commenting, but when they started talking, they were vicious. In times like those, only you and God know the whole truth. Job knew his own heart. "My prayer is pure," he said. It doesn't matter what other people think about you or your prayer life. You and God know the truth. Pray on.

Job 16:17 - "Not for any injustice in mine hands: also my prayer is pure."

D | He Hath Made Me A Proverb

This might be the most prophetic verse in the entire book of Job, buried under all the incessant talking. Job said, "He hath made me also a byword of the people," 17:6. A byword is a common saying or a proverb. 3500 years ago, Job perceived that his life was a divinely-orchestrated proverb. Who has not heard of the patience of Job? Our hard trials will be much easier to bear if we believe, as Job, that God is orchestrating something of value to HIM during our difficulties.

Job 17:8 - "Upright men shall be astonied at this."

B | Bildad Erroneously Predicts Job's Demise

Bildad disdained every word Job spoke, railing on him mercilessly. "How long will it be ere ye make an end of words? mark, and afterwards we will speak." Bildad hammered Job with predictions that God would soon kill him. But Bildad was wrong. Job lived 140 years longer and raised another family. Ignore self-appointed prophets.

Job 18:5-6,18-19 - "The light of the wicked shall be put out, ...his candle shall be put out with him. He shall be driven from light into darkness, and chased out of the world. He shall neither have son nor nephew among his people."

A | Struggling With Unanswered Prayer

Job pleaded with his friends to stop attacking him. He was overwhelmed and struggling to make sense of his trials. He rehearsed all the prayers he had prayed and all the efforts he had made to correct his mistakes and persuade God to deliver him from his plight. Sooner or later, we all get the feeling that God does not care or is not listening. But God IS listening. Just hold on a little longer, and you will see.

Job 19:7 - "Behold, I cry out of wrong, but I am not heard: I cry aloud, but there is no judgment."

A | Prayer Notes

I keep extensive notes that help me pray effectively. I use notes for preaching, for teaching, even notes for writing. Why not pray with notes?

I have hundreds of people on my prayer list, and without notes I am sure I would forget to pray for many people or things that are very important to me. But that is not all. Writing reinforces my faith and determination to have the things I ask. Writing reminds me to believe!

Job 19:23 - "Oh that my words were now written! Oh that they were printed in a book!"

D | Job Speaks Of Life After Death And His Coming Redeemer

Here is evidence in the oldest book of the Bible that Job believed in life after death. He expected to see God and prophesied that his redeemer would appear on the earth in the latter days - a clear reference to the coming of Jesus Christ.

Job 19:25-27 - "For I know that my redeemer liveth, and that he shall stand at the latter day upon the earth: And though after my skin worms destroy this body, yet in my flesh shall I see God: Whom I shall see for myself, and mine eyes shall behold, and not another."

C | The Wicked Condemn The Righteous

Even after suffering Job begged for mercy, Zophar resumed his verbal assault. Job's friends were viciously determined to prove that Job was a dirty rotten sinner and would never escape the wrath of God. This is an amazing state of mind for men who had never seen or heard of a Bible, never heard a preacher, seen a Tabernacle or Temple, or had any organized religion. That sounds like multitudes of godless people in our day who viciously condemn righteous men.

Job 20:29 - "This is the portion of a wicked man from God, and the heritage appointed unto him by God."

B | Job Says Wicked Often Prosper, Righteous Suffer

Job turned their argument back on his "friends." "Suffer me that I may speak; and after that I have spoken, mock on." Job argued that wicked men often flourish in their lifetimes. They are safe. They know no punishment. They prosper. They celebrate. They think they have no need of God. But temporal prosperity is no proof that it will go well on the Day of Judgment. Job's argument was meant to counter their assertions that his suffering was proof he was wicked.

Job 21:34 - "How then comfort ye me in vain, seeing in your answers there remaineth falsehood?"

□✓

A | Satan Accuses You To Discount Your Prayers

Eliphaz refused to stop accusing Job of sin. He heaped a long list of sins on him - refusing to feed the hungry, taking clothes from the naked, sending widows away empty, and other outrageous charges. He arrogantly told Job "acquaint now thyself with Him, and ...return to the Almighty," as if Job did not even know God. God was already hearing Job's prayers, but Satan wanted him to believe otherwise.

Job 22:27-28 - "Thou shalt make thy prayer unto him, and he shall hear thee, ...Thou shalt also decree a thing, and it shall be established unto thee."

B | The Left Hand Of God - "Where He Doth Work"

God's right hand is often mentioned in scriptures. It is "glorious in power." "From his right hand went a fiery law." "At thy right hand are pleasures forever more." "Thy right hand upholdeth me," and many more. But God also works on His left hand, where there are trials and testings, but mighty and divine nevertheless.

Job 23:8 - "Behold, I go forward, but he is not there; and backward, but I cannot perceive him: On the left hand, where he doth work, but I cannot behold him: he hideth himself on the right hand, that I cannot see him."

C | I Shall Come Forth As Gold

Job did not hide his confusion about what God was doing in his life. He yearned to stand face to face with God and "know the words which he would answer me, and understand what he would say unto me." But despite Job's profound frustration, he remained convinced that God was still working something for his eternal good. God really does see the end from the beginning. It is our task to trust Him.

Job 23:10 - "But he knoweth the way that I take: when he hath tried me, I shall come forth as gold."

D | Exalted For A While, But Gone And Brought Low

In chapter 24, Job enumerated so many felonies of evil men. They remove landmarks, steal flocks and feed, plunder the fatherless and widows, raid farmers' fields, are heartless toward the homeless, kidnap newborns, are cruel to the barren, steal food from the poor, murder, and commit adulteries. The Contemporary English Version of the Bible renders Job's conclusion thus:

Job 24:23-25 - "God may let them feel secure, but they are never out of his sight. Great for a while; gone forever! Sinners are mowed down like weeds, then they wither and die. If I haven't spoken the truth, then prove me wrong."

B | Job's "Friend," Bildad, Reveals His Fatalism

What kind of statement is this? "How then can man be justified with God? or how can he be clean that is born of a woman?" It is fatalism. Hopelessness. If Bildad's statement was true, it would be impossible to be saved. Avoid that attitude at all costs. God is righteous, and man is wicked, BUT God is also merciful.

Job 25:2 - "Behold even to the moon, and it shineth not; yea, the stars are not pure in his sight. How much less man, that is a worm? and the son of man, which is a worm?"

C | What Good Are You Doing?

Job wanted to know of his friends, "How hast thou helped him that is without power? how savest thou the arm that hath no strength?" Who do you think you are talking to? What spirit is this you are manifesting? All are good questions. Sometimes you just have to stop the critic in his tracks. It is easy to blather on with endless criticisms of others, but the real question is, "What good are you doing?"

Job 26:3 - "How hast thou counseled him that hath no wisdom? and how hast thou plentifully declared the thing as it is?"

A | The Prayers Of A Hypocrite Are Vain

After being relentlessly bombarded by merciless accusations, Job waged verbal war for his integrity. "As God liveth...," he promised to speak righteousness and avoid all reproach, to de-legitimize the countless accusations hurled at him. Job condemned hypocrisy.

Job 27:8-10,22 - "For what is the hope of the hypocrite, though he hath gained, when God taketh away his soul? Will God hear his cry when trouble cometh upon him? Will he delight himself in the Almighty? will he always call upon God? ...For God shall cast upon him, and not spare: he would fain flee out of his hand."

D | Wisdom Is Hidden In God. Fear Him To Find Wisdom.

Job contemplated wisdom. Here is what he said. Silver has its place. Gold has its place. Iron has its place. Brass has its place. Darkness has its place. The flood has its place. "But where shall wisdom be found? and where is the place of understanding?" "There is a path which no fowl knoweth, and which the vulture's eye hath not seen." "God understandeth the way thereof, and he knoweth the place thereof." Wisdom is hidden in God. Fear Him to find wisdom.

Job 28:28 - "Behold, the fear of the Lord, that is wisdom; and to depart from evil is understanding."

B | Job Remembered His "Glory" Days

Job yearned for "the good old days," when God's candle shined on him, when his children were with him, when people greeted him kindly in the streets, and great men showed him honor. He remembered when he spent his days doing good deeds for the poor, the fatherless, the widows and others. In the midst of a great trial, it is easy to think that God is not with you. But He is.

Job 29:2,5 - "Oh that I were as in months past, as in the days when God preserved me; ...When the Almighty was yet with me."

A | Job Turns Bitter, Accuses God

Job's mourning turned to bitterness. "Young people now insult me, although their fathers would have been a disgrace to my sheep dogs. ...Those worthless nobodies make up jokes and songs to disgrace me. They are hateful and keep their distance, even while spitting in my direction. ...God has destroyed me, and so they don't care what they do." "God has shrunk my skin, choking me to death. ..."God has turned brutal." You will live to regret statements like that. Just don't go there. Bite your tongue.

Job 30:31 - "My only songs are sorrow and sadness." [CEV]

C | Self-Justification Turns To Pride, Then Self-Deception

Job tried too hard to justify himself. He talked about his good morals - ("I made a covenant with mine eyes; why then should I think upon a maid?"). He spoke of his good deeds and defended his integrity. He boasted that he never sinned with a woman, never treated his servants badly, always helped the needy, spurned the love of riches, and never gloated in the sufferings of his enemies. But Job finally overstepped the boundaries of self-justification.

Job 31:37 - "I would declare unto him the number of my steps; as a prince would I go near unto him."

D | **Elihu**

A new character suddenly entered the story of Job. Elihu had not been mentioned previously. He appeared, delivered a major speech, then disappeared, never to be mentioned again in the Bible. His name meant, "My God is Jehovah." Some think Elihu was a type of Christ, but God followed his speech with, "Who is this that darkeneth counsel by words without knowledge?"

Job 32:2 - "Then was kindled the wrath of Elihu, ...against Job..., because he justified himself rather than God. Also against his three friends was his wrath kindled, because they had found no answer, and yet had condemned Job."

B | **Elihu Refutes Job And His Friends**

The three friends of Job finally stopped talking, "because he was righteous in his own eyes." When Elihu opened his mouth to speak, he was angry. The theology of all four was flawed; fixed upon the erroneous belief that only good comes to the righteous, and only evil comes to the wicked. The three insisted Job was being punished for sins, while Job argued that this was not punishment, because he was only righteous. Neither side was right. Elihu argued another perspective.

Job 32:17 - "I said, I will answer also my part, I also will shew mine opinion."

C | **There Is A Spirit In Man**

A fourth dimension. Something beyond height, width or depth. Something wiser than the human brain. The spirit dimension. Here is a controversial subject. Modern science says there is no spirit. But all the Bible, all of the Judeo-Christian belief system, is based on this most fundamental Truth. There is a spirit in man.

Job 32:7-9 - "I said, Days should speak, and multitude of years should teach wisdom. But there is a spirit in man: and the inspiration of the Almighty giveth them understanding. Great men are not always wise: neither do the aged understand judgment."

D | **Chastisement Comes To Save You In The End**

Elihu said, "The spirit within me constraineth me. ...I am according to thy wish in God's stead. ...I have heard the voice of thy words saying, I am clean without transgression, I am innocent; neither is there iniquity in me.

...he counteth me for his enemy." But Elihu argued that God has numerous valid reasons for chastising a man.

Job 33:16 - "He openeth the ears of men, and sealeth their instruction, That he may withdraw man from his purpose, and hide pride from man. He keepeth back his soul from the pit, and his life from perishing."

A | Divine Chastisement Should Lead To Effective Prayer

Elihu posited that when God chastises a man, the angel of the LORD is there to minister to him if he responds properly. The angel will deliver him from falling, and that man's prayers will become effective again; he will become contrite and repentant, and joy will soon return.

Job 33:23 - "If there be a messenger with him, ...to shew unto man his uprightness: Then he is gracious unto him, and saith, Deliver him from going down to the pit. ...He shall pray unto God, and he will be favourable unto him: and he shall see his face with joy."

A | Elihu Skillfully Indicts Job And Demands Repentance

Elihu debated against Job's self-righteous plea, demanding that God does no wrong to any man, including Job. All men eventually get what they deserve. God cannot deal unrighteously, nor put more on him than is right, but He will break a man or destroy him if necessary. Job must admit His chastening and beg forgiveness of all wrongdoing.

Job 34:36 - "My desire is that Job may be tried unto the end because of his answers for wicked men. For he addeth rebellion unto his sin, he clappeth his hands among us, and multiplieth his words against God."

B | Elihu Convicts Job Of Being Proud And Evil

Elihu hammered Job for a truthful answer, "Is your righteousness more than God's?" He pressed Job to confess whether he believed he needed cleansing from sin. He said that people ordinarily cry out to God when they are sorely oppressed, but forget God after He has helped them. Then they become proud and evil, and God refuses to answer them. That is your state, Job. You have become proud and evil.

Job 35:14 - "Although thou sayest thou shalt not see him, ...he hath visited in his anger; ...Therefore doth Job open his mouth in vain; he multiplieth words without knowledge."

C | Do Not Let God's Punishment Embitter You

Elihu exhorted, "If they obey and serve him, they shall spend their days in prosperity, and their years in pleasures. But if they obey not, they shall perish by the sword. ...But the hypocrites in heart heap up wrath: ...They die in youth, and their life is among the unclean." Elihu concluded that Job was recipient of God's wrath because of his hypocrisy. He warned him not to be further embittered because God had punished him.

Job 36:18 - "Because there is wrath, beware lest he take thee away with his stroke: then a great ransom cannot deliver thee."

D | Men Cannot Know All God's Majesty. Be Humbled.

Elihu made his closing argument against Job just before God took over the conversation. Elihu depicted the greatness of God in heaven and earth - thunder, lightning, snow, rain, whirlwinds, north winds, frost and ice. "He causeth it to come, whether for correction, or for his land, or for mercy." His point? God is too majestic to predict. Admit your failings and surrender to Him.

Job 37:23 - "Touching the Almighty, we cannot find him out: he is excellent in power, and in judgment, and in plenty of justice. Men do therefore fear him: he respecteth not any that are wise of heart."

A | Time To Talk, But Nothing To Say

Eliphaz, Bildad, Zophar and Elihu verbally assaulted Job during their nasty war of words. Suddenly, God spoke out of a whirlwind, indicting those who "darken counsel by words without knowledge." They were speechless! God then demanded that Job answer a giant list of rhetorical questions. "Where were you when I created the earth, ...when morning stars sang, ...angels shouted, ...when the ocean was set in place," ...and many more enigmas. Sometimes, speaking only exposes your foolishness. Just be quiet. Listen and learn from God.

Job 38:4 - "Where wast thou when I laid the foundations of the earth?"

B | God Quickly Humbles Job

God's questions to Job were obviously intended to diffuse his arrogance. God asked him to explain so many things like the earth, stars and constellations, clouds, ocean waves, sunrises, death, light, darkness, snow, hail, battle and war, lightning and thunder, rain and drought, lions and ravens, wild goats and hinds, the wild ass and unicorn, peacocks, horses and grasshoppers, hawks and eagles. Job could only have been stupefied. Nobody but God knows all.

Job 39:13,19 - "Gavest thou the goodly wings unto the peacocks? or wings and feathers unto the ostrich? ...Hast thou given the horse strength?"

C | Finding Fault In God Is Grave Folly

From the beginning, Satan's ambition was to provoke Job to curse God. Job never did curse God, but he lodged several complaints and foolish accusations against Him. So God confronted Job with two of His most impressive creations - Behemoth and Leviathan - largest beast and sea creature on earth. If God rules these beasts which are a terror to men, how dare any man speak evil of God! If you have a question, ask God. But insulting your Creator can be very dangerous!

Job 40:8 - "Wilt thou also disannul my judgment? wilt thou condemn me, that thou mayest be righteous?"

D | Who Then Is Able To Stand Before God?

God delivered a heart-stopping monologue to Job. Leviathan was His object lesson to illustrate that no man should resist the irresistible divine purpose. If the great beast Leviathan is too terrifying to defy, then how much more terrifying is the God who controls the great beast? You cannot win by resisting or rebelling against the purpose of God in your life. Learn from Job. Do not resist. Stop pushing against God. Surrender to His will now.

Job 41:10-11 - "None is so fierce that dare stir him up: who then is able to stand before me? ...whatsoever is under the whole heaven is mine."

A | Job Repents In Dust And Ashes

After forty-two chapters of incessant arguing, bickering and insults, God interrupted Job and his obnoxious friends with a more-than-dramatic monologue. Job was instantly and completely repentant. Job answered the LORD, "I uttered that I understood not; things too wonderful for me, which I knew not. ...Wherefore I abhor myself, and repent in dust and ashes." Immediately, God rebuked Job's friends, demanding that they offer sacrifices for their sins, and present themselves to Job for his prayers. God always has the last word.

Job 42:8 - "And my servant Job shall pray for you: for him will I accept: lest I deal with you after your folly."

B | God Turns The Captivity Of Job

God gave Eliphaz, Bildad and Zophar no choice but to humble themselves after rousing His great anger with their insolent speeches. So they prepared their sacrifice offerings and went to meet Job. Then Job prayed for his friends. God quickly began a complete renewal of all His blessings on Job. We should be impressed at how readily and how quickly God will forgive a man, and begin in him a complete restoration.

Job 42:10 - "And the LORD turned the captivity of Job, when he prayed for his friends: also the LORD gave Job twice as much as he had before."

C | Storms Never Last

This must surely be one of life's biggest lessons. Job's trial began when God licensed Satan to test him. But by the time Job's trial was over, Satan was out of the picture. That is the secret. Satan's license eventually expires. Enemies are pawns in the greater will of God. Your task is to endure. Sooner or later, the trial must end, and you will wear the victor's crown. Press on.

Job 42:12,17 - "So the LORD blessed the latter end of Job more than his beginning: ...So Job died, being old and full of days."

D | Job's Divine Destiny

In times of tragedy, it is difficult to see beyond the moment. Every stage of Job's trial must have seemed devastating. The loss of his cattle, death of his children, betrayal of his wife, agony of disease, torment of his friends, his humiliating self-defense, and finally facing God's harsh displeasure. But Job came forth as pure gold. God always knew he would.

James 5:11 - "We count them happy which endure. Ye have heard of the patience of Job, and have seen the end of the Lord; that the Lord is very pitiful, and of tender mercy."

Lessons from the Book of
PSALMS

A | David Taught Us To Delight Ourselves In The LORD

We have David to thank for most of the Psalms. His songs and lyrics articulate a broad spectrum of praise, worship, and exaltation of the LORD. The Psalms also include volumes of wise counsel and poignant prayers. What other book promotes more intimate relationship with God through prayer and praise?

Psalms 1:1 - "Blessed is the man that walketh not in the counsel of the ungodly, nor standeth in the way of sinners, nor sitteth in the seat of the scornful. But his delight is in the law of the LORD; and in his law doth he meditate day and night."

B | The Righteous Are Like A Great Tree

David was a great preacher. His exhortations are among the most quoted in all religious literature. David had profound understanding of great spiritual truths, and he articulated them well. He knew that godly people are strong and hearty because God makes them so. He compared them to a great and fruitful tree planted by a river. But sinners are like chaff that blows away. In the end of all things, the righteous will endure, but sinners and the ungodly will be banished.

Psalms 1:6 - "For the LORD knoweth the way of the righteous: but the way of the ungodly shall perish."

A | Ask Of Me, I Will Give Thee The Heathen

The psalmist asked, "Why do the heathen rage, and the people imagine a vain thing? The kings of the earth set themselves, and the rulers take counsel together, against the LORD, and against his anointed, saying, Let us break their bands asunder, and cast away their cords from us." But God in heaven will laugh at these scoffers and have them in derision and vexation. Ultimately, God will give His anointed dominion over them all.

Psalms 2:8 - "Ask of me, and I shall give thee the heathen for thine inheritance, and the uttermost parts of the earth for thy possession."

A | Prayer - A Consolation Against Adversaries

When King David fled from his evil-hearted son, Absalom, prayer became David's coping mechanism. He vented his anxieties to God: "They are increased that rise up against me," "Many say there is no help for me," and more. But David cried, "You, LORD, are a shield for me! My glory! Lifter up of my head." He rejoiced that God heard his prayers, gave him rest, sleep, and confidence to be unafraid of even ten thousands of enemies.

Psalms 3:7 - "Arise, O LORD; save me, O my God: for thou hast smitten all mine enemies upon the cheek bone."

A | Praying With Musical Accompaniment

David sent the fourth Psalm to the chief Temple musician on "Neginoth" (meaning "stringed instruments"). David wanted lyres and harps to accompany this prayer. It juxtaposes those who dishonor God and love vanities and lies, with the righteous, whom God sets apart and hears when they pray. Great truths deserve to be orchestrated. Play and sing your prayers.

Psalms 4:7-8 - "Thou hast put gladness in my heart, more than in the time that their corn and their wine increased. I will both lay me down in peace, and sleep: for thou, LORD, only makest me dwell in safety."

A | Plan to Pray

On your TO-DO list, prayer should have top priority among all the things you plan to do. If prayer is not a high priority on your daily schedule, it will almost certainly get bumped off the list entirely by the end of the day. For many years, I have forced myself to maintain a certain amount of prayer time daily. If I miss the mark, I attempt to compensate the next time.

Psalm 5:3 - "My voice shalt thou hear in the morning, O LORD; in the morning will I direct my prayer unto thee."

A | Pray Your Way Out Of Distress

Sooner or later, most of us run into some great distress. The worst distress is our own failure before Almighty God. David cried, "rebuke me not, ...neither chasten me, ...have mercy, ...heal me, ...deliver my soul, ...save me." He shooed away death and the grave as providing no relief, and discharged the groanings and tears caused by his enemies.

Psalm 6:8-10 - "Depart from me, all ye workers of iniquity; for the LORD hath heard the voice of my weeping. The LORD hath heard my supplication; the LORD will receive my prayer. Let all mine enemies be ashamed and sore vexed."

A | Console Yourself While Praying

When we recall David's fugitive years of running from King Saul, we know Saul could not hurt David because God was for him. But in the heat of the moment, David was not so sure. He prayed that God would deliver him from the lion that was tearing at his soul, "rending it in pieces." Then he consoled himself. "God is angry with the wicked every day. If he turn not, he will whet his sword; he hath bent his bow, and made it ready."

Psalms 7:13 - "He hath also prepared ...instruments of death; he ordaineth his arrows against the persecutors."

C | What Is Man?

David contemplated the heavens of God - the moon, the stars - and asked why God is mindful of mere man. It is incomprehensible that in this seemingly infinite universe, Almighty God considers such a speck as me. But He DOES!

Psalm 8:4-6 - "What is man, that thou art mindful of him? and the son of man, that thou visitest him? For thou hast made him a little lower than the angels, and hast crowned him with glory and honour. Thou madest him to have dominion over the works of thy hands; thou hast put all things under his feet."

A | Affirming God's Vindication And Judgment

David had a profound conviction that God would ultimately vindicate the righteous and judge the wicked. His countless prayers reiterate those two themes. Often targeted by jealous and hateful men, David prayed and trusted that God would sustain him in the face of sore opposition. He believed that, in the end, God would punish evil people and reward the faithful and righteous.

Psalms 9:10,17 - "They that know thy name will put their trust in thee: for thou, LORD, hast not forsaken them that seek thee. ...The wicked shall be turned into hell, and all the nations that forget God."

A | Praying Against The Wicked

David prayed hard against the wicked. He named many offenses: pride, devices, covetous desires that God abhors, spurning God, cursing, deceit, fraud, mischief, vanity, lurking to catch the weak and poor. David urged the LORD not to stand afar or hide Himself from the wicked. "Break thou the arm of the wicked and the evil man: seek out his wickedness till thou find none." We should pray relentlessly that wickedness will be overthrown and righteousness will prevail.

Psalms 10:11,18 - "Arise, O LORD; O God, lift up thine hand: ...that the man of the earth may no more oppress."

D | Upon The Wicked He Shall Rain Snares

"In the LORD put I my trust." Not many men before him spoke in such clarion terms. David confessed his total dependence upon God for his survival. Why say to my soul, "Flee as a bird to your mountain?" When the wicked draw their bows against us, "His eyes behold." "The LORD is in his holy temple, the LORD'S throne is in heaven." God's watchfulness consoles all the righteous.

Psalms 11:5 - "The LORD trieth the righteous: but the wicked and him that loveth violence his soul hateth. Upon the wicked he shall rain snares, fire and brimstone."

A | Pray For Help Against Dishonest, Threatening People

A godly person craves to see others living godly lives. But David felt as though everyone around him was dishonest or threatening. "Help, LORD; for the godly man ceaseth; for the faithful fail, ...They speak ...with flattering lips and with a double heart." When you feel oppressed by phonies, flatterers, dishonest, intimidating or threatening people, remember that God's words are purer than silver tried in a furnace and faithful for eternal generations. Though men fail, God never fails.

Psalm 12:5 - "Now will I arise, saith the LORD; I will set him in safety from him that puffeth at him."

A | How Long, O LORD?

"O LORD! How long will you forget me? How long will you hide Your face from me? How long will I search for a cure for my sorrow? How long will my enemies overpower me?" Obviously, David believed God knew the answer to those questions, or he would not have asked. Rather than die in despair, or surrender to his enemies, David forced his expectations heavenward. We should, too.

Psalms 13:5 - "But I have trusted in thy mercy; my heart shall rejoice in thy salvation. I will sing unto the LORD, because he hath dealt bountifully with me."

A | God Save Us From Fools

Sing this. "The fool hath said in his heart, There is no God." David wrote this song of Psalm 14 on that theme. Fools, corrupt, abominable, ne'er-do-good types. God sees them all. He sees how filthy they are, how they devour righteous men like bread, how they mock the wisdom of poor men. But do not fear. God will someday vindicate His righteous people.

Psalm 14:7 - "Oh that the salvation of Israel were come out of Zion! when the LORD bringeth back the captivity of his people, Jacob shall rejoice, and Israel shall be glad."

B | The Kind Of People Who Dwell In God's Holy Places

The people of God are identifiably different from the rest of the world. The world is corrupt and vile. God's people are sanctified by obedience to the will of God. What kind of person dwells in God's Tabernacle, in His holy hill? Those who walk uprightly, work righteousness, and speak the Truth. These are not backbiters. They do no evil to their neighbors. The righteous despise and scorn vile people, but honor those who fear the LORD. They keep their oaths and lend without interest.

Psalms 15:5 "He that doeth these things shall never be moved."

D | David Prophesies The Resurrection

Peter quoted extensively from Psalm 16 on the day of Pentecost. "For David speaketh concerning him, I foresaw the Lord always before my face, ...Therefore did my heart rejoice, ...Because thou wilt not leave my soul in hell, neither wilt thou suffer thine Holy One to see corruption. ...Therefore being a prophet, ...He seeing this before spake of the resurrection of Christ." David foretold Jesus' resurrection 1000 years before He was born. It could have referred to no other.

Psalms 16:10 - "For thou wilt not leave my soul in hell; neither wilt thou suffer thine Holy One to see corruption."

C | In Thy Presence Is Fulness Of Joy, Pleasures For Evermore

David contemplated with joy about his life in God and the delight of the fellowship with the saints of God. He bemoaned others who worshipped other gods and promised that he would never make sacrifices to other gods or ever speak well of them. God, he said, is my inheritance, and he will always be at the forefront of my life. "Because He is at my right hand, I shall not be moved."

Psalms 16:11 - "Thou wilt shew me the path of life: in thy presence is fulness of joy; at thy right hand there are pleasures for evermore."

A | Deliver My Soul From The Wicked

Add up all the prayers David prayed for God to deliver him from his enemies. Compare them to the many victories David won. "Keep me as the apple of the eye, hide me under the shadow of thy wings, From the wicked that oppress me, from my deadly enemies, who compass me about." Learn this lesson. David overcame many enemies because he was a prayer warrior. Declare war in your prayers. "Deliver us from all evil." Let God arise and His enemies be scattered.

Psalms 17:13 - "Arise, O LORD, disappoint him, cast him down: deliver my soul from the wicked."

A | Pray First

A predisposition is a pre-planned policy. David was predisposed to pray anytime trouble arose. Prayer should be our first recourse. It should be so embedded in our psyche that every time trouble comes, we begin to pray almost as quickly as a "knee-jerk" reaction. Pray before doing anything else. I once heard a veteran pastor say that he refused to counsel anyone unless they assure him they have already prayed earnestly about their problem.

Psalm 18:3 - "I will call upon the LORD, who is worthy to be praised: so shall I be saved from mine enemies."

B | The LORD, My Rock

David had great visions of God. Rock. Fortress. Deliverer. Strength. Buckler. Salvation. High tower. "He will save me from my enemies." All these things inspired and emboldened David. "For by thee I have run through a troop; and by my God have I leaped over a wall. ...For who is God save the LORD? or who is a rock save our God? ...He maketh my feet like hinds' feet, and setteth me upon my high places." O, magnify the LORD!

Psalms 18:46 - "The LORD liveth; and blessed be my rock; and let the God of my salvation be exalted."

C | Thy Words Are Perfect. Make Mine Acceptable.

The heavens declare the glory of God. The firmament shows His handiwork. Days speak. Nights bring knowledge. God's voice is everywhere. "His going forth is from the end of the heaven. ...The law of the LORD is perfect, converting the soul: the testimony of the LORD is sure, making wise the simple. ...More to be desired are they than gold, yea, than much fine gold: sweeter also than honey and the honeycomb."

Psalms 19:14 - "Let the words of my mouth, and the meditation of my heart, be acceptable in thy sight, O LORD, my strength, and my redeemer."

A | I Believe In Prayer

This song of David encourages and affirms prayer. "The LORD hear thee in the day of trouble; ...send thee help from the sanctuary (His temple), ...grant thee according to thine own heart, ...the LORD saveth his anointed; he will hear him from his holy heaven with the saving strength of his right hand." Pray confidently. Nothing moves God more than the prayers of the righteous.

Psalms 20:7-8 - "Some trust in chariots, and some in horses: but we will remember the name of the LORD our God. They are brought down and fallen: but we are risen, and stand upright."

B | Kingship Is Endowed By God

One of the greatest tragedies of modern times is the failure of kings and presidents to recognize the sovereignty of God over their governance. David emphatically acknowledged God's endowments upon his kingship. He rejoiced and gave thanks for God's blessings, both temporal and eternal. "For thou hast made him most blessed for ever: thou hast made him exceeding glad with thy countenance." In contrast, he declared that God will find out His enemies and remove them.

Psalms 21:7 - "For the king trusteth in the LORD, and through the mercy of the most High he shall not be moved."

D | My God, My God, Why Hast Thou Forsaken Me?

Psalm 22 contains several amazing Messianic prophecies. "My God, my God, why hast thou forsaken me? ...All they that see me laugh me to scorn: they shoot out the lip, they shake the head, saying, ...He trusted on the LORD that he would deliver him: let him deliver him, seeing he delighted in him." All were fulfilled in Jesus. The Spirit of prophecy was mightily upon David.

Psalms 22:18,22 - "They part my garments among them, and cast lots upon my vesture. ...I will declare thy name unto my brethren: in the midst of the congregation will I praise thee."

C | He Maketh Me To Lie Down

You can fly through life at rat-race speed, or you can slow down and know God. Even if you win the rat-race, you're still a rat. Slow down. Be still and know God. You won't find God in the noise, haste, or insanity. Study to be quiet. If you don't, and yet desire a relationship with God, He will have to slow you down. You may scream and kick against Him but finally discover the truth. His way is always best.

Psalms 23:2 - "He maketh me to lie down..."

C | The LORD Is My Shepherd

Every line of the 23rd Psalm contains a powerful message. As my shepherd, the LORD leads me to green pastures and still waters for rest and restoration. He leads me in righteous paths for the glory of His name. When death threatens, I am not afraid, because He is with me. He anoints me, and comforts me, and feeds me even when enemies are near. He fills my cup to overflowing.

Psalms 23:6 - "Surely goodness and mercy shall follow me all the days of my life: and I will dwell in the house of the LORD for ever."

D | The King Of Glory Shall Come In

David emphasized that the earth, its fulness, and everyone therein are the LORD's. Abraham anticipated a holy city whose builder and maker was God. David anticipated the King of Glory entering the gates of the city of Jerusalem. Those with clean hands and clean hearts will someday ascend into His holy place and see Him there.

Psalms 24:9-10 - "Lift up your heads, O ye gates; even lift them up, ye everlasting doors; and the King of glory shall come in. Who is this King of glory? The LORD of hosts, he is the King of glory."

A | Let Me Not Be Ashamed

David often prayed something like this: "Let me not be ashamed." David was profoundly ashamed of his own sins and mistakes, and frequently abased himself verbally. He asked God to cover his sins and help him stand. On the other hand, David often prayed that his enemies would be ashamed because they dared take sides against God and His anointed.

Psalms 25:2-3 - "O my God, I trust in thee: let me not be ashamed, let not mine enemies triumph over me. Yea, let none that wait on thee be ashamed: let them be ashamed which transgress without cause."

B | Contrasting Job and David

There are many similarities between Job's self-defense and David's self-defense before God. But God was not so confrontational or harsh with David as He was with Job. It appears that David was much more forthcoming to admit his mistakes. He profusely asked God to redeem him from his errors and mercifully forgive him. It is always best to quickly confess your sins and repent.

Psalm 26:1-2,9 - "Judge me, O LORD, ...Examine me, O LORD, and prove me; try my reins and my heart. ...Gather not my soul with sinners, nor my life with bloody men."

B | The House of God

No man-made building on earth is more sacred than the House of God. In these days of multi-purpose buildings, gymnasiums and recreation centers, we need a place where we can find a sanctuary, a holy, sanctified environment for prayer, praise and the preaching of the Word. Sanctify God's house.

Psalms 27:4 - "One thing have I desired of the Lord, that will I seek after; that I may dwell in the house of the Lord all the days of my life, to behold the beauty of the Lord, and to enquire in his temple."

C | God Save The Righteous, Judge The Wicked

In our world of forced political correctness, the wicked demand respect, and the righteous are assaulted. But David clearly favored the righteous who feared God. "Save thy people, and bless thine inheritance: ...and lift them up for ever."

Psalms 28:3-4 - "Draw me not away with the wicked, and with the workers of iniquity, which speak peace to their neighbours, but mischief is in their hearts. Give them according to their deeds, and according to the wickedness of their endeavours: ...Because they regard not the works of the LORD, ...he shall destroy them, and not build them up."

D | The LORD Sitteth King Forever

"The LORD sitteth King forever," David proclaimed. This should be a self-evident truth, yet multitudes of anti-God protestors would banish the

Creator from His creation if they could. But in prophetic terms, His kingship can never be challenged. David reminded us that God's voice is on the waters, in the thunder, all powerful, full of majesty, and more. He exhorts us to give to the LORD the glory due to His name. "Worship the LORD in the beauty of holiness."

Psalms 29:10-11 - "The LORD sitteth King for ever. The LORD will give strength unto his people."

A | **Joy Comes In The Morning**

David wrote a song for all the saints to sing with thanksgiving when the Temple was finally dedicated. He praised God for saving him from his foes and healing him. "His anger endures but a moment, ...weeping may endure for a night, but joy cometh in the morning." David prayed that God would spare him from early death. He knew the dead cannot praise Him or teach His Truth. The new Temple would be cause for glorious celebrations, a testimony to countless victories over unspeakable adversities.

Psalm 30:12 - "O LORD my God, I will give thanks unto thee for ever."

B | **My Times Are In Thy Hands**

We remember David as a great warrior and a mighty king, but in his day, David agonized with God. He trusted God as his rock and his fortress. "Into thine hand I commit my spirit," (a Messianic prophecy), was David's sighing resignation in the face of many griefs, reproaches and slanders. "I am like a broken vessel." His confession, "My times are in thy hands," meant that David still trusted God's guidance, though enemies threatened and times were dark.

Psalms 31:24 - "Be of good courage, and he shall strengthen your heart, all ye that hope in the LORD."

C | **Confession And Repentance Bring Blessing**

David's "Beatitudes" said, "Blessed is he whose transgression is forgiven, whose sin is covered. Blessed is the man unto whom the LORD imputeth not iniquity, and in whose spirit there is no guile." Before David confessed his sins, he said that his "bones waxed old" and his "moisture" was turned into summer drought. But when he confessed and repented, he found a hiding place in God and a song of deliverance to sing. Need energizing? Try repenting.

Psalms 32:10 - "Many sorrows shall be to the wicked: but he that trusteth in the LORD, mercy shall compass him about."

D | Blessed Is The Nation Whose God Is The LORD

In all the history of mankind, few nations have prospered as Israel and the United States. Tragically, however, we are witnessing the meltdown of a once great civilization, because the countries which were founded by men who worshipped and honored the LORD God of Abraham, Isaac and Jacob have now turned their backs on Him and gone after "strange flesh" (homosexuality) and other gods - the gods of the heathen. No power on earth can override this prophecy.

Psalms 33:12 - "Blessed is the nation whose God is the LORD; and the people whom he hath chosen for his own inheritance."

A | This Poor Man Cried, And The LORD Heard Him

In younger days, David fled from King Saul's wrath to Philistine country. He hoped to remain anonymous for safety's sake, but unfortunately, some men recognized David. He feared that the king of Gath would capture him, so in desperation, David feigned madness to convince the king that he was no threat to him. That exasperating experience later inspired David to write a marvelous song of praise, Psalm 34. Sometimes, our most terrifying experiences become the greatest sources of inspiration.

Psalms 34:6 - "This poor man cried, and the LORD heard him, and saved him out of all his troubles."

B | Guardian Angels

Virtually every major Bible character had a personal encounter with an angel of the LORD. There was at least one angel in nearly every great story. From the cherub at the gate of the Garden of Eden, including Abraham, Lot, Isaac, Jacob, Moses, Joshua, Gideon, Manoah, David, Hezekiah, Daniel, Ezekiel, Mary, Joseph, Elizabeth, Jesus, Peter, Paul and others. The angels of the LORD were there as ministering spirits to those who shall be the heirs of salvation. Yours is there right now.

Psalms 34:7 - "The angel of the LORD encampeth round about them that fear him, and delivereth them."

C | I Will Bless The LORD At All Times

Psalm 34 contains several of the most-quoted verses in the Bible, probably because David's exclamations were so relevant to all our predicaments. It is a good read and a worthy bookmark in any time of trouble. "I will bless the LORD at all times: his praise shall continually be in my mouth. My soul shall make her boast in the LORD: ...O magnify the LORD with me, and let us exalt his name together." A great chapter to memorize.

Psalms 34:8 - "O taste and see that the LORD is good: blessed is the man that trusteth in him."

D | Many Are The Afflictions Of The Righteous

Who is righteous, if not Christ? Who was afflicted, if not Christ? At Gethsemane, his heart was broken. His contrite spirit surrendered to eternal purpose. David spoke prophetically of all the righteous, but especially Christ.

Psalms 34:17-20 - "The righteous cry, and the LORD heareth, and delivereth them out of all their troubles. The LORD is nigh unto them that are of a broken heart; and saveth such as be of a contrite spirit. Many are the afflictions of the righteous: but the LORD delivereth him out of them all. He keepeth all his bones: not one of them is broken."

A | Praying For Judgment On Enemies

Jesus cursed a fig tree because it did not bear fruit according to His wishes. But His action was typological. The entire Jewish nation would be judged for rejecting their Messiah. We are obliged to give equal weight to both the goodness and severity of God. His mercy and grace is boundless to repentant seekers, but His wrath is inevitable against those who persistently oppose Him. David justifiably prayed God's judgment on those who warred against his soul.

Psalms 35:1 - "Plead my cause, O LORD, with them that strive with me: fight against them that fight against me."

B | The Battle For The Soul Of Man

The thirty-fifth Psalm demonstrates David's grave concern for his soul. "Say unto my soul, I am thy salvation." "Let them be put to shame that seek after my soul." "They hid for me their net in a pit ...for my soul." "They rewarded me evil... to the spoiling of my soul." "Rescue my soul from their destructions." David called his soul, "my darling." I must overcome the enemies of my soul at any cost. David invoked supernatural intervention.

Psalm 35:5-6 – "Let the angel of the LORD chase them. ...Let the angel of the LORD persecute them."

C | God Is The Fountain Of Life

The wicked have no fear of God. They flatter themselves and become hateful. They speak evil and deception. They reject wisdom and good deeds. They devise mischief. But God in Heaven shows His faithfulness, righteousness, judgments and lovingkindness to those who trust Him. "They shall be abundantly satisfied with the fatness of thy house; and thou shalt make them drink of the river of thy pleasures. For with thee is the fountain of life: in thy light shall we see light."

Psalms 36:10 - "O continue thy lovingkindness unto them that know thee; and thy righteousness to the upright in heart."

D | The Meek Shall Inherit The Earth

Do not fret over evildoers. Do not envy sinners. "For they shall soon be cut down like the grass, and wither as the green herb. Trust in the LORD, and do good; so shalt thou dwell in the land, and verily thou shalt be fed. Delight thyself also in the LORD; and he shall give thee the desires of thine heart. Commit thy way unto the LORD; trust also in him; ...Rest in the LORD, and wait patiently for him."

Psalms 37:9 - "For evildoers shall be cut off: but those that wait upon the LORD, they shall inherit the earth."

C | God Provides A Safety Net

Famed aerialist, Karl Wallenda died at age 73 while attempting to walk a wire suspended 123 feet in the air between two hotels in San Juan, Puerto Rico. He had no safety net. An aerialist's life depends on the safety net. One simple mistake can result in sudden death. In the same way, only one transgression against God's laws means certain death. But God's amazing grace saves our lives again and again.

Psalms 37:24 - "Though he fall, he shall not be utterly cast down: for the LORD upholdeth him with his hand."

A | **Praying Your Way Out Of Depression**

David was deeply depressed and suffering from some disease. "My wounds stink and are corrupt because of my foolishness. ...my loins are filled with a loathsome disease: and there is no soundness in my flesh. ...My lovers and my friends stand aloof from my sore." He mourned God's heavy-handed punishments for past sins. Still, he prayed for help.

Psalms 38:15, 21-22 - "For in thee, O LORD, do I hope: thou wilt hear, O Lord my God. ...Forsake me not, O LORD: O my God, be not far from me. Make haste to help me, O Lord my salvation."

B | **Jeduthun, The Chief Musician**

Jeduthun, Asaph and Heman were musicians on trumpet, cymbals, psaltries, harps and other stringed instruments. David wrote three psalms (39, 62, 77) dedicated to Jeduthun, apparently to be sung by a choir. All three songs were much longer than those we are accustomed to hearing today. But they had a richer, more poignant message than songs nowadays. Perhaps we should invest more meaning into our modern songs than seven words sung twenty times.

Psalms 39:4 - "LORD, make me to know mine end, and the measure of my days, what it is; that I may know how frail I am."

C | **An Unbridled Tongue Brings Divine Rebuke**

This song-prayer bemoans God's stroke of rebuke. David promised to be much more careful with his tongue and keep his mouth with a bridle, because he had suffered so much from his previous errors. "My heart was hot within me, while I was musing the fire burned: then spake I with my tongue." Always engage your brain before running your mouth.

Psalms 39:10-11 - "Remove thy stroke away from me: I am consumed by the blow of thine hand. When thou with rebukes dost correct man for iniquity, thou makest his beauty to consume away like a moth."

D | **I Come To Do Thy Will, O God**

Paul quoted from Psalm 40 in Hebrews 10. David prophesied of Christ. "Wherefore when he cometh into the world, he saith, Sacrifice and offering thou wouldest not, but a body hast thou prepared me: In burnt offerings and sacrifices for sin thou hast had no pleasure. Then said I, Lo, I come (in the volume of the book it is written of me,) to do thy will, O God," vs. 5-7. David spoke of the Lamb slain from the foundation of the world.

□✓

Psalms 40:7 - "Lo, I come: in the volume of the book it is written of me."

A | **Heal My Soul**

David had a sick soul. "Mine enemies speak evil of me, When shall he die, and his name perish? ...An evil disease, say they, cleaveth fast unto him: and now that he lieth he shall rise up no more." But he remembered God's goodness. "Blessed is he that considereth the poor: the LORD will deliver him in time of trouble. The LORD will preserve him, and keep him alive." Do not believe the prognosis rendered by your enemies. Talk to God.

Psalms 41:4 - "I said, LORD, be merciful unto me: heal my soul; for I have sinned against thee."

D | **Mine Own Familiar Friend, In Whom I Trusted**

At the Last Supper, Jesus sopped the bread and gave it to Judas Iscariot, who quickly betrayed Him. He said, "I know whom I have chosen: but that the scripture may be fulfilled, He that eateth bread with me hath lifted up his heel against me," John 13:18. 1000 years earlier, King David had suffered a devastating betrayal loaded with prophetic implications of the future Christ. If you have been betrayed, remember that God has a purpose.

Psalms 41:9 - "Yea, mine own familiar friend, in whom I trusted, which did eat of my bread, hath lifted up his heel against me."

C | **Deep Calleth Unto Deep**

David elaborated his hunger and thirst for God. "As the hart panteth after the water brooks, so panteth my soul after thee, O God." So, "Why art thou cast down, O my soul?" Then a curious observation, "Deep calleth unto deep at the noise of thy waterspouts." Like a dreadful monsoon or tornado dips down from the sky and siphons water from the sea, the deep of God calls to the deep of man amidst great turmoil.

Psalms 42:11 - "Why art thou cast down, O my soul? and why art thou disquieted within me? hope thou in God."

B | **Light And Truth Lead Me To Thy Holy Hill**

Despondency was a frequent visitor to David. Same enemies. Same frustrations. Same questions. But every time, David prayed to God, and his spirit revived.

Psalms 43:3 - "O send out thy light and thy truth: let them lead me; let them bring me unto thy holy hill, and to thy tabernacles. Then will I go unto the altar of God, unto God my exceeding joy: yea, upon the harp will I praise thee, O God my God. Why art thou cast down, O my soul? and why art thou disquieted within me? hope in God: for I shall yet praise him."

A | For Thy Sake We Are Killed

David was smothering in negativity. He remembered old stories - how God miraculously brought Israel from Egypt into the Promised Land, but he lamented their present defeats and woes. He confessed his confusion about why things were so bad. "For thy sake are we killed all the day long." But you should never fall out with God over a few bad days. In the long tale, God always intervenes for His people. Prayer brings change.

Psalms 44:24,26 - "Wherefore hidest thou thy face, and forgettest our affliction and our oppression? ...Arise for our help, and redeem us for thy mercies' sake."

B | David Celebrates King Jesus

"My heart is inditing a good matter," David exclaimed. Inditing means gushing or bubbling forth. He proceeded to celebrate the King. But WHAT king is he celebrating? Not himself - the verses do not fit. Some say he was celebrating his son, Solomon. Perhaps. But verses 6-7 can only refer to the Son of Man, Messiah, Jesus Christ.

Psalms 45:6-7 - "Thy throne, O God, is for ever and ever: the sceptre of thy kingdom is a right sceptre. Thou lovest righteousness, and hatest wickedness: therefore God, thy God, hath anointed thee with the oil of gladness above thy fellows."

C | Selah - Pause And Think About It

Over seventy times, a psalm ends with the word "Selah." It means "pause and think about it." Every divine Truth deserves a "selah." "Selah" occurred three times in Psalm 46, each time following an assertion that God is our refuge. Some think this psalm was written while Israel was under siege. When you feel you are under siege, take refuge in God. Selah.

Psalm 46: 1-2 - "God is our refuge and strength, a very present help in trouble. Therefore will not we fear, though the earth be removed, and though the mountains be carried into the midst of the sea."

D | There Is A River

No river flows through Jerusalem presently. But the prophets David, Isaiah (66:12), Ezekiel (47) and Zechariah (14:8), say a river will someday flow from the threshold of the Temple in Jerusalem and divide eastward to the Dead Sea and westward to the Mediterranean. It also symbolizes the peace and rest that will characterize the reign of Messiah, Jesus Christ, as He rules over all the earth from Jerusalem for 1000 years.

Psalms 46:4 - "There is a river, the streams whereof shall make glad the city of God, the holy place of the tabernacles of the most High."

D | David: Christ To Be Exalted Following Armageddon

After speaking prophetically of a river in Jerusalem, the city of God, David continued, "God is in the midst of her; she shall not be moved: God shall help her, ...The LORD of hosts is with us; ...what desolations he hath made in the earth. He maketh wars to cease unto the end of the earth." He prophesied the war to end all wars - Armageddon - followed by crowning Jesus in Jerusalem as King of Kings.

Psalms 46:10 - "Be still, and know that I am God: I will be exalted among the heathen, I will be exalted in the earth."

A | Clapping, Shouting, Singing, Praising

It is unthinkable that God, in all His glorious majesty, might not be praised by His creation. "The LORD most high is terrible; He is a great King over all the earth." He will subdue all people and all nations. He will give His people their promised inheritance. So let us all exalt Him - with a shout, with a trumpet, singing praises to the King of all the earth! Applaud Him! Cheer Him! Lift your voice in songs and praise the LORD!

Psalms 47:1 - "O clap your hands, all ye people; shout unto God with the voice of triumph."

B | The City Of The Great King

Jerusalem is "the city of our God, in the mountain of his holiness. Beautiful for situation, the joy of the whole earth, is mount Zion, on the sides of the north, the city of the great King. ...Mark ye well her bulwarks [walls, fortresses]." The UN cannot have it. The Catholic Church cannot have it. The Muslims cannot have it. Jerusalem belongs to Jehovah Savior. Jesus Christ will soon retake it at Armageddon.

Psalms 48:8 - "So have we seen in the city of the LORD of hosts, in the city of our God: God will establish it for ever."

C | You Can't Take It With You

David discounted life without hope in God. "Both low and high, rich and poor, ...They that trust in their wealth, and boast themselves in the multitude of their riches; None of them can by any means redeem his brother, nor give to God a ransom for him: ...For he seeth that wise men die, likewise the fool and the brutish person perish, and leave their wealth to others." Worldly assets are no asset at all in eternity. Put your treasures in Heaven.

Psalms 49:15 - "But God will redeem my soul from the power of the grave: for he shall receive me."

D | Asaph Prophesies Christ At Armageddon

Asaph, one of David's chief musicians, wrote the Messianic Psalm 50, of Christ with His saints at Armageddon. Here is what he said: God has shined out of Zion, the perfection of beauty, unto the whole earth. God will come. He will not keep silent. A fire will devour before Him. A great tempest will surround Him. He will call and gather all His covenant saints from heaven to earth. He will judge His people, and the heavens will declare His righteousness.

Psalms 50:5,7 - "Gather my saints together unto me; ...O Israel, ...I am God, even thy God."

B | God Rejects False Claims On His Covenant

God published a fearful warning to sinners who claim the blessings of His covenant. "Unto the wicked God saith, What hast thou to do to declare my statutes, or that thou shouldest take my covenant in thy mouth?" He blasted them for hating instructions, casting away His word, consenting with criminals, partaking with adulterers, and speaking evil and deceit. God rejects all false claims on His covenant. If you want His blessings, get your act together now.

Psalms 50:22 - "Now consider this, ye that forget God, lest I tear you in pieces, and there be none to deliver."

A | Offer Thanksgiving. Offer Praise. Call Upon Me.

The psalmist exhorted Israel to call on God. Weary of their heartless rituals, God transcended the Law to make an offer of grace. God said, "I will take no bullock out of thy house, nor he goats out of thy folds." "Offer unto God thanksgiving; and pay thy vows unto the most High: And call upon me in the day of trouble: I will deliver thee." He warned the wicked to consider, lest He tear them to pieces.

Psalms 50:23 - "Whoso offereth praise glorifieth me: and to him that ordereth his conversation aright will I shew the salvation of God."

A | David's Repentance

David's sin with Bathsheba was devastating, and Nathan prophesied grievous punishment. Psalm 51 records David's repentance.

Psalms 51:1-4 - "[A Psalm of David, when Nathan the prophet came unto him, after he had gone in to Bathsheba.] Have mercy upon me, O God, according to thy lovingkindness: according unto the multitude of thy tender mercies blot out my transgressions. Wash me throughly from mine iniquity, and cleanse me from my sin. For I acknowledge my transgressions: and my sin is ever before me. Against thee, thee only, have I sinned, and done this evil in thy sight."

C | God Will Not Despise A Broken And Contrite Heart

Nathan's rebuke mortified David, so he turned to a painful soul-searching. "I was shapen in iniquity," and conceived in sin, but God requires "truth in the inward parts," and wisdom in the hidden places. He knew he could not cleanse himself. "Purge me with hyssop, and I shall be clean. Wash me and I shall be whiter than snow. ...Create in me a clean heart, O God; and renew a right spirit within me."

Psalms 51:17 - "The sacrifices of God are a broken spirit: a broken and a contrite heart, O God, thou wilt not despise."

A | Doeg Threatened David, But David Overcame By Faith

In Psalm 52, David overcame his enemy with a bold statement of faith. To escape Saul's assassination attempts against him, David fled to the priest, Ahimelech, at Nob (1 Samuel 21), but Saul's servant, Doeg was in town and threatened him. Great men of God consistently assert their faith in God during their fearful trials.

Psalms 52:1 - "[To the chief Musician, Maschil, A Psalm of David, when Doeg the Edomite came and told Saul, and said unto him, David is come to the house of Ahimelech.] Why boastest thou thyself in mischief, O mighty man? the goodness of God endureth continually."

B | God Despises Atheists

For the second time, David declared, "The fool hath said in his heart, There is no God." But he added more. Atheists are corrupt. They commit abominable iniquities. They do no good. God looks on this and sees that they are filthy. They eat up God's people like bread. But God will scatter their bones and put them to shame because He despises them and will show His vengeance.

Psalms 53:6 - "Oh that the salvation of Israel were come out of Zion! When God bringeth back the captivity of his people, Jacob shall rejoice, and Israel shall be glad."

C | When Enemies Pursue, God Will Help

David wrote a song about his terrifying experience while running from Saul. Twice, in 1 Samuel 23 & 26, David fled Saul's wrath to the wilderness of Ziph. Both times, someone tattled on David to Saul. David's only advantage was prayer. "Save me, O God, by thy name, ...For strangers are risen up against me, and oppressors seek after my soul." When pursuing enemies are closing in, you can call on God for help.

Psalms 54:4 - "Behold, God is mine helper: the Lord is with them that uphold my soul. He shall reward evil unto mine enemies."

D | A Prophecy About Judas Iscariot In Psalms

"It was not an enemy that reproached me; then I could have borne it: neither was it he that hated me that did magnify himself against me; then I would have hid myself from him: But it was thou, a man mine equal, my guide, and mine acquaintance. We took sweet counsel together, and walked unto the house of God in company." From an intimate dinner with Jesus, to the hill of evil counsel, 1000 years earlier, God foresaw Judas.

Psalms 55:15 - "Let death seize upon them, and let them go down quick into hell: for wickedness is in their dwellings."

A | Pray Without Ceasing

You really can pray all day long. Talking to God is as simple as talking with a friend who is riding in your car. God is with you 24/7. Why not talk with Him all day long? Everything needs a "prayer covering;" more than "dinner grace." Getting a job? Talk to God. Buying a house? Talk to God. Looking for a new dentist? Talk to God. Choosing a college major? Talk to God.

Psalms 55:17 - "Evening, and morning, and at noon, will I pray, and cry aloud: and he shall hear my voice."

A | When I Cry Unto Thee, My Enemies Turn Back

Long ago, when David fled to Gath from Saul's treachery, he sought asylum for a little while. But the Philistines of Gath did not want this Jewish hero in their midst and demanded the king of Gath send David away. David was in dire straits. He cried to God, "Mine enemies would daily swallow me up: for they be many that fight against me, O thou most High. What time I am afraid, I will trust in thee."

Psalms 56:8 - "Put thou my tears into thy bottle, ..When I cry unto thee, then shall mine enemies turn back."

A | My Heart Is Fixed

When David stumbled upon Saul (who was pursuing to kill him) in a cave, David cried, "Be merciful unto me, O God, be merciful unto me: for my soul trusteth in thee: yea, in the shadow of thy wings will I make my refuge, until these calamities be overpast." A true believer spontaneously calls on God in every crisis because his heart is fixed on God.

Psalms 57:7 - "My heart is fixed, O God, my heart is fixed: I will sing and give praise. ...For thy mercy is great unto the heavens, and thy truth unto the clouds."

B | There Is A Reward For The Righteous

Do you speak righteousness? Do you judge uprightly? Is there wickedness in your heart, or violence in your hands? The wicked go astray from the womb, speaking lies, stopping their ears, like poisonous serpents. God will break them. He will melt them. He will take them away. The righteous will rejoice at God's vengeance against the wicked. Here is all the preaching you should need to hear to convert your soul: "There shall be no reward to the evil man," Proverbs 24:20. So simple, but so profound.

Psalms 58:11 - "Verily there is a reward for the righteous."

C | In Times Of Trouble, I Will Sing

Saul made a total of twenty-one attempts to kill David. David's recourse was always the same - call on God. "Deliver me from mine enemies, O my God: defend me from them that rise up against me. ...they lie in wait for my soul: the mighty are gathered against me." During his gravest dangers, David wrote poetry and sang songs to the LORD!

Psalms 59:16 - "But I will sing of thy power; yea, I will sing aloud of thy mercy in the morning: for thou hast been my defence and refuge in the day of my trouble."

D | Moab Is My Washpot

David contemplated several regional conflicts he faced and declared, "God hath spoken in his holiness; I will rejoice, I will divide Shechem, ...Gilead is mine, ...Manasseh is mine; Ephraim also is the strength of mine head; ...Moab is my washpot; over Edom will I cast out my shoe." Concerning Moab, God washed away that incestuous seed of Lot. Concerning Edom, Jews cast out their shoe when they forfeited property. God forfeited Edom (Esau's descendants) - separated from Jacob's seed.

Psalms 60:11-12 - "Through God we shall do valiantly: for he it is that shall tread down our enemies."

A | Lead Me To The Rock

When you are overwhelmed, go to the Rock. When enemies encroach, run to the strong tower. The psalmist trusted in the covert of God's wings. He said he would abide in His Tabernacle forever. He believed that God would preserve him and prolong his life. Nobody is safe alone. I call Him Jesus, My Rock.

Psalms 61:2 - "From the end of the earth will I cry unto thee, when my heart is overwhelmed: lead me to the rock that is higher than I. For thou hast been a shelter for me, and a strong tower from the enemy."

B | He ONLY Is My Rock. I Shall Not Be Moved.

A choir leader named Ethan received this song from David. It was a psalm to encourage the people to trust in God. Look at the keywords he used throughout the song to refer to God: "HE ONLY IS my rock and my salvation." My defense. My expectation. My glory. My strength. My refuge. With such a great God, "...I shall not be moved."

Psalms 62:1,8 - "Truly my soul waiteth upon God: from him cometh my salvation. ...Trust in him at all times; ye people, pour out your heart before him: God is a refuge for us. Selah."

C | Thy Lovingkindness Is Better Than Life

The Psalms were not written in one sitting; not carefully outlined; not chronological. They were concocted on countless occasions, often on the run, especially during great trials, when these declarations, praises and prayers were literally the key to David's survival. They are poignant and inspiring. Once, while David was hiding in the wilderness of Judea, this phrase popped into his head. It is pregnant with meaning. Borrow it.

Psalms 63:3 - "Because thy lovingkindness is better than life, my lips shall praise thee. Thus will I bless thee while I live: I will lift up my hands in thy name."

D | The Arrows Of God

It is an incontrovertible truth. God will ultimately settle His displeasure with the wicked. It is prophetic. No matter that the wicked are, even today, in great power. God will absolutely and finally vindicate His righteous of their enemies. They "bend their bows to shoot their arrows, ...That they may shoot in secret at the perfect: suddenly do they shoot at him, ...But God shall shoot at them with an arrow; suddenly shall they be wounded."

Psalms 64:9-10 - "And all men shall fear, and shall declare the work of God; ...The righteous shall be glad in the LORD."

A | Thou That Hearest Prayers, To Thee Shall All Flesh Come

David exalted God, pronouncing His worthiness of praise, and that men should keep their vows unto Him. "O thou that hearest prayer, unto thee shall all flesh come." He recognized the universality of sin, and how eminently important it is for all men to turn to God to have their transgressions purged. Nobody can forgive and cleanse but our Great God!

Psalms 65:4 - "Blessed is the man whom thou choosest, and causest to approach unto thee, that he may dwell in thy courts: we shall be satisfied with the goodness of thy house, even of thy holy temple."

B | The Wealthy Place

"How terrible art thou in all thy works! ...Come and see the works of God: he is terrible in his doing toward the children of men." Why does the psalmist call God "terrible"? Because His works are sometimes truly dreadful (as the parting of the Red Sea and delivering Israel from Egypt to the Promised Land). God's "terrible" acts refine men as silver in the fire, but produce priceless results.

Psalms 66:12 - "Thou hast caused men to ride over our heads; we went through fire and through water: but thou broughtest us out into a wealthy place."

A | Futile Prayer

Some prayers are just useless. If we offend God by our sins and do not resolve the problem through proper repentance, the lines of communication are down. The Lord will not withhold blessings from someone in good standing with Him, but "God is angry with the wicked every day," Psalm 7:11. It is a hard saying, but true. He essentially says, "The only prayer I want to hear right now is repentance." Fortunately, God quickly responds to true repentance.

Psalms 66:18 - "If I regard iniquity in my heart, the Lord will not hear me."

B | God Governs The Nations

Lest the world forget, David prayed that God's ways would be known upon the earth and His saving health among all nations. We cannot prosper if we deny Him. "O let the nations be glad and sing for joy: for thou shalt judge the people righteously, and govern the nations upon earth. ...let all the people praise thee." God rules in the affairs of men. Worship Him!

Psalms 67:6 - "Then shall the earth yield her increase; and God, even our own God, shall bless us. God shall bless us; and all the ends of the earth shall fear him."

C | God Setteth The Solitary In Families

The psalmist prayed, "Let God arise, let his enemies be scattered, ...But let the righteous be glad; let them rejoice before God." He is Father to the fatherless, a judge for widows, a deliverer for those in chains, and He prepares goodness for the poor. Either way you look at it, God aggregates people. He separates the wicked to their place and gathers the righteous to their place. If you trust fully in Him, He will not leave you alone. He will send someone from the family of God to help you.

Psalms 68:6 - "God setteth the solitary in families."

D | Thou Hast Led Captivity Captive

Again and again, God has shown Himself to be the LORD of hosts - a mighty warrior. "When thou didst march through the wilderness; The earth shook, the heavens also dropped at the presence of God: even Sinai itself was moved at the presence of God, the God of Israel. ...Kings of armies did flee." The psalmist waxed prophetic, speaking of Messiah's ultimate conquest. Following Calvary, Jesus delivered all the righteous souls of the Old Testament from death and the grave.

Psalms 68:18 - "Thou hast ascended on high, thou hast led captivity captive: thou hast received gifts for men."

A | Bless God

In this text, the word blessing means to kneel as in worship. Repeatedly, the psalmist says, "Blessed be the LORD, ...bless ye God in the congregations, ...Sing unto God, ...O sing praises unto the Lord, ...Blessed be God." He declared that even the enemies of God saw how "the singers went before, the players on instruments followed after; among them were damsels playing with timbrels." When you go to pray, bless God. Sing, dance, kneel, worship, praise. Bless Him. Even Kings must bless the Lord.

Psalms 68:29 - "Because of thy Temple at Jerusalem shall kings bring presents unto thee."

C | God Will See You Through The Flood

Most of us have felt desperation like David's. "Save me, O God; for the waters are come in unto my soul. ...I am come into deep waters, where the floods overflow me." Sometimes enemies threaten us, and we feel overwhelmed - like we are drowning. "Let me not sink!" Like Jesus in Gethsemane, praying for the cup of suffering to pass, we pray for grace to survive our suffocating trials. But trials are ordained. Noah survived his flood, and you can survive yours.

Psalms 69:15 - "Let not the waterflood overflow me, neither let the deep swallow me up."

D | Prophecies Of Christ's Betrayal

Nineteen Messianic psalms contain 128 prophetic facts about Jesus Christ. They also contain 72 facts about the traitor, Judas Iscariot. Psalm 69 contains several of those facts. Of Judas, "Let their table become a snare before them, ...Let their habitation be desolate; ...Let them be blotted out of the book of the living," and more. Of Christ, "They hate me without a cause, ...They gave me gall for my meat; and in my thirst they gave me vinegar to drink."

Psalms 69:20 - "Reproach hath broken my heart; ...I looked for some to take pity, ...but I found none."

A | Repetitious Prayers

Jesus said, "When ye pray, use not vain repetitions." Saying forty "Our Fathers" or twenty "Hail, Marys" is vain repetition. Worthless. Yet repetitious prayer is perfectly in order. Five times in the Psalms, David asked God to "make haste" to help him. Twenty-six times he prayed, "Deliver me." Eight times he prayed "Let them be ashamed," over his enemies. Literally dozens of phrases are oft repeated throughout the book of Psalms. Every time you have a need, pray about it, even if it is the one-hundredth time.

Psalms 70:1 - "Make haste, O God, to deliver me."

B | David Promised To Praise God

David wrote 75 of the 150 Psalms. Fifty were anonymous. The rest were written by Asaph, Heman, Solomon, Ethan, and one from Moses. Twenty Psalms are prayers of distress. Each time David cried out to God for help, for salvation, for deliverance, for protection, he also promised to praise God for His blessings. Be careful to praise God for every answered prayer.

Psalms 71:22-24 - "I will also praise thee with the psaltery, ...unto thee will I sing with the harp, ...My lips shall greatly rejoice when I sing unto thee; ...My tongue also shall talk of thy righteousness."

D | Shadows Versus Substance

Typology is the study of prefigurative symbols. Temporal, material things often reveal eternal, spiritual things. David wrote Psalm 72 "for Solomon," a prayer for his son-king. But it is mostly prophetic of the coming kingdom of Christ. Most of its context was NOT fulfilled in Solomon, lending evidence that it truly refers to Jesus.

Psalms 72:5,8,11,17 - "They shall fear thee as long as the sun and moon endure, ...He shall have dominion also from sea to sea, ...all kings shall fall down before him: all nations shall serve him, ...His name shall endure for ever."

A | It Is Good For Me To Draw Near To God

Asaph expressed his frustration with himself for envying the prosperity of the wicked and how they seemed to escape punishment. He felt that his attempts to live righteously had gone unrewarded. He reminded himself how proud, corrupt, violent and blasphemous they were. "Until I went into the sanctuary of God; then understood I their end. Surely thou didst set them in slippery places: thou castedst them down into destruction."

Psalms 73:28 - "It is good for me to draw near to God: I have put my trust in the Lord GOD, that I may declare all thy works."

D | Asaph, The Seer

Asaph, the choir and orchestra conductor and composer, wrote Psalm 50 and 73-83. Decades later, King Hezekiah called Asaph a seer (prophet). Asaph lamented great spiritual decline in Israel in Solomon's latter years. Asaph mourned the profaning of the Sanctuary and heathen insurgencies throughout the land. "We see not our signs: there is no more any prophet: neither is there among us any that knoweth how long." Asaph yearned for God to intervene.

Psalms 74:12,22 - "God is my King of old, working salvation in the midst of the earth. ...Arise, O God, plead thine own cause."

C | God Promotes And Exalts Whom He Will

Who could have known better than King David that promotion comes from the LORD? God cuts off "the horns of the wicked," and exalts "the horns of the righteous." The ancients considered horns on beasts as symbols of their strength and power. So when God exalts or cuts off the horns, He is either strengthening or weakening men at His discretion.

Psalms 75:5-7 - "Lift not up your horn on high: ...For promotion cometh neither from the east, nor from the west, nor from the south. But God is the judge: he putteth down one, and setteth up another."

B | God Is Notorious In Israel, Jerusalem And Zion

God is known, and His name is great in Israel. His Tabernacle is in Salem (Jerusalem). His dwelling place is in (Mount) Zion. God broke His enemies' weapons there. They are spoiled and in a dead sleep. "Thou art to be feared." NEVER forget that God chose Israel for Himself. Not one enemy, ancient or modern, will ever take it away from Him.

Psalms 76:11 - "Let all that be round about him bring presents unto him that ought to be feared. He shall cut off the spirit of princes: he is terrible to the kings of the earth."

A | Remind Yourself Of God's Former Works Before You Pray

The psalmists often declared that God hears prayer. "I cried unto God with my voice, ...and he gave ear unto me. In the day of my trouble I sought the Lord." Then he reflected, "I call to remembrance my song in the night." Before making new requests, it is very beneficial to remember how many great things God has already done!

Psalms 77:10-12 - "I will remember the years of the right hand of the most High. I will remember the works of the LORD: ...I will meditate also of all thy work, and talk of thy doings."

D | The Ancient Signs From God Condemn Unbelief

Asaph enumerated many miraculous works of God for Israel: the plagues in Egypt, His dividing the Red Sea, leading them with a cloud by day, and fire by night, giving them water out of rocks, "angels' food" - manna from heaven, quail for meat, and ultimately, His Law - His testimony. God's past works condemn our unbelief.

Psalms 78:32 - "For all this they sinned still, ...Therefore their days did he consume in vanity, ...When he slew them, then they sought him: ...and enquired early after God. ...And they remembered that God was their rock, and the high God their redeemer."

A | Pray During A Holocaust

The seventy-ninth Psalm is perhaps one of the most desperate prayers in the Bible. It mourns devastating losses in Jerusalem by the hands of heathen enemies. Even during a holocaust, prayer is more necessary than ever.

Psalms 79:1-3, 9 - "O God, the heathen are come into thine inheritance; thy holy temple have they defiled; they have laid Jerusalem on heaps. The dead bodies of thy servants have they given to be meat unto the fowls of the heaven. ...Help us, O God of our salvation, ...deliver us, and purge away our sins, for thy name's sake."

D | Messiah Will Save God's Vineyard

Asaph prayed while mourning God's fierce dealings with backsliding Israel. He reminded God how He "brought a vine out of Egypt: thou hast cast out the heathen, and planted it. ...and didst cause it to take deep root, and it filled the land." "O God of hosts: look down from heaven, and behold, and visit this vine; And the vineyard which thy right hand hath planted." Then he prayed for Messiah to save His vineyard.

Psalms 80:17 - "Let thy hand be upon the man of thy right hand, upon the son of man whom thou madest strong for thyself."

B | A Law And A Statue To Worship God With Music

God grieves when His people fail to praise and worship Him, but He delights to hear their praises. Throughout the ages, His prophets have urged His people to sing loudly, make a joyful noise, play musical instruments, and declare His goodness. Why? For His mighty works in our behalf from ancient days.

Psalms 81:1-4 - "Sing aloud unto God our strength: make a joyful noise unto the God of Jacob. ...bring hither the timbrel, the pleasant harp with the psaltery. Blow up the trumpet, ...For this was a statute for Israel, and a law of the God of Jacob."

C | God Is Our Source Of Justice And True Judgment

Asaph said, "I have said, Ye are gods; and all of you are children of the most High. But ye shall die like men." Asaph was correcting himself. We are no gods. At best, we are children of the Lord if we are born again of His Spirit. Only God can judge righteously among men. He exhorts us to judge justly among the poor, the fatherless, the afflicted and needy. But only as we appropriate the wisdom of God may we walk in righteous judgment.

Psalms 82:8 - "Arise, O God, judge the earth: for thou shalt inherit all nations."

A | Pray That Men May Know God Defends Israel

Asaph prayed to God, "hold not thy peace, and be not still." "Thine enemies make a tumult: ...They have taken crafty counsel against thy people, ...They have said, Come, and let us cut them off from being a nation; that the name of Israel may be no more in remembrance." Even now, as in ancient times, God alone will save Israel.

Psalms 83:17-18 - "Let them be confounded and troubled for ever; yea, let them be put to shame, and perish: That men may know that thou, whose name alone is JEHOVAH, art the most high over all the earth."

C | **God Is A Blesser**

Look at God's track record! He blessed Adam with a garden paradise. He blessed Noah with an escape route from the flood. He blessed Lot, sending angels to deliver him from Sodom. He blessed Joseph with dominion over Egypt. He blessed fleeing Israel with sensational miracles. He sent miraculous food, miraculous water, even miraculous shoes! There is no need God cannot provide. Stop thinking God cannot or will not bless you, too!

Psalms 84:11 - "...the LORD will give grace and glory: no good thing will he withhold from them that walk uprightly."

C | **Revival**

One of the greatest principles in the Bible is revival. Since creation's dawn, God was the giver of life. Not only can God create and give life, but He also has the power to resurrect that which has died. Throughout the scriptures we see examples of God raising the dead. Ezekiel saw Israel as a valley of dried bones, but the Spirit of God came on them, and they revived. Destroyed in 70 AD, Israel revived in 1948. I believe in divine revivals.

Psalms 85:6 - "Wilt thou not revive us again: that thy people may rejoice in thee?"

B | **There Is Only One God, And All Nations Will Worship Him**

In the midst of one of David's earnest prayers for God's help, he made several profound declarations concerning God. "Among the gods there is none like unto thee, O Lord; neither are there any works like unto thy works. All nations whom thou hast made shall come and worship before thee, O Lord; and shall glorify thy name." Two eternal truths are affirmed here: God is the only God, and all nations will finally worship Him. No power on earth can change that.

Psalms 86:10 - "For thou art great, and doest wondrous things: thou art God alone."

D | **The Foundation Of God Is In Zion**

The world wonders how the Middle East crisis will ever be resolved. Powerful men from powerful nations exhaust themselves daily, looking for ways to settle "the Jerusalem issue." Who will ultimately control Jerusalem? God will. He set Israel above all nations and Jerusalem above all cities. The psalmist reveals that when He (Messiah) comes to reign, multitudes will wish they were born there.

Psalms 87:1-3 - "His foundation is in the holy mountains. The LORD loveth the gates of Zion more than all the dwellings of Jacob. Glorious things are spoken of thee, O city of God."

A | Pray Like A Dying Man

People pray differently when they think they are dying. Our prayers are often too light-hearted; our intercessions fail to manifest urgency. But when we think we are dying, that changes. In the 1600s, a preacher named Richard Baxter was transformed by a series of grave illnesses. "As a dying man, my soul was the more brought to seriousness, and to preach as a dying man to dying men."

Psalms 88:2-3 - "Let my prayer come before thee: incline thine ear unto my cry; For my soul is full of troubles: and my life draweth nigh unto the grave."

D | God's Covenant With David

God promised David, "Thy seed will I establish for ever, and build up thy throne to all generations." Messiah will soon come and revive the Throne of David. "His seed also will I make to endure for ever, and his throne as the days of heaven. ...If his children forsake my law, ...Then will I visit their transgression with the rod, ...Nevertheless my lovingkindness will I not utterly take from him."

Psalms 89:34-36 - "My covenant will I not break, ...I will not lie unto David. His seed shall endure for ever, and his throne as the sun before me."

B | The Days Of Our Years Are Three-Score-And-Ten

Moses was 120 when he died. But in Moses' prayer (Psalm 90), the old prophet magnified God for being "our dwelling place in all generations. ...from everlasting to everlasting, thou art God." As God is timeless, so things on earth are increasingly short-lived - especially man. "The days of our years are threescore years and ten; and if by reason of strength they be fourscore years, yet is their strength labour and sorrow; for it is soon cut off, and we fly away."

Psalms 90:12 - "So teach us to number our days, that we may apply our hearts unto wisdom."

C | God's Angels Will Bear You Up

What is it like in God's "secret place"? His shadow and "wings" cover you. He is your refuge and fortress. He delivers you from snares and pestilence. His shield protects you. Night terrors and flying arrows do not frighten you. When the LORD is your habitation, destruction comes to others, but "there shall no evil befall thee, neither shall any plague come nigh thy dwelling."

Psalms 91:11 - "For he shall give his angels charge over thee, to keep thee in all thy ways. They shall bear thee up in their hands, lest thou dash thy foot against a stone."

A | Set Your Love Upon Him

How often do you encounter someone who has genuine affection for God? There is no more important reason for living than to give joy and pleasure to our Creator. We were created by Him, but also FOR His pleasure. He is thrilled to see us loving, worshipping, serving, even singing to Him. He promised to provide His choicest favors to those who live to please Him. Who on earth can compete with that offer?

Psalms 91:14 - "Because he hath set his love upon me, therefore will I deliver him: I will set him on high."

B | The Righteous Shall Flourish. The Wicked Shall Perish.

It is a good thing to give thanks unto the LORD and to sing praises unto His name. Sing praises to Him for His lovingkindness with stringed instruments. Brutish men or fools cannot know or understand this. The wicked "shall be destroyed forever, ...shall perish, ...shall be scattered." The righteous shall flourish like palm trees and cedars. This simple truth is nevertheless profound.

Psalms 92:13-14 - "Those that be planted in the house of the LORD shall flourish in the courts of our God. They shall still bring forth fruit in old age; they shall be fat and flourishing."

C | Holiness Becometh God's House

The LORD is "clothed with majesty; ...with strength." His Throne is established of old. He established the world. He is from everlasting. He is mightier than all the floods and waves of the sea. Of who else in the universe can these things be said? Who is great like the LORD? Everything His word declares about Him is forever settled. If anything anywhere is holy, it is God and His house. We should keep the LORD's house sanctified and never profane it.

Psalms 93:5 - "Thy testimonies are very sure: holiness becometh thine house, O LORD, for ever."

D | The LORD Will Not Cast Off His People

There is prophecy in the statement, "The LORD will not cast off his people, neither will he forsake his inheritance." Despite everything we could say about the righteous flourishing and wicked perishing, God has made covenants with Israel. After centuries of apostasy, still God has never totally written them off. At the end of this age, Jesus will come and save Israel. That is the priceless, unimaginable benefit of covenant with God who cannot lie.

Psalms 94:14-15 - "For the LORD will not cast off his people, neither will he forsake his inheritance. But judgment shall return unto righteousness."

A | Harden Not Your Heart

This Psalm admonishes us to "make a joyful noise" to the LORD; ...sing unto the LORD; ...come ...with thanksgiving; ...worship; ..bow down, ...kneel before the LORD our maker; ...For he is our God." Then, a sudden warning: Do not provoke Me as Israel did, by hardening your hearts. I will ban you from entering into My rest. If you fail to worship God as He so richly deserves, you offend Him greatly. It is grim folly to disdain your Creator.

Psalms 95:7-8 - "To day if ye will hear his voice, Harden not your heart, as in the provocation."

D | He Cometh To Judge The Earth

Throughout the Psalms, we are admonished countless times to sing and worship and praise God for all His wonders. "For the LORD is great, and greatly to be praised: he is to be feared above all gods. For all the gods of the nations are idols: but the LORD made the heavens." In addition to praising God, we are commanded to instruct the heathen that God reigns over all. "Say among the heathen that the LORD reigneth."

Psalms 96:13 - "For he cometh to judge the earth: he shall judge the world with righteousness, and the people with his truth."

C | Light Is Sown For The Righteous

The LORD reigns majestically. Clouds and darkness obscure Him. Righteousness and judgment fill His throne. Fires consume His enemies. The wonders of nature - lightning, earthquakes, volcanoes - testify to His glories. Those who serve idols and images must someday worship Him. God's people, (i.e., Zion, daughters of Judah, all His saints) will be preserved and delivered from those wicked. For those who WANT to see, God shines light, revealing His glories. All others are blinded and darkened.

Psalms 97:11 - "Light is sown for the righteous, and gladness for the upright in heart. Rejoice in the LORD, ye righteous."

B | The Right Hand Of God

No man has seen God, except allegorically in dreams or visions. The eternal Spirit dwells "in the light which no man can approach unto; whom no man hath seen, nor can see," 1 Timothy 6:16. Jesus, the fullness of God bodily, dwells at the right hand of the Majesty and is the arm, even the face of God. God reaches down to man through His Son - the man, Jesus Christ.

Psalms 98:1 - "O sing unto the LORD a new song; for he hath done marvellous things: his right hand, and his holy arm, hath gotten him the victory."

B | He Sitteth Between The Cherubims

God was literally present in Jerusalem. The psalmist said, "He sitteth between the cherubims," which were the golden angels on the mercy seat atop the Ark of the Covenant. "The LORD is great in Zion; and he is high above all the people." Isaiah described that scene years later when he saw the LORD high and lifted up, and His train filled the Temple. God was in the Temple, sitting above the Ark, on His holy hill - Mount Moriah.

Psalms 99:9 - "Exalt the LORD our God, and worship at his holy hill; for the LORD our God is holy."

A | Make A Joyful Noise Unto The LORD

This psalm needs no commentary. Just do what it says! "Make a joyful noise unto the LORD, all ye lands. Serve the LORD with gladness: come before his presence with singing. Know ye that the LORD he is God: it is he that hath made us, and not we ourselves; we are his people, and the sheep of his pasture. Enter into his gates with thanksgiving, and into his courts with praise: be thankful unto him, and bless his name."

Psalms 100:5 - "For the LORD is good; his mercy is everlasting; and his truth endureth to all generations."

C | I Will Do Right

Emulate righteous men. King David lived by these affirmations: I will sing of mercy and judgment unto thee, O LORD. I will behave myself wisely in a perfect way. I will walk within my house with a perfect heart. I will set no wicked thing before mine eyes. I will not know a wicked person. I will cut off slanderers. I will not suffer a high look and a proud heart. I will cut off wicked doers. What will YOU do?

Psalms 101:3 - "I will set no wicked thing before mine eyes: I hate the work of them that turn aside."

D | The LORD Shall Appear In His Glory In Zion

God's chosen people of Israel have suffered countless holocausts and genocide attempts for centuries. But God promised to return them to Jerusalem and rebuild Zion. No one will ever destroy Israel. Jesus will soon come and crush all their enemies at Armageddon.

Psalms 102:13, 15-16 - "Thou shalt arise, and have mercy upon Zion: for the time to favour her, yea, the set time, is come. ...So the heathen shall fear the name of the LORD, and all the kings of the earth thy glory. When the LORD shall build up Zion, he shall appear in his glory."

B | The Created Throne Of God

One of the many things that God created is His own Throne. The psalmist said, "The LORD hath prepared His throne in the heavens." "Prepared" in Hebrew means "set up, erected." God was a lone Spirit in a void universe. Eventually, He created the city of Heaven, and set up a Throne for Himself. Even in His Throne, He is invisible, because He is a Spirit, and dwells in the light whom no man hath seen, nor can see. He was an infinite Spirit before He had a Throne.

Psalm 103:19 - "The LORD hath prepared his throne in the heavens."

A | Exalt His Majesty

The psalmist waxed eloquent, attempting to paint a word-picture of God's majesty. "He is clothed with light as a garment. He stretches out the heavens like a curtain. He lays the beams of His chambers in the waters. He makes the clouds His chariots. He walks on the wings of the wind. He makes His angels spirits; His ministers a flaming fire." God's majesty (grandeur, sovereignty, power and authority) far exceeds all allegories.

Psalms 104:24 - "O LORD, how manifold are thy works! in wisdom hast thou made them all: the earth is full of thy riches."

D | God Remembers His Covenants Forever

The fulfilled prophecies and covenants of God - His mighty works in behalf of Abraham, Isaac, Jacob, Joseph, Moses, Aaron, the plagues of Egypt and the miracles in the wilderness, and more - are endless reminders that our God never fails.

Psalms 105:8 - "He hath remembered his covenant for ever, the word which he commanded to a thousand generations. Which covenant he made with Abraham, and his oath unto Isaac; And confirmed the same unto Jacob for a law, and to Israel for an everlasting covenant: Saying, Unto thee will I give the land of Canaan, the lot of your inheritance."

C | Never Make Excuses For The Miracles Of The Bible

Skeptics argue against the miraculous parting of the Red Sea, saying the Israelites crossed the "Sea of Reeds" in a dried shallow area at low tide. How then did Pharaoh's army drown in a shallow marsh when the tide came back? If Israel even reached the Red Sea, that concedes that other miracles had already occurred - the burning bush, the rod and snake, the leprosy, dreadful plagues on Egypt, and more. The Bible is unequivocally true. Only skeptics will be disproven - not God.

Psalms 106:11 - "And the waters covered their enemies: there was not one of them left."

A | Dark Trials Inspire Us To Pray

People who "sit in darkness and in the shadow of death, being bound in affliction and iron, ...cried unto the LORD in their trouble, and He saved them out of their distresses." Again, "They that go down to the sea in ships, that do business in great waters; These see the works of the LORD, and his wonders in the deep. ...they cry unto the LORD in their trouble, ...he bringeth them unto their desired haven." Affliction compels men to search out God.

Psalms 107:20 - "He sent his word, and healed them, and delivered them from their destructions."

C | He Shall Tread Down His Enemies

The verses of Psalm 108 are copied from Psalms 57 and 60. It is not uncommon for content to be repeated in the Bible. Many stories of the chronicles of the kings were told twice. The Gospels tell the story of Jesus four times. Why the repetition? Repetition is an unrivaled teaching method. So why is this psalm repeated? It emphatically reminds us that God is exceedingly worthy to be praised and does as He pleases over the cities of men.

Psalms 108:13 - "Through God we shall do valiantly: for he it is that shall tread down our enemies."

A | Adversaries And Prayer

The best way to deal with your enemies is to go to prayer first of all. It is a dangerous thing to tangle with your enemies before presenting the situation to God. A cool head, a quiet tongue and an earnest prayer is a better strategy than a carnally-minded confrontation that will almost certainly produce bad results. Pray for those who despitefully use you. Let God work on the situation before you make a big mess of it.

Psalms 109:4 - "For my love they are my adversaries: but I give myself unto prayer."

B | Melchizedek

Abraham warred against (Iraq) and (Iran) to avenge their siege on Lot and the city of Sodom. He recovered people and possessions. Melchizedek brought bread, wine and blessings for Abraham, who gave him tithes of everything recovered. This Melchizedek, "king of Salem, priest of the most high God," was not Christ, but a type. Both were king and priest of Jeru-salem. Melchizedek's offering of bread and wine portended Jesus' offering body and blood at Calvary.

Psalms 110:4 - "The LORD hath sworn, and will not repent, Thou art a priest for ever after the order of Melchizedek."

D | God Performs His Covenant

The works of the LORD are great, honorable, glorious and memorable. He gives meat to those who fear Him. He never forgets His covenant. He shows His powerful works to give His people their promised heritage, and He does so in truth and uprightness. He redeems His people and keeps His covenant. Holy and reverend is His name. We should both fear and praise a great God like that. "Praise ye the LORD."

Psalms 111:10 - "The fear of the LORD is the beginning of wisdom: a good understanding have all they that do his commandments."

B | The Righteous Man

The righteous man fears God and obeys His commandments. He is gracious, compassionate, giving, and discreet. His heart is fixed - established. He is not afraid of bad news because He trusts in the LORD. He lives to see his desire over his enemies. His generation is blessed by God, and his righteousness endures forever. In contrast, the wicked grieve and gnash their teeth at the sight of the righteous. They will melt away and not see their desires.

Psalms 112:1 - "Praise ye the LORD. Blessed is the man that feareth the LORD, that delighteth greatly in his commandments."

C | The Name Of The LORD Is To Be Praised

Hundreds of times, the scriptures urge us to praise the LORD. And the reasons are endless. "The LORD is high above all nations. ...He raiseth up the poor out of the dust, and lifteth the needy out of the dunghill; That he may set him with princes, ...He maketh the barren woman to keep house, and to be a joyful mother of children. Praise ye the LORD." Jesus - Jehovah Incarnate - deserves all praise.

Psalm 113:3 - "From the rising of the sun unto the going down of the same the LORD'S name is to be praised."

B | The Presence Of The LORD

The presence of God was so awesome in the midst of Israel as they were escaping from Egypt, the psalmist declared, "The sea saw it, and fled. The mountains skipped like rams." If God's presence could turn back the flood-waters and make the earth quake, just imagine what the presence of the LORD will do in your life!

Psalms 114:7 - "Tremble, thou earth, at the presence of the Lord, at the presence of the God of Jacob; Which turned the rock into a standing water, the flint into a fountain of waters."

B | Idols Are Nothing

The idols of the heathen are silver and gold - the work of men's hands. They have mouths that cannot speak, eyes that cannot see, ears that cannot hear, noses that cannot smell, hands that cannot hold anything, and feet that cannot go anywhere. The people who make such absurdities, or put their trust in them, are like them. Worship the one, true, living God!

Psalms 115:3,11 - "But our God is in the heavens: he hath done whatsoever he hath pleased. ...Ye that fear the LORD, trust in the LORD: he is their help and their shield."

A | Pray For Comfort In The Face Of Death

Shortly before my wife died of cancer at 51, I found Psalm 116 underlined in her childhood Bible. As a teen-ager, she had experienced a dread of dying, and these verses comforted her. "I love the LORD, because he hath heard my voice ...sorrows of death compassed me... Then called I upon the name of the LORD... thou hast delivered my soul from death, mine eyes from tears, and my feet from falling." Whether we live or die, we are the LORD's.

Psalms 116:15 - "Precious in the sight of the LORD is the death of his saints."

A | Praise The LORD

Psalm 117 has the distinction of being both the shortest chapter in the Bible AND the middle chapter in the King James Version. There are 594 chapters BEFORE and 594 chapters AFTER Psalm 117. Remember, the original texts had no chapter or verse divisions for hundreds of years. Nevertheless, the message of Psalm 117 is an appropriate centerpiece to the entire Bible.

Psalms 117:1-2 - "O praise the LORD, all ye nations: praise him, all ye people For his merciful kindness is great toward us: and the truth of the LORD endureth for ever. Praise ye the LORD."

D | The Rejected Stone Becomes The Corner Stone

This great Messianic psalm is about trusting the LORD. It speaks of "this gate of the LORD, into which the righteous shall enter," which certainly pertains to Christ. Then he says thou "art become my salvation. The stone which the builders refused is become the head stone of the corner. This is the LORD'S doing; it is marvellous in our eyes." Prophetic destiny overrules the will of men.

Psalms 118:24,26 - "This is the day which the LORD hath made; we will rejoice and be glad in it. ...Blessed be he that cometh in the name of the LORD."

C | **Adversity**

A seafood purveyor noticed that live fish stored in tanks for long periods ended up being tough and tasteless when finally eaten. What was wrong? They became too sedate, lazy, inactive. His remedy? He put a small shark in the tank. It livened up the fish and made them active again. They proved to be delicious when finally served to diners. The moral? Adversity is good for us. The sharks in our lives make us more active, stronger and healthier.

Psalms 119:67 - "Before I was afflicted I went astray: but now have I kept thy word."

D | **The Entrance Of Thy Words Giveth Light**

Humans cannot see in total darkness. Light is essential to sight. The 119th Psalm declares again and again that keeping the commandments and precepts of God gives understanding and light. The Old Testament prophets were called seers - enlightened because of the word of God in their souls. "I have more understanding than all my teachers: for thy testimonies are my meditation. I understand more than the ancients, because I keep thy precepts," Psalms 119:99-100. Want to know the future? Read the Word!

Psalms 119:130 - "The entrance of thy words giveth light; it giveth understanding unto the simple."

A | **Order My Steps In Thy Word**

The 119th Psalm is divided into sections of eight verses each, headed by each letter of the Hebrew alphabet. Some call it the "Psalm of the Word of God" because it very repetitiously emphasizes the blessings of observing and obeying the Word of God. Its key phrases are very synonymous. Walk in the Law. Keep His testimonies. Keep His precepts. Keep His statutes. Respect His commandments. Learn His righteous judgments. Delight in His statutes. Keep His word. We should be so repetitious, to observe His word all day long, every day.

Psalm 119:133 - "Order my steps in thy word."

D | **The Home Of The Enemy Who Will Attack Israel At Armageddon**

Augustine Calmet, who published a groundbreaking Bible commentary in 1707, said, "Meshec was apparently the father of the Mosquians (Islamists), who dwelt in the mountains that separate Iberia from Armenia, and both from Colchis (modern Georgia and Eastern Turkey).

This priceless clue identifies Meshech of Ezekiel 38. The warrior who will attack Israel and be defeated by Jesus Christ at Armageddon will come from Mesheck (Georgia/Southern Russia).

Psalm 120:5-7 - "Woe is me, that I sojourn in Mesech, ...My soul hath long dwelt with him that hateth peace. I am for peace: but when I speak, they are for war."

C | Divine Protection 24/7

The eternal Spirit of God is forever conscious. He is wide-awake, aware, in-touch, on-the-job. If we could comprehend the awesome magnitude of His omnipotence and omniscience, we would never doubt His ability to care for us in infinite detail. He knows the number of hairs on our head, and He discerns not only our thoughts, but also our intentions. From the farthest reaches of the universe, to the infinite depths of our heart and soul, God is aware of it all.

Psalm 121:3 - "...he that keepeth thee will not slumber."

A | Pray For The Peace Of Jerusalem

David said, "I was glad when they said unto me, Let us go into the house of the LORD. Our feet shall stand within thy gates, O Jerusalem." The tribes of Israel assembled before the Ark to give thanks unto the name of the LORD. Jerusalem is hallowed to God and His saints. He dwelled in the Temple in ancient times, and will soon return to build His Millennial Temple there.

Psalms 122:6,9 - "Pray for the peace of Jerusalem: they shall prosper that love thee. ...Because of the house of the LORD our God I will seek thy good."

A | I Lift Up My Eyes Unto The LORD

Every man and woman has need of the mercy of God to face the many adversaries and adversities of life, and we need God's help to endure the contempt, scorn and pride of those who vex our souls. Look up to heaven and call on the LORD.

Psalms 123:2-3 - "As the eyes of servants look unto the hand of their masters, and as the eyes of a maiden unto the hand of her mistress; so our eyes wait upon the LORD our God, until that he have mercy upon us. Have mercy upon us, O LORD."

C | If It Had Not Been The LORD Who Was On Our Side

If God had not fought for us against our enemies, they would have consumed us. "Then the waters had overwhelmed us, the stream had gone over our soul: ...Our soul is escaped as a bird out of the snare of the fowlers: the snare is broken, and we are escaped. Our help is in the name of the LORD, who made heaven and earth."

Psalms 124:2-3 - "If it had not been the LORD who was on our side, when men rose up against us: Then they had swallowed us up quick, when their wrath was kindled against us."

B | The Mountains Round About Jerusalem

Permanence. "They that trust in the LORD shall be as mount Zion, which cannot be removed." The mountains of Jerusalem will never remove as long as time shall be. Neither shall the goodness of God remove from those that are good and upright in heart. Those that do iniquity, however, "turn aside unto their crooked ways, the LORD shall lead them forth." God will remove them. Mentioned 154 times, Zion is God's favorite place on earth.

Psalms 125:2 - "As the mountains are round about Jerusalem, so the LORD is round about his people from henceforth even for ever."

C | They That Sow In Tears Shall Reap In Joy

"Am I dreaming?" That must have been the thoughts of thousands of Jews returning to Zion from seventy years of captivity in Babylon. They were laughing and singing, and their enemies were saying, "The LORD has done great things for them!" If you have suffered exile or hardships due to past sins, you will make a glorious comeback if you will keep the faith and do righteousness.

Psalms 126:5-6 - "They that sow in tears shall reap in joy. He that goeth forth and weepeth, bearing precious seed, shall doubtless come again with rejoicing, bringing his sheaves with him."

D | Except The LORD Build The House...

"Except the LORD build the house, they labour in vain that build it: except the LORD keep the city, the watchman waketh but in vain. It is vain for you to rise up early, to sit up late, to eat the bread of sorrows: for so he giveth his beloved sleep." God forbid David to build a temple, but ordained Solomon. Prophetically speaking, you must realize that personal ambitions cannot build the Kingdom of God. You must be led by His Spirit.

Psalms 127:1-2 - "Except the LORD build the house, they labour in vain that build it."

B | Children

Children are a God-given heritage. The fruit of the womb is His reward. Children are like arrows in the hand of a mighty man, so the more, the merrier. Those who fear the LORD and walk in His ways will eat of the labor of his hands, in happiness and wellness. His wife will be fruitful, and his children well-nurtured.

Psalms 128:5-6 - "The LORD shall bless thee out of Zion: and thou shalt see the good of Jerusalem all the days of thy life. Yea, thou shalt see thy children's children, and peace upon Israel."

D | They That Hate Zion Will Be Confounded

We live in a world boiling over with Zion-bashers and Zion-haters. Hundreds of millions of people crave to see Israel annihilated and Jerusalem totally controlled by non-Jews. It is an ancient syndrome. The psalmist reflected on the enemies of Zion. He said, "Let them be as grass that grows on housetops. It withers before it is full-grown. It can never be mown or bound in sheaves." Certainly, God will fulfill this ancient wish, and sooner than you may think.

Psalms 129:5 - "Let them all be confounded and turned back that hate Zion."

B | Songs Of Degrees

Fifteen of the psalms (120-134) are called "A Song of degrees." They are synonymously called "Songs of Ascent," "Gradual Psalms," "Songs of Steps," or "Pilgrim Songs." They were traditionally recited as the Jews ascended the steps to the Temple Mount when they came, three times each year, to worship. The kohanim, or priests, also recited them regularly in the course of ministry in the Temple.

Psalms 130:1-2 - "(A Song of degrees.) Out of the depths have I cried unto thee, O LORD. Lord, hear my voice: let thine ears be attentive to the voice of my supplications."

C | As Peaceful As A Weaned Child

David wrote this song of degrees, stating, "LORD, my heart is not haughty, nor mine eyes lofty: neither do I exercise myself in great matters, or in things too high for me. Surely I have behaved and quieted myself, as a child that is weaned of his mother: my soul is even as a weaned child." The gist of this statement is, "I have learned to be humble, peacefully quiet, and patient, and have overcome separation anxiety, knowing that I always have hope in the LORD."

Psalms 131:3 - "Let Israel hope in the LORD from henceforth and for ever."

D | The Key Of David

"The key of David" was his supernatural understanding of prophetic destiny: Messiah enthroned in His Temple on Zion. "I will not give sleep to mine eyes, ...Until I find out a place for the LORD." "We will go into his tabernacles: we will worship at his footstool. Arise, O LORD, into thy rest." "The LORD hath sworn in truth unto David; ...Of the fruit of thy body will I set upon thy throne."

Psalms 132:13-14 - "The LORD hath chosen Zion; he hath desired it for his habitation. This is my rest for ever: here will I dwell; for I have desired it."

C | Unity - The Blessing Of Life

Imagine Aaron standing in the door of the Tabernacle in a glorious priestly robe, wearing mitre and crown, waiting to be consecrated as Israel's High Priest. Moses lifted the vessel of holy anointing oil and poured it on Aaron's head until it flowed down his beard onto the skirt of his garment. When brethren dwell together in unity, that blessing is simulated. Unity is like dew anointing Mount Herman or the mountains of Zion. "There the LORD commanded the blessing, even life for evermore."

Psalms 133:1 - "How good and how pleasant it is for brethren to dwell together in unity!"

A | Lift Up Your Hands In The Sanctuary

This "Song of degrees" instructs the servants who stand by night in the house of the LORD to "lift up your hands in the sanctuary, and bless the LORD." Psalm 28 specifies lifting up hands toward the holy oracle (the

Ark of the Covenant). The next time you go to church, be sure to lift your hands and bless the LORD. He deserves your worship.

Psalms 134:1 - "Behold, bless ye the LORD, all ye servants of the LORD, which by night stand in the house of the LORD. Lift up your hands in the sanctuary, and bless the LORD."

B | Vapors, Lightnings, Winds, Tokens and Wonders

Although many of the psalms seem repetitious in their content, we need those repeated reminders to praise and bless the LORD. Everything in heaven and earth abundantly proves that He is worthy of our praise. Do not overlook the divinely majestic wonders, even in everyday thunderstorms, or forget the mighty works of God down through the ages. Praise Him!

Psalms 135:7,9 - "He causeth the vapours to ascend from the ends of the earth; he maketh lightnings for the rain; he bringeth the wind out of his treasuries. ...Who sent tokens and wonders into the midst of thee."

A | Give Thanks, For His Mercy Endureth For Ever

One of the most oft-repeated phrases in the Bible is "for His mercy endureth for ever." It is a core reason why men should praise the LORD. That phrase was sung repeatedly on the day that King David brought up the Ark of the Covenant to the Tabernacle of David. It was sung the day Solomon dedicated the First Temple. Jeremiah (33:11) prophesies that those who say "his mercy endureth for ever" will be among those who will return to Jerusalem.

Psalms 136:26 - "O give thanks unto the God of heaven: for his mercy endureth for ever."

C | Sin Will Steal Your Song

God punished the Jews for their unrepented sins. As captives along the rivers of Babylon, they hung their harps on willow trees and wept. Babylonians ordered them to sing the songs of Zion, but they could not. "How shall we sing the LORD'S song in a strange land?" Babylon will steal your song and leave you begging for Jerusalem.

Psalms 137:5 - "If I forget thee, O Jerusalem, let my right hand forget her cunning. If I do not remember thee, let my tongue cleave to the roof of my mouth; if I prefer not Jerusalem above my chief joy."

D | All The Kings Of The Earth Shall Praise Thee

In Acts 2:29-30, Peter preached that the patriarch David was a prophet. David foresaw Messiah on earth as the King of Kings, ruling over all the earth. That is why, in his day, David praised God above all the gods on earth. "Before the gods will I sing praise unto thee. I will worship toward thy holy temple."

Psalms 138:4-5 - "All the kings of the earth shall praise thee, O LORD, when they hear the words of thy mouth. Yea, they shall sing in the ways of the LORD: for great is the glory of the LORD."

C | Man Evolved?

Just what did man evolve from, if the evolutionists can say? More than seven billion humans overrun this planet. Where is one "evolving one," a halfway-there one? There should be at least a few million of them if the theory has truth in it. But it doesn't. It takes infinitely more "faith" to believe that we happened by accident than to believe God made it all. So who's the fool?

Psalms 139:14 - "I will praise thee; for I am fearfully and wonderfully made: marvelous are thy works; and that my soul knoweth right well."

B | The Evil Man

David prayed, "Deliver me, O LORD, from the evil man." He is violent, imagines mischief in his heart, is ready for war, sharpens his tongue like a serpent, has poison under his lips, purposes to overthrow me, hides a snare for me, and spreads a net by the wayside. God will destroy him.

Psalms 140:8 - "Grant not, O LORD, the desires of the wicked: further not his wicked device; ...let the mischief of their own lips cover them. Let burning coals fall upon them: let them be cast into the fire; into deep pits, that they rise not up again."

A | Prevent Me From Doing Evil

This is not an unreasonable prayer: "LORD, prevent me from doing evil." David prayed such a prayer. He asked God to set a watch - a guard - over his mouth, to stop his lips from saying evil. He asked God to prevent his heart from evil, or from collaborating, or even associating with evil men. Then he invited God to use righteous men to correct him when he needed reproof.

Psalms 141:5 - "Let the righteous smite me; it shall be a kindness: and let him reprove me; it shall be an excellent oil, which shall not break my head."

C | Thou Art My Refuge - My Safe Hiding Place

The 142nd Psalm was written while David was hiding in a cave from the evil hand of King Saul. "I cried unto the LORD. ...I showed him my trouble." It was terrifying for the young man to contemplate that the King of Israel was pursuing him with armies, threatening to kill him. "They privily laid a snare for me, ...REFUGE failed me; no man cared for my soul." David was panic-stricken. But God was his refuge. Even now, God is our safe hiding place.

Psalms 142:5 - "I cried unto thee, O LORD: I said, Thou art my refuge."

A | Deliver Me From Mine Enemies

Your enemies may get you down, but you can still call on the LORD. David did. He said, "The enemy hath persecuted my soul. ...He hath smitten my life down to the ground. ...He hath made me to dwell in darkness. ...My spirit is overwhelmed within me. ...My heart within me is desolate. ...I flee unto thee to hide me." Your enemies cannot escape when God intervenes.

Psalms 143:9,12 - "Deliver me, O LORD, from mine enemies. ...And of thy mercy cut off mine enemies, and destroy all them that afflict my soul: for I am thy servant."

B | Strange Children

David blessed the LORD for teaching his hands to war; for subduing his people under him; for being his fortress, high tower, deliverer and shield. Twice, he asked God to deliver him "from the hand of strange children. Whose mouth speaketh vanity, and their right hand is a right hand of falsehood." Simultaneously, he blessed Israel. "That our sons may be as plants grown up in their youth; that our daughters may be as cornerstones." Strange children - vain liars - enemies - will be banished. True sons of God will be blessed.

Psalms 144:11 - "Deliver me from the hand of strange children."

D | Meat In Due Season

All his life, David never ceased praising God for everything he could think of - a practically endless list. He knew that we all depend upon God for everything we have. "The eyes of all wait upon thee." "Due season" infers a prophetic certainty that He will always meet our needs according to His riches in glory. In due season, all the blessings and purposes of God will be fulfilled.

Psalms 145:15 - "The eyes of all wait upon thee; and thou givest them their meat in due season. Thou openest thine hand, and satisfiest the desire of every living thing."

C | Don't Trust In Men - Trust In God

Here is an admonition NOT to trust in princes or ordinary men in whom is no help. Men stop breathing and are buried in the earth. Look at God's record: He made heaven, earth, the sea, and everything in it. He keeps Truth forever, executes judgment for the oppressed, gives food to the hungry, loosens prisoners, opens the eyes of the blind, raises up those who are bowed down, and more and more.

Psalms 146:5 - "Happy is he that hath the God of Jacob for his help, whose hope is in the LORD his God."

D | He Hath Not Dealt So With Any Nation

"The LORD doth build up Jerusalem. He gathereth together the outcasts of Israel. ...He hath strengthened the bars of thy gates; he hath blessed thy children within thee. He makes peace in thy borders, and filleth thee with the finest of the wheat. ...He sheweth his word unto Jacob, his statutes and his judgments unto Israel." No nation in history has been so profoundly blessed of God as Israel.

Psalms 147:12 - "Praise the LORD, O Jerusalem; praise thy God, O Zion. ...He hath not dealt so with any nation: and as for his judgments, they have not known them."

B | All Creation Praises God

The psalmist called on all of Creation to praise the LORD. "Praise ye him, all his angels: ...all his hosts, ...sun and moon, ...all ye stars of light, ...heaven of heavens, ...waters above the heavens, ...earth, ...fire, and hail; snow, and vapour; stormy wind, ...mountains, and all hills, fruitful trees, and all cedars: beasts, and all cattle; creeping things, and flying fowl, ...kings of the earth, and all people, ...young men, maidens, old men and children."

Psalms 148:13 - "Let them praise the name of the LORD: for his name alone is excellent; his glory is above the earth and heaven."

B | New Songs

Traditional hymns and songs of worship are at the very core of Christian worship. But all these songs were once new and innovative. We liked them when we first heard them, and we have continued to use them for many years. But it is just as important to continue writing new songs of worship - songs that are fresh and perhaps even spontaneous. We should welcome the use of both old songs and new songs in our worship experience.

Psalms 149:1 - "Praise ye the LORD. Sing unto the LORD a new song, and his praise in the congregation of saints."

C | Praise Him In The Dance

Miriam led the people in a celebratory dance after God took them miraculously through the Red Sea. When the LORD gave Jephthah victory over the Ammonites, his daughter danced to celebrate. The women of Israel danced when David defeated the Philistines. David danced before the LORD to celebrate the arrival of the Ark of the Covenant. We should dance to celebrate God's wonderful works in our behalf.

Psalms 149:3 - "Let them praise his name in the dance: let them sing praises unto him with the timbrel and harp." Psalms 150:4 – "Praise him with the timbrel and dance."

A | Praise Him With Musical Instruments

Banning musical instruments in worship contradicts several biblical mandates. Music expresses worship from the soul - not just the music that comes from our mouths, but from our hands on musical instruments. It is as biblical as anything. Psalm 150 says to PRAISE HIM with trumpets, psalteries (guitars), harps, timbrels, stringed instruments, organs, loud cymbals, and high sounding cymbals. The music is not intended for your pleasure or your entertainment. It is for HIS pleasure and HIS entertainment. He loves it loud, energetic and boisterous!

Psalms 150:6 - "Let every thing that hath breath praise the LORD. Praise ye the LORD."

Lessons from the Book of
PROVERBS

B | The Proverbs Of Solomon

In his lifetime, Solomon spoke over 3000 proverbs and authored 1005 songs (1 Kings 4:32). His wise sayings predated every other major work of its kind. Why? His was God-given wisdom. The reasons for his proverbs were "to know wisdom and instruction; to perceive the words of understanding; to receive the instruction of wisdom, justice, and judgment, and equity; ...and discretion." He warned that to reject wisdom was to invite destruction. All the world should learn the Proverbs.

Proverbs 1:7 - "The fear of the LORD is the beginning of knowledge: but fools despise wisdom and instruction."

A | They Shall Call Upon Me, But I Will Not Answer

Solomon personified wisdom so she could speak: "Wisdom crieth, ...uttereth her voice, ...saying, Turn you at my reproof, ...I have called, and ye refused; I have stretched out my hand, ...But ye have set at nought all my counsel." If you reject wisdom, calamity will come, and wisdom cannot help you then.

Proverbs 1:27-30 - "When distress and anguish cometh upon you. Then shall they call upon me, but I will not answer; they shall seek me early, but they shall not find me: For that they hated knowledge, and did not choose the fear of the LORD."

D | I Will Laugh At Your Calamity

Solomon wrote hundreds of proverbs - wise sayings - urging men to get wisdom in the fear of the LORD. "Wisdom crieth without; she uttereth her voice in the streets: ...saying, How long, ye simple ones, will ye love simplicity? and the scorners delight in their scorning, and fools hate knowledge? ...ye have set at nought all my counsel, and would none of my reproof: I also will laugh at your calamity; I will mock when your fear cometh." Reject simplicity. Seek His wisdom.

Proverbs 1:33 - "But whoso hearkeneth unto me shall dwell safely, and shall be quiet from fear of evil."

C | The LORD Giveth Wisdom

In this morally bankrupt generation, wise men are loathed, and fools carry the day. But the future belongs to the wise. If you "incline thine ear to wisdom, and ...seek her as silver, ...the LORD giveth wisdom." "Discretion will preserve thee, understanding shall keep thee: To deliver thee from the way of the evil man, ...to deliver thee from the strange woman."

Proverbs 2:21-22 - "For the upright shall dwell in the land, and the perfect shall remain in it. But the wicked shall be cut off from the earth, and the transgressors shall be rooted out of it."

D | God Promises Rewards To Those Who Fear And Obey

Obeying God's Commandments adds long life and peace. Fearing God and departing from evil assures good health. "Honour the LORD with thy substance, and with the firstfruits of all thine increase: So shall thy barns be filled with plenty, and thy presses shall burst out with new wine. ...Happy is the man that findeth wisdom, ...Length of days is in her right hand; and in her left hand riches and honour."

Proverbs 3:5-6 - "Trust in the LORD with all thine heart; and lean not unto thine own understanding. In all thy ways acknowledge him, and he shall direct thy paths."

A | Despise Not The Chastening Of The LORD

Be careful how you talk to God about your hard trials. It is easy to forget how often we have been carnal, worldly, or offensive to His righteous will. Just as a parent bears the responsibility of disciplining a son or daughter, God has to chasten us from time to time. "My son, despise not the chastening of the LORD; neither be weary of his correction: For whom the LORD loveth he correcteth; even as a father the son in whom he delighteth."

Proverbs 3:26 - "For the LORD shall be thy confidence, and shall keep thy foot from being taken."

B | Wisdom Is The Principal Thing; Therefore Get Wisdom

The wisest man says to the children, "Hear the instruction of your father." Nobody has time to research and prove all wisdom in one short lifetime. It must be handed down from generation to generation. But a rebellious generation spurns, and thus does not possess the priceless legacy of wisdom. Simpleton, listen to your forebears! "Wisdom is the principal thing; therefore get wisdom: and with all thy getting get understanding."

Proverbs 4:20,22 - "My son, attend to my words; incline thine ear unto my sayings. ...For they are life unto those that find them, and health to all their flesh."

C | Rejoice With The Wife Of Thy Youth

The wise man repeatedly and strenuously warned his son against the strange woman. Her lips "drop as an honeycomb, her mouth is smoother than oil: but her end is bitter as wormwood, sharp as a twoedged sword. Her feet go down to death; her steps take hold on hell. ...Remove thy way far from her, and come not nigh the door of her house." Flee to your wife!

Proverbs 5:15,18 - "Drink waters out of thine own cistern, and running waters out of thine own well. Let thy fountain be blessed: and rejoice with the wife of thy youth."

D | Calamity Will Come Suddenly To The Wicked Man

We usually heed warnings in a way that is proportionate to the credibility of the person who issues the warning. If a foolish man gives a warning, we might completely ignore it. But if GOD issues a warning, His warnings are prophetic - no false alarms! Be warned!

Proverbs 6:12-15 - "A naughty person, a wicked man, walketh with a froward mouth. He winketh with his eyes, he speaketh with his feet, he teacheth with his fingers; Frowardness is in his heart, he deviseth mischief continually; he soweth discord. Therefore shall his calamity come suddenly; suddenly shall he be broken without remedy."

B | The Strange Woman

At least ten times in Proverbs, Solomon warned his son against strange women. "A woman with the attire of an harlot, and subtil of heart. ...With her much fair speech she caused him to yield, with the flattering of her lips she forced him." Be warned, mister. That woman will DESTROY you.

Proverbs 7:22-24 - "He goeth after her straightway, as an ox goeth to the slaughter, or as a fool to the correction of the stocks; Till a dart strike through his liver; as a bird hasteth to the snare, and knoweth not that it is for his life."

C | If You Hate Wisdom, You Love Death

Wisdom cries in every place, calling the sons of men to understand wisdom and receive instruction. "By me kings reign, and princes decree justice. By me princes rule, and nobles, even all the judges of the earth. I love them that love me; and those that seek me early shall find me. Riches and honour are with me." God possessed wisdom in the beginning. Crave wisdom.

Proverbs 8:35 -"For whoso findeth me findeth life, and shall obtain favour of the LORD. But he that sinneth against me wrongeth his own soul: all they that hate me love death."

A | Whoso Is Simple, Let Him Turn In Hither

Wisdom built her house, hewed pillars, killed beasts, mingled wine, furnished her table, sent forth maidens, and invited everyone to her feast. "Forsake the foolish, and live." Wisdom makes an offer you must not refuse. Whatever else you are asking God for, move it down the list. Put wisdom at the top. Postpone the other blessings until you have sought the LORD for wisdom.

Proverbs 9:4-5 - "Whoso is simple, let him turn in hither: as for him that wanteth understanding, she saith to him, Come, eat of my bread, and drink of the wine which I have mingled."

D | The Righteous Shall Never Be Removed

The contrasts between the righteous and the wicked are endless. The righteous make glad parents; the wicked cause heaviness. The righteous will not famish, but the wicked lose their substance. Blessings are on the just, but violence is on the wicked. The labor of the righteous tends toward life: the fruit of the wicked to sin. The tongue of the just is as choice silver: the heart of the wicked is little worth. Above all, God promises eternal life to the righteous.

Proverbs 10:30 - "The righteous shall never be removed: but the wicked shall not inhabit the earth."

C | Righteousness Is Right, Wickedness Is Wrong

Proverbs 11 addresses many topics. God hates false balances, but delights in a just weight. Pride brings shame. Integrity guides the upright. Righteousness directs and delivers a man. Transgressors are headed for trouble. "Where no counsel is, the people fall: but in the multitude of counselors there is safety." "The liberal soul shall be made fat: and he that watereth shall be watered also himself." The theme in all the sayings is that righteousness is always right, and wickedness is always wrong.

Proverbs 11:19 - "As righteousness tendeth to life: so he that pursueth evil pursueth it to his own death."

B | A Good Man (Loves Instruction)

Every proverb has the potential of an entire sermon. Every wise saying could be elaborated and amplified many times over. But the important thing is to learn the basics. In the end, you will either be wise or foolish, virtuous or shameful, diligent or slack, honorable or despised, true or false, good or bad. "Whoso loveth instruction loveth knowledge. He that hateth reproof is brutish." Seek to know what is right, and strive to be good. Any brute can be bad.

Proverbs 12:2 - "A good man obtaineth favour of the LORD: but a man of wicked devices will he condemn."

C | Learn To Hear Instruction

A wise son hears his father's instruction. He that fears the commandments will be rewarded. He that regards reproof will be honored. He that walks with wise men shall be wise. But scorners hear not rebuke. The way of transgressors is hard. Poverty and shame come to him that refuses instruction. Whoso despises the Word or is companion of fools shall be destroyed. Parents, discipline your child to follow instructions! God disciplines and chastens us so we will learn wisdom.

Proverbs 13:24 -"He that spareth his rod hateth his son: but he that loveth him chasteneth him."

D | Righteousness Exalteth A Nation

There is a way which seemeth right unto a man, but the end thereof are the ways of death. Without the fear of God, death and destruction are unavoidable. The fear of the LORD is a fountain of life - an escape from the snares of death. The house of the wicked shall be overthrown: but the tabernacle of the upright shall flourish. Upright men fear the LORD. What is true for the individual is true for the nation. A nation must fear God in righteousness.

Proverbs 14:34 - "Righteousness exalteth a nation: but sin is a reproach to any people."

□✓

A | The Prayer Of The Upright Is His Delight

Does God love to hear your voice? Judge your tongue. Soft answers turn away wrath. Grievous words stir up anger. The tongue of the righteous uses knowledge rightly, but the mouth of fools pours out foolishness. A wholesome tongue is a tree of life, but a perverse tongue is a breach in the spirit. The words of the pure are pleasant words, but the mouth of the wicked pours out evil things. The prayer of the upright is God's delight.

Proverbs 15:29 - "The LORD is far from the wicked: but he heareth the prayer of the righteous."

C | Pride Goes Before Destruction

Pride is a too-high or inordinate opinion of one's own dignity, importance, merit, or superiority. Paul, in Romans 12:3, admonishes every man "not to think of himself more highly than he ought to think; but to think soberly." Solomon said, "Pride goeth before destruction, and an haughty spirit before a fall. ...Better it is to be of an humble spirit with the lowly, than to divide the spoil with the proud." Humble yourself before you self-destruct.

Proverbs 16:5 - "Every one that is proud in heart is an abomination to the LORD."

A | Think Before You Speak

Your heart should govern your mouth - not the other way around. "The heart of the wise teacheth his mouth, and addeth learning to his lips. ...the sweetness of the lips increaseth learning. ...Pleasant words are as an honeycomb, sweet to the soul, and health to the bones." THINK BEFORE YOU SPEAK. "He that is slow to anger is better than the mighty; and he that ruleth his spirit than he that taketh a city." God favors a well-disciplined man.

Proverbs 16:7 - "When a man's ways please the LORD, he maketh even his enemies to be at peace with him."

B | A King And His Throne

A king, being a sovereign on earth, wields the power of life and death over men. Wise men should seek his favor. The king's word must be righteous for the sake of his throne. To fail in that is an abomination.

Proverbs 16:10-15 - "A divine sentence is in the lips of the king: ...The wrath of a king is as messengers of death: but a wise man will pacify it.

...In the light of the king's countenance is life; ...It is an abomination to kings to commit wickedness: for the throne is established by righteousness."

D | Those Who Love To See Others Suffer Will Be Punished

"A friend loveth at all times, and a brother is born for adversity." The godly virtue is to overlook others' faults as much as is possible. "He that covereth a transgression seeketh love; but he that repeateth a matter separateth very friends." Tattletales and gossips are troublemakers. "He that hath a froward heart findeth no good: and he that hath a perverse tongue falleth into mischief." God will judge you for your verbal sins. Be kind to others.

Proverbs 17:5 - "Whoso mocketh the poor reproacheth his Maker: and he that is glad at calamities shall not be unpunished."

A | Sometimes, It Is Better To Be Quiet

Paul admonished the Thessalonians to "study to be quiet." Solomon said, "Better is a dry morsel, and quietness therewith, than an house full of sacrifices with strife. ...He that hath knowledge spareth his words: ...Even a fool, when he holdeth his peace, is counted wise: and he that shutteth his lips is esteemed a man of understanding." If you can't say something good, don't say anything. "A wicked doer giveth heed to false lips; and a liar giveth ear to a naughty tongue."

Proverbs 17:7 - "Excellent speech becometh not a fool: much less do lying lips a prince."

B | The Fool And The Wise Man

The 18th chapter of Proverbs renounces fools. "A fool hath no delight in understanding." Wicked men come with contempt, disgrace and reproach. It is not good to accept a wicked person and overthrow a righteous man's judgment. A fool speaks contentious words and calls for violence. His words eventually destroy him. Talebearers wound others, slothful men are great wasters, and he that prejudges people gets folly and shame. But a man with desire separates himself and seeks and interacts with all wisdom.

Proverbs 18:15 - "The heart of the prudent getteth knowledge; and the ear of the wise seeketh knowledge."

□✓

C | Treat Other People Kindly, Show Yourself Friendly

Proverbs contains hundreds of lessons on human relations. The wise man says that a man's spirit will ordinarily sustain him, but if his spirit is wounded by another, how can he bear his infirmity? "A brother offended is harder to be won than a strong city." "Death and life are in the power of the tongue." "Contentions are like the bars of a castle." We should not offend others, but strive to be a friend and brother.

Proverbs 18:24 - "A man that hath friends must shew himself friendly: and there is a friend that sticketh closer than a brother.

C | Divine Counsel

Compare your wisdom to God's. It is a shocking comparison. He is infinite. He has seen everything and knows everything. He has witnessed every act and thought of every man who ever lived. He is omnipotent, omnipresent, and omniscient. We are finite, limited, inexperienced, ignorant and unlearned. So, why do we typically trust ourselves and don't trust HIM? That's illogical! "...it is not in man that walketh to direct his steps," Jeremiah 10:23.

Proverbs 19:21 - "There are many devices in a man's heart; nevertheless the counsel of the LORD, that shall stand."

D | Man's Goings Are Of The LORD

You will never beat God at His game. You are not your own. "All souls are mine," God says (Ezekiel 18:4). Your destiny is in God's hands. There is one destiny for the righteous and another destiny for the wicked. Rather than spend your life trying to do your own thing, why not spend your life trying to do God's will? "Say not thou, I will recompense evil; but wait on the LORD, and he shall save thee."

Proverbs 20:24 - "Man's goings are of the LORD; how can a man then understand his own way?"

A | Your Prayers Are Ignored Because You Ignore Others' Cries

God cares for the poor and requires us to care. "He that oppresseth the poor to increase his riches, ...shall surely come to want. ...Rob not the poor, because he is poor: neither oppress the afflicted in the gate: For the LORD will plead their cause, and spoil the soul of those that spoiled them," Proverbs 22:16,22-23. If you want God to hear YOUR cries, you must not ignore the cries of those in need.

Proverbs 21:13 - "Whoso stoppeth his ears at the cry of the poor, he also shall cry himself, but shall not be heard."

D | **Foresee The Evil**

What error is more inexcusable than the one we saw coming? It is one thing to make a mistake in ignorance, but when God has given explicit warnings concerning virtually every hazard a man can face, what is our excuse? One-third of the Bible is prophetic in nature. If you ignore the warnings about things to come, you are inviting disaster. That is why I am so heavily invested in understanding Bible prophecy. I want to be prepared.

Proverbs 22:3 - "A prudent man foreseeth the evil, and hideth himself: but the simple pass on, and are punished."

C | **Remove Not The Ancient Landmark**

A landmark establishes a boundary or a property line. It is often a legal instrument proving ownership. More than that, landmarks perpetuate legacies and posterities. Things which have been sacred for ages have far more wisdom in them than you can imagine. That is especially true with proven truths and precepts based on the Bible. This perverse generation would recklessly destroy priceless, holy things. Never remove boundaries that separate the Church from the world. You will sorely regret the loss.

Proverbs 22:28 - "Remove not the ancient landmark, which thy fathers have set." 23:10 - "Remove not the old landmark."

B | **Drunkards And Gluttons**

"Be not among winebibbers; among riotous eaters of flesh: For the drunkard and the glutton shall come to poverty: ...Who hath woe? who hath sorrow? who hath contentions? who hath babbling? who hath wounds without cause? who hath redness of eyes? They that tarry long at the wine; they that go to seek mixed wine. ...At the last it biteth like a serpent, and stingeth like an adder." Refuse all mind-altering substances. Righteous men must be sober, moderate and temperate.

Proverbs 23:2-3 "And put a knife to thy throat, if thou be a man given to appetite."

C | Train A Child To Be Wise

"Train up a child in the way he should go: and when he is old, he will not depart from it." You cannot have a wise child who has not been disciplined - corrected when he is wrong. "Foolishness is bound in the heart of a child; but the rod of correction shall drive it far from him. ...Withhold not correction from the child: for if thou beatest him with the rod, he shall not die. Thou shalt beat him with the rod, and shalt deliver his soul from hell."

Proverbs 23:19 - "Hear thou, my son, and be wise."

D | God's Prophetic Word Works Like His Creative Word

This reprobate generation says evil is good, and good is evil. But payday is still coming. The wicked will not survive their wickedness, and the righteous will eventually receive their reward. IT IS WRITTEN. God's prophetic word works just like His creative word. It just takes a little longer. "There shall be no reward to the evil man; the candle of the wicked shall be put out."

Proverbs 24:14 - "So shall the knowledge of wisdom be unto thy soul: when thou hast found it, then there shall be a reward, and thy expectation shall not be cut off."

B | A Man's Gift

What is that you have? The gift of God is your destiny. Moses' rod, David's sling, Elijah's mantle - every man's gift is different. "A gift is as a precious stone in the eyes of him that hath it: whithersoever it turneth, it prospereth," Proverbs 17:8. "A man's gift maketh room for him, and bringeth him before great men," Proverbs 18:16. Avoid pursuing things God has not given you to do. God gave you your gift to do His will.

Proverbs 25:14 - "Whoso boasteth himself of a false gift is like clouds and wind without rain."

B | The Fool And His Folly

Mismatches: snow in summer - rain in harvest - honor for a fool. Honoring a fool is like shooting a stone from a sling. As a whip for a horse, or a bridle for a mule, a rod is for the fool's back. A parable in the mouth of a fool is like a thorn in the hand. Fools return to their folly like dogs to their vomit. The only reason to answer a fool is to expose his self-deluded conceit.

Proverbs 26:4 - "Answer not a fool according to his folly, lest thou also be like unto him."

B | **Riches**

Riches can be a blessing or a curse. "Labour not to be rich: cease from thine own wisdom. Wilt thou set thine eyes upon that which is not? for riches certainly make themselves wings; they fly away as an eagle toward heaven." God rains His blessings on good and bad men. Wealth is not proof that God approves. Poverty is not proof God disapproves. "The rich and poor meet together: the LORD is the maker of them all." Seek first His kingdom.

Proverbs 26:10 - "The great God that formed all things both rewardeth the fool, and rewardeth transgressors."

C | **Appreciate A Friend's Rebuke**

When we need correction, as we all eventually do, it comes best from a dear friend. "Faithful are the wounds of a friend; but the kisses of an enemy are deceitful." Toss out your resentment and receive your friend's honest appraisal. "Open rebuke is better than secret love." "Ointment and perfume rejoice the heart: so doth the sweetness of a man's friend by hearty counsel. Thine own friend, ...forsake not; ...for better is a neighbour that is near than a brother far off."

Proverbs 27: 17 - "Iron sharpeneth iron; so a man sharpeneth the countenance of his friend."

A | **They That Seek The LORD Understand All Things**

The surest way to get wisdom and understanding is to seek the LORD. We must not merely ask for His blessings, but conscientiously hear and obey His instructions, whether they are ancient or current directives. "He that turneth away his ear from hearing the law, even his prayer shall be abomination." We must empty ourselves if we hope to be filled with His treasures. "He that covereth his sins shall not prosper: but whoso confesseth and forsaketh them shall have mercy."

Proverbs 28:5 - "Evil men understand not judgment: but they that seek the LORD understand all things."

A | **Confess Your Sins**

The entire book of Proverbs appeals to the young man to flee from sin and sinners. "My son, if sinners entice thee, consent thou not," Proverbs

1:10. Solomon posted warnings against keeping company with foolish men and foolish women. He admonished against pursuing the follies of riches, keeping company with mischief-makers and every kind of evil. His overriding theme was to forsake all wickedness and do righteousness. That necessarily includes admitting your sins and turning from them.

Proverbs 28:13 - "He that covereth his sins shall not prosper: but whoso confesseth and forsaketh them shall have mercy."

D | Suddenly Destroyed Without Remedy

Truth always produces the right outcome. Lies always produce the wrong outcome. Truth will prevail, even when men steadfastly ignore its warnings. Although a man may sin a thousand times without consequences, Truth says he cannot continue. When everything comes to judgment, the righteous will always outlast the wicked. "When the wicked are multiplied, transgression increaseth: but the righteous shall see their fall. ...every man's judgment cometh from the LORD." Beware, lest you foolishly presume that you are invincible.

Proverbs 29:1 - "He, that being often reproved hardeneth his neck, shall suddenly be destroyed, and that without remedy."

A | Give Me Neither Poverty Nor Riches

Here is a great prayer worth repeating. "Remove far from me vanity and lies: give me neither poverty nor riches; feed me with food convenient for me." Too much prosperity may tempt me to become self-sufficient and forget God. Too much poverty may tempt me to steal or rail against God. I prefer to have only as much as is convenient to live a modest life.

Proverbs 30:9 - "Lest I be full, and deny thee, and say, Who is the LORD? or lest I be poor, and steal, and take the name of my God in vain."

D | The Virtuous Woman

Proverbs 31 contains "the words of king Lemuel, the prophecy that his mother taught him. ...give not thy strength unto women, nor thy ways to that which destroyeth kings." She admonished him to avoid strong drink and judge righteously. Then she described the model woman - the virtuous woman - to her son. She is morally perfect, invaluable, trustworthy, good, sews, shops, cooks, gardens, is strong, wise, talented, merciful, thoughtful, well-dressed, industrious, honorable, kind, hard-working and respected. The future of such a woman is certain.

Proverbs 31:25,30 - "She shall rejoice in time to come. ...she shall be praised."

Lessons from the Book of
ECCLESIASTES

B | Ecclesiastes

The book of Ecclesiastes, "The Preacher," catalogues Solomon's frustrations with life "under the sun." "Vanity of vanities; all is vanity. What profit hath a man of all his labour which he taketh under the sun?" His observations only apply to the mortal life, not the hereafter. That agrees with New Testament teachings. James said, "For what is your life? It is even a vapour, that appeareth for a little time, and then vanisheth away," 4:14.

Ecclesiastes 1:14 - "I have seen all the works that are done under the sun; and, behold, all is vanity and vexation of spirit."

C | Earthly Possessions Are Temporary At Best

Solomon gave himself to mirth and pleasure. He got houses, vineyards, gardens, orchards, pools, servants, maidens, singers, musicians, silver, gold and peculiar treasures of kings. "Whatsoever mine eyes desired I kept not from them." "There is nothing better for a man, than that he should eat and drink, and that he should make his soul enjoy good in his labour. ...it was from the hand of God." But earthly possessions are temporary.

Ecclesiastes 2:18 - "I hated all my labour which I had taken under the sun: because I should leave it unto the man that shall be after me."

D | God Appoints Times And Seasons

God sets a time and a season for every purpose under heaven. "A time to be born, and a time to die; ...to plant, ...to pluck up; ...to kill, ...to heal; ...to break down, ...to build up; ...to weep, ...to laugh; ...to mourn, ...to dance; ...to cast away stones, ...to gather stones together; ...to embrace, ...to refrain from embracing; ...to get, ...to lose; ...to keep, ...to cast away; ...to rend, ...to sew; ...to keep silence, ...to speak; ...to love, ...to hate; ...of war, ...of peace."

Ecclesiastes 3:11 - "He hath made every thing beautiful in his time."

C | Two Are Better Than One

Solomon became cynical, watching the tears of the oppressed, observing that they had no comforter. Oppressors had power, but the poor had no comforter. The dead are better off than the living (or the unborn), he said. He marveled at men's jealousy of one another, since everyone seemed miserable anyway. Solitary men with no family worked endlessly, and for what? Vanity, he said. Those who have someone to work with, to sleep with, to walk with fare better. He argued that companions make a difference.

Ecclesiastes 4:9-10 - "Two are better than one; ...the one will lift up his fellow."

A | Abstain From Hasty Words And Rash Vows

"Be not rash with thy mouth, and let not thine heart be hasty to utter any thing before God: ...let thy words be few. ...a fool's voice is known by multitude of words." If you make a vow to God, do not fail to pay it. "Better is it that thou shouldest not vow, than that thou shouldest vow and not pay."

Ecclesiastes 5:6 - "Suffer not thy mouth to cause thy flesh to sin; neither say thou before the angel, that it was an error: wherefore should God be angry at thy voice, and destroy the work of thine hands?"

C | Law Of Diminishing Return

Life on earth has little promise. In economics, any system that requires constantly increasing input to maintain equal output is said to have a diminishing return. That law dominates this world. Alcoholics require more liquor. Drug addicts need more drugs. More money. More food. More sex. More parties. Bigger houses. Fancier cars. Solomon concluded that life is a vain pursuit. Solution? Seek God's kingdom - only God can give unlimited satisfaction with no diminishing return.

Ecclesiastes 6:7 - "All the labour of man is for his mouth, and yet the appetite is not filled."

C | Prosperity

God has pleasure in the prosperity of His servant. But sometimes, it also pleases the Lord to bruise His servant. God wants you and me to be blessed, but sometimes, for His glory, He needs us to endure some things that may drain us, even bankrupt us. Remember Job's trial. Learn how to prosper AND how to be abased.

Ecclesiastes 7:14 - "In the day of prosperity be joyful, but in the day of adversity consider: God also hath set the one over against the other, to the end that man should find nothing after him."

B | Sin, Sinners, And Their Delayed Sentence

This generation actually believes they will get by with their heinous sins - deluded by the successes of multitudes of evil people. Why abandon riotous living if there is no punishment? The truth is heart-stopping. "Because sentence against an evil work is not executed speedily, therefore the heart of the sons of men is fully set in them to do evil."

Ecclesiastes 8:12-13 - "Though a sinner do evil an hundred times, and his days be prolonged, yet surely I know that it shall be well with them that fear God, ...But it shall not be well with the wicked."

A | Some Things Will Never Be Revealed On Earth

Every Bible believer is trained to seek the LORD in prayer and supplications. But no matter how you pray, some things will never be revealed on earth. "God, give us grace to accept with serenity the things that cannot be changed, courage to change the things that should be changed, and the wisdom to distinguish the one from the other," (Reinhold Niebuhr).

Ecclesiastes 8:17 - "I beheld all the work of God, that a man cannot find out the work that is done under the sun: because though a man labour to seek it out, yet he shall not find it."

D | The Dead Know Not Things On Earth

Solomon asserted that when a man dies, his body returns to the dust. His spirit has no more awareness of what is going on in earth, "...for who shall bring him to see what shall be after him?" 3:22. "Wherefore I praised the dead... who hath not seen the evil work that is done under the sun." Human spirits are very conscious in Heaven or Hell, but not on earth.

Ecclesiastes 9:5-6 - "The living know that they shall die: but the dead know not any thing, ...Also their love, and their hatred, and their envy, is now perished."

C | Inequities

Modern culture worships overachievers. Two dozen millionaires play baseball to entertain 30,000 people in air-conditioned stadiums with television screens the size of cornfields. That mentality has migrated into religion. Mega-churches empty smaller churches with pseudo-Christian agendas - pop-culture teachings, and music played by pseudo-Christian musicians - not because they have exemplary relationships with God, but because of stellar talents and celebrity status. "Ordinary" Christians who live by their Bibles, pray and live godly lives become impertinent.

Ecclesiastes 10:7 - "I have seen servants upon horses, and princes walking as servants upon the earth."

C | Cast Thy Bread Upon The Waters

This is a curious, enigmatic statement. "Cast thy bread upon the waters: for thou shalt find it after many days." Its context reveals that it is a charge to invest, to give, to plant. "He that observeth the wind shall not sow." Give, and you shall receive. The liberal soul shall be made fat. He that soweth bountifully shall reap also bountifully.

Ecclesiastes 11:6 - "In the morning sow thy seed, and in the evening withhold not thine hand: for thou knowest not whether shall prosper, either this or that, or whether they both shall be alike good."

D | The Afterlife

It is the ultimate recall. From the moment God breathed the breath of life into Adam, man became a living soul. Since then, souls of men have been God's property. "All souls are mine," Ezekiel 18:4. Our souls do not reincarnate into plants, animals, or newborn babies. They go back to God and will be disposed of according to His plan: sinners to Hell, saints to Heaven. No other options.

Ecclesiastes 12:7 - "Then shall the dust return to the earth as it was: and the spirit shall return unto God who gave it."

Lessons from the Book of the
SONG OF SOLOMON

B | The Song Of Solomon

No one knows for certain who wrote "The Song of Solomon." It is a romantic dialogue between a greatly enamored woman and her lover - Solomon. She says, "the king hath brought me into his chambers." Sometimes, she shares her excitement with local virgins, the daughters of Jerusalem. Some Jewish scholars interpret the song as an allegory depicting the love between God and Israel. Some Christians apply it allegorically to Christ and His Church. Whether or not it was intended to be an allegory cannot be proven either way.

Song of Solomon 1:1 - "The song of songs, which is Solomon's."

A | He Speaks To Me And Bids Me Come With Him

Whether or not the Song of Solomon was intended to be an allegory representing the love between Christ and His bride, the Church, we can certainly believe that such a love affair does not misrepresent the intense love between Jesus and His saints. A modern meaning might not be found for every line in the song, but I do know that no one ever cared for me like Jesus. He has invited me to spend eternity in His presence.

Song of Solomon 2:10 - "My beloved spake, and said unto me, Rise up, my love, my fair one, and come away."

A | I Sought Him Whom My Soul Loveth

The loving bride-in-waiting said, "I sought him whom my soul loveth: ...but I found him not." She arose and went about the city streets, enquiring as she went. Soon, she found him and would not let him go. "If from thence thou shalt seek the LORD thy God, thou shalt find him, if thou seek him with all thy heart and with all thy soul," Deuteronomy 4:29.

Song of Solomon 3:2 - "I will rise now, and go about the city in the streets, and in the broad ways I will seek him whom my soul loveth."

B | My Love

The love talk between Solomon and his lover was extremely sensual and affectionate, arousing every emotion, and embellishing every feature. Each spoke flatteringly of the other's beauty, fragrance, sounds, taste and touch. Theirs was the most intimate of relationships. Contrasted with so many stoic, disaffected marriages in modern society, Almighty God, in His Word, endorses a far more loving relationship between a husband and wife, and between a Christian and his Savior.

Song of Solomon 4:10 - "Thou hast ravished my heart, ...How much better is thy love than wine! and the smell of thine ointments than all spices!"

C | **He Is Altogether Lovely**

Solomon and his lover exchanged affections, but soon he went away, and she yearned for his return. She went to the watchmen of the city and to the daughters of Jerusalem soliciting their help in finding him. They asked her why he was so important to her. The reasons for her yearning for him are so much like the reasons why we yearn for the return of the LORD Jesus Christ.

Song of Solomon 5:10,16 – [He is] "the chiefest among ten thousand. ...yea, he is altogether lovely. This is my beloved, and this is my friend."

D | **He Is Gone Away, But He Will Return**

The daughters of Jerusalem asked her, "Whither is thy beloved gone, ...that we may seek him with thee?" She answered, "My beloved is gone down into his garden, to the beds of spices, to feed in the gardens." Similarly, Jesus, lover of my soul, has gone away - to prepare a place for me. "And if I go and prepare a place for you, I will come again, and receive you unto myself; that where I am, there ye may be also," John 14:3.

Song of Solomon 6:13 - "Return, return, that we may look upon thee."

D | **His Desire Is Toward Me**

When Eve sinned against God in the Garden of Eden, He said to her, "In sorrow thou shalt bring forth children; and thy desire shall be to thy husband." But in the Song of Solomon, we see the reverse - the man expressing his desire to the woman. "How fair and how pleasant art thou, O love, for delights!" Does this prophesy the day when Jesus restores the heavenly order - the male's desire toward the woman (i.e., God's love for His bride)?

Song of Solomon 7:10 "I am my beloved's, and his desire is toward me."

C | **Love Yearns For Its Lover**

The bride expresses her intense desire for her lover to come to her, "Make haste, my beloved, and be thou like to a roe or to a young hart upon the mountains of spices." Love has an irresistible attraction. "Love is strong as death." If we truly love our LORD, our yearning to see Him

369

cannot be quenched until He returns. "The Spirit and the bride say, Come. ...Even so, come, Lord Jesus," Revelation 22:17,20.

Song of Solomon 8:7 - "Love cannot be drowned by oceans or floods; it cannot be bought, no matter what is offered." (CEV)

Lessons from the Book of
ISAIAH

B | Isaiah The Prophet

Isaiah, son of Amoz, prophesied forty-four years under Judean kings Uzziah, Jotham, Ahaz, and Hezekiah. Ancient written traditions say that Isaiah died as a martyr under the evil king Manasseh by being sawn in two, and he is probably who Paul had in mind when listing heroes of faith in Hebrews 11:37, "...they were sawn asunder." And no wonder. Isaiah was fearless to preach before kings and princes, including stinging rebukes to kings of Judah.

Isaiah 1:10 - "Hear the word of the LORD, ye rulers of Sodom; give ear unto the law of our God, ye people of Gomorrah."

B | The Book Of The Prophet Isaiah

All but seven New Testament books quote or allude to the prophecies of Isaiah. He pronounced judgments and captivity on Israel for her sins, plus judgments on many heathen (Gentile) nations, for their mistreatment of Israel and God. Isaiah prophesied the restoration of Israel under the coming Messiah.

Isaiah 1:24,28 - "Therefore saith the Lord, the LORD of hosts, the mighty One of Israel, Ah, I will ease me of mine adversaries, and avenge me of mine enemies: ...And the destruction of the transgressors and of the sinners shall be together, and they that forsake the LORD shall be consumed."

A | When You Make Many Prayers, I Will Not Hear

This is a terrifying prospect - that God would utterly refuse to hear my prayers. God was so angry about Israel's sins, He called them Sodom and Gomorrah. "To what purpose is the multitude of your sacrifices unto me? ...I am full of the burnt offerings, ...when ye spread forth your hands, I will hide mine eyes from you: yea, when ye make many prayers, I will not hear." Repentance was the only prayer God wanted to hear.

Isaiah 1:16 - "Wash you, make you clean; put away the evil of your doings from before mine eyes; cease to do evil."

A | Come Now, And Let Us Reason Together

God invites His backsliders to a hearing. "Come now, and let us reason together, saith the LORD: though your sins be as scarlet, they shall be as white as snow; though they be red like crimson, they shall be as wool. If ye be willing and obedient, ye shall eat the good of the land." God is not willing for you to perish, if you will but open up and talk to Him on His terms.

Isaiah 1:20 - "But if ye refuse and rebel, ye shall be devoured with the sword: for the mouth of the LORD hath spoken it."

D | Jerusalem - Capital Of The World

Messiah, Jesus Christ, will rule the world from Jerusalem. "The mountain of the LORD'S house shall be established in the top of the mountains, and shall be exalted above the hills; and all nations shall flow unto it."

Isaiah 2:3 - "And many people shall go and say, Come ye, and let us go up to the mountain of the LORD, to the house of the God of Jacob; and he will teach us of his ways, and we will walk in his paths: for out of Zion shall go forth the law, and the word of the LORD from Jerusalem. "

D | Neither Shall They Learn War Anymore

The United Nations claims to be the "world's last hope for peace." A huge statue at the UN depicts a man beating a sword into a plowshare. Nearby, Isaiah 2:4 is inscribed WITHOUT the phrase, "And he shall judge among the nations, and shall rebuke many people." Only Jesus Christ WILL bring peace on earth. The UN is assuming an Antichrist position by claiming that Messianic role.

Isaiah 2:4 - "...and they shall beat their swords into plowshares, and their spears into pruninghooks: nation shall not lift up sword against nation, neither shall they learn war any more."

D | **The Day Of The LORD**

Isaiah was the first to use the phrase, "the day of the LORD," but many more references followed. The simplest way to define the Day of the Lord is one word: Armageddon. Everyone who exalts himself against God will be dealt with on that day. God will come down in the body of Jesus Christ, and judge His enemies, including every soothsayer, the haughty, and all idolaters.

Isaiah 2:12 - "For the day of the LORD of hosts shall be upon every one that is proud and lofty, and upon every one that is lifted up; and he shall be brought low."

C | **God Will Have His Day**

For ages, men have exalted themselves and ignored God. But God will have His day. "The lofty looks of man shall be humbled, and the haughtiness of men shall be bowed down, and the LORD alone shall be exalted in that day. For the day of the LORD of hosts shall be upon every one that is proud and lofty."

Isaiah 2:19 - "They shall go into the holes of the rocks, and into the caves of the earth, for fear of the LORD, and for the glory of his majesty, when he ariseth to shake terribly the earth."

C | **God Will Dishonor Backsliders**

One of God's tactics in judging backsliders is to take away their power and give it to someone who will dishonor them. He said He would take away "The mighty man, and the man of war, the judge, and the prophet, and the prudent, and the ancient, The captain of fifty, and the honourable man, and the counsellor, and the cunning artificer, and the eloquent orator. And I will give children to be their princes, and babes shall rule over them."

Isaiah 3:5 - "And the people shall be oppressed, ...the child shall behave himself proudly against the ancient."

C | **Woe Unto The Wicked!**

This is a most fundamental Truth, but somehow, this generation no longer believes it. So many people no longer believe in sin, much less that there will be any punishment for sin. But be warned. Almighty God is still taking notes, and sooner or later, He will call every one of us to judgment.

Isaiah 3:10-11 - "Say ye to the righteous, that it shall be well with him: for they shall eat the fruit of their doings. Woe unto the wicked! it shall be ill with him: for the reward of his hands shall be given him."

D | Judgment Of The Daughters Of Zion

One of the most difficult tasks on earth is to convince a haughty woman of her vanity. "Because the daughters of Zion are haughty, and walk with stretched forth necks and wanton eyes, ...the Lord will take away the bravery of their tinkling ornaments about their feet, ...the chains, ...bracelets, ...ornaments, ...headbands, ...earrings, ...rings, ...nose jewels, ...changeable suits of apparel, ...fine linen..."

Isaiah 3:24 - "Instead of sweet smell there shall be stink; and instead of a girdle a rent; and instead of well set hair baldness; and instead of a stomacher a girding of sackcloth; and burning instead of beauty."

D | Only Godliest Men In Israel Survive Armageddon

God judges the daughters of Zion in the "Day of the Lord." "In that day seven women shall take hold of one man, saying, We will eat our own bread, and wear our own apparel: only let us be called by thy name, to take away our reproach." Armageddon will devastate Israel's male population. "He that is left in Zion, and ...in Jerusalem, shall be called holy, even every one that is written among the living."

Isaiah 4:2 - "In that day shall the branch of the LORD [Christ] be beautiful and glorious, and the fruit of the earth shall be excellent and comely for them that are escaped of Israel."

B | Mount Zion After Armageddon

Following Armageddon, Mount Zion will have a vast covered pavilion to protect visitors from the sun and weather. Over every building will be a glory cloud by day and flaming fire by night (similar to the Tabernacle in the wilderness).

Isaiah 4:5-6 "The LORD will create upon every dwelling place of mount Zion, ...a cloud and smoke by day, and the shining of a flaming fire by night: ...And there shall be a tabernacle for a shadow in the daytime from the heat, and for a place of refuge, and for a covert from storm and from rain."

B | Israel - God's Vineyard

God made a vineyard - Israel. He put it on a very fruitful hill, fenced it, cleared away the stones, and planted the choicest vine. He built a tower in it and made a winepress, anticipating luscious grapes. Instead, it brought forth wild grapes. He said, "What could have been done more to my vineyard, that I have not done in it?" Shortly after this prophecy, the Assyrians took the northern ten tribes of Israel into captivity.

Isaiah 5:6 - "I will lay it waste: it shall not be pruned, nor digged; but there shall come up briers and thorns."

C | Hell Hath Enlarged Herself

A reprobate is a depraved, unprincipled or wicked person. In a scriptural context, it is someone who believes that right is wrong, and wrong is right. People who abandon godly morals and virtues and give themselves to riotous living are a stench in the nostrils of God. "Therefore hell hath enlarged herself, and opened her mouth without measure: and their glory, and their multitude, and their pomp, and he that rejoiceth, shall descend into it."

Isaiah 5:20 - "Woe unto them that call evil good, and good evil; that put darkness for light, and light for darkness."

B | God's Throne Was In Jerusalem

In a vision, Isaiah saw it. So did Ezekiel (10:9). God's Throne sat inside the Temple in Jerusalem. Apparently, it came from heaven the day Solomon dedicated the Temple, and remained until God wearied of Israel's backsliding, and drove them out of Jerusalem. God will again have His Throne in Jerusalem when Jesus reconquers the city, the nation and the world (Zechariah 6:13) at Armageddon.

Isaiah 6:1 - "In the year that king Uzziah died I saw also the Lord sitting upon a throne, high and lifted up, and his train filled the temple."

A | Here Am I; Send Me

When Isaiah saw the LORD in the Temple, he cried out, "Woe is me! for I am undone; because I am a man of unclean lips, and I dwell in the midst of a people of unclean lips: for mine eyes have seen the King, the LORD of hosts." A seraphim came with a live coal from the altar and touched his lips, and purged his sin." Isaiah heard a voice saying, "Whom shall I send?" Even without knowing where God will send us, we should instantly respond.

Isaiah 6:8 - "Then said I, Here am I; send me."

A | Ask A Sign Of The LORD Thy God

The ten northern tribes, referred to as "Ephraim," allied with Syria against the kingdom of Judah. Ahaz was king of Judah. God instructed him to "Ask thee a sign of the LORD thy God," but Ahaz indignantly refused. He was embroiled in idolatry himself (2 Kings 16:4) and did not want to talk to God. Isaiah slammed him with an epic prophecy. Messiah would come, but not before both Israel and Judah had fallen.

Isaiah 7:14 - "Therefore the Lord himself shall give you a sign; Behold, a virgin shall conceive, and bear a son, and shall call his name Immanuel."

A | Should Not A People Seek Unto Their God?

Isaiah pronounced a scathing rebuke upon Judah for associating with and expecting help from Rezin, king of Syria at Damascus. God dislikes men trusting the arm of flesh instead of Him. Remember David's punishment for numbering Israel. Isaiah prophesied Rezin's demise, which soon followed.

Isaiah 8:12-13, 19 - "Say ye not, A confederacy, to all them to whom this people shall say, A confederacy; neither fear ye their fear, nor be afraid. Sanctify the LORD of hosts himself; and let him be your fear, and let him be your dread. ...should not a people seek unto their God?"

C | Messiah - A Great Light

The prophet said that when Messiah came, Israel would not be in as much darkness as it had been in former days, when they were much deeper in rebellion and sin. He used the word "dimness." Into this dimness, Messiah would be a light to Israel. He would bring joy, as in harvest time, and rejoicing, as when soldiers divide the spoil. Jesus is the Light of the World.

Isaiah 9:2 - "The people that walked in darkness have seen a great light: they that dwell in the land of the shadow of death, upon them hath the light shined."

D | Jesus - Everlasting Father

The prophets ascribed seemingly contradictory titles to Messiah - King and Prince, Father and Son, God and man. That is because Jesus has a dual nature. He is both God and man. The Spirit is the Father. The human is the Son. Same person. The divine nature is King. The human nature is Prince. The Throne of God in Heaven seats only one. God and the Lamb - the invisible Spirit and His incarnation, Jesus.

Isaiah 9:6 - "...and his name shall be called Wonderful, Counselor, The mighty God, The everlasting Father, The Prince of Peace."

D | The Government Of Christ

Lucifer wanted it and tempted Christ to surrender it, but it can't be taken. The Kingdom is Christ's forever. No other power will ever prevail. The earth is the Lord's and the fullness thereof. He shall reign forever.

Isaiah 9:7 - "Of the increase of his government and peace there shall be no end, upon the throne of David, and upon his kingdom, to order it, and to establish it with judgment and with justice from henceforth even for ever. The zeal of the LORD of hosts will perform this."

A | Prayerlessness, Even In The Face Of Judgment

God afflicted Israel in Isaiah's day for countless years of backsliding. God reminded them repeatedly that His arm was outstretched to them, to show them mercy. But nobody sought the LORD. It is tragic when God has to send calamity to wake people up to righteousness, yet they fail to move! Don't wait until God sends dreadful woes. Seek Him now!

Isaiah 9:12-13 - "For all this his anger is not turned away, but his hand is stretched out still. For the people turneth not unto him that smiteth them, neither do they seek the LORD of hosts."

C | God Will Finally Destroy Hypocrites With Great Anger

So much of modern Christianity depicts a milquetoast God - soft, timid, unassertive and spineless. But God, the Righteous Judge, will not tolerate flagrant sin and hypocrisy indefinitely. "The Lord shall have no joy in their young men, neither shall have mercy on their fatherless and widows: for every one is an hypocrite and an evildoer, and every mouth speaketh folly."

Isaiah 9:14-15 - "Therefore the LORD will cut off from Israel head and tail, branch and rush, in one day. The ancient and honourable, he is the head; and the prophet that teacheth lies, he is the tail."

B | The Assyrian - Rod Of Mine Anger

After centuries in the Promised Land, God had enough of Israel's idolatries, hypocrisies, and countless other transgressions. He ordained

Assyria to be "the rod of mine anger." "The staff in their hand is mine indignation. I will send him against an hypocritical nation, ...to tread them down." God sent the Assyrians to punish Israel, taking the northern ten tribes into captivity. Even today, God uses His enemies to punish backsliders. Then, they too will be judged.

Isaiah 10:15 - "Shall the axe boast itself against him that heweth therewith? or shall the saw magnify itself against him that shaketh it?"

D | The Last Consumption

In Moses' day, God warned Israel that if they "despise my statutes, ...abhor my judgments, ...not do all my commandments, ...break my covenant," He would put terror and consumption upon them (Leviticus 26:15). Again, in Deuteronomy 28, He threatened to "consume" them from off the land. The battle of Armageddon will be the last cleansing, performed by Jesus Christ, prior to the restoration of all things.

Isaiah 10:17 - "And the light of Israel shall be for a fire, and his Holy One for a flame: and it shall burn and devour his thorns and his briers in one day."

B | The Remnant

A remnant is a part left over after a greater part has been removed. A residue is the remains at the end of a process. God will always have a remnant of His people. When God cursed Satan in the Garden of Eden, He promised that a seed of the woman would bruise Satan's head. A remnant of that holy seed must perpetuate until Satan is defeated. Not to worry. That day is not far away.

Isaiah 10:22 - "For though thy people Israel be as the sand of the sea, yet a remnant of them shall return."

D | The Yoke Shall Be Destroyed Because Of The Anointing

Assyrians were first to conquer Israel (northern kingdom). Assyrians will also be their LAST enemy, too. Jesus Christ will destroy the Assyrians at Armageddon. "Thus saith the Lord GOD of hosts, ...be not afraid of the Assyrian: he shall smite thee with a rod, ...For yet a very little while, and the indignation shall cease, and mine anger in their destruction."

Isaiah 10:27 - "It shall come to pass in that day, that his burden shall be taken away from off thy shoulder, and his yoke from off thy neck, and the yoke shall be destroyed because of the anointing."

D | Roadmap The Antichrist Will Follow

Isaiah actually plotted the path the Assyrian Antichrist will travel from the North on his way to the battle of Armageddon at Jerusalem. "He is come to Aiath (Khirbet el-Maqatir, just east of Ramallah), he is passed to Migron, (evacuated by Israel in 2008), ...Michmash, ...Geba, ...Ramah, ...Gibeah, ..Anathoth, ...Madmenah, ...Gebim, ... Nob, ...he shall shake his hand against the mount of the daughter of Zion, the hill of Jerusalem."

Isaiah 10:33 - "The LORD of hosts, shall lop the bough with terror: and the high ones of stature shall be hewn down, and the haughty shall be humbled."

C | Messiah Will Have A Seven-fold Anointing

In Revelation 5:6, the Lamb of God had "seven eyes, which are the seven spirits of God." Isaiah prophesied Messiah's seven-fold anointing: Spirit of the LORD; Spirit of wisdom; understanding; Spirit of counsel; might; Spirit of knowledge; and of the fear of the LORD.

Isaiah 11:1-2 - "...a rod out of the stem of Jesse, and a Branch shall grow out of his roots: And the spirit of the LORD shall rest upon him, the spirit of wisdom and understanding, the spirit of counsel and might, the spirit of knowledge and of the fear of the LORD."

D | Jesus Will Rule The Earth

When Jesus returns to rule the earth for 1000 years, He will righteously judge the poor and the meek. Isaiah depicts a period when Jesus will firmly bring all the people of the world to order. He will bring justice to those who love righteousness and destroy those who are wicked.

Isaiah 11:4-5 "...with righteousness shall he judge the poor, and reprove with equity for the meek of the earth: and he shall smite the earth with the rod of his mouth, and with the breath of his lips shall he slay the wicked."

A | To It Shall The Gentiles Seek

Among all the great Messianic prophecies of the Bible are many announcements concerning His coming kingdom on earth. Isaiah called Messiah both the Root and Branch of Jesse. He is the hope of all Israel. But Isaiah made an even greater pronouncement. The Gentiles (non-Jews) would also turn to and seek after Messiah. Jesus is the answer to the whole world's problems.

Isaiah 11:10 - "And in that day there shall be a root of Jesse, which shall stand for an ensign of the people; to it shall the Gentiles seek: and his rest shall be glorious."

B | The Ensign

Six times, Isaiah called Messiah an ensign (banner, flag). God "will lift up an ensign to the nations from far, and ...they shall come with speed swiftly," 5:26. The "diaspora" (dispersed Jews) began immigrating to Israel around 1948. Jesus' return will signal worldwide "aliyah," the second and final immigration!

Isaiah 11:11-12 - "The Lord shall set his hand again the second time to recover the remnant of his people, ...He shall set up an ensign for the nations, and shall assemble the outcasts of Israel, and gather together the dispersed of Judah from the four corners of the earth."

A | Call Upon His Name

Today, Christianity is being marginalized in every nation. In America, church attendance has plummeted, and new laws forbid praying in Jesus' name in public places. An entire generation of young people know nothing about Jesus Christ. But He will come, and all the world will praise Him and call upon His name.

Isaiah 12:4 - "And in that day shall ye say, Praise the LORD, call upon his name, declare his doings among the people, make mention that his name is exalted. Sing unto the LORD; for he hath done excellent things: this is known in all the earth."

A | Draw Water Out Of The Wells Of Salvation

If you are saved, you will certainly praise God when Jesus comes. His saints will say, "O LORD, I will praise thee: though thou wast angry with me, thine anger is turned away, and thou comfortedst me. Behold, God is my salvation; ...the LORD JEHOVAH is my strength and my song; he also is become my salvation." With joy they will draw water out of the wells of salvation. Draw that salvation water now. Rejoice!

Isaiah 12:6 - "Cry out and shout, thou inhabitant of Zion: for great is the Holy One of Israel in the midst of thee."

C | God Will Destroy The Sinners Out Of The Land

Armageddon will occur when Jesus brings His saints to Jerusalem to execute the Man of Sin, the False Prophet, and every army coming to destroy Israel.

Isaiah 13:2-5, 9 - "Lift ye up a banner upon the high mountain, ...I have commanded my sanctified ones, ...The noise of a multitude in the mountains, like as of a great people; ...the LORD of hosts mustereth the host of the battle. They come from a far country, from the end of heaven, even the LORD, and the weapons of his indignation, to destroy the whole land. ...and he shall destroy the sinners thereof out of it."

C | Signs In The Heavens Will Announce Armageddon

When the LORD returns to reclaim the earth, the sun and moon and stars will bear witness. God will choreograph the most extreme drama in the heavens to announce His day of triumph.

Isaiah 13:10, 13 - "For the stars of heaven and the constellations thereof shall not give their light: the sun shall be darkened in his going forth, and the moon shall not cause her light to shine. ...I will shake the heavens, and the earth shall remove out of her place, in the wrath of the LORD of hosts, and in the day of his fierce anger."

C | I Will Punish The World For Their Evil

You can view this as a prophecy, but it is also a divine principle. Sin cannot abide in God's presence. We must put away sin, via the plan of salvation. He must either cleanse us, or destroy us.

Isaiah 13:11-12 - "I will punish the world for their evil, and the wicked for their iniquity; and I will cause the arrogancy of the proud to cease, and will lay low the haughtiness of the terrible. I will make a man more precious than fine gold; even a man than the golden wedge of Ophir."

D | The Burden Of Babylon

In "the burden of Babylon" articulated by Isaiah in chapter 13, God says that Babylon will finally be destroyed as Sodom and Gomorrah, and it will NEVER be inhabited again. This prophecy will be fulfilled when Jesus returns for the battle of Armageddon. The place in context is southern Iraq.

Isaiah 13:19-21 - "Babylon, the glory of kingdoms, the beauty of the Chaldees' excellency, shall be as when God overthrew Sodom and

Gomorrah. It shall never be inhabited, neither shall it be dwelt in from generation to generation. ...but wild beasts of the desert shall lie there;..."

D | The LORD Will Yet Choose Israel

Some people think that God permanently rejected Israel when they rejected their Messiah, Jesus Christ. But God is NOT through with Israel. In the millennium, Christ's thousand-year reign, Israelites will rule with Him in the Promised Land, while Gentiles rule as kings and priests around the world (Revelation 5:10).

Isaiah 14:1 - "For the LORD will have mercy on Jacob, and will yet choose Israel, and set them in their own land: and the strangers shall be joined with them, ...and they shall take them captives, whose captives they were; and they shall rule over their oppressors."

D | Lucifer And Babylon Will Become A Proverb

After Armageddon, both Lucifer and historical Babylon will fit this proverb: "How hath the oppressor ceased! ...The LORD hath broken the staff of the wicked, and the sceptre of the rulers. ...The whole earth is at rest, and is quiet."

Isaiah 14:9 - "Hell from beneath is moved for thee to meet thee at thy coming: ...it hath raised up from their thrones all the kings of the nations. All they shall speak and say unto thee, Art thou also become weak as we? art thou become like unto us? Thy pomp is brought down to the grave."

B | Lucifer

Isaiah revealed that Lucifer (Satan) was fallen from heaven, cut down to the ground, and was a weakener of nations. His foolish claims: "I will ...ascend into heaven, ...exalt my throne above the stars of God, ...sit upon the mount of the congregation, ...ascend above the clouds, ...be like the most High."

Isaiah 14:15-17 - "Yet thou shalt be brought down to hell, to the sides of the pit. They that see thee shall narrowly look upon thee, and consider thee, saying, Is this the man that made the earth to tremble, that did shake kingdoms; ...and destroyed the cities thereof?"

D | I Will Break The Assyrian In My Land

God says, "This is the purpose that is purposed upon the whole earth." We should pay attention to this divinely-identified purpose. "The LORD of hosts hath sworn, saying, ...I will break the Assyrian in my land, and upon my mountains tread him under foot: then shall his yoke depart from off them, and his burden depart from off their shoulders." This is an Armageddon prophecy. The Man of Sin (commonly referred to as the Antichrist) will come from the region of Assyria, and Jesus will destroy him in the mountains of Jerusalem.

Isaiah 14:27 - "For the LORD of hosts hath purposed, and who shall disannul it?"

D | Palestine Will Be Dissolved

The entire world is presently awaiting the official declaration of a Palestinian State. Israel is being stripped and deprived of its recent and ancient holdings, like Nazareth, Bethlehem, Hebron, Jericho and many Biblically significant cities. But God will not tolerate it. When Jesus comes, the Bible says that Palestine will be dissolved.

Isaiah 14:29,31 - "Rejoice not thou, whole Palestina, because the rod of him that smote thee is broken: ...Howl, O gate; cry, O city; thou, whole Palestina, art dissolved: for there shall come from the north a smoke, and none shall be alone in his appointed times. ...The LORD hath founded Zion."

B | The Burden Of Moab

The land of Moab contained the descendants of Lot's children by incest. They became enemies of Israel in Moses' day. God sent judgment upon them. Two principal cities of Moab were destroyed during the night, and great mourning and howling overcame the people. Sackcloth and weeping marked the occasion. Even Isaiah's heart cried out for sorrow. The people fled, for the crops failed, and their water supplies were spent.

Isaiah 15:3 - "In their streets they shall gird themselves with sackcloth: on the tops of their houses, and in their streets, every one shall howl, weeping abundantly."

B | Antichrist: Spoiler And Extortioner

Isaiah called the Assyrian Antichrist "the spoiler," (one who robs, ravages, plunders) and "the extortioner," (one who takes by violence, force or abuse). The Man of Sin will seize Jewish properties in the West Bank (Judea), precipitating "Jacob's trouble," the Great Tribulation. Jesus warned them that dwell in Judea to flee at that time (Matthew 24:15-16). Some believe they will flee to Petra; however no specific prophecy proves that.

Isaiah 16:4-5 - "Let mine outcasts dwell with thee, Moab; be thou a covert to them from the face of the spoil, for the extortioner is at an end."

A | **A Man Shall Look To His Maker**

In "the burden of Damascus," Isaiah prophesied a day when Syria and Damascus will be destroyed (at Armageddon) - only a remnant will survive. They will be ready to abandon their false gods and call on the Holy One of Israel, Jesus Christ.

Isaiah 17:7 - "At that day shall a man look to his Maker, and his eyes shall have respect to the Holy One of Israel. And he shall not look to the altars, the work of his hands, neither shall respect that which his fingers have made, either the groves, or the images."

C | **Forgetting God Brings A Curse**

It is great folly to forget God. God will answer your negligence by making your efforts unfruitful. You can plant your crop, but your harvest will fail. Join a multitude and make a noise of success, but God will rebuke you and blow you away.

Isaiah 17:10 - "Because thou hast forgotten the God of thy salvation, and hast not been mindful of the rock of thy strength, therefore shalt thou plant pleasant plants, ...and in the morning shalt thou make thy seed to flourish: but the harvest shall be a heap in the day of grief and of desperate sorrow."

B | **A Present To The LORD In Mount Zion**

God says (in paraphrase), "Woe to those who have taken advantage of my people in their dispersion. I will lift up my ensign/banner (Messiah) on Jerusalem's mountains, at the last trumpet. I will take my rest in the earth (1,000 years of peace under Messiah). I have often pruned my people, and they suffered many reversals, but they will finally dwell gloriously in my holy place, Mount Zion."

Isaiah 18:7 - "In that time shall the present be brought ...of a people scattered and peeled, ...to the place of the name of the LORD of hosts, the mount Zion."

A | **Egypt Will Cry Unto The LORD**

The LORD will come to Egypt upon a swift cloud at Armageddon. Civil war will start. A fierce king will rule. Egyptians will seek idols, wizards, and familiar spirits. The Nile will dry up. Agriculture, fishing, and industry will fail. In fear and terror, they will turn to God.

Isaiah 19:19-22 - "There shall be an altar to the LORD in the midst of the land of Egypt, ...they shall cry unto the LORD, ...he shall send them a saviour, ...the Egyptians shall know the LORD, ...and shall do sacrifice and oblation, ...he shall be intreated of them, and shall heal them."

C | God Speaks By Pantomime

In ancient times, without radio, television, or even the printed page, God spoke to people using various methods. Sometimes, a pantomime could get people's attention when nothing else could. A pantomime is a form of communication without words - using bodily movement, gestures or facial expression. God told Isaiah to strip down to his basics to warn Israel's enemies that the Assyrians would lead them captive, naked and barefoot.

Isaiah 20:3 - "The LORD said, ...my servant Isaiah hath walked naked and barefoot three years for a sign and wonder upon Egypt and upon Ethiopia."

A | Enquire Of The Watchman

A grievous vision caused Isaiah to panic. "My heart panted, fearfulness affrighted me." He saw a treacherous one, and a spoiler; Elam and Media. The LORD said, "Set a watchmen, and see what he says." The watchman said, "Babylon is falling! And her idols have fallen to the ground!" Isaiah was frightened by the magnitude of this revelation. He was seeing, years in advance, the overthrow of Babylon by the Medes and Persians. God planned to "thresh" Babylon.

Isaiah 21:10 - "That which I have heard of the LORD of hosts, the God of Israel, have I declared unto you."

C | God Will Judge You For Being Flippant

Isaiah was probably in the valley below the Temple Mount when his "burden of the valley of vision" came. Many of Jerusalem's men and rulers had been killed or captured, but the inhabitants were careless, tumultuous, even joyous. Isaiah mourned. "Ye have not looked unto the maker thereof, neither had respect unto him that fashioned it." God called them to mourning and sackcloth, but they flippantly said, "Let us eat and drink, for tomorrow we shall die."

Isaiah 22:14 - "It was revealed in mine ears by the LORD of hosts, Surely this iniquity shall not be purged from you till ye die."

B | The Port City Of Tyre

Isaiah prophesied the fall of the ancient merchant port city of Tyre. "Howl, ye ships of Tarshish; for it is laid waste. ...The LORD of hosts hath purposed it, to stain the pride of all glory, and to bring into contempt all the honourable of the earth." When Nebuchadnezzar of Babylon captured Jerusalem, he destroyed Tyre. "Tyre shall be forgotten seventy years." Then it would revive. Following Armageddon, Messiah will rule over Tyre.

Isaiah 23:18 - "And her merchandise and her hire shall be holiness to the LORD: ...for her merchandise shall be for them that dwell before the LORD."

B | Judgment By Fire

God will judge the inhabitants of the earth by fire. "As with the people, so with the priest; as with the servant, so with his master; as with the maid, so with her mistress; as with the buyer, so with the seller; as with the lender, so with the borrower." This dreadful purge will occur near the end of the Great Tribulation. Messiah will restore the earth immediately following Armageddon.

Isaiah 24:6 - "Therefore hath the curse devoured the earth, and they that dwell therein are desolate: therefore the inhabitants of the earth are burned, and few men left."

D | A Curse Will Devour The Earth

A curse will devour the earth (24:6) just before Armageddon. Jeremiah called it "Jacob's trouble." Daniel called it "a time of trouble, such as never was..." "The LORD maketh the earth empty, and maketh it waste, and turneth it upside down, and scattereth abroad the inhabitants thereof," Isaiah 24:1. It ends with the shaking of the olive tree (the "rapture" and resurrection of saints from all ages) and gleaning the vintage grapes (God's wrath on the wicked at Armageddon).

Isaiah 24:13 - "...there shall be as the shaking of an olive tree, and as the gleaning grapes when the vintage is done."

A | The Righteous Will Rejoice At Armageddon

Isaiah never used the word 'Armageddon,' but volumes of his prophecies pertain to Armageddon. John the Baptist said that Messiah "will throughly purge his floor, and gather his wheat into the garner; but he will burn up the chaff with unquenchable fire," Matthew 3:12. Isaiah said, "Behold, the LORD maketh the earth empty, and maketh it waste, and turneth it upside down, and scattereth abroad the inhabitants thereof." As the wicked perish, the righteous will rejoice.

Isaiah 24:14 - "They shall lift up their voice, they shall sing for the majesty of the LORD, they shall cry aloud from the sea."

D | Christ Will Cast Satan And World Rulers Into The Pit

Principalities, powers, rulers of the darkness of this world, and spiritual wickedness in high places (demon princes) heavily influence kings on earth. At Armageddon, Christ will imprison those demons and their earthly agents.

Isaiah 24:21-23 - "And it shall come to pass in that day, that the LORD shall punish the host of the high ones that are on high, and the kings of the earth upon the earth. And they shall be gathered together, as prisoners are gathered in the pit, and shall be shut up in the prison, ...when the LORD of hosts shall reign in mount Zion."

D | Messiah Will Reign Gloriously In Zion

Expect one thousand years of bliss on earth under Jesus Christ. The glory of the LORD in Zion will put to shame the light of the sun and moon. Saints from all ages will serve Jesus in His glorious Temple and have "run-of-the-earth" during that entire time. No war or terrorism. No sickness, disease, sin or Satan. No famine, pestilence, pain or death. Just a perfect world - utopia - under the perfect rule of the God who created it.

Isaiah 24:23 - "...the LORD of hosts shall reign in mount Zion, and in Jerusalem, and before his ancients gloriously."

B | Messiah's Victory Banquet

Isaiah exalted and praised God for making defensed cities into ruins and making terrible nations fear Him. He prophesied the Marriage Supper of the Lamb. "In this mountain shall the LORD of hosts make unto all people a feast of fat things, a feast of wines on the lees, of fat things full of marrow, of wines on the lees well refined. ...He will swallow up death in victory; and the Lord GOD will wipe away tears from off all faces."

Isaiah 25:9 - "It shall be said in that day, Lo, this is our God; we have waited for him."

C | Perfect Peace

The Word of God holds the universe together, and it will hold you together if you will focus on it. People's lies, doubts, fears, unbelief and all their other godless sayings corrupt our minds and sabotage our peace. Toss out everything that does not agree 100% with God's Word, even if it means sitting down and shutting up. Better to be alone in peace, than perplexed by a so-called friend's deleterious words or ways.

Isaiah 26:3 - "Thou wilt keep him in perfect peace, whose mind is stayed on Thee."

A | I Have Desired Thee In The Night

Look forward to the day when Jerusalem will be restored under Messiah. Offer a praise and a prayer with Isaiah: "In that day shall this song be sung in the land of Judah; We have a strong city; salvation will God appoint for walls and bulwarks. Open ye the gates, that the righteous nation which keepeth the truth may enter in."

Isaiah 26:9 - "With my soul have I desired thee in the night; yea, with my spirit within me will I seek thee early: for when thy judgments are in the earth, the inhabitants of the world will learn righteousness."

A | Pain Will Make You Pray

The prophet remembered other lords who had oppressed Israel, but they died, and God was erasing their memory. "Thou hast increased the nation, O LORD, ...thou art glorified." He admitted that Israel's oppressors had driven them to prayer. "LORD, in trouble have they visited thee, they poured out a prayer when thy chastening was upon them." Nothing makes you pray more than hardship and pain.

Isaiah 26:17 - "Like as a woman with child, that draweth near the time of her delivery, is in pain, and crieth out in her pangs; so have we been in thy sight, O LORD."

C | Dead Men Shall Live, Dead Bodies Shall Arise

Isaiah condemned the wicked. "They are dead, they shall not live; they are deceased, they shall not rise: therefore hast thou visited and destroyed them," 26:14. After Christ rules for 1000 years on earth, the wicked dead will be summoned to the White Throne Judgment where they will be sentenced to Hell (Revelation 20). But Christ will raise the righteous dead before the Millennium to rule with Him.

Isaiah 26:19 - "Thy dead men shall live, together with my dead body shall they arise. Awake and sing, ye that dwell in dust: ...the earth shall cast out the dead."

B | A Hiding Place For Jews During The Tribulation

Three-and-a-half years before the battle of Armageddon, God will hide 144,000 Jews from the persecution of the Antichrist. "When ye therefore shall see the abomination of desolation, spoken of by Daniel the prophet, ...let them which be in Judaea flee into the mountains," Matthew 24:16. "And the woman fled into the wilderness, where she hath a place prepared of God," Revelation 12:6.

Isaiah 26:20 - "Come, my people, enter thou into thy chambers, and shut thy doors about thee: hide thyself as it were for a little moment, until the indignation be overpast."

B | Leviathan

John, in Revelation 13:1, saw a beast rising out of the sea - the end-time world government. "The waters which thou sawest, ...are peoples, and multitudes, and nations, and tongues," Revelation 17:15. Behind this despotic, evil government rising from out of the midst of humanity will be Satan himself, in his Man of Sin. And God has, all along, planned Satan's demise at Armageddon.

Isaiah 27:1 - "In that day the LORD with his sore and great and strong sword shall punish leviathan the piercing serpent, even leviathan that crooked serpent; and he shall slay the dragon that is in the sea."

B | A Vineyard Of Red Wine

Israel, Abraham's natural descendants, have been in exile since shortly after the Church Age began. But they are still God's original vineyard, and "I the LORD do keep it; I will water it every moment: lest any hurt it, I will keep it night and day." He promises to burn any briers or thorns (enemies) that spoil His vineyard, and to smite all those who smote Israel.

Isaiah 27:6 - "He shall cause them that come of Jacob to take root: Israel shall blossom and bud, and fill the face of the world with fruit."

C | He Stayeth His Rough Wind In The Day Of The East Wind

Throughout the scriptures, an east wind was a bad omen. In the Middle East, an east wind was dry and often stormy. It parched and withered crops, brought drought and pestilence, and sometimes broke up ships at sea. Isaiah observed that when evil winds are blowing upon the wicked, God often spares His chosen people from the worst winds. "Hath he smitten him, as he smote those that smote him? or is he slain according to the slaughter of them that are slain by him?

Isaiah 27:8 - "...he stayeth his rough wind in the day of the east wind."

A | Overdue Worship

From the beginning, God planned to settle His score with Lucifer over the souls of men at Armageddon. At the Last Trump, Jesus will defeat every opposing man and angel and save every righteous soul from all of time. They will worship the LORD in His new Capital – Jerusalem!

Isaiah 27:13 - "And it shall come to pass in that day, that the great trumpet shall be blown, and they shall come which were ready to perish in the land of Assyria, and the outcasts in the land of Egypt, and shall worship the LORD in the holy mount at Jerusalem."

C | Woe To Drunkards

The prophet denounced Ephraim (Northern Kingdom of Israel) for their drunkenness. Drunkenness spoiled the priests and prophets, causing their vision to err and impairing their judgment. Ephraim's glory faded like a flower. God sent a mighty, strong one (Assyrian) like a tempest and storm to tread down Ephraim. Only Messiah can and will restore the beauty of Ephraim.

Isaiah 28:5 - "In that day shall the LORD of hosts be for a crown of glory, and for a diadem of beauty, unto the residue of his people, And for a spirit of judgment to him that sitteth in judgment."

A | Stammering Lips And Another Tongue

Paul referred to Isaiah's prophecy when he taught the Corinthians, "With men of other tongues and other lips will I speak unto this people; and yet for all that will they not hear me, saith the Lord." Since the day of Pentecost in Acts 2, the baptism of the Holy Ghost with the evidence of speaking in unknown tongues, fulfills Isaiah's prophecy.

Isaiah 28:11 - "For with stammering lips and another tongue will he speak to this people. To whom he said, This is the rest wherewith ye may cause the weary to rest; and this is the refreshing: yet they would not hear."

C | Line Upon Line, Precept Upon Precept

God continually sent His Word to Israel for centuries, but they were obstinate to hear or obey. "Whom shall he teach knowledge? and whom shall he make to understand doctrine? them that are weaned from the milk, and drawn from the breasts." Those who hear and obey it will live. Those who reject it will die.

Isaiah 28:13 - "But the word of the LORD was unto them precept upon precept, precept upon precept; line upon line, line upon line; here a little, and there a little; that they might go, and fall backward, and be broken, and snared, and taken."

C | He Will Not Always Be Threshing You

Numerous spiritual lessons can be learned in the field. A plowman does not plow merely to sow. All his labors are ultimately for a good harvest. God teaches men to be fruitful. Every kind of grain has to be harvested differently. Some grains must be beaten hard, others lightly. By that same reasoning, God never puts us through more of a trial than He knows we can endure. He is not trying to destroy you. He will not always be threshing you. His purpose is your fruitfulness.

Isaiah 28:28 - "Bread corn is bruised; because he will not ever be threshing it."

D | Neither Israel Nor Her Enemies Will Understand Armageddon

Israel will not understand the events against them which lead to Armageddon. God will blind and deafen them. They will be like a man who has a book that is sealed, or that he cannot read. Likewise, Israel's enemies, as they come to destroy Israel at Armageddon, will be like a man who dreams he is eating, but wakes up hungry; or dreams he is drinking, and wakes up famished.

Isaiah 29:10 - "The LORD hath poured out upon you the spirit of deep sleep, and hath closed your eyes: the prophets and your rulers, the seers hath he covered."

A | Beware Of Giving Lip Service To God

God said, "Forasmuch as this people draw near me with their mouth, and with their lips do honour me, but have removed their heart far from me. Therefore, behold, I will proceed to do a marvellous work among this people." If you pretend to serve God; if you serve God with your lips, but your heart is far from Him, be warned. God says that He will empty your phony heart of its wisdom and understanding. That's scary.

Isaiah 29:14 - "...for the wisdom of their wise men shall perish, and the understanding of their prudent men shall be hid."

B | Ariel (Jerusalem)

Isaiah is the only Bible writer to call Jerusalem "Ariel," meaning "Lion of God." He prophesied woes on Jerusalem to cure their pernicious hypocrisy. "There shall be heaviness and sorrow, ...thou shalt be brought down, ...it shall be at an instant suddenly, ...thou shalt be visited of the LORD of hosts with thunder, and with earthquake, and great noise, with storm and tempest, and the flame of devouring fire." This will be the fire of God's "indignation" during the Great Tribulation.

Isaiah 29:24 - "They also that erred in spirit shall come to understanding, and they that murmured shall learn doctrine."

A | Woe, For Seeking Counsel Without God

In all your inquiry, God must be your first and last source of counsel. "Woe to the rebellious children, saith the LORD, that take counsel, ...That walk to go down into Egypt, and have not asked at my mouth. ...this is a rebellious people, ...children that will not hear the law of the LORD: Which say to the seers, See not; and to the prophets, Prophesy not unto us right things, speak unto us smooth things, prophesy deceits." The jealous God wants His voice to rule all.

Isaiah 30:12,14 - "Because ye despise this word, ...he shall not spare."

A | He Will Be Very Gracious At The Voice Of Thy Cry

The book of Isaiah is weighted with rebukes for Israel, and prophetic warnings of impending judgment if they refused to reform. But with the rebukes came a generous offer of mercy if they would only turn their hearts back to God and seek Him. Fortunately for all of us, God's wrath is tempered with mercy. He WILL answer your cry!

Isaiah 30:19 - "For the people shall dwell in Zion at Jerusalem: thou shalt weep no more: he will be very gracious unto thee at the voice of thy cry; when he shall hear it, he will answer thee."

A | Ye Shall Have A Song

Sometimes, we grow silent as we wait for a much-desired victory. Like the saints in Babylon, who hung their harps on willow trees, our songs are sometimes silenced because of our hard trials. But when Jesus comes, we will suffer no more defeats. We will have victory forever. Instantly, our songs will return - to stay!

Isaiah 30:29 - "Ye shall have a song, as in the night when a holy solemnity is kept; and gladness of heart, as when one goeth with a pipe to come into the mountain of the LORD, to the mighty One of Israel."

C | The Voice Of The LORD Will Lead You

God told Israel, "In returning and rest shall ye be saved; in quietness and in confidence shall be your strength: and ye would not." He wanted them to be quiet and hear HIS voice. "Thine ears shall hear a word behind thee, saying, This is the way, walk ye in it, when ye turn to the right hand, and when ye turn to the left." The voice of the LORD will lead you right.

Isaiah 30:30-31 - "The LORD shall cause his glorious voice to be heard, ...For through the voice of the LORD shall the Assyrian be beaten down."

B | Egypt

During a famine, Abraham took his family to Egypt for supplies, but following a convoluted ordeal concerning Sarah, Pharaoh asked him to leave. God sent Abraham's descendants to the land of Goshen in Egypt, where they became slaves crying for deliverance. God was turning their hearts against any dependence on Egypt. God wants His people to put all their trust in Him.

Isaiah 31:1 "Woe to them that go down to Egypt for help; ...and trust in chariots, ...and in horsemen, because they are very strong; but they look not unto the Holy One of Israel, neither seek the LORD!"

D | As Birds Flying, The LORD Will Defend Jerusalem

Israel was exiled from Jerusalem from 70AD until 1917. In WW1, the British set out to capture Jerusalem from the Ottoman Turks and establish a homeland for the Jews. The night before the invasion, British General Edmund Allenby prayed for God's guidance. He commandeered every available aircraft for a fly-over on December 10. One pilot dropped a note demanding surrender. The Turks surrendered the city without a single shot being fired.

Isaiah 31:5 - "As birds flying, so will the LORD of hosts defend Jerusalem; defending also he will deliver it; and passing over he will preserve it."

D | A King Shall Reign In Righteousness

This wonderful prophecy depicts Jesus Christ ruling the world. "A king shall reign in righteousness, and princes shall rule in judgment. ...a man shall be as an hiding place from the wind, and a covert from the tempest; as rivers of water in a dry place, as the shadow of a great rock in a weary land."

Isaiah 32:3 - "The eyes of them that see shall not be dim, and the ears of them that hear shall hearken. The heart also of the rash shall understand knowledge, and the tongue of the stammerers shall be ready to speak plainly."

C | "Liberal" Is A Misnomer For Evil Men

In these modern times, our entire global society is afflicted with a great scourge of so-called "left-wing liberalism." This most popular political ideology of our day fights against religion and free speech, and promotes atheism, abortion, euthanasia, population control, earth worship, socialism, despotism and countless evil agendas. But God has never seen "liberalism" for anything but what it really is. "The vile person will speak villany, and his heart will work iniquity, to practise hypocrisy, and to utter error against the LORD."

Isaiah 32:5 - "The vile person shall be no more called liberal, nor the churl [rascal] said to be bountiful."

A | Ambassadors Of Peace Will Weep Bitterly When Jesus Comes

The international community invests its most talented and powerful diplomats from many nations, striving in vain to find peace on earth without God's help. But the spoilers will only be spoiled, and the treacherous will only be dealt with treacherously when men pray to God for His intervention. "O LORD, be gracious unto us; ...be thou ...our salvation also in the time of trouble. ...Behold, their valiant ones shall cry without: the ambassadors of peace shall weep bitterly."

Isaiah 33:10 - "Now will I rise, saith the LORD; now will I be exalted; now will I lift up myself."

B | The Devouring Fire

You may have heard the saying, "It won't be water, but fire next time." There will not be another flood like Noah's. But dozens of prophecies warn that God will send fire upon backslidden Israel and many of their enemies. "The Lord Jesus shall be revealed from heaven with his mighty angels, In flaming fire taking vengeance on them that know not God." 2 Thessalonians 1:7-8. "As thorns cut up shall they be burned in the fire."

Isaiah 33:14 - "Who among us shall dwell with the devouring fire? who among us shall dwell with everlasting burnings?"

B | The Righteous Person

The righteous person "...walketh righteously, ...speaketh uprightly; ...despiseth the gain of oppressions, ...shaketh his hands from holding of bribes, ...stoppeth his ears from hearing of blood, ...shutteth his eyes from seeing evil; ...shall dwell on high: ...bread shall be given him; ...his waters shall be sure, ...shall see the king in his beauty: ...behold the land that is very far off, ...shall see Jerusalem a quiet habitation." God gives us more than enough reasons to live right.

Isaiah 33:22-23 - "For the LORD is our judge, the LORD is our lawgiver, the LORD is our king; he will save us."

D | The Indignation

"The indignation of the LORD is upon all nations." Before setting up His earthly kingdom, Jesus will "utterly destroy" evil nations and peoples at Armageddon. Not only will the Beast, the False Prophet, and Lucifer be cast into the pit (Revelation 19:20; 20:10), but "all the host of heaven [principalities] shall be dissolved, ...shall fall down, as the leaf falleth off from the vine." There will be no adversaries - men or spirits - anywhere in that Millennium.

Isaiah 34:8 - "For it is the day of the LORD'S vengeance, and the year of recompences for the controversy of Zion."

C | Seek Ye Out Of The Book Of The LORD, And Read

It takes a lot of courage for a man to prophesy the bold things that Isaiah prophesied. He subjected himself to scorn, cynicism and opposition from every kind of person. But his most potent defense was (paraphrased), "If you don't believe me, ask God!" As I have mined the scriptures daily for many years, I am increasingly persuaded that men must not ignore or betray what God reveals to them by His Word.

Isaiah 34:16 - "Seek ye out of the book of the LORD, and read: no one of these shall fail, ...for my mouth it hath commanded."

D | Armageddon Will Begin In Heaven, Then In Jordan

"My sword shall be bathed in heaven." Apparently, Messiah launches Armageddon in Heaven, overthrowing demon princes [stars falling]. Next, Messiah will slaughter "Idumea [Edom]" - southern Jordan! At this writing, the King of Jordan is leading the plunder of Israel for a Palestinian State via the "Roadmap for Peace." But Southern Jordan will turn into brimstone and burning pitch. "It shall not be quenched night nor day; the smoke thereof shall go up for ever: from generation to generation it shall lie waste;" a worthless place of thorns, nettles, brambles, cormorants, bitterns, owls, ravens, vultures, and wild beasts.

Isaiah 34:17 - "They shall possess it for ever."

D | He Will Come And Save You

The return of Jesus Christ to earth will literally save the world from total destruction. Every condition will be worse than has ever been known to man. Jesus' return will precipitate the restitution of all things (Acts 3:21). The wilderness and desert will blossom like a rose. Weak hands and feeble knees will become strong. Blind eyes will see. Deaf ears will hear. The dumb will speak. Streams will break out in the desert.

Isaiah 35:4 - "Be strong, fear not: behold, your God will come with vengeance, even God with a recompence; he will come and save you."

D | The Highway Of Holiness

At least six times, Isaiah prophesied a highway in Israel, from Egypt to Assyria through Jerusalem, when Jesus reigns. "A highway for our God," 40:3. "...prepare ye the way of the people; ...gather out the stones," 62:10. No more checkpoints, barrier walls or roadside bombs. Only the righteous will travel on it.

Isaiah 35:8-10 - "An highway shall be there, and a way, and it shall be called The way of holiness; the unclean shall not pass over it; ...No lion shall be there, nor any ravenous beast shall go up thereon, ...but the redeemed shall walk there."

B | Sennacherib

Sennacherib, the king of Assyria, captured several cities of Judah. Then he sent a great army under Rabshakeh to capture Jerusalem. Rabshakeh met Eliakim, Shebna and Joah, and mocked King Hezekiah's trust in God. He tried to terrorize them with threats, then offered 2000 horses for Jerusalem's surrender. But Hezekiah had instructed them not to respond. There is a "Rabshakeh" in every believer's life. You do not have to answer to the devil.

Isaiah 36:21 - "But they held their peace, and answered him not a word: for the king's commandment was, saying, Answer him not."

A | Lift Up Thy Prayer For The Remnant

Hezekiah was sorely distressed by threats from Sennacherib and Rabshakeh to take Jerusalem. He rent his clothes and went to prayer. He sent Eliakim and Shebna to Isaiah, asking for prayer. "It may be the LORD ...will reprove the words which the LORD thy God hath heard: wherefore lift up thy prayer for the remnant that is left." God heard and promised to destroy Sennacherib. When enemies overwhelm you, call on God. He is more powerful than your enemies.

Isaiah 37:6-7 - "Isaiah said unto them, ...I will cause him to fall by the sword in his own land."

A | Prayer Saved Hezekiah From The Assyrians

King Hezekiah of Judah faced deadly hostility from Rabshakeh, warrior for Sennacherib, king of Assyria. Rabshakeh brazenly mocked Israel for believing that the LORD would deliver them from the Assyrians. Hezekiah donned sackcloth and went into the House of the LORD. Prayer saved Hezekiah and Judah that day. Prayer will save you, too.

Isaiah 37:15 - "And Hezekiah prayed unto the LORD, saying, ...hear all the words of Sennacherib, which hath sent to reproach the living God. ...save us from his hand, that all the kingdoms of the earth may know that thou art the LORD, even thou only."

C | Fighting God's People Is Fighting God

Rabshakeh send a nasty letter to Hezekiah, blaspheming God and threatening Jerusalem. Hezekiah went into the Temple and laid the letter before the LORD. "God, save us from his hand." Isaiah sent Hezekiah a prophetic word. God was incensed! "Whom hast thou reproached and blasphemed? ...even against the Holy One of Israel." God sent an angel that night and smote 185,000 Assyrians. Anybody who fights against God's people is fighting against God.

Isaiah 37:33,35 - "He shall not come into this city, ...For I will defend this city to save it for mine own sake."

A | Terminal Illness Can Be Cured Through Prayer

King Hezekiah was sick and dying, and Isaiah warned him to set his house in order. But Hezekiah turned his face toward the wall and prayed, weeping sorely. Mercifully, God sent word again by Isaiah that He would add fifteen years to Hezekiah's life. God gave him a sign to confirm His promise. The shadow on the sundial went backwards. You never know how God may answer your prayers. Just PRAY, expecting a miracle!

Isaiah 38:8 - "I will bring again the shadow of the degrees, which is gone down in the sun dial of Ahaz, ten degrees backward."

B | Death

His terminal illness moved Hezekiah to pen some provocative and sobering thoughts about death. "I am deprived of the residue of my years. ...I shall behold man no more with the inhabitants of the world. ...the grave cannot praise thee, death can not celebrate thee: they that go down into the pit cannot hope for thy truth." Life is unspeakably precious. We should cherish the moments we have while we live and spend them as best we can to the glory of God.

Isaiah 38:19 - "The living, the living, he shall praise thee, as I do this day."

C | **Your Descendants Deserve Your Intercession**

Hezekiah entertained visitors from Babylon and showed them all the royal treasures; gold, silver, spices, ointments, armor and precious treasures. Isaiah immediately prophesied that the Babylonians would return and take it all - even his sons, making them eunuchs in the king's palace. Hezekiah's response was shocking! He showed no concern for the future generation, as long as he had peace in his day. Do you care enough about your children to prevent their destruction?

Isaiah 39:8 - "Good is the word of the LORD which thou hast spoken. ...For there shall be peace and truth in my days."

D | **Israel Will Be Comforted When Jesus Comes**

The nation of Israel has rarely enjoyed any semblance of real peace on earth. The few decades of David and Solomon's reigns comprise the bulk of Israel's short-lived "golden age." But centuries of trials and tribulations at the hands of countless oppressors will suddenly end when Jesus comes.

Isaiah 40:1-2 - "Comfort ye, comfort ye my people, saith your God. Speak ye comfortably to Jerusalem, and cry unto her, that her warfare is accomplished, that her iniquity is pardoned: for she hath received of the LORD'S hand double for all her sins."

C | **Make His Path Straight**

All four Gospels record John the Baptist's quote from Isaiah 40. Every believer must make a straight path for the Savior. Come out of depression (your valleys). Tear down your pride (your hills). Put away your crookedness. Give Jesus a clear path in your life.

Isaiah 40:3-5 - "The voice of him that crieth in the wilderness, Prepare ye the way of the LORD, make straight in the desert a highway for our God. Every valley shall be exalted, and every mountain and hill shall be made low: and the crooked shall be made straight, and the rough places plain."

A | **The Voice Said, "Cry."**

God often speaks to us, but we rarely hear. Next time you are at a loss for words to pray, make this declaration. It is a divine reminder of our frailty and His strength.

Isaiah 40:6-8 - "The voice said, Cry. And he said, What shall I cry? All flesh is grass, and all the goodliness thereof is as the flower of the field:

The grass withereth, the flower fadeth: because the spirit of the LORD bloweth upon it: surely the people is grass. The grass withereth, the flower fadeth: but the word of our God shall stand for ever."

B | The Arm Of The LORD

Moses often referred to the outstretched arm of the LORD which helped Israel. Isaiah cried out to Zion, to Jerusalem, to Judah; "Behold, your God!" He declared, prophetically, the coming of Christ - the arm of the LORD *revealed.*

Isaiah 40:10-11 - "The Lord GOD will come with strong hand, and his arm shall rule for him: behold, his reward is with him, and his work before him. He shall feed his flock like a shepherd: he shall gather the lambs with his arm, and carry them in his bosom, and shall gently lead those that are with young."

C | They That Wait Upon The LORD Renew Their Strength

Our God holds the worlds in His hands. He has no counselors. Nations and idols are nothing before Him. He has no equal. He names every star. There is no searching His understanding.

Isaiah 40:29-31 - "He giveth power to the faint; and to them that have no might he increaseth strength. Even the youths shall faint and be weary, and the young men shall utterly fall: But they that wait upon the LORD shall renew their strength; they shall mount up with wings as eagles; they shall run, and not be weary; and they shall walk, and not faint.

B | Israel - A New Sharp Threshing Instrument

When Christ comes, He will empower Israel to its long-prophesied glory. "I will make thee a new sharp threshing instrument having teeth: thou shalt thresh the mountains, ...and shalt make the hills as chaff. Thou shalt fan them, and the wind shall carry them away, ...thou shalt rejoice in the LORD, and shalt glory in the Holy One of Israel."

Isaiah 41:10 - "Fear thou not; for I am with thee: be not dismayed; for I am thy God: I will strengthen thee; yea, I will help thee; yea, I will uphold thee with the right hand of my righteousness."

A | Israel Will Pray For Water

Israel will almost be annihilated before Armageddon. The surviving remnant will cry for water. Jesus will answer. "I will open rivers in high places, and fountains in the midst of the valleys: I will make the wilderness a pool of water, ...That they may see, and know, ...that the hand of the LORD hath done this, and the Holy One of Israel hath created it."

Isaiah 41:17 - "When the poor and needy seek water, and there is none, and their tongue faileth for thirst, I the LORD will hear them, I the God of Israel will not forsake them."

D | Shew Us What Will Happen

The prophetic word of the LORD cannot be faked. The LORD says to false prophets, "Shew the things that are to come hereafter, that we may know that ye are gods. ...behold, ye are of nothing, and your work of nought: and abomination is he that chooseth you. ...Who hath declared from the beginning, that we may know? ...there is none that sheweth." Unclean familiar spirits sometimes make short-term predictions accurately, but are deceptive, misleading and evil in the long-term.

Isaiah 41:29 - "Behold, they are all vanity; their works are nothing: their molten images are wind and confusion."

B | My Servant, Mine Elect

Nobody will ever accomplish the task that belongs to Messiah (Anointed One) alone. God calls Him, "my servant, ...mine elect, ...I have put my spirit upon him." He will open the eyes of the blind; set prisoners free; bring judgment and Truth to earth; not fail or be discouraged; not break a bruised reed (but heal it), nor quench a smoking flax (but renew the flame).

Isaiah 42:6 - "I the LORD have called thee in righteousness, and will hold thine hand, and will keep thee, and give thee for a covenant of the people, for a light of the Gentiles."

A | Sing Unto The LORD A New Song

What is wrong with an old song? Nothing, particularly. If it was a good song then, it is probably a good song now. But a new song reflects a fresh relationship, a living connection with the LORD. Experiencing His presence inspires spontaneous singing. The absence of a new song is a bad sign.

Isaiah 42:10 - "Sing unto the LORD a new song, and his praise from the end of the earth, ...Let the wilderness and the cities thereof lift up their voice, ...let them shout from the top of the mountains. Let them give glory unto the LORD."

D | Man Of War

God hated what the serpent did to Adam and Eve in the Garden, so He swore to send a man born of woman to deal with him. What other God among the world's religions said, "I will come down from heaven as a man, and go to war!" Jesus came to destroy the works of the devil, to destroy him that had the power of death.

Isaiah 42:13 - "The LORD shall go forth as a mighty man, ...like a man of war: he shall cry, yea, roar; he shall prevail against his enemies.

D | Messiah Will Cry Like A Woman In Travail

The coming of the LORD will be like a woman coming to childbirth after waiting nine months to be delivered. The LORD says, "I have long time holden my peace; I have been still, and refrained myself: now will I cry like a travailing woman." After waiting thousands of years to bring forth His kingdom, He will destroy EVERYTHING that has opposed it.

Isaiah 42:14,21 - "I will destroy and devour at once. I will make waste mountains and hills, ...The LORD is well pleased for his righteousness' sake; he will magnify the law, and make it honourable."

C | God Paid A Ransom For Israel

God paid a ransom for Israel to redeem them from slavery. "I gave Egypt for thy ransom, Ethiopia and Seba for thee." He said He "created," "formed," "redeemed" them, and "called" them by their name. "Thou art mine." "I am the LORD thy God, the Holy One of Israel, thy Saviour." Ransom is the price paid to deliver someone who has been captured or imprisoned. God slaughtered a generation of Egypt's firstborn to persuade Pharaoh to "let my people go."

Isaiah 43:4 - "I have loved thee: therefore will I give men for thee, and people for thy life."

B | Israel - God's Witnesses

Of all nations, God chose to reveal Himself to the world through Israel. "Bring my sons from far, and my daughters from the ends of the earth; Even every one that is called by my name: for I have created him for my glory."

Isaiah 43:10 - "Ye are my witnesses, saith the LORD, and my servant whom I have chosen: that ye may know and believe me, and understand that I am he: before me there was no God formed, neither shall there be after me. I, even I, am the LORD; and beside me there is no saviour."

C | We Have A Savior

We scarcely know the word savior outside the Biblical context of Jesus Christ. Following ancient typology, our heavenly Joshua will take us across the Jordan into the blessed Promised Land. He will deliver us once and for all from this dreadful wilderness. Now, as then, the people do not or cannot appreciate that their Savior has come. Many would pathetically go back to Egypt. Others prefer to settle their camps this side of the river. Holy Child, Jesus, save Your people from their sins!

Isaiah 43:11 - "I, even I, am the LORD; and beside me there is no saviour."

A | Prayers To Idols Are Abominations

Vain workmen who make graven and molten images - smiths and carpenters - will be ashamed. They hew cedars, cypress, oak and ash; some even salvaged from the fire - and fashion images. People fall down and worship and pray to them! "Shall I fall down to the stock of a tree?" Idolatry is an abomination against God (verse 19). God is incensed! Destroy such images before idolatry destroys you.

Isaiah 44:20 - "He feedeth on ashes: a deceived heart hath turned him aside, that he cannot deliver his soul, nor say, Is there not a lie in my right hand?"

B | I Am The First And The Last

It is not necessary for men to define God. He often defines Himself in the scriptures. "Thus saith the LORD the King of Israel, and his redeemer the LORD of hosts; I am the first, and I am the last; and beside me there is no God." This single, solitary Deity has no companions, no associates. He is a **single divine person**[6].

Isaiah 44:24 - "Thus saith the LORD, thy redeemer, and he that formed thee from the womb, I am the LORD that maketh all things; that stretcheth forth the heavens *alone;* that spreadeth abroad the earth *by myself.*"

D | Isaiah Prophesied To Cyrus 200 Years In Advance

Cyrus the Great received a divine mandate to send the Jews in Babylon back to Jerusalem to rebuild their Temple. The great historian, Josephus, wrote that Cyrus discovered it when he read his name in a prophecy in the Book of Isaiah - written 200 years earlier!

Isaiah 45:1-4 - "Thus saith the LORD to his anointed, to Cyrus, ...I, the LORD, which call thee by thy name, am the God of Israel. For Jacob my servant's sake, and Israel mine elect, I have even called thee by thy name: I have surnamed thee, though thou hast not known me."

C | I Will Give Thee The Treasures Of Darkness

God chose a pagan king, Cyrus of Persia, to pay for Israel's return to Jerusalem from captivity. "I will give thee the treasures of darkness, and hidden riches of secret places, that thou mayest know that I, the LORD, which call thee by thy name, am the God of Israel." God will reveal treasures of darkness - mysteries concerning His plan - to persuade you to obey His divine will.

Isaiah 45:21 - "Who hath declared this from ancient time? who hath told it from that time? have not I the LORD? and there is no God else beside me."

D | All Their Host Have I Commanded

The entire universe is under God's command. "I have made the earth, and created man upon it: I, even my hands, have stretched out the heavens, and all their host have I commanded. ...I will direct all his ways: he shall build my city, and he shall let go my captives, not for price nor reward." Ultimately, every person will bow before His Throne and worship Him.

Isaiah 45:23 - "I have sworn by myself, the word is gone out of my mouth in righteousness, and shall not return, That unto me every knee shall bow, every tongue shall swear."

A | Ask Of Me Things To Come

God takes pleasure in men who enquire of Him. "Thus saith the LORD, the Holy One of Israel, and his Maker, Ask me of things to come concerning my sons, and concerning the work of my hands command ye me." "Look unto me, and be ye saved, all the ends of the earth: for I am God, and there is none else." I can think of no more rewarding endeavor than to seek a word from the LORD.

Isaiah 45:24 - "Surely, shall one say, in the LORD have I righteousness and strength: even to him shall men come."

B | The Idols Of Bel And Nebo

Israel fell into gross apostasy with their foolish idols, Bel and Nebo. God mocked them because their beasts, cattle and carriages were laden down with carrying their idols. God boasted that Israel never had to carry HIM, but rather, HE had carried Israel from their first days in the womb unto their old age. He ridiculed them for their gods of gold and silver who could not possibly answer their cries. He charged them to be real men and acknowledge His divine sovereignty.

Isaiah 46:8-9 - "Shew yourselves men: ...O ye transgressors. ...for I am God, and there is none else."

D | God Declares The End From The Beginning

God boasted that He was "calling a ravenous bird from the east, the man that executeth my counsel from a far country." Nebuchadnezzar would come from Babylon to execute God's punishment on Israel. Afterward, God would "bring near my righteousness, ...and I will place salvation in Zion for Israel my glory." Sovereign God choreographs every phase of human history.

Isaiah 46:10 - "I am God, and there is none like me, Declaring the end from the beginning, and from ancient times the things that are not yet done, saying, My counsel shall stand, and I will do all my pleasure:

C | God Exploits His Enemies, Then Judges Them

God exploited His enemy, Babylon, saying, "I was wroth with my people, I have polluted mine inheritance, and given them into thine hand." Babylon "very heavily laid" a yoke on Israel, showing no mercy. Haughty Babylon boasted, "I shall be a lady forever, ...I shall not sit as a widow, neither shall I know the loss of children." But God promised both widowhood and loss of children because of their sorceries and enchantments.

Isaiah 47:5 - "Sit thou silent, and get thee into darkness, O daughter of the Chaldeans: for thou shalt no more be called, The lady of kingdoms."

A | God Foils False Sayings And False Accusations By Prophecy

God knows that apostate people say lies against Him to strengthen their evil positions, so He gives Himself the advantage by prophesying things before they happen.

Isaiah 48:5 - "Because I knew that thou art obstinate, ...I have even from the beginning declared it to thee; before it came to pass I shewed it thee: lest thou shouldest say, Mine idol hath done them, and my graven image, and my molten image, hath commanded them. ...For mine own sake, ...will I do it: for how should my name be polluted? and I will not give my glory unto another."

B | The Furnace Of Affliction

Three times, scriptures say that Israel came out of "the iron furnace," referring to Egypt. Seven times, the Bible speaks of Israel's "affliction" in Egypt. The word of the LORD by Isaiah said, "I have chosen thee in the furnace of affliction." God uses afflictions to refine us so we will have greater value to Him. "For our light affliction, which is but for a moment, worketh for us a far more exceeding and eternal weight of glory," 2 Corinthians 4:17.

Isaiah 48:10 - "I have refined thee, ...I have chosen thee in the furnace of affliction."

D | My Servant Israel

"The LORD hath called Israel from the womb." Here is prophetic double entendre. These verses apply to both the nation of Israel, and their offspring, Messiah. "He hath made my mouth like a sharp sword; ...and made me a polished shaft; in his quiver hath he hid me; And said unto me, Thou art my servant, O Israel, in whom I will be glorified." Try as they may, the world cannot destroy either one.

Isaiah 49:6 - "I will also give thee for a light to the Gentiles, that thou mayest be my salvation unto the end of the earth."

C | God Loves Israel As Much As A Mother With Child

Zion said, "The LORD hath forsaken me, and my Lord hath forgotten me." But God insisted, "Can a woman forget her sucking child, that she should not have compassion on the son of her womb? yea, they may forget, yet will I not forget thee. Behold, I have graven thee upon the palms of my hands."

Isaiah 49:23 - "And kings shall be thy nursing fathers, and their queens thy nursing mothers: they shall bow down to thee with their face toward the earth, and lick up the dust of thy feet; and thou shalt know that I am the LORD."

B | The Divorce Between God And Israel

Moses taught that a man who put away his wife should give her a bill of divorcement to set her free. God insisted that Israel show Him "the bill of your mother's divorcement, whom I have put away." He wanted them to understand that "for all the causes whereby backsliding Israel committed adultery I had put her away, and given her a bill of divorce," Jeremiah 3:8. Nevertheless, God plans to reconcile with Israel as soon as they will. He considers Himself still married to the backslider.

Isaiah 50:1 - "For your transgressions is your mother put away."

D | I Gave My Back To The Smiters

Israel sold themselves to iniquity. God put them away for their transgressions, but reminded them that He can dry up the sea, or blacken the heavens, and can still redeem and deliver Israel from sin. God gave Isaiah "the tongue of the learned," to speak to them. "Who is among you that feareth the LORD, ...trust in the name of the LORD." Isaiah's suffering as an intercessor prophetically typified Christ.

Isaiah 50:6 - "I gave my back to the smiters, and my cheeks to them that plucked off the hair: I hid not my face from shame and spitting."

A | A Reminder For Seekers

The Bishop of Lincoln in Canterbury, Robert Sanderson (1621) said, "Am not I a child of the same Adam ... a chip of the same block, with him?" Israel was a chip off the block of Abraham. "Ye that follow after righteousness, ye that seek the LORD: look unto the rock whence ye are hewn, and to the hole of the pit whence ye are digged." God's people descend from great seekers of God.

Isaiah 51:1-2 - "Look unto Abraham your father, and unto Sarah that bare you: for I called him alone, and blessed him, and increased him."

C | Sorrow And Mourning Shall Flee Away

Despite all the trials and tribulations Israel ever suffered pertaining to Jerusalem and Zion, God promised to comfort and restore them. The wilderness will become like Eden, the desert like a garden. Law and judgment will proceed from there. Heaven and earth will fade, but His righteousness will endure through every generation. Everyone who faithfully follows His Word has that same hope.

Isaiah 51:11 - "Therefore the redeemed of the LORD shall return, and come with singing unto Zion; and everlasting joy shall be upon their head: they shall obtain gladness and joy; and sorrow and mourning shall flee away."

C | God Will Turn His Fury From Israel To Their Enemies

So often in scriptures we find God speaking comforting words to His people. He pleaded with them as "my people," and "my nation," and reminded them that heaven and earth, and all things evil, will pass away. He promised to afflict their enemies as harshly as their enemies afflicted them. Only He would be their everlasting salvation.

Isaiah 51:22-23 - "I have taken out of thine hand the cup of trembling, even the dregs of the cup of my fury; thou shalt no more drink it again: But I will put it into the hand of them that afflict thee."

B | They That Publish Good Tidings Of Peace And Salvation

It is easy to become obsessed with life's oppressions and oppressors. The Bible writers certainly documented Israel's many hardships at the hands of their enemies. But God requires us to consider the day when all oppressors will cease and His name is no longer blasphemed. He commends anyone who will publish the good news of His coming kingdom. I volunteer for that task.

Isaiah 52:7 - "How beautiful upon the mountains are the feet of him that bringeth good tidings, that publisheth peace; that bringeth good tidings of good, that publisheth salvation; that saith unto Zion, Thy God reigneth!"

D | The Rereward - God's "Rear Guard"

Isaiah 58 decrees blessings upon those who do the will of God. "Thy righteousness shall go before thee; the glory of the LORD shall be thy rereward." The archaic word "rereward" simply means "rear guard." So the prophecy says that when you are led by righteousness, God will both go ahead of you, and follow behind you. He will protect you from the front and from behind. You might also interpret that as meaning that God will protect you from your past!

Isaiah 52:12 - "The LORD will go before you; and the God of Israel will be your rereward."

B | **The Marvel Of Messianic Prophecies**

In one chapter, Isaiah declared over forty-five explicit prophecies about Messiah. What are the chances that anyone can accurately prophesy forty-five unique details about a world-changing citizen who will be born 700 years from now, AND that those prophecies will be known by billions around the world? Such is the marvel of Isaiah's prophecies concerning Christ.

Isaiah 53:5,7,9 - "...wounded for our transgressions, ...bruised for our iniquities: ...with his stripes we are healed....brought as a lamb to the slaughter, ...he openeth not his mouth. ...he made his grave with the wicked, and with the rich in his death."

D | **Prophecies Nobody Else Could Fulfill**

Who is this? Tender plant. Root out of dry ground. No form, comeliness, or desirable beauty. Despised. Rejected. Man of sorrows. Acquainted with grief. Wounded for our transgressions. Bruised for our iniquities. Chastised for our peace. Bore stripes for our healing. Bore our iniquities. Taken from prison. Taken from judgment. Cut off from the living. Stricken. Did no violence. Had no deceit in His mouth. Bruised to please the LORD. An offering for sin. Poured out His soul unto death. Numbered with transgressors. NOBODY but Jesus!

Isaiah 53:11 - "My righteous servant [shall] justify many; for he shall bear their iniquities."

C | **The Glory Of Barrenness**

Believe it or not, there is glory in barrenness. Barrenness exemplifies the limitations of the flesh, but God's power overrides it. Barren Sarah bore Isaac. Rebekah bore twins. Rachel bore Joseph. Hannah bore Samuel. Elizabeth bore John. God favors the barren. He who sent Manna from the sky sends fruitfulness to the faithful.

Isaiah 54:1 - "Sing, O barren, thou that didst not bear; break forth into singing, and cry aloud, thou that didst not travail with child: for more are the children of the desolate than the children of the married wife, saith the LORD."

D | **Israel Will NEVER Be Troubled Again**

When Messiah comes to save Israel, every curse will be forever lifted. As God promised Noah there would never be another great flood, so He promised to permanently establish His people. No earthquake, tempest or weapon will ever prosper against them again. God will build them up gloriously and never rebuke them again.

Isaiah 54:11-12 - "O thou afflicted, tossed with tempest, and not comforted, behold, I will lay thy stones with fair colours, and lay thy foundations with sapphires. And I will make thy windows of agates, and thy gates of carbuncles, and all thy borders of pleasant stones."

C | Great Shall Be The Peace Of Thy Children

You who are barren and destitute, sing and rejoice! Your Creator will not leave you empty. Expand your living quarters, because He is going to bless and multiply your family. You felt shamed under His punishments, but they were necessary. Soon you will forget them, when He pours out great mercies on you.

Isaiah 54:13 - "All thy children shall be taught of the LORD; and great shall be the peace of thy children. In righteousness shalt thou be established: thou shalt be far from oppression; for thou shalt not fear: and from terror; for it shall not come near thee."

B | The Sure Mercies Of David

Any Bible-reader will soon discover that David was one of God's most favored men. God promised to establish his kingdom and Throne forever, including setting Messiah on that Throne. So if God promises you "the sure mercies of David," you should esteem that as one of His best blessings.

Isaiah 55:3-4 - "Incline your ear, and come unto me: hear, and your soul shall live; and I will make an everlasting covenant with you, even the sure mercies of David. Behold, I have given him for a witness to the people, a leader and commander to the people."

A | Seek Ye The LORD While He May Be Found

God invites the thirsty to come drink, and those with no money to buy and eat without money or price. "Seek ye the LORD while he may be found, call ye upon him while he is near." Today, you have a glorious opportunity to find favor and blessings from God. Tomorrow may be too late. No one is guaranteed another heartbeat.

Isaiah 55:7 - "Let the wicked forsake his way, and the unrighteous man his thoughts: and let him return unto the LORD, and he will have mercy upon him; and to our God, for he will abundantly pardon."

A | **Why You Should Seek The LORD**

Men pay outrageous fees to consult with lawyers, doctors, psychologists, psychiatrists, or a host of other counselors. In the end, their counsel may prove to be flawed or harmful. But God has wisdom and council that far exceeds anything any man on earth can furnish. Why not seek the LORD? He has the wisdom of eternity.

Isaiah 55:8-9 - "For my thoughts are not your thoughts, neither are your ways my ways, saith the LORD. For as the heavens are higher than the earth, so are my ways higher than your ways, and my thoughts than your thoughts."

C | **God's Word - "It Shall Not Return Unto Me Void"**

"Wherefore do ye spend money for that which is not bread? and your labour for that which satisfieth not?" Buy God's word.

Isaiah 55:10-11 - "As the rain cometh down, and the snow from heaven, and returneth not thither, but watereth the earth, and maketh it bring forth and bud, that it may give seed to the sower, and bread to the eater: So shall my word be that goeth forth out of my mouth: it shall not return unto me void, but it shall accomplish that which I please, and it shall prosper in the thing whereto I sent it."

D | **I Will Give Them An Everlasting Name [Yad Vashem]**

At the foot of Mount Herzl in Jerusalem is Yad [memorial] Vashem [name] - the Holocaust Museum. The names of known Jewish victims of the Holocaust are permanently displayed there. The name Yad Vashem is derived from Isaiah 56:5. But no honor or memorial will compare to the everlasting recognition that Jesus Christ will give when He rules in Jerusalem, to those in Israel whom He has redeemed for all the ages.

Isaiah 56:5 - "And to them will I give in my house and within my walls a memorial and a name [Yad Vashem] that shall not be cut off."

A | **I Will Make Them Joyful In My House Of Prayer**

God is always mindful of those who are righteous unto Him, regardless of their significance in the eyes of others. He remembers those who keep His judgments and do justice. He tells even the eunuchs and the strangers who are faithful not to say that they are cut off from the congregation. God promises joy to His people who come into His house to pray.

Isaiah 56:7 - "Even them will I bring to my holy mountain, and make them joyful in my house of prayer: ...for mine house shall be called an house of prayer for all people."

B | Cursed Watchmen

Watchmen must be sober and diligent. Isaiah harshly denounced them. "His watchmen are blind: they are all ignorant, they are all dumb dogs, they cannot bark; sleeping, lying down, loving to slumber." God called beasts of the field to devour His watchmen.

Isaiah 56:12 - "They are greedy dogs which can never have enough, ...shepherds that cannot understand: they all look to their own way, every one for his gain, from his quarter. Come ye, say they, I will fetch wine, and we will fill ourselves with strong drink; and to morrow shall be as this day, and much more abundant."

C | The Righteous Perisheth, And No Man Layeth It To Heart

The death of a saint is a bittersweet occasion. We will miss our loved one's godly influence on our lives, but it is impossible to appreciate what a glorious deliverance he or she has just experienced. We must continue to fight the good fight, but their battle is won.

Isaiah 57:1-2 - "The righteous perisheth, and no man layeth it to heart: and merciful men are taken away, none considering that the righteous is taken away from the evil to come. He shall enter into peace: they shall rest in their beds, each one walking in his uprightness."

A | A Broken And A Contrite Spirit

In the heart of a bombastic denouncement against Israel for their flood of sorceries and adulteries, God stopped momentarily to say that He is still merciful. Notwithstanding, "The wicked are like the troubled sea. ...there is no peace, saith God, to the wicked." Humble yourself while you can!

Isaiah 57:15 - "Thus saith the high and lofty One that inhabiteth eternity, whose name is Holy; I dwell in the high and holy place, with him also that is of a contrite and humble spirit, to revive the spirit of the humble, and to revive the heart of the contrite ones."

C | Fasting Versus Asceticism

Fasting is prescribed in the Old and New Testaments. Saints in all ages practiced fasting and prayer. Nevertheless, fasting does not buy blessings. God hates heartless rituals. Fasting crucifies the flesh.

Without prayer, fasting will only make you miserable and mean. Asceticism [self-denial] alone does not move God. Fasting needs to be accompanied by the prayer of faith.

Isaiah 58:3 - "Wherefore have we fasted, say they, and thou seest not? wherefore have we afflicted our soul, and thou takest no knowledge? Behold, in the day of your fast ye find pleasure, and exact all your labours."

A | What A Godly Fast Is NOT Supposed To Be

Here is a worthless fast: claiming to afflict your soul while you find pleasure and continue all your regular routines; fasting to justify your side of an argument, or to deal a self-righteous blow to someone, or to justify raising your voice above others; fasting to make false humility appear legitimate (head bowed, dressed in sackcloth, etc.). Godly fasting produces godly results.

Isaiah 58:6 - "Is not this the fast that I have chosen? to loose the bands of wickedness, to undo the heavy burdens, and to let the oppressed go free, and that ye break every yoke?"

A | Presumption Sabotages Prayer

The LORD rebuked His people for presumptuous praying. "Cry aloud, spare not, lift up thy voice like a trumpet, and shew my people their transgression, ...Yet they seek me daily, and delight to know my ways, ...they ask of me the ordinances of justice; they take delight in approaching to God." Sin and hypocrisy sabotages prayer. Repent first!

Isaiah 58:9 - "Then shalt thou call, and the LORD shall answer; thou shalt cry, and he shall say, Here I am. If thou take away from the midst of thee the yoke, the putting forth of the finger, and speaking vanity."

D | Fasting Invokes Promised Blessings

Fasting crucifies your flesh. Prayer strengthens your spirit. You become less carnal, more spiritual. Godly works follow; feeding the hungry, clothing the naked, housing the homeless, etc. God rewards your discipline.

Isaiah 58:12 - "The LORD shall guide thee continually, and satisfy thy soul in drought, and make fat thy bones: and thou shalt be like a watered garden, and like a spring of water, whose waters fail not. And they that shall be of thee shall build the old waste places: ...and thou shalt be called, The repairer of the breach, The restorer of paths to dwell in."

B | An Evil Generation, Separated From God

Isaiah painted a very dark, tragic picture of his generation. Hands defiled with blood. Lips speaking lies. Tongues uttering perverseness. No justice or truth. Conceiving mischief. Hatching viper eggs (poisonous imaginations). Running to do evil. Crooked paths. No peace. Obscurity. Darkness. Stumbling like blind men. Desolate like dead men. Sounds like our times.

Isaiah 59:1-2 - "The LORD'S hand is not shortened, that it cannot save; neither his ear heavy, that it cannot hear: But your iniquities have separated between you and your God, and your sins have hid his face from you, that he will not hear."

D | Jesus: The Intercessor

The sins of mankind have wreaked havoc on every generation. From the beginning, God looked for someone to turn humanity back to Him. "It displeased him that there was no judgment. And he saw that there was no man, and wondered that there was no intercessor." Then Jesus came.

Isaiah 59:16-17 - "Therefore his arm brought salvation unto him; and his righteousness, it sustained him. For he put on righteousness as a breastplate, and an helmet of salvation upon his head; and he put on the garments of vengeance for clothing, and was clad with zeal as a cloke."

C | God's People Shine When The World Is In Darkness

It is both a divine principle and prophetic destiny that God's chosen people will ultimately prevail over all the world. Whether it is national Israel or the Church of Jesus Christ, God's chosen must eventually rise above all men to rule and reign with their LORD throughout the ages.

Isaiah 60:1-2 - "Arise, shine; for thy light is come, and the glory of the LORD is risen upon thee. For, behold, the darkness shall cover the earth, and gross darkness the people: but the LORD shall arise upon thee, and his glory shall be seen upon thee."

B | Jesus: King Of ALL Kingdoms

God sets up kingdoms and takes them down. He sets kings on thrones and removes them. "He is the governor among the nations," Psalm 22:18. "His kingdom ruleth over all," Psalm 103:19. "The Son of man shall send forth his angels, and they shall gather out of his kingdom all things that offend, and them which do iniquity; and shall cast them into a furnace of fire." Matthew 13:42.

Isaiah 60:12 - "...the nation and kingdom that will not serve thee shall perish; yea, those nations shall be utterly wasted."

A | Thou Shalt Call Thy Gates "Praise"

God knows what He wants and what He does not want. He does not want to hear the sounds of violence, wasting and destruction. He DOES want to hear the sounds of His people praising Him. Today, the world is filled with a cacophony of voices that offend and infuriate God. But in that day, everyone who enters into His gates will be praising Him. Get wise. Join the praisers now.

Isaiah 60:18 - "Violence shall no more be heard in thy land, wasting nor destruction within thy borders; but thou shalt call thy walls Salvation, and thy gates Praise."

D | The Spirit Of The Lord GOD Is Upon Me

Would Israel have become an obscure people if Messiah had not come? Did He save the nation from eventual extinction? Jesus is the hope and salvation of His people, but in their unbelief, they have not yet comprehended that reality.

Isaiah 61:1-2 - "The Spirit of the Lord GOD is upon me; because the LORD hath anointed me to preach good tidings unto the meek; he hath sent me to bind up the brokenhearted, to proclaim liberty to the captives, and the opening of the prison to them that are bound; To proclaim the acceptable year of the LORD."

B | Priests Of The Lord; Ministers Of Our God

A priest is an intercessor between God and men. A minister is one who serves the Lord while serving the people. The overall weight of these prophecies in Isaiah 61 shows that Messiah will raise up Israel as priests and ministers unto the Lord. The great King must have a great people to serve Him.

Isaiah 61:6,8 - "But ye shall be named the Priests of the LORD: men shall call you the Ministers of our God: ...For I the LORD love judgment, ...and I will direct their work in truth, and I will make an everlasting covenant with them."

C | Beauty For Ashes

Jesus salvaged a discouraged nation. He came to "preach good tidings unto the meek; ...bind up the brokenhearted, ...proclaim liberty to the captives, ...open prisons, ...proclaim the acceptable year of the LORD, ...comfort all that mourn; ...give unto them beauty for ashes, ...oil of joy for mourning, the garment of praise for the spirit of heaviness." His beautiful Church came from the ashes of a fallen nation.

Isaiah 61:9 - "Their seed shall be known among the Gentiles, and their offspring among the people: all that see them shall acknowledge them, that they are the seed which the LORD hath blessed."

A | My Soul Shall Be Joyful In My God

During Jesus' thousand-year reign on earth, joy will be indescribable. Reborn Israel will be glorious, and the Church, ruling the nations as kings and priests, will be more exciting than tongue or pen can tell. I crave to see that day. What joy! What happiness!

Isaiah 61:10-11 - "I will greatly rejoice in the LORD, my soul shall be joyful in my God; for he hath clothed me with the garments of salvation, he hath covered me with the robe of righteousness, as a bridegroom decketh himself with ornaments, and as a bride adorneth herself with her jewels."

D | Jerusalem Will Be Beulah - Married; Bride Of God

God declared that He will not rest or be silent until righteousness and salvation shine brightly in Zion and Jerusalem, and all people, even all kings, see it. Jerusalem will be a royal diadem and crown of glory unto the LORD. Israel will no longer be called "forsaken and desolate, but will be called "delight (Hephzibah) and married" (Beulah). "As the bridegroom rejoiceth over the bride, so shall thy God rejoice over thee."

Isaiah 62:12 - "And they shall call them, The holy people, The redeemed of the LORD: and thou shalt be called, Sought out, A city not forsaken."

B | Messiah's Fury And The Day Of Vengeance

The seer, Isaiah, envisioned Armageddon - Messiah coming from Bozrah, Edom (southern Jordan) with His garments bloodied by war. "I have trodden the winepress alone; and of the people there was none with me: ...and their blood shall be sprinkled upon my garments, ...For the day of vengeance is in mine heart, and the year of my redeemed is come." After every "peace process" on earth has failed, Jesus will single-handedly destroy Israel's enemies.

Isaiah 63:5 - "I looked, and there was none to help; ...therefore mine own arm brought salvation unto me; and my fury, it upheld me."

C | In All Their Affliction, He Was Afflicted

Whatever God might have done with the human race (if only Adam and Eve had not sinned) may never be known. But one thing is certain. When we fail, it impacts God. We focus on our own suffering, forgetting that we also caused injury to God's kingdom. In restoring us, He restores glory to His own purposes.

Isaiah 63:9 - "In all their affliction he was afflicted, and the angel of his presence saved them: in his love and in his pity he redeemed them; and he bare them, and carried them all the days of old."

A | Look Down From Heaven, And Behold...

Despite God's miraculous works for Israel in Moses' day, "they rebelled, and vexed his holy Spirit: therefore he was turned to be their enemy, and he fought against them." Over time, Israel alternately repented, then backslid again. Isaiah instinctively went into prayer. A real intercessor cannot ignore such a need.

Isaiah 63:15-17 - "Look down from heaven, and behold from the habitation of thy holiness and of thy glory, ...O LORD, why hast thou made us to err from thy ways, and hardened our heart from thy fear? Return for thy servants' sake, the tribes of thine inheritance."

A | Oh, That Thou Would Rend The Heavens!

Isaiah 64 is a desperate prayer for the LORD to come. "...rend the heavens, ...come down, ...make thy name known to thine adversaries." Stir up volcanoes to erupt! Make the nations tremble at Your Presence! "Thou camest down, the mountains flowed down at thy presence." I pray, "Let God arise, and His enemies be scattered!" The world needs a divine wake-up call!

Isaiah 64:4 - "Since the beginning of the world men have not heard, nor perceived by the ear, neither hath the eye seen, O God, beside thee, what he hath prepared for him that waiteth for him."

C | Our Righteousness Is As Filthy Rags

You can lie to yourself until you actually believe you are a good person. But God sees all, hears all and knows all. Sooner or later, you will have to acknowledge that you are a trespasser, and confess it to God, and repent.

Isaiah 64:6 - "But we are all as an unclean thing, and all our righteousnesses are as filthy rags; and we all do fade as a leaf; and our iniquities, like the wind, have taken us away. ...But now, O LORD, thou art our father; ...Be not wroth very sore, O LORD, neither remember iniquity for ever."

B | The Vineyard That Could Not Die

God remarked about the irony. "I am sought of them that asked not for me," speaking of the Gentiles. But His beloved Israel rejected Him. "I have spread out my hands all the day unto a rebellious people." God was provoked to *destroy* Israel, but He only *punished* them, because His ancient covenant still promised them a glorious kingdom under Christ.

Isaiah 65:8 - "As the new wine is found in the cluster, and one saith, Destroy it not; for a blessing is in it: so will I do for my servants' sakes, that I may not destroy them all."

D | The New Millennial Earth

This is a delicate subject. Watch carefully. God will cleanse the heavens and earth at the beginning of the 1000-year reign of Christ. Isaiah 65 reveals much of the millennial plan. At the END of the Millennium, however, God will DISSOLVE all the elements in heaven and earth and makes all things new. On BOTH of these two separate occasions, God says He will make a new heaven and a new earth.

Isaiah 65:17 - "For, behold, I create new heavens and a new earth: and the former shall not be remembered, nor come into mind."

B | Jerusalem Rejoicing

John saw the saints from all ages coming with Jesus to earth to wage the great and final battle of Armageddon. At its conclusion, Jesus will build the Millennial Temple and rule the world from His Capital, Jerusalem. From that day, Jerusalem will be restored, renewed, and revitalized. Great rejoicing will fill the air for 1000 years.

Isaiah 65:18-19 - "...behold, I create Jerusalem a rejoicing, and her people a joy. And I will rejoice in Jerusalem, and joy in my people: and the voice of weeping shall be no more heard in her, nor the voice of crying."

D | Babies And Dying In The Millennium

Apparently, millions of humans who are not involved in the battle of Armageddon will live into the Millennium. God promises to cleanse the earth and make it new at that time. Life expectancies will multiply. Anyone dying at 100 will be considered a child. Resurrected saints from past ages will be immortal, but survivors of Armageddon will be mortal, although amazingly long-lived.

Isaiah 65:20 - "There shall be no more thence an infant of days, nor an old man that hath not filled his days: for the child shall die an hundred years old."

B | Sinners In The Millennium

Jesus will rule the world from Jerusalem for 1000 years with His resurrected saints from all ages. They will have immortal, sinless bodies. Still, the earth will be inhabited by mortals - sinners. Ancient prophecies foresee Messiah sitting on His Throne in Jerusalem, ruling the world from Israel. Not everyone will be saints. Jesus will show millions, perhaps billions of people His righteousness in those days. The knowledge of the Lord will cover the earth as the waters cover the seas.

Isaiah 65:20 - "...but the sinner being an hundred years old shall be accursed."

D | Building Homes In The Millennium

The Promised Land will be completely possessed, finally fulfilling God's ancient covenant with Abraham, Isaac and Jacob during the Millennium.

Isaiah 65:21-23 - "...they shall build houses, and inhabit them; and they shall plant vineyards, and eat the fruit of them. They shall not build, and another inhabit; they shall not plant, and another eat: for as the days of a tree are the days of my people, and mine elect shall long enjoy the work of their hands. They shall not labour in vain, nor bring forth for trouble."

A | Communications In The Millennium

If I am reading this even half-way correctly, then cell phones will be quite unimpressive in the Millennium. God says that before you call Him He will answer, and while you are speaking He will hear. If I say that we will communicate with Jesus during that time via mental telepathy, I might be correct. We will just have to wait and see. Get ready to be impressed!

Isaiah 65:24 - "...it shall come to pass, that before they call, I will answer; and while they are yet speaking, I will hear."

A | Before You Call

Did you ever receive a gift you had been wishing for, but had told no one? What a pleasant surprise to know that someone knew you well enough to know intuitively what you would like to have. God is infinitely more in touch with our needs. He knows what we have need of before we ask or think. More importantly, He begins to work in our behalf before we expect.

Isaiah 65:24 - "And it shall come to pass, that before they call, I will answer; and while they are yet speaking, I will hear."

B | Animals In The Millennium

All God's creatures will be peaceful and harmless during the Millennium; no more predators or pain. The prophets said that wolves will live with lambs. Leopards will lie down with kid goats. Calves and young lions and fatlings will be together. Cows and bears and their young will feed and lie down together. Lions will eat straw like oxen. Babies not yet weaned will play safely around asps and scorpions. Little children will lead great beasts around.

Isaiah 65:25 - "The wolf and the lamb shall feed together, and the lion shall eat straw like the bullock."

C | God Will Choose Your Delusions

God listed several complaints against Israel; for sacrifices they made to idols, for burning incense and making oblations (prayers) to them, and for delighting in all their abominations. They presumed to do as they pleased, forgetting that God always has the last word. Sin all you want, but you cannot control the outcome. God does.

Isaiah 66:4 - "I also will choose their delusions, and will bring their fears upon them; because when I called, none did answer; when I spake, they did not hear: but they did evil before mine eyes, and chose that in which I delighted not."

C | God Will Not Shut Israel's Womb

What can any man do for a God whose Throne is the heavens and the earth is His footstool? What kind of house can you build Him? What can you do to give Him rest? God will take care of Himself. He will establish Israel in Jerusalem, and nobody will stop Him. Israel has already begun bringing forth children, and you can believe that God will not shut her womb now.

Isaiah 66:9 - "Shall I bring to the birth, and not cause to bring forth? saith the LORD: shall I cause to bring forth, and shut the womb?"

A | Rejoice With Jerusalem

I have never seen such dire circumstances as now bear down on that tiny city of Jerusalem. The entire world is Hell-bent on destroying Israel and removing her from Jerusalem. But God says to rejoice, because He has a plan.

Isaiah 66:10,15 - "Rejoice ye with Jerusalem, and be glad with her, all ye that love her: rejoice for joy with her, all ye that mourn for her: ...For, behold, the LORD will come with fire, and with his chariots like a whirlwind, to render his anger with fury, and his rebuke with flames of fire."

D | After Armageddon, Carcasses Of Sinners Abhorred

The battle of Armageddon is the event that precipitates one thousand years of peace on earth. Jesus will rule a glorious earthly kingdom from Jerusalem. Saints from all ages will be kings and priests during that age. Isaiah says that the carcasses of sinners who die during that time will be left to "be an abhorring to all flesh."

Isaiah 66:24 - "...they shall go forth, and look upon the carcases of the men that have transgressed against me: for their worm shall not die, neither shall their fire be quenched; and they shall be an abhorring unto all flesh."

Lessons from the Book of
JEREMIAH

A | Jeremiah's Conversation With God

Jeremiah, son of Hilkiah, received the word of the LORD in the days of kings Josiah, Jehoahaz, Jehoiakim, Jehoiachin, and Zedekiah. God said, "Before I formed thee in the belly I knew thee; and before thou camest forth out of the womb I sanctified thee, and I ordained thee a prophet unto the nations." Jeremiah objected, "Ah, Lord GOD! behold, I cannot speak: for I am a child."

Jeremiah 1:7 - "But the LORD said unto me, Say not, I am a child: for thou shalt go to all that I shall send thee, and whatsoever I command thee thou shalt speak."

C | God Knows, Sanctifies, And Ordains You Before Birth

The foreknowledge of God is unimaginable. Before you are even conceived, God knows all about you. Before you are born, God ordains your purpose. From the womb, God's hand is on your life. Tragically, many people betray their calling and never live up to their divinely ordained purpose. You will never accomplish anything more worthwhile than the will of God. Abandon your will for His.

Jeremiah 1:5 - "Before I formed thee in the belly I knew thee; and before thou camest forth out of the womb I sanctified thee, and I ordained thee a prophet unto the nations."

A | God Will Answer Your Objections

God had a very dramatic, very dangerous role for Jeremiah to play as prophet to the nations. Jeremiah voiced strong objections. The LORD answered, "Be not afraid of their faces: for I am with thee to deliver thee." Faint not! God will not only answer you, He will also embolden, enable and encourage you, too.

Jeremiah 1:9-10 - "Behold, I have put my words in thy mouth. See, I have this day set thee over the nations and over the kingdoms, to root out, and to pull down, and to destroy, and to throw down, to build, and to plant."

B | The Rod Of An Almond Tree

The word of the LORD assured Jeremiah that God was with him. A vision appeared. "Jeremiah, what seest thou? And I said, I see a rod of an almond tree." In Moses' day, a company of rebels tried to overthrow Aaron the High Priest. God made every tribe lay a wooden rod on the ground. Overnight, "the rod of Aaron ...brought forth buds, and bloomed blossoms, and yielded almonds." As God quickly vindicated Aaron, so He promised to vindicate Jeremiah.

Jeremiah 1:12 - "Then said the LORD unto me, Thou hast well seen: for I will hasten my word to perform it."

D | The Seething Pot

Jeremiah's second vision was of a seething (boiling) pot facing northward, from which direction an evil calamity would come. It was a prophecy foretelling the invasion of the Babylonians, who eventually attacked from the north. Israel was going to "boil" in Nebuchadnezzar's "pot." It happened just a few years later, in Jeremiah's lifetime. If you persist in your sins, God is going to judge you.

Jeremiah 1:16 - "I will utter my judgments against them touching all their wickedness, who have forsaken me, and have burned incense unto other gods, and worshipped the works of their own hands."

C | God Makes His Prophet Invincible

God told Jeremiah, "I have this day set thee over the nations and over the kingdoms, to root out, and to pull down, and to destroy, and to throw down, to build, and to plant." "...speak unto them all that I command thee: be not dismayed at their faces..."

Jeremiah 1:19 - "I have made thee ...a defenced city, ...an iron pillar, ...brasen walls against the whole land, against the kings, ...the princes..., the priests..., ...the people. ....they shall fight against thee; but they shall not prevail against thee; for I am with thee, saith the LORD, to deliver thee."

C | Never Stop Asking "Where Is The LORD?"

Jeremiah did not want to pronounce judgments on his countrymen, but God required him to. After all God's kindnesses - deliverance from Egypt, and countless miracles in the wilderness and in the Promised Land - the people stopped inquiring of the LORD and turned to idols. It is a frightening, foolish mistake to forget God. Seek Him always!

Jeremiah 2:5 - "What iniquity have your fathers found in me, that they are gone far from me, ...Neither said they, Where is the LORD that brought us up out of the land of Egypt, ...The priests said not, Where is the LORD?"

B | Israel Was Holiness Unto The LORD

The LORD was grieved over Jerusalem when He said, "I remember thee, the kindness of thy youth, the love of thine espousals, when thou wentest after me in the wilderness, in a land that was not sown. ISRAEL WAS HOLINESS UNTO THE LORD, and the firstfruits of His increase." In a similar way, He must now grieve over the Church because so much of it is no longer holiness unto the LORD.

Jeremiah 2:7 - "I brought you into a plentiful country, to eat the fruit thereof and the goodness thereof; but when ye entered, ye defiled my land, and made mine heritage an abomination."

C | The Fountain Of Living Water, Or Broken Cisterns?

Israel forsook the Water of Life for broken cisterns when they turned to idols. "Hath a nation changed their gods, which are yet no gods? but my people have changed their glory for that which doth not profit. Be astonished, O ye heavens, at this, and be horribly afraid, be ye very desolate, saith the LORD." Our generation is doomed for committing the same folly - forsaking the living God for other gods.

Jeremiah 2:13 - "For my people have committed two evils; they have forsaken me the fountain of living waters, and hewed them out cisterns, broken cisterns, that can hold no water."

C | Thine Own Wickedness Shall Correct Thee

Jeremiah rebuked Israel for forsaking the LORD, allowing themselves to be spoiled by their enemies, and adopting the ways of the Egyptians and Assyrians. "Thine own wickedness shall correct thee, and thy backslidings shall reprove thee." Sometimes, the best rebuke comes from the shame, humiliation and sheer pain that occurs when you wake up and realize what a fool you have been, and what tragic circumstances your disobedience has caused.

Jeremiah 2:26 - "As the thief is ashamed when he is found, so is the house of Israel ashamed; they, their kings, their princes, and their priests, and their prophets."

A | Will You Not Cry Unto Me?

Spiritual adultery was Israel's great offense against God. "Thou hast played the harlot with many lovers." "Lift up thine eyes unto the high places, and see where thou hast not been lien with." "...and committed adultery with stones and with stocks [idols]." Nevertheless (and astonishingly) God asked them to return and repent! Oh, marvelous grace!)

Jeremiah 3:1,4 - "If a man put away his wife, and she go from him, and become another man's, shall he return unto her again? ...yet return again to me, saith the LORD. ...Wilt thou not from this time cry unto me?"

B | God Divorced Israel, But Not Judah

The northern ten tribes of Israel fell into idolatry immediately after Solomon died. The tribes of Benjamin and Judah in Jerusalem had a few righteous kings like Jehoshaphat, Josiah, and Hezekiah, who literally saved Judah from destruction by their righteousness. God divorced Israel, but not Judah. Once Judah backslid, only the coming of Messiah could save them all.

Jeremiah 3:8 - "And I saw, when for all the causes whereby backsliding Israel committed adultery I had put her away, and given her a bill of divorce; yet her treacherous sister Judah feared not, but went and played the harlot also."

D | The Ark Of The Covenant Will Be In Heaven

The Ark of the Covenant vanished when Nebuchadnezzar of Babylon captured Jerusalem. It will not be in Jerusalem when Jesus reigns 1000 years. It will be in Heaven (Revelation 11:19; 15:5). God's glory is now in Jesus, the true Ark.

Jeremiah 3:16-17 - "In those days, saith the LORD, they shall say no more, The ark of the covenant of the LORD: neither shall it come to mind: neither shall they remember it; neither shall they visit it; neither shall that be done any more. At that time they shall call Jerusalem the throne of the LORD."

D | Jerusalem Will Be The Throne of the LORD

Let all the world come against Jerusalem. Let them set themselves against Israel and their God. Let them amass all their political and military might. Let them terrorize and plunder. Yet God has declared it shall be His, and nothing shall stop the Holy One of Israel.

Jeremiah 3:17 - "At that time they shall call Jerusalem the throne of the LORD; and all the nations shall be gathered unto it, to the name of the LORD, to Jerusalem: neither shall they walk any more after the imagination of their evil heart."

A | **Return, Ye Backsliding Children**

Throughout the book of Jeremiah, God exploited the people's backsliding, sharply reminding them that the chaos, war, and tragic losses they were experiencing were their own fault. His intention was to motivate them to repentance, but they completely failed to appease Him. Sin becomes so vile that men sometimes become incapable of repenting. Take great care never to reach that place.

Jeremiah 3:20,22 - "Surely as a wife treacherously departeth from her husband, so have ye dealt treacherously with me, O house of Israel, saith the LORD. Return, ye backsliding children, and I will heal your backslidings."

C | **Break Up Your Fallow Ground**

Jeremiah's rebukes against Israel seemed almost rhetorical. They were not listening. Calls to put away their abominations and swear, "The LORD liveth, in truth, in judgment and in righteousness," fell on deaf ears and hard hearts; like sowing seed on hard ground. God said, "Break up your fallow ground." He admonished them to blow trumpets and call the people together, but they would not. Judgment had to fall.

Jeremiah 4:7 - "The lion [Nebuchadnezzar] is come up from his thicket, and the destroyer of the Gentiles [Babylon] is on his way; ...thy cities shall be laid waste, without an inhabitant."

B | **Watchers From A Far Country**

Jeremiah and Daniel use the term "watchers" to describe heavenly agents who carry out God's judgments. Daniel 4 chronicles the downfall of Nebuchadnezzar at the hands of "watchers." Jeremiah prophesied divine judgment on the people of Judah by the "watchers." Beware, lest watchers visit you in your sins.

Jeremiah 4:16-17 - "Make ye mention to the nations; behold, publish against Jerusalem, that watchers come from a far country, and give out their voice against the cities of Judah. As keepers of a field, are they against her round about; because she hath been rebellious against me, saith the LORD."

D | The Earth Without Form

Jeremiah's heart and bowels were suffering as he contemplated the spoil and destruction that he saw coming to the "foolish, ...sottish" people. "I beheld the earth, and, lo, it was without form, and void; and the heavens, and they had no light. ...there was no man, ...the fruitful place was a wilderness, ...the cities thereof were broken down at the presence of the LORD." The prophecies depicted the land after Nebuchadnezzar's armies captured, burned, and destroyed Judah.

Jeremiah 4:24 - "Thus hath the LORD said, The whole land shall be desolate; yet will I not make a full end."

A | Travail In Prayer, Or Travail In Judgment

Many people disdain the seemingly unsavory task of travailing in prayer. In over forty years of ministry, I have known precious few people who relish true, travailing prayer. But it is a divinely-ordained occupation. If we fail to agonize in prayer for victory over the world, the flesh and the devil, we will someday agonize because we did not.

Jeremiah 4:30 - "When thou art spoiled, what wilt thou do? ...For I have heard a voice as of a woman in travail, and the anguish as of her that bringeth forth her first child, ...saying, Woe is me now!"

D | Judah Sentenced To Serve Strangers In Another Land

Their prophets prophesied falsely and "became wind." The people loved it. God told Jeremiah, "I will make my words in thy mouth fire, and this people wood, and it shall devour them." He warned that lions, wolves and leopards would spoil the land after a mighty, ancient nation "whose language thou knowest not" [Babylon] impoverished their cities.

Jeremiah 5:19 - "Wherefore doeth the LORD our God all these things unto us? then shalt thou answer them, Like as ye have forsaken me, and served strange gods in your land, so shall ye serve strangers in a land that is not yours.

B | The Sins Of Judah Which Led To Captivity

Jeremiah assaulted Judah's sins and backslidings: Adulteries, whoredoms, chasing women, idolatry, false gods, not seeking Truth or God's ways, swearing falsely, foolishness, wickedness, getting rich and fat through deceit, rebellious, denying punishment, refusing correction or to return to the LORD, treacherous against God, not grieved when stricken, not fearing of God, forsaking God, not executing judgment, trusting in their cities, lying wait, setting snares, trapping and catching men, ignoring the fatherless and needy.

Jeremiah 5:29 - "Shall I not visit for these things? saith the LORD: shall not my soul be avenged on such a nation as this?"

C | Be Thou Instructed, Lest I Make Thee Desolate

Even after God irrevocably determined to send Nebuchadnezzar to capture Jerusalem, He urged the people to flee in advance. "O ye children of Benjamin, gather yourselves to flee out of the midst of Jerusalem, ...for evil appeareth out of the north, and great destruction." It was God's last-ditch effort to save them. "Be thou instructed, O Jerusalem, lest my soul depart from thee; lest I make thee desolate."

Jeremiah 6:10 - "To whom shall I speak, and give warning, that they may hear? ...the word of the LORD is unto them a reproach; they have no delight in it."

A | Ask For The Old Paths

While you are praying, ask God to show you the old paths. The world hates the path of righteousness. It hates the ancient Truth of God's Word. It hates the people of God. But their way is NOT better. Walk in the old paths. It is the good way. You will find rest for your soul.

Jeremiah 6:16 - "Thus saith the LORD, Stand ye in the ways, and see, and ask for the old paths, where is the good way, and walk therein, and ye shall find rest for your souls. But they said, We will not walk therein."

A | Gird Thee With Sackcloth, Make Thee Mourning

What better can a preacher do, than convince the people of their sins and persuade them to repent? Yet some refuse to do just that. God denounced the false prophets and priests who deceived the people. "They have healed also the hurt of the daughter of my people slightly, saying, Peace, peace; when there is no peace. Were they ashamed when they had committed abomination? nay, they were not at all ashamed."

Jeremiah 6:26 - "O daughter of my people, gird thee with sackcloth, and wallow thyself in ashes: make thee mourning, ...for the spoiler shall suddenly come upon us."

A | **Useless Prayer**

Most people will not acknowledge that "God is angry with the wicked every day," Psalm 7:11. Unrepented sin separates us from Him. It really cuts off our communications with God. The only prayer God really wants to hear from a sinner is repentance. Sincere repentance opens His heart and ears again.

Jeremiah 7:9,10 - "Will ye steal, murder, and commit adultery, and swear falsely, and burn incense unto Baal, and walk after other gods whom ye know not; and come and stand before me in this house, which is called by my name?"

B | **Shiloh - Go, See What I Did To It**

God advised sinful Judah to go to Shiloh and learn a lesson about how He judges wickedness. Shiloh is where Eli the High Priest allowed his sons to misuse holy offerings and commit whoredoms in the Tabernacle. Their evils were demoralizing Israel. God suddenly killed Hophni, Phinehas and Eli in one day, and the Ark of the Covenant was stolen. Learn from their mistakes.

Jeremiah 7:12 - "Go ye now unto my place which was in Shiloh, where I set my name at the first, and see what I did to it for the wickedness of my people Israel."

C | **Cut Off Thine Hair; The LORD Hath Rejected Thee**

Jeremiah said, "Cut off thine hair, ...cast it away." Cutting off a woman's hair, or plucking a man's beard, symbolized humiliation, shame, disgrace and reproach. God concluded them all in disgrace for their abominations.

Jeremiah 7:29-30 - "Cut off thine hair, O Jerusalem, and cast it away, and take up a lamentation on high places; for the LORD hath rejected and forsaken the generation of his wrath. For the children of Judah have done evil in my sight, saith the LORD: they have set their abominations in the house which is called by my name, to pollute it."

D | **Tophet Shall Be Called The Valley Of Slaughter**

Judah made cakes to "the queen of heaven" and poured drink offerings to other false gods. Outrageously, they set idols in the House of the LORD, built evil altars in Tophet (the Valley of Hinnom), and burned their children in the fire. God's response was to prophesy the utter slaughter of those who were guilty.

□✓

Jeremiah 7:32 - "The days come, ...that it shall no more be called Tophet, ...but the valley of slaughter: for they shall bury in Tophet, till there be no place. And the carcases of this people shall be meat for the fowls of the heaven."

D | Scattering Judah's Bones To The Sun, Moon And Stars

In worshipping the sun, moon and stars, Judah exhausted God's longsuffering. In retaliation, God ordered the Babylonians to desecrate their graves.

Jeremiah 8:1 - "At that time, saith the LORD, they shall bring out the bones of the kings of Judah, and the bones of his princes, and the bones of the priests, and the bones of the prophets, and the bones of the inhabitants of Jerusalem, out of their graves: And they shall spread them before the sun, and the moon, and all the host of heaven, whom they have loved, and whom they have served."

B | The Stork, Turtle, Crane And Swallow Know Better

Deception is worse than a brain disease. When people reject His wisdom, "God shall send them strong delusion, that they should believe a lie: That they all might be damned who believed not the truth, but had pleasure in unrighteousness," 2 Thessalonians 2:11-12. Why did Judah perish? "They hold fast deceit, ...The wise men ...have rejected the word of the LORD."

Jeremiah 8:7 - "The stork in the heaven knoweth her appointed times; and the turtle and the crane and the swallow observe the time of their coming; but my people know not the judgment of the LORD."

C | The Preacher's Heart Is Broken When People Resist

A preacher spends his entire life trying to save people from their sins. But when their hearts are of stone and judgment cannot be averted, the preacher is the one whose heart is broken, whose cry cannot cease.

Jeremiah 8:18,20-22 - "When I would comfort myself against sorrow, my heart is faint in me. ...The harvest is past, the summer is ended, and we are not saved. For the hurt of the daughter of my people am I hurt; I am black; astonishment hath taken hold on me. Is there no balm in Gilead; is there no physician there?"

A | Oh That My Eyes Were A Fountain Of Tears

Jeremiah's tears were of suffocating grief, after Judah finally provoked the fatal wrath of God. When someone you love has died, the tears are so painful. Weep now, while your prayers can make a difference.

Jeremiah 9:1 - "Oh that my head were waters, and mine eyes a fountain of tears, that I might weep day and night for the slain of the daughter of my people! Oh that I had in the wilderness a lodging place of wayfaring men; that I might leave my people, and go from them! for they be all adulterers, an assembly of treacherous men."

B | Liars

God has a big problem with liars. Some people are so corrupted, they would tell a lie even when the truth is more convenient. What is a lie, but a perversion of reality, a cancerous mental condition, a spiritual tumor that begs to be excised? All liars will have their part in the lake of fire.

Jeremiah 9:3,5 - "They bend their tongues like their bow for lies: but they are not valiant for the truth upon the earth; ...they will deceive every one his neighbour, and will not speak the truth: they have taught their tongue to speak lies."

C | Do Not Trust A Deceiver

I cannot understand why men engage in deception. The entire universe stands on Truth. Nothing stands on deception. Everything built on deception falls. Society crumbles when men deceive one another. "Trust ye not in any brother: for every brother will utterly supplant, and every neighbour will walk with slanders." God hates deception. Stop the lies now. Stand up for Truth.

Jeremiah 9:6 - "Thine habitation is in the midst of deceit; through deceit they refuse to know me, saith the LORD. Their tongue is as an arrow shot out; it speaketh deceit: ...Shall I not visit them for these things?"

C | Glory In The LORD

"Who is the wise man, that may understand this? ...I will send a sword after them, till I have consumed them." Neither wisdom, might, nor riches compare with understanding the will of God. Your only glory is to understand Him.

Jeremiah 9:23-24 - "Thus saith the LORD, Let not the wise man glory in his wisdom, neither let the mighty man glory in his might, let not the rich man glory in his riches: But let him that glorieth glory in this, that he understandeth and knoweth me, that I am the LORD which exercise lovingkindness, judgment, and righteousness."

C | The Counsel Of The LORD Shall Stand

Compare your wisdom to God's. Well, that's not a fair comparison. He is infinite. He has seen everything and knows everything. He has witnessed every act and thought of every man and woman who ever lived. He is omnipotent, omnipresent, and omniscient. We are finite, limited, inexperienced, ignorant and unlearned. Still, we trust ourselves, and don't trust HIM? That's illogical! "There are many devices in a man's heart; nevertheless the counsel of the LORD, that shall stand," Proverbs 19:21.

Jeremiah 10:23 - "...it is not in man that walketh to direct his steps."

A | Oh LORD, Correct Me

Jeremiah contemplated the gross vanities of the heathen, especially how they inexplicably made gods out of wood and silver and gold. He surmised that men were brutish [beastlike, carnal], and grievously foolish. He charged God's people, "Learn not the ways of the heathen." In frustration, he declared, "O LORD, I know that the way of man is not in himself: it is not in man that walketh to direct his steps." Man is nothing without divine correction and judgment.

Jeremiah 10:24 - "O LORD, correct me, but with judgment; not in thine anger, lest thou bring me to nothing."

D | I Will Bring Evil They Shall Not Be Able To Escape

Israel tragically ignored the enormous reality that their very existence came from the covenant God made with them in Egypt. In that covenant, God said, "If you will obey me, and keep my commandments, I will bring you into the land which floweth with milk and honey." But all those years later, they forgot where their prosperity came from and went whoring after other gods.

Jeremiah 11:11 - "Therefore thus saith the LORD, Behold, I will bring evil upon them, which they shall not be able to escape; and though they shall cry unto me, I will not hearken unto them."

A | Pray Not!

I began to pray for a man, but the Holy Spirit pressed me not to. I didn't know why at first, but soon learned that he had a long history of sternly resisting God. In most scriptural cases, the people grieved the Lord with persistent, hardened sins. God determined not to listen to prayers made in their behalf.

Jeremiah 11:14 - "Therefore pray not thou for this people, neither lift up a cry or prayer for them: for I will not hear them in the time that they cry unto me for their trouble."

D | God Had To Destroy His Green Olive Tree

Judah's idolatries sorely provoked God. "What hath my beloved to do in mine house, seeing she hath wrought lewdness with many?" Once, God called Judah "a green olive tree, fair, and of goodly fruit." But their sins infuriated God. "With the noise of a great tumult he hath kindled fire upon it, and the branches of it are broken." You may have once been a green tree in God's favor, but if you persist in your sins, He will destroy you.

Jeremiah 11:16-17 - "For the LORD of hosts, that planted thee, hath pronounced evil against thee."

B | The Men Of Anathoth

The men of Anathoth threatened Jeremiah, saying, "Prophesy not in the name of the LORD, that thou die not by our hand." "I was like a lamb or an ox that is brought to the slaughter; and I knew not that they had devised devices against me." Jeremiah prayed, "O LORD... let me see thy vengeance on them." Never threaten God's anointed.

Jeremiah 11:22-23 - "I will punish them: the young men shall die ...their sons and their daughters shall die ...there shall be no remnant of them: for I will bring evil upon the men of Anathoth."

A | Jeremiah's Prayer

You may find yourself asking the same questions Jeremiah asked. "Wherefore doth the way of the wicked prosper? wherefore are all they happy that deal very treacherously? Thou hast planted them, yea, they have taken root: they grow, yea, they bring forth fruit: thou art near in their mouth, and far from their reins." God may not explain why He allows the wicked to prosper, but your questions prove that you believe He knows why. And He does.

Jeremiah 12:1 "Righteous art thou, O LORD, when I plead with thee: yet let me talk with thee of thy judgments."

D | Horses, Jordan, And The Last Days

The four horsemen of Zechariah 6 and Revelation 6[7] are four spirits traversing the earth, loosed in the last days near the Euphrates River for a cataclysmic "clash of civilizations" (Sixth Trumpet War, Revelation 9). At this writing, King Abdullah of Jordan leads the call for these world powers to create a Palestinian State opposing Israel.

Jeremiah 12:5 - "If thou hast run with the footmen, and they have wearied thee, then how canst thou contend with horses? and if in the land of peace, wherein thou trustedst, they wearied thee, then how wilt thou do in the swelling of Jordan?"

C | Horsemen Will Come, Jordan Will Swell

Jeremiah was distressed by the apostasy he saw all around him. He sought God for understanding. "Why...? How long...? and many other questions. But God's response was sobering, even breath-taking. "If thou hast run with the footmen, and they have wearied thee, then how canst thou contend with horses? and if in the land of peace, wherein thou trustedst, they wearied thee, then how wilt thou do in the swelling of Jordan?" When sin persists, things can only get worse.

Jeremiah 12:7 - "I have given the dearly beloved of my soul into the hand of her enemies."

B | The Lion And The Speckled Bird

God accused Judah of being like a lion in the forest, roaring threateningly against Him. He also compared them to a speckled bird of prey waiting to devour a fallen beast, while other birds compete against her. God's "heritage" had become hateful and bloodthirsty people.

Jeremiah 12:8-9 - "Mine heritage is unto me as a lion in the forest; it crieth out against me: therefore have I hated it. Mine heritage is unto me as a speckled bird, the birds round about are against her; come ye, assemble all the beasts of the field, come to devour."

A | My Vineyard, My Portion, Desolate, Mourneth Unto Me

It reminds me of Abel's innocent blood crying out to God from the ground. When God saw His Holy Land desolate like a wilderness, it mourned unto Him. His fierce anger rose up. He promised to pluck His people out of the land, then send the sword of the LORD to devour - "utterly pluck up and destroy" - His enemies from one end of the land to the other. Then He would re-plant His people. If God hears the land mourn, He surely hears your cry.

Jeremiah 12:11 - "They have made it desolate, and being desolate it mourneth unto me."

B | The Marred Girdle

God told Jeremiah to get a linen girdle, wear it for a while, then take it down to the Euphrates River and hide it in the hole of a rock. Later, God told him to go back and retrieve it. It was ruined, no longer useful. This object lesson demonstrated how God would punish Judah for their pride.

Jeremiah 13:10 - "This evil people, which refuse to hear my words, which walk in the imagination of their heart, and walk after other gods, to serve them, and to worship them, shall even be as this girdle, which is good for nothing."

D | To The King And Queen: Judah Shall Be Carried Away

King Jehoiachin and his queen-mother bore the guilt for Judah's downfall. Kings must give account to God for their rule. Then, Nebuchadnezzar captured Judah. Next time, the Antichrist will execute God's punishment.

Jeremiah 13:18-22 - "Say unto the king and to the queen, Humble yourselves, sit down: for your principalities shall come down, even the crown of your glory. ...Judah shall be carried away captive all of it. ...where is the flock that was given thee, thy beautiful flock? ...And if thou say in thine heart, Wherefore come these things upon me? For the greatness of thine iniquity."

C | Can The Leopard Change His Spots?

It is a sad day when Almighty God says to you, in effect, "You will never change. I am finished with you." A hardened heart is worse than death. Strive to keep your heart tender and pliable before God.

Jeremiah 13:23-24,27 - "Can the Ethiopian change his skin, or the leopard his spots? then may ye also do good, that are accustomed to do evil. Therefore will I scatter them as the stubble that passeth away by the wind of the wilderness. ...Woe unto thee, O Jerusalem! wilt thou not be made clean? when shall it once be?"

☐✓

A | Empty Cries

Because of their sins, the people were languishing. No water. No food. The fields were bare. Cattle were perishing. "The cry of Jerusalem is gone up." But it was an empty cry. Nobody but Jeremiah even tried to repent, and God rejected his intercession.

Jeremiah 14:10-12 - "Then said the LORD unto me, Pray not for this people for their good. When they fast, I will not hear their cry; and when they offer burnt offering and an oblation, I will not accept them: but I will consume them by the sword, and by the famine, and by the pestilence."

C | God Will Destroy False Prophets

I remember reading Jeremiah 14 when I was a small child. The LORD said, "The prophets prophesy lies in my name: I sent them not, neither have I commanded them, neither spake unto them: they prophesy unto you a false vision and divination." I tremble when a man prophesies flippantly, "Thus saith the LORD..." He should be absolutely certain!

Jeremiah 14:15 - "Therefore thus saith the LORD concerning the prophets that prophesy in my name, and I sent them not, yet they say, Sword and famine shall not be in this land; By sword and famine shall those prophets be consumed."

D | A Great Breach, A Very Grievous Blow

False prophets will certainly meet their doom, but not them alone. God says that He is going to pour out their wickedness on all the people who love to hear the false prophets. God told them to weep night and day, because "the people to whom they prophesy shall be cast out in the streets" because of famine and sword.

Jeremiah 14:17,19 - "... for the virgin daughter of my people is broken with a great breach, with a very grievous blow ...we looked for peace, and there is no good; and for the time of healing, and behold trouble!"

A | Not Even Moses Or Samuel Could Dissuade God

The LORD told Jeremiah, "Though Moses and Samuel stood before me, yet my mind could not be toward this people: cast them out of my sight." This is very terrifying. But it illustrates the fact that even people who have previously been effective intercessors do not necessarily carry more weight with God. God operates on divine principle. If you have finally sinned away your day of grace, it doesn't matter who tries to convince God otherwise.

435

Jeremiah 15:5-6 - "For who shall have pity upon thee, O Jerusalem? or who shall bemoan thee? ...I am weary with repenting."

B | Unbreakable Northern Iron And Steel

Jeremiah was nigh unto despair, trapped between the unrepented sins of the people and the judgments of God. The women would soon be widows and childless as God sentenced their men to Nebuchadnezzar's sword. Jeremiah had to obey God in pronouncing dreadful judgments, but he knew the people hated him for it. They cursed and threatened him. Nevertheless, the iron will of the people could not break the heavenly iron and steel in Jeremiah's soul. The strength of the righteous is greater than the strength of the wicked.

Jeremiah 15:12 - "Shall iron break the northern iron and the steel?"

A | The Preacher Seeks Refuge

Jeremiah was feeling quite overwhelmed by the downfall of his nation. God made it clear that He was not going to change His mind about their overthrow by Nebuchadnezzar. In desperation, Jeremiah pleaded with God for his personal survival. "O LORD, ...remember me, and visit me, and revenge me of my persecutors; take me not away in thy longsuffering: know that for thy sake I have suffered rebuke." Even if the whole world fails, you can still be saved!

Jeremiah 15:16 - "Thy word was unto me the joy and rejoicing of mine heart: for I am called by thy name."

C | Take The Precious From The Vile

God answered Jeremiah's personal plea for help with a challenge. "If thou take forth the precious from the vile, thou shalt be as my mouth: let them return unto thee; but return not thou unto them." Nothing is more effective than isolating the precious things of truth, righteousness, and holiness from all the contaminants of sin. God will be delighted.

Jeremiah 15:21 - "I will make thee unto this people a fenced brasen wall: and they shall fight against thee, but they shall not prevail against thee: for I am with thee to save thee and to deliver thee."

B | The Unmarried And Childless Prophet

The word of the LORD told Jeremiah not to take a wife or to have sons or daughters. They would only die grievous deaths and would neither be buried nor mourned. God took all peace, lovingkindness and mercies from the people, to provoke them to ask why the LORD pronounced all this great evil on them. Eventually, God will force every sinner to stand face to face with his sins.

Jeremiah 16:11 - "Because your fathers have forsaken me, saith the LORD, and have walked after other gods, and have served them, and have worshipped them, and have forsaken me."

D | I Will Send For Many Fishers; They Shall Fish Them

Just as God closed up shop in Jerusalem, and liquidated His apostate people from His Holy Land, He spoke intriguingly to the future, prophesying that "Gentiles shall come unto thee from the ends of the earth." Then He added the strangest statement: "They shall fish them." How can you read that and not remember Jesus telling Peter, "I will make you to become fishers of men"? Ages ago, God knew the only way Israel would ever be saved is by the Gospel of Christ.

Jeremiah 16:16 - "I will send for many fishers, saith the LORD, and they shall fish them."

C | Unrepented Sins Will Never Be Forgiven

God told Judah that her pernicious sins "have kindled a fire in mine anger which shall burn forever." God will forever be angry that Judah turned their backs on Him and brought down the great nation that He wanted to bless. Future generations might find redemption in the blood of Jesus, but that generation's sins will never be blotted out and never forgiven.

Jeremiah 17:1 - "The sin of Judah is written with a pen of iron, and with the point of a diamond: it is graven upon the table of their heart, and upon the horns of your altars."

B | A Heath In The Desert, Or A Tree By A River?

"Cursed be the man that trusteth in man, and maketh flesh his arm, and whose heart departeth from the LORD. For he shall be like the heath in the desert, and ...shall inhabit the parched places in the wilderness." You can forsake God and trust only human abilities, but you cannot escape divine destiny. Ultimately, you can ONLY prosper if you trust the LORD.

Jeremiah 17:7-8 - "Blessed is the man that trusteth in the LORD, and whose hope the LORD is. For he shall be as a tree planted by the waters, ...neither shall cease from yielding fruit."

C | The Heart Is Deceitful Above All Things

It is impossible for you or me to know someone else's heart. We cannot even know our own heart. It is deceitful. A man who pursues the riches of this world while ignoring God is like a partridge sitting on eggs that never hatch. Your heart can make you trust folly and doubt wisdom. Only God can accurately search your heart and "try your reins." He will give you what is right, according to what He finds in your heart.

Jeremiah 17:9 - "The heart is deceitful above all things, and desperately wicked: who can know it?"

B | Pastors: Leaders Of Israel

Jeremiah is the only Old Testament prophet who called Israel's leaders "pastors." They "transgressed against me," 2:8; "they have become brutish, and have not sought the LORD," 10:21; "destroyed my vineyard, ...trodden my portion underfoot," 12:10; "...scattered my flock, and driven them away, " 23:2. Jeremiah sensed his own solemn responsibilities as a prophet-pastor.

Jeremiah 17:15-16 - "They say unto me, Where is the word of the LORD? let it come now. As for me, I have not hastened from being a pastor to follow thee: ...that which came out of my lips was right before thee."

A | Heal Me. Save Me.

"Heal me, O LORD, and I shall be healed; save me, and I shall be saved." Jeremiah had no one but God. The people resisted his prophecies. "They say unto me, Where is the word of the LORD? let it come now." The prophet reminded God of how diligently he attempted to follow the LORD, and speak what He required. A track-record of obedience goes well with earnest, expectant prayer. He WILL save!

Jeremiah 17:18 - "Let them be confounded that persecute me, but let not me be confounded: let them be dismayed, but let not me be dismayed."

D | Unclaimed, Expired Prophecies

There are literally hundreds of prophecies in the Bible that will never come to pass, because God's people did not meet the terms of the prophecies: curses that will not be fulfilled because they made amends; blessings that might have been if they had only repented. "Thus said the LORD unto me; Go and stand in the gate of the children of the people, ...And say unto them, Hear ye the word of the LORD."

Jeremiah 17:23 - "But they obeyed not, neither inclined their ear, but made their neck stiff, that they might not hear, nor receive instruction."

B | The Potter's House

God told Jeremiah to go to the potter's house, because He would speak to him there. So he went, and the potter "wrought a work on the wheels. And the vessel that he made of clay was marred in the hand of the potter: so he made it again another vessel, as seemed good to the potter to make it." God can destroy everything you are and start over.

Jeremiah 18:6 - "O house of Israel, cannot I do with you as this potter? ...as the clay is in the potter's hand, so are ye in mine hand."

D | IF...

It is the biggest little word in the English language: IF. It is also the biggest little word in the Bible. So many of the prophecies that God has ever uttered are contingent on that big little word: IF. Not, "IF GOD...," but "IF YOU..."

Jeremiah 18:8,10 - "If that nation, against whom I have pronounced, turn from their evil, I will repent of the evil that I thought to do unto them. ...If it do evil in my sight, that it obey not my voice, then I will repent of the good, wherewith I said I would benefit them."

A | Hearken To The Voice Of Them That Contend With Me

As soon as you take God's part, you inherit His enemies. Ask Jeremiah. They oppose you because they oppose Him. You can never overcome them alone, because they are not just flesh and blood adversaries, but principalities and powers - spiritual wickedness in high places. "Then said they, Come, and let us devise devices against Jeremiah." When adversaries strengthen themselves against you, strengthen yourself in prayer. God will be there.

Jeremiah 18:19,23 - "Give heed to me, O LORD, and hearken to the voice of them that contend with me, ...thou knowest all their counsel against me to slay me."

D | Judah Was To Be Broken Like A Potter's Bottle

For the second time, God told Jeremiah to prophesy that **Tophet (the Valley of Hinnom)**[8] would become "the valley of slaughter." "Get a potter's earthen bottle, ...go forth unto the valley of the son of Hinnom,

...break the bottle in the sight of the men." This pantomime foretold Judah's destruction by Nebuchadnezzar.

Jeremiah 19:11 - "Say unto them, Thus saith the LORD of hosts; Even so will I break this people and this city, as one breaketh a potter's vessel, that cannot be made whole again: and they shall bury them in Tophet, till there be no place to bury."

C | People Resist God's Messenger To Their Own Hurt

Jeremiah stood in the court of the LORD's house and prophesied divine judgments on the people in the name of the LORD. When Pashur, chief governor in the house of the LORD, heard Jeremiah prophesy these things, he smote Jeremiah and put him in stocks. When he was released the following day, Jeremiah prophesied again.

Jeremiah 20:6 - "And thou, Pashur, and all that dwell in thine house shall go into captivity: and thou shalt come to Babylon, and there thou shalt die, and shalt be buried there, thou, and all thy friends, to whom thou hast prophesied lies."

A | His Word Was As A Burning Fire Shut Up In My Bones

Jeremiah complained bitterly to the LORD for the persecution he was suffering as a prophet of doom. "I am in derision daily, every one mocketh me. ...I cried violence and spoil; because the word of the LORD was made a reproach unto me. ...Then I said, I will not make mention of him, nor speak any more in his name." Complaining to God will not release you from your responsibility.

Jeremiah 20:9 - "But his word was in mine heart as a burning fire shut up in my bones, and I was weary with forbearing, and I could not stay."

A | Let Me See Thy Vengeance On Them

The prophet had often prayed for his enemies, that they would repent and return to God. After years of persecution and rejection, however, he blessed the LORD, but cursed the day he was born. Then he asked the LORD to show him His vengeance on them.

Jeremiah 20:10,12 - "For I heard the defaming of many, fear on every side. ...All my familiars watched for my halting, saying, Peradventure he will be enticed, and we shall prevail against him, and we shall take our revenge on him. ...O LORD of hosts, ...let me see thy vengeance on them."

A | Zedekiah Calls On Jeremiah To Pray

As the end drew near for Jerusalem and Judah, Zedekiah wanted Jeremiah the prophet to enquire of the LORD what the outcome would be. Jeremiah was not nice. He prophesied copiously against Zedekiah - that God would utterly foil his efforts to fight Nebuchadnezzar, and "I myself will fight against you with an outstretched hand and with a strong arm, even in anger, and in fury, and in great wrath." Oh, don't wait too late to pray!

Jeremiah 21:7 - "And afterward, saith the LORD, I will deliver Zedekiah king of Judah ...into the hand of Nebuchadrezzar king of Babylon."

B | Z for Zedekiah - The Last King In Ancient Israel

As Z is the last letter in the alphabet, so Zedekiah was Israel's last king. The nation fell in 586 BC. Jeremiah was absolutely right.

Jeremiah 21:9-10 - "He that abideth in this city shall die by the sword, and by the famine, and by the pestilence: but he that goeth out, and falleth to the Chaldeans that besiege you, he shall live, ...For I have set my face against this city for evil, and not for good, saith the LORD: it shall be given into the hand of the king of Babylon, and he shall burn it with fire."

D | Many Nations Shall Pass By This City

Millions of tourists from around the world visit Jerusalem every year, to see the ancient sites and rehearse the Bible stories. God said that would be the case.

Jeremiah 22:5, 8-9 - "If ye will not hear these words, I swear by myself, saith the LORD, that this house shall become a desolation. ...And many nations shall pass by this city, and they shall say every man to his neighbour, Wherefore hath the LORD done thus unto this great city? Then they shall answer, Because they have forsaken the covenant of the LORD their God, and worshipped other gods."

B | Josiah - Shallum - Jehoiakim - Jehoiachin - Zedekiah

Josiah, the last righteous king, died in 609 BC. His evil son, Jehoahaz (Shallum), ruled only three months before being taken to Egypt and murdered - as prophesied. His brother, Eliakim (Jehoiakim), ruled eleven years under Egyptian tribute. He died when Nebuchadnezzar seized Jerusalem. His uncle, Jehoiachin (Jeconiah), ruled three months before he was taken to Babylon. Finally, Zedekiah resisted the Babylonian siege for eleven years, until Judah was utterly destroyed in 586 BC.

Jeremiah 22:11 - "Thus saith the LORD touching Shallum the son of Josiah king of Judah, ...he shall die in the place whither they have led him captive."

D | The Prophesied Death Of Jehoiakim

It makes no sense when a righteous man's son becomes extremely evil. Josiah was one of Judah's most righteous kings, but his son, Jehoiakim, was vain, selfish, and wickedly unjust. God said, "thine eyes and thine heart are not but for thy covetousness, and for to shed innocent blood, and for oppression, and for violence." God sentenced him to death without a proper burial - no one knows where.

Jeremiah 22:18-19 - "Thus saith the LORD... They shall not lament for him, ...He shall be buried with the burial of an ass, drawn and cast forth beyond the gates of Jerusalem."

C | Hear The Word Of The LORD

Many Old Testament books open similarly, "The word of the Lord came to..." [whoever]. God's Word came to many men either audibly or in visions: Noah, Abraham, Jacob, Moses, Balaam, Joshua, Samuel, Saul, Nathan, Gad, David, Solomon, Shemaiah, Jeroboam, Jehu, Elijah, Elisha, Micaiah, Jonah, Isaiah, Hezekiah, Jeremiah, Cyrus, Ezekiel, Hosea, Joel, Amos, Jonah, Micah, Zephaniah, Haggai, Zerubbabel, Zechariah, Malachi, John the Baptist, Peter, Paul. The world would be completely righteous if everyone would hear the Word of the Lord.

Jeremiah 22:29 - "O earth, earth, earth, hear the word of the LORD."

D | Jehoiachim (Jeconiah) Cut Out Of Messianic Line

King Josiah's grandson, Jehoiachim (also called Jeconiah, or Coniah) was removed from the Messianic line because of his sins! "As I live, saith the LORD, though Coniah ...were the signet upon my right hand, yet would I pluck thee thence; ...I will cast thee out." Coniah's descendants (including Jesus' step-father, Joseph) were denied kingship. God abandoned Solomon's descendants. Through David's son, Nathan, Mary descended, passing kingship to Jesus.

Jeremiah 22:30 - "Thus saith the LORD, Write ye this man childless, ...for no man of his seed shall prosper, sitting upon the throne of David, and ruling any more in Judah."

C | Woe To Pastors That Scatter The Flock

If you are a leader, beware! "Woe be unto the pastors that destroy and scatter the sheep of my pasture! saith the LORD. ...Ye have scattered my flock, and driven them away, and have not visited them: behold, I will visit upon you the evil of your doings." God vowed to feed them with wormwood and gall (bitterness). You will be replaced. God will find someone right for the job.

Jeremiah 23:4 - "I will set up shepherds over them which shall feed them: and they shall fear no more, nor be dismayed, neither shall they be lacking, saith the LORD."

B | The Righteous Branch Of David

David's life was awfully tainted by personal sins. His sons' lives were fraught with shameful and evil behavior. Solomon scarcely inherited the throne, and in later life, gravely reproached it. Nevertheless, God immortalized David's diligent efforts to please his God by promising to raise up a righteous branch to his posterity. Messiah would descend from him - a King of Kings and Savior for all mankind.

Jeremiah 23:5 - "Behold, the days come, saith the LORD, that I will raise unto David a righteous Branch, and a King shall reign and prosper, and shall execute judgment and justice in the earth."

A | Prayerlessness - Like A Canary In A Coal Mine

In the old days, coal miners carried a canary in a cage with them, down into the mines. The canary was a sign to them. If the canary died, it was a signal that toxic gases might be present, and they needed to quickly escape. Prayerlessness is like that. Any time you notice that nobody around you is praying, you should find another place, because death is in the midst.

Jeremiah 23:22 - "But if they had stood in my counsel, ...then they should have turned them from their evil way, and from the evil of their doings."

A | I Have Heard What The Prophets Said

You do not have to be praying for God to be listening. He hears EVERYTHING you say. God condemned the false prophets. "I have not sent these prophets, ...I have not spoken to them, yet they prophesied." "I have heard what the prophets said, that prophesy lies in my name, saying, I have dreamed." Using your tongue to prophesy without divine unction can land you in BIG trouble with God.

Jeremiah 23:26,31 - "They are prophets of the deceit of their own heart;...I am against the prophets, saith the LORD, that use their tongues, and say, He saith."

C | The Burden Of The LORD

God demands that His burden (His strong desire) should never be misrepresented. If a prophet has a dream or a word from the LORD, he should accurately represent it. But God is adamantly opposed to anyone who presumes to declare the burden of the LORD inaccurately. This is a real indictment against many of the so-called prophetic ministries that are illegitimate.

Jeremiah 23:38-40 - "Because ye say this word, The burden of the LORD, and I have sent unto you, saying, Ye shall not say, The burden of the LORD; ...I will ...cast you out of my presence."

B | Two Baskets Of Figs

The LORD showed Jeremiah a vision of two baskets of figs sitting in front of the Temple, after Nebuchadnezzar began taking Judah away to Babylon. One basket contained good figs, and it represented the Jews who cooperated with their captors. God promised to bring them again to Jerusalem after the captivity was over. The other basket contained "naughty" figs - evil, because they resisted God's punishments.

Jeremiah 24:10 - "And I will send the sword, the famine, and the pestilence, among them, till they be consumed from off the land that I gave unto them and to their fathers."

D | Seventy Years Of Captivity Prophesied

The captivity of the Jews under Nebuchadnezzar in Babylon is one of the most significant prophecies in the Bible. Daniel 4-5 documents its fulfillment.

Jeremiah 25:11-13 - "And this whole land shall be a desolation, and an astonishment; and these nations shall serve the king of Babylon seventy years. And it shall come to pass, when seventy years are accomplished, that I will punish the king of Babylon, and that nation, saith the LORD, for their iniquity, and the land of the Chaldeans, and will make it perpetual desolations, ...all that is written in this book, which Jeremiah hath prophesied."

□✓

D | Jeremiah Prophesies Global Calamity At Armageddon

The LORD showed Jeremiah a time far beyond the Babylonian captivity when He would finally bring every evil nation to judgment. He foresaw Jesus Christ destroying the grapes of wrath at the battle of Armageddon.

Jeremiah 25:29-30,33 - "I will call for a sword upon all the inhabitants of the earth, saith the LORD of hosts. ...The LORD shall roar from on high, ...as they that tread the grapes, against all the inhabitants of the earth. ...And the slain of the LORD shall be at that day from one end of the earth even unto the other end of the earth."

A | They Should Have Prayed Instead Of Threatening The Prophet

When Jeremiah prophesied the destruction of Jerusalem, "the priests and the prophets and all the people took him, saying, Thou shalt surely die." But the princes of the city defended Jeremiah, arguing that King Hezekiah did not kill the prophet Micah when he prophesied similarly. Instead, Hezekiah "besought the LORD." Resisting God is always futile. Prayer, including repentance, is always a better solution.

Jeremiah 26:19 - "Did Hezekiah king of Judah and all Judah put him at all to death? did he not fear the LORD, and besought the LORD, and the LORD repented him of the evil which he had pronounced against them?"

C | Some Live, Some Die For The Cause

There was another prophet, named Urijah, saying the same things that Jeremiah was saying. King Jehoiakim wanted him killed, so Urijah fled to Egypt. Unfortunately, the king sent men to Egypt to bring him back. Jehoiakim personally killed the prophet with a sword and had his body cast into a commoners' grave. God oversees a unique plan for every man. Urijah had to die. Jeremiah had to live.

Jeremiah 26:24 - "Nevertheless the hand of Ahikam the son of Shaphan was with Jeremiah, that they should not give him into the hand of the people to put him to death."

C | God Made The Earth, And Gives It To Whom He Pleases

God instructed Jeremiah to send messengers to all the neighboring kings to deliver a word from the LORD. He informed them that changes were coming. To this very day, kings and nations fail to recognize (to their own hurt) that the destiny of all men is carefully in the hand of God.

Jeremiah 27:5 - "Thus saith the LORD of hosts, the God of Israel; ...I have made the earth, the man and the beast that are upon the ground, by my great power and by my outstretched arm, and have given it unto whom it seemed meet unto me."

B | The Yoke Of Babylon

God often instructed Jeremiah to use pantomime. This time, He told him to make several yokes and send them by messengers to the kings of Edom, Moab, Ammon, Tyre, Zidon, and Zedekiah of Judah. The messengers conveyed a message from the LORD. Every nation is under God's control.

Jeremiah 27:6-8 - "I have given all these lands into the hand of Nebuchadnezzar the king of Babylon, ...and all nations shall serve him, and his son, and his son's son, ...that the nation and kingdom which will not serve the same Nebuchadnezzar ...will I punish, ...until I have consumed them."

C | Cooperate With Your Captors

Jeremiah instructed every king in the region to cooperate with Nebuchadnezzar, for in doing so, God would guarantee their safety. But if they resisted Nebuchadnezzar, they would surely die. He also gave this word to his own king, Zedekiah. Jesus taught a similar principle in His day: "Agree with thine adversary quickly, whiles thou art in the way with him; lest [he] deliver thee to the judge, ...and thou be cast into prison," Matthew 5:25.

Jeremiah 27:9 - "Bring your necks under the yoke of the king of Babylon, and serve him and his people, and live."

A | False Prophets Should Pass A Prayer Test

False prophets told the people that the vessels of the Temple would quickly be brought back from Babylon, although Jeremiah had prophesied "seventy years." "They shall be carried to Babylon, and there shall they be until the day that I visit them, saith the LORD." Jeremiah challenged them to a prayer test to prove they actually had power with God.

Jeremiah 27:18 - "If they be prophets, and if the word of the LORD be with them, let them now make intercession to the LORD of hosts, that the vessels which are left ...at Jerusalem, go not to Babylon."

B | Hananiah - Jeremiah's Vicious Adversary

Hananiah defied Jeremiah in the Temple. "Thus speaketh the LORD, ...I have broken the yoke of the king of Babylon." He prophesied the soon return of the Temple vessels and Jehoiakim. Jeremiah argued that time would prove the true prophet. Hananiah grabbed the yoke Jeremiah wore and broke it, prophesying that Nebuchadnezzar's yoke would break in two years. God told Jeremiah to make new yokes of iron to depict Babylon's hard yoke. Jeremiah told Hananiah:

Jeremiah 28:16-17 - "This year thou shalt die, because thou hast taught rebellion against the LORD. So Hananiah the prophet died the same year."

D | After 70 Years, I Will Turn Your Captivity

Jeremiah wrote a letter to the captives in Babylon - the kings, queens, priests, prophets, eunuchs, princes, carpenters, smiths, and all the other people who were taken in the days of Kings Jeconiah and Zedekiah. He admonished them to build houses, plant gardens, marry wives, bear children, raise families, and seek the peace of Babylon. If they would obey, God promised to bring them back home.

Jeremiah 29:10 - "For thus saith the LORD, That after seventy years be accomplished at Babylon I will visit you, and perform my good word toward you, in causing you to return to this place."

A | I Know The Thoughts I Think Toward You

NEVER think that God does not want to hear your prayers. Even while in Babylonian captivity, God told His people that He WANTED a right relationship with them! He WANTED them to pray!

Jeremiah 29:11-13 - "I know the thoughts that I think toward you, saith the LORD, thoughts of peace, and not of evil, to give you an expected end. Then shall ye call upon me, and ye shall go and pray unto me, and I will hearken unto you. And ye shall seek me, and find me, when ye shall search for me with all your heart."

A | The Process of Prayer

Prayer is a process with many components: praise, worship, adoration, thanksgiving, confession, contrition, repentance, supplication, intercession, and more. Which component can you afford to neglect? Some people go weeks, months, even years without "covering all the bases." Yet they spend hundreds of hours watching television, chatting on the phone, surfing the Internet, and countless less-worthy pastimes. Uninhibited prayer is an extremely worthy activity. We owe it to ourselves to pray.

Jeremiah 29:12 - "Then shall ye call upon me, and ye shall go and pray unto me, and I will hearken unto you."

B | Three Men Cursed - Ahab, Zedekiah, And Shemaiah

Two men, Ahab and Zedekiah, committed villainy and adulteries, and prophesied lies to the people. Jeremiah prophesied that Nebuchadnezzar would "slay them before your eyes," AND that their names would become a curse: "The LORD make thee like Zedekiah and like Ahab, whom the king of Babylon roasted in the fire." Similarly, a man named Shemaiah overthrew Jehoiada the priest and tried to imprison Jeremiah.

Jeremiah 29:32 - "Thus saith the LORD; ...I will punish Shemaiah... he shall not have a man to dwell among this people; ...neither shall he behold the good that I will do for my people."

C | Travail

Ordinarily, the word "travail" speaks of the pain and agony of childbirth. In Israel's case, they were so ensnared by their sins, their punishment and subsequent deliverance was like an agonizing travail. To a Christian, overcoming the world, the flesh and the devil can sometimes be enormously painful. But a new life cannot be had without travail!

Jeremiah 30:6 - "Ask ye now, and see whether a man doth travail with child? wherefore do I see every man with his hands on his loins, as a woman in travail, and all faces are turned into paleness?"

D | The First Prophecy Concerning "Jacob's Trouble"

Both Jeremiah and Daniel prophesied "Jacob's trouble," the last and worst trial Israel will ever face. We also call it "The Great Tribulation." Messiah will save them from it.

Jeremiah 30:7-9 - "Alas! for that day is great, so that none is like it: it is even the time of Jacob's trouble; but he shall be saved out of it. For it shall come to pass in that day, saith the LORD of hosts, that I will break his yoke from off thy neck, and will burst thy bonds, and strangers shall no more serve themselves of him."

D | David Will Rule Under Christ In The Millennium

This is one of my favorite prophecies in the Bible. David will reign as a king in Israel, and as a prince under Jesus Christ (King of Kings) during the Millennium. "I the LORD will be their God, and my servant David a prince among them," Ezekiel 34:24. "Their nobles shall be of themselves, and their governor shall proceed from the midst of them; and I will cause him to draw near, and he shall approach unto me."

Jeremiah 30:9 - "They shall serve the LORD their God, and David their king, whom I will raise up unto them."

A | The Voice Of Them That Make Merry

Joy springs from hope. Hopeless people have no joy. People who have hope have joy. When God promises good things to us, hope is renewed, and we rejoice.

Jeremiah 30:18-19 - "Thus saith the LORD; Behold, I will bring again the captivity of Jacob's tents, and have mercy on his dwellingplaces; and the city shall be builded upon her own heap, and the palace shall remain after the manner thereof. And out of them shall proceed thanksgiving and the voice of them that make merry: and I will multiply them, and they shall not be few."

D | A Great Whirlwind

Together, Isaiah and Jeremiah prophesied five times of a coming whirlwind. The term refers to the fury of the battle of Armageddon. Armies from all nations will clash with Jesus Christ at His coming - like a whirlwind!

Jeremiah 30:23-24 - "Behold, the whirlwind of the LORD goeth forth with fury, a continuing whirlwind: it shall fall with pain upon the head of the wicked. The fierce anger of the LORD shall not return, until he have done it, and until he have performed the intents of his heart: in the latter days ye shall consider it."

C | I Have Loved Thee With An Everlasting Love

In 3000 years of volatile history, Israel both served and spurned the LORD. The chosen nation experienced countless upheavals; blessings and cursings; prosperity and failure. Repeatedly, they provoked God's fury, incurring His wrath. But in the end, Israel will be saved. Nothing but an everlasting divine love can explain that.

Jeremiah 31:3 - "Yea, I have loved thee with an everlasting love: therefore with lovingkindness have I drawn thee. ...I will turn their mourning into joy, and will comfort them, and make them rejoice from their sorrow. ...and my people shall be satisfied with my goodness, saith the LORD."

B | Waymarks

God often spoke to His people about their return from Babylonian captivity. "They shall come with weeping, and with supplications will I lead them: ...He that scattered Israel will gather him." But the way home needed guide-posts - waymarks. I think waymarks can be compared to the ancient landmarks. They are the old ways, the old righteous paths that were once the stuff of our joy. Let us bring back the waymarks.

Jeremiah 31:21 - "Set thee up waymarks, make thee high heaps: set thine heart toward the highway, ...O virgin of Israel, turn again to these thy cities."

D | A New Covenant

Israel breached their ancient Covenant with God irreparably. By its terms, God vowed to scatter them from His land. It finally happened. But mercifully, God vowed to make a new, spiritual covenant, writing His Law in their hearts. It began on the Day of Pentecost in Acts 2.

Jeremiah 31:31 - "The days come, ...that I will make a new covenant with the house of Israel, ...Not according to the covenant that I made with their fathers, ...But ...I will put my law in their inward parts, and write it in their hearts; and will be their God, and they shall be my people."

B | Jerusalem Eternal

God first revealed His interest in Jerusalem when He sent Abraham to Mount Moriah. God also sent an angel to meet King David there and told Him to buy the place where they stood. Then God sealed His promise when Solomon dedicated the Temple. As long as time shall be, Jerusalem is the LORD's. NOBODY will EVER change that!

Jeremiah 31:38-40 - "Behold, the days come, saith the LORD, that the city shall be built to the LORD, ...[it] shall be holy unto the LORD; it shall not be plucked up, nor thrown down any more for ever."

A | Praying To Make Sure You Did The Right Thing

Jeremiah prophesied the destruction and the 70-year captivity of Judah, but he also prophesied their return from Babylon, and the rebuilding of Jerusalem. God told Jeremiah that his uncle, Hanameel, would come to sell his property to Jeremiah. He instructed him to buy it. Jeremiah, in great faith, bought the land. Then he prayed, asking God if He would surely bring them back to the land.

Jeremiah 32: 27, 37-38 - "I am the LORD, ...is there any thing too hard for me? ...I will bring them again unto this place, and I will cause them to dwell safely."

A | Call Unto Me

Angelita's brother and his family visited our Church for the first time. Their little daughter was legally blind. "Please pray for her," she requested. The guest minister invited them to come forward for prayer. As they came, the Holy Spirit spoke and said, "I am Jehovah Rapha, the Lord that healeth. Tonight I will heal you." Immediately, the young child cried, "I can see!" Within days, her doctor confirmed the dramatic miracle. She could see excellently.

Jeremiah 33:3 - "Call unto me, and I will answer thee, and shew thee great and mighty things."

A | The Voice Of Joy, Gladness And Praise Shall Return

Jeremiah was in prison when the word of the LORD came to him. God reiterated that Judah could not escape His judgments in Babylon, but He promised again that He would eventually bring them health and cure, and would "...reveal unto them the abundance of peace and truth, ...cause the captivity to return, and ...pardon all their iniquities."

Jeremiah 33:9,11 - "Again there shall be heard in this place, ...The voice of joy, and the voice of gladness, ...the voice of them that shall say, Praise the LORD of hosts: for the LORD is good; for his mercy endureth for ever."

C | Divine Covenants Cannot Be Broken

The Old Testament Covenant did not fail. Israel failed. God sent them to Babylon because the terms of the Covenant promised their dispersion. Other divine Covenants still stand. They will be fulfilled in the Millennium.

Jeremiah 33:20-21 - "Thus saith the LORD; If ye can break my covenant of the day, and my covenant of the night, and that there should not be day and night in their season; Then may also my covenant be broken with David my servant, that he should not have a son to reign upon his throne; and with the Levites the priests, my ministers."

C | Just Obey God. Don't Renege. Don't Revert Back.

Jeremiah prophesied to King Zedekiah that Nebuchadnezzar would take him to Babylon, but would not kill him. Realizing that Judah was genuinely being overthrown, Zedekiah ordered the people to free all slaves and servants to fend for themselves. The Jews released their slaves, but quickly had a change of heart and made them return. That further angered God, and He heaped more judgments on them.

Jeremiah 34:20,22 - "I will even give them into the hand of their enemies, and into the hand of them that seek their life: and I will make the cities of Judah a desolation."

B | The Rechabites

God ordered Jeremiah to call the Rechabites to a Temple chamber and give them wine to drink. Jeremiah prepared wine pots and cups, saying "Drink ye wine." But they utterly refused. Their forefathers had commanded them never to drink wine, never build permanent houses, nor plant permanent crops. The Rechabites faithfully obeyed. The LORD told Jeremiah to reprimand the men of Judah. "They obeyed their fathers, but you will not obey ME!"

Jeremiah 35:19 - "Thus saith the LORD of hosts, the God of Israel; Jonadab the son of Rechab shall not want a man to stand before me for ever."

A | It May Be They Will Present Their Supplication

The LORD told Jeremiah to write all his prophecies in a book. Jeremiah dictated his book to a scribe named Baruch, then sent Baruch into the Temple to read it out loud to the people on a feast day while there was a crowd in attendance. The supreme purpose of God's written Word is to call us back to Him. If you have read the Bible, but have not yet repented, you have missed the point!

Jeremiah 36:7 - "It may be they will present their supplication before the LORD, and will return every one from his evil way."

D | Jeremiah Prophesies The End Of Jehoiakim's Line

Jeremiah's scribe, Baruch, read the book of prophecies to the king's princes, and they were frightened. They instructed Michaiah to read the scroll to King Jehoiakim, who cut up the book with a penknife, threw it into the fireplace, and called for Jeremiah and Baruch. But the LORD hid them, and Jeremiah prophesied against Jehoiakim.

Jeremiah 36:29-32 - "Thus saith the LORD of Jehoiakim king of Judah; He shall have none to sit upon the throne of David: and his dead body shall be cast out in the day to the heat, and in the night to the frost."

A | Some People Want Prayer, But Will Not Listen To God

Zedekiah was the last king of Judah. Nobody in Judah would hear the word of the LORD from Jeremiah. Ironically, the king sent men to Jeremiah, asking him to pray for them. But Jeremiah had only bad news. The Egyptians, who had come to help Zedekiah, would return to Egypt, and the Chaldeans (Babylonians) would take the people and burn the city. People always want the prophet to prophesy good things, even when they are completely evil.

Jeremiah 37:9 - "Thus saith the LORD; Deceive not yourselves, saying, The Chaldeans shall surely depart from us: for they shall not depart."

B | Jeremiah - Man Who Refused To Change His Message

Nobody could make Jeremiah change his message. "Though ye had smitten the whole army of the Chaldeans, ...and there remained but wounded men among them, yet should they rise up... and burn this city with fire." A captain raised up false charges against Jeremiah, which put him in prison many days.

Jeremiah 37:17 - "Then Zedekiah the king sent, and took him out: and the king asked him secretly in his house, and said, Is there any word from the LORD? And Jeremiah said, There is: for, said he, thou shalt be delivered into the hand of the king of Babylon."

C | Take A Stand - Pay The Price

From the earliest days of his ministry, Jeremiah faced threats on his life for his unpopular preaching. After a while, he found himself in and out of jail. Even the king wanted him silenced. But by the grace of God, he survived all their attempts. If you take a stand, you have to be ready to pay a price. God will help you.

Jeremiah 37:21 - "Then Zedekiah the king commanded that they should commit Jeremiah into the court of the prison, and that they should give him daily a piece of bread out of the bakers' street."

B | The Princes Of Judah Wanted To Kill Jeremiah

Jeremiah prophesied extensively that God would save Judah if they surrendered to seventy years of captivity under Nebuchadnezzar. But if they resisted, God would cause Nebuchadnezzar to utterly destroy them. "Therefore the princes said unto the king, We beseech thee, let this man be put to death: ...this man seeketh not the welfare of this people, but the hurt." You can kill the prophet, but you cannot stop the Word of the LORD.

Jeremiah 38:6 - "Then took they Jeremiah, and cast him into the dungeon ...And in the dungeon there was no water, but mire: so Jeremiah sunk in the mire."

C | Whatever You Have To Endure, Just Do It!

Whether you are Jeremiah or John Doe, the will of God will take you through unbelievable adversities. King Zedekiah permitted Jeremiah's adversaries to throw him into a lifeless dungeon, bogged in mire with no food. He nearly died. Suddenly, the king's eunuch, Ebedmelech, interceded, and Zedekiah had him lifted out. Just as suddenly, Jeremiah was standing, counseling the king. Whatever you have to endure, just do it!

Jeremiah 38:14 - "Then Zedekiah the king sent, and took Jeremiah the prophet unto him ...and the king said unto Jeremiah, I will ask thee a thing; hide nothing from me."

D | Zedekiah Rejected Prophecy, But It Came To Pass

Straight from the miry dungeon, Jeremiah stood fearfully, face-to-face with King Zedekiah, who sought his counsel. "Wilt thou not surely put me to death? and if I give thee counsel, wilt thou not hearken unto me?" Zedekiah swore not to hurt him. As often before, Jeremiah advised the king to cooperate with Nebuchadnezzar. If he resisted him, Judah would be destroyed. Zedekiah rejected that counsel, and Jeremiah saw it come to pass.

Jeremiah 38:28 - "So Jeremiah abode in the court of the prison until the day that Jerusalem was taken: and he was there when Jerusalem was taken."

B | Nebuzaradan - The Man Who Burned Solomon's Temple

Few people recognize his name, but he should be infamous. He burned down Solomon's Temple and Palace. He carried away the majority of the

Jews to Babylon. Miraculously, Nebuzaradan also delivered Jeremiah from prison. Nebuzaradan recognized a capable Jewish leader named Gedaliah and made him governor of the sparsely populated land of Judah. He gave the vineyards and fields to the remaining poor, to provide for their support.

Jeremiah 39:13-14 - "Nebuzaradan the captain of the guard sent, ...and took Jeremiah out of the court of the prison, and committed him unto Gedaliah."

A | **God Favors An Intercessor**

The Babylonians dealt the fatal blow to Jerusalem. The men of war fled. Zedekiah stood before Nebuchadnezzar and watched as his sons and nobles were killed. Then they put out his eyes. But the eunuch who interceded for Jeremiah, saving him from the miry dungeon, received a miraculous deliverance from the LORD. God favors intercessors!

Jeremiah 39:17-18 - "Thou shalt not be given into the hand of the men of whom thou art afraid. For I will surely deliver thee, and thou shalt not fall by the sword, ...because thou hast put thy trust in me, saith the LORD."

D | **The Babylonian Guard Recognized Prophecy Fulfilled**

Nebuzaradan was taking Jewish captives from Ramah to Babylon. Jeremiah was among them, in chains. Nebuzaradan told Jeremiah, "The LORD thy God hath pronounced this evil upon this place. ...because ye have sinned against the LORD." He apparently knew Jeremiah had prophesied it. Nebuzaradan removed Jeremiah's chains and promised to treat him well if he came to Babylon, but told him he could stay if he wished.

Jeremiah 40:4-5 - "I loose thee this day from the chains which were upon thine hand. ...So the captain of the guard gave him victuals and a reward, and let him go."

C | **Wise Counsel Is Worth Repeating**

Nebuzaradan appointed a great Jew, Gedaliah, to be the governor of Judea. That encouraged the remnant who had fled to quickly return. Jeremiah cooperated with Gedaliah, because all along, he had admonished everyone to cooperate with Nebuchadnezzar. His was not only prophetic, but wise counsel, and Gedaliah repeated it, too.

Jeremiah 40:9 - "Gedaliah ...sware unto them ...Fear not to serve the Chaldeans: dwell in the land, and serve the king of Babylon, and it shall be well with you, ...gather ye wine, and summer fruits, and oil, and put them in your vessels, and dwell in your cities that ye have taken."

C | Major Threat Is Past; Beware Minor Threats!

With Gedaliah as the newly-appointed Governor of Judah, the Jews who had been in hiding quickly returned and began to prosper in the vineyards and fields. Johanan came to Gedaliah to warn him that trouble was brewing among the Ammonites. "The king of the Ammonites hath sent Ishmael the son of Nethaniah to slay thee." Johanan asked permission to slay Ishmael, but Gedaliah refused. Sometimes, we think our only threat is the BIG enemies. Satan will exploit your naiveté. Be watchful!

Jeremiah 40:16 - "Gedaliah ...said unto Johanan, ...Thou shalt not do this thing: for thou speakest falsely of Ishmael."

B | Ishmael Kills Gedaliah; Johanan Defends Judah

Just as hope sprang up in the hearts of the remnant of Judah, the Ammonite king persuaded Ishmael, son of Nethaniah of David's seed royal, to kill their governor, Gedaliah. Ishmael killed Gedaliah, his men of war at Mizpah, and eighty more men. Then, he kidnapped the women of Mizpah. But Johanan raised an energetic counter-attack against him and rescued all the hostages. Ishmael fled back to the land of Ammon. Even if you have just faced the greatest trial of your life, you have to keep on fighting.

Jeremiah 41:17 - "They departed, and dwelt ...by Bethlehem."

A | The Remnant Ask Jeremiah To Pray For Them

After the Babylonians left, the remnant of Jews saw that opposition from a few rebels threatened to destroy them. They all appeared before Jeremiah and said, "Pray for us unto the LORD thy God, even for all this remnant; ...That the LORD thy God may shew us the way wherein we may walk, and the thing that we may do." Good move. Earnest prayer should always be your first action. Jeremiah agreed to pray. They promised to obey.

Jeremiah 42:5-6 - "Whether it be good, or whether it be evil, we will obey the voice of the LORD."

D | God Promised Blessing In Judah, Cursing In Egypt

The people asked Jeremiah to pray for them, so Jeremiah prayed. Ten days later, the LORD answered. He promised to build them up if they stayed in Judah, but they would all die by sword, or famine, or pestilence if they fled to Egypt.

Jeremiah 42:13-14,18 - "If ye say, We will not dwell in this land, neither obey the voice of the LORD your God, ...Saying, No; but we will go into the land of Egypt, where we shall see no war, ...so shall my fury be poured forth upon you, when ye shall enter into Egypt."

A | A Dishonest Prayer Will Only Bring Trouble

Jeremiah told Judah, "Ye dissembled in your hearts, when ye sent me unto the LORD your God, saying, Pray for us unto the LORD, ...all that the LORD our God shall say, ...we will do it." They "dissembled;" gave a false, misleading, hypocritical, camouflaged statement to God. They would not obey the LORD, and He knew it the moment they said it. You can never pull off a scam with God. He knows your phony heart the moment you have it.

Jeremiah 42:22 - "Now therefore know certainly that ye shall die ...in the place whither ye desire to go."

A | Why Pray, If You Will Not Heed The Answer?

The people of Judah promised they would do whatever the LORD told them if Jeremiah would pray. But they reneged. You will never win like that.

Jeremiah 43:1-4 - "When Jeremiah had made an end of speaking unto all the people all the words of the LORD their God, ...then spake Azariah ... and all the proud men, saying unto Jeremiah, Thou speakest falsely: the LORD our God hath not sent thee to say, Go not into Egypt to sojourn there. ...So Johanan ...and all the people, obeyed not the voice of the LORD, to dwell in the land of Judah."

B | Johanan Betrays Jeremiah, Takes The Remnant To Egypt

Johanan was the hero who defeated Ishmael, who tried to overthrow the remnant of Judah. Johanan recaptured every hostage Ishmael had taken. But Johanan wanted everybody to flee to Egypt. He hated the Word of the LORD from Jeremiah, forbidding them to flee to Egypt. Johanan and his crowd accused Jeremiah of delivering Judah to the

Chaldeans to die. You should be TERRIFIED of wanting your will more than God's will.

Jeremiah 43:5,7 - "Johanan ...took all the remnant of Judah, ...So they came into the land of Egypt: for they obeyed not the voice of the LORD."

D | Nebuchadnezzar Will Raze Egypt Like Stones In A Brick Kiln

Almost everybody hated Jeremiah's prophecies, but it did not stop them from coming to pass. When the remnant of Judah fled to Egypt against God's orders, God told Jeremiah to hide stones inside of clay in a brick kiln at the entrance of Pharaoh's house. He prophesied that Nebuchadnezzar would come and smite Egypt, and capture and kill with sword and with fire.

Jeremiah 43:12 - "And I will kindle a fire in the houses of the gods of Egypt; and he shall burn them, ...and the houses of the gods of the Egyptians shall he burn with fire."

C | Why Commit This Great Evil Against Your Soul?

When people do wrong things, they often do not believe they are doing wrong. The remnant of Judah saw their brethren horrifically judged and taken captive to Babylon. Nevertheless, they justified their own sins with "logical" arguments. But sin is just as evil for one man as it is another. None of our "reasons" will stop the judgment of God. If you sin against God, you do so at the peril of your eternal soul.

Jeremiah 44:7 - "Therefore now thus saith the LORD, ...Wherefore commit ye this great evil against your souls, ...to leave you none to remain?"

C | Evil Spirits Will Encourage Your Defiance

The rebellious Jews immediately committed idolatries and worshipped Egypt's false gods. Jeremiah argued that God made their brethren desolate for committing such abominations in Judah. Jeremiah prophesied that these Jews would be utterly consumed in Egypt. Their reply was shocking! They boasted that since they began burning incense and making offerings to the queen of heaven, they had marvelously prospered, and when they halted, they "wanted all things." Satan powerfully deludes multitudes with prosperity.

Jeremiah 44:16 - "As for the word that thou hast spoken unto us in the name of the LORD, we will not hearken unto thee."

B | The Abominable "Queen Of Heaven"

God's people went to Egypt and worshipped and burned incense to "The Queen of Heaven." Today, one billion Catholics burn incense to "The Queen of Heaven," - "The Blessed Virgin Mary."

Jeremiah 44:17 - "We will certainly do whatsoever thing goeth forth out of our own mouth, to burn incense unto the queen of heaven, and to pour out drink offerings unto her, as we have done, we, and our fathers, our kings, and our princes, in the cities of Judah, and in the streets of Jerusalem: for then had we plenty of victuals, and were well, and saw no evil."

D | Jeremiah Curses Worshippers of "Queen Of Heaven"

God's people had just broken their vows to Jehovah, God of Abraham, Isaac and Jacob. In Egypt, they made new vows to the "Queen of Heaven." "We will surely perform our vows that we have vowed, to burn incense to the queen of heaven, and to pour out drink offerings unto her."

Jeremiah 44:26-29 - "Therefore hear ye the word of the LORD, ...all the men of Judah that are in the land of Egypt shall be consumed by the sword and by the famine, ...that ye may know that my words shall surely stand against you for evil."

B | Baruch - Jeremiah's Scribe

Baruch transcribed Jeremiah's prophecies, but they terrified him. He reacted, "Woe is me! The LORD has added grief to my sorrow!" But Jeremiah prophesied, " ...The LORD saith, ...that which I have built will I break down, and that which I have planted I will pluck up." Being a mouth-piece for God can overwhelm a man with its seriousness. But God will reward that man for obeying.

Jeremiah 45:5 - "Seekest thou great things for thyself? seek them not: for, behold, I will bring evil upon all flesh, ...but thy life will I give unto thee for a prey."

A | Crying Without Praying

More than two dozen times, Jeremiah spoke of the cries of people facing the judgments of God. They are the cries of pain, anguish and agony in dreadful circumstances that accompany divine punishment. Why would they not simultaneously utter a PRAYER for mercy to the God of heaven? But prayerlessness is, from the beginning, a rudimentary cause for their judgment. A righteous prayer could have alleviated their cry.

Jeremiah 46:12 - "The nations have heard of thy shame, and thy cry hath filled the land: for the mighty man hath stumbled against the mighty, and they are fallen both together."

D | Jeremiah Prophesies Judgments Upon Egypt

Jeremiah published prophecies against the Gentiles, beginning with Egypt. The guiding principle of these prophecies is that wherever the Jews go to be punished, whether Babylon or Egypt, God will eventually deliver the Jews, and eventually punish their oppressors. God used Babylon and Egypt to punish backsliding Judah, but at last, Egypt and Babylon were still idolatrous enemies of God.

Jeremiah 46:25 - "The LORD of hosts, the God of Israel, saith; Behold, I will punish the multitude of No, and Pharaoh, and Egypt, with their gods, and their kings; even Pharaoh, and all them that trust in him."

C | God Will Correct His People In Measure

I am always amazed at God's counter-offers. Almost every time God rages against His people, He also points to the door of mercy. Regardless of how furious God becomes, He is not willing that any should perish. The Righteous Judge will have mercy!

Jeremiah 46:27-28 - "Fear not thou, ...O Israel, ...I will save thee from afar off, and thy seed from the land of their captivity; and Jacob shall return, and be in rest and at ease, and none shall make him afraid. ...I will not make a full end of thee, but correct thee in measure."

D | God Judges The Philistines At Gaza And Ashkelon

Gaza and Ashkelon are infamous coastal towns near the Egyptian border, homeland of the Philistines, and source of so very much of Israel's grief for many centuries. The word of the LORD by Jeremiah prophesied their ruin by Nebuchadnezzar and his horses and chariots.

Jeremiah 47:6-7 - "O thou sword of the LORD, how long will it be ere thou be quiet? put up thyself into thy scabbard, rest, and be still. How can it be quiet, seeing the LORD hath given it a charge against Ashkelon, and against the sea shore? there hath he appointed it."

C | God Will Judge False-god Worshippers In Cruel Mockery

Moab worshipped Chemosh and held Israel in derision - a laughing-stock and mockery. But God will have ALL false-god-worshippers in divine

□✓

derision and mockery in the end. "For the LORD, whose name is Jealous, is a jealous God," Exodus 34:14.

Jeremiah 48:26-27,35,39 - "Moab ...shall be in derision. For was not Israel a derision unto thee? ...I will cause to cease in Moab, saith the LORD, him that offereth in the high places, and him that burneth incense to his gods. ...so shall Moab be a derision and a dismaying to all them about him."

B | The Calamity Of Moab

The history of Moab is fraught with wickedness, beginning with an incestuous birth. The Moabite king hired the prophet Balaam to curse Israel. Moabite women enticed Israel with adulteries and idolatries (Numbers 25). Moab warred with Kings Saul and David. Moabite women brought their false god Chemosh into Solomon's household. God punished Moab with Babylonian captivity.

Jeremiah 48:46-47 - "Woe be unto thee, O Moab! the people of Chemosh perisheth: for thy sons are taken captives, ...Yet will I bring again the captivity of Moab in the latter days, saith the LORD. Thus far is the judgment of Moab."

B | Amman, Jordan - The Ammonites

All these prophets cursed the Ammonites [now known as Amman, Jordan]: Jahaziel, Nehemiah, David, Isaiah, Jeremiah, Daniel, Amos, and Zephaniah. Some of the calamities they prophesied were fulfilled in ancient days, but others will be finalized when Jesus comes at Armageddon. King Abdullah, who now rules in Amman, Jordan, is the primary Arab voice who demands that Israel give up much of the Holy Land to create a Palestinian State. Do you think anyone can survive who tries to steal God's Promised Land?

Jeremiah 49:1 - "Concerning the Ammonites, ...the days come, saith the LORD, ...it shall be a desolate heap."

D | Prophecies About Edom's Extinction

The descendants of Esau, Jacob's twin brother, were known as the Edomites. Edom, or Idumea, was the land south of Israel, primarily in the Negev Desert and south of the Red Sea. The Edomites were hostile to Israel and warred with them often. The prophets had nothing good to say about Edom. According to the prophecies, the Edomites became extinct following the Babylonian captivity.

461

Jeremiah 49:7,13,17 - "Concerning Edom, thus saith the LORD of hosts; ...all the cities thereof shall be perpetual wastes. ...Edom shall be a desolation: every one that goeth by it shall be astonished."

D | Prophecies About Damascus

Jewish historian, Josephus, claimed that "Abraham reigned at Damascus, ...but after a long time, he got him up and removed from that country, ...and went into the land then called the land of Canaan." In centuries to follow, Damascus conducted many wars against the descendants of Abraham. Damascus fell to Nebuchadnezzar in 572BC, then to the Persians under Cyrus in 538BC.

Jeremiah 49:23-24,26 - "Damascus is waxed feeble, ...fear hath seized on her: ...her young men shall fall in her streets, and all the men of war shall be cut off in that day, saith the LORD of hosts."

B | God's Throne In Elam (Babylon)

At the Temple dedication, God told Solomon, "Now have I chosen and sanctified this house, ...and mine eyes and mine heart shall be there perpetually. ...But if ye turn away, ...this house, ...will I cast out of my sight." Isaiah saw God's Throne in the Temple (6:1). When Israel went into Babylonian captivity, Ezekiel saw the Throne leave the Temple toward the east (10:1-18). God told Jeremiah that He would rule from Elam for a while.

Jeremiah 49:38 - "I will set my throne in Elam, and will destroy from thence the king and the princes, saith the LORD."

C | When God Turns Your Captivity

God judged evil nations in two devastating ways. In some cases, God utterly destroyed them, as He did at Sodom and Gomorrah. In other cases, He punished them, sending them into captivity. Then, after a while, He promised to "turn your captivity," or "bring again your captivity. Such was the case in ancient times for Israel, Moab, Ammon, Elam, and even Egypt. In the end, however, all enemies will go the way of Sodom.

Jeremiah 49:39 - "It shall come to pass in the latter days, that I will bring again the captivity of Elam, saith the LORD."

C | Publish The News Of What God Is Doing

The big news of the day was that Babylon had overthrown Jerusalem and taken Judah captive. But God had another, more important announcement. He would send the Medes and Persians and overthrow Babylon! Let no man err. God IS ALWAYS in control!

Jeremiah 50:2 - "Declare ye among the nations, and publish, and set up a standard; publish, and conceal not: say, Babylon is taken, Bel is confounded, Merodach is broken in pieces; her idols are confounded, her images are broken in pieces. For out of the north there cometh up a nation against her, which shall make her land desolate."

A | They Will Seek The LORD After Their Punishment

Although the LORD sentenced His people to seventy years in Babylon, He promised they would return home. God would send Medo-Persians to overthrow Babylon, and Israel would again seek the LORD.

Jeremiah 50:4 - "In those days, and in that time, saith the LORD, the children of Israel shall come, they and the children of Judah together, going and weeping: they shall go, and seek the LORD their God. They shall ask the way to Zion with their faces thitherward, saying, Come, and let us join ourselves to the LORD in a perpetual covenant that shall not be forgotten."

B | The Lost Sheep Of Israel

Here is one of the most powerful and profound allegories in the Bible. God called Israel His "lost sheep." From the time Israel was cast out of the Promised Land, until Jesus Christ establishes His earthly kingdom, Israel is indisputably displaced and "lost." Jesus said, "I am not sent but unto the lost sheep of the house of Israel." He instructed His disciples, "Go not into the way of the Gentiles, ...But go rather to the lost sheep of the house of Israel."

Jeremiah 50:6 - "My people hath been lost sheep: their shepherds have caused them to go astray."

C | The Punisher Must Be Punished

How often in world history has Almighty God drafted a heathen nation to punish His own chosen people? He drafted Assyrians to remove the ten northern tribes of Israel. Then He drafted Babylonians to remove the remaining tribes of Benjamin and Judah in Jeremiah's day. But there is mysterious irony in His workings. After they have punished God's people, they too will be punished - "Because ye were glad, because ye rejoiced, O ye destroyers of mine heritage."

Jeremiah 50:15 - "...for it is the vengeance of the LORD: take vengeance upon her; as she hath done, do unto her."

D | God Will Bring Israel Back Home And Pardon Them

God punished Assyria and Babylon for punishing Israel. "First the king of Assyria hath devoured him; and last this Nebuchadrezzar king of Babylon hath broken his bones. Therefore thus saith the LORD, ...I will punish the king of Babylon ...as I have punished the king of Assyria. And I will bring Israel again to his habitation." Messiah will then pardon their sins.

Jeremiah 50:20 - "In those days, and in that time, saith the LORD, the iniquity of Israel shall be sought for, and there shall be none; ...they shall not be found: for I will pardon them whom I reserve."

B | Cyrus And The Medes

Once Judah had endured its seventy-year captivity, God ordained the Medes, under Cyrus, to violently overthrow Babylon. In Jeremiah 51, the Medes are referred to as a destroying wind, fanners (as winnowing or threshing a harvest), an invasion of caterpillars, and spoilers. Babylon could not possibly stand.

Jeremiah 51:1-2,14,53 - "Thus saith the LORD; Behold, I will raise up against Babylon, ...a destroying wind; ...and will send unto Babylon fanners, that shall fan her, and shall empty her land: ...I will fill thee with men, as with caterpillers; ...from me shall spoilers come unto her."

D | Israel - My Battle Axe

God hated the brutish idols of Babylon. "They are vanity, the work of errors: ...they shall perish. The portion of Jacob [the LORD] is not like them; ...Israel is the rod of his inheritance." Under Messiah, Israel - His "battle axe," "the rod of His inheritance," will conquer all nations at Armageddon.

Jeremiah 51:20,24 - "Thou art my battle axe and weapons of war: for with thee will I break in pieces the nations, and with thee will I destroy kingdoms. ...I will render unto Babylon ...all their evil that they have done in Zion in your sight, saith the LORD."

C | Our Rock Is Greater Than All The World's Mountains

In the book of Daniel, Nebuchadnezzar dreamed of a statue representing the greatest kingdoms of men. He saw a rock, hewn out of a mountain, representing Messiah, come and crush the statue - crushing all the kingdoms of men. The rock became a great "mountain," a kingdom throughout the whole earth. Jeremiah affirmed that Babylon, the great "destroying mountain" would be totally destroyed. Our Rock is greater than all the world's mountains.

Jeremiah 51:26 - "They shall not take of thee a stone for a corner, nor a stone for foundations; but thou shalt be desolate for ever, saith the LORD."

D | Babylon Will Die Drunk!

In Daniel 5, Belshazzar, king of Babylon, made a great feast for a thousand of his lords. He and his Princes profanely drank wine in golden vessels from the Holy Temple of God at Jerusalem. Suddenly, God wrote their death sentence on the wall. Jeremiah's prophecy from years earlier was perfectly fulfilled.

Jeremiah 51:39,57 - "I will make their feasts, and I will make them drunken, that they may rejoice, and sleep a perpetual sleep, and not wake, saith the LORD. ...I will make drunk her princes, and her wise men, her captains, and her rulers, and her mighty men."

B | Throw The Book Into The River

Over the years, Jeremiah dictated to Baruch and Seraiah an entire book of prophecies. He instructed Seraiah to read it when he got to Babylon and remember that the LORD foretold these desolations. Jeremiah told him to throw the book into the river to symbolize the disappearance of Babylon.

Jeremiah 51:63-64 - "When thou hast made an end of reading this book, that thou shalt bind a stone to it, and cast it into the midst of Euphrates: And thou shalt say, Thus shall Babylon sink, and shall not rise from the evil that I will bring upon her."

C | Prophecies Really Do Come True

Jeremiah recounted the fall of Jerusalem and the end of the kingdom of Israel. King Jehoiachin was taken to Babylon in the first stage of Nebuchadnezzar's siege. Zedekiah, the last king, was evil and rebelled against Babylon. Nebuchadnezzar seized Jerusalem, slew its leaders, burned the Holy Temple, the palace and houses, broke down the walls, and carried thousands of residents to Babylon. Years later, in Babylon, Nebuchadnezzar's son, Evil-Merodach, mercifully released Jehoiachin from prison.

Jeremiah 52:3 - "Through the anger of the LORD it came to pass in Jerusalem and Judah, till he had cast them out from his presence."

Lessons from the Book of
LAMENTATIONS

B | Jeremiah - The Weeping Prophet

No one but a true man of God can comprehend the bitterness of failing to win the souls of a people. For twenty-five years, Jeremiah stood in the courts of the Temple and in the streets of Jerusalem, begging the people to get right with God. But they utterly rejected his ministry. Over and over again, Jeremiah cried, "She has no one to comfort her!"

Lamentations 1:16 - "For these things I weep; mine eye, mine eye runneth down with water, because the comforter that should relieve my soul is far from me: my children are desolate, because the enemy prevailed."

A | Praying Too Late

Thousands of Jerusalem residents woke up captive in Babylon and realized that everything Jeremiah had prophesied was coming to pass. Jerusalem was desolate, the people wept sorely in the night, and there were none to comfort them. They knew their adversary had prevailed because of their iniquities. Their prayers were short-winded, almost breathless. It was too late to pray. Seventy years of captivity were divinely determined.

Lamentations 1:9,11,20 - "O LORD, behold my affliction: for the enemy hath magnified himself. ...see, O LORD, and consider; for I am become vile. ...Behold, O LORD; for I am in distress."

D | God's Footstool - The Place Of His Feet

David said the earth is God's footstool. Specifically, God wanted to plant His feet in Jerusalem. In Ezekiel, God called the coming millennial Temple, "the place of the soles of my feet." Isaiah prophesied that God would beautify the place of His sanctuary, "and I will make the place of my feet glorious." No wonder Jeremiah was so distraught that God had removed His feet from His footstool in Jerusalem.

Lamentations 2:1 - "How hath the Lord ...cast down from heaven unto the earth the beauty of Israel, and remembered not his footstool in the day of his anger."

A | Let Tears Run Down Like A River Day And Night

Jeremiah was flooded with unbearable sorrow after the Babylonians finished destroying Jerusalem and Judah. His "Lamentations" articulated the profound grief that all the captives were experiencing. Nothing provokes a Niagara of prayer like a devastating calamity. Don't wait until tragedy strikes to pray.

Lamentations 2:18-19 - "Their heart cried unto the Lord, ...let tears run down like a river day and night: give thyself no rest; let not the apple of thine eye cease. Arise, cry out in the night: in the beginning of the watches pour out thine heart like water before the face of the Lord."

A | Prayer Warriors Never Stop Praying

For twenty-five years, Jeremiah stood in the gap for Judah; preaching, praying and prophesying. The people resisted every effort to save them from destruction. But even in defeat, after desolation came, and their souls were oppressed by their captors, Jeremiah never stopped pleading with God. Prayer warriors never stop praying.

Lamentations 2:20-22 - "Behold, O LORD, and consider to whom thou hast done this. ...shall the priest and the prophet be slain in the sanctuary of the Lord? The young and the old lie on the ground in the streets: ...thou hast slain them in the day of thine anger."

C | Sorrow Has Many Metaphors

Jeremiah used just about every metaphor and allegory he could think of to describe his anguish for failing to convert Judah and avert their overthrow. His sorrow was overwhelming. "I am the man that has seen affliction..."

Lamentations 3:1-16 - "...the rod of His wrath, ...dark places ...His hand against me ...my flesh and skin made old ...broken my bones ...gall and travail ...hedged me about ...my chain heavy ...He as a bear lying in wait ...as a lion in secret places ...bent His bow ...made me drunken with wormwood ...broken my teeth with stones ...covered me with ashes."

C | Hope Is Confidence In An Unseen Portion

I was a young preacher preparing a sermon on "Faith, Hope, and Love," and searching for a meaningful biblical definition of hope. I found Jeremiah saying, "The LORD is my portion, ...therefore will I hope in him." Everything Jeremiah could see had failed. Jerusalem was destroyed. His people were captives in Babylon. Then Jeremiah remembered that he still had an unseen portion. I discovered that you need never lose hope. God is always there.

Lamentations 3:21 - "This I recall to my mind, therefore have I hope. ...The LORD is my portion, saith my soul; therefore will I hope in him."

C | Great Is Thy Faithfulness

Isaiah prophesied of a day to come when God will consume wickedness from the earth. "For I have heard from the Lord GOD of hosts a consumption, even determined upon the whole earth," Isaiah 28:22. But for now, His grace is sufficient to save you and me. Today is our day of salvation. His compassions never fail. He is greatly faithful to help. He is our merciful Savior.

Lamentations 3:22-23 - "It is of the LORD'S mercies that we are not consumed, because his compassions fail not. They are new every morning: great is thy faithfulness."

A | Let Us Lift Up Our Hands Unto God In The Heavens

Jeremiah rehearsed thirty-two lamentations; things that grieved and distressed him while in captivity. Suddenly, he interjected, "Let us lift up our heart with our hands unto God..." It is as if Jeremiah knew that he could plug into God's power source and be renewed. If he would reach up to God, he knew God would reach down to him. God said that if we would seek Him, we would find Him!

Lamentations 3:41,50 - "Let us lift up our heart with our hands unto God in the heavens. ...Till the LORD look down, and behold from heaven."

A | Tell God You Remember His Great Deliverance

It is easy to forget how great the trials were that God delivered us from. But in captivity, Jeremiah remembered terrifying days in Jerusalem when God saved his life. He blessed the LORD.

Lamentations 3:52-55,57 - "Mine enemies chased me sore, like a bird, without cause. They have cut off my life in the dungeon, and cast a stone upon me. Waters flowed over mine head; then I said, I am cut off. I called upon thy name, O LORD, out of the low dungeon. ... Thou drewest near in the day that I called upon thee: thou saidst, Fear not."

A | Praying For Obvious Results

When Jeremiah surveyed the devastating, tragic consequences of Judah's rebellion, he prayed that God would deal harshly with those who fought so hard against his prophetic warnings. God certainly would have anyway.

Lamentations 3:60-61,64-66 - "Thou hast seen all their vengeance and all their imaginations against me. Thou hast heard their reproach, O LORD, and all their imaginations against me; ...Render unto them a recompence, O LORD, according to the work of their hands. Give them sorrow of heart, thy curse unto them. Persecute and destroy them in anger from under the heavens of the LORD."

D | He Hath Abhorred His Sanctuary

From the day God's glory first appeared in Solomon's Temple, God had warned Israel: "If ye shall at all turn from following me, ...Then will I cut off Israel out of the land which I have given them; and this house, which I have hallowed for my name, will I cast out of my sight." Jeremiah lived to see that day come. "He hath violently taken away his tabernacle, ...The Lord hath cast off his altar, he hath abhorred his sanctuary.

Lamentations 4:1 - "...the stones of the sanctuary are poured out in the top of every street."

B | Judah Commits Cannibalism

"The precious sons of Zion," once like fine gold, became "as earthen pitchers." Their Nazarites, who had been "purer than snow" became "blacker than a coal." But that was nothing compared to their ultimate sins. Moses prophesied in his day that if Israel forsook the LORD, "Ye shall eat the flesh of your sons, and the flesh of your daughters shall ye eat," Leviticus 26:29. It really happened in Jeremiah's day. Cannibalism!

Lamentations 4:10 - "The hands of the pitiful women have sodden their own children: they were their meat in the destruction of the daughter of my people."

A | Keep On Praying, Even Under Divine Affliction

"Remember, O LORD, what is come upon us: ...our inheritance is turned to strangers, ...We are orphans and fatherless, ...Our necks are under persecution: ...Servants have ruled over us, ...they ravished the women in Zion, ...Princes are hanged up by their hand: ...They took the young men to grind, ...The joy of our heart is ceased; our dance is turned into mourning. ...woe unto us, ...we have sinned!" Keep on praying!

Lamentations 5:21-22 - "Turn thou us unto thee, O LORD, ...renew our days as of old. But thou hast utterly rejected us; thou art very wroth against us."

Lessons from the Book of
EZEKIEL

A | Ezekiel - The Seer Who Listened

Something conspicuous characterizes Ezekiel. Almost two dozen times, Ezekiel wrote about things that "I saw," or "I heard," from the LORD. Only one time did Ezekiel ever say, "I said." Ezekiel seemed to have very little to say for himself, but again and again, he heard the voice of God and saw the visions of God. We will learn more from God if we watch and listen more attentively, and NOT do all the talking.

Ezekiel 1:1 - "As I was among the captives by the river of Chebar, that the heavens were opened, and I saw visions of God."

B | The Book Of The Prophet Ezekiel

Ezekiel, a priest and prophet, was obsessed with the subject of the presence of the Lord in Jerusalem. In forty-eight chapters, he covers the ancient sins of Israel, the glory of God departing Jerusalem, God's judgments on Israel's enemies, Israel's restoration to their land, Armageddon, and the millennial kingdom of Messiah. Ezekiel rebuked the shepherd-kings of Israel for allowing their sins, abominations, and enemy oppressors. God promised to shepherd them by His Prince, David.

Ezekiel 1:3 - "The word of the LORD came expressly unto Ezekiel the priest, ...and the hand of the LORD was there upon him."

C | Ezekiel's Revelations Are Not Mystical

In Jewish history, Ezekiel's descriptions of the Throne of God are called the "Merkabah." After the Second Temple was destroyed in 70AD, certain rabbinical groups decided that Ezekiel should not be read or studied by ordinary people, arguing that it contained mysteries that could only be understood by adept scholars. This was the earliest form of Cabbalism, a perverse twisting of the Word of God into occultic, esoteric interpretations contrary to the face-value of the Bible.

Ezekiel 1:4 - "I looked, and, behold, a whirlwind came out of the north, a great cloud, and a fire infolding itself."

D | Four Living Creatures - The Chariot Of God

Four living creatures like men had four faces (man, lion, ox, eagle), straight feet like calves, four wings, hands under each wing (two reached high, touching the next one; two covered their bodies). Sparkling, burning fires and lightnings went up and down them. Beside each creature was a wheel in the middle of a wheel, with eyes in their rims. The very Throne of God sat on a crystal firmament over their heads. They moved in unison - the living Chariot of God.

Ezekiel 1:24-25 - "I heard ...the voice of the Almighty, the voice of speech. ...a voice from the firmament that was over their heads."

C | A Wheel In The Middle Of A Wheel

The concept of wheels within wheels is generally perceived to refer to secrets behind a façade. Some truths are outward - they are obvious. Other truths are inner, concealed truths. Such is certainly the case about God. Countless great truths can be seen and known about God. But for every observable truth, there is an infinite substructure of hidden truths. Hence, the wheels beneath God's Throne depict all Truth, seen and unseen. His Throne is undergirded by infinite Truth - both revealed and hidden.

Ezekiel 1:16 - "Their work was as it were a wheel in the middle of a wheel."

B | Ezekiel Saw The Throne Of God Leave Jerusalem

Ezekiel saw God's Throne in the Temple in Jerusalem. Apparently it had been there since Solomon dedicated the Temple. Isaiah had seen it there (Isaiah 6:1). Because of Israel's sins, the cherubims lifted it up and moved it eastward to Elam - Babylon (See Ezekiel 10:18, 11:23, Jeremiah 49:38).

Ezekiel 1:26 - "...over their heads was the likeness of a throne... and... the appearance of a man above upon it." Ezekiel 10:19 - "...the cherubims lifted up their wings... and every one stood at the door of the east gate of the LORD's house; and the glory of the God of Israel was over them above."

A | I Fell On My Face

Ezekiel saw the Throne of God on a sapphire pavement above the crystal firmament, carried by the four living creatures. The form of a Throne, with the form of a man, was all engulfed in amber-colored fire. An emerald rainbow shone above it. This vision represented the glorious, otherwise invisible presence of God in the Temple. Ezekiel fell on his face. You would, too.

Ezekiel 1:28 - "So was the appearance of the brightness round about. This was the appearance of the likeness of the glory of the LORD. And when I saw it, I fell upon my face."

B | Ezekiel Sent To A Rebellious Nation

Ezekiel was a boy when he was carried to Babylon in the first exile with King Jehoiachin, around 598BC. In those days, Jeremiah was already prophesying in Jerusalem. Ezekiel began receiving visions from the LORD along the banks of the river Chebar in Babylon. Then God sent him to prophesy to His people for more than twenty years. In the first twenty-four chapters, Ezekiel prophesied the impending judgments of God on Jerusalem and Judah.

Ezekiel 2:7 - "Thou shalt speak my words unto them, whether they will hear, or whether they will forbear: for they are most rebellious."

C | Eat The Book, Speak The Word

God sent Ezekiel to a "nation that hath rebelled against me: ...impudent children and stiffhearted." A roll of a book was spread, "...written therein lamentations, and mourning, and woe." God said, "Son of man, eat that thou findest; eat this roll, and go speak unto the house of Israel." Every man of God must eat the Word before he speaks.

Ezekiel 3:3 - "Then did I eat it; and it was in my mouth as honey for sweetness. And he said unto me, Son of man, go, get thee unto the house of Israel, and speak with my words unto them."

C | God Makes His Prophets Hard-Headed

Ezekiel's audience was already in captivity. They did not want to hear from God. But God required Ezekiel to prophesy to them anyway. God warned him, "...the house of Israel will not hearken unto thee; for they will not hearken unto me." They were "impudent and hardhearted." But God made his face strong against their faces, his forehead strong against their foreheads. "Tell them... whether they will hear ...or forebear."

Ezekiel 3:9 - "As an adamant [i.e., diamond] harder than flint have I made thy forehead: fear them not, neither be dismayed at their looks, though they be a rebellious house."

D | The Noise Of The Throne Being Moved

Do not allow the detailed imagery of these visions to distract you from the real message. What is most important is NOT why a man had a lion's face, or feet like a calf. The bigger picture is of God on His Throne being moved from one place to another by this living Chariot of God. God was abandoning Jerusalem because Israel was a rebellious house.

Ezekiel 3:13 - "I heard also the noise of the wings of the living creatures that touched one another, and the noise of the wheels over against them, and a noise of a great rushing."

D | Watchman, Their Blood Will Be On Your Hands

Ezekiel sat for seven days studying his captive brethren by the river Chebar. The LORD said, "I have made thee a watchman" over them. "Give them warning from me."

Ezekiel 3:20 - "When a righteous man doth turn from his righteousness, and commit iniquity, and I lay a stumblingblock before him, ...because thou hast not given him warning, he shall die in his sin, ...but his blood will I require at thine hand. Nevertheless if thou warn the righteous man, that the righteous sin not, and he doth not sin, he shall surely live, ...also thou hast delivered thy soul."

A | Go To The Plain, I Will Speak To You There

After ordaining him a watchman, God called Ezekiel to the plain for a private discussion. "I will there talk with thee." When he went, "the glory of the LORD stood there," as he had seen at Chebar. "I fell on my face." The Spirit said, "Go, shut thyself within thine house." God warned him not to go among the people because they planned to bind him up.

Ezekiel 3:26 - "I will make thy tongue cleave to the roof of thy mouth, that thou shalt be dumb, and shalt not be to them a reprover: for they are a rebellious house."

C | God Uses Object Lessons And Illustrated Sermons

One picture is worth a thousand words. God told Ezekiel to draw Jerusalem on a clay tile, then build a fort around it, lay siege and set battering rams against it. Then, he was to set an iron pan as a wall and pretend to attack the city. This was to warn the people that Jerusalem would be attacked and seized, which soon happened.

Ezekiel 4:1-3 - "Take thee a tile, and lay it before thee, and pourtray upon it the city, even Jerusalem: and lay siege against it, ...This shall be a sign to the house of Israel."

D | 430 Years Of Iniquity

Counting backwards 430 years from the end of the Babylonian captivity (537BC) is 967BC - the year Solomon became king. God tore the kingdom from Solomon because of his idolatries (1 Kings 11). Ezekiel pantomimed 430 years of iniquity, lying on his side, one day for one year.

Ezekiel 4:5-6 - "I have laid upon thee the years of their iniquity, ...three hundred and ninety days: so shalt thou bear the iniquity of the house of Israel. ...lie again on thy right side, and thou shalt bear the iniquity of the house of Judah forty days: ...each day for a year."

B | Ezekiel's Bread

God directed Ezekiel to make bread that would be his diet for a 430-day prophetic vigil. Its ingredients were mixed and baked. Amazingly, scientists discovered that when these six grains and legumes are sprouted and combined, one of the highest quality proteins is created, rivaling the protein in milk and eggs. Ezekiel bread includes eighteen amino acids, including nine essential to the human diet. Only God could have known those benefits. We receive many blessings unknowingly.

Ezekiel 4:9 - "Take thou also unto thee wheat, and barley, and beans, and lentiles, and millet, and fitches, ...make thee bread thereof."

A | Ezekiel Prayed Not To Be Defiled

God instructed Ezekiel to act out a pantomime that he just dreaded to do. While Ezekiel lay in the streets, illustrating 430 years in which iniquity was "laid upon" Israel, God wanted him to eat defiled bread - bread baked over human dung. Ezekiel pleaded against that. God consented for him to bake it over cow dung instead.

Ezekiel 4:14 - "Then said I, Ah Lord GOD! behold, my soul hath not been polluted: for from my youth up even till now have I not eaten of that which dieth of itself, ...neither came there abominable flesh into my mouth."

B | The Sign Of The Barber's Razor

God told Ezekiel to shave his head and beard, and demonstrate object lessons in the midst of the city. He would burn one-third of the hair, symbolizing the upcoming burning of Jerusalem. He would smite one-third with a knife, symbolizing being captured by the sword. The remaining one-third of the people would die of pestilence and famine.

Ezekiel 5:1 - "And thou, son of man, take thee a sharp knife, take thee a barber's razor, and cause it to pass upon thine head and upon thy beard: then take thee balances to weigh, and divide the hair."

D | Prophecies Foretell Cannibalism Among Apostates

In Deuteronomy 28:49, Moses prophesied that if Israel forsook God, He would send enemies to take them captive, "and thou shalt eat the fruit of thine own body, the flesh of thy sons and of thy daughters (v 53)" - cannibalism! They did commit cannibalism in the days following Ahab and Jezebel, and in Lamentations 4:10 - Jeremiah's and Ezekiel's days. Gross sins and godlessness inevitably culminate in unspeakable perversions.

Ezekiel 5:10 - "Therefore the fathers shall eat the sons in the midst of thee, and the sons shall eat their fathers; and I will execute judgments in thee."

C | God Will Always Have A Remnant

This is no small matter. The fact that God miraculously sustains and perpetuates a remnant throughout all generations is awesome. How many times might the godly have been driven into total extinction by powerful and hostile forces in this world? But God will never allow that to happen. Nobody but God can provide that kind of insurance.

Ezekiel 6:7-10 - "The slain shall fall in the midst of you, and ye shall know that I am the LORD. Yet will I leave a remnant, ...some that shall escape the sword among the nations ...you shall remember me among the nations."

C | **The Land Is God's, And He Will Cleanse It**

God spoke to the land - the mountains, hills, rivers, valleys, even the trees - "Hear the word of the Lord GOD." He declared that He would make the entire place desolate. He would send the sword and slay all those who attended the altars of idols and strew their bodies. He would then destroy all the altars and high places. The land was God's, and He determined to cleanse it.

Ezekiel 6:14 - "So will I stretch out my hand upon them, and make the land desolate, ...in all their habitations: and they shall know that I am the LORD."

D | **The Worst Of The Heathen Shall Possess Their Houses**

The Word of the LORD said, "the end is come upon thee, ...I will pour out my fury, ...I will judge thee, ...I will recompense thee for all thine abominations, ...neither will I have pity, ...and ye shall know that I am the LORD that smiteth."

Ezekiel 7:3,8-9,21,24 - "And I will give it into the hands of the strangers for a prey, and to the wicked of the earth for a spoil; and they shall pollute it. ...Wherefore I will bring the worst of the heathen, and they shall possess their houses: ...and their holy places shall be defiled."

A | **They Shall Seek Peace, A Vision, The Law, Counsel**

The Word of the LORD came to Ezekiel, listing a catalogue of horrific woes soon to come upon Israel. Worst of all, God promised He would not hear any appeals from them. God's Spirit will not always strive with men. Seek Him now, while He will have mercy.

Ezekiel 7:18-26 - "They shall also gird themselves with sackcloth, ...My face will I turn also from them, ...and they shall seek peace, and there shall be none. ...then shall they seek a vision of the prophet; but the law shall perish from the priest, and counsel from the ancients."

B | **The Image Of Jealousy And The Chambers Of Imagery**

In a vision, God lifted up Ezekiel by the hair of the head and stood him at the north entrance of the Temple to reveal "the seat of the image of jealousy, which provoketh to jealousy." Seventy elders of Israel were burning incense to idols and abominable beasts INSIDE the Holy Temple. God was enraged! He will FURIOUSLY judge everyone who worships false gods.

Ezekiel 8:12 - "Hast thou seen what the ancients of the house of Israel do in the dark, every man in the chambers of his imagery? for they say, The LORD seeth us not."

A | Though They Cry With A Loud Voice, I Will Not Hear

The hand of the Lord GOD fell on Ezekiel in the plain. He saw a likeness of His Glory, a bright, fiery, amber-colored appearance. God brought him in a vision to the north, inner gate of Jerusalem, and showed him the seventy elders committing abominations near the place of the Glory of the LORD, and others committing idolatries and worshipping the sun. God will show His worst fury on such a crowd.

Ezekiel 8:18 - "Therefore will I also deal in fury: ...and though they cry in mine ears with a loud voice, yet will I not hear them."

A | God Marks Those Who "Sigh And Cry" Against Sin

In a vision, God told Ezekiel to gather the city rulers with their weapons. Six men came. One had a writer's inkhorn at his side. God told him to mark everyone in Jerusalem who grieved about the abominations of the people. He told the others to slay everyone who did not receive the mark. God will only save those who hate sin and grieve over it. Do you?

Ezekiel 9:4 - "Go through Jerusalem and set a mark on the foreheads of the men that sigh and cry for all the abominations that be done in the midst thereof."

B | Is Blue God's Favorite Color?

The High Priest wore a blue ephod robe and blue lace on his mitre. God prescribed blue cloth coverings for several Tabernacle furnishings. The Tabernacle entrance and the Holy of Holies entrance was one-third blue. Israelites wore blue ribbon fringes on their garments. Moses saw the Spirit of God over a blue sapphire pavement. Ezekiel saw a blue sapphire stone under the Throne. The Israeli flag is now blue on white.

Ezekiel 10:1 - "Above the head of the cherubims there appeared over them as it were a sapphire stone, as the appearance of the likeness of a throne."

B | The Living Creature And The Throne

You can get lost in the details of Ezekiel 10. The firmament, the cherubims, the Throne on a sapphire stone foundation, the glory cloud, the man in linen, the wheels, the coals of fire, the threshold of the

Temple. Ezekiel observed a complex multi-creatured living creature that forms the chariot of God's Throne, lifting up toward the East. As Judah was carried off to Babylon, God prepared to leave Jerusalem, too. This was a rare glimpse at the holiest site in the universe – God's Throne.

Ezekiel 10:20 - "This is the living creature that I saw by the river of Chebar."

A | What Happens When You Reach For The Throne?

God called the man in linen to approach the Throne of God. "Go in between the wheels, even under the cherub, and fill thine hand with coals of fire from between the cherubims." One cherub reached into the fire and handed the coals to the man. Immediately, the glory of God filled the place. When you boldly reach for the Throne, your life will be filled with the glory of God.

Ezekiel 10:3-4- "When the man went in; ...the house was filled with the cloud, and the court was full of the brightness of the LORD'S glory."

D | God Halts The Cauldron

The Spirit showed Ezekiel twenty-five men devising mischief in the East Gate of the LORD'S house. They said, "Let us build houses. Jerusalem is a cauldron, a boiling pot. Its people are the meat." God hated their murderous ways. They turned Jerusalem into a cauldron for slain flesh. Their rulers had become blood-thirsty. God vowed to bring an end to it in harsh judgment - removing them to Babylon.

Ezekiel 11:11 - "This city shall not be your caldron, neither shall ye be the flesh in the midst thereof; but I will judge you in the border of Israel."

A | Wilt Thou Make A Full End Of The Remnant?

Sometimes in our worst trials we really wonder if there will be any survivors. Ezekiel reached that point. He saw a man named Pelatiah devising mischief in the Temple. As he prophesied, Ezekiel saw Pelatiah fall dead. In shock, Ezekiel cried out, "Ah LORD God! Wilt thou make a full end of the remnant of Israel?" But God consoled him there. God will ALWAYS have a remnant. He will be their sanctuary.

Ezekiel 11:16 - "Although I have scattered them among the countries, yet will I be to them as a little sanctuary in the countries where they shall come."

D | I Will Give You The Land Of Israel

"I will put a new spirit within you; and I will take the stony heart out of their flesh, and will give them an heart of flesh: That they may walk in my statutes, ...and they shall be my people, and I will be their God." This will happen IN THE LAND OF ISRAEL. No terrorist organization or world government can prevent it.

Ezekiel 11:17 - "Thus saith the Lord GOD; I will even gather you from the people, and assemble you out of the countries where ye have been scattered, and I will give you the land of Israel."

D | Coals Of Fire And Sparkling Ice

The creatures which transport the Throne of God move like lightning. Four beryl-colored (blue-green) wheels, full of eyes, beneath four cherubim, all move and function as one. The spirit of the living creature was even in the wheels. They held up a firmament of "terrible crystal," possibly translated "sparkling ice (CEV)," with a sapphire blue pavement supporting the Throne. Below it, between the wheels were coals of fire. God's carriage appears to be a random sampling of everything He has created.

Ezekiel 11:22 - "...and the glory of the God of Israel was over them above."

B | The Throne Passes Over The Mount Of Olives

"Then did the cherubims lift up their wings, and the wheels beside them; and the glory of the God of Israel was over them above. And the glory of the LORD went up from the midst of the city, and stood upon the mountain which is on the east side of the city." This documents God's Throne passing over the Mount of Olives toward Babylon (Elam, or Chaldea; see Jeremiah 49:38).

Ezekiel 11:24 - "Afterwards the spirit took me up, and brought me in a vision by the Spirit of God into Chaldea, to them of the captivity."

C | Rebellion Causes Blindness And Deafness

Isaiah once said, "He hath shut their eyes, that they cannot see; and their hearts, that they cannot understand," 44:18. When people resist God, He hardens their hearts, blinds their eyes, and deafens their ears. Rebellion is a fatal malady. It causes you to lose all sense of God. Submit to Him now.

Ezekiel 12:1-2 - "The word of the LORD also came unto me, saying, Son of man, thou dwellest in the midst of a rebellious house, which have eyes to see, and see not; they have ears to hear, and hear not: for they are a rebellious house."

D | Ezekiel Prophesies Zedekiah's Blindness

God instructed Ezekiel to act out another pantomime to illustrate the flight from Jerusalem. He was to prepare his stuff and remove by day in their sight. "It may be they will consider, though they be a rebellious house." He was told to dig through the wall, with his face covered, so he could not see the ground. Ezekiel probably did not realize it, but he was prophesying the blindness of King Zedekiah (2 Kings 25:7).

Ezekiel 12:10,13 - "This burden concerneth the prince in Jerusalem. ...I will bring him to Babylon ...yet shall he not see it."

C | God Will Make Foolish Proverbs To Cease

It is the nature of rebellion and unbelief to deny the Truth of God's Word. God challenged the false proverbs in Israel which said, "The days are prolonged, and every vision faileth." They foolishly surmised, "The vision that he seeth is for many days to come, and he prophesieth of the times that are far off." No! God's Word will be fulfilled exactly in its time. Denial is a foolish practice.

Ezekiel 12:28 - "There shall none of my words be prolonged any more, but the word which I have spoken shall be done, saith the Lord GOD."

A | You Have Not Gone Up Into The Gaps

The false prophets in Israel said, "The LORD saith," but the LORD had not sent them. Their motives were diabolical. It is evil to promise peace when God has promised judgment. People who lie are never true intercessors. They do not have the people's best interest at heart. Only the love for Truth drives genuine intercession.

Ezekiel 13:4-5 - "O Israel, thy prophets are like the foxes in the deserts. Ye have not gone up into the gaps, neither made up the hedge for the house of Israel to stand in the battle in the day of the LORD."

C | Daubing The Wall With Untempered Morter

Never daub a broken wall with untempered morter [slime]. It cannot stand. Never prophesy with false prophecies. They fix NOTHING. False prophecies - "prophesying out of their own hearts," "seeing vain visions," "speaking lying divinations," saying "the LORD saith," when the LORD did not say; they SEDUCE the people. They love them, but they incur the wrath of God!

Ezekiel 13:14 - "So will I break down the wall that ye have daubed with untempered morter [slime], and bring it down to the ground, so that the foundation thereof shall be discovered, and it shall fall, and ye shall be consumed in the midst thereof."

B | False Prophetesses Cursed For Making Kerchiefs, Pillows

Much conjecture has arisen about the meaning of false prophetesses making kerchiefs and sewing pillows to armholes. One thing is certain. They did so to win people to themselves, instead of speaking the Truth of God. They prophesied peace when God had declared judgment. With pillows, kerchiefs and lies, they endeavored to save souls that should not live and slay souls that should not die. God cursed them.

Ezekiel 13:23 - "Therefore ye shall see no more vanity, nor divine divinations: for I will deliver my people out of your hand: and ye shall know that I am the LORD."

A | The Stumblingblock Of Their Iniquity

God said that the men of Israel had set up idols – called "stumblingblocks of their iniquity" - in their hearts. "Should I be enquired of at all by them? ...They are all estranged from me through their idols." Outrageously, they continued to inquire of the prophets! But predictably, God refused to hear them. "I will set my face against that man, ...and I will cut him off from the midst of my people." Your prayers will not be answered while idols are in your heart.

Ezekiel 14:6 - "Repent, and turn yourselves from your idols; and turn away your faces from all your abominations."

C | The LORD Deceives Compromising Prophets

God operates by principle. The people entertained idols in their heart, yet they came to the prophets for counsel. God could not allow that. He made sure the prophets deceived them. "If the prophet be deceived when he hath spoken a thing, I the LORD have deceived that prophet, and I will stretch out my hand upon him, and will destroy him." You just cannot mix sin with righteousness and win.

Ezekiel 14:10 - "They shall bear the punishment of their iniquity: the punishment of the prophet shall be even as the punishment of him that seeketh unto him."

B | Not Even Noah, Daniel Or Job Could Save Israel

"By trespassing grievously," Israel caused God to stretch out His hand upon the land. He "broke the staff of the bread," sent famine, pestilence, the sword, and "noisome beasts" to spoil the land. Amazingly, God said, "Though these three men, Noah, Daniel, and Job, were in it, they should deliver but their own souls." Lot's family could not save perverse Sodom. Neither could Noah, Daniel or Job save perverse Israel.

Ezekiel 14:18 - "Though these three men were in it, as I live, saith the Lord GOD, they shall deliver neither sons nor daughters, but they only shall be delivered themselves."

D | I Have Not Done Without Cause All That I Have Done

Again, as so often before, God paused in the midst of His great wrath to declare that He would yet save a remnant in Israel. God assured Ezekiel that "they shall comfort you, when ye see their ways and their doings: and ye shall know that I have not done without cause all that I have done in it." Proverbs 26:2 says, "The curse causeless shall not come." God curses sin and exalts righteousness for His eternal glory.

Ezekiel 14:22 - "Yet, behold, therein shall be left a remnant that shall be brought forth, both sons and daughters."

D | God Cast His Vine Tree Into The Fire

Israel was God's vineyard, but because of their sins, it was no longer of value to Him. He could do no work with it. It was not good for wooden fixtures. He decided to cast it into the fire.

Ezekiel 15:6-7 - "As the vine tree among the trees of the forest, which I have given to the fire for fuel, so will I give the inhabitants of Jerusalem. And I will set my face against them; they shall go out from one fire, and another fire shall devour them; and ye shall know that I am the LORD."

B | The Story Of How Jerusalem Was Chosen

After Moses died, Jerusalem had been the first city to attack Joshua and Israel at Gibeon. Joshua defeated them - the day the sun and moon stood still. That may be one reason why God determined to claim Jerusalem above other cities. The tribe of Judah captured Jerusalem in

Judges 1:8. Ezekiel said that God found Jerusalem as a cast-off newborn infant with its umbilical cord not yet cleaned. God took an ill-fated city and made it the choicest on earth.

Ezekiel 16:6 - "...when I passed by thee, and saw thee polluted in thine own blood, ...I said unto thee..., Live."

B | God Claimed Orphan Jerusalem From The Amorites

In Moses' day, the once-Canaanite land was ruled largely by Amorites (closely identified with Babylonians). The children of Israel met several Amorite adversaries: Og, Bashan and Sihon. Five Amorite kings, led by Adonizedec, king of Jerusalem, waged war against Joshua at Gibeon - and lost! Under pagan Amorites, God saw Jerusalem as a hopeless, cast-off, abandoned orphan, its umbilical cord not cut or cleaned. "None pitied thee... to have compassion on thee." God alone ordained greatness for Jerusalem.

Ezekiel 16:7 - "I have caused thee to multiply as the bud of the field, and thou hast increased and waxen great."

D | God Judged Jerusalem For Their Whoredoms

Jerusalem, God's beloved city, committed spiritual adultery with other nations and other gods. "Thou hast also committed fornication with the Egyptians, ...Thou hast played the whore also with the Assyrians, ...multiplied thy fornication in the land of Canaan unto Chaldea; ...thou givest thy gifts to all thy lovers." God requires His people to be separate from the rest of the world.

Ezekiel 16:37-42 - "I will gather all thy lovers, ...with all them that thou hast hated; I will even gather them round about against thee, ...and execute judgments upon thee, ...So will I make my fury toward thee to rest."

C | God Requires Faithfulness, Judges Spiritual Adultery

God prospered and made Jerusalem beautiful. "Thus wast thou decked with gold and silver; and thy raiment was of fine linen, and silk, and broidered work; thou didst eat fine flour, and honey, and oil: and thou wast exceeding beautiful, and thou didst prosper into a kingdom. ...But thou didst trust in thine own beauty, and playedst the harlot. ...a wife that committeth adultery, which taketh strangers instead of her husband!" For His love, God demands faithfulness!

Ezekiel 16:38 - "O harlot, ...I will judge thee, as women that break wedlock, ...thou shalt not commit this lewdness above all thine abominations."

B | Sisters: Jerusalem, Samaria, Sodom

God called Samaria "thine elder sister," and Sodom "thy younger sister." The sins of Sodom were pride, fullness of bread, idleness, neglecting the poor and needy, haughtiness. Moreover, they "committed abominations" (gross immoralities). But Jerusalem "wast corrupted more than they in all thy ways. ...neither hath Samaria committed half of thy sins." God said that Samaria and Sodom would someday be restored (verse 53), and Jerusalem would be ashamed that she had been worse than they. All three will be restored when Jesus returns.

Ezekiel 16:61 - "Thou shalt remember thy ways, and be ashamed, when thou shalt receive thy sisters, thine elder and thy younger."

D | The Riddle And Parable Of Two Eagles

God gave Ezekiel a riddle, or parable and interpreted it. A great eagle represented Nebuchadnezzar. He took "the highest branch of the cedar" (King Jehoiachin), cropped off the top of its young twigs (captured his princes) and carried them to Babylon. He planted the remaining seed (remnant) which grew into a vine, in covenant to Nebuchadnezzar. That vine (under Zedekiah) rebelled toward another eagle (Pharaoh) for protection from Babylon. But God sent Nebuchadnezzar to capture Pharaoh and Zedekiah. Finally, a Messianic prophecy foretells Christ planted, ruling Israel.

Ezekiel 17:23 - "In the mountain of the height of Israel will I plant it."

C | The Soul That Sinneth, It Shall Die

Israel had a proverb which said, "The fathers have eaten sour grapes, and the children's teeth are set on edge." God hates that proverb. They said, "Doth not the son bear the iniquity of the father?" God said, "No." "All souls are mine; as the soul of the father, so also the soul of the son is mine: the soul that sinneth, it shall die." Nobody goes to Hell for somebody else's sins.

Ezekiel 18:5,9 - "If a man be just, and do that which is lawful and right, ...he shall surely live, saith the Lord GOD."

B | The Definition Of A Just Man

A just man does what is lawful and right. He does not participate in idolatrous practices. He is morally upright, is not an oppressor, pays his obligations, is not violent, is benevolent, does not lend on usury or take unjust gains. He withdraws his hand from iniquity. God blesses him. The man who fails in these things will die in his sins.

Ezekiel 18:8-9 - "He that ...hath executed true judgment between man and man, Hath walked in my statutes, and hath kept my judgments, to deal truly; he is just, he shall surely live, saith the Lord GOD."

C | No So-Called "Eternal Security"

God's ways are equal. If the wicked turn from wickedness and do what is lawful and righteous, he will live. All his wickedness shall not be mentioned. But if the righteous turn from righteousness and commit iniquity, He will die in his sins. All his righteousness shall not be mentioned. There is no so-called "eternal security." If you return to your sins, you will die in them. Today's sin cancels yesterday's righteousness.

Ezekiel 18:20 - "For I have no pleasure in the death of him that dieth, saith the Lord GOD: wherefore turn yourselves, and live ye."

A | Repent, So Iniquity Shall Not Be Your Ruin

As I have mined the scriptures from Genesis to Revelation, I never cease to be amazed at the conspicuous absence of prayer in times of sin and judgment. It is something like a vitamin deficiency. In almost all cases, sickness that is caused by vitamin deficiency can be quickly remedied by administering the needed vitamin. Such is the case in times of sin and judgment. The administration of effectual, fervent prayer can quickly remedy the situation. Prayer should always be our first remedy.

Ezekiel 18:30 - "Repent, and turn yourselves from all your transgressions; so iniquity shall not be your ruin."

B | The Lioness And Her Young Lions

Ezekiel lamented the princes of Israel, "young lion whelps," born of a lioness (Israel). First, King Jehoahaz, "the nations also heard of him; he was taken in their pit, and they brought him with chains unto the land of Egypt." Next, King Jehoiakim "laid waste their cities; ...by the noise of his roaring. ...They put him in ward in chains, and brought him to the king of Babylon." Finally, the lioness was cast down.

Ezekiel 19:14 - "She is planted in the wilderness, in a dry and thirsty ground. ...she hath no strong rod to be a sceptre to rule."

A | Sin Prevents Answered Prayer

There will be times when you go to pray that God will stop you in your tracks. "The elders of Israel came to enquire of the LORD, and sat before me. Then came the word of the LORD unto me, saying, Son of man, speak unto the elders of Israel, and say unto them, ...Are ye come to enquire of me? As I live, saith the Lord GOD, I will not be enquired of by you." God requires us to confront our sins before He answers prayer.

Ezekiel 20:4 - "Cause them to know the abominations of their fathers."

C | God Saves Sinners For His Name's Sake

God made a verbose complaint against Israel, saying (in paraphrase), "I made myself known to you in Egypt and brought you out to a land flowing with milk and honey. I gave you my Law, but you despised it. You would not keep it. You rebelled again and again, provoking me to pour out my fury." Logically, God should have destroyed Israel, but He saved them to preserve His own good name.

Ezekiel 20:22 - "Nevertheless I withdrew mine hand, and wrought for my name's sake, that it should not be polluted in the sight of the heathen."

A | Bamah

Israel chose high hills, built altars to idols, made sweet savors, poured drink offerings, passed their children through the fire, and polluted themselves with abominations. God said, "What do you call this place?" They said, "Bamah" - the same high place where Balak worshipped Baal, and took Balaam (Numbers 22:41). They grossly offended the only God who could really hear them.

Ezekiel 20:31-33 - "Shall I be enquired of by you? ...As I live, saith the Lord GOD, I will not be enquired of by you. ...with a mighty hand, ...and with fury poured out, will I rule over you."

D | God Will Foil The Backsliders' Plans

Sinners erroneously presume that they can take their lives out of the hands of God and do whatever they want, forgetting that God says "all souls are mine." Although Israel persisted in gross sins and idolatries for centuries, God reminded them He would always be in control.

Ezekiel 20:32,37-38 - "That which cometh into your mind shall not be at all, that ye say, We will be as the heathen, as the families of the countries, to serve wood and stone. ...I will cause you to pass under the rod, ...and ye shall know that I am the LORD."

A | Sighing

If Jeremiah was the weeping prophet, then Ezekiel was the sighing prophet. "Sigh therefore, thou son of man, with the breaking of thy loins; and with bitterness sigh before their eyes." We should also mourn the divine judgments soon coming on this world.

Ezekiel 21:7 "When they say unto thee, Wherefore sighest thou? that thou shalt answer, For the tidings; because it cometh: and every heart shall melt, and all hands shall be feeble, and every spirit shall faint, and all knees shall be weak as water: behold, it cometh, and shall be brought to pass, saith the Lord GOD.

C | God Sends The Sword

The Word of the LORD said, "prophesy against the land of Israel, ...I am against thee, and will draw forth my sword out of his sheath, and will cut off from thee the righteous and the wicked. ...A sword is sharpened, ...to make a sore slaughter." The sword may come at the hands of men, but it is God who sends it.

Ezekiel 21:12 - "Cry and howl, son of man: for it shall be upon my people, it shall be upon all the princes of Israel: terrors by reason of the sword shall be upon my people."

D | I Will Draw My Sword And Remove Thy Diadem

The LORD told Israel, "I am against thee, and will draw forth my sword out of his sheath, and will cut off from thee the righteous and the wicked. ...from the south to the north." The prophecy called the sword of Nebuchadnezzar to Judah on his right and to the Ammonites on his left. It also called for the crown of King Zedekiah and the promotion of Gedaliah in his place.

Ezekiel 21:26 - "And thou, profane wicked prince of Israel, ...Remove the diadem, and take off the crown: ...exalt him that is low, and abase him that is high."

B | The House Of Israel Became Dross

God told the prophet to show the "bloody city" (Jerusalem) their abominations. The list was long: shedding blood, making idols, dishonoring fathers and mothers, oppressing strangers, vexing fatherless and widows, despising holy things, profaning Sabbaths, eating food offered to idols, committing lewdness, incest, adulteries, extortion, usury, forgetting God, making dishonest gain. God swore to blow them away, as dross from silver.

Ezekiel 22:18 - "The house of Israel is to me become dross: ...even the dross of silver. ...I will gather you, and blow upon you in the fire of my wrath, and ye shall be melted in the midst thereof."

B | Prophets, Priests, Princes Like Lions, Wolves Ravening Prey

God ordered Ezekiel to tell Jerusalem that there was a conspiracy of her prophets, priests and princes; like lions and wolves ravening their prey. "They have devoured souls; ...taken the treasure and precious things; ...made her many widows, ...priests have violated my law, ...profaned mine holy things, ...put no difference between the holy and profane, ...and I am profaned among them." Their leaders despised God and plundered Israel for personal gain, to their own damnation. Sounds like today.

Ezekiel 22:27 - "Her princes in the midst thereof are like wolves ravening the prey, to shed blood, and to destroy souls, to get dishonest gain."

A | Make Up The Hedge And Stand In The Gap

Men and women of God who will pray and intercede in behalf of God and men are the most precious commodity on earth. In their absence, entire nations are lost. "I sought for a man among them, that should make up the hedge, and stand in the gap before me for the land, that I should not destroy it: but I found none." Will you not **pray with me**[9] one hour?

Ezekiel 22:30-31 - "Therefore have I poured out mine indignation upon them; I have consumed them with the fire of my wrath: ...saith the Lord GOD."

D | Aholah And Aholibah - Cursed Sisters

God concluded that both Samaria (capital of the Northern Kingdom of Israel) and Jerusalem (capital of the Southern Kingdom) were both whores. Spiritual whores. God renamed Samaria, Aholah, and Jerusalem, Aholibah. Both names insinuated that they were tents or sanctuaries for idolatry and whoredom. He was incensed that instead of being sanctified unto Him, they had played the harlot with Assyria, Egypt, Babylon and other surrounding nations. Thus, they condemned themselves.

Ezekiel 23:22 - "I will raise up thy lovers against thee, from whom thy mind is alienated, and I will bring them against thee on every side."

C | You Will Eventually Hate Your Sinful Past

After Israel was polluted and vile from her whorish relationships with her illicit lovers (Assyria, Egypt, Babylon, etc.), "her mind was alienated from them." That meant "severed, dislocated, abandoned." She hated her former lovers. That is the way sin is. At some point, sin becomes repulsive, repugnant, and distasteful, and you wish you had never got involved with it. Unfortunately, you still have to pay the penalty.

Ezekiel 23:28 - "I will deliver thee into the hand of them whom thou hatest, into the hand of them from whom thy mind is alienated: And they shall deal with thee hatefully."

D | Scum And Filth In The Seething Pot

God gave Ezekiel a parable about a seething pot. Meat and bones were boiled until they were burned into scum and filth. It represented divinely-sent woes and judgment upon the "bloody city," Jerusalem, for her lies, lewdness and filth.

Ezekiel 24:12-13 - "She hath wearied herself with lies, and her great scum went not forth out of her: her scum shall be in the fire. In thy filthiness is lewdness: because I have purged thee, and thou wast not purged, thou shalt not be purged from thy filthiness any more, till I have caused my fury to rest upon thee."

A | God Can Take Away Your Desire To Pray

Prayer is a universal solution. When nothing else can change a situation, you can pray. But persistent sin can antagonize God, and He can take away your desire to pray. That is a most frightening prospect. Take great care not to exceed His longsuffering, or push God too far.

Ezekiel 24:16-17,23 - "I take away from thee the desire of thine eyes with a stroke: yet neither shalt thou mourn nor weep, neither shall thy tears run down. Forbear to cry, make no mourning for the dead, ...ye shall pine away for your iniquities, and mourn one toward another."

B | Death Of Ezekiel's Wife Symbolized Loss Of The Holy Temple

God warned Ezekiel, "I take away from thee the desire of thine eyes with a stroke." That evening, his wife died. God forbade him to mourn or weep. People asked him why, and God answered, "I will profane my sanctuary, the excellency of your strength, the desire of your eyes, ...your sons and your daughters whom ye have left shall fall by the sword. And ye shall do as I have done." Divine judgment would leave them in shock - speechless.

Ezekiel 24:24 - "Ezekiel is unto you a sign: according to all that he hath done shall ye do."

C | God Will Judge All Nations With Israel

The first twenty-four chapters of Ezekiel pronounce judgments on Israel. But in chapter twenty-five, God begins naming heathen nations that He will also judge. The whole earth is the LORD's, and He will judge every nation.

Ezekiel 25:2,11-17 - "Set thy face against the Ammonites, and prophesy against them; ...I will execute judgments upon Moab; ...I will also stretch out mine hand upon Edom, ...I will stretch out mine hand upon the Philistines, and I will cut off the Cherethims, ...they shall know that I am the LORD, when I shall lay my vengeance upon them."

B | Tyre - World Commerce Center Versus Jerusalem

Tyre consisted of a mainland community and a heavily-populated, strongly-fortressed island. Historians say that Tyre was first to navigate the Mediterranean and populate colonies on its coasts. Tyre was a world-class shipping and merchant port in ancient times, with every conceivable kind of merchandise in its stores. But they were godless pagans who gloated in the demise of Jerusalem.

Ezekiel 26:2 - "Son of man, because that Tyrus hath said against Jerusalem, Aha, she is broken that was the gates of the people: she is turned unto me: I shall be replenished, now she is laid waste."

D | The Judgment Of Tyrus (Tyre)

Ezekiel declared the Word of the LORD, "I am against thee, O Tyrus, and will cause many nations to come up against thee, as the sea causeth his waves to come up." Over many centuries, Tyre was besieged by Nebuchadnezzar, Alexander, and many renowned conquerors. In 1322, Ibn Batutah visited Tyre and found nothing but a mass of ruins, and wrote: "It was formerly proverbial for its strength, being washed on three sides by the sea. Of the ancient walls and port, traces remain."

Ezekiel 26:4 - "And they shall destroy the walls of Tyrus, and break down her towers."

C | The World At Its Best Is Condemned

The judgment of Tyre was monumental. Tyre represented the pinnacle of worldly ambition, success and prosperity. Its strategic location on the Mediterranean, its impregnable fortress, and its international shipping and commercial center made it the ancient equivalent of Wall Street and New York. No wonder its king was typecast as the earthly version of Lucifer himself. "O Tyrus, thou hast said, I am of perfect beauty. ...thy builders have perfected thy beauty."

Ezekiel 27:27 - "Thy riches, and thy fairs, thy merchandise, thy mariners, and thy pilots, ...shall fall into the midst of the seas in the day of thy ruin."

B | Important Facts About Lucifer

It is important to know that Lucifer was SINLESS when he first appeared "perfect in thy ways" in the Garden of Eden. Lucifer sinned AFTER God made the Garden of Eden. Therefore, there was no pre-Adamite world inhabited by sinful angels. All sins of men and angels began in the Garden.

Ezekiel 28:13-15 - "Thou hast been in Eden the garden of God; ...thou wast upon the holy mountain of God; ...in the midst of the stones of fire. Thou wast perfect in thy ways from the day that thou wast created, till iniquity was found in thee."

C | Men And Devils Corrupt Wisdom

Both Lucifer and men under his counsel (ironically) possess astonishing wisdom. God said of Lucifer, "Behold, thou art WISER THAN DANIEL; there is no secret that they can hide from thee: With thy wisdom and with thine understanding thou hast gotten thee riches. ...thou sealest up the sum, FULL OF WISDOM." But "THOU HAST CORRUPTED THY WISDOM by reason of thy brightness." Men and devils pervert wisdom (remember Solomon's decline). Tenaciously hold divine wisdom in sacred safe-keeping.

Ezekiel 28:16 - "Thou hast sinned: therefore I will cast thee as profane out of the mountain of God: and I will destroy thee, O covering cherub."

D | **The King Of Tyre Mirrored Lucifer**

The arrogance of the King of Tyre mirrored that of Lucifer. Ezekiel prophesied curses on both the mortal king and Lucifer. Some of these prophecies could only apply to the man Tyrus: "...thou shalt be a man, and no God, in the hand of him that slayeth thee." Other prophecies could only apply to Luficer. "Thou hast been in Eden the garden of God; every precious stone was thy covering." Some addressed both.

Ezekiel 28:17 - "Thine heart was lifted up because of thy beauty, thou hast corrupted thy wisdom by reason of thy brightness: I will cast thee to the ground."

B | **A Snapshot Of Tyre**

The luxurious Mediterranean island-city had everything. World-class pilots and mariners operated ships of fine firs, oak and cedars, some with ivory benches. Its fairs traded in mercenary soldiers, horsemen, slaves, military equipment, shields, helmets, chariot uniforms, horses, mules, lambs, rams, goats, precious stones, emeralds, coral, agate, ivory, ebony, gold, silver, brass, bright iron, tin, lead, fine linens, embroidered linens, cedar chests, wine, wool, spices, wheat, honey, oil, balm and more. But God condemned it all for sinning against Israel. Ancient Tyre is now in ruins.

Ezekiel 28:19 - "Thou shalt be a terror, and never shalt be any more."

D | **No More Pricking Brier Or Grieving Thorn Around Israel**

Isaiah declared the Word of the LORD against Tyre and Sidon. "Who would set the briers and thorns against me in battle? I would go through them, I would burn them together." Ezekiel identified Tyre and Sidon as briers and thorns that God would judge. In the last days, when Israel is fully restored to the Promised Land, these antagonists will no longer torment Israel.

Ezekiel 28:24 - "And there shall be no more a pricking brier unto the house of Israel, nor any grieving thorn of all that are round about them, that despised them; and they shall know that I am the Lord GOD."

B | **Egypt Faces Ruin By God's Decree**

Ezekiel spent four full chapters prophesying against Egypt, the first and greatest empire on earth. Egypt resisted Jehovah, although God dealt severely with them many times. Abraham, Joseph and Moses all made profound impressions upon Egypt in their days. Joseph literally saved

Pharaoh and Egypt from ruin by the Word of the LORD, and Moses demonstrated the greatest miracles ever in Pharaoh's presence. Still, the Pharaohs never truly worshipped God, but instead, declared themselves deities.

Ezekiel 29:2 - "Son of man, set thy face against Pharaoh king of Egypt, and prophesy against him, and against all Egypt."

D | Pharaoh - Dragon In The Midst Of The River

The Egyptians greatly feared the crocodiles that infested the Nile River. Crocodiles can attack and kill humans swiftly without warning. In ridiculous arrogance, each Pharaoh blasphemously claimed to be the Dragon-God of the Nile, infuriating God.

Ezekiel 29:3-5 - "Thus saith the Lord GOD; Behold, I am against thee, Pharaoh king of Egypt, the great dragon that lieth in the midst of his rivers, which hath said, My river is mine own, and I have made it for myself. ...I will bring thee up out of the midst of thy rivers, ...I will leave thee thrown into the wilderness."

D | Egypt Shall Be Desolate

Egypt is larger than Texas and California combined, yet it is a desolate place. 99% of its population of 76 million lives on 5% of its land, along the banks of the Nile. Prophecy fulfilled.

Ezekiel 29:9-10 - "And the land of Egypt shall be desolate and waste; and they shall know that I am the LORD: because he hath said, The river is mine, and I have made it. Behold, therefore I am against thee, ...and I will make the land of Egypt utterly waste and desolate, from the tower of Syene even unto the border of Ethiopia."

C | God Sometimes Scatters Those Who Anger Him

At the tower of Babel, God confounded the languages of the people, thereby dividing the people. But since that time, God has used other methods to divide an evil society. After Israel exhausted His longsuffering, He scattered them from their land to other lands. Three times in the book of Ezekiel, God promised to scatter the Egyptians for their evil ways. Many people believe that is why millions of Egyptians were sold into slavery in the centuries that followed.

Ezekiel 29:12;30:26 - "I will scatter the Egyptians among the nations, and will disperse them through the countries."

C | God Rules All Empires

The nations of this world are pawns on God's chessboard. Jeremiah (43:10-3; 44:30) and Ezekiel (29) emphatically prophesied the fall of Egypt and Pharaoh to Nebuchadnezzar and the Babylonians. "He shall smite the land of Egypt." Adam Clark's Commentary refers to the ancient writings of Herodotus in "Euterpe" for documentation that Pharaoh was greatly weakened by one of his generals, Amasis, forcing Pharaoh into exile. Nebuchadnezzar quickly moved on this unstable situation, and took control of Egypt. God rules all empires.

Ezekiel 29:19 - "I will give the land of Egypt unto Nebuchadrezzar king of Babylon."

B | The Tower Of Syene = Migdol To Syene

God pronounced desolations "from the tower of Syene even unto the border of Ethiopia." The prophecy seemed to refer only to Syene (modern Aswan) in extreme southern Egypt, near Ethiopia. But "tower" came from the Hebrew word "Migdol." That makes a big difference. Migdol was a huge gate at Medinet Habu, near Luxor (ancient Thebes), in the heart of central Egypt. Therefore, the prophecy cursed the entire southern half of Egypt.

Ezekiel 30:6 - "...the pride of her power shall come down: from the tower [Migdol to] Syene shall they fall in it by the sword, saith the Lord GOD."

C | Self-Proclaimed Deities Succumb To The One True God

Almighty God called an end to the Pharaohs' dynasties. For centuries, Pharaohs ruled Egypt, the most powerful nation on earth. God ended that. First, He called in Nebuchadnezzar with the sword to "take away her multitude, and her foundations shall be broken down. ...and there shall be no more a prince of the land of Egypt: and I will put a fear in the land of Egypt." When Babylon fell, the Persians conquered Egypt. Egypt never again attained its former power.

Ezekiel 30:19 "Thus will I execute judgments in Egypt: and they shall know that I am the LORD."

D | As Assyria Fell Like A Great Cedar, So Would Egypt

The prophecies against Egypt said, "It shall be the basest of the kingdoms; neither shall it exalt itself any more above the nations: for I will diminish them, that they shall no more rule over the nations," Ezekiel 29:14-15. Egypt would fall like the great Assyrian Empire, which was once like a great cedar, envied by the trees of the forest. Assyria fell to Babylon, as Egypt soon would.

Ezekiel 31:18 - "To whom art thou thus like in glory and in greatness among the trees? ...This is Pharaoh and all his multitude, saith the Lord GOD."

C | Evil Nations Accompany Each Other To The Grave

God instructed Ezekiel to pronounce lamentations over the downfall of Pharaoh and Egypt. Though Pharaoh was like a lion, or a great sea monster, God promised to catch him and all of Egypt in a net and give them to the fouls of heaven. Kings and nations would be aghast at Egypt's downfall. Egypt would take its place among other great but fallen nations: Asshur, Elam, Meshech, Tubal, Edom, Zidon, and others.

Ezekiel 32:23 - "Her company is round about her grave: all of them slain, fallen by the sword, which caused terror in the land of the living."

B | The Watchman's Solemn Responsibilities

God spoke forcefully about the solemn responsibilities of a watchman. "I have set thee a watchman unto the house of Israel; therefore thou shalt hear the word at my mouth, and warn them from me." Men of God in every generation must fulfill their sacred duty to warn people of God's judgments. All men must heed divine warnings, but preachers who fail to declare those warnings will be punished.

Ezekiel 33:6 - "If the watchman see the sword come, and blow not the trumpet, and the people be not warned; ...his blood will I require at the watchman's hand."

C | Watchman, How Should We Then Live?

The sacred, solemn role of a watchman is necessitated by the fact that the righteous will be rewarded, and the wicked will be punished. If there were no consequences for our living, we should need no warnings, no watchman. But "if our transgressions and our sins be upon us, ...how should we then live?"

Ezekiel 33:11 - "Say unto them, As I live, saith the Lord GOD, I have no pleasure in the death of the wicked; but that the wicked turn from his way and live: turn ye, turn ye from your evil ways; for why will ye die?"

B | The Chronicles Of Ezekiel

Most readers would quickly skim over the numerous references that Ezekiel gives to the exact years, months, and days in which certain prophecies and events took place. But the specific dates Ezekiel provided in chapters 1,8,20,24,26,29,30,31,32, and 33 provide scholars with enormous abilities to accurately know when major historical events took place. Nothing is incidental with God.

Ezekiel 33:21 - "And it came to pass in the twelfth year of our captivity, in the tenth month, in the fifth day of the month, that one that had escaped out of Jerusalem came unto me, saying, The city is smitten."

D | The Tragic Consequences Of Breaking Covenant

Jews who escaped the final capture of Jerusalem argued that Abraham inherited the land, so it was theirs. Ezekiel retorted that they worshipped idols, shed blood, worked abominations, and committed adulteries. "SHALL YE POSSESS THE LAND?" But they deafly ignored Ezekiel's solemn warnings.

Ezekiel 33:32-33 - "Thou art unto them as a very lovely song of one that hath a pleasant voice, and can play well on an instrument: for they hear thy words, but they do them not. And when this cometh to pass, (lo, it will come,) then shall they know that a prophet hath been among them."

B | The Great Shepherd Takes Flock From Evil Shepherds

God scourged the evil shepherds for feeding themselves instead of the flock, eating the fat, clothing themselves with their wool, neglecting the diseased, and abandoning the lost. "I am against the shepherds; ...I will deliver my flock from their mouth, that they may not be meat for them." "I will seek that which was lost, and bring again that which was driven away, and will bind up that which was broken, and will strengthen that which was sick."

Ezekiel 34:14 - "I will feed them in a good pasture, and upon the high mountains of Israel shall their fold be."

D | David In The Millennium

Ezekiel foresaw into the Millennium, that a magnificent recreated Israel will span the ancient Holy Land, encompassing every square mile originally promised to the patriarchs. Jerusalem will be larger and more glorious than at any time before. Jesus will reign on earth as King of

Kings. Under Christ, many righteous kings will rule the earth. In Israel, David will return to the Throne, as a prince under Christ.

Ezekiel 34:24 - "And I the LORD will be their God, and my servant David a prince among them; I the LORD have spoken it."

D | Mount Seir Shall Be Desolate

The history of Mount Seir traces back to Deuteronomy, when Moses explicitly designated that the sons of Esau were to possess it. Israel was never to take it from them. Notwithstanding, the people of Mount Seir hated Israel for many centuries. Finally, God cursed the place. That entire region around Petra has been desolate for about 2000 years. "Because thou hast had a perpetual hatred, and hast shed the blood of the children of Israel..."

Ezekiel 35:9 - "I will make thee perpetual desolations, and thy cities shall not return: and ye shall know that I am the LORD."

A | God Hears Everything You Say

God not only hears your prayers, but also every word you speak. If you pray, God hears you. But if you blaspheme, He hears that, too. God pronounced curses upon the people of Mount Seir because they blasphemed the house of Israel. Guard your mouth and your lips. Anything you say can be held against you.

Ezekiel 35:12-15 - "I have heard all thy blasphemies which thou hast spoken against the mountains of Israel, ...with your mouth ye have boasted against me, and have multiplied your words against me: I have heard them. ...I will make thee desolate. ...O mount Seir."

C | The Chosen Land Is Witness To God's Great Plan

God's chosen Holy Land outlasts generations of saints and sinners. He promised to avenge the LAND of the enemies who desecrated it with abominations and made it desolate. "Thus saith the Lord GOD to the mountains, and to the hills, to the rivers, and to the valleys, to the desolate wastes, and to the cities that are forsaken."

Ezekiel 36:8,12 - "O mountains of Israel, ye shall shoot forth your branches, and yield your fruit to my people of Israel; for they are at hand to come. ...I will cause men to walk upon you, even my people Israel."

C | God Has Pity For His Own Holy Name

God saves us, not because we are good, but because He is. "I had pity for mine holy name. ...I do not this for your sakes, O house of Israel, but for mine holy name's sake, which ye have profaned among the heathen. ...I will... gather you out of all countries, and will bring you into your own land."

Ezekiel 36:25 - "Then will I sprinkle clean water upon you, and ye shall be clean: ...A new heart also will I give you, and a new spirit will I put within you: ......and cause you to walk in my statutes."

D | Israel Will Be Like The Garden Of Eden

After Jesus defeats all His enemies at Armageddon, Israel will become a paradise on earth. Its borders will extend beyond its historical boundaries, fulfilling the ancient Abrahamic covenant - from the Euphrates to the Nile River. God will have forgiven all Israel's sins, and multitudes of Jews will live throughout the land.

Ezekiel 36:33,35 - "In the day that I shall have cleansed you from all your iniquities I will also cause you to dwell in the cities, and the wastes shall be builded,...And they shall say, This land that was desolate is become like the garden of Eden."

A | Then Will I Be Enquired Of By You

Although God harshly refused to be enquired of by Israel during the days of Jeremiah and Ezekiel, He promised the day would come when Israel would be restored to their land, and He would again be enquired of by them. Our God is a God of second chances. By His grace, we have hope!

Ezekiel 36:36-38 - "I will yet for this be enquired of by the house of Israel, to do it for them; I will increase them with men like a flock. As the holy flock, ...and they shall know that I am the LORD."

B | The Valley Of Dry Bones

In the context of the entire book of Ezekiel, the valley of dry bones is the logical conclusion to Israel, following a litany of divine scourges, curses and punishments. All of it came about because of Israel's incorrigible, sinful ways. But again, as so many times before, Almighty God cannot, will not utterly forget His people. He called the prophet.

Ezekiel 37:4-5 - "He said unto me, Prophesy upon these bones, and say unto them, O ye dry bones, hear the word of the LORD. ...Behold, I will cause breath to enter into you, and ye shall live."

A | **Speak To The Dry Bones**

Here is an incomparable word-picture! A valley full of dry bones. The LORD asked Ezekiel, "Can these bones live?" He replied, "LORD, thou knowest!" "Prophesy upon these bones - 'hear the word of the LORD'." God's Word can raise up an army from a field of dry bones. Jeremiah said that God's Word is like fire in a man's bones. Look at your valley. What needs resurrecting? Speak the Word of the Lord to it.

Ezekiel 37:5 - "Thus saith the Lord GOD unto these bones; Behold, I will cause breath to enter into you, and ye shall live."

A | **Say To The Wind, "Breathe Upon These Slain"**

The power of the spoken word is inestimable when God says "speak." In a vision, Ezekiel prophesied to a valley full of dry bones, and they all came together, and sinews of flesh came upon them. The LORD said, "Say to the wind, Thus saith the Lord GOD; Come from the four winds, O breath, and breathe upon these slain, that they may live." When God says speak, SPEAK!

Ezekiel 37:10 - "So I prophesied as he commanded me, and the breath came into them, and they lived, and stood up upon their feet, an exceeding great army."

D | **Jesus Will Resurrect All Of Israel**

In a vision, Ezekiel prophesied unto a valley of dry bones. They all came together and came to life as a mighty army. That prophecy was symbolically fulfilled in 1948 when the State of Israel again became a sovereign nation after 2500 years in exile. Still, more literally, Jesus will return and resurrect all Jews, and return them all to the Promised Land.

Ezekiel 37:11-12 - "These bones are the whole house of Israel: ...O my people, I will open your graves, and cause you to come up out of your graves, and bring you into the land of Israel."

B | **Israel Will Be Born Again**

Jesus will resurrect all Israel from the dead. "...they shall look upon me whom they have pierced," Zechariah 12:10. "So all Israel shall be saved: as it is written, There shall come out of Sion the Deliverer, ...this is my covenant unto them, when I shall take away their sins," Romans 11:26-27. They will repent, confess that Jesus is LORD, and be filled with His Spirit.

Ezekiel 37:13-14 - "Ye shall know that I am the LORD, when I have opened your graves, O my people, ...And shall put my spirit in you, and ye shall live."

D | One Stick

Every Jew who ever lived will be resurrected from the grave and brought to Israel. Tribal roots and genealogical lineage will be easily traceable. Under the Kingship and Lordship of Jesus Christ, Israel will become one undivided nation.

Ezekiel 37:16-20 - "Son of man, take thee one stick, ...For Judah, ...then take another stick, and write upon it, For Joseph, the stick of Ephraim ...And join them one to another into one stick; ...Behold, I will take the stick of Joseph, ...and will put them with him, even with the stick of Judah, and make them one stick."

C | Restoration

Nobody can heal and restore like Jesus. The nation that was torn from its homeland and scattered to the four corners of the earth for thousands of years will miraculously come together and be healed. Despite its long history of profound divisions and schisms, Israel will be a single, unified nation in that day.

Ezekiel 37:22 - "I will make them one nation in the land upon the mountains of Israel; and one king shall be king to them all: and they shall be no more two nations, neither shall they be divided into two kingdoms any more at all."

C | Perfect Compliance With His Statutes

During the Millennium, Jesus Christ will ascertain that Israel will keep His statutes. Although Israel committed every conceivable breach against God throughout its history, this will be 1000 years of perfect compliance.

Ezekiel 37:23 - "Neither shall they defile themselves any more with their idols, nor with their detestable things, nor with any of their transgressions: but I will save them out of all their dwellingplaces, wherein they have sinned, and will cleanse them: so shall they be my people, and I will be their God. ...they shall also walk in my judgments, and observe my statutes, and do them."

B | The Throne Of David Under Christ

Jesus, King of Kings, will rule from His Throne in His new Temple at Jerusalem during the Millennium. His saints will rule cities, states and nations as kings and priests under Him (Revelation 5:10). David will rule in Jerusalem, as the King of Israel, and as a Prince under Christ.

Ezekiel 37:24-25 - "David my servant shall be king over them; and they all shall have one shepherd: And they shall dwell in the land that I have given unto Jacob my servant, wherein your fathers have dwelt; ...and my servant David shall be their prince for ever."

C | For Evermore

Revelation 20 reveals that Messiah will rule the world from Jerusalem for 1000 years. Afterward, the old heavens and earth will be dissolved (2 Peter 3:10-12; Matthew 24:35; Daniel 7:14). The wicked will be judged at the White Throne and sent to Hell. The righteous will then enter Heaven for eternity. "The Lord God Almighty and the Lamb are the temple of it," Revelation 21:22. Ezekiel's "Millennium" prophecies extended to "for evermore."

Ezekiel 37:25-28 - "David shall be their prince for ever, ..they shall dwell therein, ...forever; ......my sanctuary shall be in the midst of them for evermore."

B | The Tabernacle In The Millennium

The millennial Tabernacle is not the sanctuary. The sanctuary refers to the Temple. But the Tabernacle will be a vast covered pavilion in Jerusalem, built to protect visitors - "...a tabernacle for a shadow in the daytime from the heat, and for a place of refuge, ...a covert from storm and from rain," Isaiah 4:6. In an even larger sense, Messiah is the Tabernacle. "The tabernacle of God is with men, and he will dwell with them," Revelation 21:3.

Ezekiel 37:27 - "My tabernacle also shall be with them: ...I will be their God, ...they shall be my people."

D | Messiah Will Build The Millennial Sanctuary

The third Temple will be built during the first half of the last seven years. The Antichrist will commit the Abomination of Desolation there. That will NOT be the millennial Temple. Jesus will build a new Temple for His 1000-year reign. "Even he shall build the temple of the LORD; and he shall bear the glory, and shall sit and rule upon his throne," Zechariah 6:13, for as long as time shall be.

Ezekiel 37:28 - "The heathen shall know that I the LORD do sanctify Israel, when my sanctuary shall be in the midst of them for evermore."

B | Gog, Magog, Meschech, Tubal

Ezekiel prophesied against Gog, the land of Magog, "the chief prince of Meshech and Tubal." "Gog" comes from the Hebrew "nesi rosh," or "leader." Josephus said that Gog was Scythia (southern Russia and Georgia). Descendants of Meshech and Tubal, sons of Japheth, settled near the Black Sea (Meskhiti mountains, Meskhi tribes) now Tbilisi, Georgia. Many Georgians claim to be descendants of Meshech. **See a full explanation.**[10]

Ezekiel 38:2 - "Son of man, set thy face against Gog, the land of Magog, the chief prince of Meshech and Tubal, and prophesy against him."

C | God Knows The End From The Beginning

Isaiah said that God declares the end from the beginning. That proves that He KNOWS the end already - every detail. We should be very impressed that, 2500 years ago, God revealed that Russia (Gog, Magog) would lead a coalition of nations against Israel at Armageddon through Georgia (Meshech and Tubal). In 2009, Russia forcefully took control of two of Georgia's northern provinces - South Ossetia and Abkhazia. They are already staging the battle of Armageddon.

Ezekiel 38:4 - "And I will ...put hooks into thy jaws, and I will bring thee forth, and all thine army."

D | The Armageddon Coalition: Russia, Iran, Ethiopia, Libya, Turkey

Russia will descend on Israel at Armageddon with a coalition of nations. Gomer and Togarmah is modern Turkey. Persia is modern Iran. "Be thou a guard unto them." Russia defends Iran at the UN. Russia builds up Iran's military and nuclear programs. These nations will precipitate **Israel's worst nightmare ever.**[11]

Ezekiel 38:5-7 - "Persia, Ethiopia, and Libya with them; all of them with shield and helmet: Gomer, and all his bands; the house of Togarmah of the north quarters, and all his bands: and many people with thee. Be thou prepared, ...and be thou a guard unto them."

D | Russia And Iran Will Invade Israel, Starting Armageddon

It could hardly be stated any more clearly in an ancient prophecy. "In the latter years thou shalt come into the land that is brought back from the sword, and is gathered out of many people, against the mountains of Israel, which have been always waste: but it is brought forth out of the nations." Gog (Russia) and Persia (Iran) will invade Israel in this run-up to Armageddon.

Ezekiel 38:9 - "Thou shalt ascend and come like a storm, thou shalt be like a cloud to cover the land, thou, and all thy bands, and many people with thee."

B | The Spoil - The Hook

God said He would put a hook in the jaw of Gog (Russia) to draw them to Armageddon. Iran and Syria are major client states of Russia, but Russia wants Palestine as its client, also. The terrorists in that region (Iranian Guard, Hezbollah and Hamas) are already supplied by Russia. The theft of the Promised Land - Palestine - and dominance in the Middle East, is the spoil, the hook.

Ezekiel 38:10 - "Thou shalt think an evil thought: And thou shalt say, I will go up to the land of unwalled villages; ...To take a spoil, and to take a prey."

D | Saudi Arabia Objects To Russian Invasion

When Russia, Iran, and their coalition nations come against Israel for the battle of Armageddon, Saudi Arabia (Ancient Sheba and Dedan) will verbally challenge them, but do nothing to stop them. Why? Saudi Arabia verbally pretends to be a Mideast peacemaker on the world stage, while stealthily perpetrating a deleterious Muslim agenda against Israel. See **"Roadmap For Peace"**[12] for details.

Ezekiel 38:13 - "Sheba, and Dedan, and the merchants of Tarshish, with all the young lions thereof, shall say unto thee, Art thou come to take a spoil? hast thou gathered thy company to take a prey?"

C | Checkmate

In the game of chess, "checkmate" occurs when one player's "King" is under direct attack and cannot avoid being captured. Since the Garden of Eden, God has planned the capture of the Prince of this World. When Russia and its cohorts descend on Israel, Jesus will come, and all kings and kingdoms will fall to Him. Checkmate.

Ezekiel 38:18,23 - "When Gog shall come against the land of Israel, ...my fury shall come up in my face. ...and I will be known in the eyes of many nations, and they shall know that I am the LORD."

B | Communist Russia - Aggressor At Armageddon

Communism was created largely by Cabalistic Jews. Karl Marx and his "Communist Manifesto" ascended amidst "The League of Just Men" and the "Jacobins," secret orders evolved from ancient Talmudic-Babylonian-Freemasonic-Illuminati societies. Communism would utterly enslave mankind to the New World Order. 20th-Century Russia (Gog) suffered Communism's blood-lust - the very evil that will assault Israel at Armageddon. God vows to destroy them.

Ezekiel 39:3-4 - "I will smite thy bow out of thy left hand, and will cause thine arrows to fall out of thy right hand. Thou shalt fall upon the mountains of Israel."

C | All Men Will Know The LORD After Armageddon

At Armageddon, Almighty God will finally unleash all His fury and settle His differences with His enemies once and for all. When He is done, ALL His enemies will be vanquished for 1000 years.

Ezekiel 39:7-8 - "So will I make my holy name known in the midst of my people Israel; and I will not let them pollute my holy name any more: and the heathen shall know that I am the LORD, the Holy One in Israel. Behold, it is come, and it is done, saith the Lord GOD; this is the day whereof I have spoken."

D | The Supper Of The Great God

Vultures and beasts will feast on the war dead at Armageddon (while the saints of God begin feasting in Jerusalem at the marriage supper of the Lamb). In Revelation 19, John called it "the supper of the great God." "I will give thee unto the ravenous birds of every sort, and to the beasts of the field to be devoured."

Ezekiel 39:18,20 - "Ye shall eat the flesh of the mighty, and drink the blood of the princes of the earth, ...Thus ye shall be filled at my table ...with all men of war, saith the Lord GOD."

C | Even The Heathen Understand That Israel Is Being Punished

People live in denial of infallible Truth, but it does not pay to lie to yourself. If you sin against God, be sure your sins will find you out. Israel deceived themselves into thinking they could prosper while in rebellion against God. But anybody in their right mind knows better than that.

Ezekiel 39:23 - "And the heathen shall know that the house of Israel went into captivity for their iniquity: because they trespassed against me, therefore hid I my face from them, and gave them into the hand of their enemies: so fell they all by the sword."

A | **Neither Will I Hide My Face Any More From Them**

God has complete sovereignty over who He will bless or curse, and when He will hear a people's prayers. After centuries of unrepented sins, God stopped listening to Israel. But in the coming restoration, God promises to hear and bless.

Ezekiel 39:28-29 - "Then shall they know that I am the LORD their God, which caused them to be led into captivity among the heathen: but I have gathered them unto their own land, ...Neither will I hide my face any more from them: for I have poured out my spirit upon the house of Israel, saith the Lord GOD."

B | **The Face Of God Will Be Revealed**

At first reading, it appeared that God was reassuring Israel that He would no longer refuse to hear their prayers. But there was much more meaning in His promise. When God said, "Neither will I hide my face any more from them," He promised that for evermore, Israel would be able to SEE the FACE of GOD - something they could not do in Old Testament days. They will see the face of God in JESUS CHRIST.

Ezekiel 39:28-29 - "Then shall they know that I am the LORD their God, ...Neither will I hide my face any more from them."

B | **Ezekiel's Vision Of The Future Temple Mount**

In Babylon, Ezekiel received a vision of the Jerusalem during the Millennium under Messiah, Jesus Christ. He stood on a high mountain (probably Zion) while a man who shone like brass measured everything with a line of flax for cubits (roughly two feet), and a ten-foot reed for longer measurements. **Here is one artist's concept.**[13]

Ezekiel 40:4 - "And the man said unto me, Son of man, behold with thine eyes, and hear with thine ears, and set thine heart upon all that I shall shew thee; ...declare all that thou seest to the house of Israel."

A | **Ministering To The LORD In The Millennial Temple**

Beginning in chapter 40, Ezekiel describes in great detail all the features of the city of Jerusalem and the new Temple, built by Christ for His glorious thousand-year rule on earth. In that Temple, certain priests will directly minister to Jesus Christ.

Ezekiel 40:46-47 - "The chamber whose prospect is toward the north is for the priests, the keepers of the charge of the altar: these are the sons of Zadok among the sons of Levi, which come near to the LORD to minister unto him. So he measured the court, ...and the altar that was before the house."

C | **God Retains Creative Control Over His Dwellingplace**

God does not leave it to mortal men to design His dwelling place. He meticulously defined the millennial Temple Mount in great detail: the house, building, gates, porches, steps, chambers, posts, courts, windows, arches, pavements, ornaments, tables, altars and more. Everything strongly resembled the original Temple as described in 1 Kings 6 and 2 Chronicles 4.

Ezekiel 40:49 - "The length of the porch was twenty cubits, and the breadth eleven cubits; and he brought me by the steps whereby they went up to it: and there were pillars by the posts, one on this side, and another on that side."

B | **Measurements Of The Millennial Temple**

The messenger in the vision showed Ezekiel the future Temple in which Jesus Christ will rule for 1000 years. He measured the posts, the doors, the most holy place, the walls, surrounding chambers, windows, galleries, porches, and the height and thickness of the walls. The Temple will be 70x100 cubits (roughly 140x200 feet) inside a walled courtyard that will be about 200 feet wide.

Ezekiel 41:1,4 - "Afterward he brought me to the temple, ...he measured the length thereof, twenty cubits; and the breadth, twenty cubits, before the temple: and he said unto me, This is the most holy place."

D | **The Man And The Young Lion In The Temple**

Ezekiel described the doors, posts, windows, galleries (three stories high), and wooden ceilings of the Temple. Above the doors and walls were ornamental cherubims and palm trees. Every cherubim had two faces - a man and a young lion. Was that a symbol of the man Jesus, lion of Judah?

Ezekiel 41:18-19 - "A palm tree was between a cherub and a cherub; and every cherub had two faces; so that the face of a man was toward the palm tree on the one side, and the face of a young lion toward the palm tree on the other side."

C | The Separate Place

Seven times, Ezekiel spoke of "the separate place." This was a large marginal area - a free space - that separated the Temple proper from the remaining chambers and structures. In spiritual terms, it reminds us that we should have a clear distance between the holy things in our lives and the profane things of this world.

Ezekiel 42:1-2 - "And he brought me into the chamber that was over against the separate place, and which was before the building toward the north. Before the length of an hundred cubits was the north door, and the breadth was fifty cubits."

A | Priests Approach The LORD In The Millennial Temple

It is not for us to contradict the divine purpose of Christ sitting in the Holy Place of the millennial Temple. Priests will minister to Him there, where the Ark of the Covenant might have been. Jesus is now the Ark of the Covenant.

Ezekiel 42:13 - "The north chambers and the south chambers, ...they be holy chambers, where the priests that approach unto the LORD shall eat the most holy things: there shall they lay the most holy things, and the meat offering, and the sin offering, and the trespass offering; for the place is holy."

D | The Enlarged Temple Mount - One Mile Square

Ezekiel reported that the outer court of the millennial Temple will be 500 reeds (5000 feet) square - almost one mile square. Early versions, including the Septuagint, have no word for reed, leading some scholars to argue that it should instead read 500 cubits, or about 1000 feet square, but it is not unreasonable to envision the entire Temple Mount site expanded to one mile square. The Temple Mount is presently about 1000x1500 feet.

Ezekiel 42:20 - "He measured it by the four sides: ...five hundred reeds long, and five hundred broad, to make a separation between the sanctuary and the profane place."

B | The Earth Will Shine When Jesus Comes From The East

The glory of God came to the first Temple when Solomon dedicated it. Isaiah saw God sitting high on His Throne in the Temple. God abandoned Jerusalem when He gave it to the Babylonians. Ezekiel saw the cherubims remove the Throne from the Temple across the Mount Olivet to the east. But Jesus will bring the glory AND the Throne back to Jerusalem for 1000 years.

Ezekiel 43:2 - "The glory of the God of Israel came from the way of the east: and his voice was like a noise of many waters: and the earth shined with his glory."

D | Bowing Down When Jesus Returns

In a vision, Ezekiel stood in the Eastern Gate of the Temple Mount. "Behold, the glory of the God of Israel came from the way of the east: and his voice was like a noise of many waters: and the earth shined with his glory. ...and I fell upon my face." Every born-again believer will be there, bowing down, when Jesus returns through the Eastern Gate.

Ezekiel 43:4-5 - "The glory of the LORD came into the house by the way of the gate whose prospect is toward the east. ...the glory of the LORD filled the house."

C | The LORD, His Throne, His Name Never Again Defiled

Ezekiel heard the LORD speaking to him out of the Temple, saying, "Son of man, the place of my throne, and the place of the soles of my feet, where I will dwell in the midst of the children of Israel for ever, and my holy name, shall the house of Israel no more defile, neither they, nor their kings." NEVER again will the name of the LORD (Jesus Christ) or His house be defiled or profaned. Jesus' 1000-year reign will be completely glorious.

Ezekiel 43:9 - "...and I will dwell in the midst of them for ever."

C | God's Great Plan Should Shame Us For Transgressing

As God revealed His plan for the glorious future Temple Mount to Ezekiel, He instructed him to show the whole form and fashion of it to all Israel, "that they may be ashamed of their iniquities, ...that they may keep the whole form thereof, and all the ordinances thereof, and do them." If we could see the glorious future that God has planned for the righteous, we would be ashamed that we ever transgressed against Him.

Ezekiel 43:10 - "Thou son of man, shew the house to the house of Israel, that they may be ashamed of their iniquities."

D | Israel Will Keep Ordinances During The Millennium

It is difficult for Christians to understand why Jews will be required to keep ordinances during the Millennium. Israel will observe and practice many laws, including making sacrifices and offerings in the Temple. Keeping ordinances will not save them. Jesus will have saved them already. It will apparently be to honor the LORD and to teach them the powerful doctrines they failed to learn in the past.

Ezekiel 43:11 - "If they be ashamed of all that they have done, ...write it in their sight, that they may keep the whole form thereof, and all the ordinances thereof, and do them."

C | The Law Of The House - The Most Holy Mountain

Six times, Ezekiel beheld the glory of the LORD and fell on his face. Nowadays, multitudes stand for hours in "St. Peter's Square" in Rome to see the false prophet, the Pope. But in the Millennium, the Temple Mount will be the viewing place to see Jesus Christ. Mount Moriah will be the most holy site on earth. God calls it "the law of the house."

Ezekiel 43:12 - "This is the law of the house; Upon the top of the mountain the whole limit thereof round about shall be most holy. Behold, this is the law of the house."

B | The Millennial Altar

Christians should not recoil at this fact. Jews must offer blood sacrifices on the altar in the millennial Temple. Yes, Jesus' blood is the ONLY BLOOD that can cleanse our sins. But Israel failed to learn that. They never believed the animal sacrifices symbolized the Lamb of God, Jesus Christ. So, for 1000 years, they must offer sacrifices IN HIS PRESENCE.

Ezekiel 43:18-19,27 - "Thus saith the Lord GOD; These are the ordinances of the altar in the day when they shall make it, to offer burnt offerings thereon, and to sprinkle blood thereon. ...for a sin offering."

D | The Eastern Temple Gate Will Open Only On Sabbaths

In the vision, Ezekiel saw that the eastern gate of the new millennial Temple was shut. For hundreds of years, the eastern gate on the Jerusalem wall has been closed. An earthquake will open it at Armageddon. Christ will enter Jerusalem right there. But the Temple gate is a different gate, which will be closed, except on Sabbath days, for people to behold Jesus Christ.

Ezekiel 44:2 - "This gate shall be shut, ...and no man shall enter in by it; because the LORD, the God of Israel, hath entered in by it, therefore it shall be shut."

B | David Will Have Daily Meals With Jesus Christ

David, the prince of Jerusalem, will be the only person to use the eastern gate of the Temple for six days each week. The prince will sit and eat with Jesus Christ regularly. On Sabbath days, that gate will open for public audiences with Jesus. Unsanctified or uncircumcised mortals who survive Armageddon will never enter the sanctuary (verse 9).

Ezekiel 44:3 - "It is for the prince; the prince, he shall sit in it to eat bread before the LORD; he shall enter by the way of the porch of that gate, and shall go out by the way of the same."

D | Idolatrous Levites Banned From Millennial Priesthood

According to Ezekiel 37:11-14, Christ will resurrect all Jews from every age. According to Romans 11:26. they will repent and be filled with His Spirit. But one group of Jews will be punished in the Millennium - the Levites who led Israel into idolatry. "Because they ministered unto them before their idols, and caused the house of Israel to fall into iniquity; ...they shall bear their iniquity."

Ezekiel 44:13 - "They shall not come near unto me, to do the office of a priest unto me, nor to come near to any of my holy things."

B | The Elite Millennial Priesthood

In the millennial Temple, Jesus Christ will have priests ministering to Him at all times. This most elite group of Levites, sons of Zadok, will be comprised exclusively of Levites who were faithful to keep the charge of the Old Testament sanctuary in ancient times when all of Israel were going astray. This should inspire us today to be especially faithful to God in these times of general apostasy. God is a rewarder.

□✓

Ezekiel 44:16 - "They shall enter into my sanctuary, and they shall come near to my table, to minister unto me, and they shall keep my charge."

C | Teaching Holy Vs. Profane, Clean Vs. Unclean

Resurrected Levites who were idolatrous in ancient times will not serve Messiah as priests in the millennial Temple. "They shall slay the burnt offering and the sacrifice," and be "keepers of the charge of the house, for all the service thereof." Levite sons of Zadok will minister to Christ in compliance with several Old Testament regulations - hair, apparel, abstention from wine and defilements, etc. They must teach the people what is holy, versus profane.

Ezekiel 44:23 - "They shall teach my people the difference between the holy and profane, and cause them to discern between the unclean and the clean."

D | Millennium Divisions Of The Land Of Israel

Jerusalem will be a sixty mile square of land given to the holy service of the LORD. "Ye shall offer an oblation unto the LORD, an holy portion of the land." 24x60 miles will go to the priests and the Temple Mount. 24x60 miles will go to other Levites. A 12x60 mile strip will be suburbs of Jerusalem. The Prince will have two 12x12 mile plots east and west of Jerusalem. The twelve tribes will divide the remainder of Israel.

Ezekiel 45:8 - "The rest of the land shall they give to the house of Israel according to their tribes."

B | The Millennial Princes Of Israel

Israel's "Garden of Eden" (36:35) will be inhabited by many millions of mortal Jews who will be ruled by Messiah's rod of iron (Revelation 2:26-27;12:5;19:15). Jesus the Messiah will require the princes of Israel to execute judgment and justice while removing violence and spoil.

Ezekiel 45:8-9 - "My princes shall no more oppress my people; and the rest of the land shall they give to the house of Israel according to their tribes. Thus saith the Lord GOD; ...O princes of Israel: remove violence and spoil, and execute judgment and justice."

D | Millennial Jews Must Reconcile With Christ

Dead Jews and Gentiles who are IN CHRIST will rise immortal when Jesus comes (1 Corinthians 15:42,51-53). Unregenerate Jews who are NOT IN CHRIST will resurrect (37:13) as mortals (44:22,25 speaks of

511

widows and dying family members). They must be saved from their sins (37:23), filled with His Spirit (37:14), and perform select O.T. sacrifices to reconcile with Christ.

Ezekiel 45:15,17 - "...meat offering, ...burnt offering, ...peace offerings, to make reconciliation for them, saith the Lord GOD. ...it shall be the prince's [David's] part to give burnt offerings, and meat offerings, and drink offerings."

A | Worshipping The LORD At The Eastern Gate

During the Millennium, the eastern gate of the INNER court (not the main Eastern Gate) will be closed six days, accessible only to the earthly prince who rules under Christ. However, that gate will open every Sabbath for people to come and worship the LORD Jesus Christ.

Ezekiel 46:1-3 "The gate of the inner court that looketh toward the east shall be shut the six working days; but on the sabbath it shall be opened. ...The people of the land shall worship at the door of this gate before the LORD in the sabbaths and in the new moons."

A | You Won't Leave The Way You Came

During the Millennium, those who worship the LORD in His Temple will leave by a different direction than they came. When you worship God, you will leave different.

Ezekiel 46:9 - "When the people of the land shall come before the LORD, ...he that entereth in by the way of the north gate to worship shall go out by the way of the south gate; and he that entereth by the way of the south gate shall go forth by the way of the north gate: he shall not return by the way of the gate whereby he came in."

C | David Will Open Sabbath Worship Events

In the Millennium, Jesus will have an outdoor audience with the public every Sabbath at the Eastern Gate. David, prince of Israel, will enter, and priests will prepare his offerings. "He shall worship at the threshold of the gate: ...The people of the land shall worship at the door of this gate before the LORD in the sabbaths and in the new moons." Non-public sacrifices will be made daily in the Temple.

Ezekiel 46:13 - "Thou shalt daily prepare a burnt offering unto the LORD of a lamb of the first year without blemish: thou shalt prepare it every morning."

B | Things Absent, Things Present In The Millennial Temple

There will be no veil over the holiest place in the millennial Temple, because the veil was rent when Jesus died. No table of shewbread - Jesus is the bread of life. No menorah - Jesus is the light. No Ark of the Covenant - God is in Christ. But holy priests will offer sacrifices unto Messiah; NOT to save sinners (Jesus saved them), but as a holy ordinance for 1000 years.

Ezekiel 46:14-15 - "Thou shalt prepare a meat offering for it every morning, ...by a perpetual ordinance unto the LORD, ...every morning for a continual burnt offering."

B | Boiling Places

One cannot escape the fact that Ezekiel repeatedly established that there will be blood sacrifices in the Millennium. However that may seem to contradict the doctrine of the blood of Jesus and salvation by grace, the reality is that Jesus will be in the midst of the Jews AS THEIR SAVIOR, yet Jews will be required to make these sacrifices before Him in the Temple. Ezekiel called it reconciliation (45:15).

Ezekiel 46:20 - "This is the place where the priests shall boil the trespass offering and the sin offering, where they shall bake the meat offering; ...to sanctify the people."

C | The Water Of Life

Water is one of the greatest symbols of life, both in the physical world and in the spiritual world. When Moses, by the hand of God, brought water out of the rock, it was a type of Christ. Jesus said that His Spirit in a man is like a well of living water. In the Millennium, a river of water will proceed from the Temple of Jesus Christ to give life to the Dead Sea. In the New Jerusalem that comes from Heaven, a river will proceed from the Throne of God.

Ezekiel 47:1 - "Behold, waters issued out from under the threshold of the house eastward."

C | Resurrection Life

Jesus was the firstfruit from the dead and the firstborn among many brethren. His resurrection was the first of countless resurrections. All Israel will be resurrected when He comes. All the dead in Christ will be resurrected when He comes. Even the Dead Sea will be resurrected!

Ezekiel 47:8-9 - "These waters ...go down into the desert, and go into the sea: ...whithersoever the rivers shall come, shall live: and there shall be a very great multitude of fish, because these waters shall come thither: for they shall be healed; and every thing shall live whither the river cometh."

B | From Engedi To Eneglaim

At Jesus' coming, a river will begin flowing from the Temple westward to the Mediterranean and eastward to the Dead Sea. Engedi and Eneglaim will be major fishing centers, suggesting that the river will continue flowing southward from the Dead Sea to the Gulf of Aqaba on the Red Sea. The old salt marshes will remain a rich source of minerals.

Ezekiel 47:10 - "Fishers shall stand upon it from Engedi even unto Eneglaim; they shall be a place to spread forth nets; their fish shall be according to their kinds, as the fish of the great sea, exceeding many."

D | Sanctuary River Will Provide Fish, Fruit, Medicine

A river will flow from Jerusalem to the Mediterranean and the Dead Sea. At Armageddon, Jesus will stand on the Mount of Olives (Zechariah 14), and it will cleave into a huge east-to-west valley, and a river will begin to flow to both seas. The Dead Sea will be healed and will come alive with every fish species found in the Mediterranean.

Ezekiel 47:12 - "And by the river ...shall grow all trees for meat, ...because their waters they issued out of the sanctuary: and the fruit thereof shall be for meat, and the leaf thereof for medicine."

D | The Final And Divinely Ordained Borders Of Israel

When Jesus returns, prince David, his family, the priests and Levites will inherit Jerusalem and its environs. Considering all Bible prophecies, Israel's west border will be the Mediterranean Sea; its east border, the Jordan River. The north border will reach above Tripoli and Beirut, Lebanon to the Euphrates River in Syria. The southern border will extend from below the Dead Sea to the Egyptian Nile.

Ezekiel 47:13-14 - "Thus saith the Lord GOD; This shall be the border, whereby ye shall inherit the land, ...concerning the which I lifted up mine hand to give it unto your fathers."

C | Everyone Will Inherit Exactly What God Promised

Every tribe of Israel will receive land stretching from western to eastern borders of the country. Beginning in the north, the order of the tribes is: Dan, Asher, Naphtali, Manasseh, Ephraim, Reuben, and Judah. The "most holy oblation" surrounding Jerusalem belongs to David, his family, the priests and Levites. The southern tribes will be Benjamin, Simeon, Issachar, Zebulun and Gad. Jerusalem will have twelve gates named after the tribes. "The name of the city from that day shall be, The LORD is there."

Ezekiel 48:29 - "This is the land which ye shall divide by lot unto the tribes of Israel."

Lessons from the Book of
DANIEL

B | Daniel And The Three Hebrews

The prophesied siege of Jerusalem by the Babylonians began when Nebuchadnezzar captured King Jehoiakim. He took the vessels of the holy Temple back home to his own idolatrous temple in Shinar. He also captured the finest young princes of Israel, including the king's seed; "children in whom was no blemish, but well favoured, and skilful in all wisdom, and cunning in knowledge, and understanding science, and such as had ability in them to stand in the king's palace." Even in the midst of tragedy, God has big plans for His chosen people.

Daniel 1:6 - "Among these were of the children of Judah, Daniel, Hananiah, Mishael, and Azariah."

C | Courage To Be Different

Where are the souls who will dare to be different from the world? Does anybody go against what is popular anymore? How can God be pleased with our living when we are no different from the rest of the world? God, give us **courage like Daniel had**[14], to buck the trends and be different for righteousness' sake.

Daniel 1:8 - "But Daniel purposed in his heart that he would not defile himself with the portion of the king's meat, nor with the wine which he drank: therefore he requested of the prince of the eunuchs that he might not defile himself."

C | **Modesty And Sobriety Are Better**

While preparing to serve the king in Babylon, Daniel and his fellows were appointed a daily provision of the king's meat and wine for three years. Daniel did not want to be defiled by royal indulgences. He asked the prince of the eunuchs to be excused, but the prince was afraid Daniel would appear unhealthy. Daniel challenged him to prove the Hebrews with vegetables and water for ten days.

Daniel 1:15 - "At the end of ten days their countenances appeared fairer and fatter in flesh than all the children which did eat the portion of the king's meat."

D | **God Gave Daniel Supernatural Knowledge And Skills**

Daniel was profoundly spiritually insightful, and was one of Israel's most important and influential prophets. He served under four pagan kings because Almighty God carefully endued him with knowledge and skill to serve His eternal purpose. God works that way. He will enable you to do His will.

Daniel 1:17,19 - "As for these four children, God gave them knowledge and skill in all learning and wisdom: and Daniel had understanding in all visions and dreams. ...the king enquired of them, he found them ten times better than all the magicians and astrologers that were in all his realm."

B | **Nebuchadnezzar Dreamed A Dream**

This story is reminiscent of Pharaoh and Joseph. The Egyptian Pharaoh had a dream that was interpreted by a Hebrew (Joseph), who had a divine gift for interpreting dreams. **Nebuchadnezzar also dreamed a dream,**[15] and the Hebrew (Daniel) possessed the divine gift to interpret it. In both cases, God was setting the stage to reveal His sovereign power. In the end, it became apparent that God sent the dream, and God sent the interpreter.

Daniel 2:1 "In the second year of the reign of Nebuchadnezzar Nebuchadnezzar dreamed dreams, wherewith his spirit was troubled, and his sleep brake from him."

A | They Desired Mercies Of The God Of Heaven

Nebuchadnezzar could not remember the dreams that troubled him, so he demanded his magicians, astrologers and sorcerers to reveal and interpret them. Naturally, they could not, so Nebuchadnezzar ordered them all to be put to death. But Daniel begged time to show the answer. "Then Daniel went to his house, and made the thing known to Hananiah, Mishael, and Azariah, ...That they would desire mercies of the God of heaven concerning this secret." Fortify your prayers with strong desire.

Daniel 2:19 - "Then was the secret revealed unto Daniel in a night vision. ...what we desired of thee."

D | God Sets Up And Removes Kings

Daniel had the keenest awareness that everything going on in Babylon, including everything going on with Nebuchadnezzar, was under the perfect control of Almighty God. That truth is the heart and soul of Bible prophecy. Prophecy is simply the declaration of what God is going to do. Never doubt that God has EVERYTHING under control, and it is ALL working for HIS good. You should want to be perfectly allied with Him.

Daniel 2:20-21 - "Blessed be the name of God for ever and ever: ...he changeth the times and the seasons: he removeth kings, and setteth up kings."

A | Don't Forget To Give Thanks

None of King Nebuchadnezzar's counselors could reveal his troubling dreams to him, so he ordered them all to be killed. But by intercessory prayer, Daniel obtained a revelation from God which answered the King's wishes and saved the lives of Daniel and his brethren. Daniel immediately gave thanks and praise to God.

Daniel 2:23 - "I thank thee, and praise thee, O thou God of my fathers, who hast given me wisdom and might, and hast made known unto me now what we desired of thee: for thou hast now made known unto us the king's matter."

C | God Reveals Secrets Of The Latter Days

The wisest men in Babylon had no clues about the future. Nebuchadnezzar would have killed them for their ignorance. But all wisdom and knowledge comes from the LORD, and wise men of God like Daniel save many lives. God knows EVERYTHING. Daniel saw things 2500 years in the future.

Daniel 2:27-28 - "Daniel answered... The secret which the king hath demanded cannot the wise men, the astrologers, the magicians, the soothsayers, shew unto the king; but there is a God in heaven that revealeth secrets, and maketh known to the king Nebuchadnezzar what shall be in the latter days."

B | God Tutored Nebuchadnezzar, Pagan King

When all else had failed, the man of God, Daniel, had the answers that Nebuchadnezzar could find nowhere else. Nebuchadnezzar was the most powerful man on earth in his day, ruling over the sprawling Babylonian Empire. But he did not have a clue about the future. God decided to teach him a few things.

Daniel 2:29 - "As for thee, O king, thy thoughts came into thy mind upon thy bed, what should come to pass hereafter: and he that revealeth secrets maketh known to thee what shall come to pass....Thou, O king, sawest, and behold a great image."

D | Nebuchadnezzar's Image

God gave the dream to Nebuchadnezzar. He saw a great statue of a man. It was bright, excellent and terrible, and foretold the sequence of coming world empires. Its golden head represented the current Babylonian Empire; its silver breast and arms represented the successor Medo-Persian Empire. Brass thighs prophesied of Greece. Iron legs foresaw the Roman empire; **iron and clay feet, the Holy Roman empire.**[16] Jesus Christ will come and crush them.

Daniel 2:45 - "...the stone was cut out of the mountain without hands, and... brake in pieces the iron, the brass, the clay, the silver, and the gold"

B | God Of Gods, Lord Of Kings

Nebuchadnezzar fell on his face and worshipped Daniel for his ability to describe the dream he had forgotten, and to interpret it. He ordered his officers to offer an oblation and sweet odors to Daniel. He made him a great man, gave him many great gifts, made him ruler over the whole province of Babylon, and chief of the governors. People can recognize that our God is the greatest.

Daniel 2:47 - "Of a truth it is, that your God is a God of gods, and a Lord of kings, and a revealer of secrets, seeing thou couldest reveal this secret."

A | We Will Worship No Other God

King Nebuchadnezzar made an image of gold over one hundred feet high and ordered everyone in Babylon to bow down and worship it, on threat of death. But three Hebrew princes said no. If you really know God, you will worship no other.

Daniel 3:17-18 - "Our God whom we serve is able to deliver us from the burning fiery furnace, and he will deliver us out of thine hand, O king. But if not, be it known unto thee, O king, that we will not serve thy gods, nor worship the golden image which thou hast set up."

C | You Can Survive Your Trial Without Loss

Not only did Shadrach, Meshach and Abed-nego survive the fiery furnace, but there was also no physical evidence they had even been in the fire. God can take you through your trial completely unharmed. Trust Him.

Daniel 3:26-27 - "Then Shadrach, Meshach, and Abednego, came forth of the midst of the fire. And the princes, governors, and captains, and the king's counsellors, being gathered together, saw these men, upon whose bodies the fire had no power, nor was an hair of their head singed, neither were their coats changed, nor the smell of fire had passed on them."

D | God Sent His Angel

What did Nebuchadnezzar see in the furnace with the three Hebrews - a man, the son of God or an angel? First, he called it the fourth man - "I see four men loose." Next, in the Hebrew text, he said that he "resembles a son of the gods." We cannot believe that this was the man Christ, because the man Christ would not be born of Mary until almost six centuries later. It was an angel.

Daniel 3:28 - "Nebuchadnezzar spake, and said, Blessed be the God of Shadrach, Meshach, and Abednego, who hath sent his angel, and delivered his servants."

A | Nebuchadnezzar Blesses God

When Shadrach, Meshach and Abednego walked out of the fiery furnace without even the smell of smoke on them, Nebuchadnezzar realized that he and all his officials had witnessed an astonishing miracle. When God-fearing people take a stand, God is glorified, and the world takes note.

Daniel 3:28-30 - "Nebuchadnezzar spake, and said, Blessed be the God of Shadrach, Meshach, and Abednego, who hath sent his angel, and delivered his servants that trusted in him, ...there is no other God that can deliver after this sort. Then the king promoted Shadrach, Meshach, and Abednego, in the province of Babylon."

C | No Other God Can Deliver After This Sort

How many times will you ever have the opportunity to watch three men walk out of a fiery inferno unscathed? That furnace was so hot that the guards who approached it died. Nobody but our God can deliver after this sort. You can have a miracle, too. Believe.

Daniel 3:29 - "Therefore I make a decree, That every people, nation, and language, which speak any thing amiss against the God of Shadrach, Meshach, and Abednego, shall be cut in pieces, and their houses shall be made a dunghill: because there is no other God that can deliver after this sort."

B | Nebuchadnezzar's Testimony

Again, Nebuchadnezzar dreamed a dream. Again, his magicians, astrologers, and soothsayers could do nothing to interpret it. Again, by God's help, Daniel interpreted the dream and saved the day. This, and every major Bible story has a miraculous component; sign, wonder, miracle, angel, etc. When you trust God, your story will be miraculous, too.

Daniel 4:1 - "Nebuchadnezzar the king, unto all people, nations, and languages, that dwell in all the earth; ...I thought it good to shew the signs and wonders that the high God hath wrought toward me. How great are his signs! and how mighty are his wonders!"

C | God Sets Up The Basest Of Men

God sent Nebuchadnezzar out to pasture as punishment for his pride, "by the decree of the watchers, and the demand by the word of the holy ones" - angelic messengers. God can abase the most powerful man on earth, or exalt the basest of men. God can send a righteous leader to a righteous people, or a fool to fools. He is the King of kings.

Daniel 4:17 - "That the living may know that the most High ruleth in the kingdom of men, and giveth it to whomsoever he will, and setteth up over it the basest of men."

D | Nebuchadnezzar - The Great Tree Hewn Down

Nebuchadnezzar dreamed about a great tree in the earth. It had fair leaves, much fruit for everyone, beasts resting under it, and birds nesting in it. But "watchers" - heavenly agents - hewed it down, leaving only a stump. Daniel interpreted it. God would judge Nebuchadnezzar. He must be converted from his evil ways.

Daniel 4:25-28 - "They shall drive thee from men, ...thy dwelling shall be with the beasts of the field, ...they shall make thee to eat grass as oxen, ...till thou know that the most High ruleth in the kingdom of men, and giveth it to whomsoever he will."

D | Nebuchadnezzar's Seven-Year Insanity

An ancient clay tablet in the British Museum (BM34113) describes Nebuchadnezzar's insane behavior: "His life appeared of no value to him... he gives an entirely different order... he does not show love to son or daughter... family and clan does not exist." The Expositor's Bible Commentary reports that "There is no record of acts or decrees by the king during 582 to 575 BC." Daniel prophesied it four times (4:16,23,25,32).

Daniel 4:32 - "Thy dwelling shall be with the beasts of the field: they shall make thee to eat grass as oxen, and seven times shall pass over thee."

A | Blessing And Praising God After Being Hewn Down

After dreaming that he was a great tree, hewn down by a watcher from heaven, Nebuchadnezzar experienced a devastating and traumatic reality check. God sent the great king into the fields where he lost his mind. After the ordeal ended, Nebuchadnezzar greatly feared and reverenced God. God knows how to sober you up and make you recognize His greatness.

Daniel 4:34-35 - "At the end of the days I Nebuchadnezzar lifted up mine eyes unto heaven, and mine understanding returned unto me, and I blessed the most High, and I praised and honoured him that liveth for ever, whose dominion is an everlasting dominion."

A | None Can Say, "What Doest Thou?"

The parameters of prayer are mostly unlimited. Jesus said, "If ye shall ask any thing in my name, I will do it," John 14:14. But one area that is off-limits is opposing God's sovereign will. Nebuchadnezzar learned the hard way that God is always in charge. Not even a king is big enough to override His final answer. Learn to accept His judgments.

Daniel 4:35 - "He doeth according to his will in the army of heaven, and among the inhabitants of the earth: and none can stay his hand, or say unto him, What doest thou?"

C | **Kings Quickly Rise And Fall**

"Nebuchadnezzar the Great," who conquered Jerusalem and ruled Babylon from 605-562BC, experienced a profound divine rebuke when God drove him to insanity for seven years. Nebuchadnezzar's successors were minor figures who could not maintain the empire. His son, Amel-Marduk was killed by his brother-in-law, Neriglissar, who was subsequently deposed by his son Labas-Marduk, who was immediately removed in a coup by Belshazzar, who shared power with his father, Nabonidus, who was mentally ill.

Daniel 5:1 - "Belshazzar the king made a great feast to a thousand of his lords, and drank wine before the thousand."

B | **Handwriting On The Wall Abruptly Ends The Party**

Belshazzar defiled the sacred vessels from the Holy Temple in Jerusalem at an idolatrous, drunken party for all his courtiers. God sent a mysterious hand to write judgments on the wall.

Daniel 5:5-6 - "In the same hour came forth fingers of a man's hand, and wrote over against the candlestick upon the plaister of the wall of the king's palace: and the king saw the part of the hand that wrote. Then the king's countenance was changed, and his thoughts troubled him, so that the joints of his loins were loosed, and his knees smote one against another."

B | **Belteshazzar**

The name Daniel means "El (God) is my judge." Nebuchadnezzar gave Daniel a Chaldean name - Belteshazzar - meaning "Prince of Bel." His Hebrew name identified him with EL - (i.e., Elohim, El Shaddai). His Babylonian name referred to Bel, Babylon's false god. The world will try to change your identity into something compatible with their way of thinking. But in all his first-person writings, Daniel never mentioned his given name, Belteshazzar, without reminding the reader that he was also Daniel. Don't let the world steal your godly identity.

Daniel 5:12 - "...Daniel, whom the king named Belteshazzar."

A | Do Not Waste Time Calling Astrologers Or Soothsayers

When King Belshazzar of Babylon profaned the holy vessels of the Jewish Temple in a drunken party, God sent a message to him by mysterious handwriting on the wall. He called for his astrologers and soothsayers to interpret the writing, but they were powerless. The Queen urged him to call for Daniel. She knew about Daniel's interpreting of Nebuchadnezzar's dreams by the power of God. The world has no substitute for a true man of God.

Daniel 5:15 - "The wise men, the astrologers, have been brought in before me, ...but they could not shew the interpretation of the thing."

C | You Should Learn From Your Forefathers

Daniel 5:13 called Nebuchadnezzar the father of Belshazzar. "The king spake and said, ...Art thou that Daniel, ...whom the king my father brought out of Jewry?" Daniel said, "The most high God gave Nebuchadnezzar thy father a kingdom..." 5:18. Herodotus identified a Queen Nitocris as Nebuchadnezzar's daughter, and other sources say Belshazzar was her grandson. Even if Nebuchadnezzar was, at best, a "forefather," Belshazzar should have feared God who dealt so profoundly with him. Tragically, he did not.

Daniel 5:22 - "And thou his son, O Belshazzar, hast not humbled thine heart, though thou knewest all this."

D | Mene, Mene, Tekel, Upharsin

Daniel indicted Belshazzar for lifting up himself "against the Lord of heaven," drinking from the holy vessels, praising non-existent gods, "and the God in whose hand thy breath is, and whose are all thy ways, hast thou not glorified." Then, he interpreted the handwriting. "Mene, Mene, Tekel, Upharsin."

Daniel 5:26-31 "God hath numbered thy kingdom, and finished it. ...Thou art weighed in the balances, and art found wanting. ...Thy kingdom is divided, and given to the Medes and Persians. In that night was Belshazzar the king of the Chaldeans slain. Darius the Median took the kingdom."

B | Darius And Daniel

When the Persians came to power in Babylon, following the fall of Belshazzar, Daniel not only survived the transition, but was also immediately promoted for his excellence. In the real world, most officials are thrown out in a regime change. But Almighty God had His hand on Daniel. Darius had three presidents and 120 princes, and Daniel was over them ALL. God will keep you in power as long as He wants to.

Daniel 6:3 - "Daniel was preferred above the presidents and princes, because an excellent spirit was in him; and the king thought to set him over the whole realm."

A | Pray, Even Under Threat Of Death

God prospered Daniel in Babylon so profoundly that his jealous pagan counterparts wanted him dead. They created an outrageous law to sentence him to death for PRAYING! But you know the story. Daniel continued praying, and God took miraculous care of him. Let nothing stop your praying.

Daniel 6:7 - "All the presidents of the kingdom, the governors, and the princes, the counsellors, and the captains, have consulted together to establish a royal statute, ...that whosoever shall ask a petition of any God or man for thirty days, save of thee, O king, he shall be cast into the den of lions."

A | Communion With God In Prayer Is Worth Every Risk

I would rather be in a lion's den if God is there, than to live in a luxurious castle without God. Obviously, Daniel felt that way, too. Never let anybody interfere with your relationship with God.

Daniel 6:10-11 - "Now when Daniel knew that the writing was signed, he went into his house; and his windows being open in his chamber toward Jerusalem, he kneeled upon his knees three times a day, and prayed, and gave thanks before his God, as he did aforetime. Then these men assembled, and found Daniel praying and making supplication before his God."

A | Will Prayer Become A Crime?

Daniel's adversaries were ambitious to prosecute him for praying three times a day to his God. Will such a day ever come for you or me? One of my readers wrote to say that military soldiers in his country invaded their church service and shot up a dozen people. Two of them died. Their crime? Practicing Christianity. Everyone else was warned to abandon all Christian practices within thirty days or be prosecuted. Will you keep on praying if and when that time comes?

Daniel 6:16 - "Then the king commanded, and they brought Daniel, and cast him into the den of lions."

D | God Shut The Lions' Mouths And Saved His Prophet

Daniel's insanely jealous peers tricked King Darius, who painfully regretted Daniel's being thrown into the lion's den. But God was not finished with His prophet. When Darius visited the lion's den early in the morning, Daniel was miraculously quite well.

Daniel 6:20-22 - "O Daniel, servant of the living God, is thy God, whom thou servest continually, able to deliver thee from the lions? Then said Daniel unto the king, O king, live for ever. My God hath sent his angel, and hath shut the lions' mouths, that they have not hurt me: forasmuch as before him innocency was found in me."

C | God Will Vindicate The Righteous

Daniel's foes passed legislation to criminalize prayer. The same thing is happening nowadays. But Daniel prayed anyway, and God delivered him from dying in the lion's den. Moreover, the king cast Daniel's enemies into the lion's den - with their wives and children. They all died. Darius then issued a decree throughout his kingdom that men should fear the God of Daniel.

Daniel 6:27-28 - "He delivereth and rescueth, and he worketh signs and wonders in heaven and in earth. ...So this Daniel prospered in the reign of Darius, and in the reign of Cyrus the Persian."

D | Four Winds Striving On The Great Sea

Soon after Belshazzar came to power, Daniel dreamed a very disturbing dream. He wrote it down and told what he saw. The first thing he saw was four winds striving on the great sea. These winds correspond to the four horsemen of Revelation 6 and Zechariah 6:5, "These are the **four spirits of the heavens,**[17] which go forth from standing before the Lord of all the earth." The great sea represents the human masses (Revelation 17:15).

Daniel 7:2 - "I saw in my vision by night, and, behold, the four winds of the heaven strove upon the great sea."

B | Four Great Beasts Came Up From The Sea

While four great winds blew upon the great sea of humanity (Revelation 17:15), Daniel saw four great beasts coming up from the sea. Grieved and troubled, Daniel asked for "the truth of all this." "These great beasts, which are four, are **four kings, which shall arise out of the earth.**[18] But the saints of the most High shall take the kingdom, and possess the kingdom for ever, even for ever and ever." Daniel dreamed of four great kingdoms on earth when Jesus returns.

Daniel 7:3 - "Four great beasts came up from the sea, diverse one from another."

D | A Lion With Eagle's Wings

We cannot correctly interpret **Daniel's four beasts using ancient empires,**[19] as most Bible commentators do. This lion must be a modern empire, as must be the eagle's wings. Anybody in the 21st Century should know that the British Lion and the American Eagle are universally recognized symbols. America was originally a British colonial possession until the wings were plucked in 1776 by their Declaration of Independence. 2500 years ago, Daniel saw America being born.

Daniel 7:4 - "The first was like a lion, and had eagle's wings: I beheld till the wings thereof were plucked."

D | A Bear With Three Ribs In Its Mouth

Virtually everybody on earth recognizes the symbol of the Russian Bear. Nothing in Russia's history is more significant than **the Yalta Conference of 1945,**[20] when Joseph Stalin met with Winston Churchill and Franklin D Roosevelt ("The Big Three" ribs), took control of Eastern Europe and created the socialistic United Nations.

Daniel 7:5 - "Another beast, a second, like to a bear, and it raised up itself on one side, and it had three ribs in the mouth of it between the teeth of it: and they said thus unto it, Arise, devour much flesh."

D | A Four-Headed Leopard

No nation on earth is more closely associated with the symbol of a LEOPARD than Germany. And amazingly enough, it has had **FOUR HEADS - four Reichs**[21] - 1. The Holy Roman Empire; 2. The German Empire; 3. Hitler's Third Reich; 4. The European Union. Through the centuries, Germany has had a symbiotic relationship with France, whose symbol is a FOWL - the Rooster!

Daniel 7:6 - "After this I beheld, and lo another, like a leopard, which had upon the back of it four wings of a fowl; the beast had also four heads; and dominion was given to it."

D | The Dreadful Beast

This is **the most powerful beast that Jesus Christ will confront at Armageddon**[22]. Out of this ten-horned beast, a LITTLE HORN will come - the Man of Sin (2 Thessalonians 2) who will commit the Abomination of Desolation in the Third Temple. This will be a vicious totalitarian world government, probably a future form of the United Nations.

Daniel 7:7 - "Behold a fourth beast, dreadful and terrible, and strong exceedingly; and it had great iron teeth: it devoured and brake in pieces, and stamped the residue with the feet of it: and it was diverse from all the beasts that were before it; and it had ten horns."

D | The Little Horn

The prophets saw a Ten-Horned Beast; a world-government driven by ten mighty kings just before Armageddon. We cannot know beforehand exactly who this will be. I suspect that the **Iron and Clay Holy Roman Empire**[23] (now European Union) will be the provisor of a new ten-member power structure in unprecedented submission to the United Nations. The LITTLE HORN, a rising nation (I suspect Turkey), will drive three others out of that federation. The Man of Sin, from that region of Ancient Assyria, will commit the Abomination of Desolation. He will almost certainly be Muslim, sanctioned by the U.N. and the Vatican.

Daniel 7:7-8 - "...there came up among them another little horn, before whom there were three of the first horns plucked up by the roots."

B | The Ancient Of Days

Is the Ancient of Days an old, white-haired man? Is the Lamb of God a four-legged sheep with seven horns and seven eyes? (Revelation 5:6) No. John 1:18 says, "No man hath seen God at any time." "No man hath seen, nor can see" Him. I Timothy 6:16. The King is "eternal, immortal, invisible," I Timothy 1:17. The white-haired man is an allegory, a metaphor, symbolic. **Jesus is the only "image of the invisible God,"**[24] Colossians 1:15.

Daniel 7:9 - "The Ancient of days did sit, ...the hair of his head like the pure wool."

D | The Judgment Of The Beast And The Little Horn

The four beasts of Daniel 7 reveals the four empires most hostile to Israel AND Christian saints on earth just before Jesus Christ comes to Armageddon. In the vision, Daniel saw their demise. "I beheld till the thrones were cast down, and the Ancient of days did sit, ...the judgment was set, and the books were opened." From Heaven, God pronounced **judgment on the Man of Sin**[25].

Daniel 7:9-11 - "I beheld then because of the voice of the great words which the horn spake: I beheld even till the beast was slain, and his body destroyed, and given to the burning flame."

C | God Keeps A Record

Daniel showed that God will judge the Little Horn (the Man of Sin) out of the record-books. God keeps records on every man and woman, boy and girl. David said his wanderings, his tears, his substance, and "all my members" were in His book. Malachi 3:16 said there is "a book of remembrance." John said, "I saw the dead, small and great, stand before God; and the books were opened: ...and the dead were judged out of those things," Revelation 20:12. Be careful how you live. God keeps a record.

Daniel 7:10 - "The judgment was set, and the books were opened."

B | The Burning Flame

Put this in its correct time-frame. This verse will be fulfilled immediately after Armageddon. Jesus will have just returned to earth with His newly resurrected saints. He will defeat all His foes in the Battle of all Battles - Armageddon. He will destroy the Little Horn and the False Prophet. The setting is Jerusalem. In the sight of vast multitudes of Israelites and Christians, He will cast the Man of Sin and the False Prophet into a flaming pit. See Revelation 19:20.

Daniel 7:11 - "I beheld even till the beast was slain, and his body destroyed, and given to the burning flame."

C | God Will Repossess All Dominion

There is no earthly dominion that is not a gift from God. If a king has any kingdom, God gave it - and He can just as easily take it back. That is what the **Parable of the Husbandman**[26] (Matthew 21:33) is all about. If God gives you a vineyard and you do not take care of it, He will take it back. At Armageddon, Jesus will repossess all earthly kingdoms and give them to His saints.

Daniel 7:12 - "Concerning the rest of the beasts, they had their dominion taken away: yet their lives were prolonged for a season and time."

□✓

D | The Kingdom To Come

Jesus prayed, "Thy Kingdom come, thy will be done on earth as it is in heaven." Jesus will soon return to set the world in holy order after the battle of Armageddon. The demonic global government will be destroyed, and Satan will be cast into Hell. Jesus will command all nations from Jerusalem for 1000 years.

Daniel 7:14 - "...there was given him dominion, and glory, and a kingdom, that all people, nations, and languages, should serve him: his dominion is an everlasting dominion, which shall not pass away, and his kingdom that which shall not be destroyed."

D | Heaven and Earth Shall Pass Away

Matthew, Mark and Luke record the identical words of Jesus, "Heaven and earth shall pass away..." John saw it prophetically in Revelation 21:1, "I saw a new heaven and a new earth: for the first heaven and the first earth were passed away." Like it or not, this world is not going to last. God is going to destroy it (2 Peter 3:12). Only those in His eternal kingdom will survive (2 Corinthians 5:1).

Daniel 7:14 - "...his dominion is an everlasting dominion, which shall not pass, and his kingdom that which shall not be destroyed."

A | Ask God For The Truth Of All This

God showed Daniel an amazing vision of four spirits striving on the earth, four great beasts creating horrors, and the Ancient of Days giving kingdoms and dominion unto the Son of Man. Daniel could not understand, so he asked for help. Ask for the Truth. God will show it to you.

Daniel 7:15-16 - "I Daniel was grieved in my spirit in the midst of my body, and the visions of my head troubled me. I came near unto one of them that stood by, and asked him the truth of all this. So he told me, and made me know the interpretation of the things."

B | The Saints And Their Eternal Kingdom

The world hates the saints of God, but they are most precious to God. His saints are the primary reason why we have a Bible. God could easily have withheld creating the earth and the things therein. But He made the earth and created mankind, then sent a Savior, so He would have an eternal people for Himself. We will inherit the entire earth as kings and priests for 1000 years, then inherit the New Jerusalem forever.

529

Daniel 7:18 - "The saints of the most High shall take the kingdom, and possess the kingdom for ever, even for ever and ever."

B | Ten Horns On The Dreadful Beast

The fourth beast Daniel saw had ten horns. This will almost certainly be a European-dominated United Nations. Its ten horns will be newly designated, powerful nations, including Britain (Lion), Russia (Bear), and Germany (Leopard), (Revelation 13:1-2), perhaps comprising the UN Security Council. An eleventh horn (perhaps Islamic Turkey) will rise to become the Little Horn, removing three previous horns (kings/kingdoms).

Daniel 7:20 - "Of the ten horns that were in his head, and of the other which came up, and before whom three fell; even of that horn that had eyes, and a mouth that spake very great things, whose look was more stout than his fellows."

C | The Earth Is The LORD's

No man, devil, or Antichrist will ever wrest the earth from God. He created it, owns the title deed, and will give it to whosoever He pleases - namely, His saints, to rule and reign for 1000 years. Exodus 9:29; Deuteronomy 10:14; Psalms 24:1; 1 Corinthians 10:26 - "The earth is the Lord's, and the fulness thereof."

Daniel 7:21-22 - "The same horn made war with the saints, and prevailed against them; Until the Ancient of days came, and judgment was given to the saints of the most High; and the time came that the saints possessed the kingdom."

D | The Truth Of The Fourth Beast

Daniel said that the fourth beast will be diverse from all the others, exceeding dreadful. It will have iron teeth. In Nebuchadnezzar's statue, iron represented Rome, or Europe. Brass represented Grecia, which includes Turkey. Brass nails suggest the inclusion of Turkey and Islam in the fourth beast. It will devour, break in pieces and stamp the residue with its feet of a bear – (Russia and Communism). Here appears to be a terrifying monstrous European, Turkish, Communistic world government.

Daniel 7:23 - "The fourth beast ...shall devour the whole earth, and shall tread it down, and break it in pieces."

B | The Ten-Horned Beast

The ten-horned beast will not be manifest until very shortly before Armageddon, so we cannot yet know for certain who it will be. It will be a World-Government, "diverse from all kingdoms, and shall DEVOUR THE WHOLE EARTH, and shall tread it down, and break it in pieces." It is a future form of what is now the United Nations. But Jesus and His saints will conquer it at Armageddon.

Daniel 7:27 - "And the kingdom and dominion, and the greatness of the kingdom under the whole heaven, shall be given to the people of the saints of the most High."

C | Keep The Matter In Your Heart

I have been teaching about Bible prophecies for the last days for almost four decades. I am truly disturbed by the tendency most people have for "burying their head in the sand" and ignoring the signs of the times. Daniel was very different from most of us. Even though the dreams and visions DEEPLY troubled him, he KEPT THEM IN HIS HEART. Everything God reveals is important.

Daniel 7:28 - "Hitherto is the end of the matter. As for me Daniel, my cogitations much troubled me, and my countenance changed in me: but I kept the matter in my heart."

B | The Palace At Shushan in Elam (Iran)

Some of Daniel's visions and dreams occurred while he was in the palace at Shushan, in the province of Elam. Elam was named after the son of Shem, son of Noah. Nehemiah later served in the palace at Shushan, and Esther became the queen there. It is now Shush, Iran - east of the Tigris River. Daniel's tomb is there.

Daniel 8:1-2 - "In the third year of the reign of king Belshazzar a vision appeared unto me, ...I was at Shushan in the palace, which is in the province of Elam; ...and I was by the river of Ulai."

B | The Ram and The He-Goat

Daniel had another vision in which a he-goat with a notable horn attacked a great ram with two horns. The he-goat became great after smiting the ram in great fury, destroying him. God was showing Daniel the epic overthrow of the Medo-Persian Empire by Alexander the Great of Greece about 250 years before it would happen (in 331 BC)!

Daniel 8:20-21 - "The ram which thou sawest having two horns are the kings of Media and Persia. And the rough goat is the king of Grecia: and the great horn that is between his eyes is the first king."

B | The "He-Goat" Kingdom Of Greece Would Be Divided Four Ways

After the he-goat with the notable horn (Alexander the Great and the Grecian Empire) defeated the ram with two horns (the Medo-Persian Empire), Daniel saw prophetically that Alexander's Empire would eventually be divided into four parts. That actually happened when Alexander died in 323 BC. The four divisions were Egypt, Seleucia (Middle East), Pergamon (Turkey), and Macedonia (Greece). Rome later conquered all four divisions.

Daniel 8:8 - "The he goat waxed very great: and when he was strong, the great horn was broken; and for it came up four notable ones toward the four winds of heaven."

D | The Little Horn (The Man of Sin) Will Banish Temple Sacrifices

One of the four remnant kingdoms of ancient Grecia (I suspect Turkey) will produce a Little Horn (Daniel 8:8) – the Man of Sin! He will be strong toward the south (Egypt?), east (Iran?), Palestine (8:9), and even demon principalities - overthrowing and crushing them (8:10). The Little Horn (Man of Sin) will rise up against "the prince of the host [of Heaven]" (Michael, guardian of Israel). He will halt daily sacrifices in the Third Temple and cast down the place of the sanctuary - Jerusalem! (Revelation 11:2b). Multitudes of evil ones will support his actions.

Daniel 8:12 - "An host was given him against the daily sacrifice... , and it cast down the truth to the ground; and it practised, and prospered."

C | God Sends Angels To Help His Saints

Angels! "Are they not all ministering spirits, sent forth to minister for them who shall be heirs of salvation?" Hebrews 1:14. When Daniel was dumbfounded by marvelous visions from the LORD, Gabriel came and made him understand how God's indignation would end.

Daniel 8:15-17 - "Behold, there stood before me as the appearance of a man. And I heard a man's voice, ...which called, and said, Gabriel, make this man to understand the vision. So he came near where I stood: and ...said unto me, Understand, ...for at the time of the end shall be the vision."

C | The End Of The Indignation (The Wrath Of God)

There is no more universal theme in scriptures than that of the FINAL DAY OF GOD'S WRATH at Armageddon. Since the first sins of Lucifer, Adam and Eve, God has been INDIGNANT - angry, resentful, infuriated, mad. As soon as all these prophecies of the last days are fulfilled, God will no longer be indignant. At Armageddon, Jesus Christ will unleash all His fury against Lucifer, the Beast, the False Prophet and all evil nations.

Daniel 8:19 - "I will make thee know what shall be in the last end of the indignation: for at the time appointed the end shall be."

C | The World Is Headed For Unprecedented Evil

Every thinking person should come to terms with the reality that, apart from the Word of God, and Jesus Christ, this world is utterly, hopelessly headed for unrestrained evil. By the time the Little Horn Man of Sin emerges, there will be no turning back. Run to the Rock while you can.

Daniel 8:23-24 - "A king of fierce countenance, and understanding dark sentences, shall stand up. And his power shall be mighty, but not by his own power: and he shall destroy wonderfully, and shall prosper, and practise, and shall destroy the mighty and the holy people. ...by peace shall destroy many."

B | The Fiercest King In History

Many prophecies describe the coming Man of Sin, and the view is never pretty. The "Little Horn" that will lead the final one-world dictatorship will "destroy wonderfully." He will "destroy the mighty and the holy people." His policies will "cause craft [deception] to prosper in his hand." This most demon-possessed world-wide dictator in history will crush everything he can crush, until Jesus Christ returns and crushes HIM.

Daniel 8:24 - "And his power shall be mighty, but not by his own power: ...he shall also stand up against the Prince of princes; but he shall be broken without hand."

C | We Must Trust God When He Refuses To Explain

Sometimes God's greatest works in our lives leave us profoundly distressed. Daniel fainted and was sick for days when God showed him the vision. When he finally returned to work, he still did not understand. We must trust God.

Daniel 8:26-27 - "The vision of the evening and the morning which was told is true: wherefore shut thou up the vision; for it shall be for many days. And I Daniel fainted, and was sick certain days; afterward I rose up, and did the king's business; and I was astonished at the vision, but none understood it."

C | Go By The Book

Daniel calculated exactly how much longer Judah would be in captivity, by studying the book of Jeremiah. Consequently, Daniel knew what to expect and was able to prepare himself mentally, physically and spiritually. If we would go by the Book, we would know where we are headed.

Daniel 9:2-3 - "I Daniel understood by books the number of the years, whereof the word of the LORD came to Jeremiah the prophet, that he would accomplish seventy years in the desolations of Jerusalem. And I set my face unto the Lord God, to seek by prayer and supplications, with fasting."

A | Daniel Repented In Behalf Of All Israel

In the days of King Darius the Mede, Daniel contemplated Jeremiah's prophecies concerning SEVENTY YEARS of DESOLATION in Jerusalem. "I set my face unto the Lord God, to seek by PRAYER and SUPPLICATIONS, with FASTING, and SACKCLOTH, and ASHES." Daniel knew that Moses had prophesied judgments upon Israel if they became godless and prayerless. Daniel made intercession for Israel that day.

Daniel 9:16 - "Lord, ...let thine anger and thy fury be turned away from thy city Jerusalem, thy holy mountain: because for our sins, ...hear the prayer of thy servant, ...cause thy face to shine upon thy sanctuary that is desolate."

A | Angels Respond to Prayer

The Bible records that almost every major character in the Bible was visited by an angel. Angels are ministering spirits for those who will be the heirs of salvation. Do you think no angels work in your behalf? Daniel prayed, and Gabriel came to give him skill and understanding. Keep praying! You may receive a surprise visitor!

Daniel 9:21 - "...whiles I was speaking in prayer, even the man Gabriel, whom I had seen in the vision at the beginning, being caused to fly swiftly, touched me about the time of the evening oblation."

A | At The Beginning Of Thy Supplications...

We often feel like God does not hear our prayers because we do not get the answer we want as quickly as we want it. When Daniel began to pray for Israel, Gabriel instantly appeared with an answer. Angels rarely appear when we pray, but never doubt that God hears and will answer in His own good time.

Daniel 9:22-23 - "O Daniel, I am now come forth to give thee skill and understanding. At the beginning of thy supplications the commandment came forth, and I am come to shew thee; for thou art greatly beloved: therefore understand the matter."

B | Seventy Weeks Of Years To Finish The Transgression

In Leviticus 26:21,28, God warned that if Israel did not respond when chastened, He would multiply their punishment SEVEN TIMES. So when seventy years of punishment in Babylonian captivity failed to turn their hearts, Daniel prophesied SEVEN TIMES SEVENTY - 490 years (70 weeks of years) of punishment to finish their transgressions.

Daniel 9:24 - "Seventy weeks are determined upon thy people and upon thy holy city, to finish the transgression, and to make an end of sins, and to make reconciliation for iniquity, and to bring in everlasting righteousness, and to seal up the vision and prophecy, and to anoint the most Holy."

D | Finishing The Transgression - Israel's Last Sins

Secular Zionism is blood-brother to the New World Order, the International Banking System, and Communism. All were created in large part by cabalistic Jews who abandoned Biblical truth for Talmudic-Babylonian-Freemasonic-Illuminati perversions. Their Antichrist system will introduce the Mark of the Beast. Communism was created to enslave humanity. Zionists would rule the world in defiance of Jehovah. But Jehovah, embodied in Jesus Christ, will hook the jaw of their own monster - Communist Russia - and destroy it at Armageddon.

Daniel 9:24 - "Seventy weeks are determined upon thy people, ...to make an end of sins, ...and to anoint the Most Holy."

B | Sixty-Nine Weeks = 483 Years - Nehemiah To Calvary

Nehemiah asked Artaxerxes to "send me unto Judah, unto the city of my fathers' sepulchres, that I may build it. ...And the king granted me." Artexerxes commandment started the clock that counted 483 years until the crucifixion of Jesus Christ, which fulfilled Daniel's 69-week prophecy. A MOST AMAZING prophecy!

Daniel 9:25 - "From the going forth of the commandment to restore and to build Jerusalem unto the Messiah the Prince shall be seven weeks, and threescore and two weeks: the street shall be built again, and the wall, even in troublous times. And after threescore and two weeks shall Messiah be cut off."

C | Never Doubt The Accuracy Of Bible Prophecies

Around 550 BC, Daniel prophesied of King Artaxerxes of Persia commissioning Nehemiah to return to Jerusalem to rebuild the streets and walls in troublous times - which happened a century later (445 BC). Nehemiah documented his troubles with Assyrians, Sanballat and Tobiah. Daniel prophesied that Messiah would die 483 years later. He did. An awesome prophecy was precisely fulfilled.

Daniel 9:25 - "From the going forth of the commandment to restore and to build Jerusalem unto the Messiah the Prince shall be seven weeks, and threescore and two weeks: the street shall be built again, and the wall, even in troublous times. ...[afterward] shall Messiah be cut off."

D | After 62 Weeks Shall Messiah Be Cut Off

When did Daniel say Messiah would be cut off? After 62 weeks, or after 69 weeks? The fact is that the first seven weeks PRECEDED the second 62 weeks. Therefore, if Messiah was cut off AFTER 62 weeks, it was ALSO at the END of 69 weeks. Both answers are the same date. Messiah (Jesus) WAS cut off (from Israel) by His crucifixion, "but not for Himself." Christ can NEVER be cut off from His divine purpose! All prophecy WILL be fulfilled!

Daniel 9:26 - "And after threescore and two weeks shall Messiah be cut off, but not for himself."

B | The People Of The Prince That Shall Come - ROME!

In Daniel 10, the heavenly messenger revealed to Daniel the spiritual, heavenly warfare between Michael (the archangel) and the Prince of Persia and the Prince of Grecia. When the Prince of Persia fell. the Persian Empire failed. When the Prince of Grecia prevailed, Alexander the Great built the great Grecian Empire. Next, the Roman Empire conquered Greece, and also conquered Israel. Corresponding to the iron legs in Nebuchadnezzar's Image, Daniel foresaw Jerusalem and the Temple overthrown by **the PRINCE OF ROME!**[27]

Daniel 9:26 - "...and the people of the prince that shall come shall destroy the city and the sanctuary."

D | Daniel's Seventieth Week

A "week of years" in prophecy is seven years. Several prophecies indicate **an event-packed SEVEN YEAR PERIOD**[28] immediately before Armageddon. A seven-year Covenant will be put forward by a Rome-influenced European power-broker who will install the Assyrian Man of Sin in Jerusalem (Isaiah 14:25-26; 2 Thessalonians 2:3-4). The time-line is firm. Exactly seven years after the Confirmation of the Covenant, Jesus will return with His saints to Jerusalem at Armageddon and will destroy this Man of Sin. Jesus' 1000-year Kingdom will begin immediately.

Daniel 9:27 - "And he [the Prince of Rome] shall confirm the covenant with many for one week..."

B | The Confirmation Of The Covenant

"He shall confirm the covenant..." Who is "HE"? The previous verse answers, "the Prince that shall come." **The Prince of Rome.**[29] Both the **IRON and the CLAY in Nebuchadnezzar's Image**[30] are Roman. The Seven-Headed, Ten-Horned Beast and the Pope of the Roman Catholic Church will make a Seven-Year Covenant pertaining to the future of Israel. I expect them to install an Assyrian over Palestine.

Daniel 9:27 - "He shall confirm the covenant with many for one week: and in the midst of the week he shall cause the sacrifice and the oblation to cease."

B | The Sacrifice And The Oblation

Here is one of the most important prophesied events in the Bible: the taking away of the Sacrifice and the Oblation from the Third Temple in Jerusalem. Shortly after the Third Temple is built and sacrifices resumed, the Man of Sin will enter the Holy Place and halt all sacrifices. This event will trigger the final 42 months leading to the battle of Armageddon – called the Great Tribulation in Matthew 24:15,21, and Jacob's Trouble in Daniel 12:1 and Jeremiah 30:7.

Daniel 9:27 - "In the midst of the week he shall cause the sacrifice and the oblation to cease, and for the overspreading of abominations he shall make it desolate."

D | The Consummation Of Israel

The Man of Sin will terminate the offerings of sacrifices in the Third Jewish Temple "even until the CONSUMMATION." What does that mean? From Joshua's day, God warned, "If ye forsake the LORD, and serve strange gods, then he will turn and do you hurt, and CONSUME you," Joshua 24:20. The horrifying events leading to the battle of Armageddon will CONSUME Israel, except for 144,000 divinely-protected Jews. If those days were not shortened, no flesh would be saved. At Armageddon, Jesus will save and restore Israel.

Daniel 9:27 - "...he shall make it desolate, even until the consummation."

D | The Abomination Of Desolation

The Antichrist will defile the Third Temple by standing in the Holy Place and demanding the daily sacrifices be halted. That will make the Temple desolate. Under the Old Testament scheme, the sacrifices were the heart of every activity in the Temple. Without sacrifices, the Temple is useless. Desolate. The Temple will remain desolate 42 months - 3 1/2 years, until everything is consumed at Armageddon (the consummation), and Jesus begins the restitution of all things (Acts 3:20-21).

Daniel 9:27 - "...he shall make it desolate, even until the consummation, and that determined shall be poured upon the desolate."

C | You Cannot Know God Without Supernatural Assistance

Bible scholars and biblical scholarship alone cannot discover God. Many brilliant men have undertaken to know the scriptures and the will of God, yet have never come to the true knowledge of God. God reveals Himself supernaturally. Dreams, visions, angels, miracles, signs, wonders, are indispensable components of divine revelation.

Daniel 10:1,7 - "A thing was revealed unto Daniel, ...and he understood the thing, and had understanding of the vision. ...I Daniel alone saw the vision: for the men that were with me saw not the vision; but a great quaking fell upon them, so that they fled to hide themselves."

A | Daniel's Fast

Daniel fasted for twenty-one days. Finally, the angel Gabriel brought him a spectacular revelation of the plan of God for the last days. We could have stupendous results if we could discipline ourselves to fast. It does not always have to be an absolute fast, although a total food-fast is advisable. Daniel abstained from "pleasant bread," "flesh" (meat), and "wine." Do your very best. God will honor your best effort.

Daniel 10:3 - "I ate no pleasant bread, neither came flesh nor wine in my mouth, neither did I anoint myself at all, till three whole weeks were fulfilled."

B | **The Man Clothed In Linen**

A man appeared to Daniel in his vision. He was an angel of the LORD. He and Israel's chief prince, Michael, had been withstanding the demon prince of Persia.

Daniel 10:5 - "I lifted up mine eyes, and looked, and behold a certain man clothed in linen, whose loins were girded with fine gold of Uphaz: His body also was like the beryl, and his face as the appearance of lightning, and his eyes as lamps of fire, and his arms and his feet like in colour to polished brass, and the voice of his words like the voice of a multitude."

C | **Divine Revelations Are Personal And Private**

When God showed Daniel the vision, other men stood by, but did not see it. They fled because it scared them so badly, they were "quaking." A similar situation occurred when God spoke to Saul in Acts 9. He heard the voice of the LORD, but "the men which journeyed with him stood speechless, hearing a voice, but seeing no man." God usually deals very personally with a man when giving a great revelation.

Daniel 10:7 - "I Daniel alone saw the vision: for the men that were with me saw not the vision; but a great quaking fell upon them, so that they fled to hide themselves."

A | **From The First Day, Thy Words Were Heard**

Daniel prayed about everything, it seemed. Toward the end of Israel's captivity, he undertook an extended fasting and prayer vigil, that he might have understanding of his visions. On his last fast day, an angel woke him from a deep sleep, putting him on his hands and knees. Then he told him to stand to receive his answer. God hears - the minute you call.

Daniel 10:12,14 - "From the first day that thou didst set thine heart to understand, ...thy words were heard. ..., I am come to make thee understand what shall befall thy people in the latter days."

C | **Spiritual Warfare In The Heavens**

The man-clothed in linen was an angel of the Lord. He explained to Daniel that he and the angel Michael had been warring in heaven against the spirit prince of Persia. That explains why the Persians ultimately sponsored the reconstruction of Jerusalem, and were then overthrown by the mighty Grecian, Alexander the Great. The angel warned that "when I am gone forth, lo, the prince of Grecia shall come."

Daniel 10:13 - "The prince of the kingdom of Persia withstood me one and twenty days: but, lo, Michael, one of the chief princes, came to help me; and I remained there with the kings of Persia."

B | **The Princes Of Persia And Grecia**

This is a rare view of how things happen in the spirit world. The angel revealed to Daniel that he and Michael, the angel-prince of Israel, were at war with the demon prince of Persia. When they overthrew the demon, the Persian Empire fell, and another prince (Grecia) came.

Daniel 10:13,20-21 - "The prince of the kingdom of Persia withstood me, ...now will I return to fight with the prince of Persia: and when I am gone forth, lo, the prince of Grecia shall come, ...there is none that holdeth with me in these things, but Michael your prince."

C | **God Follows An Ancient Plan In These Latter Days**

The heavenly visitor explained to Daniel that his vision was all about "the latter days." OUR days! Almighty God decreed the future from millennia past. Now, these ARE the latter days. Now, you and I will see with our eyes, hear with our ears, and UNDERSTAND hundreds of elaborate prophecies from thousands of years past. Obscure prophecies will no longer be obscure, but clearly understood, albeit shocking headlines in our daily news.

Daniel 10:14 - "Now I am come to make thee understand what shall befall thy people in the latter days: for yet the vision is for many days."

A | **When You Don't Feel Like Praying**

As the angel narrated Daniel's vision of coming epic events in the last days, Daniel literally quaked and trembled. He had no strength and objected to the angel that he could not speak. The angel touched him and said, "O man greatly beloved, fear not: ...be strong." When you feel too faint to pray, God will help you.

Daniel 10:19,21 - "And when he had spoken unto me, I was strengthened, and said, Let my lord speak; for thou hast strengthened me. [the angel replied] ...I will shew thee that which is noted in the scripture of truth."

C | Visions Are Often Given For Events Far In The Future

In the days of Cyrus, King of Persia, Daniel received revelations from God for which "the time appointed was long." While Daniel was on a three-week fasting and prayer vigil, a heavenly visitor showed him "what shall befall thy people in the latter days: for yet the vision is for many days." Let all the atheistic detractors in the world know that God knows the end from the beginning. Fulfilled ancient prophecies comprise irrefutable evidence of the eternal power and foreknowledge of God. The testimony of Jesus Christ is the Spirit of Prophecy.

Daniel 10:21 - "I will shew thee that which is noted in the scripture of truth."

C | Angels Strengthen And Weaken Empires

Daniel's angel visitor continued to explain how things happen in the heavens. After explaining how he and Michael had fought with the prince of Persia, and would next fight with the prince of Grecia, he revealed that it was he who had helped the Persians conquer the Babylonians. So the angels presided over the fall of Babylon, the rise of Media-Persia, the fall of Persia, and rise of Grecia. God's angels rule in the heavens.

Daniel 11:1[31] - "Also I in the first year of Darius the Mede, even I, stood to confirm and to strengthen him."

C | Prophecies Are A Revelation Of Truth

Daniel 11 contains complex prophecies covering a long saga of events between the Old and New Testaments. Daniel accurately prophesied dozens of VERY DETAILED events that would happen between the King of the North - Syria (and the Seleucian Empire) and the King of the South - Egypt (and the Ptolemaic Empire). These prophecies SHOULD have ASTONISHED the Jews who lived in the days of Jesus Christ, and totally convinced them of HIS MESSIAHSHIP, since Daniel also prophesied the VERY YEAR Messiah would die. For heaven's sake - PAY ATTENTION TO PROPHECY!

Daniel 11:2 - "And now will I show thee the truth."

D | Gabriel: The Fourth Persian King Will Oppose Grecia

The angel Gabriel (8:16; 9:1) explained to Daniel, then serving King Cyrus of Persia, that the fourth Persian king would engage the Grecians in a major war. Certainly enough, after Cyrus the Great came Cambyses, then Darius I (the Great), then Xerxes, who, with an army of two million (according to Herodotus), fulfilled the prophecy of Daniel 11:2.

Daniel 11:2 - "There shall stand up yet three kings in Persia; and the fourth shall be far richer than they all: and by his strength through his riches he shall stir up all against the realm of Grecia."

D | Daniel Prophesied The Rise Of Alexander The Great

Gabriel had already revealed that the Prince of Grecia would come (10:20; 11:2). Daniel then prophesied that "a mighty king" with "great dominion" would "do according to his will." TWO CENTURIES LATER, Alexander the Great of Greece conquered the Persians and all of Eurasia. When he died, his vast empire split into four separate kingdoms - perfectly fulfilling Daniel's prophecies. Utterly awesome!

Daniel 11:3-4 - "A mighty king shall stand up, that shall rule with great dominion, and do according to his will. And when he shall stand up, his kingdom shall be broken, and shall be divided toward the four winds of heaven."

B | King Of The North (Syria), King Of The South (Egypt)

Daniel prophesied that the empire of Alexander the Great would split four ways. It did. 1. Egypt 2. Seleucia (Syria, Iran, Iraq, Eastern Turkey) 3. Pergamon (Western Turkey) 4. Macedonia (Greece). In the prophecies of Daniel 11, Seleucia (Syria) is called the "King of the North," and Egypt is called the "King of the South."

Daniel 11:5-6 - "The king of the south [Egypt] shall be strong, And in the end of years they shall join themselves together; for the king's daughter of the south shall come to the king of the north [Syria] to make an agreement."

B | Meet Ptolemy I Of Egypt, Seleucus Of Syria

Meet Ptolemy I and Seleucus. Ptolemy I claimed Egypt when Alexander the Great died. Seleucus eventually joined him, but soon rose from there to conquer Gaza, Babylon, and Syria. His empire became larger than Ptolemy's. Two centuries beforehand, Daniel prophesied amazing details of their rise to power, which would not occur until about 325-281 BC.

☑✓

Such astonishingly accurate prophecies should make believers out of everyone!

Daniel 11:5 - "The king of the south shall be strong, and one of his princes; and he shall be strong above him, and have dominion; his dominion shall be a great dominion."

⋄ | Meet Berenice, Daughter Of Ptolemy II Of Egypt

The successor of Ptolemy I in Egypt was Ptolemy II. The successor of Seleucus in Syria was Antiochus. Antiochus made war with Ptolemy II. To settle their differences, Antiochus married the daughter of Ptolemy II. That ended the war. Daniel prophesied it all by divine revelation, two centuries before it happened. WOW!

Daniel 11:6 - "In the end of years they shall join themselves together; for the king's daughter of the south shall come to the king of the north to make an agreement: but she shall not retain the power of the arm; neither shall he stand, nor his arm."

⋄ | The Fate Of Syrian And Egyptian Royalty Prophesied

The vast Seleucid Empire, ruled from Syria by Antiochus, made peace with Ptolemy II of Egypt when he married Ptolemy's daughter, Berenice. Antiochus divorced his first wife, Laodice, to marry Berenice. But Ptolemy died, and Antiochus divorced Berenice to return to his first wife. In rage, Berenice poisoned him. Then Laodice poisoned Berenice and her son, the crown prince. All was prophesied by Daniel.

Daniel 11:6b - "She shall be given up [Berenice divorced], and they that brought her [Antiochus died], 'and her child' (YLT Version) [crown prince died], and he that strengthened her in these times [Ptolemy II died]."

⋄ | The Overthrow Of Syria By Egypt in 241 BC

When Egypt's Ptolemy II died, Antiochus of Syria divorced Ptolemy's daughter, Berenice, and returned to his first wife, Laodice. Berenice murdered Antiochus, so Laodice murdered her. Berenice's brother raised an Egyptian army and invaded Syria. Egypt attained the height of its world power. Daniel prophesied it 200 years earlier.

Daniel 11:7-8 - "Out of a branch of her [Egyptian] roots shall one stand up in his estate [her brother], which shall come with an army, and shall enter into the fortress of the king of the north [Syria], and shall deal against them, and shall prevail."

B | Antiochus III Loses Syria To Ptolemy IV In 217 BC

In the third generation of the Seleucid (Syrian) Empire, Antiochus III waged the "Fourth Syrian War," taking Israel, and attacking Ptolemy IV of Egypt. But Egypt won and took Syria. Daniel foretold that 300 years earlier. We should be impressed.

Daniel 11:10-12 - "His [Antiochus II] sons shall be stirred up, and shall assemble a multitude of great [Syrian] forces: ...the king of the south [Ptolemy IV] shall be moved with choler, and shall come forth and fight with him, even with the king of the north [Syria] ...and he shall cast down many ten thousands: but he shall not be strengthened by it."

D | Antiochus The Great Regroups, Retakes Syria, 198 BC

After losing Syria to the Egyptians, Antiochus III (the Great) went back east and regrouped. He formed an alliance with Philip of Macedonia, and together they attacked and conquered Ptolemy V and Egypt - 350 years after Daniel prophesied it. At that time, they also gained control of Palestine.

Daniel 11:13-14 - "The king of the north [Syria] shall return, and shall set forth a multitude greater than the former, and shall certainly come after certain years with a great army and with much riches. And in those times there shall many stand up against the king of the south."

C | God Controls The Destinies Of All People

Daniel prophetically depicted Egypt as "robbers" with a vision to take Palestine. His prophecy that Syria would defeat Egypt and consume "the glorious land" was fulfilled in 198 BC.

Daniel 11:14b-16 - "The robbers of thy people [Egyptians] shall exalt themselves to establish the vision; but they shall fall. So the king of the north [Syria] shall come, ...and the arms of the south [Egypt] shall not withstand, neither his [God's] chosen people, ...he that cometh against him [Syria] will do according to his own will, ...he [Syria] shall stand in the glorious land, which by his hand shall be consumed."

C | Ultimately, All The Prophecies Point To Israel

No matter how complex the Bible prophecies are, they all eventually run in a full circle back to the nation of Israel. Whether the subject is Babylon, Rome, Syria, Egypt, Beasts or False Prophets, everything eventually points to God, His people, and His land. The other characters only play roles in testing and trying Israel until Jesus Christ returns to HIS LAND and HIS PEOPLE.

Daniel 11:16 - "He that cometh against him shall do according to his own will, and none shall stand before him: and he shall stand in the glorious land, which by his hand shall be consumed."

B | Prophecies About Cleopatra The Syrian

Antiochus of Syria contemplated invading Egypt. Instead, he gave his daughter Cleopatra to marry Ptolemy V in 193 BC, hoping to subvert Egypt through her. But Cleopatra proved loyal to her Egyptian husband. When he died, she became the first sovereign Ptolemaic queen. Egyptians called her "The Syrian." Daniel prophesied it over three centuries earlier.

Daniel 11:17 - "He [Antiochus] shall also set his face to enter with the strength of his whole kingdom, and upright ones with him; thus shall he do: and he shall give him the daughter of women [Cleopatra], corrupting her: but she shall not stand on his side, neither be for him."

D | Daniel Prophesied The Romans' Victory Over Syria

Antiochus the Great refocused his military efforts from controlling Egypt to conquering Greece and the islands of the Mediterranean. Unfortunately for him, the Roman general Scipio Asiaticus launched a counter-attack and prevented Antiochus from his conquest. Antiochus' Seleucid (Syrian) Empire crumbled in 188 BC, and the Roman Empire began emerging.

Daniel 11:18 - "After this shall he [Antiochus] turn his face unto the isles, and shall take many: but a prince for his own behalf [Scipio the Roman] shall cause the reproach offered by him to cease; without his own reproach he shall cause it to turn upon him."

D | Antiochus The Great Falls, Son Seleucus Taxes Israel

The prophecy said that Antiochus the Great would "turn his face toward the fort of his own land: but he shall stumble and fall, and not be found." Following a defeat by the Roman Scipio, Antiochus returned to his fort in Antioch, and soon afterward, died in another war, fulfilling prophecy. His son, Seleucus II, imposed harsh taxes on his kingdom, including Israel, to pay tributes to the Romans. He was poisoned. That also fulfilled a 300-year-old prophecy.

Daniel 11:20 - "Then shall stand up in his [Antiochus'] estate a raiser of taxes [Seleucus II] ...but within few days he shall be destroyed."

B | Antiochus Epiphanes - Prototype Of The Coming Man Of Sin

Daniel 11:21-32 prophesies of one of the most infamous men in the Bible - the Old Testament prototype of the New Testament Man of Sin. He committed the Abomination of Desolation in the Temple during the Maccabean period - between the Old and New Testaments. His name was never mentioned in the Bible, but it was Antiochus Epiphanes, king of Syria.

Daniel 11:21,28,31 - "...[there] shall stand up a vile person, ...his heart shall be against the holy covenant; ...and they shall pollute the sanctuary of strength, and shall take away the daily sacrifice, and they shall place the abomination that maketh desolate."

C | Flattery - Trademark Of The Man Of Sin

The wise man in Proverbs 29:5 said, "A man that flattereth his neighbour spreadeth a net for his feet." People use flattery to snare you. The Man of Sin will use flattery to obtain power in the world. Always beware of silver-tongued oratory that is full of flattery - "excessive, insincere praise." It is poisonous.

Daniel 11:21,32,34 - "He shall come in peaceably, and obtain the kingdom by flatteries. ...And such as do wickedly against the covenant shall he corrupt by flatteries: but the people that do know their God shall be strong, ...but many shall cleave to them with flatteries."

C | God Knows His Enemies

How can we read all these amazing prophetic details about seemingly obscure events without realizing that God knows His enemies intimately? Every spy agency and intelligence organization on earth would crave to know the thoughts and intentions of their enemies years in advance the way God knows. God not only knows every thought, but He also knows every movement of every person on earth BEFORE they make it.

Daniel 11:28 - "Then shall he return into his land with great riches; and his heart shall be against the holy covenant; and he shall do exploits, and return to his own land."

D | The Kingdom Of The Coming Man Of Sin

This fellow, Antiochus Epiphanes, king of Syria from 171-167 BC, was a foreshadow of the future Man of Sin. Both come from the ancient Syrian Empire (reaching from Turkey on the west to Iran on the east). It is one of four divisions of Alexander's Grecian Empire. It is the "little horn" of Daniel 8:9. Antiochus defiled the Temple then, as will the coming Man of Sin.

Daniel 11:31 - "And arms [armies] shall stand on his part, and they shall pollute the sanctuary of strength, and shall take away the daily sacrifice, and they shall place the abomination that maketh desolate."

B | The Maccabeans

Before the Roman (iron legs) periods of Nebuchadnezzar's image was a period involving the four divisions of the Grecian Empire. One division was Syria, called the "king of the north." Antiochus Epiphanes of Syria invaded Judea, deposed Onias the High Priest ("[Onias] shall be broken"), placed a statue of Zeus in the Temple, and offered swine flesh on the altar. Mattathias, the successor High Priest, and his son, Judas Maccabeus, raised an army [the Maccabeans] and fought valiantly against the Syrians.

Daniel 11:32 - "The people that do know their God shall be strong, and do exploits. ...yet they shall fall by the sword."

C | They That Understand Shall Instruct Many

Much has been said about the power of one. One person can make a difference. When the entire Syrian Empire was against Jerusalem, one man, Judas Maccabeus, rallied an army of God-fearing Jews who were willing to die for a righteous cause - defending all that is holy from a tyrant. The Maccabean revolt is a historical phenomenon, a glorious example of men of clear understanding standing up and speaking out. Now, more than ever, righteous men must be heard, even if they must die for the cause.

Daniel 11:33 - "They that understand among the people shall instruct many."

D | Some Will Be Tried, To The Time Of The End

Suddenly, the prophecies in Daniel 11 turned from ancient events to future coming events in the last days - "the time of the end." Verses 21-34 described ancient events between the Jews and the Syrian King

Antiochus Epiphanes, (an Old Testament type of the Antichrist) who committed abominations in the Temple. But beginning in verse 35, the prophecies refer to a future Assyrian (Turkey, Syria, or Iran) king, the coming Man of Sin. Daniel specifically said that these prophecies pertain to the time of the end.

Daniel 11:35 - "...even to the time of the end: because it is yet for a time appointed."

C | **Saints, Heroes, And Martyrs In The Last Days**

Daniel's prophecies (11:21-32) described the struggles that eventually occurred between Syrian king Antiochus Epiphanes and saintly Jewish heroes, the Maccabeans, who resisted the Syrians under Antiochus for committing abominations in the Temple (around 170 BC). Similarly, great saints in the last days will make a brave stand against the final Man of Sin as he defiles and opposes everything divine and holy. Many will be purged and purified during that time.

Daniel 11:35 - "Some of them of understanding shall fall, to try them, and to purge, and to make them white, even to the time of the end."

C | **White Means Purified In Tribulation**

In Revelation 3:18, an angel delivered a message for the Church to John saying, "I counsel thee to buy of me gold tried in the fire, that thou mayest be rich; and WHITE RAIMENT, that thou mayest be clothed." "These are they which came out of great tribulation, and have washed their ROBES, and made them WHITE in the blood of the Lamb," Revelation 7:14.

Daniel 11:35 - "Some of them of understanding shall fall, to try them, and to purge, and to make them WHITE," 12:10 - "Many shall be purified, and made WHITE, and tried."

B | **The Man Of Sin: The Assyrian**

Israel never had a more persistent enemy than Assyria. Assyria took the northern ten tribes of Israel into captivity, beginning in 740 BC under Tiglathpileser, then Shalmaneser, and then Sargon II. Later, Sennacherib of Assyria also threatened King Hezekiah of Judah. Hundreds of years later, after Judah returned from Babylonian captivity, the Assyrian, Antiochus Epiphanes profaned the Temple in Jerusalem. Daniel revealed that the final Man of Sin will be the king of Assyrians (I suspect modern Turkey, but possibly Syria or Iran).

Daniel 11:36 - "The king shall do according to his will; and he shall exalt himself, and magnify himself above every god."

D | The Man Of Sin Will Prosper Till God's Anger Is Satisfied

The self-willed Man of Sin from somewhere in the Turkey/Syria/Iran region will exalt and magnify himself above and against every god, even the God of gods. God has determined this evil man's fate since the beginning of time. The Man of Sin will prosper until God's indignation (anger) with Israel is satisfied.

Daniel 11:36 - "The king shall do according to his will; and he shall exalt himself, and magnify himself above every god, and shall speak marvelous things against the God of gods, and shall prosper till the indignation be accomplished: for that that is determined shall be done."

B | The God Of The Man Of Sin

Who is the God of the Antichrist? Himself! He will not honor Jehovah or any other god. We would expect a man from the region of Turkey, Syria or Iran to be a Muslim who honors Allah. But if the Man of Sin does not honor any other god, he could not be a Muslim, UNLESS he claims to be the INCARNATION of Allah. Muslims refer to their expected "Mahdi" as "the last REPOSITORY of ALLAH."

Daniel 11:37 - "Neither shall he regard the God of his fathers, nor the desire of women, nor regard any god: for he shall magnify himself above all."

D | The Man Of Sin And His Strange God - Lucifer!

The Man Of Sin will completely deny the Jehovah of Abraham, Isaac and Jacob. He will violently hate Jehovah, Jesus, Jews and Christians. His "strange god" will be God's worst enemy. Who else? Lucifer will absolutely possess this terrifying man – the Man of Sin! The world has never seen such evil. Islam's purported "Mahdi"!

Daniel 11:37-39 - "Neither shall he regard the God of his fathers, ...nor regard any god: for he shall magnify himself above all. ...a god whom his fathers knew not shall he honour. ...Thus shall he do in the most strong holds with a strange god, whom he shall acknowledge and increase with glory."

C | **The "Estate" Of The Man Of Sin**

Even the devil has his own place. The Antichrist will have his own place. "In his estate," means, "in his place, his base." The Man of Sin will probably have a fortified installation that he operates from. The real news here is that God determines and grants everybody a place until everything ultimately comes to judgment. Remember how Jesus granted Judas, "What thou doest, do quickly." Ever since Lucifer sinned in the Garden of Eden, God has granted him a place. But his final place will be in Hell.

Daniel 11:38 - "In his estate shall he honour the God of forces."

B | **The Man Of Sin And His Defense System**

The Antichrist will honor the "God of forces." In dozens of other Old Testament verses, the Hebrew word "maoz" is translated "strength" or "stronghold." It also has a connotation of "defense systems." Will the Antichrist stand behind the world's most dangerous defense system? Will he possess a threatening nuclear arsenal? I suspect that he will.

Daniel 11:38-39 - "But in his estate shall he honour the God of forces: ...with gold, and silver, and with precious stones, and pleasant things. Thus shall he do in the most strong holds, ...and he shall cause them to rule over many."

D | **The Man Of Sin Will Rule Israel During Last 42 Months**

During the forty-two months after he desecrates the Jewish Temple (by standing inside it, claiming to be God), the Man of Sin will set about to rule the world as the most evil king in all of human history. As "the king of the north," he will quickly engage in war with Egypt and take over ALL Israel.

Daniel 11:39,41,45 - "...he shall cause them to rule over many, and shall divide the land for gain. ...He shall enter also into the glorious land, ...And he shall plant the tabernacles of his palace between the seas in the glorious holy mountain."

C | **All Biblical Prophecies Have Purpose**

I have not found a more difficult chapter in the Bible than Daniel 11. But despite its apparent complexity and difficulty, it contains some of the most important prophetic information in the Bible. To ignore Daniel 11 is to deprive ourselves of several INDISPENSABLE pieces of the prophetic puzzle. If we want to understand what will happen in the last days, or accurately identify the coming Antichrist, we must understand Daniel 11.

Daniel 11:40 - "At the time of the end shall the king of the south push at him: and the king of the north shall come against him."

B | Antichrist Will Take Egypt

Egypt made peace with Israel in 1979 when President Anwar Sadat signed the Israel-Egyptian Peace Treaty with Israeli President Menachem Begin. Egypt hosts the headquarters of the 22-nation Arab League. Egypt will initially stand against the Man of Sin, but will later be defeated by him.

Daniel 11:40,42-43 - "At the time of the end shall the king of the south [Egypt] push at him: and the king of the north [Antichrist] shall come against him like a whirlwind, ...and the land of Egypt shall not escape. But he shall have power over ...all the precious things of Egypt."

C | The Man Of Sin Will Have Money And Power

The Antichrist will have more earthly power than any man who ever lived. He will also control the earth's wealth. Nevertheless, his power and money cannot stand against the sovereign power of Almighty God. Jesus Christ will come and take it all from him.

Daniel 11:40-45 - "He [Man of Sin] shall enter into the countries, and shall overflow and pass over. ...many countries shall be overthrown: ...He shall stretch forth his hand also upon the countries: ...he shall have power over the treasures of gold and of silver, ...yet he shall come to his end, and none shall help him."

D | The Man Of Sin Will Overthrow Many Countries

This Assyrian (from either Turkey, Syria or Iran) Man of Sin will be a vicious enemy of Israel, and probably all Western civilization. He will have no tolerance for moderate Arabs. Jordan will escape his terrible control, but Egypt, Libya and Ethiopia will not. He will overthrow MANY countries.

Daniel 11:41-43 - "Many countries shall be overthrown: but these shall escape out of his hand, even Edom, and Moab, and the chief of the children of Ammon [Jordanians]. He shall stretch forth his hand also upon the countries: and the land of Egypt shall not escape. ...the Libyans and the Ethiopians shall be at his steps."

B | "Great Fury" - Islamic Antichrist Warring Against Communism?

The Man of Sin will conquer Israel, Egypt, and many other nations. This Assyrian monster will do everything he wants until trouble comes from the north and east. I suspect that Communists from Russia (north) and China (east) will try to terminate this Islamic Mahdi's global conquest, provoking the worst war in history: Islam trying to deal a death-blow to Communism. The Sixth Trumpet War of Revelation 9. One-third of mankind will die. The Man of Sin will survive until Armageddon. He has an appointment with Jesus Christ.

Daniel 11:44 - "Tidings out of the east and out of the north shall trouble him: therefore he shall go forth with great fury to destroy, and utterly to make away many."

C | Paradise Gained, Paradise Lost

Lucifer, possessing the Man of Sin, will finally realize one of his most-longed-for dreams. Lucifer said in Isaiah 14:13, "I will sit also upon the mount of the congregation, in the sides of the north." But God answered him back in Ezekiel 28:16. "I will cast thee as profane out of the mountain of God: and I will destroy thee, O covering cherub." Lucifer will finally sit in power on the Holy Mount in Jerusalem, but Jesus will violently overthrow him.

Daniel 11:45 - "And he shall plant the tabernacles of his palace between the seas in the glorious holy mountain; yet he shall come to his end, and none shall help him."

D | The Archangel Michael And The Great Tribulation

It appears that the tandem Iron and Clay entity of Europe and the Roman Catholic Church will install an Assyrian Man of Sin in his palace in Jerusalem. The Great Tribulation will begin when he commits the Abomination of Desolation in the Third Temple, and it will continue for 42 months. Michael the archangel will stand up for Israel. 144,000 godly Jews will be sealed and delivered.

Daniel 12:1 - "At that time shall Michael stand up, the great prince which standeth for the children of thy people: and there shall be a time of trouble, such as never was since there was a nation even to that same time."

□✓

B | Everyone That Shall Be Found Written In The Book

According to Revelation 12, God will seal 144,000 Jews - 12,000 for each of the twelve tribes - at the very beginning of the Great Tribulation. This will be the remnant, "which keep the commandments of God, and have the testimony of Jesus Christ," mentioned in Revelation 12:17. The unspoken conclusion is that they will be the only Jews to survive the Great Tribulation. The rest will apparently be destroyed or enslaved during the Antichrist's 42-month rule in Jerusalem.

Daniel 12:1 - "At that time thy people shall be delivered, every one that shall be found written in the book."

D | Saints Will Resurrect First, Sinners 1000 Years Later

The FIRST resurrection will occur when Jesus returns to earth. The dead in Christ will rise, and living saints will be caught up to meet them in the air (I Thessalonians 4:16-17). "The rest of the dead [the wicked] lived not again until the thousand years were finished," Revelation 20:4-5. Daniel foresaw both resurrections. Sinners will be resurrected and judged at the White Throne (Revelation 20:11) AFTER the Millennium.

Daniel 12:2 - "And many of them that sleep in the dust of the earth shall awake, some to everlasting life, and some to shame and everlasting contempt."

C | The Righteous Will Shine Forever

Only the mighty God of all things can make this true. If the universe is godless, or only evil, then righteous men will finally perish. But there is a God in Heaven, a righteous God whose people are righteous. His cause is righteous. EVERYTHING evil will someday be destroyed, and every man, woman, boy and girl who has embraced and stood for the eternal Truth of this living, almighty God will live forever.

Daniel 12:3 - "And they that be wise shall shine as the brightness of the firmament; and they that turn many to righteousness as the stars for ever and ever."

B | Transportation and Education In The Last Days

"Many shall run to and fro." Daniel could never have imagined how accurate that would be in a world with 800 million cars, 50,000 airline flights daily, and nearly two billion airline passengers annually. "And knowledge shall be increased." As of June, 2009, about 1.7 billion people were using the Internet and 350 million students worldwide attended school regularly. Globally, information is growing at about 66% annually, and that rate is accelerating exponentially.

Daniel 12:4 - "Seal the book, even to the time of the end: many shall run to and fro, and knowledge shall be increased."

C | The Words Are Closed Up And Sealed Until The End

God presides over His mysteries and only reveals them whenever and to whomever He wants. Although Daniel received volumes of the most amazing prophecies ever given, most of them made absolutely no sense to him at the time. You and I must also realize that God often works that way in our lives.

Daniel 12:4, 8-9 - "O Daniel, shut up the words, and seal the book, even to the time of the end: ...I heard, but I understood not: ...He said, Go thy way, Daniel: for the words are closed up and sealed till the time of the end."

D | Lucifer And The Antichrist

What is the relationship between Lucifer and the Antichrist? One and the same. Every diabolical plan Lucifer ever concocted will be manifested in the Antichrist. Antichrist will be Lucifer's human puppet. This man will be absolutely Lucifer-possessed like nothing ever seen before. If you see one, you've seen them both. Whereas Michael and Gabriel fought personally with the princes of Babylon, Persia, Grecia and Rome, only Jesus Christ will confront the Syrian Antichrist – completely possessed by Lucifer.

Daniel 12:7 - "When he shall have accomplished to scatter the power of the holy people, all these things shall be finished."

D | The Final Destruction Of Israel During Jacob's Trouble

In Daniel's vision, someone asked the man clothed in linen "how long shall it be to the end of these wonders?" The angel raised both hands to heaven and swore that it would be a time, times, and half a time (42 months or 3.5 years in other related prophecies). The Great Tribulation, or Jacob's Trouble runs from the Abomination of Desolation until Israel is essentially wiped off the map, and Jesus comes with vengeance at Armageddon.

Daniel 12:7 - "When he shall have accomplished to scatter the power of the holy people, all these things shall be finished."

□✓

A | What Shall Be The End Of These Things?

God gave so many spectacular revelations to Daniel concerning the last days, he was literally overwhelmed with it all. But as in every previous situation of his life, Daniel sought for an answer by praying. When things around you are confusing and distressing, talk to God about it. He is the Great Comforter.

Daniel 12:8-9 - "And I heard, but I understood not: then said I, O my Lord, what shall be the end of these things? And he said, Go thy way, Daniel: for the words are closed up and sealed till the time of the end."

C | None Of The Wicked Will Understand, But The Wise Will

This may be one of the most amazing things in the Bible. A person who walks with God, knows the Word of God, and understands the will of God will recognize and understand the rise of the Antichrist, the Great Tribulation, and events leading to Armageddon. But ungodly people DO NOT HAVE A CLUE! Prophetic events mean nothing - darkness - to ungodly men. RIGHT NOW, STUDY to show yourself approved unto God!

Daniel 12:10 - "Many shall be purified, and made white, and tried; but the wicked shall do wickedly: and none of the wicked shall understand; but the wise shall understand."

D | The Extra 45 Days - Armageddon

What is the purpose of the extra 45 days at the end of the Great Tribulation? I suspect that is how long the battle of Armageddon will be. I believe the war between Israel and its enemies will rage for days or weeks before Jesus returns. As the enemies nearly destroy Israel, Jesus will finally arrive to finish that epic Battle by destroying all His enemies. Multitudes will die. Blessed are those who survive Armageddon.

Daniel 12:11-12 - "From the time that the daily sacrifice shall be taken away, and the abomination that maketh desolate set up, there shall be a thousand two hundred and ninety days. Blessed is he that waiteth, and cometh to the thousand three hundred and five and thirty days."

Lessons from the Book of
HOSEA

B | Hosea And His Wife Of Whoredoms

Hosea was contemporary with Isaiah, during the reigns of Uzziah, Jotham, Ahaz and Hezekiah, kings of Judah. The northern ten tribes of Israel were already completely apostate, and Judah was in the process of backsliding. God instructed the prophet to engage in a provocative pantomime before the people. He was to marry a prostitute and adopt the children of her whoredoms. The pantomime dramatized the appalling unfaithfulness of His whorish people.

Hosea 1:2 - "The LORD said to Hosea, Go, take unto thee a wife of whoredoms and children of whoredoms: for the land hath committed great whoredom, departing from the LORD."

C | The Sin Of Unfaithfulness – Spiritual Adultery

It is a foolish thing to presume that God does not notice our unfaithfulness. When God sees us being intimate with the world, He views it as infidelity – spiritual adultery! God requires His people to love Him purely, and never compromise themselves with the world, the flesh or the devil. No man can serve two masters. If you are torn between two lovers, you are an adulterer, a whoremonger in God's eyes. Love not the world, neither the things that are in the world. Love the LORD your God.

Hosea 1:2 - "...the land hath committed great whoredom, departing from the LORD."

B | Gomer, Jezreel, Loruhamah, and Loammi

Gomer was the "wife of whoredoms" that Hosea took, as per God's instructions. She bore him three children. God gave Hosea the names of all three. Jezreel - "God will scatter" - was to notify Israel and King Jehu that God would soon judge them. A daughter was named Loruhamah - "no more mercy." The second son was named Loammi - "not my people." Nevertheless, God prophesied a future day of mercy.

Hosea 1:10 - "In the place where it was said unto them, Ye are not my people, there it shall be said unto them, Ye are the sons of the living God."

D | The Day Of Jezreel - Armageddon

Hosea was one of the first prophets to appear in the days of the divided kingdom of Israel, even before Isaiah. His "doomsday" prophecies concerning Jezreel alluded to the dreadful battle of Armageddon, and the complete regathering and restoration of a united Israel afterward, under one King – (Jesus Christ).

Hosea 1:10-11 - "The number of the children of Israel shall be as the sand of the sea, ...Then shall the children of Judah and the children of Israel be gathered together, and appoint themselves one head, and they shall come up out of the land: for great shall be the day of Jezreel."

C | That Which Is Not Shall Be

In the first chapter, God named two of Hosea's children Lo-Ammi and Lo-Ruhamah, meaning "not my people," and "no more mercy," respectively - words of condemnation. But because of the wondrous and incomprehensible love of God for His people, He commanded them to be renamed, "my people," and "obtained mercy." If God was like men, He would have permanently cast away His adulterous people. But God truly loved Israel and would not ultimately disown them. We should be profoundly encouraged by such inexplicable mercy.

Hosea 2:1 - "Say ye unto your brethren, Ammi; and to your sisters, Ruhamah."

D | Israel Turned Into Dry Wilderness Land

Mark Twain described his visit to the Holy Land in 1867. "Palestine sits in sackcloth and ashes. Over it broods the spell of a curse that has withered its fields and fettered its energies... Palestine is desolate and unlovely... It is a hopeless, dreary, heartbroken land... [a] desolate country ...given over wholly to weeds - a silent mournful expanse." God often warned Israel that unrepented sin would bring this judgment.

Hosea 2:2-3 - "Plead with your mother, plead: ...let her therefore put away her whoredoms ...her adulteries ...Lest I ...make her as a wilderness, and set her like a dry land."

C | Illicit Lovers Cannot Compare To True Love

Gomer - Hosea's "wife of whoredoms" symbolized Israel, who "played the harlot," saying, "I will go after my lovers, that give me my bread and my water, my wool and my flax, mine oil and my drink." For worshipping and burning incense to Baal, God cut off His blessings from Israel.

Hosea 2:8 - "Then shall she say, I will go and return to my first husband; for then was it better with me than now. For she did not know that I gave her corn, and wine, and oil, and multiplied her silver and gold, which they prepared for Baal."

B | **Earrings And Other Jewelry**

When God first brought Israel out of Egypt, He blessed them with riches in jewelry. But after they turned their jewelry into golden calves and worshipped them (Exodus 32:2-3), **God ALWAYS hated jewelry after that.**[32] In Numbers 31, the people gave all their jewelry to Moses and Eleazar for a sin offering. God views jewelry with great disdain.

Hosea 2:13 - "I will visit upon her the days of Baalim, wherein she burned incense to them, and she decked herself with her earrings and her jewels, and she went after her lovers, and forgat me, saith the LORD."

B | **After Valley Of Achor (Trouble); Ishi (Husband), Baali (Master)**

God called Israel, His unfaithful wife, back to Him. "I will give her the valley of Achor for a door of hope." In Joshua's day, the place where Achan sinned became known as the "valley of trouble." God said to Israel, in effect, "I give you a valley full of trouble, and it will be your doorway back to God - your hope. Then you will love Me as a spouse, instead of a slave-master."

Hosea 2:16 - "At that day, saith the LORD, that thou shalt call me Ishi [Husband]; and shalt call me no more Baali [Master]."

A | **God Will Hear His Unfaithful Lover If She Will Return**

God drafted the prophet Hosea to portray a divine moral lesson, by marrying a harlot. Hosea's corrupted marriage symbolized God's own spoiled relationship with whoremongering Israel. God denounced Israel for taking other lovers, and determined to break her evil habits. He begged her to quit her whoremongering and promised mercy in exchange for her faithfulness.

Hosea 2:21 - "I will hear, saith the LORD, ...I will have mercy upon her that had not obtained mercy; and I will say to them which were not my people, Thou art my people; and they shall say, Thou art my God."

D | **Many Days Without A King**

God has the power and the ability to dismantle everything you put your trust in, other than Him. He warned Israel that He would completely dismantle their nation, their government and their religion if they did not repent. That happened exactly as they were warned. They suffered about 2000 years under that sentence of judgment.

Hosea 3:4-5 - "For the children of Israel shall abide many days without a king, and without a prince, and without a sacrifice, and without an image, and without an ephod, and without teraphim. Afterward shall [they] seek the LORD... and David their king."

A | Israel Will Seek The LORD In The Latter Days

God instructed Hosea to purchase an adulteress harlot and love her, to symbolize how He had to buy Israel's love. They loved other gods and strong drink. But God's blessings do not always buy people's love for Him. Israel's relationship with God was failing. He would make them "abide many days without a king, and without a prince," and love them from afar until their hearts turned back to Him.

Hosea 3:5 - "Afterward shall the children of Israel return, and seek the LORD their God, ...and shall fear the LORD and his goodness in the latter days."

C | My People Are Destroyed For Lack Of Knowledge

This oft-quoted passage is a frightening rebuke from God. "Hear the word of the LORD, ye children of Israel: for the LORD hath a controversy with the inhabitants of the land, because there is no truth, nor mercy, nor knowledge of God in the land." All Israel committed grievous sins: swearing, lying, stealing, adulteries, and murders. "Thou shalt fall, ...and the prophet ...with thee." Surely, this modern generation must also face the same judgments. O, hear the word of the LORD!

Hosea 4:6 - "My people are destroyed for lack of knowledge: because thou hast rejected knowledge, I will also reject thee."

A | My People Ask Counsel At Their Stocks

Hosea prophesied during the same general time-frame as did Isaiah; concurrent with Kings Uzziah, Jotham, Ahaz and Hezekiah. During that time, Jeroboam led the northern ten tribes into gross idolatry. We cannot fully appreciate the intense fury that God feels when His people pray to other gods - which are no gods. Few things provoke God any worse than idolatry.

Hosea 4:12 - "My people ask counsel at their stocks [idols], and their staff [divining rods] declareth unto them: for the spirit of whoredoms hath caused them to err, and they have gone a whoring from under their God."

A | They Shall Seek Him And Not Find Him

Most people cannot comprehend the concept of spiritual adultery. They do not realize how seriously God is offended when they are spiritually engaged with evil spirits. It is spiritual whoredom - spiritual adultery. Like Achan who had "goodly Babylonish" treasures hidden in his tent (in Joshua's day), men died because there was sin in the camp. Do not foolishly presume that God will receive you while you are in love with forbidden things.

Hosea 5:6 - "They shall go with their flocks and with their herds to seek the LORD; but they shall not find him; he hath withdrawn himself from them."

D | Ephraim Must Pay For Their Bad Example

God leveled criticism and condemnation upon Ephraim (representing the northern tribes) because of their evil influence. "Judgment is toward you, because ye have been a snare on Mizpah, and a net spread upon [Mount] Tabor." They were "profound to make slaughter." God said "the spirit of whoredoms is in the midst of them, and they have not known the LORD."

Hosea 5:12,14 - "Therefore will I be unto Ephraim as a moth, and to the house of Judah as rottenness. ...I will be unto Ephraim as a lion, ...I will tear and go away; ...and none shall rescue him."

C | Return Unto The LORD - He Hath Torn, He Will Heal

In so many prophecies, God used metaphor and simile. Comparing Israel to a broken vessel, God promised to make them over, as a meticulous potter would. Comparing Israel to a valley of dry bones, God promised to raise them and make them live again. Like a smoking flax, God will not quench, but fan it into flames. And like a bruised reed, God will not break it, but mend it.

Hosea 6:1 - "Come, and let us return unto the LORD: for he hath torn, and he will heal us; he hath smitten, and he will bind us up."

D | After Two Days He Will Revive Us

The Apostle Peter declared that "one day is with the LORD as a thousand years, and a thousand years as one day," 2 Peter 3:8. So God relegated Israel to TWO DAYS (two thousand years) of suffering and discipline (following their rejection of their Messiah), followed by ONE DAY (one thousand years) of glorious living in their Promised Land under the perfect rule of Jesus Christ - King of Kings and Lord of Lords.

Hosea 6:2 - "After two days will he revive us: in the third day he will raise us up, and we shall live in his sight."

B | The Former Rain And The Latter Rain

Jeremiah, Hosea and Joel prophesied former and latter rains. Most Israeli crops grow in winter. Most rain falls between November and May. Early rains sprout the plants, and latter rains finish the crops. Typologically, the Old Testament works of God were the first rain **(Joel 2:23,28)**. The Holy Ghost outpouring on the New Testament Church is the latter rain.

Hosea 6:3 - "Then shall we know, if we follow on to know the LORD: his going forth is prepared as the morning; and he shall come unto us as the rain, as the latter and former rain unto the earth."

B | A Lament For Ephraim

Hosea was one of the first to mourn for the loss of the northern ten tribes of Israel. The idolatries and adulteries they began to do in Samaria and Shechem under the leadership of King Jeroboam never stopped for over 200 years (ca. 930-730 BC). The Assyrians finally carried them away. Hosea lamented their demise, which he witnessed with his own eyes. All their goodness fled away, like clouds and morning dew.

Hosea 6:4 - "O Ephraim, what shall I do unto thee? ...for your goodness is as a morning cloud, and as the early dew it goeth away."

C | God Brands Persistent Sinners, Refuses To Forget

God branded all the sinful northern ten tribes of Israel as "Ephraim," because it was an Ephraimite - King Jeroboam - who led them into idolatry and Baal-worship. "Jeroboam, who made all Israel to sin" is often repeated in the Bible. Unless you fully repent of your sins, they will follow you to your grave.

Hosea 7:11-12 - "Ephraim also is like a silly dove without heart: they call to Egypt, they go to Assyria. When they shall go, I will spread my net upon them; I will bring them down as the fowls of the heaven; I will chastise them."

B | The Calf Of Samaria

If God has flash-backs, He must have had one when Jeroboam set up two golden calves in Samaria and led Israel into idolatry. It was the same outrageously foolish stunt that Aaron did hundreds of years earlier, for which God almost killed the entire nation.

Hosea 8:4-6 "...of their silver and their gold have they made them idols, that they may be cut off. Thy calf, O Samaria, hath cast thee off; mine anger is kindled against them: ...the workman made it; therefore it is not God: but the calf of Samaria shall be broken in pieces."

C | Sow To The Wind, Reap The Whirlwind

One of the greatest miracles in all God's creation is the miracle of the seed. Everything living has its seed within itself. But the seed is for reproduction after its kind. The seed is not to be defiled, profaned, or sown in vain. That is at the very heart of all morality. God despises all those who "sow to the wind;" those who frivolously squander their lives on riotous living. He guarantees that bad will come of it. Sow your life unto God.

Hosea 8:7 - "For they have sown the wind, and they shall reap the whirlwind."

D | Reaping The Whirlwind

The whirlwind was a prophetic term used by several prophets in pronouncing judgment on Israel. It symbolized the coming of Armageddon - God's Day of Wrath - when Israel's sin will be finished. God's indignation will finally pass, and Messiah will begin the restitution of all things. Despite all that Israel has ever suffered, the worst is yet to come. Jacob's trouble, the Great Tribulation, will surpass anything they have ever known.

Hosea 8:14 - "For Israel hath forgotten his Maker, ...Judah hath multiplied fenced cities: but I will send a fire upon his cities, and it shall devour the palaces thereof."

D | They Shall Return To Egypt

God drove Ephraim (the northern tribes) out of the Holy Land for their sins. "They shall not dwell in the LORD'S land; but Ephraim shall return to Egypt, and they shall eat unclean things in Assyria," Hosea 9:3. Hosea prophesied around 735 BC. Most of Israel was originally taken captive by Assyria, but Josephus, the historian records that around 320 BC,

Ptolemy I took 120,000 Jews to Egypt from all over Syria and Palestine. As late as 1922 AD, 80,000 Jews lived in Egypt.

Hosea 9:6 - "Egypt shall gather them up, Memphis shall bury them."

B | Fruitful Grapes And Figs

God created mankind to be fruitful, as a husbandman expects fruit from his vineyards and orchards. God expected to gather fruit from His chosen people, Israel, whom He often likened unto grapes on the vine, or figs on the tree. But the prophets often lamented the failure of His people to bear fruit. God wants us to bear fruit unto righteousness, not evil.

Hosea 9:10 - "I found Israel like grapes in the wilderness; I saw your fathers as the firstripe in the fig tree at her first time: but they went to Baalpeor, and separated themselves unto that shame."

C | The Days Of Visitation

"The days of visitation are come." That is frightening news. These are days when God recompenses sin. In Isaiah, they are associated with desolation. In Jeremiah, they are associated with evil, darkness, falling, being cast down, perishing, and the day of calamity. When sinners face their days of visitation, it is over. "The prophet is a fool, the spiritual man is mad, ...the prophet is the snare of a fowler." The game is over.

Hosea 9:15,17 - "For the wickedness of their doings I will drive them out of mine house, ...they shall be wanderers among the nations."

B | Israel - An Empty Vine

It is not good to present yourself empty-handed to the LORD, especially if you have given lavishly to self-gratification. God weighs your priorities. If you give your life, your talents, and your energies to selfish, worldly living, He will remember it harshly when you come to judgment.

Hosea 10:1-2 - "Israel is an empty vine, he bringeth forth fruit unto himself: according to the multitude of his fruit he hath increased the altars; ...they have made goodly images. Their heart is divided; now shall they be found faulty: he shall break down their altars, he shall spoil their images."

C | **Unrepentant People Only Grow Worse**

Hosea recalled a long-past event, when Jews in Gibeah raped and murdered an innocent woman in the days of the Judges, resulting in a civil war that cost thousands of lives. He declared that Israel had only become more evil since then, adding idolatry and worshipping golden calves to their sins. He prophesied that God swore to shame them by giving their "god" AND the people over to the Assyrians.

Hosea 10:6 - "It shall be also carried unto Assyria for a present to king Jareb: Ephraim shall receive shame, and Israel shall be ashamed of his own counsel."

A | **It Is Time To Seek The LORD**

Just a little earlier, the prophet had denounced the people for their sins and concluded that they would seek the LORD and would not find Him, because "He hath withdrawn Himself from them," Hosea 5:6. Then, in a sudden about-face, he said, "It is time to seek the LORD." God may sometimes withdraw from you because you provoked His anger, but that is all the more reason why you should seek Him until He responds.

Hosea 10:12 - "Break up your fallow ground: for it is time to seek the LORD, till he come and rain righteousness upon you."

D | **Backsliding Israel Sent To Serve The King Of Assyria**

God said that He loved Israel when he was young, and called him out of Egypt. But they worshipped other gods and graven images. God taught them the ways of life in His Law and His Word, and He lovingly compelled them by helping them and providing for them. But they would not turn back to Him. So, instead of sending them back to Egypt, He sent them first to Assyria to serve the Assyrian king.

Hosea 11:7 - "My people are bent to backsliding from me: though they called them to the most High, none at all would exalt him."

C | **God's Heart Would Not Let Him Utterly Destroy Israel**

God's wrath was thoroughly kindled against Israel, but He knew that if He loosed His fiercest anger, they would disappear forever. He remembered Admah and Zeboim, cities that were destroyed with Sodom and Gomorrah (Genesis 14:2), and His heart was turned to mercy.

Hosea 11:8-9 - "How shall I give thee up, Ephraim? how shall I deliver thee, Israel? how shall I make thee as Admah? how shall I set thee as

Zeboim? ...I will not execute the fierceness of mine anger, ...for I am God, and not man; the Holy One in the midst of thee."

A | **Pray Like The Patriarchs**

Hosea reminded Israel of their patriarch Jacob, in his efforts to turn them back to righteousness. Jacob was the "heel-grabber" who fought to gain position and favor with God. "He had power over the angel, and prevailed." Hosea struggled to inspire the people to pray. Did you have godly ancestors who were more prayerful than yourself? Remember, and follow their example.

Hosea 12:4,6 - "He wept, and made supplication unto him: he found him in Bethel, and there he spake with us; ...Therefore turn thou to thy God: keep mercy and judgment, and wait on thy God continually."

D | **God Reinforced The Ministry Of Prophets Over Israel**

God indicted Ephraim(northern tribes of Israel) as a deceitful merchant and an oppressor, boasting of riches, smug in self-confidence, and denying all wrong-doing. But God restated His sovereign rights to them, which He had exercised as far back as their exodus from Egypt. He vowed to continue to put forward His prophets with visions and similitudes to speak to and govern them.

Hosea 12:9-10,14 - "I that am the LORD thy God from the land of Egypt... I have also spoken by the prophets, ...by a prophet the LORD brought Israel out of Egypt, and by a prophet was he preserved."

A | **Kissing Calves And Smoking Chimneys**

The pagan, idolatrous abominations that became commonplace in Israel defied the best rebukes. Hosea grasped for word-pictures to persuade the people to abandon their loathsome practices. Those who kiss idols, he said, God will blow away like clouds and smoke.

Hosea 13:2-3 - "They ...have made them molten images, ...they say of them, Let the men that sacrifice kiss the calves. Therefore they shall be as the morning cloud, and as the early dew that passeth away, as the chaff that is driven with the whirlwind out of the floor, and as the smoke out of the chimney."

B | **A Lion, A Leopard, And An Angry Bear**

I do not want God to pursue me as would a lion, a leopard, or an angry bear. But if personal sin threatens me with eternal damnation, I want God to do whatever it takes to startle me to my senses. The fear of God is the beginning of wisdom. Scare me.

Hosea 13:7-9 - "Therefore I will be unto them as a lion: as a leopard by the way will I observe them: I will meet them as a bear that is bereaved of her whelps, ...O Israel, thou hast destroyed thyself; but in me is thine help."

B | Israel's True King Is God

God was always jealous of Israel trusting earthly kings more than Himself. "I will be thy king; where is any other that may save thee?" 13:10. At first, God gave them Saul, but removed him for insubordination. In reality, nobody can truly govern mankind but God. Earthly kings could not keep Israel from gross and unrestrained sins. Only an all-knowing King can uncover and penalize hidden sin.

Hosea 13:12-14 - "The iniquity of Ephraim [Israel] is bound up; his sin is hid. The sorrows of a travailing woman shall come upon him: he is an unwise son."

A | Take With You Words

I cannot estimate how much of the Old Testament writings consist of rebukes for Israel's backsliding, but it certainly is a major segment. The prophets never stopped trying to awaken the people to righteousness. Again and again, they laid out patterns for approaching God in contrition and repentance. Start by opening your mouth and speaking humbly and honestly to God.

Hosea 14:1-2 - "O Israel, return unto the LORD thy God; for thou hast fallen by thine iniquity. Take with you words, and turn to the LORD: say unto him, Take away all iniquity, and receive us graciously."

D | Miraculous, Ultimate Fullness

All the allegories God ever used to describe His people will be epitomized when He returns to save them. Their "vine" will flourish, as will their roots, their branches, even their scent! Only God our Savior can impute miraculous, ultimate fullness.

Hosea 14:5-7 "I will be as the dew unto Israel: he shall grow as the lily, and cast forth his roots as Lebanon. His branches shall spread, and his beauty shall be as the olive tree, ...they shall revive as the corn, and grow as the vine: the scent thereof shall be as the wine of Lebanon."

Lessons from the Book of

JOEL

C | Tell Your Children And Your Children's Children

Joel offered no previews about what he was about to say. He simply served notice, especially on the old men, and then to all the inhabitants of the land, to report everything he was about to prophesy to everyone. Our modern Christian leaders preach only carefully selected things that they feel will be well-accepted or popular. But EVERYTHING GOD SAYS needs to be repeated for everyone to hear.

Joel 1:1,3 - "The word of the LORD that came to Joel... Tell ye your children of it, and let your children tell their children, and their children another generation."

B | The Palmerworm, Locust, Cankerworm, And Caterpillar

All four insects mentioned by Joel are voracious creatures that devastate foliage, fruit of trees and vegetative crops. These migratory pests can move into a field, strip it bare, destroy its crops, and disappear. The prophet Joel compared their work to the ruin that the armies of Babylon would leave when they captured the land of Israel.

Joel 1:6-7 - "For a nation is come up upon my land, strong, and without number, ...He hath laid my vine waste, and barked my fig tree: he hath made it clean bare, and cast it away; the branches thereof are made white."

A | Sanctify A Fast

Joel spoke of devastating plagues of locusts devouring everything in the land, leaving everyone in great desolation. From 1:6, we surmise that the locusts symbolized a nation (apparently Babylon) coming to seize Israel. "For a nation is come up upon my land, strong, and without number." ANYTIME calamity comes, we should immediately seek the LORD.

Joel 1:13-15 - "Lament, ...howl, ...lie all night in sackcloth, ...Sanctify ye a fast, call a solemn assembly, gather the elders and all the inhabitants of the land into the house of the LORD your God, and cry unto the LORD."

C | **Blow The Trumpet. Sound An Alarm. Warn Jerusalem.**

"Blow the trumpet in Zion [the heart of Jerusalem]." "Sound an alarm in my holy mountain [Temple Mount]." "Let all the inhabitants of the land tremble: for the day of the LORD cometh, for it is nigh at hand." This prophesied war can only refer to Armageddon. "There hath not been ever the like, neither shall be any more after it," verse 2. We are facing Armageddon in the very near future. Do you realize how near? It is nearer than you think!

Joel 2:2 - "A day of darkness and of gloominess, a day of clouds and of thick darkness."

D | **Messiah's Immortal Army Will Fight At Armageddon**

Here are the important keywords that reveal a supernatural (immortal) army of saints led by Messiah at Armageddon: Thick Darkness. Earthquake. Gloominess. Clouds. A great, strong people set in battle array. Fire devouring before and behind them, leaving a desolate wilderness. The appearance of horses and horsemen. The noise of chariots leaping in the mountains. Running like mighty men, not breaking rank. They shall not be wounded. Nothing shall escape them.

Joel 2:6,11 - "Before their face the people shall be much pained: all faces shall gather blackness. ...And the LORD [Jesus Christ] shall utter his voice before his army."

A | **The Prospect Of Armageddon Calls For Prayer**

Joel articulated one of the clearest prophecies in the Bible about how events will unfold at the battle of Armageddon - both dreadful and exciting. But with Armageddon in mind, the prophet published a clarion call to the people.

Joel 2:12-13 - "Therefore also now, saith the LORD, turn ye even to me with all your heart, and with fasting, and with weeping, and with mourning: And rend your heart, and not your garments, and turn unto the LORD your God: for he is gracious and merciful, slow to anger, and of great kindness, and repenteth him of the evil."

D | **The Bridegroom And The Bride Go Forth**

Immediately following Joel's depiction of Armageddon, he called for Israel to repent and prepare for that epic event. He added, "Let the bridegroom go forth of his chamber, and the bride out of her closet." Here, "coincidentally," is a prophetic call for the saints from all ages (the bride, the Lamb's wife) to meet their bridegroom (Jesus Christ) immediately before Armageddon.

Joel 2:16 - "Gather the people, sanctify the congregation, assemble the elders, gather the children, and those that suck the breasts: let the bridegroom go forth of his chamber, and the bride out of her closet."

A | Weep Between The Porch And The Altar

Joel counseled the priests to "weep between the porch and the altar." He even gave them words to pray. From the church-house porch to the altar - cry and pray for mercy! When sin and Satan overwhelm, try this formula!

Joel 2:17-19 - "Let the priests, the ministers of the LORD, weep between the porch and the altar, and let them say, Spare thy people, O LORD, and give not thine heritage to reproach, that the heathen should rule over them, ...Then will the LORD be jealous for his land, and pity his people. Yea, the LORD will answer."

B | The Northern Army

At Armageddon, the LORD Jesus Christ will drive out "the northern army," described in Ezekiel 37. Gog, prince of Magog, Gomer and Togarmah are the ancient identities of modern Russia, Turkey, Syria and western Iran. Jesus and His army will utterly desolate them.

Joel 2:20 - "I will remove far off from you the northern army, and will drive him into a land barren and desolate, with his face toward the east sea, and his hinder part toward the utmost sea, and his stink shall come up, and his ill savour shall come up, because he hath done great things."

C | Fear Not. Be Glad. Rejoice.

After Joel finished his discourse about Armageddon, and the sore defeat of Israel's enemies at that time, he shifted to a more present place and time, encouraging the people and prophesying a great work that God would yet do sometime in the interim before Armageddon. God knows that His people must have hope, and He always gives us a reason to hope. Regardless of how bad the world situation becomes, a righteous person has countless reasons NOT to be afraid.

Joel 2:21 - "Fear not, O land; be glad and rejoice: for the LORD will do great things."

D | **A National Spiritual Revival For Israel**

Joel's prophecies about Armageddon were only part of his overall message. Joel also had much to say about a great national spiritual revival that would come to Israel before the end of the age. The Apostles remembered Joel when God's Spirit fell on the Day of Pentecost in Acts 2.

Joel 2:23 - "Be glad then, ye children of Zion, and rejoice in the LORD your God: for he hath given you the former rain moderately, and he will cause to come down for you the rain, the former rain, and the latter rain in the first month."

C | **God Will Restore His People After They Are Tried**

Too often, people excuse themselves from making a commitment to God or the Bible because they have a dark opinion of how God really is. Many people perceive God as only harsh, judgmental, condemning, demanding and cruel. Nothing could be further from the truth. God has unimaginably wonderful plans for everyone who believes in Him, obeys His word, and faithfully follows wherever He leads.

Joel 2:24,26 - "The floors shall be full of wheat, and the fats shall overflow with wine and oil. ... And ye shall eat in plenty, and be satisfied, and praise the name of the LORD your God."

C | **God's Armies Punish The Wicked, Reward The Righteous**

Joel spoke of the indestructible, immortal army of the LORD coming to Armageddon, with soldiers (saints) who would not break rank and could not be injured. In contrast, God also said that the locusts, cankerworms, caterpillars and palmerworms, (metaphors for the Assyrians and Babylonians) were "my great army which I sent among you." God commands ALL ARMIES. His armies punish the wicked and deliver the righteous. Someday, God will reward all His saints who suffered in His wars.

Joel 2:25 - "I will restore to you the years that the locust hath eaten, the cankerworm, and the caterpiller, and the palmerworm."

D | **Israel Will Never Be Ashamed Again**

For nearly 2500 years, Israel has endured hardships and humiliation as the most hated people on earth. But God promised that when they finish their iniquity, and He finishes His indignation, they will never be ashamed again.

Joel 2:26-27 - " Ye shall eat in plenty, and be satisfied, and praise the name of the LORD your God, that hath dealt wondrously with you: and my people shall never be ashamed. And ye shall know that I am in the midst of Israel, and that I am the LORD your God, and none else: and my people shall never be ashamed."

D | The Outpouring Of The Holy Spirit Prophesied

Joel prophesied two seasons of rain (spiritual blessings) on the people. He said that God had already given them the former rain moderately. That means that the mighty works and miracles of God in the Old Testament were the first rain. The Holy Ghost outpouring on the New Testament Church (beginning at Pentecost in Acts 2) which continues to this day is the latter rain.

Joel 2:28-29 - "It shall come to pass afterward, that I will pour out my spirit upon all flesh; ...upon the servants and upon the handmaids in those days will I pour out my spirit."

B | Dreams, Visions And Prophesying

Throughout history, God has spoken to His people by dreams, visions and prophecies. In virtually every story in the Bible, either a dream, a vision, or a prophecy is a major factor in that story. Many today say that these works have ceased, but God said that He would continue to use these methods until the end of the age. Quench not the Spirit (I Thessalonians 5:19).

Joel 2:28 - "I will pour out my spirit upon all flesh; and your sons and your daughters shall prophesy, your old men shall dream dreams, your young men shall see visions."

B | Blood, Fire, Pillars Of Smoke

"Before the great and terrible day of the LORD [Armageddon] comes,", God will show wonders in the heavens and in the earth. When you compile everything that all the prophets wrote about the last 42 months, (the Great Tribulation or Jacob's Trouble), the Sixth Trumpet War of Revelation 9 seems to coincide with it. Apparently, there will be a nuclear holocaust which will exactly fulfill these prophecies.

Joel 2:30 - "I will shew wonders in the heavens and in the earth, blood, and fire, and pillars of smoke. The sun shall be turned into darkness, and the moon into blood."

C | **Deliverance**

Here is a prophecy and a principle. When Jesus returns for the battle of Armageddon, He will defeat His enemies and the enemies of His people, and will recapture Mount Zion, which is in Jerusalem. Anyone and everyone who calls on His name at that time will be delivered. That has always been true. Call on Him!

Joel 2:32 - "And it shall come to pass, that whosoever shall call on the name of the LORD shall be delivered: for in mount Zion and in Jerusalem shall be deliverance, as the LORD hath said, and in the remnant whom the LORD shall call."

D | **Armageddon: Death For Dividing Land, Scattering Jews**

God says that He will bring "ALL NATIONS" down to the valley of Jehoshaphat (which runs along the eastern wall of the Temple Mount) and will "plead with them" (Hebrew: "judge, punish") because they drove the Jews out of Israel and divided the land. That is EXACTLY what the United Nations is trying to do right now!

Joel 3:2 - "I will also gather all nations, and will bring them down into the valley of Jehoshaphat, and will plead with them there for my people and for my heritage Israel, whom they have scattered among the nations, and parted my land."

D | **Punishment For Enslaving, Prostituting, Trafficking Jews**

God never forgets unrepented crimes against His chosen people. He has not forgotten that Roman Emperor Titus murdered 1.9 million Jews, and his soldiers cast lots to own 97,000 Jews as slaves. God has not forgotten that Mohammed besieged the Jewish community of Banu Qurayzah, beheaded hundreds of men, and sold about 1000 women and children into slavery. At Armageddon, Jesus will punish countless nations, ancient and modern, for crimes against His people.

Joel 3:3 - "They have cast lots for my people; and have given a boy for an harlot, and sold a girl for wine, that they might drink."

B | **Palestine**

Joel portrayed Palestine as an enemy of God. Who could have imagined how true that would be in these days? Since Israel was reborn in 1948, "Palestinians" (people who never in the history of the world had their own state) have agitated most of the Arab-Muslim world to destroy Israel and declare a Palestinian state.

Joel 3:4 - "Yea, and what have ye to do with me, O Tyre, and Zidon, and all the coasts of Palestine? will ye render me a recompence? and if ye recompense me, swiftly and speedily will I return your recompence upon your own head."

D | God Will Judge Israel's Enemies, Let Jews Rule Them

Jews have often been conquered, plundered, captured and killed; by Assyrians, Babylonians, Grecians, Romans, Moslems, and more. Jesus will resurrect Israel and give them dominion over them all.

Joel 3:5-8 - "Because ye have taken ...my goodly pleasant things: The children also of Judah and the children of Jerusalem have ye sold ...that ye might remove them far from their border. ...I will raise them out of the place whither ye have sold them, and will return your recompence upon your own head: And I will sell your sons and your daughters into the hand of the children of Judah."

D | God Declares War: Meet Me At Jerusalem

Six thousand years of human rejection is enough. God will soon demand the heathen nations to meet Him AT JERUSALEM for the war to end all wars - Armageddon!

Joel 3:9-12 - "Proclaim ye this among the Gentiles; Prepare war, wake up the mighty men, let all the men of war draw near; ...Beat your plowshares into swords, and your pruninghooks into spears: let the weak say, I am strong. Assemble yourselves, ...all ye heathen, and gather yourselves together round about: ...come up to the valley of Jehoshaphat: for there will I sit to judge all the heathen round about."

C | Divine Harvest

The Bible clearly teaches two divine harvests (Revelation 14:14-20). There will be a wheat harvest, symbolizing the righteous souls that God will resurrect or rapture before Armageddon. But there will also be a harvest of the grapes of wrath. God will gather heathen from all nations at Armageddon and tread them down in the winepress of His anger. Saints will be in the first harvest; sinners in the second.

Joel 3:13 - "Put ye in the sickle, for the harvest is ripe: come, get you down; for the press is full, the fats overflow; for their wickedness is great."

B | **The Valley Of Decision**

Joel 2:32 says that at Armageddon, "whosoever shall call on the name of the LORD shall be delivered: for in mount Zion and in Jerusalem shall be deliverance." It appears to me that anyone who calls on the name of Jesus at Armageddon will be delivered from destruction. Is that why it is called "the valley of decision"? WHY, when faced with certain destruction, do multitudes yet refuse to call on the name of the LORD?

Joel 3:14 - "Multitudes, multitudes in the valley of decision: for the day of the LORD is near in the valley of decision."

C | **The LORD Is The Hope And Strength Of His People**

It is impossible to exaggerate how terrifying the world will become in the last days of the Great Tribulation. The Sixth Trumpet War of Revelation 9 will apparently kill one-third of the world population. "The sun and the moon shall be darkened, and the stars shall withdraw their shining." No flesh would be saved, except that Jesus will come!

Joel 3:16 - "The LORD also shall roar out of Zion, and utter his voice from Jerusalem; and the heavens and the earth shall shake: but the LORD will be the hope of his people, and the strength of the children of Israel."

B | **God Says That Zion Is MY Holy Mountain**

All the world had better prepare for this day. Jesus Christ is coming to take absolute control of Israel, of the city of Jerusalem, and of the Temple Mount. Nobody, but nobody can stop Him - not the UN, the EU, NATO, Russia, Fatah, Hamas, Hezbollah, the Iranian Revolutionary Guard, or the Muslim Brotherhood. Not even the Antichrist. Nobody. Even the Dome will go. You will see.

Joel 3:17 - "So shall ye know that I am the LORD your God dwelling in Zion, my holy mountain: then shall Jerusalem be holy, and there shall no strangers pass through her any more."

B | **A New River In Israel**

Although the land of Palestine has been largely wasteland for centuries, Israel's Messiah, Jesus Christ, will transform everything about the place. Israel will become like the Garden of Eden (Isaiah 51:3; Ezekiel 36:35). A new river will flow from the Temple Mount.

Joel 3:18 - "And it shall come to pass in that day, that the mountains shall drop down new wine, and the hills shall flow with milk, and all the rivers of Judah shall flow with waters, and a fountain shall come forth of the house of the LORD, and shall water the valley of Shittim."

C | All God's Enemies Will Be Made Desolate

This lesson could be drawn from countless examples in the Bible. Forget for a moment that the world is spinning totally out of control politically, economically, morally, and spiritually. Remember that the earth is the LORD's, and He rules ALL the affairs of men. There is a great day of reckoning just around the corner. Make a list of His enemies. They will EVERY ONE be left desolate.

Joel 3:19 -" Egypt shall be a desolation, and Edom shall be a desolate wilderness, for the violence against the children of Judah, because they have shed innocent blood in their land."

B | Jerusalem: Throne Of Jesus Christ

The last line in the prophecies of Ezekiel says, "the name of the city from that day shall be, The LORD is there." The last line of the prophecies of Joel says, "the LORD dwelleth in Zion." Until time is no more (Revelation 10:6); until the earth and firmaments melt, and everything is dissolved (2 Peter 3:12), Judah and Jerusalem will be home to Jesus Christ.

Joel 3:20-21 - "Judah shall dwell for ever, and Jerusalem from generation to generation. For I will cleanse their blood that I have not cleansed: for the LORD dwelleth in Zion."

Lessons from the Book of
AMOS

C | God Uses Ordinary People Greatly

God specializes in using ordinary people. Amos was the first prophet to appear after the kingdom of Israel was divided by Jeroboam, preceding even Isaiah and Hosea. He was not a priest or Levite. "I was no prophet, neither was I a prophet's son; but I was an herdman, and a gatherer of sycomore fruit: And the LORD took me as I followed the flock, and the LORD said unto me, Go, prophesy unto my people Israel," 7:14-15. Prepare yourself, Mr. Nobody. God may want to use you.

Amos 1:1 - "The words of Amos, who was among the herdmen of Tekoa."

C | I Will Not Turn Away The Punishment

"For three transgressions... and for four, I will not turn away the punishment thereof..." God pronounced this judgment EIGHT TIMES in the first two chapters of Amos; on Damascus, Gaza, Tyre, Edom, Ammon, Moab, Judah and Israel. The punishment was similar for each nation except Israel. God said He would send a fire, devour their palaces, cut off their inhabitants, and cut off their rulers (kings, princes, etc.). Unrepented sins against the righteous God cannot go unpunished.

Amos 1:3 - "Thus saith the LORD; For three transgressions of Damascus, and for four, I will not turn away the punishment thereof."

B | The Sins Of Israel In Amos' Day

Amos made a list of the sins for which God was going to punish Israel: 1. Selling the righteous for silver, and the poor for a pair of shoes - SLAVERY. 2. Man and father taking the same maid - INCEST. 3. Profaning my holy name - BLASPHEMY. 4. Pledging by every altar and drinking wine in the house of their god - IDOLATRY. 5. Giving Nazarites strong drink and forbidding prophets to prophesy - REBELLION. They literally piled up sins on top of sins against God.

Amos 2:13 - "I am pressed under you, as a cart is pressed that is full of sheaves."

D | Amos Prophesied That Israel Would Have No Strength

Amos prophesied what would happen to Israel. Flight would perish from the swift. The strong could not strengthen himself. The mighty could not deliver himself. The archer could not stand. The runner could not flee. The horseman could not deliver himself. The courageous would flee away naked. These prophecies eventually led to the total ruin of Israel when Assyrians took them helplessly away from their homeland. Before you sin, remember: God can take your strength.

Amos 2:14 - "The flight shall perish from the swift, and the strong shall not strengthen his force, neither shall the mighty deliver himself."

D | God Had To Punish His Favorite Family

Israel was the only family on earth that God had ever been intimate with. "You only have I known of all the families of the earth." But they ceaselessly transgressed against Him, and sin always separates men from God. Amos delivered a divine warning. "Hear this word that the LORD hath spoken against you, O children of Israel."

Amos 3:2,6 - "Therefore I will punish you for all your iniquities. ...Shall a trumpet be blown in the city, and the people not be afraid? shall there be evil in a city, and the LORD hath not done it?"

C | **Can Two Walk Together, Except They Be Agreed?**

Israel's sins made God's favorite family His hated enemy. Instead of comparing their relationship to a Father and His beloved children, the analogy depicted a lion roaring and a fowler setting snares for his prey. Where did the love go? The people forsook their LORD.

Amos 3:3,9-10 - "Can two walk together, except they be agreed? ...Assemble yourselves upon the mountains of Samaria, and behold the great tumults in the midst thereof, and the oppressed in the midst thereof. For they know not to do right, saith the LORD, who store up violence and robbery in their palaces."

B | **Why Does A Lion Roar?**

People say that a lion is the king of the jungle. Few things on earth strike terror like the roar of a lion. Lions roar to drive off competitors and to terrify their prey. So when God roars, it means that the King of heaven and earth is warning His enemies and His prey.

Amos 3:4,8 - "Will a lion roar in the forest, when he hath no prey? will a young lion cry out of his den, if he have taken nothing? ...The lion hath roared, who will not fear? the Lord GOD hath spoken, who can but prophesy?"

B | **Palaces**

Many mighty rulers throughout history attempted to immortalize themselves by building great buildings - palaces, temples, mosques, and shrines - as magnificent, permanent testimonials to their earthly powers. But Amos prophesied that Almighty God would devour the palaces of His enemies. Even Jerusalem's palaces would be spoiled because of Israel's sins. Messiah will construct new palaces and a new Temple when He comes.

Amos 3:11,15 - "Thy palaces shall be spoiled. ...And I will smite the winter house with the summer house; and the houses of ivory shall perish, and the great houses shall have an end, saith the LORD."

D | Led Away Like Cows - The Cows Of Bashan

Amos referred to backsliding Israel as "ye kine of Bashan, that are in the mountains of Samaria." The tribe of Manasseh, one of the first tribes to apostatize, dwelled in the region of Bashan. "Kine" is a word for cows. For Israel's sins, God declared that enemies [Assyrians] would break down their walls and their fences, and they would be led away like lines of cows breaking through a fence, instead of through the gates, with dignity.

Amos 4:2 - "And ye shall go out at the breaches, every cow at that which is before her."

A | Yet Have Ye Not Returned Unto Me

The prophet Amos, contemporary with Hosea, Isaiah and King Uzziah, saw Israel apostatize under King Jeroboam. Amos lived in Judah, but preached to the northern tribes. He listed so many punishments God had sent to them because of their sins, "yet have ye not returned unto me," the LORD said. Insolent people ignore God's chastisements to their own great hurt.

Amos 4:6-10 - "I also have given you ...want of bread, ...withholden the rain, cities wandered ...to drink water, ...blasting and mildew, ...slain with the sword, ...taken away your horses, ...yet have ye not returned unto me, saith the LORD."

C | Prepare To Meet Thy God

Men and women in every generation have spurned their Creator. Although He deals with them forcefully in terrible works upon earth, they still ignore Him. Even when God moved drastically, as at Sodom and Gomorrah, men still refused to repent. This may be your final warning.

Amos 4:12-13 - "...Prepare to meet thy God, O Israel. For, lo, he that formeth the mountains, and createth the wind, and declareth unto man what is his thought, that maketh the morning darkness, and treadeth upon the high places of the earth, The LORD, The God of hosts, is his name."

A | Seek Me, And Ye Shall Live

If more people would seek the LORD, the world would be a much better place. Why are we so enamored with celebrities, actors, athletes, entertainers, or rich and famous personalities, and NOT GOD? Why must we hear sermons in our pulpits about football coaches and basketball players? Seek the LORD!

Amos 5:4,6,8 - "Seek ye me, and ye shall live: ...Seek the LORD, and ye shall live; ...Seek him that maketh the seven stars and Orion, ...that calleth for the waters of the sea, and poureth them out upon the face of the earth: The LORD is his name."

C | **Hate Evil. Love Good.**

Just about every prophet in the Bible toiled at exposing the sinfulness of sin. That is the work of true men of God. As sin multiplies rampantly, however, men of God are increasingly ignored. "Therefore the prudent shall keep silence in that time; for it is an evil time." Regardless of the times, however, God always favors those who hate evil and love good.

Amos 5:14-15 - "Seek good, and not evil, that ye may live: and so the LORD, the God of hosts, shall be with you, as ye have spoken. Hate the evil, and love the good."

D | **The Day Of The LORD Is Darkness, And Not Light**

The prophets prophesied "the day of the LORD" numerous times in reference to coming judgments. Amos was first to warn Israel that Assyrians would capture them. They mistakenly believed that the Day of the LORD would be a day of blessing. Amos had bad news.

Amos 5:18-19 - "Woe unto you that desire the day of the LORD! to what end is it for you? the day of the LORD is darkness, and not light. As if a man did flee from a lion, and a bear met him; or ...leaned his hand on the wall, and a serpent bit him."

B | **The Songs And Music Of Sinners**

Oh, God detests just about everything sinners do. He really is angry at the wicked every day. But sinners have a way of entertaining themselves as a way of smothering their guilt and conscience. You can sing, and dance and play your music, while you defy God and His holiness, but all of your frivolous music is going to end one of these days.

Amos 5:23-24 - "Take thou away from me the noise of thy songs; for I will not hear the melody of thy viols. But let judgment run down as waters, and righteousness as a mighty stream."

D | Fiddling While Rome Burns

Legend says that Emperor Nero stood on his balcony and played the lyre as he watched the city of Rome burn in 64 AD. Hence the popular phrase, "fiddling while Rome burns." Hundreds of years earlier, the prophet Amos cried, "Woe to them that are at ease in Zion, ...That chant to the sound of the viol, and invent to themselves instruments of musick, like David; ...but they are not grieved for the affliction of Joseph." AND... It is happening again today! Judgment is coming!

Amos 6:1,5 - "Therefore now shall they go captive with the first that go captive."

B | Remember Calneh, Hamath and Gath

Calneh was a great city founded by Nimrod [also called Ctesiphon, on the river Tigris] that was captured by the Assyrians and eventually fell into ruins. Hamath was another great city that fell to the Assyrians in Amos' day. Gath was a city taken by Hazael, king of Damascus shortly before Amos' day. Amos warned Israel that they would likewise fall into ruin unless they turned from their sins.

Amos 6:2 - "Pass ye unto Calneh, and see; and from thence go ye to Hamath the great: then go down to Gath of the Philistines: be they better than these kingdoms?"

C | Self-Delusion Is Fatal

The prophet targeted the self-delusions of Israel: "ye put far away the evil day," (procrastination, denial and excuse-making), lying on ivory beds, stretching on couches, eating, drinking, making music and living in luxury (taking false comforts). Their prosperity and successes became an abomination to God. Beware the self-delusion of trusting in temporal comforts when divine judgments are certain to come. Every generation will answer to God.

Amos 6:8 - "The Lord GOD hath sworn by himself, ...I abhor the excellency of Jacob, and hate his palaces: therefore will I deliver up the city with all that is therein."

C | Judgment Turned Into Gall, Righteousness Into Hemlock

In God's economy, intangible precepts are far more important and more valuable than tangible possessions or physical strength. Amos prophesied a death plague that would empty the houses of Israel for trusting in the "horns [of] our own strength." They despised righteous judgment - it was gall and hemlock (poison) to them. Our modern generation is exactly the same, and similarly cursed.

Amos 6:12 - "...ye have turned judgment into gall, and the fruit of righteousness into hemlock: ...behold, I will raise up against you a nation, O house of Israel, saith the LORD the God of hosts; and they shall afflict you."

B | No Grasshoppers, No Fire, But A Plumbline

The LORD showed Amos that grasshoppers would devour the fall crops of Israel, but Amos pleaded with God for mercy, and God called off the grasshoppers. Then God threatened judgment by fire, and Amos again repented in behalf of the people. Finally, the LORD showed him a plumbline. As a carpenter judges his work by a plumbline, God judged Israel by His straight measure - and rejected them.

Amos 7:8-9 - "I will set a plumbline in the midst of my people Israel: ...And the high places of Isaac shall be desolate, and the sanctuaries of Israel shall be laid waste."

D | What Makes A Prophet?

What makes a prophet? The word of the LORD turns a man into a seer. Supernaturally, he sees the will of God clearly, as other men cannot. He overflows with divine understanding that he cannot contain. He must declare what he sees. King Amaziah tried to silence Amos, but he could not.

Amos 7:12-17 - "Amaziah said unto Amos, O thou seer, go, flee thee away ...prophesy not again any more, ...[Amos said] Thou sayest, Prophesy not against Israel, ...Therefore thus saith the LORD; ...thy sons and thy daughters shall fall by the sword, and thy land shall be divided."

B | A Basket Of Summer Fruit

God showed Amos a basket of summer fruit and said, "The end is come upon my people of Israel." Apparently, the basket of fruit represented the LAST HARVEST of the season. God expected to receive no more good out of Israel at that time. Surely enough, the northern ten tribes NEVER had another righteous king. They are now called the "lost tribes of Israel."

Amos 8:2 - "And he said, Amos, what seest thou? And I said, A basket of summer fruit. Then said the LORD unto me, The end is come upon my people of Israel; I will not again pass by them any more."

C | Sinners Want To Get Out Of Church Early

The people lived like they did not have time for God. "When will the new moon be gone, that we may sell corn? and the sabbath, that we may set forth wheat?" They wanted Sabbath to pass so they could get back to their cheating, thieving and taking advantage of others. If you are stingy with God, He will become stingy with you.

Amos 8:9-10 - "I will cause the sun to go down at noon, and I will darken the earth in the clear day: And I will turn your feasts into mourning, and all your songs into lamentation."

D | God Promised A Famine Of His Word Upon Israel

Amos pronounced some of the first doomsday prophecies against Israel, including the ruin of the Temple and dead bodies throughout Jerusalem. "I will never forget any of their works," the LORD said. If you refuse to hear God's word, He may utterly stop speaking to you.

Amos 8:11-12 - "The days come, saith the Lord GOD, that I will send a famine in the land, not a famine of bread, nor a thirst for water, but of hearing the words of the LORD: ...they shall run to and fro to seek the word of the LORD, and shall not find it."

B | The Sword Of The LORD

In a vision, Amos saw the Lord standing on the altar in the Temple, commanding the door posts to shake, and that His sword should pursue those who had committed all the aforementioned evils against Him. He swore that they could not escape His sword, though they sought refuge in Heaven or Hell, in the mountains or in the seas, even captive among their enemies.

Amos 9:4 - "Though they go into captivity before their enemies, thence will I command the sword, and it shall slay them: and I will set mine eyes upon them for evil, and not for good."

C | Sifting Divides Nations

God often punishes people by dispersing them. God divided their tongues at Babel. They dispersed, and their little empire collapsed. God divides people physically and geographically to diffuse their evildoing. Sinful Israel became "as Ethiopians to me," [like people outside His covenant], so God decided they must either die, or be scattered like corn from a sieve.

Amos 9:9-10 - "I will sift the house of Israel among all nations, like as corn is sifted in a sieve, ...All the sinners of my people shall die by the sword, which say, The evil shall not overtake nor prevent us."

D | I Will Raise Up The Tabernacle Of David That Is Fallen

Amos remembered how King David inspired the people to worship. The Tabernacle [tent] that David pitched for the Ark of the Covenant was inaugurated with the joyous music of harps, psalteries, timbrels, cornets, trumpets, cymbals and choirs of singers. Amos prophesied that God would punish Israel, and afterward, He would raise up the Tabernacle of David again. James said that the Church born at Pentecost fulfilled that prophecy (see Acts 15:16).

Amos 9:11 - "In that day will I raise up the tabernacle of David that is fallen, ...and I will build it as in the days of old."

B | The Remnant Of Edom And Of All The Heathen

Here is a prophetic treasure completely overlooked by most commentators. Since James, in Acts 15:16, said the New Testament Church is the restored Tabernacle of David, then the next prophecy pertains to the Church: "...that they may possess the remnant of Edom, and of all the heathen, which are called by my name." The Church, called by the name of Jesus, will rule the heathen during the millennial Kingdom of Christ.

Amos 9:12 - "That they may possess the remnant of Edom, and of all the heathen, which are called by my name, saith the LORD that doeth this."

D | Bumper Crops In The Millennium

As soon as Jesus Christ establishes His earthly Kingdom at Jerusalem, after destroying all His enemies at Armageddon, Israel will begin flourishing like the Garden of Eden.

Amos 9:13-15 - "The plowman shall overtake the reaper, and the treader of grapes him that soweth seed; and the mountains shall drop sweet wine, ...they shall plant vineyards, and drink the wine thereof; they shall also make gardens, and eat the fruit of them. And I will plant them upon their land, and they shall no more be pulled up out of their land which I have given them, saith the LORD."

Lessons from the Book of
OBADIAH

B | **The Book Of Obadiah**

The entire "book" of Obadiah is only one page long. It is a prophecy given somewhere around 835 BC about the coming destruction of Edom. Edom was the homeland of the descendants of Esau, who were relentless enemies of Israel, located on the south and southeast of Israel, around Mount Seir. The area is famous for the magnificent stone-carved community of Petra, which is now extinct. The prophecies came to pass.

Obadiah 1:1 - "The vision of Obadiah. Thus saith the Lord GOD concerning Edom; ...thou that dwellest in the clefts of the rock, ...thence will I bring thee down."

C | **God Controls Whether A Nation Will Be Small Or Great**

As far back as the book of Numbers 24, the prophet Balaam foretold the coming of Messiah, "a star out of Jacob," who would take possession of the land that once belonged to the descendants of Esau - obstinate enemies of Israel. Jesus will reclaim that territory for Israel. "Edom shall be a possession, [Mount] Seir also shall be a possession for his enemies; and Israel shall do valiantly." From the very beginning, God intentionally prevented Edom from ever becoming a major force in the earth.

Obadiah 1:2 - "Behold, I have made thee small among the heathen: thou art greatly despised."

C | **There Is No Security Without God - Nothing Is Hidden**

It is impossible to make something of lasting value for yourself if you are in conflict with God. The Edomites, Esau's descendants, were proud of their accomplishments - the beautiful city of Petra. But God said, "the pride of thine heart hath deceived thee." Set yourself as high as an eagle's nest - yet God will bring you down. Robbers will invade, and you will not be able to stop them. Grape gatherers will do as they please in your vineyards.

Obadiah 1:6 - "How are the things of Esau searched out! how are his hidden things sought up!"

D | Prophecies Against The Edomites And Temanites

The Edomites dwelt peaceably with the Temanites and Amalekites - descendants of Esau's first son, Eliphaz - but they hatefully refused to live peaceably with Israel, their cousins. God will fiercely judge the belligerent adversaries of His people.

Obadiah 1:7-9 - "The men of thy confederacy have brought thee even to the border: the men that were at peace with thee have deceived thee, and prevailed against thee; ...Shall I not in that day, saith the LORD, even destroy the wise men out of Edom, and understanding out of the mount of Esau? And thy mighty men, O Teman, shall be dismayed."

C | As Thou Hast Done, It Shall Be Done Unto Thee

God hated the way the Edomites treated His people. They rejoiced in Israel's calamities and captivity, and took advantage of them in their downfall. "For thy violence against thy brother Jacob shame shall cover thee, and thou shalt be cut off for ever." The rule of God is "touch not mine anointed," Psalm 105:15. God will certainly get even with those who harm His people.

Obadiah 1:15 - "For the day of the LORD is near upon all the heathen: as thou hast done, it shall be done unto thee: thy reward shall return upon thine own head."

D | House Of Jacob A Fire, House Of Esau For Stubble

Almighty God is interminably committed to Israel and will NEVER forfeit His holy Mount Zion in Jerusalem. Every enemy of Israel, ancient and modern will be made utterly desolate, and Israel will flourish and have glorious dominion in their Promised Land under the kingship of Jesus Christ and His saints.

Obadiah 1:18,21 - "The house of Jacob shall be a fire, ...and the house of Esau for stubble, and they shall kindle in them, and devour them; ...And saviours shall come up on mount Zion to judge the mount of Esau; and the kingdom shall be the LORD'S."

Lessons from the Book of
JONAH

B | Jonah - Running From The Call Of God

What would YOU do if God told you to go to the largest, most evil city in the world and march through the streets announcing their destruction from the hand of God? Jonah ran away, but found that it is impossible to escape the call of God.

Jonah 1:3 - "Jonah rose up to flee unto Tarshish from the presence of the LORD, and went down to Joppa; and he found a ship going to Tarshish: so he paid the fare thereof, and went down into it, to go with them unto Tarshish from the presence of the LORD."

A | The Prayers Of Godless Men

The mariners on board Jonah's ill-fated voyage were frightened and called on their many gods. They urged Jonah to call on his God, but there is no record that Jonah did so. Maybe if Jonah had taken their good advice, he could have saved himself and his fellows the nightmarish experience.

Jonah 1:5-6 - "Then the mariners were afraid, and cried every man unto his god, ...So the shipmaster came to him, and said unto him, What meanest thou, O sleeper? arise, call upon thy God, if so be that God will think upon us, that we perish not."

C | Rebels Cannot Answer The Hard Questions

A mighty tempest nearly broke up their ship, and the mariners were afraid. They decided that Jonah was the cause of their misfortune. The shipmaster woke Jonah from his sleep and asked, "What meanest thou, O sleeper?" The other mates had questions, too. "Tell us... for whose cause this evil is upon us; What is thine occupation? and whence comest thou? what is thy country? and of what people art thou?" Jonah said, "I am an Hebrew; and I fear the LORD, the God of heaven." Then came their BEST question:

Jonah 1:10 - "Why hast thou done this?"

A | When Saints Fail, Ungodly Men Fear And Pray

The men onboard ship with Jonah cast lots to determine who was causing their misfortunate storm. (Casting lots was a deciding factor in several Bible stories.) The lot fell on Jonah. Jonah admitted that he was running from God.

Jonah 1:13-15 - "Wherefore they cried unto the LORD, and said, We beseech thee, O LORD, ...let us not perish for this man's life, and lay not upon us innocent blood: for thou, O LORD, hast done as it pleased thee. So they took up Jonah, and cast him forth into the sea: and the sea ceased from her raging."

B | The Whale Of God

The LORD "prepared a great fish to swallow up Jonah." (Jesus called it a whale in Matthew 12:40 KJV). God sent the whale at the perfect moment, because He was preaching Jesus' death, burial and resurrection centuries in advance. God pre-ordains all your trials, and every detail has divine purpose.

Jonah 1:15,17 - "They took up Jonah, and cast him forth into the sea: and the sea ceased from her raging. ...Now the LORD had prepared a great fish to swallow up Jonah. And Jonah was in the belly of the fish three days and three nights."

A | Then Jonah Prayed

Nothing is more typical of people's relationship with God. Like Jonah, they run from God, avoiding and evading all responsibility and obedience to Him - until calamity strikes. Jonah ran full-speed ahead in his own direction until God arrested him, and his fellow shipmates threw him into the sea. God had prepared a great fish to swallow him. He knows how to get you on your knees.

Jonah 1:17-2:1 - "Jonah was in the belly of the fish three days and three nights. Then Jonah prayed unto the LORD his God out of the fish's belly."

A | I Cried By Reason Of My Affliction

God cast Jonah into the deep, stormy billows. Encompassed by waters, with weeds wrapped about his head, Jonah promised to seek toward the Holy Temple. From the bottoms, as his soul fainted, Jonah's prayer came up with a sacrifice of thanksgiving and renewed vows. God heard

Jonah's desperate prayer and saved him. "The LORD spake unto the fish, and it vomited out Jonah upon the dry land."

Jonah 2:2 - "I cried by reason of mine affliction unto the LORD, and he heard me; out of the belly of hell cried I, and thou heardest my voice."

D | Jonah's Return From Death

Did Jonah die in the whale? "Out of the belly of hell (sheol - place of the departed) I cried," he said. "The waters compassed me about, even to the soul. ...the earth with her bars was about me for ever: yet hast thou brought up my life from corruption. ...My soul fainted within me." If he was to be a type of Christ, he must have died and been miraculously raised.

Jonah 2:1,10 - "Then Jonah prayed unto the LORD his God out of the fish's belly, ...And the LORD spake unto the fish, and it vomited out Jonah."

B | Jonah - First Of The Major And Minor Prophets

Chronologically, Jonah was the first of the four major and twelve minor prophets who appeared at the end of the Old Testament. That is significant, because it illustrates God's priority in dealing with the people of Nineveh - the Assyrians - ahead of all the other prophecies of all the other prophets. Assyria later destroyed ten tribes of Israel. Punishing the Assyrian Man of Sin in Jerusalem will be Jesus' first priority at Armageddon.

Jonah 3:1-2 - "The word of the LORD came unto Jonah the second time, saying, Arise, go unto Nineveh, that great city, and preach unto it the preaching that I bid thee."

D | The Prophet Is God's Messenger And Intercessor

Jonah exemplifies countless men who have delayed to do the will of God. Even Jesus Christ prayed that He might be released from drinking the bitter cup assigned to Him. God nevertheless extracted the ultimate obedience from Him. In His sovereign purpose, God must have a man - an intercessor. How can they believe upon Him of whom they have not heard? How can they hear except it be preached? Even if he cannot understand what God is doing, the prophet must preach the Word.

Jonah 3:2 - "Arise, go... and preach unto it the preaching that I bid thee."

C | **God Gives A Warning Before His Worst Judgments**

Why was Nineveh on God's "Hit List"? From ancient days of Nimrod and Asshur, Nineveh was a stronghold of pagan idolaters - Ishtar worshippers. God called Jonah to warn them of coming judgment. They repented at that time, but a century later, ca. 740BC, Sennacherib, the Assyrian of Nineveh, captured the northern ten tribes of Israel, and tried to destroy Judah, too. King Hezekiah prayed, and an angel of the LORD killed 185,000 Assyrian soldiers. But the record shows that they had been warned.

Jonah 3:3 - "So Jonah arose, and went unto Nineveh, according to the word of the LORD."

A | **Nineveh Repented With Fasting When Jonah Preached**

The second time God commanded, Jonah went quickly to Nineveh and preached the Word of the LORD. "Yet forty days, and Nineveh shall be overthrown." He gave no call to repentance, no call to action - just a warning. But "the people of Nineveh believed God, and proclaimed a fast, and put on sackcloth, from the greatest of them even to the least of them."

Jonah 3:10 - "God saw their works, that they turned from their evil way; and God repented of the evil, that he had said that he would do unto them; and he did it not."

A | **Jonah Prays To Die, Scorns 120,000 Souls**

Jonah became very angry when God forgave Nineveh, because he originally argued that God would be merciful to Nineveh and claimed that was the reason he did not want to go preach there. Jonah angrily asked God to take his life. Interestingly, God grew a gourd to provide a shade over Jonah's head. As soon as Jonah enjoyed the shade, God smote the gourd, and it died. Jonah again wished to die. God rebuked Jonah for loving the gourd more than the 120,000 inhabitants of Nineveh.

Jonah 4:10-11 - "Should not I spare Nineveh, that great city?"

Lessons from the Book of
MICAH

B | Micah - A Major "Minor" Prophet

Micah prophesied at about the same time as the prophet Isaiah, during the reigns of Jotham, Ahaz and Hezekiah. A century later, Jeremiah prophesied doom over Israel in the tradition of Micah. The elders of Israel would have killed Jeremiah, except that they recognized a legal precedent inasmuch as Micah had also prophesied doom, but King Hezekiah did not kill him. This "minor" prophet was a major prophet.

Micah 1:1 - "The word of the LORD that came to Micah the Morasthite in the days of Jotham, Ahaz, and Hezekiah, kings of Judah, which he saw concerning Samaria and Jerusalem."

C | Prophecies Are Historic, Noteworthy, And Highly Significant

Joel and Amos had been the first of the minor prophets to pronounce clear and articulate Messianic prophecies, foretelling a day when Israel would be mightily revived, and the LORD Himself would rule on earth. A generation later, more historic, epochal prophecies were penned by Micah and Isaiah.

Micah 1:2-3 - "Hear, all ye people; hearken, O earth, and all that therein is: and let the Lord GOD be witness against you, the Lord from his holy temple. For, behold, the LORD cometh forth out of his place, and will come down, and tread upon the high places of the earth."

D | Earthquakes And Volcanic Eruptions When Jesus Comes

Micah's prophecies pertained to Samaria (the northern capital of Israel) and Jerusalem (the southern capital of Judah). His prophecies said that God would come to earth and do great destruction because of the sins of the people. This unfulfilled prophecy will occur when Jesus comes to Armageddon.

Micah 1:3-4 - "The LORD cometh forth out of his place, and will come down, and tread upon the high places of the earth. And the mountains shall be molten under him, and the valleys shall be cleft, as wax before the fire, and as the waters that are poured down a steep place."

D | Micah Prophesied Israel's Rejection, Ruin And Revival

What other nation in the world had such a line-up of prophets who simultaneously denounced its citizens for their evil ways, condemned and cursed them into captivity and near oblivion, then prophesied an eventual rebirth and re-establishment of that nation, including the rise of an eternal King who would be no less than Almighty God incarnate? Only Israel.

Micah 1:5,12-13 - "For the transgression of Jacob is all this, and for the sins of the house of Israel. ...evil came down from the LORD unto the gate of Jerusalem ...for the transgressions of Israel were found in thee."

B | Samaria's Contagious Sins

The word of the LORD by Micah warned that He would make a heap of Samaria for its idolatries and whoredoms. "All the graven images thereof shall be beaten to pieces, and all the hires [harlots] thereof shall be burned with the fire," verse 7. Micah wailed, howled and stripped himself in mourning, sorely lamenting that the sins of Samaria had spread to Jerusalem. We have all the same reasons to mourn for our generation.

Micah 1:9 - "For her wound is incurable; for it is come unto Judah; he is come unto the gate of my people, even to Jerusalem."

C | God Will Judge The Small As Surely As The Great

Micah mourned several small towns in Israel. Gath - keep silent, do not weep. Aphrah - roll in the dust. Saphir - go away ashamed and naked. Zaanan - will not be mourned. Lachish - a swift beast pulling a chariot symbolizes her aggressive sins. Achzib - will deceive the king. Mareshah - baldness symbolizes the loss of his children. God will judge the small, the insignificant, and the obscure just as surely as He will the rich and famous.

Micah 1:16 - "Make thee bald, and poll thee for thy delicate children; enlarge thy baldness as the eagle; for they are gone into captivity from thee."

C | God Devises Affliction Upon Those Who Afflict

Micah prophesied divine retaliation against insolent Jews who devised evil [Hebrew: affliction] against their own people, scheming in their beds at night, practicing evil by day, coveting and stealing houses, stealing garments from soldiers returning from war, casting women out of their houses, depriving children of their inheritance, and demanding that prophets not prophesy against them.

Micah 2:3 - "Thus saith the LORD; Behold, against this family do I devise an evil, from which ye shall not remove your necks; neither shall ye go haughtily: In that day shall one take up a parable against you, and lament with a doleful lamentation."

D | Lying Prophets Cannot Negate The Spirit Of Prophecy

The prophets of God have always had to contend with phony prophets. The people almost always prefer someone who will prophesy smooth things. "If a man walking in the spirit and falsehood do lie, saying, I will prophesy unto thee of wine and of strong drink; he shall even be the prophet of this people." But they reject the prophets of doom. "PROPHESY NOT!" they say. Foolish error! God will ALWAYS have the last say.

Micah 2:7 - "Is the spirit of the LORD straitened [curtailed, discouraged]? ...do not my words do good to him that walketh uprightly?"

A | They Shall Cry - He Will Not Hear Them

Again and again, the prophets warned Israel that God would cease to hear their prayers if they did not repent. God complained against them because they "hate the good, and love the evil," and persecuted the righteous. Take note of this frightening threat. If you continually contradict God with sinful beliefs, He may decide to ignore or oppose you the next time you call.

Micah 3:4 - "Then shall they cry unto the LORD, but he will not hear them: he will even hide his face from them at that time, as they have behaved themselves ill in their doings."

B | The Prophets That Make My People Err

Prophets who deceive the people of God are like the serpent who beguiled Eve in the Garden. God condemns them all to darkness.

Micah 3:5-7,11-12 - "Thus saith the LORD concerning the prophets that make my people err, ...night shall be unto you, that ye shall not have a vision; and it shall be dark unto you, ...the sun shall go down over the prophets, ...Then shall the seers be ashamed, and the diviners confounded: ...the prophets thereof divine for money: ...Therefore shall Zion for your sake be plowed as a field, and Jerusalem shall become heaps."

B | The Mountain Of The House Of The LORD

Jesus will soon come to live on Mount Zion in Jerusalem for 1000 years. "In the last days... The mountain of the house of the LORD shall be established... and it shall be exalted above the hills; and people shall flow unto it." Many nations will come to the mountain and house of Jehovah. He will teach them His ways, and they will walk in His paths. He will rule the world from Jerusalem (not Moscow, New York, Brussels, or Beijing).

Micah 4:2 - "For the law shall go forth of Zion, and the word of the LORD from Jerusalem."

D | The Whole Earth Will Be At Peace Under Christ

Micah and Isaiah echoed a similar theme. When Messiah (Jesus Christ) makes His home in Jerusalem, there will be no end of His government and power. The whole world will be at peace.

Micah 4:3-4 - "And he shall judge among many people, and rebuke strong nations afar off; and they shall beat their swords into plowshares, and their spears into pruninghooks: nation shall not lift up a sword against nation, neither shall they learn war any more. But they shall sit every man under his vine and under his fig tree; and none shall make them afraid."

C | Sin's Debt Must Be Paid Before Restoration And Blessing

Three great truths propel Micah's prophecies. 1) Messiah will gloriously rule the earth. 2) Israel will fully recover from their former reproaches and have great dominion in the earth under Christ. 3) Israel must first suffer punishment for their sins.

Micah 4:7,10 - "I will make her that halted a remnant, and her that was cast far off a strong nation: and the LORD shall reign over them in mount Zion... for now shalt thou go forth out of the city, ...thou shalt go even to Babylon; ...there the LORD shall redeem thee from the hand of thine enemies."

D | God Will Trap The Nations Who Try To Take Jerusalem

The lustful nations that are right now trying to take Jerusalem and Israel are falling into God's trap. "Many nations are gathered against thee, that say, Let her be defiled, and let our eye look upon Zion. But they know not the thoughts of the LORD, neither understand they his counsel: for he shall gather them as the sheaves into the floor." Jesus will crush them all at Armageddon. Israel will rule the nations.

Micah 4:13 - "Arise and thresh, O daughter of Zion: ...thou shalt beat in pieces many people: and I will consecrate their gain unto the LORD."

B | Bethlehem - Messiah Will Come From You

Micah prophesied, "they shall smite the judge of Israel with a rod upon the cheek." That was fulfilled in Matthew 27:30. "They ...took the reed, and smote him on the head." Micah also prophesied that He would come from Bethlehem. "Jesus was born in Bethlehem of Judaea in the days of Herod the king," Matthew 2:1.

Micah 5:2 - "But thou, Bethlehem Ephratah, though thou be little among the thousands of Judah, yet out of thee shall he come forth unto me that is to be ruler in Israel; whose goings forth have been from of old, from everlasting."

C | God Sometimes Gives Up On People

Nobody anywhere is more longsuffering than God. But there is a point of no return when God takes His hand off of a situation, and leaves fools to their folly. After centuries of rebellion and apostasy, God abandoned Israel to their own devices, until His appointed time comes to finish the work and regather them in righteousness. Take heed lest relentless sin causes God to give up on you.

Micah 5:3 - "Therefore will he give them up, until the time that she which travaileth hath brought forth: then the remnant of his brethren shall return unto the children of Israel."

D | Jesus Will Deliver Israel From The Assyrian Man Of Sin

Jesus will come "in the majesty of the name of the LORD." He shall "be great unto the ends of the earth" (King of Kings), and overthrow the Assyrian Man of Sin (Antichrist). "I will break the Assyrian in my land, and upon my mountains tread him under foot: ...This is the purpose that is purposed upon the whole earth," Isaiah 14:25-26.

Micah 5:5 - "This man [Christ] shall be the peace, when the Assyrian shall come into our land: and when he shall tread in our palaces ...thus shall he deliver us from the Assyrian, when he cometh into our land."

B | Seven Shepherds And Eight Principal Men With Christ

Israel will be given to "the Assyrian." European powers and the Roman Catholic Church (The Beast and False Prophet of Revelation 13), via the United Nations, will apparently mandate a Muslim government in Jerusalem. 42 months of Great Tribulation will follow, until Jesus comes at Armageddon. Seven kings or nations and eight principal men will stand with Israel against Assyria until Christ comes to finish the job.

Micah 5:5-6 - "Then shall we raise against him seven shepherds, and eight principal men. And they shall waste the land of Assyria with the sword, and the land of Nimrod ...thus shall he deliver us from the Assyrian, when he cometh into our land."

C | God's People Are Like Dew From The LORD

In this godless global society, God says that the presence of Jews is like dew from the LORD. The hope of civilization is based on God's covenant with Abraham, Isaac, and Jacob. God also depicts them as lions who conquer their adversaries.

Micah 5:7 - "The remnant of Jacob shall be in the midst of many people as a dew from the LORD, as the showers upon the grass, And the remnant of Jacob shall be among the Gentiles ...as a lion among the beasts of the forest, who ...both treadeth down, and teareth in pieces, and none can deliver."

D | Armageddon: Vengeance Such As They Have Not Heard

At the battle of Armageddon, Jesus will lead an army comprised of resurrected Israel (Ezekiel 37:11-12), the saints of all the ages (1 Thessalonians 4:16-17), and seven earthly nations (Micah 5:5) against an attempted "final solution" - the utter annihilation of Israel, by an international army led by Russia, Turkey, Iran, Libya and Ethiopia (**see "Ezekiel's War"**)[33].

Micah 5:9,15 - "Thine hand shall be lifted up upon thine adversaries, and all thine enemies shall be cut off. ...And I will execute vengeance in anger and fury upon the heathen, such as they have not heard."

C | Do Justly. Love Mercy. Walk Humbly With Thy God.

Micah retrogressed from his prophesying to do a little preaching. He told Israel that God had a controversy with them. He reminded them of God's awesome mercies throughout history - deliverance from Egypt, from false prophets like Balaam, giving great leaders like Moses, Aaron and

Miriam, and the Law. God demanded that they show what He had done to them to make them hate Him.

Micah 6:8 - "He hath shewed thee, O man, what is good; and what doth the LORD require of thee, but to do justly, and to love mercy, and to walk humbly with thy God?"

B | Treasures Of Wickedness In The House Of The Wicked

Micah reminded Israel that God knows what you have hidden in your house, and He knows what sins you have been doing. He knows when you have cheated or deceived someone. He knows your lies, your violence, your idolatries. He is sworn to casting down your evils, and He most certainly will.

Micah 6:10,13-15 - "Are there yet the treasures of wickedness in the house of the wicked? ...I make thee sick in smiting thee, in making thee desolate because of thy sins. Thou shalt eat, but not be satisfied; ...Thou shalt sow, but thou shalt not reap."

A | My God Will Hear Me

Micah was one of the earliest prophets to condemn the gross apostasy in Israel. Before the days of Hezekiah of Judah, Micah saw that "the good man is perished out of the earth; there is none upright." He saw blood-lust and violence, extortions, endless mischief, sons and daughters dishonoring their fathers and mothers. Then, as now, the only consolation is to call on the LORD for His favor. That is what we must do today.

Micah 7:7 - "Therefore I will look unto the LORD; I will wait for the God of my salvation: my God will hear me."

C | When I Fall, I Shall Arise

Countless times throughout the Bible, the prophets scathed the people for their abominable sins, leveling judgments against them in the name of the LORD. Just as consistently, they looked with hope to the day when God, in His mercy would save Israel.

Micah 7:8-9 - "Rejoice not against me, O mine enemy: when I fall, I shall arise; when I sit in darkness, the LORD shall be a light unto me. I will bear the indignation of the LORD, because I have sinned against him, ...he will bring me forth to the light, and I shall behold his righteousness."

D | Israeli Security Walls Signal Antichrist Will Soon Appear

Security walls are now being built throughout Israel. "In the day that thy walls are to be built, ...In that day also he shall come even to thee from Assyria, and from the fortified cities, ...and from sea to sea, and from mountain to mountain." The Assyrian Man of Sin will soon appear, but soon thereafter, Jesus Christ!

Micah 7:16-17 - "The nations shall see and be confounded at all their might: they shall lay their hand upon their mouth, their ears shall be deaf. ...they shall be afraid of the LORD our God, and shall fear because of thee."

B | Who Is A God Like Unto Thee?

Where will you find a god like our God? He pardons iniquities. He passes by the sins of the remnant of His people. He does not stay angry longer than He should, because He delights in mercy. We will worship no other but Him.

Micah 7:19-20 - "He will turn again, he will have compassion upon us; he will subdue our iniquities; and thou wilt cast all their sins into the depths of the sea. Thou wilt perform the truth to Jacob, and the mercy to Abraham, which thou hast sworn unto our fathers from the days of old."

Lessons from the Book of
NAHUM

B | Nahum – The Prophet Against Nineveh

Nahum came along a century after Jonah, prophesying again the destruction of Nineveh. Yes, Nineveh repented in Jonah's day, and God spared them at that time. But in Nahum's days, the sins of Nineveh again overflowed the cup, provoking God again. The city is now extinct, a pile of ruins outside the city of Mosul, Iraq.

Nahum 1:1,14 - "The burden of Nineveh. The book of the vision of Nahum the Elkoshite ...And the LORD hath given a commandment concerning thee, that no more of thy name be sown: ...I will make thy grave; for thou art vile."

C | God Is Jealous Of His Enemies

God is as good as anyone can possibly declare. But His righteous indignation toward His enemies is perfectly justified. Everything in the universe was created by Him, and lives, moves, and has its being in Him. It makes NO sense that God should even have enemies. Let Him do whatever He pleases with them.

Nahum 1:2-3 - "God is jealous, and the LORD revengeth; ...the LORD will take vengeance on his adversaries, and he reserveth wrath upon His enemies. The LORD is slow to anger, and great in power, and will not at all acquit the wicked."

D | God Promised To Destroy Vile Nineveh And Its Idolatry

Nineveh was once the capital of Assyria, a vast middle-eastern empire for hundreds of years, north and east of Israel. Nineveh was famous for its idols and temples and worship of various gods: Sin, the moon god; Nergel and Shamash, sun gods; and most of all, Ishtar, goddess of sex and fertility.

Nahum 1:14 - "And the LORD hath given a commandment concerning thee, that no more of thy name be sown: out of the house of thy gods will I cut off the graven image and the molten image: I will make thy grave; for thou art vile."

B | Him That Bringeth Good Tidings, That Publisheth Peace

Jesus Christ will stand upon the Mount of Olives in Jerusalem (Zechariah 14:4), and from that moment, Israel will never know another threat. The Prince of Peace (a.k.a. "The LORD of Hosts) will overthrow every adversary once and for all, and for 1000 years, Israel and the rest of the world will live in perfect peace.

Nahum 1:15 - "Behold upon the mountains the feet of him that bringeth good tidings, that publisheth peace! O Judah, keep thy solemn feasts, perform thy vows: for the wicked shall no more pass through thee; he is utterly cut off."

D | Nahum Accurately Prophesied The Fall Of Nineveh

God sent scarlet-robed warriors with shields and chariots against Nineveh in 612 BC. King Nabopolassar, who had only recently conquered Babylon, led an army of Medes and Babylonians in the final overthrow of Nineveh.

Nahum 2:1,8,13 - "He that dasheth in pieces is come up before thy face: keep the munition, watch the way, ...But Nineveh is of old like a pool of water: yet they shall flee away. ...Behold, I am against thee, saith the LORD of hosts, and I will burn her chariots in the smoke, and the sword shall devour thy young lions."

C | Woes For Lies, Robbery, Whoredom, And Witchcraft

God is no respecter of persons (Acts 10:34). The soul that sinneth, it shall die (Ezekiel 18:20). The wicked shall be turned into Hell, and every nation that forgets God (Psalm 9:17). Great Nineveh was not great enough to defy those eternal precepts of the Holy One of Israel.

Nahum 3:1,4,7 - "Woe to the bloody city! it is all full of lies and robbery; ...that selleth nations through her whoredoms, and families through her witchcrafts, ...all they that look upon thee shall flee from thee, and say, Nineveh is laid waste: who will bemoan her?"

D | O King Of Assyria, Thy People Is Scattered

Nineveh was the capital of the Assyrian empire. Renowned Assyrian kings included Shalmaneser I, Tiglath-Pileser I, and Sennacherib. Its palace, at 794 feet x 1650 feet, had no rival. The city had elaborate streets, canals and aqueducts, as many as 150,000 citizens. But God said, "no more."

Nahum 3:18-19 - "Thy shepherds slumber, O king of Assyria: thy nobles shall dwell in the dust: thy people is scattered upon the mountains, and no man gathereth them. There is no healing of thy bruise; thy wound is grievous: ...for upon whom hath not thy wickedness passed continually?"

Lessons from the Book of
HABAKKUK

B | Habakkuk - A Final Warning To Judah

Habakkuk is one of only four Bible writers who referred to themselves as a prophet (others were Isaiah, Jeremiah, and Haggai). He certainly was a seer of things to come. At least twenty years before the fact, Habakkuk prophesied that the Chaldeans (Babylonians) would capture and destroy Jerusalem. Judah should have given heed and repented.

Habakkuk 1:1;2:1 - "The burden which Habakkuk the prophet did see. ...I will stand upon my watch, and set me upon the tower, and will watch to see what he will say unto me, and what I shall answer when I am reproved."

A | Why Do You Show Me Iniquity, Spoiling And Violence?

No one knows for certain when the prophet Habakkuk lived, but historical statements in the book of Habakkuk suggest that he lived around 605 BC, shortly before Nebuchadnezzar began invading Israel and Jerusalem. Habakkuk would have witnessed the historic downfall of Nineveh and the Assyrian Empire. Habakkuk cried to God for the meaning of those epic events. Impressively, God often answers sincere inquiries and grants prophetic wisdom.

Habakkuk 1:3-4 - "Why dost thou shew me iniquity, and cause me to behold grievance? for spoiling and violence are before me: ...the wicked doth compass about the righteous; therefore wrong judgment proceedeth."

C | I Will Work A Work Which Ye Will Not Believe

Men underestimate the power of God. Nobody ever overstated God's abilities to perform. Whether it was calling down Babylonian armies to punish Judah, or raising Christ from the dead (Acts 13:30-41), God has more power than you can imagine.

Habakkuk 1:5-6 - "Behold ye among the heathen, and regard, and wonder marvellously: for I will work a work in your days, which ye will not believe, though it be told you. For, lo, I raise up the Chaldeans, that bitter and hasty nation, which shall march through the breadth of the land, to possess the dwellingplaces."

B | Them That Deal Treacherously

Habakkuk cried unto the LORD for justice against "them that deal treacherously." They "devour the man that is more righteous," "make men as fishes of the sea ...catching them in their net." Then, "they sacrifice unto their net." Evil men worship the evil devices that get them their power. Habakkuk simultaneously mourned Judah's sins and the fact that their enemies were overpowering them. Fortunately, God will eventually judge the enemies of His people and offer to save His own.

Habakkuk 1:12 - "O LORD, thou hast ordained them for judgment; and, O mighty God, thou hast established them for correction."

☑

C | Write The Vision, That He May Run That Readeth It

When God shows you something, write it down. If God is in a thing, it WILL come to pass. (You do not have to force a prophetic revelation to come to pass.) Whoever it was meant for will run with it.

Habakkuk 2:2-3 - "The LORD answered me, and said, Write the vision, and make it plain upon tables, that he may run that readeth it. For the vision is yet for an appointed time, but at the end it shall speak, and not lie: though it tarry, wait for it; because it will surely come, it will not tarry."

D | A Prophetic Curse Against Those Who Cause Drunkenness

Habakkuk sharply rebuked the people of Judah for their drunkenness, pride, covetousness, violence and corruption. They did not keep their homes; they had insatiable desires and wanted more power over more people. God's people degenerated into a pathetic, shameful people. ANY people invite divine judgment on themselves for such living.

Habakkuk 2:15-16 "Woe unto him that giveth his neighbour drink, that puttest thy bottle to him, and makest him drunken also, that thou mayest look on their nakedness! Thou art filled with shame for glory: ...the cup of the LORD'S right hand shall be turned unto thee."

A | O LORD, Revive Thy Work In The Midst Of The Years"

Habakkuk cared more about affirming God's holiness than defending the nation of Israel. "Thou art of purer eyes than to behold evil, and canst not look on iniquity: wherefore lookest thou upon them that deal treacherously, and holdest thy tongue when the wicked devoureth the man that is more righteous than he?" 1:13. But Habakkuk realized that God is more merciful than we are, so he appropriately asked God to revive the people.

Habakkuk 3:2 - "O LORD, revive thy work in the midst of the years, in the midst of the years make known; in wrath remember mercy."

B | Habakkuk Recalls Israel's Deliverance From Egypt

The prophet remembered the glory days of Israel, when God brought them out of Egypt, through Teman (Edom) and Mount Paran. He recalled the pestilences in Pharaoh's courts, how God opened the sea, and afflicted those who stood in the way. "Thou wentest forth for the salvation of thy people." Habakkuk trembled because God was about to judge them sorely.

Habakkuk 3:16 - "When I heard, my belly trembled; my lips quivered at the voice: rottenness entered into my bones, and I trembled in myself, ...when he cometh up unto the people, he will invade them with his troops."

A | **Although The Fig Tree Shall Not Blossom...**

"Although the fig tree shall not blossom, neither shall fruit be in the vines; the labour of the olive shall fail, and the fields shall yield no meat; the flock shall be cut off from the fold, and there shall be no herd in the stalls: Yet I will rejoice in the LORD, I will joy in the God of my salvation." EVERY believer in God should memorize and quote this regularly!

Habakkuk 3:19 - "The LORD God is my strength, and he will make my feet like hinds' feet, and he will make me to walk upon mine high places."

Lessons from the Book of
ZEPHANIAH

B | **Zephaniah - The Clarion Call**

Zephaniah was a great-great-grandson of King Hezekiah of Judah, who lived in the days of King Josiah, the last righteous king of Judah. Doomsday prophecies were at fever pitch. Jonah, Joel, Amos, Hosea, Isaiah and Micah had already prophesied and died. Zephaniah witnessed the nauseating corruption of Manasseh and knew that godly Josiah was having limited success at turning the people back to righteousness. Zephaniah's prophecies were quick and to the point.

Zephaniah 1:1-2 - "The word of the LORD which came unto Zephaniah ...I will utterly consume all things from off the land, saith the LORD."

D | **The LORD Will Cleanse The Land By Consumption**

This major prophecy is rooted in Leviticus 26:15 and Deuteronomy 28. Isaiah and Daniel declared it. God will cleanse the land by consumption at Armageddon. Will there be a nuclear holocaust?

Zephaniah 1:2-6 - "I will utterly consume all things from off the land, saith the LORD. ...man and beast; ...fowls ...fishes ...stumblingblocks ...the wicked; ...I will cut off man from off the land, ...Judah, ...inhabitants of

Jerusalem; ...remnant of Baal ...them that worship the host of heaven ...that ...swear by the LORD ...that swear by Malcham; ...that are turned back from the LORD; ...that have not sought the LORD."

C | God Sacrifices The Wicked For The Righteous

God must and will destroy the wicked for the sake of the Righteous. Righteousness will be universal.

Zephaniah 1:7-8,15-16 - "The day of the LORD is at hand: for the LORD hath prepared a sacrifice, he hath bid his guests. ...in the day of the LORD'S sacrifice, that I will punish... That day is a day of wrath, ...trouble and distress, ...wasteness and desolation, ...darkness and gloominess, ...clouds and thick darkness, ...trumpet and alarm. ...the whole land shall be devoured by the fire of his jealousy: for he shall make even a speedy riddance of all them."

A | Under Terrifying Prophecies, Seek The LORD

The prophet Zephaniah ministered in the days of King Josiah - last righteous king of Judah. His prophecies were as harsh and terrifying as any of the prophets'. He declared "the day of the LORD," when everything evil would be utterly consumed (the battle of Armageddon). But, as is consistent with all the prophets, Zephaniah nevertheless pleaded with the people to seek the LORD.

Zephaniah 2:3 - "Seek ye the LORD, all ye meek of the earth, which have wrought his judgment; seek righteousness, seek meekness: it may be ye shall be hid in the day of the LORD'S anger."

D | The Land Will Be Desolate - No Inhabitant

Zephaniah prophesied that Gaza, Ashkelon, Ashdod, and Ekron will be forsaken, emptied and desolate. All of Canaan (the Holy Land) will be uninhabited. Moab and Ammon (modern Jordan) will be as Sodom and Gomorrah (v9). All this sounds like a nuclear holocaust may occur at Armageddon, clearing the land for Messiah's resurrected, immortal ones.

Zephaniah 2:4-5 - "Gaza shall be forsaken, and Ashkelon a desolation: they shall drive out Ashdod at the noon day, and Ekron shall be rooted up. ...the word of the LORD is against you; O Canaan, ...I will even destroy thee, that there shall be no inhabitant."

C | **Perpetual Desolation**

DESOLATION is an oft-repeated term describing the future of God's enemies. God promised Abraham that He would bless those who blessed him and curse those who cursed him. The nations of the world choose to forget that covenant, ignore it, disbelieve it, or defy it. But that sacred covenant will forever stand, and God and Israel's enemies will utterly come to naught.

Zephaniah 2:9-11 - "...a perpetual desolation: ...This shall they have for their pride, because they have reproached and magnified themselves against the people of the LORD of hosts. The LORD will be terrible unto them."

D | **He Shall Famish All The Gods Of The Earth**

Most Bible commentators ascribe the second chapter of Zephaniah to ancient events against Assyria and Nineveh, which could only be partially true. Several of these cities have never been totally destroyed, so the prophecies must be fulfilled in future events. Zephaniah also clearly said that the LORD would famish ALL the gods of the earth, and men would worship HIM. That is an ultimatum of great finality - a powerful Messianic prophecy about His millennial kingdom.

Zephaniah 2:11 - "...for he will famish all the gods of the earth; and men shall worship him, ...even all the isles of the heathen."

D | **Assyria And Nineveh At Armageddon**

The Man of Sin will come to rule Palestine from Assyria (most likely Turkey, but possibly Syria, Iran or Iraq). I expect European powers and the Roman Catholic Church (The Beast and the False Prophet of Revelation 13) to install an Assyrian Muslim in Jerusalem, who will crush Israel until Jesus comes at Armageddon. Jesus will destroy Assyria and Nineveh. Mosul, in the province of Ninewah, Iraq has recently been a Sunni Islamic - Al Qaeda stronghold dedicated to the destruction of Israel.

Zephaniah 2:13 - "He [God] will stretch out his hand against the north, and destroy Assyria; and will make Nineveh a desolation."

B | **The Fire Of My Jealousy**

Zephaniah denounced Jerusalem, the "filthy and polluted ...[and] oppressing city" that disobeyed and trusted not God. He denounced their princes, judges and prophets for pathetic sins. God cut off nations and made them desolate, trying to persuade Israel to fear Him. Despite it all, they persisted in their sins. Consequently, God has determined to purge the earth with fire.

Zephaniah 3:8 - "My determination is to gather the nations, that I may assemble the kingdoms, to pour upon them mine indignation, even all my fierce anger: for all the earth shall be devoured with the fire of my jealousy."

B | A Pure Language: Hebrew?

What language will be spoken in Israel during the Millennium? Is there any doubt that it will be Hebrew? The Old Testament is written in "classical" Hebrew. Jesus spoke to the Apostle Paul from Heaven, speaking in Hebrew. Nearly extinct for 2000 years, conversational Hebrew, "The Holy Tongue," is now spoken by about 7 million people. Does this prophecy indicate that it will become a universal language in the Millennium?

Zephaniah 3:9 - "For then will I turn to the people a pure language, that they may all call upon the name of the LORD, to serve him with one consent."

C | The LORD Thy God In The Midst Of Thee Is Mighty

All kings, nations and men are pawns in the hands of the only Sovereign God. "I will take away ...them that rejoice in thy pride, ...I will ...leave ...an afflicted and poor people, ...I will gather them that are sorrowful, ...I will undo all that afflict thee: ...I will save her that halteth, ...I will get them praise and fame ...[I] will bring you again, ...I will make you a name and a praise among all people."

Zephaniah 3:17 - "The LORD thy God in the midst of thee is mighty; he will save, he will rejoice over thee with joy."

Lessons from the Book of

HAGGAI

C | The LORD's House Should Be Built

Zerubbabel and Joshua the priest returned from Babylonian captivity to rebuild Jerusalem. The LORD rebuked the people through Haggai, because they neglected to rebuild the Temple. God demands that we put Him first.

Haggai 1:2,4,8 - "This people say, The time is not come, the time that the LORD'S house should be built. ...Is it time for you, O ye, to dwell in your cieled houses, and this house lie waste? ...Go up to the mountain, and bring wood, and build the house; and I will take pleasure in it, and I will be glorified, saith the LORD."

C | There Is No True Prosperity Apart From God's Plan

Every man must make God his priority. If you fail, your life will come to naught. You will sow much, but bring in little. You will eat and drink, but never be full; be clothed, but never warm; earn wages to put into a bag with holes. "Why? saith the LORD of hosts. Because of mine house that is waste, and ye run every man unto his own house." Seek first His kingdom. Fullness can only come from God.

Haggai 1:10-11 - "Therefore the heaven over you is stayed from dew, and the earth is stayed from her fruit. And I called for a drought..."

B | Haggai - An Encourager From The LORD

The encouraging ministry of Haggai to the Jews returning from exile exemplifies the way God sends His Word to help and heal those who are in need.

Haggai 1:13-14 - "Then spake Haggai the LORD'S messenger in the LORD'S message unto the people, saying, I am with you, saith the LORD. And the LORD stirred up the spirit of Zerubbabel ...governor of Judah, and the spirit of Joshua ...the high priest, and the spirit of all the remnant of the people; and they came and did work in the house of the LORD of hosts, their God."

D | The Desire Of All Nations Will Come

Haggai published one of the great Messianic prophecies. "The desire of all nations shall come." Men may not realize it, but Jesus will fulfill mankind's deepest cravings. But before He comes, God will have to shake the heavens and earth.

Haggai 2:6-7 - "Thus saith the LORD of hosts; Yet once, it is a little while, and I will shake the heavens, and the earth, and the sea, and the dry land; And I will shake all nations, and the desire of all nations shall come: and I will fill this house with glory, saith the LORD of hosts."

D | The Glory Of The Latter House Will Be Greater

Only the oldest Jews remembered the Temple as it was before the Babylonians destroyed it seventy years earlier. Haggai prophesied that it would yet be far more glorious than it was. Eventually, Herod reconstructed a much larger and more lavish Temple. But still much greater, Jesus will build a new Temple there and live in it during His 1000-year reign in Jerusalem - the ultimate glory.

Haggai 2:9 - "The glory of this latter house shall be greater than of the former, saith the LORD of hosts: and in this place will I give peace, saith the LORD of hosts."

B | Blasting, Mildew And Hail - Tools Of God's Punishment

The LORD told Haggai to ask the priests to confirm that they knew that there were consequences for defiling themselves, such as contaminating holy meat by touching unholy items, or priests becoming unclean by touching a dead body. "So is this nation before me, saith the LORD; and so is every work of their hands." God cursed Israel's harvests. Twenty measures diminished to ten, and fifty vessels diminished to twenty.

Haggai 2:17 - "I smote you with blasting and with mildew and with hail in all the labours of your hands; yet ye turned not to me, saith the LORD."

C | When Rebukes Bring Blessings

The rebukes that Haggai handed down to the returning remnant were not intended to ostracize or banish them from God, but to correct their errors and move them forward on the right track. Haggai actually reversed their misfortune and pronounced a rich blessing on them. Don't assume that a rebuke from the LORD is a bad thing. Whom He loves, He chastens.

Haggai 2:19 - "Is the seed yet in the barn? yea, as yet the vine, and the fig tree, and the pomegranate, and the olive tree, hath not brought forth: from this day will I bless you."

D | Zerubbabel Will Be Prominent In Kingdom Of Christ

Bible commentaries offer many exotic theories about the meaning of Haggai 2:21-23, but it is best taken at face value. Just as David will rule in Jerusalem under Christ following Armageddon, God promised Zerubbabel a prominent role in His Millennial Kingdom.

Haggai 2:21-23 - "I will shake the heavens and the earth; ...I will overthrow the throne of kingdoms, and I will destroy the strength of the kingdoms of the heathen; ...In that day, ...will I take thee, O Zerubbabel, my servant, ...and will make thee as a signet: for I have chosen thee, saith the LORD."

Lessons from the Book of
ZECHARIAH

B | Zechariah - Prophet And Priest

Haggai and Zechariah were the two lone prophets of Israel in the days when Darius of Persia released the captive Jews to return to Jerusalem. Their influence on Zerubbabel, governor of Judah, and Joshua, the High Priest was observable. Zechariah was born into the priesthood. Several of his prophecies foretold the millennial Temple of the Messiah. Zechariah prophesied extensively about the LORD coming to earth, including enlightening details about His Millennial Kingdom.

Zechariah 1:1 - "In the second year of Darius, came the word of the LORD unto Zechariah, the son of Berechiah, the son of Iddo the prophet."

C | Turn Unto Me And I Will Turn Unto You

This is God's perennial proposition. "Turn to me, and I will turn to you." The premise is that the fathers have turned their backs on God, and the sons must rectify the breach by turning back to God. As long as we continue in sin, God, of necessity, must remain aloof. But He will instantly respond to our first overture.

Zechariah 1:2-3 - "The LORD hath been sore displeased with your fathers. Therefore say thou unto them, Thus saith the LORD of hosts; Turn ye unto me, ...and I will turn unto you, saith the LORD of hosts."

D | Spirit-Messengers Report To God How Israel Fares

Zechariah prophetically saw men riding horses among myrtle trees outside Jerusalem. The riders told an angel, "We have walked to and fro through the earth, ...all the earth sitteth still, and is at rest." God responded, "I am very sore displeased with the heathen that are at ease: ...they helped forward the affliction." God was angry because no one helped Jerusalem after their return from captivity.

Zechariah 1:16 - "I am returned to Jerusalem with mercies: my house shall be built in it, ...My cities through prosperity shall yet be spread abroad; and the LORD shall yet comfort Zion."

B | Four Horns And Four Carpenters

Zechariah saw four horns and enquired of the angel. "These are the horns which have scattered Judah, Israel, and Jerusalem," the angel replied. Previous to this prophecy, four great empires (horns) had displaced Israel: Babylon, Medo-Persia, Egypt and Assyria (Daniel 11). Then Zechariah saw four carpenters (builders). Zerubbabel, Joshua (the High Priest), Ezra and Nehemiah would rebuild Jerusalem and Judah around the time of this prophecy. God ordained a national revival.

Zechariah 1:21- "But these are come to fray them, to cast out the horns of the Gentiles, which lifted up their horn over the land of Judah to scatter it."

C | God Is Not Limited By Human Boundaries

Zechariah saw a man with a measuring line going to measure the length and breadth of Jerusalem. He heard one angel tell another, "Run, speak to this young man, saying, Jerusalem shall be inhabited as towns without walls for the multitude of men and cattle therein." The measurements of Jerusalem were insignificant at that time because God planned to vastly expand Jerusalem. That can only be fulfilled by a miracle.

Zechariah 2:5 - "For I, saith the LORD, will be unto her a wall of fire round about, and will be the glory in the midst of her."

B | The Apple Of God's Eye

The enemies of Israel might just as easily pluck out the eyes of God than to destroy Israel. God made an everlasting covenant with Abraham, Isaac and Jacob, in which He obliged Himself to Israel's perpetuation. He often punished them, but vowed never to annihilate them.

Zechariah 2:6-8 - "Come forth, and flee from the land of the north, saith the LORD: for I have spread you abroad as the four winds of the heaven, saith the LORD. Deliver thyself, O Zion, that dwellest with the daughter of Babylon. ...for he that toucheth you toucheth the apple of his eye."

A | Sing, Rejoice! The LORD Shall Inherit The Holy Land!

Zechariah prophesied exciting things about the coming kingdom of Christ, and commanded the people to rejoice!

Zechariah 2:10-12 - "Sing and rejoice, O daughter of Zion: for, lo, I come, and I will dwell in the midst of thee, saith the LORD. And many nations shall be joined to the LORD in that day, and shall be my people: and I will dwell in the midst of thee, and thou shalt know that the LORD of hosts hath sent me unto thee. And the LORD shall inherit Judah his portion in the holy land, and shall choose Jerusalem again."

D | Silence Before The LORD Following Armageddon

In Revelation 8:1, when the Seventh Seal is opened, there will be thirty minutes of silence in Heaven. Since the Sixth Seal is "The Day of His Wrath," (Armageddon), John apparently saw the same thing that Zechariah foresaw - silence in the presence of the LORD after He won His great victory over all His enemies. When Jesus finishes His final war at Armageddon, all creatures in Heaven and earth will stand in silent awe for half an hour.

Zechariah 2:13 - "Be silent, O all flesh, before the LORD: for he is raised up out of his holy habitation."

A | Joshua The High Priest, The Angel Of The LORD, And Satan

After Israel's 70 years in Babylon, Joshua the High Priest finally stood in the Holy Place in Jerusalem before the angel of the LORD for the first service. Zechariah saw Satan resisting him - spiritual warfare! But the LORD rebuked Satan. When YOU come to intercede, the LORD will rebuke YOUR devourer.

Zechariah 3:1-2 - "He shewed me Joshua the high priest standing before the angel of the LORD, and Satan standing at his right hand to resist him. And the LORD said unto Satan, The LORD rebuke thee, O Satan; even the LORD that hath chosen Jerusalem rebuke thee."

C | Like A Fiery Brand, Ministers Make Their Mark On Men

The High Priest stood before the angel of the LORD. On his right hand, Satan resisted him, but the LORD rebuked Satan and warned him that the High Priest was "a brand plucked out of the fire." As a fiery brand burns its mark, God's fire-tested ministers are victorious over Satan and are tools used by God to govern the people.

Zechariah 3:7 - "Thus saith the LORD of hosts; If thou wilt walk in my ways, and if thou wilt keep my charge, then thou shalt also judge my house, and shalt also keep my courts."

D | I Will Bring Forth My Servant - The BRANCH

Isaiah prophesied that a branch would come out of the stem of Jesse. Jeremiah prophesied that the LORD would raise a righteous branch unto David. Zechariah prophesied to Joshua the High Priest that God would bring forth His servant called THE BRANCH. Henceforth, Jesus Christ would be called not only A branch, but one of His names is also now THE BRANCH. All life is in THE BRANCH.

Zechariah 3:8 - "Hear now, O Joshua the high priest, thou, and thy fellows that sit before thee: for they are men wondered at: for, behold, I will bring forth my servant the BRANCH."

B | 7 Lamps, 7 Candles, 7 Eyes, 7 Spirits, 7 Churches

"Seven lamps shall give light." Numbers 8:2 described the candlestick in Moses' Tabernacle. In Revelation, John saw "seven lamps of fire burning before the throne, ...the seven Spirits of God," 4:5, and "...a Lamb ...having ...seven eyes, which are the seven Spirits of God sent forth into all the earth," 5:6. A stone (Rock/Christ) had seven eyes. "...the eyes of the LORD, which run to and fro through the whole earth," 3:9; 4:10. "...the seven Spirits which are before his throne," Revelation 1:4.

Zechariah 3:9 - "The stone that I have laid before Joshua; upon one stone shall be seven eyes."

C | **Christ With His Church Will Save Israel At Armageddon**

A stone with seven eyes will remove the iniquity of the land in one day. The stone represents the rock, Christ Jesus. The seven eyes represent the seven Spirits of God that are sent forth into all the earth. Moses' Tabernacle had seven lamps, which foreshadowed the early Church, also symbolized by seven candlesticks (the seven churches of Asia; Revelation 1:20). In one day, Jesus will save Israel when He and His Church arrive at Armageddon.

Zechariah 3:9 - "Upon one stone shall be seven eyes: ...and I will remove the iniquity of that land in one day."

D | **Thou, Great Mountain, Shall Become A Plain**

When Zerubbabel, born in Babylon, returned to Jerusalem, the Holy Temple built by Solomon had been completely destroyed. The Temple Mount (Moriah, altitude 2428') was covered with charred heaps of debris, with a small plateau on the northern end, and a steep decline on the southern slope. By the time Jesus was born, that ragged mountain had become a giant 35 acre level platform. Part of the Antonian hill on the north had also been annexed, and the area between was filled up with landfill.

Zechariah 4:7 - "Who art thou, O great mountain? before Zerubbabel thou shalt become a plain."

B | **The Second Temple, Built By Zerubbabel**

Ezra recorded the fulfillment of Zechariah's prophesies. "Then rose up Zerubbabel the son of Shealtiel, and Jeshua the son of Jozadak, and began to build the house of God which is at Jerusalem: ...And this house was finished on the third day of the month Adar, ...the sixth year of the reign of Darius the king," Ezra 5:2;6:15.

Zechariah 4:7-9 "And he shall bring forth the headstone [capstone] thereof with shoutings, ...Moreover the word of the LORD came unto me, saying, The hands of Zerubbabel have laid the foundation of this house; his hands shall also finish it."

C | **Not By Might, Nor By Power, But By My Spirit**

When Zechariah saw the candlestick and the two olive trees, the angel explained, "This is the word of the LORD unto Zerubbabel, saying, Not by might, nor by power, but by my spirit, saith the LORD of hosts." Zerubbabel, governor of Judah, had no might, no power to revive Israel.

But God, by His Spirit, would do the work. That principle is still true today.

Zechariah 4:9 - "The hands of Zerubbabel have laid the foundation of this house; his hands shall also finish it; and thou shalt know that the LORD of hosts hath sent me unto you."

C | Do Not Despise Small Beginnings

It must have been profoundly discouraging to see the devastation where Solomon's glorious Temple once stood. Not one stone was where it should be. But God challenges us not to despise small beginnings. When you see the general contractor setting his plumb line, you will see that God performs His promises. The eyes of the LORD scan the earth to make certain that His will is done.

Zechariah 4:10 - "For who hath despised the day of small things? for they shall rejoice, and shall see the plummet in the hand of Zerubbabel with those seven [eyes of the LORD]."

D | Grace, Grace Unto It!

The prophetic word of the LORD to Zerubbabel said, "Who art thou, O great mountain? before Zerubbabel thou shalt become a plain: and he shall bring forth the headstone thereof with shoutings, crying, Grace, grace unto it." God promised to give Zerubbabel the grace he needed to rebuild Jerusalem. In a larger sense, GRACE would finish God's great work and build the New Testament Church - heavenly Jerusalem, the "mother of us all" Galatians 4:26.

Zechariah 4:10 - "For who hath despised the day of small things? for they shall rejoice, and shall see the plummet in the hand of Zerubbabel."

B | Two Olive Trees - The Two Witnesses

An angel showed Zechariah a golden candlestick having seven lamps, with two olive trees beside it providing golden oil through golden pipes. Zechariah asked, "What are these, my lord?" The lamps were the eyes of the LORD (called seven spirits of God in Revelation 5:6), running to and fro through the whole earth. Revelation 11:3 says, "I will give power unto my two witnesses, ...These are the two olive trees." The identity of these two preachers will be revealed during the Great Tribulation.

Zechariah 4:14 - "These are the two anointed ones, that stand by the Lord of the whole earth."

B | A Flying Roll - God's Word - Curses Evildoers

Zechariah saw a FLYING ROLL, roughly 40 x 20 feet in dimension. The angel said it was a CURSE going across the whole earth, upon everyone that steals or swears falsely by the name of God. The Word of God covers the earth with either blessings or curses.

Zechariah 5:1,3-4 - "Behold a flying roll. ...Then said he unto me, This is the curse that goeth forth over the face of the whole earth: ...it shall enter into the house of the thief, and into the house of him that sweareth falsely by my name: ...and shall consume it."

C | Sign Of The Stork - Uncleanness Leads To Bondage

In Leviticus and Deuteronomy, Moses declared the stork unclean and unfit to eat. Nevertheless, Psalm 104 lists the unclean stork as one of many things that have appointed places in creation. "As for the stork, the fir trees are her house." Jeremiah added, "The stork in the heaven knoweth her appointed times; ...but my people know not the judgment of the LORD." Zechariah saw two evil women with wings of a stork, carrying Israel away into bondage. Uncleanness (sin) always leads to bondage.

Zechariah 5:9 - "There came out two women, ...they had wings like the wings of a stork."

D | Woman In A Basket Carried To Shinar (Babylon)

The angel showed Zechariah an ephah (basket) with a heavy lead lid. Inside sat a woman called "wickedness" (presumably Israel). Two women, with wind in their wings, carried the basket to Shinar (Babylon). Ezekiel 23 describes two women as the apostate cities of Samaria and Jerusalem. This prophecy came AFTER the Babylonian captivity, so must indicate another, future Jewish exile to Babylon, probably when the Antichrist overthrows Israel during the Tribulation.

Zechariah 5:10-11 - "Then said I... Whither do these bear the ephah? And he said unto me, To build it an house in the land of Shinar."

D | Four Horses - Four Spirits Of The Heavens

Have you heard of the Four Horsemen of the Apocalypse? Two great prophets spoke of them: Zechariah (Chapter 6) and John (Revelation 6). Chariots and horses - a red one, a white one, a black one and a strange colored one. They are the four prevailing spirits on earth in the last days and have ENORMOUS prophetic significance. You need to understand this prophecy! **See "The Four Horsemen of Revelation."**[34]

Zechariah 6:5 - "And the angel answered and said unto me, These are the four spirits of the heavens, which go forth from standing before the Lord of all the earth."

D | Crowns For The Royal Priesthood

Joshua the High Priest worked with Zerubbabel, governor of Judah, to build the Holy Temple following the Babylonian exile. God instructed Zechariah to make gold and silver crowns for Joshua and his fellow priests - Helem, Tobijah, Jedaiah, and Hen. Likewise, the LORD promises a "crown of righteousness," "...of life," "...of glory" for all His saints - His Royal Priesthood (1 Peter 2:9).

Zechariah 6:9 - "The word of the LORD came unto me, saying, ...take silver and gold, and make crowns, and set them upon the head of Joshua, ...Helem, ...Tobijah, ...Jedaiah, and ...Hen, ...for a memorial in the temple of the LORD."

B | The Millennial Temple

At Armageddon, Jesus will take permanent ownership of Jerusalem. The Islamic Dome of the Rock will have to go. He will build a new Temple more glorious than ever before. His Throne will sit where the Ark of the Covenant once sat, and He will rule as King and High Priest of Israel and the entire world.

Zechariah 6:13 - "He shall build the temple of the LORD; and he shall bear the glory, and shall sit and rule upon his throne; and he shall be a priest upon his throne: and the counsel of peace shall be between them both."

C | You Will Know That God Sent The Prophets

The world is suffocating from atheism and unbelief. But that fact cannot prevent the prophesied plan of Almighty God from coming to pass. When God's people finally see the millennial Temple being constructed and Jesus Christ standing in His place on the Temple Mount as King and Priest in His newly-constructed Temple, the world will know forever that the prophets were truly sent from God.

Zechariah 6:15 - "They that are far off shall come and build in the temple of the LORD, and ye shall know that the LORD of hosts hath sent me unto you."

A | A Rebuke Against Phony Fasting And Weeping

Zechariah was one of three prophets who ministered after the Babylonian captivity (Haggai and Malachi were the other two.) Some of the Jews who had returned to Jerusalem came to Zechariah to enquire whether they should continue practicing fasting as they had during captivity. Zechariah used the occasion to rebuke them for hypocritical fasting, without even being mindful of God. Ritual fast days are worthless. Fasting and prayer must be personal before the LORD. Do not stop fasting. Just do it properly.

Zechariah 7:5-6 - "When ye fasted and mourned ...did ye at all fast unto me, even to me?'"

A | He Cried, They Would Not Hear. They Cried, He Would Not...

God's warnings should not be taken lightly. In these modern times, we WILL see a repetition of this spiritual law. If God cries out, WE MUST HEAR! If we refuse to hear HIM, HE will eventually refuse to hear US!

Zechariah 7:11-13 - "But they refused to hearken, and pulled away the shoulder, and stopped their ears, that they should not hear. ...therefore came a great wrath from the LORD of hosts. Therefore it is come to pass, that as he cried, and they would not hear; so they cried, and I would not hear, saith the LORD of hosts."

B | Jerusalem Will Be Called The City Of Truth

The LORD told Zechariah that He would return to Jerusalem, "and will dwell in the midst of Jerusalem: and Jerusalem shall be called a city of truth; and the mountain of the LORD of hosts the holy mountain." He said that old men and old women would dwell there, and the streets would be full of boys and girls playing. Jerusalem will be unimaginably glorious under Christ.

Zechariah 8:8 - "I will bring them, and they shall dwell in the midst of Jerusalem: and they shall be my people, and I will be their God, in truth and in righteousness."

A | Prayer In The Millennium

Jesus Christ will resurrect Israel and His born-again Church to establish a 1000-year kingdom on earth. Sinners who survive the horrors of the Great Tribulation and Armageddon will repopulate the earth with mortals. Jesus will rule that world with a rod of iron.

Zechariah 8:21-22 - "The inhabitants of one city shall go to another, saying, Let us go speedily to pray before the LORD, and to seek the LORD of hosts: I will go also. Yea, many people and strong nations shall come to seek the LORD of hosts in Jerusalem, and to pray before the LORD."

C | God Keeps A List Of His Enemies

Born-again Christians enjoy the comfort of knowing that God will never remember their sins against them again. But such is not the case with unrepentant sinners. Not one of the wicked will be accidentally overlooked. When Jesus comes, judgment will be meted out to everyone who trespassed against Him. Zechariah listed just enough names to remind us that God never forgets who His enemies were.

Zechariah 9:1 - "The burden of the word of the LORD in the land of Hadrach, ...Damascus, ...Hamath, ...Tyrus, ...Zidon, ...Ashkelon, ...Gaza, ...Ekron, ...Ashdod, ...but he that remaineth, even he, shall be for our God."

D | The King Cometh, Riding Upon The Foal Of An Ass

Zechariah prophesied the grand entrance of Messiah in Jerusalem. 500 years later, Matthew 21:9 documented the fulfillment. "The multitudes that went before, and that followed, cried, saying, Hosanna to the Son of David: Blessed is he that cometh in the name of the Lord; Hosanna in the highest." Just as certainly, Jesus will fulfill prophecies of His second coming!

Zechariah 9:9 - "Rejoice greatly, O daughter of Zion; shout, O daughter of Jerusalem: behold, thy King cometh unto thee: he is just, and having salvation; lowly, and riding upon an ass, and upon a colt the foal of an ass."

B | Israel Will Be As Stones In The LORD's Crown

Zechariah called the northern and southern kingdoms of Israel Ephraim and Jerusalem, and prophesied that the LORD will be seen over them; His arrow shall go forth as lightning, and His trumpet will blow. Jesus will come and save them from their sins, and they will be as stones in His crown.

Zechariah 9:16-17 - "The LORD their God shall save them in that day as the flock of his people: for they shall be as the stones of a crown, lifted up as an ensign upon his land. For how great is his goodness, and how great is his beauty!"

A | Ask Of The LORD Rain In The Time Of The Latter Rain

If you simply want to waste a lot of your time, pray to a stone or rock, or a wood-carving, or any man-made image. How can anybody in their right mind explain the logic in praying to an idol? If you need a miracle, you should go to the only power in the universe Who can give you a miracle. Call Jesus.

Zechariah 10:1 - "Ask ye of the LORD rain in the time of the latter rain; so the LORD shall make bright clouds, and give them showers of rain, to every one grass in the field."

C | In Jesus Christ, Failures Become Mighty Men

The LORD looked at Israel and saw idolaters, diviners, false dreamers, and a scattered flock. But He said that He would make them as good horses in battle, as mighty men who tread down their enemies. By the blood of His covenant (9:6), through Jesus Christ, men who have been failures can become mighty men.

Zechariah 10:5 - "And they shall be as mighty men, which tread down their enemies in the mire of the streets in the battle: and they shall fight, because the LORD is with them, and the riders on horses shall be confounded.

D | They Shall Be As Though I Had Not Cast Them Off

The return of Israel to the Holy Land in 1948 was considered to be an exciting fulfillment of Bible prophecy. But that was miniscule compared to what God will soon do. He has only begun to regather Israel. When Jesus comes, He will raise them from their graves and gather every living Jew from every nation.

Zechariah 10:6,12 - "I will strengthen the house of Judah, and I will save the house of Joseph, and I will bring them again to place them; for I have mercy upon them: and they shall be as though I had not cast them off."

B | Lebanon - No More Pity

Zechariah pronounced doom on Lebanon - fires will devour its cedars, fir trees will fall, and its oaks will come down. The glory of its shepherds (kings and rulers) will be spoiled. The modern state of Lebanon is infiltrated and controlled by rabidly anti-Jewish radical Islamic extremists and terrorists. No wonder this prophecy is in the Book.

☐✓

Zechariah 11:1-3,6 - "O Lebanon, ...the cedar is fallen; ...the mighty are spoiled: ...There is a voice of the howling of the shepherds; for their glory is spoiled. ...For I will no more pity the inhabitants of the land, saith the LORD."

C | Broken Staves, Beauty And Bands, Covenant And Unity

A shepherd's staff became an object lesson for Israel. God said that He carried two staves, one called Beauty, the other called Bands, all the while He shepherded Israel. But when they forsook Him, He BROKE both staves. BEAUTY represented the Old Testament Covenant (verse 10). With that broken, a New Testament would have to be made. The second, BANDS, represented the brotherhood of Judah and Israel (verse 14). Their separate identities were lost in the Diaspora (dispersion). Both were divine punishments.

Zechariah 11:7 - "I took unto me two staves; the one I called Beauty, and the other I called Bands."

D | Israel's Redeemer-King Sold For Thirty Pieces Of Silver

Israel despised the Covenant of God, so He broke it, as illustrated in the broken staff named Beauty. Zechariah published this breathtaking prophecy 500 years before Judas Iscariot fulfilled it: "I said unto them, If ye think good, give me my price. ...So they weighed for my price thirty pieces of silver." Judas sold Jesus (Matthew 27), and they took Him and crucified Him. That day, the Old Covenant ended, the New Covenant began, and Judas' guilt destroyed him.

Zechariah 11:13 - "And I took the thirty pieces of silver, and cast them to the potter in the house of the LORD.

B | A Foolish Shepherd (Antichrist)

A foolish shepherd with a sword (Islamic?) and an evil eye, and will completely betray Israel. This Assyrian Man of Sin will be destroyed by Jesus at Armageddon. His sword and his evil eye will stopped.

Zechariah 11:15-17 - "Take unto thee yet the instruments of a foolish shepherd. For, lo, I will raise up a shepherd in the land, which shall not visit those that be cut off, neither shall seek the young one, nor heal that that is broken, ...Woe to the idol shepherd that leaveth the flock! the sword shall be upon his arm, and upon his right eye: his arm shall be clean dried up, and his right eye shall be utterly darkened."

C | Prophets Carry The Burden Of The Word Of The LORD

Isaiah called the Word of the LORD against Babylon a "burden." He called the word of the LORD for Moab a "burden." Then there was the "burden" of Damascus, then Egypt, Arabia, Tyre and several others. Jeremiah often called it "the burden of the LORD." Nahum, Habakkuk, Zechariah and Malachi all mentioned their burden. Any time God gives a preacher a heavy word of prophecy, especially a message of doom or a dire warning, it is a heavy burden. The preacher can only relieve his burden by preaching.

Zechariah 12:1 - "The burden of the word of the LORD for Israel..."

B | Jerusalem - Cup Of Trembling - Burdensome Stone

God brought Abraham to Mount Moriah to make a Covenant. God also brought David to Moriah and told him to buy the place. God chose that mountain. Satan said, "I will sit on that mountain." God said, "I will destroy you in that mountain." The Assyrian Man of Sin (Antichrist) will die on that mountain. Jerusalem is a death trap for anybody who denies those truths.

Zechariah 12:2-3 - "I will make Jerusalem a cup of trembling unto all the people round about, ...In that day will I make Jerusalem a burdensome stone for all people: all that burden themselves with it shall be cut in pieces."

C | Nobody - Not Even Everybody - Can Stop God

God said that Jerusalem would be a cup of trembling and a burdensome stone for ALL people that contend with it - "though all the people of the earth be gathered together against it." ALL THE PEOPLE OF THE EARTH? If seven billion people in chorus cannot stop God from doing as He pleases, then why should one single man ever resist God? You cannot win. "Submit yourselves therefore to God," James 4:7.

Zechariah 12:3 - "Jerusalem... all that burden themselves with it shall be cut in pieces, though all the people of the earth be gathered together against it."

D | Governors Of Judah Like A Hearth Of Fire Among Wood

When the enemy armies of Israel gather around Jerusalem for the final battle of Armageddon, God said He would smite every horse with blindness and every rider with madness. "I make the governors of Judah

☑

like an hearth of fire among the wood, and like a torch of fire in a sheaf; and they shall devour all the people round about."

Zechariah 12:8-9 - "In that day shall the LORD defend the inhabitants of Jerusalem; and he that is feeble among them at that day shall be as David; ...I will seek to destroy all the nations that come against Jerusalem."

D | They Shall Look Upon Me Whom They Have Pierced

The Assyrian Man of Sin (Antichrist) will kill or displace most of the Jews. But by God's Spirit of grace and supplications, the Savior will come. They will mourn when they realize that Jesus was their Messiah all along.

Zechariah 12:10-11 - "And they shall look upon me whom they have pierced, and they shall mourn for him, as one mourneth for his only son, and shall be in bitterness for him, as one that is in bitterness for his firstborn. In that day shall there be a great mourning in Jerusalem, as the mourning of Hadadrimmon in the valley of Megiddon."

B | The Mourning Of Hadadrimmon In The Valley Of Megiddon

The last righteous and beloved king of Israel, Josiah, died tragically in the crossfire of a fight between the king of Egypt and the king of Carchemish "in the valley of Megiddo. ...and all Judah and Jerusalem mourned for Josiah," 2 Chronicles 35:22,24. When Messiah comes to Armageddon, and the surviving remnant of Israel realizes their Savior is the One their fathers killed, they will mourn their error as the death of a firstborn son.

Zechariah 12:11 - "In that day shall there be a great mourning in Jerusalem, as the mourning of Hadadrimmon in the valley of Megiddon."

C | Nearest Of Kin Are Most Grief-stricken

When Jesus comes, the proper lineage and ancestry of all Jews will become known. Those who were direct ancestors of Messiah (from David) and those who were in the priesthood (the Levites) will grieve the long years since their fathers crucified Jesus Christ.

Zechariah 12:12-13 - "The land shall mourn, every family apart; the family of the house of David apart, and their wives apart; the family of the house of Nathan apart, and their wives apart; the family of the house of Levi apart, and their wives apart; the family of the Shimeites apart, and their wives apart."

B | False Prophets Will Not Be Tolerated In The Millennium

In the Millennium, Christ will rid His Holy Land of all idols and false prophets. False prophets will not be tolerated, but will be put to death in accordance with the ancient laws of God. No man will want to admit that he has been prophesying, knowing that he faces the death penalty.

Zechariah 13:4-5 - "The prophets shall be ashamed every one of his vision, when he hath prophesied; neither shall they wear a rough garment to deceive: But he shall say, I am no prophet, I am an husbandman; for man taught me to keep cattle from my youth."

C | Wounded By A Friend

Betrayal is one hallmark of the godly life. "Mine own familiar friend, in whom I trusted, which did eat of my bread, hath lifted up his heel against me," Psalms 41:9. Judas came to Jesus and kissed Him. Jesus said to him, "Friend..." "Betrayest thou the Son of man with a kiss?" Matthew 26:49-50 and Luke 22:48. No enemy can hurt you as much as a dear friend who betrays you. If you have never been betrayed, brace yourself. It is coming.

Zechariah 13:6 - "I was wounded in the house of my friends."

D | Smite The Shepherd, The Sheep Shall Be Scattered

This prophecy said that the Shepherd would be smitten, and the sheep would be scattered. Both were fulfilled. Jesus, the Chief Shepherd of Israel (1 Peter 5:4) was scourged, smitten, and crucified at Calvary. The sheep were scattered shortly after Calvary, when Romans destroyed Jerusalem in 70 AD, and the Jews were dispersed to the four winds. Jesus pointed out this prophecy to His disciples shortly before He was taken and crucified (Matthew 26:31; Mark 14:27).

Zechariah 13:7 - "Awake, O sword, against my shepherd, ...smite the shepherd, and the sheep shall be scattered."

D | Under Antichrist, 2/3 Of Jews In Israel Will Die

When Israel finally calls on the name of Jesus, two-thirds of the people will have recently died. In the forty-two months under the Assyrian Man of Sin (Antichrist), only one third of all Jews living in Israel will survive.

Zechariah 13:8-9 - "In all the land, saith the LORD, two parts therein shall be cut off and die; but the third shall be left therein. And I will bring the third part through the fire, and will refine them as silver is refined, and will try them as gold is tried: they shall call on my name, and I will hear them."

A | When They See His Wounds, They Will Pray

Zechariah prophesied of a day that would come when Israel would look upon Jesus Christ and say, "What are these wounds in thine hands?" He will answer, "Those with which I was wounded in the house of my friends." In that day there will a fountain of mercy and salvation opened to the house of David, and to the inhabitants of Jerusalem for cleansing from sin and uncleanness.

Zechariah 13:9 - "They shall call on my name, and I will hear them: I will say, It is my people: and they shall say, The LORD is my God."

C | Earthly Spoils Will Go To God's People

The earth is the LORD's, and He promised that the meek will inherit it. Although Satan and sinners have exercised dominion over the earth for thousands of years, "the day of the LORD" will remedy that wrong forever. When all the armies of earth come against Jerusalem to render their final, fatal blow to Israel, Christ will come and destroy them. All that was theirs will become God's. He will divide His spoils of war to His holy people.

Zechariah 14:1 - "Behold, the day of the LORD cometh, and thy spoil shall be divided in the midst of thee."

D | Jerusalem Will Be Divided Violently

As I write this, world powers are calling for a Palestinian State with Jerusalem as its capital. Jerusalem will be divided. Prophecies say that hostile forces will go from house to house, raping and plundering Jews, violently driving them out of Jerusalem. That will provoke the second coming of Jesus Christ.

Zechariah 14:2 - "I will gather all nations against Jerusalem to battle; and the city shall be taken, and the houses rifled, and the women ravished; and half of the city shall go forth into captivity, and the residue of the people shall not be cut off from the city."

B | The Battle Of Armageddon

A prominent TV evangelist declared, "There is no battle of Armageddon" mentioned in the Bible. He is wrong. It will be "the day of the LORD."

Jesus Christ will make war with His adversaries. Zechariah 14:1-15 details several events during that battle.

Zechariah 14:2-3 - "For I will gather all nations against Jerusalem to battle; and the city shall be taken, and the houses rifled, and the women ravished; and half of the city shall go forth into captivity, ...Then shall the LORD go forth, and fight against those nations, as when he fought in the day of battle."

B | The Mount Of Olives

Jesus surrendered to Satan and Judas Iscariot while standing on the Mount of Olives. But soon He will stand there again in electrifying victory. He will conclude the final battle of Armageddon on that very spot.

Zechariah 14:4 - "His feet shall stand in that day upon the mount of Olives, which is before Jerusalem on the east, and the mount of Olives shall cleave in the midst thereof toward the east and toward the west, and there shall be a very great valley; and half of the mountain shall remove toward the north, and half of it toward the south."

B | Earthquake Will Provide Jews Escape Route To Christ

Armies of the Antichrist will be in the process of annihilating the Jews when Jesus arrives on the Mount of Olives. An earthquake will cleave the mountain open, and terrified Jews will flee to Christ through that new valley.

Zechariah 14:4-5 - "His feet shall stand in that day upon the mount of Olives, ...before Jerusalem on the east, and [it] shall cleave in the midst thereof..., there shall be a very great valley; and half of the mountain shall remove toward the north, and half of it toward the south. And ye shall flee to the valley of the mountains."

D | All The Saints Will Come With Christ

Jesus Christ will gather all His saints, living and dead, to the great climax at Armageddon. "Immediately after the tribulation of those days... They shall see the Son of man coming in the clouds of heaven with power and great glory. And he shall send his angels with a great sound of a trumpet, and they shall gather together his elect from the four winds, from one end of heaven to the other," Matthew 24:29-31. "They lived and reigned with Christ a thousand years" Revelation 20:4.

Zechariah 14:5 - "The LORD my God shall come, and all the saints with thee."

☑

C | It Shall Be Light In The Evening Time

This is one of the great divine paradoxes. When the world faces its darkest hour, it shall be light. When sin, hatred and war reach their very worst, Jesus will come, and the people who sit in darkness will see a Great Light - the Light of the World!

Zechariah 14:6-7 - "It shall come to pass in that day, that the light shall not be clear, nor dark: But it shall be one day which shall be known to the LORD, not day, nor night: but it shall come to pass, that at evening time it shall be light."

D | Living Waters Shall Go Out From Jerusalem

Several prophets called the LORD the fountain of life, or the fountain of living waters. It only makes sense that when Jesus moves into His new Temple in Jerusalem, a new fountain will spring up from beneath the sanctuary, creating a new river that will run throughout Israel from the Mediterranean to the Dead Sea (bringing it to life).

Zechariah 14:8 - "And it shall be in that day, that living waters shall go out from Jerusalem; half of them toward the former sea, and half of them toward the hinder sea: in summer and in winter shall it be.

B | There Shall Be One LORD, And His Name One

God has been known by many names throughout the centuries. The Bible gives us many of them: Elohim (God), Jehovah [Yhwh] (the Self-Existent One), El Shaddai (God Almighty), Jehovah Jireh (Provider), Jehovah Nissi (Banner of War), Jehovah Shalom (Peace), Jehovah Rapha (Healer), Jehovah Tsidkenu (Our Righteousness), and others. But when Messiah comes to earth, we will only know God by one name from then on. He will be known as Jesus (Yehoshua - Jehovah Savior).

Zechariah 14:9 - "And the LORD shall be king over all the earth: in that day shall there be one LORD, and his name one."

D | All Who Fight Against Jerusalem Will Suffer A Plague

Many Bible prophecies speak of fiery judgment from God during the Sixth Trumpet War AND the battle of Armageddon. From the description that Zechariah gave, it appears that a nuclear holocaust will come to the Middle East. Look at these symptoms:

Zechariah 14:12,15 - "This shall be the plague wherewith the LORD will smite all the people that have fought against Jerusalem; Their flesh shall consume away while they stand upon their feet, and their eyes shall consume away in their holes, and their tongue shall consume away in their mouth. ...And so shall be the plague of ...all the beasts."

A | **The Nations Will Worship The LORD, Or Get No Rain**

During the millennial rule of Jesus, all nations must come yearly to worship the LORD in Jerusalem, or they will get no rain. O, worship the LORD!

Zechariah 14:16-17 - "Every one that is left of all the nations which came against Jerusalem shall even go up from year to year to worship the King, the LORD of hosts, and to keep the feast of tabernacles. And it shall be, that whoso will not come up of all the families of the earth unto Jerusalem to worship the King, the LORD of hosts, even upon them shall be no rain."

C | **HOLINESS UNTO THE LORD**

The world we live in is vile and profane - NOT the world that God created it to be. Sin has taken its toll and left its ugly mark. But when Jesus comes, He will be King over all the earth. There will be no more destruction, and Jerusalem will be safely inhabited. The whole land of Israel will be restored to beauty. Everything will be HOLY.

Zechariah 14:20 - "In that day shall there be upon the bells of the horses, HOLINESS UNTO THE LORD; ...every pot in Jerusalem and in Judah shall be holiness unto the LORD of hosts."

Lessons from the Book of
MALACHI

C | **"I Loved Jacob, And I Hated Esau"**

This verse is problematic for those who claims that God loves every person unconditionally. I know that God so loved the world that He gave His only begotten Son. But I also know that God is angry with the wicked every day. God loves you until you sin against Him for the last time. Then He will judge you without mercy. God will have righteousness. Righteousness is bigger than love.

Malachi 1:2-3 - "Was not Esau Jacob's brother? saith the LORD: yet I loved Jacob, And I hated Esau, and laid his mountains and his heritage waste for the dragons of the wilderness."

B | The LORD's Reputation Goes Beyond Israel's Borders

The Edomites were the descendants of Esau and historical enemies of the children of Israel. They were determined to rebuild and strengthen themselves in defiance of the God of Israel, but they could not. God greatly impoverished them, and finally made their place a desolate place. The ancient nation no longer exists. Far beyond Israel's borders, our God reigns.

Malachi 1:4 - "They shall call them, The border of wickedness, and, The people against whom the LORD hath indignation for ever. And your eyes shall see, and ye shall say, The LORD will be magnified from the border of Israel."

C | God Deserves Honor More Than Fathers Or Masters

Malachi, who is only mentioned by name one time in the Bible, had the unsavory task of pronouncing the judgments of God on the Jews returned from Babylonian captivity. Despite the amazing grace of God to return them to their homeland, they nevertheless failed to honor and fear God. They fell into the same sins of their forefathers.

Malachi 1:6 - "A son honoureth his father, and a servant his master: if then I be a father, where is mine honour? and if I be a master, where is my fear? saith the LORD of hosts unto you."

A | Effectual Prayer Requires Right Relationship With God

The foremost important factor in effectual prayer is not faith. It is right relationship with God. It is possible to have faith without right relationship. Prayer will not work, no matter how much faith you have, if you are not in right standing with God. Malachi rebuked Israel for dishonoring God, having no fear of God, and offering polluted and blemished sacrifices.

Malachi 1:8-10 - "Will he be pleased with thee, or accept thy person? ...will he regard your persons? ...I have no pleasure in you, saith the LORD of hosts, neither will I accept an offering at your hand."

B | **Polluted Bread And Contemptible Sacrifices**

So you do not think that God cares about the quality of your living sacrifice? Will you give Him a half-hearted life, tainted with carnality or worldliness? That kind of self-deception cost Israel their relationship with God. Instead of pure, excellent sacrifices, they brought polluted bread and blind, lame, torn and sick animals.

Malachi 1:13-14 - "Should I accept this of your hand? saith the LORD. But cursed be the deceiver, which ...sacrificeth unto the Lord a corrupt thing: for I am a great King, saith the LORD of hosts, and my name is dreadful among the heathen."

A | **Give Glory To His Name**

We commonly ask much from God, only talking to Him when we have a problem that only He can solve. Change your priorities. Glorify Him daily with praises.

Malachi 2:2,13,17 - "If ye will not ...give glory unto my name, ...I will even send a curse upon you, and I will curse your blessings: ...And this have ye done again, covering the altar of the LORD with tears, with weeping, and with crying out, insomuch that he regardeth not the offering any more, or receiveth it with good will at your hand. Ye have wearied the LORD with your words."

C | **Priests Must Keep Covenant With God**

God reminded the priests of His covenant with their ancestor, Levi. "My covenant was with him of life and peace; ...The law of truth was in his mouth, and iniquity was not found in his lips: he ...did turn many away from iniquity." God rebuked them for corrupting that covenant, causing many to stumble with their errors. "The LORD will cut off the man that doeth this, the master and the scholar."

Malachi 2:7 - "The priest's lips should keep knowledge, and they should seek the law at his mouth: for he is the messenger of the LORD of hosts."

D | **Malachi Prophesies John The Baptist And Christ**

This is one of the truly great prophecies of the Old Testament, the one that John the Baptist fulfilled. John was the LORD's messenger. He prepared the way for Jesus. Jesus suddenly appeared to the multitudes, and straightaway, was seen in the Temple in Jerusalem, preaching the Gospel of the New Covenant.

Malachi 3:1 - "Behold, I will send my messenger, and he shall prepare the way before me: and the Lord, whom ye seek, shall suddenly come to his temple, even the messenger of the covenant, whom ye delight in: behold, he shall come, saith the LORD of hosts."

B | A Refiner's Fire And A Fuller's Soap

The coming of the LORD will not be a quiet, inconspicuous event. It will be the biggest, most dramatic event in human history. Jesus Christ will "throughly purge His floor," Matthew 3:12. He will come in judgment, making a swift witness against the sorcerers, adulterers, false swearers, oppressors, and every worker of evil. Even the rich and powerful will be terrified and will try to hide from His Presence.

Malachi 3:2 - "But who may abide the day of his coming? and who shall stand when he appeareth? for he is like a refiner's fire, and like fullers' soap."

D | Israel's Offerings Will Again Be Pleasant Unto The LORD

In the olden days of the Tabernacle and Sanctuary, daily sacrifices made on the holy altar were the heart and soul of the people's relationship with God. As they presented their offerings to the LORD, their sins were atoned, and God was pleased. When the people backslid, that entire system broke down. God yearns for the day when the children of Israel will once again honor Him with their offerings (Ezekiel 45:17).

Malachi 3:4 - "Then shall the offering of Judah and Jerusalem be pleasant unto the LORD, as in the days of old, and as in former years."

C | God Never Changes

God is forever the same - in mercy and judgment; in goodness and severity. What He loves, He will always love. What He hates, He will always hate. His longsuffering and mercy affords us the opportunity to be saved. His judgment and wrath assures us that Heaven will be eternally pure and righteous.

Malachi 3:6-7 - "I am the LORD, I change not; therefore ye sons of Jacob are not consumed. Even from the days of your fathers ye are gone away from mine ordinances, and have not kept them. Return unto me, and I will return unto you."

B | The Tithe

Abraham was the first on record to offer a tithe (tenth) of his income - to the priest of Salem, Melchizedek. Jacob vowed to give his tithe to the LORD. God prescribed that all of Israel should tithe into the Tabernacle for the support of the priesthood. Without the tithe, the ministry would have been starved out of business. God curses those who refuse to tithe.

Malachi 3:8 - "Will a man rob God? Yet ye have robbed me. But ye say, Wherein have we robbed thee? In tithes and offerings. Ye are cursed with a curse: for ye have robbed me."

D | Tithing Activates A Prophesied Blessing

Paying tithes sets into motion the promises of God. God wants His people to support the ministry. When you underwrite the work of God, God will underwrite you. Besides, He says the first ten percent is His (verse 8). NEVER spend God's money on yourself.

Malachi 3:10 - "Bring ye all the tithes into the storehouse, that there may be meat in mine house, and prove me now herewith, saith the LORD of hosts, if I will not open you the windows of heaven, and pour you out a blessing, that there shall not be room enough to receive it."

C | Tithers Are Very Important People

Who can you turn to for this kind of security? Nobody but your Creator can make this offer. The tithers - God's people who faithfully return to Him the first-fruits of their labors - become the VIP's in this world. God's Very Important People. "I will rebuke the devourer for your sakes, and he shall not destroy the fruits of your ground; neither shall your vine cast her fruit before the time in the field."

Malachi 3:12 - "And all nations shall call you blessed: for ye shall be a delightsome land, saith the LORD of hosts."

B | A Book Of Remembrance For His Jewels

Imagine yourself in God's place, looking down on a world full of God-haters, and only a tiny number of God-fearing men and women. THOSE are your precious jewels. Write them in a Book. Save THEM.

Malachi 3:16-17 - "Then they that feared the LORD spake often one to another: and the LORD hearkened, and heard it, and a book of remembrance was written before him for them that feared the LORD, and that thought upon his name. And they shall be mine, saith the LORD of hosts, in that day when I make up my jewels."

A | A Warning To Speak Kindly About God

Malachi indicted the people for their "stout words" - brazen, defiant words against God. "Your words have been stout against me, ...Ye have said, It is vain to serve God: and what profit is it that we have kept his ordinance?" He reminded them that God separates His friends from His enemies. "Then they that feared the LORD spake often one to another: and the LORD hearkened, and heard it, and a book of remembrance was written before him for them that feared the LORD."

Malachi 3:17 - "I will spare them, as a man spareth his own son that serveth him."

D | The Day That Shall Burn As An Oven

Almost every book in the Bible mentions the fire of God's judgment in one way or another. One of the most recurrent prophecies is that God will judge the earth by fire shortly before Jesus establishes His earthly kingdom at Armageddon.

Malachi 4:1-3 - "The day cometh, that shall burn as an oven; and all the proud, yea, and all that do wickedly, shall be stubble: and the day that cometh shall burn them up, ...the wicked ...shall be ashes under the soles of your feet in the day that I shall do this, saith the LORD of hosts."

C | There Is Healing In His Wings

Six thousand years of human history are littered with horrific calamities, pain, sorrow, sickness and death. Nobody but God can measure the suffering that men have borne for their sins through the ages. But there is exciting hope for those who fear and trust in God. He will arise as the Sun of righteousness, and heal us and make us strong again. O, happy day!

Malachi 4:2 - "Unto you that fear my name shall the Sun of righteousness arise with healing in his wings; and ye shall go forth, and grow up as calves of the stall."

D | Elijah Will Come Before The Day Of The LORD

The angel told Zacharias that his wife Elisabeth would bear a son named John. "He shall go before [Christ] in the spirit and power of Elias, to turn the hearts of the fathers to the children." Jesus said, "Elias is come already, ...and the disciples understood that he spake unto them of John the Baptist."

Malachi 4:5-6 - "I will send you Elijah the prophet before the coming of the great and dreadful day of the LORD: And he shall turn the heart of the fathers to the children, and the heart of the children to their fathers."

"Now being made free from sin,
and become servants to God,
ye have your fruit unto holiness,
and the end everlasting life,"
Romans 6:22.

☐✓

ENDNOTES:
For additional information on noted topics, see these articles online...

1 http://kenraggio.com/KRPN-SevenTrumpets.htm
2 http://kenraggio.com/KR-Islam.html
3 http://kenraggio.com/KR-MaleFemale.htm
4 http://kenraggio.com/KR-ParableOfTheHusbandman.htm
5 http://kenraggio.com/KR-FatherSpirit.htm
6 http://kenraggio.com/KR-Oneness.htm
7 http://kenraggio.com/KRPN-CathComCap.htm
8 http://kenraggio.com/KRPN-ValleyOfHell.html
9 http://kenraggio.com/KR-IGiveMyselfUntoPrayer.html
10 http://kenraggio.com/KRPN-EzekielsWar.htm
11 http://kenraggio.com/KRPN-EzekielsWar.htm
12 http://kenraggio.com/KRPN-Quartet.html
13 http://kenraggio.com/Temple-Ezekiel-Millennium.jpg
14 http://kenraggio.com/KR-Daniel.html
15 http://kenraggio.com/KRPN-Statue-Of-Nebuchadnezzar.html
16 http://kenraggio.com/KRPN-IronAndClayFeet.html
17 http://kenraggio.com/KRPN-CathComCap.htm
18 http://kenraggio.com/KRPN-DreadfulBeast.htm
19 http://kenraggio.com/KRPN-Four-Beasts-Of-Daniel.html
20 http://kenraggio.com/KRPN-Four-Beasts-Of-Daniel.html
21 http://kenraggio.com/KRPN-Four-Beasts-Of-Daniel.html
22 http://kenraggio.com/KRPN-DreadfulBeast.htm
23 http://kenraggio.com/KRPN-IronAndClayFeet.html
24 http://kenraggio.com/KR-Oneness.htm
25 http://kenraggio.com/KRPN-ValleyOfHell.html
26 http://kenraggio.com/KR-ParableOfTheHusbandman.htm
27 http://kenraggio.com/KR-SpiritualWar.htm
28 http://kenraggio.com/KRPN-Daniels-Seventy-Weeks.html
29 http://kenraggio.com/KR-SpiritualWar.htm
30 http://kenraggio.com/KRPN-IronAndClayFeet.html
31 http://kenraggio.com/KR-Daniel-Chapter-11.html
32 http://kenraggio.com/KR-OrnamentsOfJewelry.htm
33 http://kenraggio.com/KRPN-EzekielsWar.htm
34 http://kenraggio.com/KRPN-CathComCap.htm

□✓

635

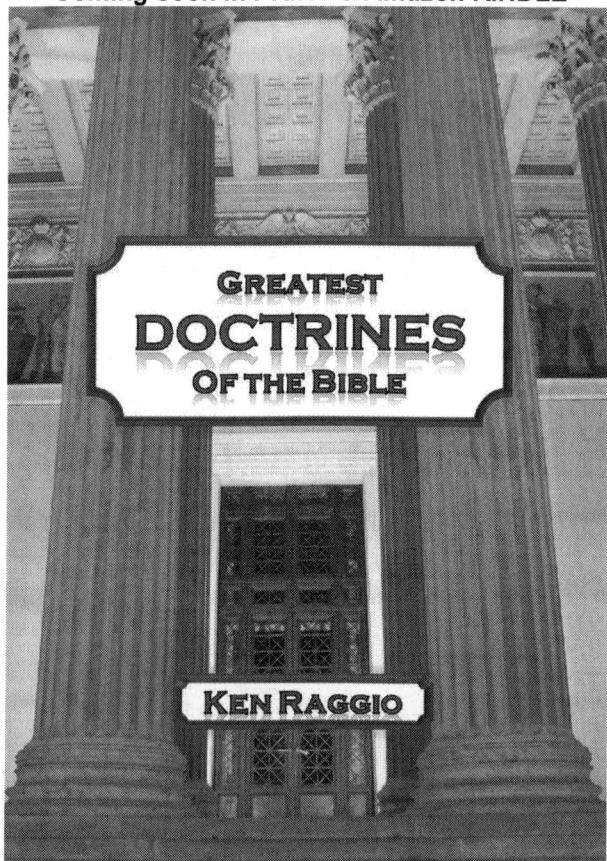

Coming soon in PRINT & Amazon KINDLE

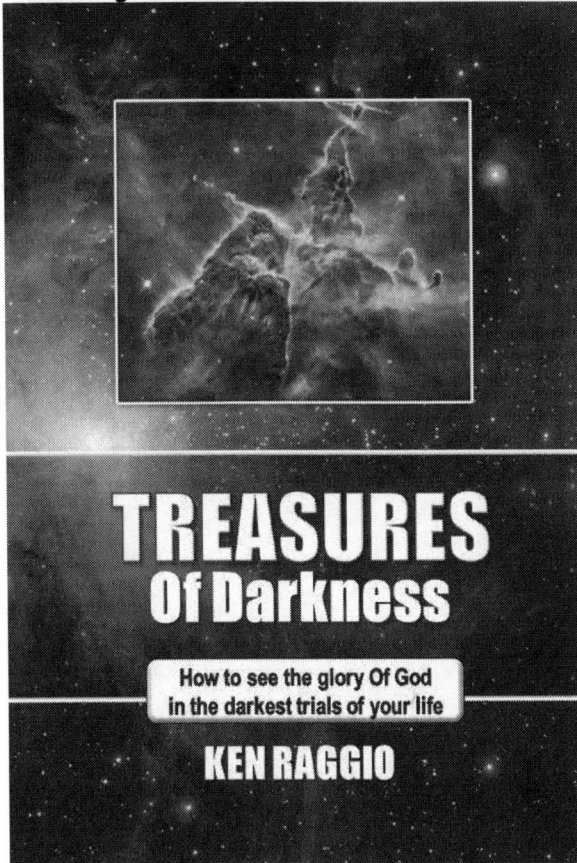

TREASURES OF DARKNESS

How to see the glory of God in the darkest trials of your life.

This book was born in the furnace of a great personal trial, and is nothing short of a revelation of how God works behind the scenes during your greatest difficulties. God wants you to be able to see clearly in the dark. This book is a fascinating journey into the world of the Spirit, and will definitely enhance your night vision, and show you how to see the **Treasures of Darkness!**

Chapters include"
Blinded By The Light | God Plays Hide-And-Seek | Let There Be Light | Dark Matter | String Theories and Spin | and much, much more.

TO ORDER, VISIT http://kenraggio.com

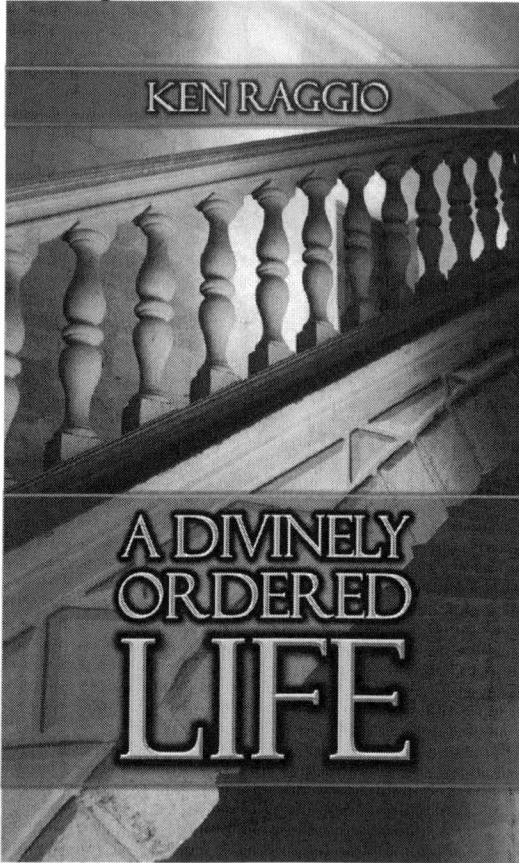

☐✓

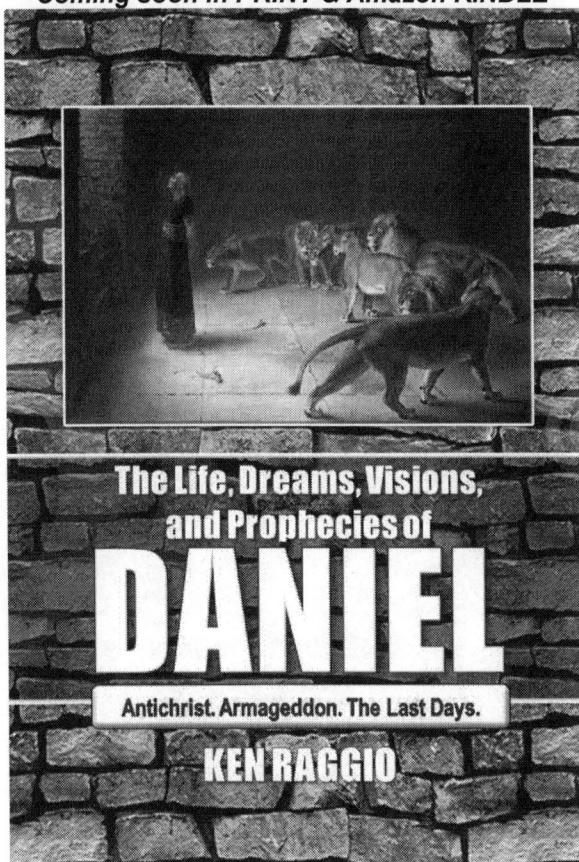
THE LIFE, DREAMS, VISIONS AND PROPHECIES OF DANIEL

A rich, in-depth look at the life and prophetic essence of the prophet Daniel. It includes a close-up character study of Daniel's life, followed by a point-by-point examination of each dream, vision and prophecy.

Includes MAJOR Last-Days Prophecies you need to understand. Nebuchadnezzar's Image | The Four Beasts Of Daniel | The Iron and Clay Feet and the Four-Headed Leopard | Daniel's Dreadful Beast | Daniel's Seventy Weeks Prophecy | Daniel Chapter 11 (Revelation of the coming Man of Sin), and much more. This is a very powerful book.

TO ORDER, VISIT http://kenraggio.com

NOW AVAILABLE! $4.95 PRINT | $2.95 KINDLE

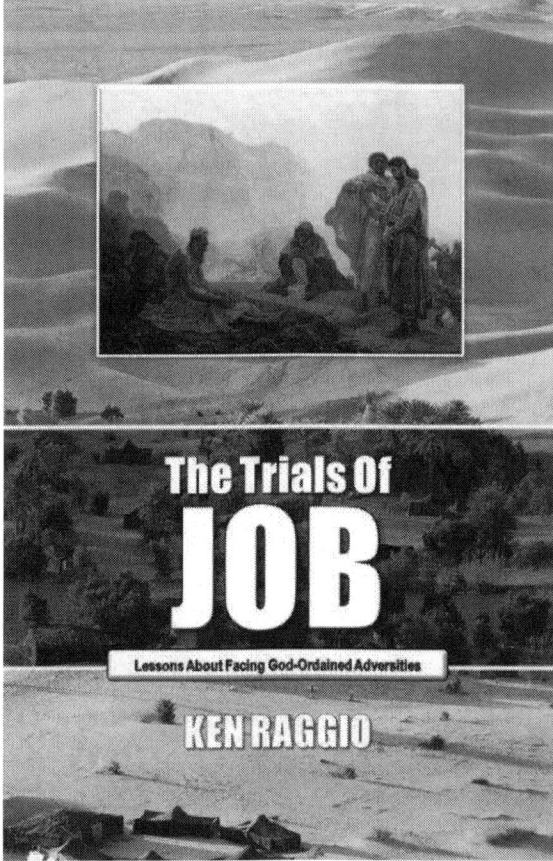

THE TRIALS OF JOB
Lessons about facing God-ordained adversities.

Before going to press with MY DAILY BIBLE COMPANION, I felt that it would be good to introduce this work in a sample version.

Since the Book of Job is probably the oldest book in the Bible, and since it contains many priceless and poignant life lessons, I decided to extract the 58 mini-lessons from the Book of Job and publish them ahead of the major work. This is only a tiny sampling of over 4,800 lessons in the MDBC. This MINI-BOOK is an excellent way to introduce your friends to the larger work, MY DAILY BIBLE COMPANION.

Order PAPERBACK Version here: https://www.createspace.com/3827423
Order the KINDLE E-Book here: http://amzn.com/B007M8A1H0

"FRIEND" ME on FACEBOOK! Click here!

Read my Daily Inspirational Posts!

ALSO...
JOIN the KEN RAGGIO FACEBOOK "FANPAGE"
Ken Raggio – Bible Resources – Lessons – Sermons - Prophecy

Read the daily PROPHECY MINI-LESSONS on my FB Fanpage!
Click "LIKE" at this site.

□✓

"FOLLOW ME" on TWITTER!

Daily Power Quotes, Mini-Lessons, and Prophecy Updates

Twitter ID:

kenraggiocom

VISIT KENRAGGIO.COM

Thousands of pages of
Bible Studies – Sermons – Lessons – Prophecy Articles

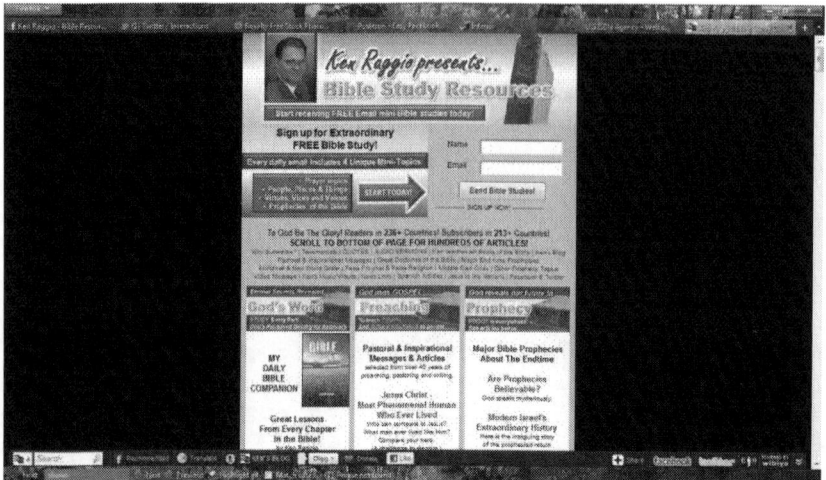

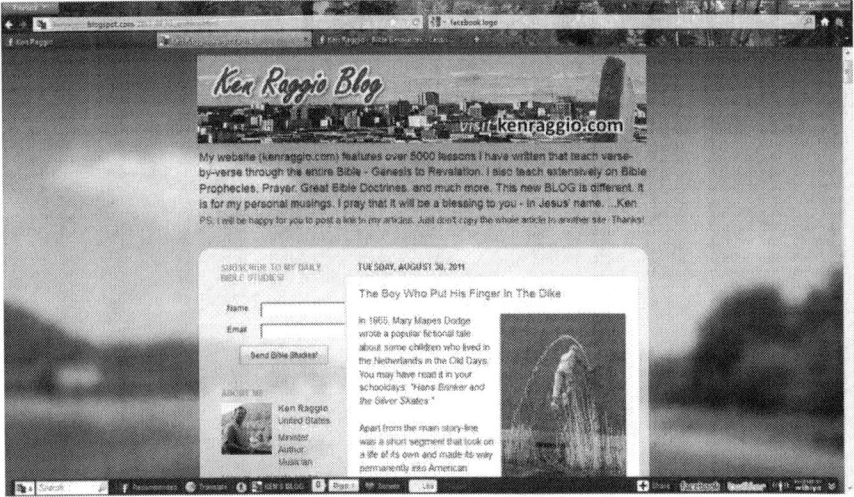

VISIT MY BLOG!

Personal Musings On God, Religion, and Daily Christian Living

kenraggio.blogspot.com

SUBSCRIBE to "Today's Bible Study"
FREE! - BY E-MAIL

Four 100-Word Mini-Bible Lessons Each Day in your Email Box

Subscribe here: kenraggio.com

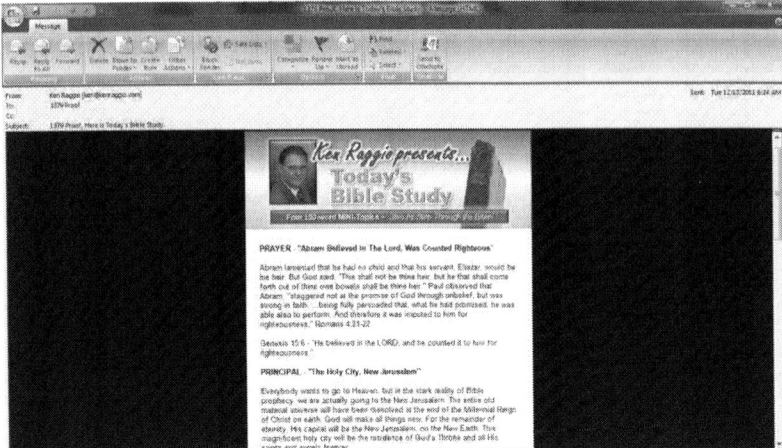

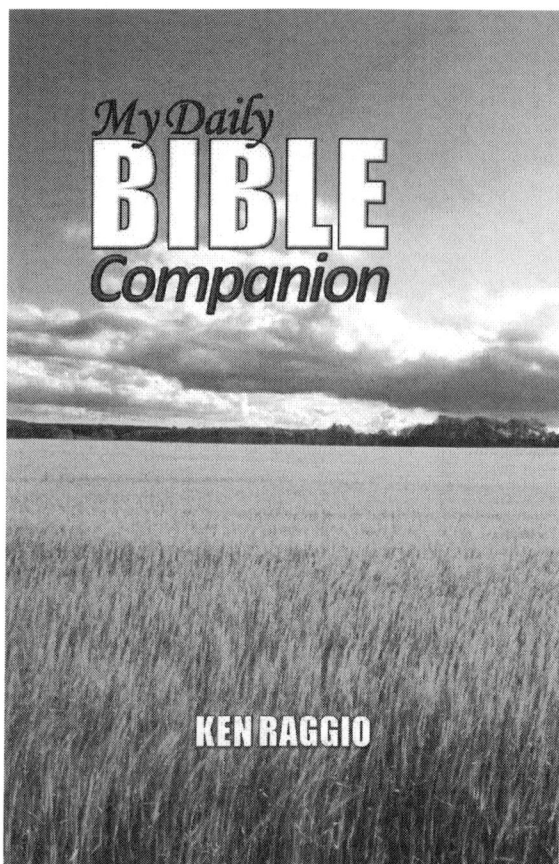

MY DAILY BIBLE COMPANION

Over 4,800 Point-by-Point Mini-Lessons through the entire Bible!

KEEP THIS AWESOME 1400+ PAGE BOOK BY YOUR FAVORITE EASY CHAIR, OR ON YOUR NIGHTSTAND. It is a unique Daily Reader that is packed with amazing Genesis-to-Revelation Bible lessons. Read as many as you want each day: 2, 3, 4 or more. Presented in easily understandable 100-Word topics in four general categories:

- **PRAYER**   Illustrations, Examples, Lessons about Prayer
- **PRINCIPALS**   People, Places and Things in the Bible
- **PRINCIPLES**   Virtues, Vices, Values in the Bible, Great Precepts
- **PROPHECIES** 1200+ Prophecies (Fulfilled and Unfulfilled) Explained

Order Vol. 1 Old Testament – 650 pgs: https://www.createspace.com/3839857
Order Vol. 2 New Testament – 788 pgs: https://www.createspace.com/3856644

Order KINDLE e-Book (Entire Bible): http://amzn.com/ Search "Ken Raggio"

□✓

Dear Friend,

For almost six years, I have worked feverishly, researching and writing in excess of 50 hours every week to produce, first of all, my major life-work, this 1438-page Bible Commentary entitled "MY DAILY BIBLE COMPANION."

It is the compilation of over 4,800 100-word mini-Bible lessons, written for "TODAY'S BIBLE STUDY," most of which have already been read in every nation on earth. My subscribers are in 214 nations at this writing. Having written step-by-step, point-by-point Bible lessons from Genesis to Revelation, virtually every topic in the Bible has been dealt with. I have already received literally thousands of testimonial letters from around the world expressing thanks and appreciation for these daily lessons. Letters continue to arrive daily. I hope and pray that you will enjoy them, too.

Because it is quite comprehensive in going point-by-point through the entire Bible, it became necessary to publish the work in two volumes.

Volume 1 contains lessons from the **Old Testament**.
Volume 2 contains lessons from the **New Testament**.

The E-Book (Kindle) contains the entire book in ONE volume.

In addition, I will soon release several other books that I have been writing: a powerful book on PRAYER, a book on the GREATEST BIBLE DOCTRINES, a MAJOR work on BIBLE PROPHECY, and at least three other inspirational books in the coming year or so.

Thank you for purchasing this book. I pray that God will bless the teaching of His Word to you.

Please visit my website (kenraggio.com) and enjoy the vast FREE Bible resources that you will find there.

God bless you.
Sincerely,

Ken Raggio

ABOUT THE AUTHOR

A Pentecostal minister since 1966, Ken Raggio has been a Pastor, Evangelist, Singer, Songwriter, Musician, Broadcaster, Journalist, Editor and Author. Ken has maintained a major Internet presence since 1996 at **kenraggio.com** and has many thousands of subscribers in 214 nations to **"Today's Bible Study,"** a daily email containing four 100-word mini-Bible-lessons. He is now focused on writing and producing video ꞇaching series.

COVER PHOTO: Wheat Field

"So is the kingdom of God, as if a man should cast seed into the ground; And should sleep, and rise night and day, and the seed should spring and grow up, he knoweth not how. For the earth bringeth forth fruit of herself; first the blade, then the ear, after that the full corn in the ear. But when the fruit is brought forth, immediately he putteth in the sickle, because the harvest is come," Mark 4:26-29.

"He that soweth the good seed is the Son of man; The field is the world; the good seed are the children of the kingdom; ...the harvest is the end of the world; and the reapers are the angels," Matthew 13:37-39.

"The harvest truly is plenteous, but the labourers are few; Pray ye therefore the Lord of the harvest, that he will send forth labourers into his harvest," Matthew 9:37-38.

"And [John] looked, and behold a white cloud, and upon the cloud one sat like unto the Son of man, having on his head a golden crown, and in his hand a sharp sickle. And another angel came out of the temple, crying with a loud voice to him that sat on the cloud, Thrust in thy sickle, and reap: for the time is come for thee to reap; for the harvest of the earth is ripe. And he that sat on the cloud thrust in his sickle on the earth; and the earth was reaped," Revelation 14:14-16.

"Whose fan is in his hand, and he will throughly purge his floor, and
  gather his wheat into the garner; but he will burn up the chaff with
  unquenchable fire," Matthew 3:12.

Made in the USA
Middletown, DE
12 September 2018